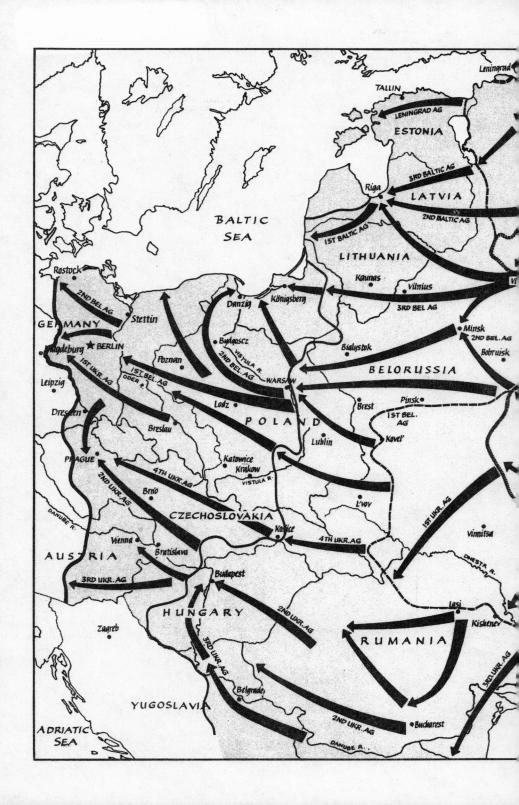

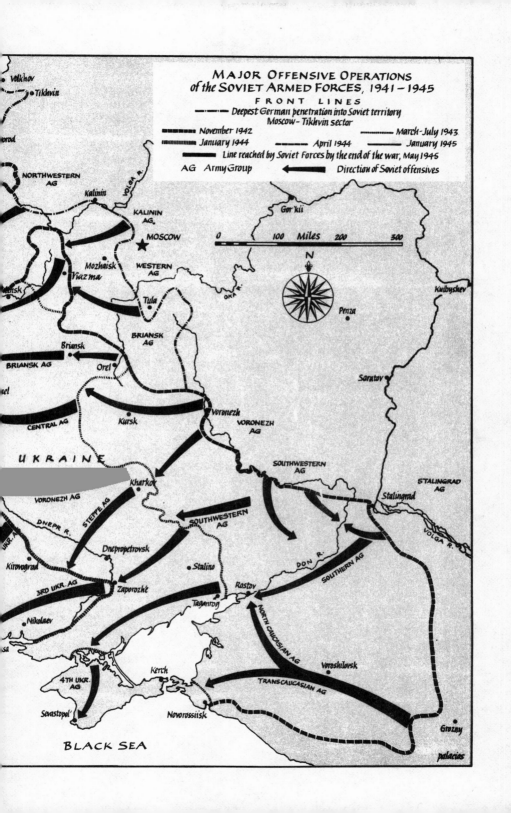

STALIN and his GENERALS

A Westview Encore Reprint

—————————————————————

STALIN
AND HIS
GENERALS

SOVIET MILITARY MEMOIRS
OF WORLD WAR II

Edited by
Seweryn Bialer

Westview Press / Boulder and London

This book was prepared under the auspices of the Research Institute on Communist Affairs, Columbia University.

Published in 1984 in the United States of America by Westview Press, Inc., 5500 Central Avenue, Boulder, Colorado 80301; Frederick A. Praeger, President and Publisher

First published in 1969 by Western Publishing Company, Inc.

Library of Congress Catalog Card Number: 84-50411

ISBN 0-86531-610-4

Printed and bound in the United States of America

6   5   4   3   2

CONTENTS

6   **Contents**

Chapter IV LEADERSHIP

Chapter V EPILOGUE

MAPS

Cartography by Rafael Palacios

PREFACE TO THE 1984 WESTVIEW ENCORE REPRINT EDITION

World War II remains one of the most significant events in Soviet history. It is difficult to overestimate the importance of the Nazi-Soviet conflict in decisively shaping the Soviet reality with which we contend today. Victory marked a crucial turning point for the Soviet Union. It confirmed the legitimacy of Stalin's rule, at least for the dominant Slavs of the country. It presaged the emergence of the Soviet Union as a global superpower. It created the East European empire that profoundly affected Soviet international conduct over the last four decades. The very experience of war significantly influenced the mental outlook of present Soviet political, managerial, and military elites. The centrality of that war even today may be measured by the degree to which Soviet leaders actively perpetuate its memory. Indeed, the unrelenting concentration on the wartime experience continues to provide a key device for socializing the Soviet people.

If knowledge of that wartime experience is essential to an accurate understanding of Soviet reality, we in the West have yet to apply the scholarly energies it surely warrants. When this book first appeared in 1969, it drew on abundant Soviet source materials to explore the key relations between Soviet political and military elites during World War II. Surprisingly, research over the last decade and a half has added little to our knowledge in the West of the war in the East, apart from several popular, general accounts and a few well-documented books on particular battles or episodes of the war.

Although social scientists have long known that the working of political systems is most productively studied during the critical periods when their very survival is threatened, no major work has yet treated the entire period of this perilous trial for the Soviet people and their leaders. And this is so despite the fact that Soviet primary and secondary sources on this period are more accessible to Western scholars than those on any other period of Soviet history. All these considerations argue for making this book again available to those who would return to the Nazi-Soviet war for deeper insight into Soviet values and structures.

The flood of war memoirs has not abated during the last fifteen years. Most of the new publications, however, present the recollections of middling and lesser commanders who can add little to our knowledge of Stalin and his generals. Of more relevance are the revised editions of the works by senior commanders, many of the originals of which were first excerpted in English on these pages. Careful examination of the new editions merely reinforces the assessment conveyed in this introduction. Already by 1969, in the fifth year of Brezhnev's rule, there was clearly discernible in the memoir literature a "cleansing" process that moderated or expunged the most simplistic and denigrating attacks on Stalin's wartime role, a principal ingredient of Khrushchev's anti-Stalin campaign. That process has continued, and readers will no longer find in "corrected" and "reworked" editions entire passages from, for example, Starinov, Batov, and Azarov that originally appeared here. The reissued memoirs of senior commanders contributed to the search for a more balanced evaluation of Stalin's wartime role, an evaluation that served and still serves the professional aspirations of the military and the political needs of Khrushchev's successors. These reissued memoirs do not in fundamental and striking ways alter the portrait of Stalin as war leader that is presented in this book.

The portrait was nevertheless significantly altered during the later years of Brezhnev's rule. In some accounts of the war Stalin was, for all intents and purposes, entirely rehabilitated. That this task was executed not in military memoirs but rather in documentary fiction suggests that the military's professional posture and the political needs of at least some leaders did not coincide. There are two striking examples of a technique that combines selective reporting of genuine archival materials and personal interviews about senior leaders with fictionalized dramas about more modest, "positive" war heroes. Aleksandr Chakovskii, one of the most prominent writers on the war, recounts the story of Leningrad in his three-volume *Blokada (Blockade)*.[1] Ivan Stadniuk, a well-known Ukrainian writer, chooses the four months between the Nazi invasion and the Battle of Moscow for his novel, *Voina (War)*.[2] The more detailed, explicit, and dramatic reinstatement of Stalin's supreme role is that of Stadniuk, all the more amazing and important because of its party sponsorship. Readers who are familiar with the sources on which *Stalin and His Generals* was based will discover in Stadniuk's novel radical departures at significant points in the story told on these pages.

Stadniuk reproduces in considerable detail entire episodes from meetings of the Politburo, the Main Defense Committee, and Supreme Headquarters. Stalin appears in political and personal terms as a giant,

[1](Moscow: *Izvestiia*, 1975)
[2](Moscow: Voenizdat, 1981).

as the demiurge of the Soviet nation and armed forces at war. Particularly significant is the sympathetic treatment of Stalin's role in the initial phase of war. From the beginning, according to Stadniuk, Stalin personally directed the military effort. Stadniuk denies Stalin's isolation and depression in the first week of crushing defeat. He stresses the failure of communications between field commanders and the General Staff to minimize responsibility and to justify, among other things, the execution of Commander Pavlov of the Western Army Group and his associates. He attributes to Stalin personally, and not to the General Staff or to Zhukov, the key decisions in the first months of war that led to slowing the German advance. Not once does he mention the Great Purge or lesser persecutions of senior army commanders. Stalin's relations with military aides of the General Staff and People's Commissariat of Defense are depicted as civilized and professional, the meetings of the Politburo and Main Defense Committee as collegial. He presents Chief Commissar of the Red Army Mekhlis, the leader most hated by professional army officers, as a man of great integrity and will power and a source of considerable help to Stalin in the early months of war; the head of Stalin's private Secretariat, Poskrebyshev, second only to Beria in his instigation of butchery, emerges as a reasonable and devoted intermediary between Stalin and his generals. Stadniuk does not question the wisdom of Stalin's accumulation in the first months of war of those positions that formalized his unrestricted power as war leader—Prime Minister, Secretary General of the Party, People's Commissar of Defense, Chairman of the Main Defense Committee, and Supreme Commander in Chief.

Stadniuk's celebration of Stalin's war leadership virtually returns to the starting point of the war. Thus, the political line has moved from extravagant glorification while Stalin lived to brutal assault on the idol under Khrushchev, to muted criticism during Brezhnev's early years, to renewed exaltation of Stalin, if not as a living god at least as the great leader who inspired miraculous feats of heroism, the herculean war mobilization effort, and the exhilarating victory over Nazi Germany.

From time to time a note of realism returns to writings on the war. Konstantin Simonov, for example, in his most recently published diary of a war correspondent,[3] reminds us who Stalin really was, what morbid suspicion and mortal danger surrounded him, how costly to the Soviet people was his total, uncontested and viciously abused power. More prominent in official literature today, however, is the portrait of

[3]*Raznye dni voiny. Dnevnik pisatelia* (Moscow: "Molodaia gvardiia," 1975).

a complicated and contradictory leader, but one who was great by any standard. If Stalin were alive, he would have scant reason to dispute this introduction to a new generation of Soviet readers who do not remember World War II.

S. B.
J. A.
Wendell, Massachusetts
3 November 1983

ACKNOWLEDGMENTS

Grateful acknowledgment is made to the Research Institute on Communist Affairs for supporting the preparation of this book, and, in particular, to its director, Professor Zbigniew Brzezinski, for encouraging the labors of its editor. The reader should know that while the conception and organization of the book and the choice of materials were mine, the analytical introductions and the final draft of translations were undertaken as a common effort with my wife, Joan Afferica, professor of history at Smith College.

Mrs. Christine Dodson, secretary of the Institute, provided generous assistance on many occasions. The draft of most translations was prepared by Miss Diane Gosslin, Mrs. Mary Mackler, Mrs. Cerisa Shopkow, and Mr. Theodore Guerchon. The manuscript was typed by Mrs. Hilda McArthur, Mrs. Norma Lepine, and Mrs. Mildred O'Brien. Mrs. E. Arensburger helped check the accuracy and consistency of military terminology.

S. B.

INTRODUCTION

The Politics of Soviet War Literature

No MORE destructive and gigantic land battles were fought during the Second World War than those on the Eastern Front where the survival of the Soviet Union and perhaps even the very outcome of the war were at stake. The immense scope and significance of these battles entitle them to greater attention than they have yet received in the voluminous Western war literature. Even those books concerned primarily with the Nazi-Soviet theater of operations tend often to portray the German protagonist more vividly, a natural consequence of their authors' dependence primarily on German sources.* This reliance on German accounts cannot be attributed to a deliberate attempt to discredit the Soviet contribution to the common victory over Nazi Germany. In most cases failure to utilize a comparable amount of Soviet source material reflects less an anti-Soviet bias than the relative scarcity and dubious reliability of Soviet documents and eyewitness accounts.

Until recently a thorough and many-sided treatment of Soviet participation in the war has been denied the Soviet citizen as well as the Western reader. Despite the fact that the war experience was undoubtedly crucial in forming what is today the political, economic, scientific, cultural, and military elite in the Soviet Union, the four decisive war years—

---

*The two most noteworthy among recently published books concerning the Nazi-Soviet war, to both of which these remarks apply are: Alan Clark, *Barbarossa: The Russian-German Conflict, 1941–45* (New York: William Morrow and Co., 1965); Paul Carell, *Hitler Moves East 1941–43* (Boston: Little, Brown and Co., 1964).

Of books which concentrate on the Soviet conduct of war one should mention first the pioneering study of Raymond L. Garthoff, *How Russia Makes War* (Glencoe, Illinois: The Free Press, 1953) and the superb and very thorough study of John Erickson, *The Soviet High Command* (Boulder: Westview Press, 1984). Of the more popular books recently published Alexander Werth's *Russia at War 1941–45* (New York: E. P. Dutton and Co., 1964) makes extensive use of Soviet sources and the author's own experience in Russia during the war.

the so-called "Great Patriotic War of the Soviet People"—remained virtually untouched by scholars and participants alike until some ten years ago. While the military officer had access to highly technical literature, the ordinary citizen could choose only between a limited number of history books, uniformly rich in slogans and poor in facts;° a sizable outpouring of newspaper and magazine articles dedicated to various war anniversaries; and, of course, the collection of Stalin's war speeches and orders of the day that revealed more about the propaganda requirements of conducting a total war than about the facts and judgments upon which actions were based.

After Stalin's death in 1953 and, more specifically, after Khrushchev's disclosure in 1956 of Stalin's alleged wartime errors, there was a rapid increase and far-reaching qualitative improvement in Soviet writing on the war period. Military professionals and historians concentrated on preparing general histories of the war and individual monographs about key battles and campaigns. By far the most impressive result of their collective efforts was the six-volume official *History of the Great Patriotic War of the Soviet Union, 1941–1945*, which was published from 1960 to 1965.† At the same time, the general histories were supplemented by personal accounts of eyewitnesses, both officers and men, industrial managers and diplomats, war correspondents and writers. The publication of war memoir literature grew from a trickle in 1956–57 to a flood of over 150 full-length books and several hundred articles by 1967. It was as if the Soviet Union were trying at long last to match the phenomenal torrent of German, British, and American memoirs which appeared in the late 1940's and the 1950's.

°During the 1945–52 period the entire output of Soviet publications on the overall history of the Nazi-Soviet war was virtually limited to one pamphlet of 71 pages (Professor I. I. Mints, *Velikaia Otechestvennaia voina Sovetskogo Soiuza* [Moscow, 1947]) and one book (S. Golikov, *Vydaiushchiesia pobedy Sovetskoi Armii v Velikoi Otechestvennoi voine* [Moscow, 1952]). To this one should add twenty-odd books and pamphlets on individual military operations of the 1941–45 period.

†*Istoriia Velikoi Otechestvennoi voiny Sovetskogo Soiuza 1941–45* (6 vols.; Moscow: Voenizdat, 1960–65).

    I (1960):   Period prior to German invasion of June 22, 1941. 533 pp.
    II (1961):   From German invasion to start of Soviet counteroffensive at Stalingrad (June 1941–November 1942). 679 pp.
    III (1961): From start of Stalingrad counteroffensive to end of 1943. 659 pp.
    IV (1962): Offensive operations of 1944. 731 pp.
    V (1963):   Conclusion of war with German and Soviet operations against Japan in 1945. 655 pp.
    VI (1965): Summary analysis of war. 612 pp.

This collective work by more than 30 historians and military experts led by Iu. P. Petrov was supervised by an editorial committee of the Party's Institute of Marxism-Leninism headed by one of the Party's chief ideologists, P. N. Pospelov.

While the appearance and burgeoning of Soviet war memoirs in the post-Stalin period cannot be ascribed to any single factor, they are closely connected with the transformation of the Soviet order during the past fifteen years from a rigorous totalitarian regime to a less tightly integrated political system, which, while remaining highly autocratic, displays more flexibility and rationality. This relationship between the emergence of memoir literature and political change has been explicitly acknowledged by Soviet writers. In the words of one Soviet critic:

There was a time when memoirs seemed out of place in the smoothly arranged prospectus of [our] history. . . . Any complication made one watchful, the word 'contradictions' sounded almost synonymous with the word 'defects,' and from this point of view memoirs created only additional difficulties, they complicated carefully prepared schemes. We have moved far away from these times. Our conception of history has become broader. Slowly, gradually, we are freeing ourselves from preconceived judgments, from a fragmentary and selective approach, from the beautification of facts, and from shaping the facts in accordance with ready-made standards.*

Political changes in post-Stalin Russia, however, in no way alter the general Soviet approach to war history as an instrument of policy. Stalin's successors, like their late leader, have manipulated war history for political purposes, not the least of which has been the inculcation of specific attitudes in the population. Yet the Stalin and post-Stalin periods differ in three principal respects which affect both the quantity and the quality of writing on the Second World War. They differ with regard to the interpretations by their respective leaders of the system's ideological and political needs and, therefore, of the purposes for which history is used. They differ in the extent to which they are willing to ignore the harmful effects of a lack of free inquiry on the expertise, the professionalism of their managerial groups. They differ in their willingness and ability to regulate the appearance, the substance, and the form of historical writing. In all three respects, the situation in the post-Stalin period has been more conducive to historical research and to the emergence of memoir literature than it was in the preceding period.

Prior to 1953 Soviet war history served the cult of the leader. Its object was to demonstrate Stalin's infallibility and omnipotence, to illumine yet another aspect of his genius—his mastery of military art—by means of a highly schematic and simplified treatment of the war which could be widely disseminated in the controlled press. Endless repetition was intended to dull the memories of participants whose personal experi-

*V. Katanian, "On the Creation of Memoirs," *Novyi Mir*, 1964, No. 5, p. 227.

ence might contradict the official version, and destruction always threatened those who would exhibit more confidence in what they remembered than in what they read. If there was no place for history which would consider wartime errors, difficulties, and policy alternatives, there was still less need for memoirs which might diminish in some way the indivisible glory of the supreme leader. While combat adventure stories abounded, no serious accounts of operational planning or high-level decision making appeared. Since the war was regarded merely as an appendage to one man's biography, memoir writing by military commanders was rendered superfluous, not to say dangerous.*

Soon after 1953 war history came to serve the cult of the Party. The infallibility of the institution replaced that of the individual leader. Weighty considerations compelled Stalin's successors to deny the necessity and the utility of perpetuating the myth of the dead leader and the possibility of retaining the system of personal dictatorship and terror on which it was based. In part their decision reflected an agreement among themselves as well as the desire of the elite as a whole to ban terroristic methods from the areas of political struggle and bureaucratic competition in the interest of their own minimal security, so long denied them. In part it reflected the inability of Stalin's successors to find any alternative to dividing his supreme power. In part it reflected an admission that Stalin's system was hampering efficient administration and was militating against further economic advance in a country emerging from its iron age of industrialization. In part it reflected the strength of pressures to correct Stalin's abuses, pressures emanating not only from various groups within the elite and from the intelligentsia, but also from the population at large. In part, finally, it reflected the exploitation of anti-Stalinism by Khrushchev in his bid to achieve and maintain himself in power.†

The destruction of Stalin's cult placed the new leaders in the difficult

---

*The type of military war memoirs published during Stalin's lifetime is best exemplified by the reminiscences of two fighter pilots, top Soviet war aces, Colonel A. I. Pokryshkin (*The Wings of a Fighter* [Moscow; Voenizdat, 1948]) and Colonel I. N. Kozhedub (*I Serve the Motherland* [Moscow: Gosizdat, 1950]), and a tank commander, Captain G. I. Penezhko (*Notes of a Soviet Officer* [Moscow: Sovetskii Pisatel', 1949]). Typical war adventure stories, they could well have been fictional accounts for all the value of the material presented. As a matter of fact, several fictional accounts based on the writers' personal experiences which were published under Stalin provided a much more valuable insight into the Soviet conduct of war than these "authentic" stories. See, for example, Victor Nekrasov's *In the Trenches of Stalingrad* (Moscow, 1946), Alexander Beck's *The Volokolamsk Highway* (Moscow, 1944), or Beck's, Grossman's, and Simonov's essays from the front where they served as war correspondents.

†For an extensive analysis of the origins, development, and underlying causes of the anti-Stalin campaign in the Soviet Union, see Wolfgang Leonhard, *The Kremlin After Stalin* (New York: Frederick A. Praeger, 1962).

position of defending the superiority and vitality of the Soviet system while at the same time denouncing major policies of the past thirty years and, by implication, questioning the judgment of the implementors of those policies, many of whom had subsequently advanced to positions of the highest responsibility. The criticism of Stalin unleashed by Khrushchev and the confusion over the desirable limits of "de-Stalinization" substantially weakened or destroyed traditions on which popular loyalties had previously been based and at the same time exacerbated the friction between generations which already reflected the contrast between the hard childhood environment of "fathers" and the relative comfort of "sons." Stalin's successors thus faced the critical problem of substituting for the past they destroyed new positive traditions that would legitimize their rule, create a bond between the elite and the population at large, and, especially, attract the allegiance of young citizens.

The new leaders seized upon two heroic experiences in Soviet history which were deemed capable of generating powerful emotional bonds of allegiance to the Communist Party—revolution and war. A major effort was made to recall and romanticize the founding of the Soviet state and to venerate the cult of its founder, Lenin. Another was made to perpetuate the memory of war victory as the supreme achievement of the Soviet state, its leadership, and its people. To the outside observer it would appear that of the two efforts the latter would in the long run bring greater rewards. The revolution, remote in time, cannot elicit the same emotional response as the war which scarred every family alive in the Soviet Union. The revolution, moreover, divided the Russian people, while World War II united them. Indeed, two major elements regarded by Soviet leaders as essential to legitimacy may be illustrated by the war experience—the strength of the Soviet system of government and the invincibility of the nation unified, the theme of nationalism. Still further, the war experience serves to heal the breach in generations, for the patriotic self-denial of the fathers, creators of victory, warrants the respect and emulation of their sons.° To keep fresh the memories of the older generation and to make the war a part of the experience of the younger generation, veterans meet, pioneers tread their fathers' paths over old battlegrounds, former heroes retell their feats in the press—and all on a scale previously unknown.

°That Soviet editors are aware of the utility of war history for reconciling the young to their fathers can be seen in the following quotation from Marshal M. V. Zakharov's introduction to a book on the battle of Moscow: "The pages of the anthology will be read with emotion by the war veterans, the people of the older generation. But they are of special interest and instructive for young people who did not go through the harsh school of war and who strive to learn as much as possible about the heroic deeds of their fathers and grandfathers." *Proval gitlerovskogo nastupleniia na Moskvu* (Moscow: "Nauka," 1966), p. 14.

Stress on the war as the supreme achievement of the Soviet people united under Party leadership opened the way for a new kind of war history which tolerated complexity and invited reminiscence. No longer were errors, miscalculations, and shortcomings in the conduct of war totally concealed by subterfuge or silence. There was a tendency to expose them in some detail for the purpose of enhancing the achievement of the nation which overcame them and of denigrating the myth of Stalin. No longer was the ultimate victory attributed to one man. It was the glory of the nation as a whole and of the Party that led it. Writers of memoirs and historians heaped blame on Stalin where previously there had been only praise. They described the individual and collective merits of those who organized victory, of those, that is, who compose the broad strata of the Soviet elite today.

If the political needs of the post-Stalin leadership encouraged the growth of war literature, so also did the military requirements of great power status. Of the various managerial groups whose professional competence was sacrificed under Stalin to political conformity, the military establishment suffered most from the subordination of historical research on World War II to narrow propagandistic and ideological schemes. A primitiveness and stagnation of military thinking ensued which the new leaders, highly sensitive to the Soviet role in world affairs, were made gradually to recognize under the prodding of their military experts as dangerous to military preparedness. High standards of professional competence require analysis, exploration, and discussion of the main source of knowledge concerning warfare—combat experience. While available technical literature sufficed for tactical training, officers were denied the possibility of confronting larger questions of strategy in other than a schematic way for a period of almost ten years following the war. They were, for example, not permitted to analyze seriously the causes of the Soviet disaster in 1941 or the mistakes of the Soviet High Command in 1942 which led to the calamitous retreat as far as Stalingrad. In acknowledging as a valid national need the encouragement of research into war history, Soviet leaders assured not only an increase in the amount of literature but an improvement in its quality and, incidentally, in its reliability as well. There has been, in other words, "a marriage between utility and truth."°

Considerations of political need or military utility may underlie the decision of Soviet leaders to permit the appearance of war literature, but they cannot explain the scope of its subsequent development. Pressures from various groups in Soviet society, specifically from the intelligentsia and the military, reinforced one another and often succeeded in expanding the

°This is the apt expression of Matthew Gallagher in his book *The Soviet History of World War II* (New York: Frederick A. Praeger, 1963), p. x.

limits of permissible historical inquiry and memoir writing. The post-Stalin leaders were neither as willing nor as able as Stalin to control these pressures.

For the intelligentsia, the pressure to speak the truth about World War II was part of its larger struggle for a renewal of the nation's spiritual values, virtually extinguished in the Stalin period. The war was perhaps the deepest emotional experience for an entire generation of Soviet intellectuals. Some of them—the writers—sought to describe and to demand explanations for what they saw and felt. Emotions pent up for a decade of enforced silence erupted in the post-Stalin period. The most courageous presented the new leaders with a long postponed claim in the name of the Soviet people—that their suffering and sacrifice during World War II had earned them the right to a better spiritual and material life.°

The questions asked, the explanations demanded by writers acted to broaden the field of research and discussion. They stimulated and at times compelled professional historians, military men, and politicians to enter a discussion and even to confront questions which they perhaps preferred to ignore. In a situation where mass terror had been abandoned, the writers, while risking persecution, could hope to test the limits of discussion without fear of automatic martyrdom for transgressing clearly prescribed rules. Indeed, the ability of the Party to control the discussion was hampered by the inability of leaders themselves to agree on its limits and by their sensitivity to international communist opinion which condemned persecution of intellectuals. In such circumstances the Party's position vis à vis the writers oscillated irregularly between attack and retreat, victory and defeat, freeze and thaw.

Even more crucial than pressure from the intelligentsia in expanding public discussion of the war was the pressure which originated among the managers of Soviet military power. While it would be incorrect to equate the goals of military officers with those of liberal intellectuals, the interest of these two groups coincided with regard to the necessity for the discussion if not the beneficiary of the discussion.† The Soviet military establishment was striving to restore its honor and its wartime legacy of

---

°Of the most noteworthy fictional accounts of the war to appear in the Soviet Union after Stalin's death one should mention Konstantin Simonov's *Zhivye i mertvye* (1958) and *Soldatami ne rozhdaiutsia* (1964). Especially interesting among the most recent books are G. Baklanov's *Iiul' 41 goda* (1965) and V. Bykov's *Mertvym ne bol'no* serialized in the monthly *Novyi Mir* in 1966 (Nos. 1, 2).

†The incompatibility of the military and literary "revisionism" can best be seen from the fact that both during the Khrushchev years and after his ouster, senior military leaders, including the Minister of Defense, were publicly denouncing the liberal writers for their alleged lack of balance in describing the war.

popularity. During Stalin's lifetime it had been forced to tolerate an unprecedented slander of its tradition. It had to accept from the time of the Great Purge the intolerable accusation of treason and sabotage leveled against the highest commanders and a large part of the officer corps. It had to remain silent about the terrible disasters of 1941 and 1942 which Stalin encouraged the Soviet public to associate with the stupidity, conservatism, and incompetence of the military. It had to consent to attribute the entire credit for the greatest military victory in Russian history to one man.

Military men possessed more formidable weapons in the quest for their goal than did the intellectuals. Their control of the armed forces assured them a hearing from Party leaders so long as their demands did not challenge the preeminence of the Party in the Soviet state. And when Party leaders acquiesced to their demand for a broad discussion of wartime experience, the military establishment disposed of a powerful organization of mass communications media through which to conduct it. One vehicle which was well suited to the military's purpose was the war memoir. Military men turned to it eagerly in order not only to rehabilitate the traditions of the group as a whole but also to serve private aims—to popularize their own individual exploits and to settle old scores.

The Utility of Soviet War Literature

While the Western reader can welcome the proliferation of what appears to be a singular source for the study of Soviet war history, he cannot but question the reliability of this material in view of the political uses to which war history is put in the USSR. The Soviet writer is plagued both by hazards common to memoirists of all nationalities and by those peculiar to Soviet conditions. As to the former, all personal accounts of historic events, while they often surpass the most painstaking scholarly research in their ability to convey atmosphere and detail, to describe at first hand the motives and thoughts of participants, suffer, despite their authors' most scrupulous search for objectivity, from the vagaries of human memory, the intrusion of private prejudices, and the inability to distinguish carefully between what happened at the moment, how the participants behaved and why, and evaluations guided by additional information and later reflection. Soviet generals, no less than their German and other counterparts, succumb to the temptation to embellish, conceal, justify, and invent their roles in historical events. Were one to trust the protestations of Soviet military authors, for example, one would conclude that they all had premonitions about the imminence of war,

they all were dissatisfied with the state of Soviet military preparedness, they all attempted to rectify the situation prior to the Nazi invasion—all, that is, except Stalin and those who have not composed their memoirs.

While many Soviet writers boast of their objective reconstruction of wartime episodes, others—like Marshal Meretskov, for example—take cognizance of the pitfalls of memoir writing. Comparing the memoir writer to a witness in court who is obliged to tell the truth, Marshal Meretskov explored the difficulties of telling the truth about remote events, of describing any given event with accurate perspective, chronology, and shading. In the last analysis, he concluded, the truthfulness of an account can only be verified by written and oral evidence. "There are documents, and they will grip the boaster by the arm. There are archives preserving these documents, and falsehood cannot stand against them. Lastly, there are eyewitnesses to what you have described."° No Western historian would quarrel with this conclusion. He would only maintain that it is just the absence of suitable counterweights that prejudices the reliability of Soviet memoirs to a greater extent than that of their Western counterparts.

The documents that "grip the boaster by the arm" lie out of reach in Soviet archives. More than three-fourths of the original documents relating to World War II published in the principal Soviet journal of military history from its inception in 1958 are either captured German documents or reprints from British and American sources. As for eyewitnesses who could verify memoir accounts, their freedom to dispute the printed accounts depends upon the political situation. Falsehood will stand in the Soviet Union so long as this suits the Party leadership which controls the archives, the publishing houses, the careers of writers and their personal safety.

Distortion can, of course, assume many forms—from patent falsehood to silence. Even the most casual reader of Soviet war memoirs will detect distortion which can be traced either to the general hazards of memoir writing or, more noticeably, to ideological or political demands made upon the author that he respects unconsciously, voluntarily, or under duress. There are two principal types of bias in Soviet war literature with which the reader of Western war histories will be unfamiliar. The first derives from the explicit character and monopolistic role of ideology in the Soviet system. The second derives from the dictates of a changing internal and international situation, from changing policies and politics of the Soviet government.

The first type of bias imposes a highly standardized approach to

---

°K. A. Meretskov, "Dorogami srazhenii," *Voprosy istorii,* 1965, No. 10, pp. 107–108.

important general questions concerning the war, an approach which reflects the Soviet communist world view, the basic outlook of the ruling Communist Party. Without variation, Soviet memoir writers and war historians adhere to certain dogmas which are highly resistant to the transformation of Soviet policies, methods, and goals and scarcely influenced by historical research. Soviet writers, for example, derive the policies of all "capitalist" governments from the interests of the "exploiting classes" which these governments allegedly represent. They will not differentiate decisively between the systems of government of the Axis and the Western Allies; the "just" character of the war against Nazi Germany will commence with the entrance of the USSR, prior to which the war will be regarded as "imperialist," at least on the part of the governments concerned. Furthermore, Soviet writers insist that their victory derived from the superiority of the Soviet "socialist" system over that of other belligerents, enemies and allies alike; that their method of mobilizing resources for war and the morale of their soldiers were superior to their "capitalist" counterparts because they were "socialist." Soviet memoir writers uniformly practice distortion deriving from ideological dogmas, and from this point of view their works are virtually indistinguishable.

The second type of distortion adjusts the historical past to conform with present policies. Whereas the first type of distortion exhibits a certain stability and constancy and thus is often predictable, the second type displays a wide range of flexibility and durability, from those distortions which may survive major changes in leadership and policy to those which appear to shift constantly and thus appear chaotic and often contradictory. Regardless of their duration, however, these distortions are clearly related to current policies and politics in a system which demands that all social endeavor serve a political function.

Among those distortions which have survived changes in leadership are those that adjust the past to spare the present leadership embarrassment. The Nazi-Soviet Nonaggression Pact of 1939 is a case in point. Not once has any Soviet memoir writer (or professional historian) admitted the existence of the secret protocol of August 27, 1939, which decided the fate of Poland and delineated spheres of German and Soviet interest in Eastern Europe prior to the outbreak of World War II. One Soviet writer astonishes the reader with his patently false statement that the Nazi-Soviet Pact was concluded *after* the war started and *after* Poland had been defeated.[°]

°A. S. Iakovlev, one of the highest executives of the Soviet aircraft industry, writes: "As is known, the negotiations [between England, France, and Russia in August 1939] were unsuccessful. The representatives of the English and French governments were not striving for success—they wanted above anything else to sound out the Soviet side. . . .

Still another topic which invites distortion in Soviet memoirs over a sustained period concerns the character and extent of the Allied contribution to end the war with Germany. The Lend-Lease program is seldom acknowledged or credited with serious aid to the Soviet Union; more often it is dealt with derisively, as when American tinned meat is called "the second front," or it is dismissed explicitly as unimportant. Similarly, not only are the contributions of the United States and Great Britain to Hitler's defeat seldom detailed, but Soviet writers seem to feel that an adequate picture of Russia's enormous contribution cannot be secured unless Allied efforts are debunked and Allied motives impugned. Indeed, from a reading of Soviet war memoirs it would appear that the West European or African theater of operations existed solely as the German High Command's source of reserves for the Eastern Front.

Particularly susceptible to more frequent change in the memoir literature is the treatment of military and political leaders whose current standing in the Soviet hierarchy determines their past performance in wartime. The metamorphosis of Marshal Zhukov's place in war history is the most striking case in point. The Marshal did not simply fall into disfavor and disappear in the postwar period. He did so a number of times—from 1946 to 1952 and again from 1957 to 1964. During one period of eclipse (1964) a book edited by his wartime chief of staff, Marshal Sokolovskii, appeared. It concerned the battle of Moscow during which Zhukov served as commander in chief of the capital's defense. Zhukov's name was mentioned in a perfunctory manner a mere four times on 428 pages, while the name of General Belov, commander of a horse cavalry corps, warranted 45 mentions and General Guderian, commander of the key German tank group at Moscow, warranted 22 mentions.† Two years later, in 1966, a book was published on the occasion of the twenty-fifth anniversary of the battle. Marshal Zhukov, his star again shining, not only figured prominently but wrote one of the principal contributions.‡

Today it is already known that the English government had simultaneously conducted secret negotiations with Hitler offering him a pact of nonaggression and an agreement on the division of spheres of influence. The English government of that period, kowtowing to Hitler, offered him no more and no less than the partition of the territory of China[!] and the Soviet Union. . . . The lessons of the war between Germany and the West European countries had confirmed the correctness of the political line of the Soviet government which tried to delay its inevitable clash with Germany. Immediately after the defeat of Poland the Minister of Foreign Affairs of Nazi Germany, Ribbentrop, flew to Moscow. He came with a proposal to conclude a pact of nonaggression between the Soviet Union and Germany. The Soviet Government, having exhausted all possibilities in the fruitless negotiations with France and England about common action against the aggressor, was forced to accept the German offer." (*Tsel' zhizni* [Moscow, Politizdat, 1966], pp. 207–208.)

†*Razgrom nemetsko-fashistskikh voisk pod Moskvoi* (Moscow, Voenizdat, 1964).

‡*Bitva za Moskvu* (Moscow, "Moskovskii rabochii," 1966).

All the frustrations confronting the would-be writer of military history in the Soviet Union can be conveniently illustrated by one example. In 1961 Marshal Eremenko, commander of an Army Group during the battle of Stalingrad, published a bulky memoir in the course of which he described the organization of a Soviet counterblow that was to be carried out by the 2nd Guards Army in order to prevent the armies of German Field Marshal von Manstein from freeing the encircled armies of Field Marshal von Paulus. The original plan for the counterblow prepared by the Chief of the General Staff, Marshal Vasilevskii, who supervised the operation, was deemed by the author unsuitable and was criticized. In Eremenko's words:

> One should note that Comrade Vasilevskii has taken the criticism as befits a communist and right then and there requested that I explain my own plan. I gave a succinct report on the essence of my idea. . . . "All right then"—Comrade Vasilevskii said after hearing me out—"You are the Army Group Commander, and you should decide as you see fit."*

Eremenko leaves no doubt that the successful counterblow was carried out according to his plan.

For five years this version of the operation went unchallenged. Marshal Vasilevskii, known to be alive, did not break the silence of his involuntary retirement. In 1966, however, he published a blistering denunciation of Eremenko's version or rather "the unjust and unfounded insinuations invented for who knows what reason."† In a footnote Vasilevskii informs his readers that he thought it necessary to seek corroboration for his own version from the commander of the 2nd Guards Army, then Minister of Defense, Marshal Malinovskii. Malinovskii is quoted as saying, "I was very amazed by [Eremenko's] incorrect explanation of events, but owing to the fact I was busy, I have been unable to refute it in writing. . . ." Throughout those "busy" five years Malinovskii held the post of Minister of Defense.

An observer of the Soviet scene cannot, of course, accept Marshal Malinovskii's plea of business to explain five years of silence. The whole matter becomes more clear with the addition of an important detail in Eremenko's account. Eremenko wisely shared his distinction as author of the counterblow plan with his political commissar, no other than N. S. Khrushchev.

> I was vigorously supported [in the critique of Vasilevskii's plan] by Nikita Sergeevich. . . . N. S. Khrushchev's support played a decisive role in the adoption of my plan. Comrade Khrushchev, evaluating the operational situation with

*A. I. Eremenko, *Stalingrad* (Moscow, Voenizdat, 1961), p. 414.

†A. Vasilevskii, "Nezabyvaemye dni," *Voenno-istoricheskii zhurnal*, 1966, No. 3, p. 36.

speed and precision, arrived at the decision which most correctly corresponded to conditions of the moment, and he defended it with a Party-like principle-mindedness and straightforwardness. This is how very often Nikita Sergeevich decisively and unhesitatingly cast aside anything that did not help our cause and supported that which contributed to rapid movement toward our goal.*

Not until Eremenko's patron was overthrown could Marshals Vasilevskii and Malinovskii speak up.

One could easily lengthen the list of dogmas, taboos, biases, and deletions that prejudice the reliability of Soviet war memoirs. Yet certain factors mitigate the dangers of distortion for the cautious Western reader. Party policy tends to distinguish between "neutral" and "non-neutral" areas of war history. Once removed from non-neutral considerations of grand policy and strategy, the memoir writer is less inhibited in his expression of remembered events. Consideration of technical and tactical questions is not closely regulated, and to an increasing extent major operational decisions are escaping the homogenous treatment imposed by Party directive, and, indeed, the entire neutral area would appear to be expanding gradually if haltingly.

Moreover, in the so-called non-neutral areas one has the impression that Party directives prohibit rather than instruct. The memoir writer is pressured by the Party less to commit deliberate falsehood than to remain silent. From a long and thorough reading of memoir literature it would appear that silence or, more precisely, selectivity accounts for the largest percentage of distortion in the memoir literature. If this impression is valid, individual episodes may be taken as factually correct, while the larger context of these episodes may be distorted. It would appear also that submission to Party sensitivities affects less the basic facts than the derogatory, ironic, or positive descriptions and emotive meanings attached to them.

Of course, memoirs can never replace authentic documents concerning the adoption and implementation of decisions by Soviet leaders during World War II. As long as such documents are not published, there will be no history of the Nazi-Soviet war comparable to the histories of other theaters of operation despite almost 5,000 books and articles on the war which have appeared so far in the USSR.† In this situation war memoirs are one of the most important primary sources for exploring the Soviet side of the bitter struggle. Once the reader takes into account the weaknesses of this form of Soviet literature he is more able to extract a considerable body of factual information and insight

* A. I. Eremenko, *loc. cit.*
† *Voenno-istoricheskii Zhurnal*, 1966, No. 5, pp. 4–5.

into the Soviet system and the thought of military professionals and political leaders.° (And not the least of their additions to our body of knowledge about the Soviet Union is the inadvertent material offered by men who try carefully to tread the prescribed political path.)

In the fifteen years since Stalin's death Party prescriptions have changed; the limitations and exaggerations of memoir literature from one period have often been "corrected," counterbalanced, or at least supplemented by the limitations and exaggerations of another; the whole becomes more than a mere sum of its individual parts. The "layers" of information thus provided over periods of intense political change since 1953 provide a possibility for a more complete and reliable judgment than could hitherto be made on the basis of Soviet sources concerning the question central to this anthology, the theme of Soviet war leadership and, particularly, the role of Stalin as Supreme Commander in Chief.

Stalin's Fate Under Khrushchev and After

The very phrase "post Stalin period" to describe the years from 1953 to the present indicates how central is the issue of Stalin in Soviet politics. Eight years after his death, for example, the announcement that his body would be removed from its place beside Lenin in the Mausoleum on Red Square could overshadow virtually all other transactions at the XXII Party Congress, and Khrushchev, the most powerful of Stalin's successors to date, would be remembered more for his denunciation of Stalin and his system than for any coherent formulation of a positive alternative to it.

If the issue of Stalin can be seen as a major orientation point around which social and political development takes place in the Soviet Union, the issue of Stalin's war role assumes major importance both because it became so central to the mythology which grew around Stalin's name and because attempts to utilize the war experience to help legitimize the new regime forces a confrontation with the undeniable fact of Stalin's enormous significance during it. Indeed, Stalin's merit as a victorious war leader was perhaps the most readily acceptable part of the propagation of his cult, even to those who had grave misgivings about the Stalinist system. Thus it is not surprising that Stalin's war role occupied so significant a place in the first dramatic official attack on Stalin personally and through him on the major abuses of the system he was seen to personify.

°Of the translated memoirs the most notable are Il'ia Ehrenburg, *The War 1941-45,* Vol. V of *Men, Years—Life* (London: MacGibbon & Kee, 1964), A. V. Gorbatov, *Years Off My Life* (New York: W. W. Norton & Co., Inc., 1965), and V. I. Chuikov, *The Battle for Stalingrad* (New York: Holt, Rinehart and Winston, 1964).

Khrushchev built the framework for subsequent discussion of Stalin's war leadership in his so-called Secret Speech to the XX Party Congress in 1956. Tnere he recalled for the delegates—military men and civilians alike—the tedium and ignominium they had witnessed for almost a decade following the end of World War II, as their leader appropriated all wartime glory and enforced the uniform view that "all victories gained by the Soviet nation during the Great Patriotic War were due to the courage, daring, and genius of Stalin and no one else."° Few in Khrushchev's audience had not been subjected to the relentless line disseminated prior to 1953 that credited Stalin with unique responsibility for victory; few had not been told, contrary to their own direct experience, that Stalin had not only grasped the conditions favorable for victory but had created them, implying that the disastrous rout and defeats of 1941 and 1942, referred to during Stalin's lifetime as "active defense," were nothing other than a well-calculated aspect of an omniscient leader's plan to ensnare and destroy the Germans at Stalingrad. In the magnification of Stalin's image during his lifetime, the phrase *"s initsiativy Stalina"*—"thanks to Stalin's initiative"—had come to precede every account of every skirmish which entered the published war histories and had been extended into all areas of Soviet life until no event was too humble to merit this ritualistic blessing.

To attack this massive creation of an undeniably formidable leader was Khrushchev's aim in 1956, an aim which reflected a desire to undermine the authority for Stalin's myth and his system of terror and at the same time a desire to manipulate this crucial issue as a weapon in a personal struggle to secure power. The singlemindedness with which Khrushchev concentrated on his goal and the specific traits of his personality led him to seek not comprehension, not rectification, but destruction of Stalin's role as war leader, both in its actual and its mythological aspects. "We have to analyze this matter [of Stalin's war leadership] carefully [Khrushchev said] because it has a tremendous significance not only from the historical point of view, but especially from the political, educational, and practical points of view." Khrushchev's attack focused on a number of aspects of this war leadership which formed with periodic shifts in emphasis, in intensity, and embellishment—depending on Khrushchev's political needs—the basic content of the discussion from 1956 to 1964.

Khrushchev criticized Stalin for empty boasting about Russia's ability to fight a war, for gross failure to heed clear warnings of Nazi hostility in word and deed long before and immediately on the eve of the inva-

---

° *The Crimes of the Stalin Era. Special Report to the 20th Congress of the Communist Party of the Soviet Union by Nikita S. Khrushchev.* Supplement to *The New Leader,* 1956, p. 3.

sion. He accused Stalin of grossly mismanaging the time and resources available for the mobilization and adequate supply of Soviet armed forces, of failing to modernize outdated military equipment, particularly tanks, artillery, and planes, of neglecting border defenses in a misguided effort to avoid "provocations." He decried the disastrous annihilation of military cadres during the purge period 1937–41. He alleged that with the outbreak of war Stalin did not direct Soviet military operations and "ceased to do anything whatever." He stressed Stalin's nervousness and even hysteria which was said to vitiate the responsible efforts of military commanders to stem the force of the initial disaster. He challenged Stalin's qualifications as strategist and tactician, accusing him of gross blunders which sacrificed innumerable lives and demonstrated rank ignorance of elementary principles of military art, as for example at the time of the Khar'kov operation in 1942. How could Stalin understand the situation at the front, Khrushchev continued, when during the entire course of the war, he visited it but once, and then "for one short ride on the Mozhaisk highway during a stabilized situation at the front"? Khrushchev criticized Stalin for denigrating his military commanders after the victory, particularly Marshal Zhukov, for minimizing if not denying altogether the contributions to the great victory over Nazi Germany of military commanders, the Politburo, the government, and the nation as a whole. In place of uniform praise for all successes, Khrushchev substituted uniform blame for all shortcomings. Victory now belonged to the collective efforts of Party, government, military, and people.

Less than a year followed Khrushchev's ouster in October 1964 before signs of change in the official attitude toward Stalin began to appear. By 1966 these signs added up to a definite departure from Khrushchev's policy of public attack on Stalin and a marked change in official assessment of the dictator's person and his significance. To cite a few examples— Brezhnev publicly acknowledged Stalin's wartime chairmanship of the State Defense Committee for the first time in many years, a reference which, incidentally, an audience of Party activists greeted with demonstrative applause; the publication of literature concerning concentration camps ceased and its most renowned practitioner, Aleksandr Solzhenitsyn, fell under sustained attack; the formula "victims of the cult of the personality of Stalin" which had hitherto explained the deaths of rehabilitated purge victims now disappeared, although biographical articles about military leaders rehabilitated by Khrushchev still appeared on anniversaries of their birth and death and new rehabilitations took place.°

°For an account of the political line of the post-Khrushchev leadership see Leonard Schapiro, "The Twenty-Third CPSU Congress," *Survey*, No. 60, July 1966, pp. 72–84, and Robert Conquest, "Immobilism and Decay," *Problems of Communism*, Vol. 15, No. 5, Sept.–Oct., 1966, pp. 35–37.

What characterizes the general attitude toward Stalin can be discerned also in references to Stalin's war leadership published since 1964. Descriptions of the terror employed by Stalin before and during the war have been drastically reduced. The derogatory tone, the invective, the repetition of phrases from Khrushchev's anti-Stalin speeches have largely disappeared. Details of the wartime activities of the Soviet High Command, including Stalin, have expanded substantially. The discussion of war strategy, the evaluation of campaigns and battles occupy even more space in the literature and provide more material for considering Stalin's significance as a war leader. Stalin himself could be treated with relative matter-of-factness instead of unrelieved disparagement.

The demonstrable reduction in published attacks and public utterances against Stalin fostered among observers within and without the Soviet Union the fear that the new Soviet leaders were effecting a gradual rehabilitation of Stalin and perhaps even a "restalinization" of the Soviet system. While such danger cannot be minimized or discounted, it would appear that it has been exaggerated, that the evidence does not support such a conclusion at least with regard to historical research. What is taking place in the writing of Soviet history and, in particular, Soviet war history can be described more appropriately as an end to the anti-Stalin campaign rather than the beginning of a new campaign to rehabilitate Stalin, although elements of the latter do in fact exist. Had Stalin's rehabilitation been the intention of the new leaders, the post-Khrushchev war literature would have been characterized by a different kind of change in factual content and tone than that which actually occurred. Second editions of earlier works critical of Stalin would not have been reprinted or would have appeared only after careful excisions.° Indictments of Stalin's behavior would not have continued to appear and, indeed, been expanded as is the case in the new memoirs of Bagramian, Iakovlev, and Emelianov.† This distinction between decline of official anti-Stalinism and inauguration of officially sponsored rehabilitation is no idle play of words but a crucial indication of the policies of Khrushchev's successors.

The abandonment of strident anti-Stalinism is one consequence of the key policy choice of present Soviet leaders—to seek political stability, to avoid "rocking the boat." After 1953 all Stalin's successors located the

°The most noteworthy recent second editions of memoirs which had originally appeared before Khrushchev's ouster are S. S. Biriuzov, *Surovye gody* (Moscow, "Nauka," 1966), which incorporates two earlier books (*Kogda gremeli pushki* [Moscow, Voenizdat, 1961] and *Sovetskii soldat na balkanakh* [Moscow, Voenizdat, 1963], and P. I. Batov, *V pokhodakh i boiakh* (Moscow, Voenizdat, 1966; 1st ed. 1962). While derogatory remarks about Zhukov were excised or weakened, the critical remarks about Stalin remained almost unchanged, although the language in a few places was somewhat tempered.

†See below, pp. 384–401, 86–8, 166–71, 104–114.

major long-range danger to the regime in the stagnation resulting from politically redundant and economically counter-productive policies and methods of rule and recognized that terror could no longer substitute for rational control over administrators. After 1964 they saw the danger in the organizational, political, and ideological flux associated with the name of Khrushchev. The present leaders in the Soviet Union ousted Khrushchev because they objected to his political ambitions, his international failures, and his personal style, but first and foremost his perpetual tinkering with the administrative structure and his unsuccessful efforts to reverse the deterioration of economic performance. In place of Khrushchev's erratic, exaggerated, and largely disappointing policies the new leaders sought a less ambitious, more moderate approach to achieving political stability and renewed economic advance.°

With regard to the writing of war history, political pressure to elimi-nate the disruptive effects of Khrushchev's anti-Stalin campaign acted to reduce truthfulness insofar as the terroristic aspects of Stalin's leadership were no longer discussed. If this were the only pressure affecting the current output of war literature, one would have to speak of a regression from the time of Khrushchev. Another pressure, however, emanating from the military, acts conversely to correct those imbalances in the depiction of war events which resulted from the purpose, style, and character of Khrushchev's anti-Stalin campaign. Both the political and military pres-sures for change in the writing of war history were reactions to Khru-shchev—the former a reaction to the political results of his campaign, the latter a reaction to by-products of the campaign which were considered offensive to military traditions and achievements.

While the military establishment generally supported Khrushchev's efforts to revise war history, it could not accept certain important ele-ments of the revision. First, while exposing Stalin's errors and crimes, Khrushchev at the same time attempted to erase Stalin's wartime achieve-ments altogether. He found himself denying Stalin's responsibility for victory at the same time as he insisted that Stalin did after all make the decisions; he found himself attributing the victory to the Party's leader-ship of the nation at the same time as he admitted that the Party leaders around Stalin were not consulted or heeded.† While military leaders

---

°It seems that the centrism of the post-Khrushchev Soviet leadership, their one step forward–one step backward policy, should be seen also as a result of the lack of a strong leader or a stable majority within the collective leadership, which makes a con-sensus possible only in the case of halfway measures.

†The inherent contradiction in Khrushchev's position led sometimes to such amusing results as asserting on one and the same page of the official war history that the Central Committee of the Party led the Soviet war effort and that during the whole war only

were interested in sharing Stalin's glory, they were not necessarily desirous of obliterating it. Many military men had a genuine allegiance to their wartime Commander in Chief, and others realized that to destroy ex post facto the authority of the leader made their loyal obedience to his orders throughout the war look unflattering to say the least.

Secondly, in Khrushchev's effort to elevate the wartime glory of the Party, he expounded the superiority of the Party over the professional military establishment in the broadest possible terms, which even asserted the fact and desirability of Party intervention in the formation of military doctrine and strategy. Military writers would on the one hand contest the right and the capacity of the Party to intrude in this area and on the other hand deny that wartime strategy and doctrine had ultimately been the creation of the Party and not the military.°

Thirdly, Khrushchev attempted to weaken Stalin's authority by elevating the significance of the wartime leadership of field commanders at the Army Group level as compared to that of Supreme Headquarters and the General Staff, Stalin's closest associates. It was, of course, easier to prove the contribution of the Party elite on the field level rather than at the center. No less important, perhaps, Khrushchev himself served during the war in the field, not at the center. This line of argument was repugnant not only to military officers who served at Supreme Headquarters or the General Staff during the war but also to those wartime field commanders presently serving at the center whose interest now calls for enhancing the past and present prestige of the professional brain of the army in Moscow.†

If anything, the efforts of military writers to correct the picture of Stalin's wartime leadership presented by Khrushchev to a large extent corroborate the factual truthfulness of this picture. While these writers have at times irately attacked Khrushchev for his exaggerations—for example, they refuse to accept Khrushchev's avowal that Stalin planned operations on a globe—they attack Khrushchev's one-sidedness, his lack of perspective rather than his factual evidence of Stalin's mismanagement,

one meeting of the Central Committee took place (in 1944) and even that meeting was not concerned with the conduct of the war.

°For an analysis see Raymond Garthoff, *Soviet Military Policy, A Historical Analysis* (New York: Frederick A. Praeger, 1966) and Thomas W. Wolfe, *Soviet Strategy at the Crossroads* (Cambridge, Mass.: Harvard University Press, 1964).

†One of the most astute observers of the Soviet military scene, John Erickson, makes the following observation: "After the death of Stalin, the Soviet Army, in pressing for the 'rehabilitation' of its murdered generals and for a reappraisal of wartime history, had sought to salvage its honor; since the fall of Khrushchev, it has worked to rescue its professional reputation." (John Erickson, "Russians on Soviet Strategy," *Problems of Communism*, July–August 1966, p. 59.)

miscalculation, and wilfulness. Often their descriptions of wartime events reinforce and amplify those of Khrushchev, even though the use of the same facts may lead to different interpretations of their significance.

The fact that the treatment of Stalin goes well beyond questions of historical truth and in many cases serves to signal intentions or preferences concerning present policies or as a unifying symbol for political pressures does not contradict the contention that an evolution has taken place in the post-Khrushchev period toward a more accurate description of the Second World War. Soviet war histories, both scholarly and popular, despite their political uses and, indeed, because of their political uses, are today in the majority of cases the most objective accounts of the war which have been written since 1945, with the explicit reservation for some aspects of Stalin's policy which were treated with greater candor and honesty under Khrushchev, in particular, the Great Purge. Indeed, one may argue that the sum total of writings in the Khrushchev period together with their correctives and amplifications in the post-Khrushchev period afford the fullest opportunity yet available in the Soviet Union to form a balanced judgment on the nature of Soviet wartime leadership and, particularly, on the role of Stalin as Supreme Commander in Chief.

Stalin As War Leader

From the years of World War II until Stalin's death the Soviet dictator was most often portrayed in a simple military tunic, adorned only with the gold star of a Hero of the Soviet Union, his country's most coveted military decoration. Stalin's role in World War II more than any other single aspect of his long leadership gave him the authority which together with the system of terror permitted him to dominate the minds and lives of his people as perhaps no other leader in the twentieth century.

Soviet war memoirs testify to Stalin's complete control over the political, industrial, and military aspects of the Soviet war effort. Not content to exercise merely formal control, the Soviet dictator personally made every wartime decision of any importance. He alone seems to have possessed the power to impose his will on both civilian and military associates alike. From all accounts Stalin's domination over his civilian associates was complete. Changes in administrative nomenclature during the war in no way altered the prewar distribution of authority between the leader and his closest associates in the Politburo whose pattern of docile response to and anticipation of Stalin's wishes had already been clearly established from the time of the Great Purge. The accounts of the People's Commissar of the Navy Kuznetsov, of Academician Emelianov, of Deputy People's Commissar of the Aviation Industry Iakovlev, and others show that Stalin seldom conducted their business without the presence of Politburo members, yet his queries—"Well, Comrades, shall we decide the issue?" and "What will be our decision, Comrades?"— were purely rhetorical and ritualistic. Stalin's wartime relations with military professionals, however, were bound to be more complex since military advisers were more indispensable to him at this time than civilian advisers. It is in the matter of Stalin's associations with military commanders that the war memoirs have the most to offer the reader, for, while continually underlining the total character of his control, they illuminate the particular areas of his interest and talent, the extent and nature of his participation in decision-making, and the manner in which he exercised his unique authority.

The two principal levels of military leadership where Stalin's strength impressed and surprised Western military men, diplomats, and journalists concerned grand strategy and tactical detail. With regard to the former it appeared to them that Stalin had an extraordinary grasp of war goals and major long-range plans for conducting the war and a talent for adjusting the conduct of military operations to political realities.* While Stalin's judgment proved erroneous in a number of instances, it nevertheless evoked the admiration of his Allied partners, who may have been led by the unexpectedness and the extent of his success to exaggerate his skill in attaining it.

On the second level, that of tactical and technical expertise, Western observers were struck by Stalin's mastery of detail, his attention to the purely professional aspects of waging war. Their descriptions are corroborated in the memoirs of Soviet commanders and industrial managers. Accounts of Kremlin meetings before and during the war reveal Stalin's constitutional inability to distinguish between primary and tertiary military matters. Considerable time was devoted to discussing details of

*One may mention for example Churchill's impression from talking to Stalin in August 1942 when the Soviet leader was presented the Anglo-American plan "Torch"—the invasion of North Africa:

"At this point Stalin seemed suddenly to grasp the strategic advantages of 'Torch.' He recounted four main reasons for it: first, it would hit Rommel in the back; second, it would overawe Spain; third, it would produce fighting between Germans and Frenchmen in France; and fourth, it would expose Italy to the whole brunt of the war.

"I was deeply impressed with this remarkable statement. It showed the Russian Dictator's swift and complete mastery of a problem hitherto novel to him. Very few people alive could have comprehended in so few minutes the reasons which we had all so long been wrestling with for months. He saw it all in a flash."

(Winston S. Churchill, *The Second World War, Vol. IV: The Hinge of Fate* [London: Cassell and Co., Ltd.; Boston: Houghton Mifflin Co.], p. 434.)

arms production, to questioning and instructing field commanders in details of combat tactics. Stalin demanded very detailed information from
his subordinates about the situation at the front and throughout the country. He zealously exercised his prerogative to approve every plan of action
in its smallest particulars; he frequently interfered in the actual conduct
of combat operations to insist on changing petty details or to challenge a
field commander who under pressure of circumstances departed from the
approved plan and timetable of action. In a word, Stalin appropriated the
responsibilities that another leader would have delegated to his Chief of
Staff, his Chief of Supply, his Chief of Personnel, and even his Chief
Clerk. While technical knowledge was indispensable to Stalin if his decisions were to be anything but random selection from existing alternatives,
it would appear that personality needs rather than military exigencies
were best served by his fascination with detail.

The task of military leadership is located to an overwhelming extent,
however, at a level between the comprehension of generalized outlines
required by grand strategy and the grasp of technical detail, in the area
of operational leadership which involves planning and control of large-
scale military operations—battles and campaigns. In this middle area, the
quintessence of military leadership, the war memoirs convincingly demonstrate that Stalin made no real contribution. When he did participate he
made major errors, and for the most part he left operational planning to
his marshals. Stalin's crucial contribution to victory did not derive from
his ability to perform as a military leader, especially in the operational
area, but rather from his ability to organize and administer the mobilization of manpower and material resources. Even when he dealt directly
with military operations, he did so more as an administrator, an organizer,
than as an initiator or planner of military action.

Stalin, it would appear from the memoirs, regarded his role as that
of arbiter and ultimate judge of his generals' strategic plans and operational designs. His major asset as a military leader was the ability to select
talented commanders and to permit them to plan operations, while reserv-
ing for himself the ultimate power of decision. It would appear that Stalin
often withheld his own views in discussion until most of his military advisers had spoken, perhaps the one sure way of eliciting their honest
evaluations of given situations. If Stalin's leadership improved over the
course of the war—and it did considerably—it did so not so much because
he was more willing to listen but because the quality of the group to
which he listened improved. The improvement of Stalin's leadership was
in large part a function of the improvement in the quality and operational
skill of the Soviet military professionals themselves.°

Khrushchev recognized Stalin's vulnerability in the crucial operational area and attempted to discredit the late dictator's entire war leadership by demonstrating the weakness of one of its parts. His protracted attack in the Secret Speech, echoed in the military memoirs, centered on three key strategic or operational blunders: the fatal delay in permitting the Kiev group in late summer and early fall 1941 to withdraw and thereby avoid encirclement and annihilation; the dispersal of the Soviet offensive capacity after the successful counteroffensive at Moscow in winter 1942; and the erroneous prediction of the major direction of the German summer offensive in 1942 together with an overly optimistic assessment of the relation of forces on the Nazi-Soviet front. Of course ultimate responsibility rests with ultimate power of decision, but the memoirs clearly indicate that Stalin's fault is shared in each case by some of his highest professional military advisers—in the first case, as Marshal Bagramian writes, by the Chief of the General Staff, Marshal Shaposhnikov; in the second case, as Marshal Zhukov writes, by a member of the High Command, Marshal Timoshenko; in the third case, as Marshal Vasilevskii admits. by the entire Soviet High Command.†

The memoirs criticize other decisions of Stalin which belong properly to the category of tactical errors, localized in importance, some of which Stalin shared with his military experts but most of which were his alone.

---

*Soviet memoirs which testify to Stalin's fallibility in the operational area and to his reliance on professional military judgment patently contradict the most well known Western assessment of Stalin's wartime leadership, that of Isaac Deutscher in his biography of the Soviet dictator (*Stalin, A Political Biography* [New York: Vintage Books, 1960]). Scant Soviet documentation or eyewitness reports on the wartime High Command were available to Deutscher when he stressed Stalin's operational skill, and were it not for Deutscher's insistence on this view in the foreword to the expanded second edition in 1966, even after acquainting himself with the new literature, one would refrain from disputing him here. Where Deutscher sees in the first months of war a coherent strategy on Stalin's part to "make the best of a disastrous situation, to gather new forces, to avoid decisive battles, to extricate his forces from successive encirclements, to wait for the moment when Hitler's armies had overreached themselves, and then to strike back at their overextended flanks and lines of communication" (p. 472), the Soviet generals point to Stalin's direct contribution to the disastrous situation and particularly to the catastrophic encirclement of his troops in the Ukraine. Where Deutscher locates the source of Stalin's military mistakes in an "excess of caution and prudence" and attributes the Soviet victory at Moscow to Stalin's "quick eye for that lack of prudence in the Fuehrer" (*ibid.*) on which his own plan of action was based, the Soviet generals (particularly Marshal Zhukov) record Stalin's continuous and stubborn underestimation of German capabilities, his lack of caution and prudence up to the very start of the battle when, as all Soviet accounts agree, the German offensive caught him by surprise and was not even accepted by him as fact for a number of days. Soviet generals bear witness to little of what Deutscher calls Stalin's "primitive, oriental, but unfailing shrewdness."

†See below, pp. 402–5.

Still other decisions, the result of petty, capricious intrusions into the direction of combat operations by field commanders or personal emissaries, can be blamed on him alone, as, for example, when at the height of the battle for Moscow, he ordered the commander in chief, Marshal Zhukov, to organize personally the recapture of a small village.

While Soviet generals aired their alleged wartime misgivings about Stalin's judgment and behavior in military matters, they never enthusiastically pursued Khrushchev's image of an almost unified military leadership opposed to the errors of their wartime commander in chief, on the model of their German counterparts who wished to dissociate themselves from Hitler's guilt. How could they, indeed? The memoirs clearly show that many of them regarded their leader with genuine respect, admiration, or awe—sentiments which sometimes were expressed even in memoirs written during the height of the anti-Stalin campaign°—while none of them ever dared to engage in vociferous, protracted, or active opposition. One can assume that Soviet generals would not have hesitated to record such behavior during the anti-Stalin campaign.

Clearly the Soviet generals feared Stalin more than they feared the Germans. No more stunning proof can be found than the conduct of commanders on the eve of the Kiev debacle in 1941. As the situation of the encircled Soviet armies deteriorated hourly, the command of the Southwestern Army Group addressed one feeble request after another to Moscow for permission to withdraw, each of them refused. Only General Tupikov, chief of staff of the Southwestern Army Group, judged the danger to his troops from German guns greater than the danger to himself from Stalin's displeasure. He addressed a dramatic telegram to Moscow which neither the Army Group commander, General Kirponos, nor the political commissar Burmistenko agreed to sign, although they fully concurred with its contents. Whether or not Stalin would have been moved by the unanimous and determined request of his commanders, the fact is that top field commanders, responsible for close to 700,000 troops who faced almost sure annihilation, refused to risk the possibility, the probability, or even the certainty of Stalin's anger in return for a chance, however remote, to save the lives of their soldiers and of themselves as well!† This evidence of paralysis, which appears frequently if somewhat less dramatically in

---

°See for example the memoirs of Chief Marshal of Artillery N. N. Voronov, *Na sluzhbe voennoi* (Moscow, Voenizdat, 1963).

†It should be stressed that this particular kind of cowardice was displayed by people who more often than not demonstrated personal courage on the battlefield. Incidentally, Kirponos, Burmistenko, Tupikov, and most of the senior officers of the Southwestern Army Group were killed or captured by the Germans while trying to fight their way out of the Kiev pocket.

the memoirs, conveys the atmosphere around the Soviet High Command in this period of war and illustrates the virtually limitless acquiescence to Stalin's will of which the Soviet military establishment was capable.*

The fresh memory of the Great Purge reinforced by the fate of frontier commanders executed for alleged treason at the start of the war contributed to a situation where not only sabotage of Stalin's orders was considered unthinkable, but even legitimate questions concerning the wisdom of operational decisions in the planning stage were risked by few generals and pursued after rejection by almost none. The striking account of Marshal Rokossovskii's opposition to Stalin over the 1944 Belorussian campaigns provokes an even more intense reaction because it stands all but alone in the midst of uniform acceptance of Stalin's orders.† The opposition disclosed by writers of military memoirs was confined to the drafting of respectful, often timid memoranda and requests to Stalin or to attempts by field commanders or Supreme Headquarters' representatives in the field to contact Stalin personally and to influence him by factual arguments. Khrushchev recounts his vain efforts to persuade the then Deputy Chief of the General Staff, Marshal Vasilevskii, to urge Stalin to abandon the ill-fated operation to recapture Khar'kov in the summer of 1942 or to get through by telephone to Stalin himself. While one cannot always rely on Khrushchev's accounts and while no military writer repeats this pattern, it would appear that field commanders, men of unquestionable personal courage in battle, did not often try to approach their supreme commander when they disagreed with his orders. Of the many episodes in the memoirs which tend to support this argument, one can mention the behavior of Marshal Eremenko, commander of an Army Group, who when ordered to prepare a planned major offensive in an absurdly short period of time, preferred to start the offensive as scheduled, despite the predictable cost in lives, rather than seek a delay from Stalin.‡ It should be said that in the majority of known

---

*A German writer's comment concerning Hitler's generals seems equally justified in the case of Stalin's generals:

"It is astonishing that the generals always speak only of their military duty toward their superiors but not of their duty to the soldiers entrusted to them, most of whom were the flower of the people. One can certainly not require anyone to kill the tyrant, if his conscience forbids him to do so. But must not one require of these men that they expend the same care and scrupulousness on the life of every single man among their subordinates? The reproach of not having prevented the slaughter of many hundreds of thousands of German soldiers must weigh heavily on the conscience of every single German general."

(Helmut Lindemann, 'Die Schuld der Generäle,' *Deutsche Rundschau*, January 1949, quoted in Gordon A. Craig, *The Politics of the Prussian Army 1640–1945* [New York, Oxford University Press, 1964], p. 502.)

†See below, pp. 459–61.

‡See below, pp. 414–17.

cases the appeals and suggestions concerning corrections in approved
plans were made by an extremely narrow group of military leaders who
occupied key posts in the General Staff itself or who served as Stalin's
representatives in preparing and supervising major combat operations in
the field. In most cases, as the memoirs show, Stalin accepted their suggestions, although often with bad grace or wrath. When Stalin refused
them, however, the matter was closed. Marshal Zhukov relates how he
disagreed with Stalin's decision to launch a full-scale winter offensive in
1942 and vainly argued for a more limited and concentrated offensive
thrust. The man who held the title of First Deputy Supreme Commander
in Chief, who enjoyed at that period an influence and independence
greater than that achieved by any military figure previously or since, who
knew that certain of his colleagues supported his opposition, apparently
never pleaded his alternate plan with Stalin a second time.*

Stalin's critics have raised doubts about the dictator's actual control
at only two points in the course of the war—the first at the very beginning
of the war, the second during the defensive stage of the battle for Moscow
in the fall of 1941. Khrushchev first attributed to Stalin after the invasion
the despairing words—"All that Lenin created we have lost forever"—
and went on to say:

> After this Stalin for a long time did not actually direct military operations
> and ceased to do anything whatever. He returned to active leadership only when
> some members of the Politburo visited him and told him that it was necessary
> to take certain steps immediately in order to improve the situation at the front.†

The memoirs provide indirect support for Khrushchev's version of
the first days by alluding to Stalin's nervousness, gloom, and inability
either to grasp or to cope with what had happened. Stalin's first public
speech took place on July 3, ten days after the invasion, and he only
assumed formal leadership of the general headquarters of the armed forces
one month after the invasion and took the title Supreme Commander in
Chief even later. Admiral Kuznetsov mentions that Stalin appeared at
general headquarters only in the second week of war and took an active
part in directing the struggle only after his speech on July 3. Chief Marshal of Artillery Voronov saw Stalin seldom in the first days and remarked
on his nervousness and depression, but at the same time he indicated that

---

*See below, pp. 331–32.
†*The Crimes of the Stalin Era,* op cit., p. 40.

Stalin attempted to direct military operations, assigning missions to field commanders with, however, scant regard for actual possibilities at the front. His evidence concerning the unreality of orders emanating from headquarters is augmented in the accounts of Generals Tiulenev and Boldin and Marshal Bagramian. Appointees to key field positions, including such important commanders as Marshal Eremenko, head of the Western Army Group, departed from the capital without seeing Stalin, although later in the war Stalin saw personally almost every appointee to a field army command and even below. The inconclusive evidence, however, does not suggest that Stalin temporarily lost control over his subordinates in Moscow but rather that he lost control over the direction of events at the front. It suggests that Stalin sulked and saw only his closest associates, that he grasped the magnitude of the disaster slowly and vented his anger against the hapless commanders of frontier armies whom he summarily accused of treason and had executed.

The second occasion when Stalin's unchallenged role as leader has been questioned concerns the defensive stage of the battle of Moscow when Marshal Zhukov, according to the accounts of General Belov and Marshal Rokossovskii, displayed an independence which no other military commander or Zhukov himself enjoyed in later periods. According to General Belov, who describes a meeting with the Supreme Commander: "It looked as if Zhukov were really the superior officer here. And Stalin accepted this as proper."° It would appear that Stalin experienced his greatest bitterness, depression, and uncertainty at this time, a mood that the memoirs would have us believe did not reappear with the same intensity even during the summer crisis of 1942 and the early stages of the critical battle for Stalingrad.

While Zhukov's own account of the battle of Moscow testifies to Stalin's meddling with the conduct of operations and his continual requests for information from field commanders, it also unmistakably shows Stalin's self-doubts about the prospects for a successful defense and his reliance and sometimes even dependence on Zhukov's leadership of the battle. Indeed, one has the impression that Stalin's fits of anger and abuse against Zhukov, which the latter records in his memoirs, stemmed exactly from Stalin's recognition and dislike of a dependence so contrary to his previous experience. In the defensive stages of the Moscow battle Stalin was in command but Zhukov commanded. It seems that the extent and substance of Stalin's leadership during the battle are very well summarized in the following statement by Zhukov:

°See below, pp. 295–96.

I am often asked: "Where was Stalin during the battle for Moscow?"

Stalin was in Moscow, organizing men and matériel for the destruction of the enemy at Moscow. He must be given his due. . . . He performed an enormous task in organizing the strategic reserves and the material-technical means needed for armed struggle. By means of his harsh exactitude he continued to achieve, one can say, the well-nigh impossible.*

The character of Stalin's military leadership and its relative weight in his overall direction of the Soviet war effort differed significantly from that of Hitler. The two dictators did not exercise the same measure of control over their military establishments, nor did they rely to a similar extent upon the judgment of their military professionals. The differences in control over and dependence upon the generals derived in part from the origins of the army, in part from contrasting temperament, talent, and interest. A comparison of Soviet and German war memoirs cannot but convince the reader that these differences in military leadership profoundly affected the performance of the Soviet and German war machines.

When Hitler attained power in Germany, he confronted a powerful, cohesive officer corps which implicitly or explicitly challenged his pre-eminence in military matters and aimed to preserve its traditional independence of civilian control. The success of Hitler's political designs depended to a large extent on his ability to subordinate the military establishment to his will. Stalin started the war with an army which was his creation from the lowest command levels to the highest during the years of the Great Purge and after; never was his effective control over Red Army commanders in doubt.

While Hitler had less control and power over the military than Stalin, he relied less on the military than Stalin. Of the many facets of wartime leadership, ranging from the symbolic to the administrative, Hitler was increasingly drawn to military planning and operational command. With the progress of the war his contempt for and isolation from his generals, his reliance on his own initiative and judgment concerning military operations grew until it became in the last stages of the war the dominant aspect of his leadership. An inordinate self-confidence fed on the exhilaration of early victories achieved over the skepticism and protests of his military professionals. Stalin, as the war memoirs show, never considered the conception and planning of military operations his paramount strength, his major interest, or the measure of his absolute authority. He was more willing to listen to his generals, more willing to correct his errors (while, of course, refusing to acknowledge them). This crucial difference in the two leaders' respective attitudes toward their military asso-

*See below, p. 336.

ciates enabled Stalin to benefit more than Hitler from the improvement in the professional quality of officer cadres which both sides witnessed over the course of the war with experience and the promotion of talented commanders. Hitler's generals exercised less influence on the decisions of their High Command at the moment they were most able to act effectively; Stalin's generals exercised more.

If Hitler's preoccupation with professional military concerns outweighed other aspects of his wartime leadership, how relevant was the matter of military leadership to the final outcome of the war? The two leaders exercised their strategic and operational leadership with a vastly different margin of permissible error, miscalculation, and misjudgment. For Hitler the military aspects of leadership were much more crucial to victory than for Stalin. Hitler had to utilize to the utmost every advantage of the superior skill, conditioning, experience, and technique of his army in order to surmount the disadvantages of fighting an adversary potentially superior in manpower and resources. Not only could the Germans simply not afford to commit errors, they could count on victory with even the most refined tactical, operational, and strategic planning only in as far as their adversaries failed to mobilize their potentially superior resources and to conduct an even moderately successful defense. The major hope of Hitler and his associates for victory over the Soviet Union was based on the assumption that the Soviet system and Stalin's political power would crumble under the impact of major military defeats; in other words, they counted on the stunning and incapacitating effects of blitzkrieg.

What in the long run would bring victory to the Soviet Union did not depend on the excellence of Stalin's military leadership. While skillful military leadership was crucial to Hitler's success even though it did not guarantee it, all that was required of Stalin's strategic and operational leadership was to see that all factors working in his favor were not squandered. If Stalin committed errors, if he gravely underestimated the German capacity to wage a blitzkrieg, he paid for this by losing battles, his nation paid by the sacrifice of millions of lives. If Hitler underestimated the Soviet economic, political, military, and psychological capacity to wage a total struggle, he paid for this by losing the war. Once the blitzkrieg bogged down, once Hitler's gamble did not pay off, once Russia survived the threat of internal paralysis and political collapse, time worked for the Soviet side.

Thus what was crucial to Soviet survival and eventual victory was Stalin's ability to mobilize Soviet manpower and economic resources over a sustained period, his ability to assure the political stability of his armed forces and the population at large despite disastrous initial defeats, and his ability to recognize and reward superior military talent at all levels under his command. This is why in evaluating the role of Stalin in leading the Soviet war effort, the weight of his performance as Supreme Commander in Chief is not of key importance, either when his military leadership was a failure in that it contributed to defeats owing to his poor judgment or the ineptitude and inexperience of his military advisers or when it contributed to success because both he and his advisers learned the business of war. It was in just the area of Russia's greatest need that Stalin showed his greatest strength. A systematic, pedantic, indefatigable worker, he found greatest satisfaction in organizational matters. He was above all an administrator better suited to directing the gigantic military and civilian bureaucracy than to initiating and formulating military plans.

If Hitler's chance depended on the rapid collapse of the Soviet system and Stalin's political power, Russia's chance to survive the initial disaster, to mobilize its resources, and finally to gain the upper hand depended, once the war had begun, on preserving the authority of the government in power, the authority of Stalin as a symbolic rallying point for national resistance to foreign invasion and as the real center of war mobilization with the power and the desire to wield it in the interest of maintaining wartime economic priorities and political controls. It is not a moral judgment but a judgment of the realities of power to insist that once the war had begun the centralization of authority in Stalin's hands served to bring into play the superior weight of Soviet manpower and resources. It seems doubtful that the Soviet system could have survived an extraordinary internal shock, such as the disappearance of Stalin, while at the same time facing the unprecedented external blow of the Nazi invasion.

NOTE ON SELECTION AND ARRANGEMENT

MILITARY men have contributed the overwhelming majority of Soviet war memoirs. Their writings can be divided according to the individual author's wartime command and responsibility into five groups. In the first group are memoirs written by members of the Soviet High Command, the close associates of Stalin, who discuss the planning and control of military operations from Moscow. In addition, given the system of Soviet war command, these authors were simultaneously engaged as Stalin's representatives in supervising in the field the preparation and conduct of key operations; some even assumed command of key front sectors during decisive battles. This group of memoirs is perhaps the most valuable because of the insight it offers into the work habits and relations within the Soviet High Command. It includes, most notably, the memoirs of Marshal Vasilevskii, Chief of Operations and later Chief of the General Staff; Colonel General Shtemenko, Deputy Chief and later Chief of Operations of the General Staff; Chief Marshal of Artillery Voronov, a member of the Supreme Command and Commander in Chief of Artillery and of Anti-aircraft Defense; Admiral Kuznetsov, Commander in Chief of the Navy; and Colonel General Khrulev, Quartermaster General of the Red Army.[*]

One remarks in this group of memoirs, the least numerous, significant hiatuses in the published writings of some important military leaders and omissions owing to the silence of others. In some cases the authors concentrate narrowly on their field commands during individual operations rather than on their overall experience as members of the High Command. Marshal Zhukov, for example, who began the war as Chief of the General Staff and throughout the war held the title of First Deputy Supreme Commander in Chief, has written about his command in the 1941 battle of Moscow and the 1945 battle of Berlin but has nowhere related his experience during the first months of war and his work at Supreme Headquarters or as Supreme Headquarters representative in the field. Nor have the war memoirs of Marshals Timoshenko and Shaposhnikov appeared. The

[*]For information on memoirs mentioned here, see the Selected Bibliography of Soviet War Memoirs at the back of this book.

former served as People's Commissar of Defense from May 1940 to July 1941 and during the first half year of war was responsible, as a member of the Supreme Command, for coordinating operations first in the Western and then the Southern Strategic Sectors. He has allegedly refused numerous invitations to publish. In 1966–67 the posthumous memoirs of Marshal Shaposhnikov, Chief of the General Staff from 1937 to 1940 and again from July 1941 to November 1942, appeared in the Soviet *Journal of Military History,* but they concern only the period of his service in the tsarist army. It is not known whether memoirs relating to the 1937–42 period survive.

Of the various service branches of the armed forces, the air force is poorly represented in this group of memoirs. Numerous accounts have been written by wartime commanders of large air combat formations, but to our knowledge no extensive account of activities in the Central Staff of the air force is available. The wartime chief of the air force, Chief Air Marshal Novikov, is dead, and his close associates in the Central Staff have written very little about their wartime activities.

The second group of memoirs includes the reminiscences of commanding personnel of "Fronts," the Soviet equivalent of Army Groups. Five Army Groups existed at the beginning of the war, ten to fifteen at later stages in the war. The Army Group command was responsible for combat operations in a field sector varying from 100 to 150 miles in length; it disposed of several combined-arms Armies, separate artillery, armor, cavalry, and air formations, as well as supporting units. Overall size of the Army Group ranged from a quarter of a million to over a million troops, depending on the period and the importance of the front sector. In the first period of war it disposed of several hundred or even fewer tanks and aircraft; in the closing period, of several thousand. Throughout most of the war, Army Group commands were directly responsible to Supreme Headquarters. They were the crucial operational link in the chain of military leadership. Although they exercised much less freedom of action in comparison with their German and Allied counterparts, both German and Western experts consider their radical improvement in the later stages of the war a basic factor in Soviet military success.

The authors of this group of memoirs include commanders of Army Groups, their chiefs of staff, and in some cases the chiefs of Army Group artillery, armor, air, etc. Their talent and fitness for the command positions they attained and retained were harshly tested in combat by a powerful adversary. Military leaders at this level and the one immediately below have shaped the outlook of the Soviet military establishment throughout the entire postwar period and continue to occupy key command, staff, and training positions in the Soviet armed forces.

These writers of course deal primarily with those aspects of the battles and campaigns in which their respective Army Groups participated and for which they were responsible, but in many cases they also discuss relations with Supreme Headquarters, with Stalin's representatives in the field, and with Stalin personally, as well as deal with general problems. Among the most interesting accounts in this group are the memoirs of Marshals Konev and Rokossovskii, the most famous wartime Army Group commanders, who relate their experiences in the battle of Moscow, the 1944 offensive operations in Belorussia, and the 1945 campaign that took Soviet troops from the Vistula to Berlin and Prague. They include also Marshal Eremenko, Army Group commander from the start to the finish of the war, who writes of the initial months of war and the battle of Stalingrad; Marshal Meretskov, who directed Soviet troops in the northernmost sector of the Soviet-German front; Marshal Bagramian, best known for his command of 1944–45 battles in the Baltic area; the late Marshal Malinovskii, Soviet Minister of Defense from 1957 to 1967, who from 1943 commanded Army Groups in the southern sector of the front and eventually participated in the capture of Budapest, the occupation of Austria, and the final march into Czechoslovakia; Marshal Biriuzov, chief of staff of Army Groups which fought in Rumania, Bulgaria, and Yugoslavia; General of the Army Kazakov and Colonel General Sandalov, Army Group chiefs of staff for most of the war; and Admirals Golovko and Tributs, commanders of the Northern and Baltic Fleets, respectively. Many authors in this group occupied positions below the Army Group level in the early period of the war, and, in some cases, their memoirs for the earlier period exceed in interest those concerned with their experience of greater authority. Marshal Bagramian, for example, provides a more interesting discussion of summer and early fall 1941, when he served as Chief of Operations of the Kiev Military District and later of the Southwestern Army Group in the Ukraine, than of the later period when he commanded an Army Group.

It should be said that the most important Army Groups, their most prominent commanders, and their most spectacular achievements are adequately represented in this abundant material. The closing campaign of the Nazi-Soviet war (January–May 1945), for example, has been described in articles or books by the commanders or chiefs of staff of all nine Army Groups active along the 1,600 mile Eastern Front.

Memoirs in the third group were written by generals who commanded the basic Soviet operational unit, an Army (or a Corps, the intermediate unit between Army and Division). A typical full-strength combined-arms Army consisted of five divisions with supporting units and numbered over 100,000 troops. The total number of Armies throughout the war varied from twelve on the Western frontiers in the first, second, and third echelons on the day of the Nazi invasion to thirty-six Armies active in the final campaign.

The following commanders figure prominently in this category: Marshal Chuikov, whose two book-length accounts describe his command of the 62nd Guards Army which took the brunt of the Nazi assault at Stalingrad and ended the war with a frontal assault on Berlin; General of the Army Batov, who for most of the war commanded the 42nd Army which first reached the German frontiers in East Prussia; Generals of the Army Belov and Pliev, commanders of the horse cavalry which earned special fame during the 1941 winter counteroffensive; General of the Army Fediuninskii, at first corps commander on the Soviet frontier, later commander of the 42nd Army which defended Leningrad and of the 2nd Assault Army which participated in the final campaigns; and Marshal of Armored Troops Katukov, commander of the 1st Guards Tank Army, the most celebrated Soviet armored unit of the war.

The fourth group includes reminiscences of commanders and staff officers on the division, brigade, and regiment levels. While these memoirs follow a stilted and standardized pattern and seldom transcend the level of typical war adventure stories, they sometimes afford insights into hierarchical relationships within the army, supplement knowledge about individual war episodes, and illustrate the divergent perspectives of subordinates and their superiors who are represented in group three.

Political commissars are the authors of the memoirs in the fifth and final group. Set apart from military professionals by their political orientation, these officers functioned as representatives of the Party machine responsible for the loyalty of professional officers and for strict supervision over the implementation of Party directives in military units. Despite their preoccupation with the propagandization of Party values, their contribution to war literature is slender. Perhaps the principal reason for this situation can be found in the fact that the most important war commissars on the Army Group and Army level and to a large extent on lower levels were not what one can call professional political commissars. They were for the most part Party leaders from Moscow and the provinces who were assigned to political work in the armed forces. They returned to civilian duties either after the Germans were expelled from Soviet territory or after the war ended. While their subsequent fates varied from one case to another, one generalization is in order: the largest group of high-ranking war commissars was disgraced, dismissed, or relegated to oblivion in the fierce leadership struggle after 1953 (for example Bulganin); others climbed to high positions and even to the top (for example Khrushchev until 1964 and Brezhnev). Either fate was scarcely conducive to the writing of memoirs. In the case of the successful commissars, their recourse to the written word may have been discouraged by lack of time, lack of wartime distinction commensurate with their present fame, or lack of tolerance on the part of colleagues who have come to suspect self-advertisement. Certainly, the composition of memoirs had not been in the tradition of Soviet political leaders. As a result, accounts of their activities have been left, at least in the case of top leaders, to the disparagers or the sycophants among the professional military.

Those few extensive memoirs by political commissars that are available were written by career politicians permanently in uniform. Two books have been written by Lieutenant General Popel', the commissar assigned to Marshal of Armored Troops Katukov. Other authors include Major General Lobachev, the commissar of Marshal Rokossovskii; Vice Admiral Azarov, one of the main naval commissars who served with the troops defending Odessa in 1941; and Lieutenant General Telegin, commissar of the Moscow Defense Zone during the battle for Moscow and commissar with Marshal Zhukov during the battle for Berlin.

In recent years the published experiences of military men during the immediate prewar and war years have been refuted, confirmed, and supplemented by civilian accounts which, unfortunately, are very few in number. These have been written by industrial managers like the Soviet aircraft designer and wartime Deputy Minister of the Aviation Industry Iakovlev; the academician Emelianov, who served both before and during the war as a high executive in the Soviet defense industry; the scientist Golovin who describes research leading to the development of Soviet atomic weapons; by diplomats like Ambassador Maiskii in London and First Secretary Berezhkov in Berlin; by war correspondents and writers like Il'ia Ehrenburg, Polevoi, and Simonov. Yet the one group of civilians most capable of offering highly significant reminiscences is conspicuously absent from the memoir literature; not one member of the State Defense Committee, the supreme ruling body during the war, has made his experiences available to the public.

Stalin himself, as far as is known, left no memoirs, and the record of his "table talks," should they exist, are securely stored in Soviet archives. None of Stalin's close associates permitted himself more than the penning of panegyrics while Stalin lived, and given their fate as a group, the likelihood of their appearing in print under the aegis of state publishing houses has been reduced virtually to nil. To review the fate of the eight members who served on the Committee under Stalin's chairmanship— Voznesenskii was executed on Stalin's orders in 1949; Beria was executed by his peers in the 1953 succession struggle; Molotov, Malenkov, Kaganovich, and Bulganin fell in the late 1950's, and of them only one, Molotov, is known with certainty to be alive; Voroshilov was partially disgraced during the succession struggle and divides the remainder of his public life between reminiscences about the Russian Civil War and attendance at anniversary celebrations; and finally Mikoyan, the most tenacious, lost his executive positions in 1966 and now lives in semi-retirement. There is no indication that any Soviet politicians, high or low, retired or active, will benefit from the encouragement or grudging tolerance of the present leadership in order to indulge the human urge, common to politicians of all nations, to commit their public experiences to paper. It would appear that the story of Soviet war leaders a quarter of a century ago is still considered too central to the political and ideological self-image of the Soviet Union, too divisive in present political alignments in the Soviet elite, too explosive in the current restless state of Soviet society to accord them more generous treatment in the memoirs that are now being published and to allow them to speak for themselves.

The military memoirs range in size from single or multi-volume works to chapters in anthologies and articles in journals. Articles which were not later reprinted as books or incorporated in anthologies account for at least a quarter of all memoir literature. The memoirs can be divided into four groups according to the author's focus of interest. One group contains fairly comprehensive autobiographies in which the immediate prewar and war period occupy only a part, such as Colonel General A. T. Stuchenko's *Our Envious Fate* or A. S. Iakovlev's *The Aim of Life*. Secondly, there are extensive accounts of the author's experience throughout the war or during some particular stage. If memoirs of this type appear in two volumes, the first usually concerns the period of retreat and the second, the period when strategic initiative passed from German to Soviet forces, as, for example, the two-volume memoirs of Lieutenant General N. K. Popel', *In Difficult Times* and *The Tanks Turned Westward*. In the third type accounts are limited to a single operation or campaign, such as Marshal I. V. Konev's *The Year 1945*, or are devoted to a particular aspect of war leadership or to a profile of an individual war leader. Typical here are Colonel General A. S. Shtemenko's articles concerning procedures and work habits in the Office of Operations of the Soviet General Staff and his reminiscences about General of the Army A. I. Antonov, acting Chief of the General Staff during the second half of the war. The last, most fragmentary type consists of personal reminiscences interjected into analytical articles or monographs on war history or military art. An example of this type are fragments of Marshal Malinovskii's memoirs which appear in the anthology *Budapest-Vienna-Prague*, which is aptly subtitled *A History-Memoir-Work*.

The tone of the memoirs can vary from the highly personal and

emotionally charged account, such as that by Colonel I. T. Starinov, a top
demolition expert, *The Mines Await Their Hour,* to the driest, official kind
of reports, such as Marshal K. Meretskov's "On the Battleroads." As for
style, military training and the bureaucratic career seldom serve as a
satisfactory school. With scant exceptions, such as Marshal Biriuzov's
When the Guns Were Roaring, the military memoirs are characterized
by dull and limited vocabulary, confused syntax, repetitiousness, and often
the standardized blend of cliché and jargon familiar to the readers of
Pravda.

If the war memoirs do not excel in literary quality, they will reward
the scrupulous reader with information and explanations concerning key
military operations of the Nazi-Soviet war which substantially supplement
official Soviet war histories as well as accounts published in the West.
The underlying assumption of this book, however, is that the significance
of Soviet war memoirs far transcends their immediate relevance to the
study of military history, that in the absence of any other Soviet memoir
literature on the Stalin years, these personal records serve in effect as a
rare firsthand source for the study of political mores among the Soviet
elite in the period 1938–45. The editor did not have the intention of
preparing a military history of the Second World War or of presenting
a balanced or representative sample of the memoir literature, a purpose
which not only space but the quantity, variety, and character of the
memoirs themselves precluded.

The main purpose of the anthology is to present to the general reader
and the student of military and Soviet affairs the greatest variety of materials relevant to one highly significant problem—the character of relations within the command group of the Soviet military establishment
shortly before and during the Second World War and, more particularly,
the relations among members of the Soviet High Command echelon and
Stalin, their chief. Since even this principle of selection did not serve to
reduce the quantity of available material to the spacial limits of this book,
it was further necessary to choose the most interesting, novel, or typical
additions of fact, episode, impression, and evaluation pertinent to our
knowledge about and understanding of Stalin's behavior and the relationships within the command structure.

Excerpts from the memoirs are grouped in five chapters, each unified
by a common theme. All but the fourth chapter can easily be placed within
the chronology of the Nazi-Soviet conflict and identified with a single issue
or event of the war. Chapter One concentrates on the state of Soviet
military preparedness in the period 1938–41, on the policies and events
which in the last analysis determined in what condition the Soviet armed
forces faced the Nazi attack in the summer of 1941. Chapter Two con-

cerns the days and hours directly before and after the moment on June 22 when Nazi forces violated the Soviet frontier from the Black to the Northern Seas. Its principal focus is the level of combat readiness in Red Army field units, the behavior of the Soviet command structure on the eve of and during this fateful night, and Soviet leadership in the initial days of war.

Chapter Three centers on Soviet leadership during one of the most decisive encounters of the Second World War—the battle for Moscow in the fall and winter months of 1941–42, when Hitler's assault, intended as the final stage of successful blitzkrieg in the East, became the first major ground defeat of the Nazis in the Second World War. Chapter Five deals with the final Soviet offensive in 1945 which brought Soviet troops from the Vistula River to Berlin.

Chapter Four deals with the question of Soviet war leadership in a topical way and casts light on the personalities of members of the Soviet High Command, their mutual relations, and the behavior of Stalin. An attempt is made here to present a general picture of the system of Soviet war leadership, its performance and evolution.

Each chapter and subchapter is preceded by the editor's introduction. The notes of memoir authors are indicated by asterisks and reproduced at the bottom of the page. The editor's notes, numbered consecutively for each chapter and printed at the end of the book, can be divided into four general types: those which explain terms and words presumably unfamiliar to the reader; those which identify the background or circumstances of described events, especially in cases where only small fragments of the original memoirs are reproduced; those which supply either additional information from Soviet sources concerning war episodes discussed in the memoirs or data from German sources, particularly where discrepancies exist; and those which provide pertinent excerpts from Soviet memoirs that are not included in the anthology. Military or political figures are identified for the reader only where a name first appears. Brief biographies of memoir authors and of military and political figures who played a prominent role in the Soviet conduct of war or who are frequently mentioned in the memoirs can be found in the Biographical Appendix. Military and political terms employed throughout the anthology and questions of translation and transliteration are explained in the following Note on Transliteration. An annotated bibliography presents those Soviet war memoirs—books and anthologies—which the editor selected on the grounds of particular interest or importance from available Soviet memoir literature.

NOTE ON TRANSLITERATION, TRANSLATION, TERMS

THE SYSTEM of transliteration is based on that used by the Library of Congress. Familiar Russian proper names, however, have been spelled in accordance with common English usage (e.g., Beria, Mikoyan).

An effort has been made to translate all Russian terms into appropriate English equivalents and to avoid the abbreviations customarily used in the Russian text.

It seems necessary to explain the choice of words to translate a number of vexing Russian terms.

Front: This military term in its general meaning corresponds to the English "front" and in its specific meaning corresponds to what in Western military terminology is called "Army Group." "Front" was used except where clear reference to the identification of specific military formations was intended (e.g., 1st Belorussian Army Group).

Soedinenie, chast': The former term is used in Russian to designate field forces of brigade, division, and corps strength. The latter is used for field forces up to and including regimental strength. To convey this distinction the translation "unit" is used for the former term and "formation" for the latter.

Operativnyi: The adjective "operational" is used in Russian as an intermediary term between tactical and strategical. "Operational" skill, for example, refers to more than the conduct of battles but less than the overall conduct of war. It is properly applied to the conduct of military operations on the army or army group level. An attempt has been made to preserve this distinction, and the word "operational" has been used throughout the book solely as a translation of this Russian adjective.

Napravlenie: This term—literally "direction"—is translated variously as "direction" or "axis" (of advance or retreat). It also has a second meaning with reference to the three field commands, each consisting of a number of army groups, which existed in the first stage of the Nazi-Soviet war—i.e., Northwestern, Western, Southwestern; in this sense the word was translated as "sector" (e.g., Northwestern Sector Command).

Stavka (verkhovnogo glavnokomanduiushchego vooruzhennykh sil SSSR): Headquarters of the Supreme Commander in Chief of the Soviet Armed Forces to which the People's Commissariats of Defense and Navy and the General Staff of the Soviet Army were subordinated. Throughout the text this term is translated as "Supreme Headquarters."

It is likely that any terms unfamiliar to the reader will be explained either in footnotes or in chapter introductions where they first appear.

CHAPTER ONE

The Prelude

INTRODUCTION

SELDOM is the vitality of a nation, a system, a leader tested more severely than in time of war. In large measure the capacity to survive the test depends on the sustained preparations of many years, on the correctness of assessments made long before the outbreak of hostilities, and on the wisdom of decisions taken to anticipate events. The issue and the cost of many a military encounter have been decided long before the first shot, as Soviet experience in World War II merely corroborates. To discover the sources of both the Soviet military disaster in 1941 and the extraordinary victory in 1945, one must look to the conduct of Soviet leaders not only on the eve of hostilities or during them, but in years well before the Nazi attack.

The magnitude and speed of German victories in the summer of 1941 were astounding. For years the conduct of the Soviet government and its widely disseminated explanations of this conduct had convinced Russians and foreign observers alike that no war would catch the Soviet Union unprepared. Unlike the Western democracies, which devoted a meager share of their vast resources to defense during the 1930's, the Soviet Union had openly reiterated the need for military preparedness, had actively mobilized its industrial capacities for military production, and had zealously engaged in the psychological conditioning of its population for war.

While the major determinant of Soviet foreign policy in the 1930's had been the resolution to shun involvement in a large war, the major determinant of Soviet domestic policy had been to prepare for it. Determination to end Russia's traditional weakness once and for all underlay the tremendous economic expansion of the decade. Stalin voiced this determination in 1931:

> One feature of the history of old Russia was the continual beatings she suffered for falling behind, for her backwardness. She was beaten by the Mongol khans. She was beaten by the Turkish beys. She was beaten by the Polish and Lithuanian gentry. She was beaten by the British and French capitalists. She was beaten by the Japanese barons. All beat her—for her backwardness; for military backwardness, for cultural backwardness, for political backwardness for industrial backwardness, for agricultural backwardness. She was beaten

57

because to do so was practicable and could be done with impunity. They beat her, saying, "You are abundant, for one can enrich oneself at your expense!" They beat her, saying, "You are poor and impotent, so you can be beaten and plundered with impunity." You are backward, you are weak—therefore you are wrong; hence, you can be beaten and enslaved. You are mighty—therefore you are right; hence, we must be wary of you. That is why we must no longer lag behind.°

Some six years later it appeared that Russia would never again tolerate another beating. Both economically and psychologically the nation was being prepared to defend its great power status. Economic development in the 1928–1937 period was impressive by any standards. In 1937 the USSR accounted for about 10 percent of the world's industrial production. It led in the production of synthetic rubber; yielded to the United States only in machine building, tractor manufacture, and oil production; and occupied third place after the USA and Germany as a producer of electrical energy, pig iron, steel, and aluminum. Expansion of military potential was accompanied by psychological preparation of the population for war. Young men and women were taught in military and paramilitary organizations, in voluntary sports associations, sharpshooting circles, aviation clubs, and evening nursing courses that their primary duty lay in defending the Soviet homeland from foreign attack. All Soviet citizens were taught that hostile powers encircled their country, that war could come at any time—indeed, that war was inevitable.

The prospect of war had haunted Soviet leaders from the very moment they seized power. Even after the last foreign enemies were expelled from Soviet territory in 1921, their ideological orientation led them to expect a unified crusade of capitalist powers against the first socialist state. This nightmare of the 1920's was succeeded in the 1930's by another, no less frightening—that the Soviet Union would be left to face Hitler alone, while European and American capitalists celebrated the mutual destruction of Bolshevism and Nazism. When war did come to Europe in 1939, the Soviet Union was spared, as if by a miracle. The conclusion of the Nazi-Soviet Nonaggression Pact not only postponed Soviet participation in the conflagration for twenty-two months, it also satisfied Soviet territorial aspirations in Poland, the Baltic states, and northern Rumania and encouraged the hope that Japanese expansion in the Far East would continue at the expense of Hitler's new enemies, not his new ally. The war in Europe involved all the principal potential enemies of the Soviet Union and removed, for a time at least, the practical danger of individual attack

°I. V. Stalin, *Sochineniia* (Moscow, 1951), XII, 38–39.

or common crusade. It was, from the Soviet point of view, the best of all possible wars.

The signing of the Nazi-Soviet Pact did not interrupt Soviet war preparations. Indeed, the pace of the campaign to mobilize all human and material resources for total war accelerated during the period of uneasy alliance with Germany. Where then were the sources of the 1941 disaster? Of the many short and long term factors which contributed to it, several of the most important will be discussed: some were the direct responsibility of Soviet leaders; others were beyond their control.

The ability of the Soviet armed forces to repulse the German invaders had been undermined years earlier by Soviet policies, the deleterious consequences of which could not be repaired even during the period of the Nazi-Soviet Pact. Perhaps the most crucial of these was the unprecedented reign of terror, the Great Purge, which decimated the officer corps. Before the violent attack on the military establishment had subsided, no less than one third of the Red Army officer corps had been executed, imprisoned, or dismissed from active service, including three of five Soviet marshals, all eleven Deputy People's Commissars of Defense, and thirteen of fifteen Generals of the Army. According to official Soviet histories, all commanders of military districts, all corps commanders, almost all brigade and division commanders, about half of all regiment commanders, and all but one fleet commander were purged, if not shot.

The Great Purge, moreover, contributed to a decline in the rate of industrial growth and engendered throughout Soviet society chronic fear and uncertainty which all but destroyed initiative and independence in the exercise of responsibility. Before the wholesale arrests of skilled civilians had ceased, large numbers of technical personnel employed in key defense industries, in factories and design bureaus went to prisons, labor camps, and graves. Although the Purge was not the sole cause of the first decline in the rate of Soviet industrial growth since the start of the industrialization program in 1928, it nevertheless contributed to the industrial slow down and drop in labor productivity. The 1939 production of pig iron, steel, and rolled metal, for example, fell below 1938 levels by 132,000 tons, 493,000 tons, and 529,000 tons, respectively, and had not recovered 1938 levels by the beginning of 1941. The drop in ferrous metal production was followed by another in machine building. Production of automobiles and tractors in 1940 declined 28 and 25 percent in relation to 1939 figures. A decisive upturn could be remarked only in the first half of 1941 on the eve of war.

Responding to the decline in industrial performance as well as to heightened awareness of the imminence of war, the Soviet government acted to increase labor productivity and defense spending. In the summer of 1940 harsh new labor laws restricted freedom of movement, punished absenteeism as a criminal offense, and substituted an eight-hour work day and six-day week for a seven-hour day and five-day week, while Soviet factories remained in constant operation seven days a week. The relative weight of defense spending in the total state budget increased sharply from about 12 to 38 percent in the middle and late 1930's to 43 percent in 1941. By late 1940 the production of war equipment and the expansion of war industries, especially in eastern regions, assumed the proportions of a crash program.

While Soviet leaders energetically pursued the policy of purge as if the survival of the country depended upon its success, they delayed in adopting a decision on which survival did in fact depend. By 1939 the Soviet leadership recognized that the Red Army's guns, tanks, and planes were rapidly becoming obsolete. The tardiness with which the decision to modernize Soviet military equipment was taken could not be offset by the gigantic effort made during the period of the Nazi-Soviet Pact to meet international standards. During these months, Soviet defense industries coped with a three-fold task of modernization—simultaneously to design and test new equipment, to shift defense production from old to new models, and to develop serial or mass production of new equipment in quantities sufficient for a complete rearmament of Soviet units in the field. When the German invasion occurred, the defense industries had largely succeeded in the first, were in the middle of the second, and only beginning the third. The chief Soviet economic planner of the period, N. A. Voznesenskii, admitted that "the war caught Soviet war industry in the process of assimilating a new technology; the mass production of modern military equipment was not yet organized." In June, 1941, 78 percent of the airplanes and more than 50 percent of the tanks in border military districts were obsolescent and/or obsolete. These districts, no doubt, had been re-equipped on a top priority basis.

The baleful effects of the Great Purge and of the delayed decision to modernize Soviet military equipment were compounded by the consequences of erroneous decisions regarding the composition, organization, training, and strategic deployment of the armed forces, the location of stores and equipment, and the plan of mobilization. The doctrine espoused and implemented by military leaders during the period of the Nazi-Soviet Pact clearly betrayed a patent failure to assimilate and adjust to the demonstrable successes of German blitzkrieg warfare. A few examples of grievous errors and miscalculations will suffice for illustration.

The entire Soviet program of combat training and staff preparation at all levels invited disaster in 1941 because it was geared primarily to offensive operations. Neither the costly Finnish war nor the stunning German victory on the European continent dissuaded military planners from the view that Soviet defensive operations would be merely tactical, localized in scope, and short in duration; that a strategic offensive against invading armies along the entire front line would follow a brief initial period of defensive action. The major slogan of the 1930's—"The Red Army will win any future war with little expenditure of blood and will carry the fight into the enemy's own territory"—permeated the thinking and conditioned the expectations of the military professional and left the soldier ill-prepared psychologically for the war he was soon to fight.

The deployment plan for troops in the frontier defense zone invited disaster in 1941 because it provided for concentrating the bulk of forces in the first echelon zone and the bulk of first echelon troops in the border area with scant provision for the development of secondary defense lines and for the concentration of mobile reserves in depth. It was expected that forces deployed in the border zone would suffice to permit mobilization and deployment of major forces in the interior which would provide the basis for a strategic offensive. In general, Soviet estimates of enemy mobility on the ground and striking power in the air owed more to the experience of World War I than to a grasp of blitzkrieg principles applied for two years in the West. The planned and actual deployment facilitated quick, deep penetration by German armies, afforded the Germans an opportunity to attack Red Army units while they were on the march, and led to the dissipation of Soviet reserves in hole-plugging operations.

A vacillating attitude toward armored units in the years before the war invited disaster in 1941. Among the first to organize large independent armored units in 1932, Soviet military leaders had recognized the expanded role of armor in modern warfare and the need to regard tank and mechanized formations as more than a simple appendage of the infantry. Yet in 1939 large armored units were disbanded; a scant two years prior to the Nazi attack the largest armored unit in the Red Army was a brigade, comparable in strength to a German tank regiment. In late 1940 the tank corps was reintroduced, but for all intents and purposes Soviet tank formations were effectively organized only in the middle of the war. Those Soviet tank and mechanized units which battled the massive, well-coordinated Panzer groups had no experience in mass maneuvers; their commanders had no established procedures for directing large formations.

The condition of frontier fortifications invited disaster in 1941 because Soviet leaders committed the unpardonable blunder of disarming and virtually dismantling their painstakingly built border defense following the incorporation in 1939 and 1940 of the three Baltic states, eastern Poland, and part of Rumania before they had constructed the new fortified line

130–200 miles westward. Since their plans for the new line required several years to complete, the Soviet army faced the invading enemy in 1941 without a fortified border defense—almost no sector of the new line was combat-ready—and without a secondary fortified line behind which to withdraw.

The relocation of equipment and supplies in the 1939–41 period also invited disaster. The main ordnance and supply depots situated close to the old frontier in Belorussia, the Ukraine, and Smolensk province prior to the incorporation of new territories were shifted to border military districts where they fell an easy prize to the invaders or went up in smoke at the time of the Soviet retreat.

If Soviet leaders bear direct responsibility both for policies which built up the country's war potential and for decisions which weakened and misused it, they could neither control nor deal with another major factor which, in the last analysis, sealed the fate of Soviet armies in 1941. While the Soviet leaders built, erred, and tried belatedly to recover from the consequences of their mistakes, the German adversaries did not stand still. If part of the Soviet rationale behind signing a pact with Germany had been the prospect of a long, exhausting war in the West which would sap Nazi resources and morale prior to any possible Nazi-Soviet confrontation, then here, too, the Soviet statesmen erred. They failed to anticipate the impressive expansion of German military might which accompanied the unprecedented conquest of virtually the entire European continent. At the end of it the number of German divisions and armored strength had increased one and a half times; the German war machine exploited the labor resources and industrial capacities of almost all Europe; the critical shortage of raw materials, particularly oil, was alleviated. Above all else, however, German armed forces had acquired invaluable combat experience, tactical and strategic skill, a fighting spirit and a faith in their invulnerability which no peacetime training could ever achieve.

It is not difficult to locate adequate explanations for the Soviet disaster of summer and fall 1941. Soviet leaders misjudged the strength of the Nazi military machine and erred grievously in their predictions concerning the course of war in Europe. Even had they made better use of the time at their disposal, it is not likely that the country could have escaped severe initial defeats. The disaster, however, was not inevitable. At its source lay the Soviet leaders' inefficient utilization of material resources and their mismanagement of human resources, particularly of professional cadres.

PART I THE PURGE

Introduction

No SINGLE factor contributed more to undermine Soviet military leadership during the first phase of the Nazi-Soviet war than the Great Purge. This unprecedented terror crippled all sectors of Soviet society but struck with special virulence the professional military establishment. Arrests of senior Red Army officers in late autumn 1936 commenced the assault against the military. In April and May 1937 a group of the highest-ranking Soviet officers were arrested, allegedly tried in camera, and convicted as foreign agents; on June 12, 1937 they were shot. Arrests and executions probably reached their high point at the end of 1937 or the beginning of 1938. Nevertheless, accusations, arrests, imprisonments, and executions continued through 1938 and even after the disappearance of the "lord high executioner" himself, the head of the Soviet secret police Ezhov. The last known execution of a senior military officer prior to the outbreak of the Nazi-Soviet war took place a scant two weeks before the invasion; the victim was General Smushkevich, Chief of the Soviet Air Force.

The Soviet military establishment sustained unbelievable losses, the magnitude of which was already indicated in the general introduction to this chapter. Many more senior officers were killed during the Great Purge than during four years of war against Nazi Germany. Moreover the professional competence of the Red Army, not to speak of morale and stability,

deteriorated enormously. As of May 1, 1940, about one fifth of the positions of unit and sub-unit commanders were vacant. Military schools could not fill vacancies, not to speak of providing reserves. The level of military training for professional officers fell disastrously. In spring 1940, 68 percent of platoon and company level officers had completed only a five-month course for junior lieutenants. As of summer 1941, only 7 percent of Soviet officers had received higher military education and 37 percent had not even completed intermediate military training; 75 percent of all Soviet officers had occupied their posts for less than one year.

The four excerpts which follow expose the tensions of the Purge years. None of the authors was himself arrested during these years, and the accounts, therefore, are of a different nature than the reminiscences of General of the Army I. E. Gorbatov,[*] who recounts his arrest, investigation, and the years he spent in prison and concentration camp. Aside from Gorbatov, no senior Soviet officer who survived arrest during the Purge (such as Marshal Rokossovskii) has yet published an account of his experiences. Yet the following excerpts perhaps provide a more valuable introduction to the tragic effects of Purge on the military establishment precisely because their authors spent those years on active duty.

[*]*Years of My Life* (New York: W. W. Norton and Co., Inc., 1966).

The first and longest excerpt was written by Colonel I. T. Starinov, an expert on mines and guerrilla warfare, who was sent to Spain in 1936 as a Soviet "volunteer." He trained Republican troops and took part in numerous actions on the front and behind enemy lines. In autumn 1937 he was ordered to return home. His memoirs begin with his arrival by ship in Leningrad.

The author of the second excerpt, Colonel General A. T. Stuchenko, spent the Purge years as a student in the Frunze Military Academy in Moscow. Prior to this assignment he served as Chief of the Operations Section of a cavalry division. The Purge struck Soviet military schools no less hard than field units. Stuchenko's description of the atmosphere in the major Soviet military academy calls into question the value of military education during these years. The case of General Poplavskii, whose life might well have been saved by the advice of Stuchenko—a Party member and an officer—to flee Moscow and hide from the authorities, is just one example of the breakdown of all established codes of behavior and loyalty.

Marshal S. S. Biriuzov, author of the third fragment, describes the situation in a rifle division to which he was appointed chief of staff following his graduation from the Frunze Military Academy. Of special interest is his testimony concerning the permanent scars which affected the military performance of senior Soviet officers who were released from camp during the war and returned to active service. In the last excerpt, A. S. Iakovlev, famous designer of Soviet military aircraft, recounts how the Central Moscow Aeroclub was for all intents and purposes disbanded as a result of the Purge. He also reveals how influential friends were able at times to secure the release of Purge victims.

Colonel I. T. Starinov
Homecoming

THE CARGO SHIP passed Kronstadt. Ahead the familiar contours of the Admiralty and the Fortress of Peter and Paul were visible in the haze of the unusually fine autumn day. Several of us were returning from Spain. We felt happy and excited as we gazed at the dark green water of our own Gulf of Finland and the golden needle of the spire we knew so well. . . .

The ship dropped anchor and touched the pier lightly. Our first footsteps on land were timid and unsure. The land seemed about to slip from underfoot, like a ship's deck. But this did not last long. The earth was firm as it should be.

All the way from the port to the hotel I felt overwhelmed by the permanency of things. Everything I loved, everything I held dear, had remained the same. It was as if I had departed from this unique city only yesterday. . . .

"Staying long?" the hotel clerk asked.

"One day."

I did not bother telling her that even this one day was on my conscience and that I would have to answer for it. But I just could not bring myself to leave Leningrad the minute I stepped on its soil.

It began with the telephone.

It may be hard to believe, but my memory retained the home and office numbers of many of my acquaintances and colleagues. So now that I was alone I literally "saddled" the telephone.

But I was disappointed! Every number I called was answered by strangers.

Surely, I couldn't have got all the numbers wrong! Nothing like that had ever happened to me before.

Hesitating, I dialed the number of the military commandant of the Moscow Railway Station in Leningrad.

"Commandant's assistant Cherniugov on duty!"

I. T. Starinov, *Miny zhdut svoego chasa* (Moscow, 1964), pp. 149–66.

At last, a familiar voice! True, the voice sounded different somehow. Formerly Cherniugov, a clerk at the time, used to answer the phone in a loud and cheery voice. Now that he had become the commandant's assistant he seemed to have grown timid. That was of no importance now however.

"Good Morning, Comrade Cherniugov. This is Starinov speaking."

There was silence for a moment. Then Cherniugov inquired uncertainly:

"Which Starinov? Comrade Army Engineer third rank?" [1]

"Yes, of course, don't you recognize my voice?"

Silence.

"Do you hear me, Comrade Cherniugov?"

"Yes, I hear you. Where are you, Comrade Army Engineer?"

"In a hotel," I laughed, recognizing the characteristic intonations of Cherniugov's voice and amused at his puzzlement. Perhaps he thought I'd been killed? I hastened to reassure him: "I'm fine. All in one piece. How are you all there?"

"Everything's normal, Comrade Army Engineer."

"Listen, Comrade Cherniugov, the real reason I'm calling is to find out how to get in touch with Boris Ivanovich Filippov."

No answer.

"Do you hear me?"

Yes, Cherniugov heard me.

"He is now at a health resort." Cherniugov's voice seemed to contain a note of indulgence, or was it contempt?

I heard another telephone ringing on his desk.

"Excuse me, someone is calling."

After holding the silent receiver for a while, I slowly lowered it.

True, Boris Ivanovich had chosen an inappropriate time to go on a vacation. Sensible people do not go south at the end of October. Still, Cherniugov's tone of voice was too disrespectful. Or had the poor man's head been turned by his promotion?

I shrugged my shoulders and started phoning again. This time I rang up Kolia Vasil'ev at the Army Transport Administration of the October Railroad. We had been in the same regiment. He'd explain everything!

That was when I first heard those short, terrible words:

"They took him!"

Took him? Boris Ivanovich arrested? Nice Boris Ivanovich Filippov who had always trembled before his superiors? Kind-hearted, unassuming Boris Ivanovich?

Unbelievable!

From the newspapers I knew that Iakir, Tukhachevskii, Uborevich,

Kork, and Primakov had confessed their guilt in full.[2] Apparently, they had really betrayed something to the enemy, had been plotting something.

But what could Boris Ivanovich have betrayed or plotted?

The most he would have dared to do was, perhaps, to get extra resort accommodations for his wife. And even then he'd have made sure he had a paper from a physician because "a paper, my friend, is a force!"

Unbelievable!

So his friendliness, his solicitude, his simplicity had all been a horrible camouflage?

Immediately I felt disgusted with myself. Whatever was happening? Or was I scared? How dared I doubt Filippov's honesty?

And at once the merciless voice of my conscience asked:

"Yet you do doubt Iakir, whom you also knew! Filippov has been arrested by the same agencies. Why don't you believe it now? Or do you think that this, too, is a mistake? Come off it! This is exactly how you reacted when you first heard about Iakir's arrest!"

Really confused now, I decided to ring up another friend—N. S. Frumkin. Frumkin had met me at the pier and had seemed very sad for some reason. He replied that he would come over to my hotel, but he would not be drawn into a conversation over the telephone.

I left the telephone alone after that.

Now I understood why strangers had answered to familiar telephone numbers.

So the obscure rumors about mass arrests in my country were true! Rumors that had reached even Spain!

I left the hotel and roamed the city for a long time, trying to understand what was happening.

My head buzzed with the persistent thought: "Tomorrow I must go to Moscow. What news is waiting for me there?"

I returned to my hotel room late at night. I could not face being alone with the black telephone.

The ground was slipping from underfoot again.

The next day, while I was waiting for the train, my impatience got the upper hand and I looked in at the Moscow Railway Station commandant's office. Cherniugov locked the door behind me and informed me in a whisper that Appoga, chief of the Red Army's military communications, and Brigadier Kartaev, chief of Leningrad district military communications, had been arrested that summer.

"Enemies of the people!" Cherniugov declared in a frightened voice. "And Filippov was Kartaev's accomplice."

I saw that Cherniugov was burning with a desire to give me more "details," but I had had enough.

I could not fall asleep all the way to Kalinin.

Tired after a sleepless night and exhausted both physically and mentally, I reported my return to my superiors in Moscow. I was put up in a hotel and told that I would be sent for. I took a pill and went to sleep.

I awoke late in the afternoon. An oppressive silence filled the hotel corridors. Then I had an idea. I would go at once to see Ivan Georgievich Zakharov, my former superior in Kiev and a close friend. I could tell him all my fears; he would clear up my doubts.

I gave the chambermaid my key, ran down the stairs, caught a passing taxi, and drove to the Zakharovs, buying a bottle of wine and a cake on the way.

But in my friend's house I found tragedy. His wife met me in tears and in mourning. The story she told me was horrible. Ivan Georgievich had been full of anxiety the past few weeks. He anticipated the worst. Two of his direct superiors had been arrested. His family and theirs had been friends. He was frightened by every rustle; he had become irritable and sullen.

One morning at dawn there came a hurried and persistent knock on their door. Ivan Georgievich started to get up but groaned and fainted. He died of heart failure. As it turned out, it was merely the duty officer from the unit with an urgent telephone message.

I do not remember how many hours I wandered aimlessly through the city. Suddenly I saw that I was standing in front of the house of another old friend, one with whom I had served in the same regiment for eight years.

With difficulty I climbed to the fifth floor of the old house, fearful that I might encounter tears here too, fervently hoping to find my friend alive and well.

I rang the bell and heard soft footsteps inside. They died down at the door. A minute later a low voice asked:

"Who's there?"

"A friend," I cried joyfully.

"What friend?"

"It is I, Starinov!"

"Starinov? Oh! Wait a minute, Il'ia, I'll open up right away."

Bolts creaked. One, then another, and a third. At last the door opened a bit.

"Come in," my friend said, peering behind my back anxiously.

After he had closed the door he gave a sigh of relief, offered me his hand, and smiled. But his face grew long again at once.

"Where are you coming from?"

"From a special mission."

"Why are you wearing foreign-made clothes?"

"Because I was abroad. I haven't had a chance to change them yet."

"Oh, is that so! Abroad!"

We were standing in the hall. He had not asked me to take off my coat.

"What's the matter? Have I come at an inconvenient time?"

My friend was carefully inspecting the toes of his house slippers.

"Pardon me, Il'ia—but you know, at a time like this— By the way, some of our regimental pals were arrested recently. Iuvko and Lermontov were taken. And they didn't belong to any opposition groups. They always followed the general Party line."

He bent his head so far that his chin touched his chest.

"I see," I said. "They hadn't belonged to any opposition groups, hadn't traveled abroad— Sorry!"

Nobody tried to detain me. The door shut without a sound.

As I went down the stairs, I felt I could hardly breathe.

I stepped onto the sidewalk.

"Il'ia, wait!" My friend was running after me, buttoning his overcoat as he went. He looked apologetic and unhappy. "Il'ia!" he seized my hand convulsively. "Don't be angry! Try to understand. If you had come from the Far East— But God knows where you have come from. I work with secret documents. All my official forms say that none of my relatives has ever visited or lived abroad! Please understand!"

"Go home. Someone may see us talking together."

"Do you understand?"

"Go!"

The night had turned cold. The streets were emptying quickly. Only in the center and near the motion picture theaters and restaurants were there the usual crowds. Liubov' Orlova smiled down from a poster, touching her hand to a captain's hat: "Volga-Volga" was playing at the Metropole.

Ivan Georgievich Zakharov was gone.

My best friend had not let me into his house.

Marshal of the Soviet Union K. E. Voroshilov received me three days later.[3] I came to the interview with a major of the state security forces, S. G. Gendin. After hearing what I had to say about Spain and about how I had trained soldiers of special units, Voroshilov thanked me for my devotion to my military duty.

"You deserve a high award," the Marshal said. "Comrade Division Commander (that is how he addressed S. G. Gendin),[4] I think that Starinov has also earned a promotion. He should be given an important post in his field."

Voroshilov came from behind his desk and clasped my hand firmly. "Expect an appointment, Comrade Starinov!"

For a while the interview with the People's Commissar of Defense set my mind at ease and cheered me up. After all, I hadn't any sins on my conscience, and no one was attributing any to me; I had even been thanked for my service!

However, I could see that by calming myself in this manner I was reneging, as it were, on my old comrades. I was betraying the memory of the dead who had not, perhaps, committed the monstrous deeds attributed to them. So I became very depressed again and more confused than ever.

Time passed. No one sent for me and no one offered me an "important post."

On the other hand, each day brought some more cheerless news.

I visited the family of Konstantin Shinkarenko, former commander of a regiment in Kotovskii's legendary brigade.[5] Shinkarenko, who was one of my friends in a partisan school in Kiev,[6] had been among the first people in the republic to be awarded a Combat Order of the Red Banner and a Weapon of Honor.[7] Shinkarenko had been arrested, too.

From his wife I learned that many of Kostia's friends had been arrested—partisan commanders whom I knew and with whom we had worked to set up concealed bases for use in case of war.

"Kostia is an honest man. He was not connected with any enemies of the people. I wrote a letter to Comrade Stalin. I'll get Comrade Voroshilov to see me," Shinkarenko's wife repeated over and over, sobbing.

But she did not get anywhere. Only after Stalin's death was Konstantin Shinkarenko released and his good name restored. He came out of camp in poor health. His strength lasted only long enough for him to reach his native Moldavia. There he died suddenly.

Meanwhile clouds were gathering above me, too.

Finally I was summoned. But not by the People's Commissariat of Defense. I was summoned by the People's Commissariat for Internal Affairs [NKVD].

The light shone in my eyes, as was the practice, while the investigator's face was in shadow.

"Calm yourself," I heard. "We have only called you as a witness. All that is required of you is that you testify honestly. That is in the state's interest and your own."

"But what am I supposed to testify about?"

"Can't you guess?"

"No."

"All right. We'll help you."

I do not recall the exact sequence of the interrogation. He kept asking where I had served, how well I knew one individual or another, had I seen M. P. Zhelezniakov and A. I. Baar often.[8]

I replied without hesitation. Yes, I knew the persons mentioned. Yes, I had carried out their orders. Naturally. They were orders of direct superiors.

"So. And why did you set up secret partisan bases thirty to one hundred kilometers from the border? Why did you train so-called partisan detachments far from the border?"

I understood what the investigator was getting at. If I replied inconsistently or evasively, I'd immediately become a defendant instead of a "witness." He wanted me to admit that the measures carried out in the thirties were criminal, and thereby to discredit my former chiefs.

From what the wives of arrested comrades had told me, I already knew that the partisans we had trained were being charged with two things: "lack of faith in the power of the socialist state" and "preparation for enemy activity in the rear of Soviet armies."

The investigator was looking at me almost with affection. No doubt, a pike does not feel any special anger toward the carp that it considers doomed, either.

"It is true that bases were set up one hundred kilometers from the border, too. But, after all, fortifications were also built one hundred and more kilometers away, and they cost hundreds of millions or billions of rubles!"

"Leave the fortifications alone. They have nothing to do with this."

"How is that? If so much money is spent on their construction, that means that the possibility the enemy may reach that line is taken into consideration. And if this is so, then it is also logical to make all the necessary preparations for developing a partisan struggle between the border and the fortified regions. I trained partisans to fight the enemy. The measures under discussion were carried out in the interests of the defense of the Homeland."

This account of the three-hour-long interrogation is brief. I find it extremely unpleasant to recall, and the details are really not so important. Apparently, the investigator did not have the authority to arrest me. As he pushed away the papers and signed my pass, he said:

"For today we shall part. In consideration of your combat record we shall leave you alone. But—perhaps we shall meet again. Think about this. I advise you to put down in writing everything you know about the participants in the cases of Iakir, Baar, Zhelezniakov, and the rest of that company. Do not conceal anything. That way you will simplify your own position."

After that "talk" at the NKVD I understood that all partisan bases and partisan detachments which had been prepared in advance for the contingency of war had been liquidated; partisan cadres had been destroyed; and anyone who had been associated with this matter was regarded as an enemy of the people or an accomplice of enemies of the people.[9]

I was suddenly frightened, frightened as I had never been either on the battlefield or behind enemy lines. At war I had risked my own life; here everyone dear, everything sacred, was in danger.

The only thing to do was to appeal to the People's Commissar of Defense, to tell him my doubts, and to ask for protection against unfounded accusations.

Voroshilov received me. But this time he was stern and withdrawn.

"What is the matter? What did you want to tell me?"

Nervously and confusedly, I told the Marshal of my troubles.

"Comrade People's Commissar, we were carrying out a Central Committee assignment to prepare for a partisan struggle, and the stores of arms were set up on your instructions."

The People's Commissar of Defense was embarrassed.

"Do calm down—"

Then, after some hesitation, he picked up the telephone:

"How are you, Nikolai Ivanovich [Ezhov].[10] Listen, I have a certain Starinov here who recently got back from Spain. He was interrogated about carrying out Iakir's and Berzin's assignments for training bandits and storing arms for them."

There was a pause. An unnaturally high voice came from the receiver. Voroshilov spoke again:

"Yes, I know he carried out assignments of enemies of the people. But he was a little man and may not have known the substance of the matter."

Another pause. Then the Marshal spoke again:

"But he distinguished himself in Spain and has expiated his guilt to a considerable extent. Leave him alone. We'll take the necessary measures ourselves."

I need not comment on this scene.

On literally the third day after I had seen K. E. Voroshilov, I was summoned by Brigade Commander A. E. Kriukov, Chief of the Red Army's Military Communications.

I was very nervous about the forthcoming meeting.

Aleksandr Evdokimovich Kriukov and I had served together for many years in the 4th Korosten Red Banner Railway Regiment.[11] How would he receive me?

Would he understand that all my thoughts and deeds had long been dedicated to the partisans? Would he be pleased that I was returning to the railway troops after such a long absence?

Hardly!

In my anxiety all kinds of thoughts came to my head. But I could not possibly have foreseen what actually happened.

The brigade commander received me in the presence of the commissar of his headquarters, Barinov.

"Splendid!" said Kriukov, smiling broadly. "The prodigal son has returned! Very well, we shall decide on your appointment."

Pausing deliberately and casting a meaningful glance at the commissar, Kriukov said:

"Comrade Barinov and I have discussed the matter and decided to offer you the post of district chief of military communications."

For a moment I was struck dumb and could merely move my lips soundlessly. Finally I recovered the power of speech:

"But Comrade Brigade Commander, what kind of district chief of military communications can I make?! I am a railway troops commander, a mine specialist; I trained partisans; and I was sent to military communications units against my will after graduating from the military academy. I cannot cope with the job you have offered me."

"That is no answer, Comrade Army Engineer third rank!" Barinov interrupted. "Only six months ago Comrade Brigade Commander here (he nodded toward Kriukov) was in command of a railway regiment, and now he is chief of military communications for the entire Red Army. And he's doing very well! We are short of cadres, and we must promote young commanders to leading positions."

He uttered the last sentence solemnly, as if reproaching me for faintheartedness.

This was a most ridiculous situation. On the one hand, the post of district chief of military communications was a promotion beyond my wildest dreams. On the other, I knew that I could not cope with the job; I had neither the knowledge nor the inclination for it. And what can be worse for a commander and his subordinates than when he's not right for the job?!

"What's on your mind?" the brigade commander asked worriedly. "You will have two railway regiments under you. Directing the military communications service of two railways, you will be able to live in a big city."

"If there is no other way, then better appoint me commander of one of the railway regiments," I implored.

"That's enough modesty, Il'ia Grigor'evich!" Kriukov shook his head.

"Many of your age group are already chiefs of railways and of district military communications, and you talk about a regiment! We have army school graduates of the class of 1930 in command of regiments, and you graduated in 1922. They were platoon commanders when you and I commanded companies."

"But can't you understand? I'm not suited for that role!"

"There you go—'not suited, not suited.' All right. Since you are so stubborn we'll drop the district. But you won't get by with a regiment! The least we can offer you is the post of chief of the Central Experimental Proving Ground. Does that suit you? But consider, the proving ground is far from big cities; it is in a forest."

One must choose the lesser of two evils. I thought a while and consented to become chief of the proving ground.

"That's the way we'll write it." Kriukov was pleased.

Barinov and I rose and went toward the door.

"Oh, Comrade Starinov, stay a minute," Kriukov called.

The two of us were left alone.

"Come over to my place tonight," Aleksandr Evdokimovich said, using the familiar "thou" as in the old days. "I haven't seen you for a hundred years. And my wife and sons will be delighted. . . ."

That evening at the Kriukovs' dinner table Aleksandr Evdokimovich and I had a heart-to-heart talk. At first we talked about Spain. But imperceptibly we went on to other things. We had a few drinks, and Kriukov asked directly:

"Do you think it is easy for me to be chief of Red Army communications? Ah, Il'ia! You know I'm a line officer and don't have any experience in administering military communications. There are reefs all around—one false step and you are shipwrecked. And now one person after another turns out to be an enemy of the people. The ranks are thinning. And so I go round in circles like a squirrel in a treadmill. You've probably done the right thing to choose the proving ground. We're sending a group of academy graduates there—bridge builders, equipment specialists. You'll be able to spread your wings."

"But the proving ground is a whole town in the forest with a large plant of its own. I'm afraid that administration will get me down," I confessed.

"No, it won't! You've got deputies and assistants for that. They'll take care of the administration, and you'll concentrate on technology and on your mines. Nobody will interfere with you. A large number of scientific projects have had to be dropped at the proving ground now; you don't have to be told why. You'll find both the required funds and time there."

Kriukov said all this cheerlessly. There was obvious anxiety, bitterness, puzzlement, and, I thought, fear in his voice and in his eyes.

It wasn't so much his words as the tone of voice that prompted me to open up to him. Agonizing doubts were a heavier burden than ever on me that evening. I pushed away my drink.

"Aleksandr Evdokimovich! How can it be that men should have served Soviet power for twenty years and then suddenly sold themselves? And what men! Men who received everything, absolutely everything, from the state! And now they are enemies of the people. Who are they? Bourgeois? Not at all. They are the first Red Guards,[12] the first Red Army commanders. What did they count on when they sold themselves? What? Why should you and I pretend with one another? We knew many of them; we fought by their sides at the front, and we worked with them."

Aleksandr Evdokimovich sighed heavily:

"Not another word, Il'ia! Comrade Stalin has taken charge of cadres himself. He took this chore on himself, and he will not let innocent people be wronged. It is not for nothing that he made Ezhov head of the NKVD— Isn't that right? Why are you silent—like a stone? Come, let us rather have a drink!" he suggested in the same cheerless voice and added: "After all, this isn't a funeral."

Kriukov leaned over the table and I saw tears on his cheeks. He took my hand.

"You saved my son's life once. I'll trust you with a family secret. My brother, Lieutenant Colonel Andrei Kriukov, was discharged from the Red Army at the end of last year. I'm certain it is a mistake. He is an honest man. I am convinced it will be cleared up and he will be reinstated. But you can imagine how I feel!"

I was astonished at Aleksandr Evdokimovich's frankness and could not reply at once.

Kriukov recovered first.

"Let's have a drink, Il'ia, to Comrade Stalin's health. He won't let the innocent be wronged!"

On February 17, 1938 I was promoted to the rank of colonel and on March 20 of the same year, that is, four months after my return from Spain, I was appointed chief of the Red Army's Central Experimental Railway Proving Ground. . . .

I did not go to the proving ground at once. Before setting out for my new job I was to take a course of medical treatment at Kislovodsk.

Before my departure (I still lived in a hotel) I decided to take my things over to Evsevii Karpovich Afon'ko, a very old friend with whom I had worked back in 1926–1930 to prepare the fortification of Ukrainian border regions. Since 1932 Evsevii Karpovich had worked on the Moscow subway construction. He was the same cheerful strongman I had known in the army.

"Leave it, leave your junk!" Afon'ko said. "You can pick it up when you get back. But, mind you, I won't keep it for nothing. You owe me a bottle of dry Caucasian wine."

When I got back from the resort I hurried over to Evsevii Karpovich's, first thing.

Afon'ko's wife stood in the doorway, her arms hanging limply down the sides of her thin body.

"It can't be?" was all I could say.

I did not see Evsevii Karpovich until twenty years later. I brought him a bottle of dry Caucasian wine then.

"A little late," Afon'ko joked. "However, I accept it. You owe it to me, after all!"

My friend's cheerful tone and appearance astonished me. He had hardly changed in all those years. His eyes were young and his hand-clasp was like iron.

"What? Surprised? Want me to lift a thirty-five-pound weight with my little finger?" Afon'ko laughed. "No, brother, I did not give in to the camps!"

We opened the cherished bottle.

"I've lived through so much, Il'ia, that it's better not to think about it. But I do think about it. You cannot forget that sort of thing!"

Evsevii Karpovich had suffered a great deal in prison.

His reaction to the first bastard-interrogator who raised a hand against him was that of a partisan; he had knocked him off his feet with one blow.

For that he got twenty days in solitary confinement. But he with-stood the icy punishment cell and the subsequent interrogations. Every ten days during his confinement in Lefortovo Prison where the NKVD investigation department was officially permitted to torture the prisoners,[13] Evsevii Karpovich used to write (this was also permitted): "Dear Iosif Vissarionovich [Stalin], prisoners are being tortured; they break down and make up lies about themselves; then they are required to name their associates, and those who break down make up lies about their acquaintances. Then these are arrested and they too, unable to endure it, 'confirm everything.' Why should it be so?"

He was not punished for writing such letters!

No torture or torment could make Afon'ko give false testimony. And although there was not even the semblance of a crime, he was thrown into a camp for eight years without trial for "espionage for an unknown state."

"And then, brother, I stopped writing to the 'great leader,'" Evsevii Karpovich said bitterly. "I stopped because I realized that Stalin knew exactly what was going on."

.   .   .   .

I arrived at my new post at the end of April 1938 and was immediately reminded that Colonel Chumak, the former proving ground chief, had been arrested as an enemy of the people. True, no one knew what crime he had committed.

"Has there been a big reorganization since Chumak?"

"Hmm— His house over there with the veranda has been turned over to the kindergarten."

I started to familiarize myself with the work of the proving ground, with the subjects of the testing of equipment for railway troops, with the training program. No, the house with the veranda was not the only thing that had been changed! I was alarmed to discover that work had been stopped on a number of models of new equipment. The inventors and designers of these new models had also been declared enemies of the people. Their names had been crossed off the work program. Their models of new equipment were often crossed off, too.

There was no logic to this. But to whom could you go? To whom could you talk? Apparently, what was happening everywhere else was happening at the proving ground.

When I think back to that time, I wonder whether this was not the reason why it took so very long to finish up many excellent models of new equipment in the years before the war? Whether this was not the reason why, when war broke out with Hitlerite Germany, the Red Army did not have many excellent types of weapons that had been nearly ready for mass production?

And I reply: yes, that is the reason.

True, not all valuable specialists were sent to dig gold in Kolyma or to build brushwood roads in the swamps of Siberia. Some were permitted to work in prison too. These "lucky ones" worked and perfected their projects in solitary cells, cut off from the world. Over them hung the threat that any mistake would be called sabotage and any failure would worsen their prison regimen. It was difficult for them to obtain important scientific data, to learn the latest scientific and technological achievements. It was not a creative atmosphere, to say the least!

The prisoner specialists were brought to proving and testing grounds under heavy escort. Only the chief of the proving ground, the commissar, and the special section representative[14] were informed of their arrival.

I remember when an aircraft designer was brought to us in this manner in the spring or summer of 1939. No one knew his name. The coach with the arrested man and the escort was rolled onto the spur of a track behind the proving ground. By that time security men had set up tents in a small forest clearing and encircled them with a high double barbed wire fence.

Only in 1943 when I met V. M. Petliakov, the designer of a remarkable dive bomber,[15] did I discover that he had been my "guest" at the proving ground then.

But even in those difficult conditions the collective of the proving ground worked smoothly and harmoniously. This was due in great measure to Commissar Aleksandr Vasil'evich Denisov, who knew how to get to the bottom of things and how to unite people. However, even our harmonious collective was thrown into a fever at times.

Soon after my arrival Dmitrii Ivanovich Vorob'ev, my assistant for material and technical supplies, was accused of having connections with Trotskyites. The only pretext for this accusation was Vorob'ev's friendship with Colonel N. M. Ipatov, chief engineer of the construction of the Saratov railway bridge, who had been declared an enemy of the people not long before.

Engineer P. I. Martsinkevich and Vorob'ev's assistant, V. N. Nikitin, a cavalier of the Combat Order of the Red Banner, tried to defend him at the Party meeting. But there were ill-wishers present; Vorob'ev was expelled from the Party.

Soon afterward Ezhov was replaced by Beria as People's Commissar of Internal Affairs.[16] Arrests began inside the NKVD itself, and no one now had time to bother with people like Vorob'ev. Nine months later Dmitrii Ivanovich's Party card was returned to him.

Danger threatened Aleksandr Evdokimovich Kriukov, too. I received a request from the General Staff personnel bureau to send them a detailed Party evaluation of Party member A. E. Kriukov, with special mention of his behavior during the intra-Party discussions.[17]

I sent them a highly favorable evaluation.

Aleksandr Evdokimovich survived, although in September 1939 he was removed from his post.

Commissions of all kinds and individuals used to come to the proving ground from the chief of the Military Communications Directorate of the Red Army. These were all novices who started to work in the central apparatus in 1937–1938. As a rule they not only lacked experience, but often the requisite knowledge.

To the credit of many of them, I must say, they realized that they could not help us in any way and tried not to interfere.

However, there were still others—"inspectors" who considered it their primary task to display their authority somehow. Since they did not have sufficient knowledge to do anything else, they would interfere in administrative matters and write statements and reports about who reported for work late (they didn't notice that we often worked till late at night!), which objectives were poorly guarded, and so forth.

Incidentally, these novices should not be condemned either. They had not asked for jobs in the central apparatus. Many were sincerely upset by their ambiguous positions; they studied hard, and by the outbreak of the war they knew their work well.

Our common misfortune was that the most experienced personnel had all left the stage at nearly the same time, and the continuity of replacement had been violated. Only after the Twentieth Party Congress did we realize the full extent of that completely unjustified disaster.[18] During the years of repressions, however, people already sensed that something was wrong.

I remember the following instance. There was a fireman at the proving ground. He was brave and completely without guile. Once in a while this knight of the fire would drink a little more than was good for him. One day, as he philosophized with his drinking buddies, he asked a profound question:

"What do you think, brothers? Today we nominated Ezhov for the Supreme Soviet. What if he turns out to be an enemy like Iagoda?"[19]

The fireman could not immediately understand why he suddenly found himself all alone. When he did, he broke out into a cold sweat. The incident was reported to the commissar of the proving ground. Denisov took a big chance by ordering the man discharged at once. In this manner he saved the poor fellow from inevitable arrest. The fireman turned out to have been right!

Colonel General A. T. Stuchenko
In the Frunze
Military Academy

I BEGAN to attend the M. V. Frunze Academy[20] in May of 1936. . . .

The course of studies was fascinating. Everything was new and interesting. The lectures were given by highly qualified instructors. Especially memorable were those of Brigade Commander Korsun on the his-

A. T. Stuchenko, *Zavidnaia nasha sud'ba* (Moscow, 1964), pp. 62–69.

tory of military strategy, those of Captain Leosheni on military engineering, those of Army Commander second rank Vatsetis[21] on the history of the Civil War, and those of Major Tsvetkov on staff work. Things did not go well, however, with Brigade Commander Sveshnikov's course on the history of ancient military strategy. You'd listen to a lecture of his and not be able to make head or tail of it. His exposition was unsystematic and disconnected. At the end of his lectures our heads would ache, but no information would remain.

We attempted to bring pressure on him through the director and commissar of our class, as well as through the director of the academy, Army Commander second rank Kork, and the commissar of the academy, Shchadenko, but to no avail. When Sveshnikov was arrested, we could not help thinking: "for teaching which amounted to sabotage."

After him, however, other instructors also began to disappear. A day did not pass that some instructor was not arrested. Many were taken straight from class. That's how it was with Vatsetis. We listened to him for an hour, and after the break the lecture was not resumed. Kashcheev, the commissar of our class, announced:

"Comrades! The lecture will not continue. Lecturer Vatsetis has been arrested as an enemy of the people."

We sat there stunned, without even a whisper. It was incredible that a man who had fought all through the Civil War for Soviet power was— an enemy of the people.

Something incomprehensible was taking place. The wave of arrests constantly swelled. Finally, it even began to reach out for the students. Our "Spaniard," Major Arman, who had fought valiantly in the International Brigade at Madrid and received the decoration of Hero of the Soviet Union for it, suddenly vanished.[22]

A new required item was introduced into our service and Party dossier concerning our zeal in the struggle against "enemies of the people." There were those who were ready to see an enemy in every one of their comrades and who hastened to inform on them in order to demonstrate their "zeal in the struggle." How much harm this did! Student Kuznetsov, for example, former battery commander in our 6th Cavalry Division, had turned to Gamarnik, the chief of the Main Political Administration,[23] for help in getting into the academy (after doing poorly on the entrance examination). In an expansive moment, Kuznetsov confided to his roommate: "Gamarnik is a good man! It was he, you know, who helped me get into the academy. I'm grateful to him!"

That was sufficient. When Gamarnik shot himself, Kuznetsov's roommate, unable to withstand being baited by the Beria-ites, lost no time in reporting the student's connections with the "enemy of the people."

Kuznetsov was expelled from the Party and the academy and was saved from arrest only by a miracle.

It was a terrifying time. People began to fear one another. Anything might serve as grounds for arrest: national origin, failure on the job, or even an incorrect interpretation of some word. It was particularly dangerous to be suspected of having connections with "enemies of the people." Such suspicion often took a wild, phantasmagoric form. For a student to be subjected to a working-over, not at one but at several Party meetings, to be expelled from the Party, and finally to be arrested, it was sufficient to discover that he had served prior to entering the academy in a unit the commander of which had been arrested. The working-over at Party meetings was just the preliminary stage. We kept that in mind when student S. G. Poplavskii (now a General of the Army) was expelled from the Party and the academy. I immediately advised him to leave Moscow without delay. Whether it was my advice or his own decision, I do not know. But he left. That saved him. About eighteen months later, Poplavskii returned to the capital, was readmitted to the Party, and was graduated from the academy. During the Great Patriotic War he proved himself a talented commander, commanding a division, a corps, and an army. After the war he was Deputy Minister of Defense of our ally, Poland.[24]

But not everyone succeeded in executing such a maneuver. They didn't have the time.

Our Party group held together. We did not look for "enemies of the people" among ourselves and firmly resisted all attacks from outside. We even began to be accused of a loss of revolutionary vigilance, and our sectional Party organization was threatened with disbandment. Leva, as we called Dovator [our Party group organizer], often returned from the class commissar looking upset.[25]

After the Central Committee's plenary meeting, which changed the situation somewhat,[26] that same class commissar, Kashcheev, praised us:

"Now those are fine communists in the cavalry section! A close-knit bunch, they held together. Their good, solid Party organization can serve as an example to everyone."

.   .   .   .

Student Nikolai Shvedov (who died in 1941 while commanding a cavalry regiment) once told a group of friends that he had drunk tea with his school director, Shmidt, when he was a squadron sergeant at the Elizavetgrad Cavalry School. When Shmidt was arrested, one of the students informed the Party Bureau of Shvedov's connections with the "enemy of the people." He repeated this at a Party meeting.

Shvedov listened to this as if on pins and needles. No sooner was he permitted to speak, than he jumped up and ran to the center of the hall.

"Comrades! I am accused of having connections with Shmidt. But put yourselves in my place: what would you do, if you received an invitation from such an important chief? You know that each of you would consider it an honor, just as I considered it an honor when I, a sergeant, was invited to have tea with the school director, a hero of the Civil War. And he invited me because he considered me a good sergeant. So what wrong have I done? Suppose the man sitting here in this presidium, the academy director Comrade Kork, invited me to visit. Would I dare refuse such an honor? Would any of you refuse, for that matter? Do I speak the truth, comrades?"

"It's the truth!" Friendly voices and applause answered him.

The academy director wiped his glasses in embarrassment. A deep sorrow could be read in his eyes. He already sensed that clouds were gathering over his head. He was soon arrested, and he perished like many other innocent comrades.

Trouble overtook my relatives also. At the end of 1937, my cousin, Aleksandr Petrovich Bragin, was arrested. He had been a commissar of the 33rd Kuban' Division during the Civil War, and later, after receiving the necessary education, he became a prominent specialist in diesel engines. For a long time, he worked as a consultant to Kaganovich,[27] with whom he had a very friendly relationship. Aleksandr was also friends with M. N. Tukhachevskii's family. Perhaps that was what led to his arrest. I was extremely shocked that Kaganovich, who knew my cousin well, did not lift a finger to save him. . . .

I had to write a report to the Party bureau of my class about my cousin's arrest. It was simply preposterous to believe that he was an enemy of Soviet power. I believed that he had suffered only for his friendly relations with M. N. Tukhachevskii and his family, which in those days was quite sufficient for a person to be arrested. No doubt I would have gotten the same, except for the Central Committee's plenary meeting in February, which condemned unfounded arrests.

The arbitrariness and violations of socialist legality which were spawned by Stalin's personality cult caused us to lose many experienced military comrades. The critical shortage of commanders began to be felt by the troops.

Graduations from military academies began to be speeded up. We learned that some of us also would be graduated in November and December, six months ahead of time. . . . We were graduated without diplomas, with the assurance that in April 1939 we would be called in to take state examinations, after which we would receive our diplomas. Anticipating events, let me say that it happened just that way: we came to Moscow, spent two weeks taking exams, received diplomas, and returned to our posts.

Friends went their separate ways. My own appointment was delayed for a long time. I had the following interview in the Main Bureau of Personnel regarding my previous service in the 24th Cavalry Division.

"Yes, it's not a bad division, only it was commanded by enemies of the people—," my interviewer said pensively.

"What enemies?"

"Antonov, for example. The division commander. He always acted so quietly and smiled at everyone. But he turned out to be a son of a bitch. He has long since been arrested and shot."

"What are you saying? I never would have thought that. I knew him well—"

"And Nichiporovich? Also an enemy of the people and also arrested."

"Impossible! What kind of enemy is he—"

"What is this," said the personnel officer, flaring up at once. "Don't you know that he destroyed many horses by deliberately creating conditions so they would catch pneumonia?"

"It's not true! He didn't create those conditions. It was the fault of whoever decided to build the stables in a swamp. The horses were in a damp place all year round; they caught colds and then pneumonia. I know how hard Nichiporovich took the loss of the horses. Whenever it was cold, we didn't get one night's rest from him. We spent our own money to get straw in the neighboring villages to save the horses." . . .

I tried again and again to prove Nichiporovich's innocence.[28]

"Hm— You don't say— Well, all right, go home," said the personnel officer coldly. "We will call you when necessary."

And that's how it began. I had to appear at the personnel bureau almost every day, sit for hours outside the office door, then fill out a questionnaire and leave. I filled out many questionnaires. They ordered me to list everyone I knew, from what year I knew them, and who knew me from what year. They were especially interested in knowing who among my relatives and close acquaintances had been arrested, when, and why. My cousin Bragin's name came up endlessly.

Only after a detailed examination lasting several weeks was I appointed chief of the operations section with the staff of the 3rd Cavalry Corps in Minsk. I lost no time in leaving for my new post.

Marshal S. S. Biriuzov
In the 30th
Red-Banner Division

ALONGSIDE such energetic figures as Berzarin, we also had a very different kind of general, the kind who was too meek and inconspicuous. The chief of staff of the 5th Shock Army belonged to this category.[29] He always tried to stay in the shadows, "out of the way of the authorities." . . .

In the ranks of the Soviet Army from the moment of its creation, he was commanding an artillery battalion by 1919. After the Civil War, he graduated from two military academies and acquired rich experience of high level staff work. Suddenly in 1939 he was arrested and sentenced to twenty years in prison. Why? No substantial charges were brought. There was just the usual formula for those years: "enemy of the people." An important military specialist, an honest Soviet citizen was put on the same level with hardened criminals.

After some time in a hard-labor camp, he was assigned to bathhouse duty. During his tour, a scoundrel stole some underwear. He was brought to trial again. They added five years to his sentence. The Civil War hero, wounded in battle eleven times, was morally crippled. And this, it would seem, affected him for a long time to come. Not everyone recovers from such traumas by any means. Even when he was released in 1943 and appointed to the high post of Army Chief of Staff, he remained a broken man.

Unfortunately, this case was not unique. We had quite a few victims of Stalin's arbitrariness among our high ranking officers. They had come to field formations straight from prison. Some of them later became remarkable military leaders, commanding troops with skill. But some lost forever the capacities of full-fledged commanders. The moral and often serious physical traumas that they suffered in jails and camps destroyed the will power, initiative, and decisiveness so necessary to a military man. . . .

I recalled with a shudder the years of 1937–1938. During that dismal period, I studied at the M. V. Frunze Academy. . . . After graduation I was appointed to the 30th Irkutsk Red-Banner Division. There, an even more stupefying picture unfolded before me.

When I arrived at division headquarters in Dnepropetrovsk I found

S. S. Biriuzov, *Sovetskii soldat na Balkanakh* (Moscow, 1963), pp. 137–43.

a situation which defied the imagination. I had already been told in the commandant's office at the railroad station that the division at present had no leadership "strictly speaking": The commanding officer, the commissar, the chief of staff, and the service chiefs had all been arrested.

The chauffeur, whom the commandant ordered to take me to my post, added the following dreary information:

"At least you still have some people left in the 30th [Division], but in corps headquarters, every last chief from the lowest to highest was swept out. What bastards these enemies of the people are! They had everything in their control."

I broke out in a cold sweat at these words. "Who commands the division, then?"

"Why nobody," answered the chauffeur. "Except the chief of the first section, Major Etsov, is still kicking."

I went directly to the office of the chief of staff without being met by anyone. There sat a captain. Raising his weary eyes and looking at me indifferently, he waited silently for what I would say or order. I in turn looked at him, not knowing what to say.

But I had to break the silence first. "Where is the division commander?"

"Where should he be, but in his office—" answered the captain reluctantly.

"Who are you?" I asked.

"How can I put it—sort of a division chief of staff, but actually the chief of the fourth section."

"And who commands the division?"

"The chief of the first section."

I asked whether there had been an order from the People's Commissar of Defense or, at least, from the military district commander allowing Major Etsov to carry out the duties of division commander.

"What kind of orders do you expect?" said the captain mournfully. "We act according to regulations: when one chief leaves the ranks, he's replaced by the next in command. Just like wartime."

And he immediately became watchful, realizing that he had been far too frank with a total stranger. He stood at attention and asked in a dry, official tone: "Who are you?"

"Chief of staff of the division, by order of the People's Commissar of Defense," I answered in the same tone.

"Well, then, let's go to our so-called division commander," the captain smiled.

Major Etsov, curly-haired and hook-nosed, sat at a desk. When we came in, he did not rise to meet us but merely turned his gloomy face in our direction and asked: "What do you want?"

I handed him my order. As he skimmed through the paper, the major brightened up at once: "Well, finally, the legitimate commander is here. What a load off my shoulders— For God's sake, here's a chair, here's your seal—now you're in business!"

My administration began with an order to seal up the division commander's office for the time being. That was the first order I gave in the 30th Irkutsk Division.

Lieutenant General A. S. Iakovlev
In the Moscow
Aeroclub

THE AERIAL RACES represented a serious examination and a test of the state of our light aviation and served as a reliable criterion for selecting the best sports planes for mass production.

The Moscow-Sevastopol'-Moscow flight route totaled 2,815 km. Out of the nine airplanes that returned to Tushino on the same day, only five fully met the conditions of the competition. . . . The results of the flight for my design bureau were wonderful.[30]

The percentage of planes that had gone out of commission, however, was high, and this adversely affected the fate of the leaders of the Central Aeroclub. It should not be forgotten that this was 1937 In those days, failure on the job or an error could be assessed as deliberate sabotage. The label "saboteur" and, subsequently, "enemy of the people" could be assigned not only in the case of failure but even on the basis of suspicion.[31]

The wave of distrust and suspicion of sabotage descended both on individuals and on entire organizations. Such was the case with the Central Aeroclub.

The fact that not all of the nineteen airplanes that had taken off returned to Moscow on the same day came to be regarded as something ill-intentioned even though, as similar undertakings abroad show, races are races precisely because some participants win, some do not win, and some simply go out of commission.

The tragic deaths of two [women] parachutists—Liubov' Berlin and

A. S. Iakovlev, *Tsel' zhizni* (Moscow, 1966), pp. 130–32.

Tamara Ivanova—were also recalled. They had been competing in making a delayed jump and, trying to outdo one another, opened their parachutes too late, and were both killed.

Certain other failures in the work of the Aeroclub—things that in my opinion are absolutely unavoidable in such a complex and exacting matter as aviation sport—were also questioned.

The chief of the Aeroclub, Brigade Commander Maks Deich—a capable officer, a wonderful organizer, and the soul of the Aeroclub—asked me to talk to Lev Zakharovich Mekhlis,[32] the editor of *Pravda* and a member of the Central Committee, to get him to use his authority to halt the destruction of the Aeroclub. To my astonishment, Mekhlis, who had helped the Aeroclub in the past, now began to insist on the necessity of investigating why Chkalov[33] had succeeded in flying across the North Pole without incident, while they had been unable to fly from Moscow to Sevastopol' without accidents.

The Central Aeroclub became one of the victims of *Ezhovshchina*. Its leaders were arrested. For a certain time, the Aeroclub for all intents and purposes existed only on paper.

Evgenii [Zhenia] Riabchikov, a reporter for *Komsomol'skaia pravda*,[34] also suffered in connection with the Aeroclub "affair." Zhenia loved aviation, had learned to fly, and was an ardent propagandist of aviation.

My relations with Zhenia Riabchikov were not limited to official ones. Sometimes he was a guest in my home, and one day in 1937 he invited me to his birthday [party]. Many journalists were there, and the evening was very festive. We went home at one o'clock in the morning.

But imagine my horror when in the morning I learned that on the same night Zhenia had been arrested as an enemy of the people. I simply couldn't believe it!

The eventual fate of Zhenia Riabchikov became known only much later. At the end of the war, Susanna Mikhailovna Kropacheva, the chief engineer of a plant in Noril'sk[35] where the exiled Riabchikov worked, came to me; at that time I was Deputy People's Commissar of the Aircraft Industry. She described everything that had happened to Zhenia. He was serving a sentence because of a slanderous accusation. Susanna Mikhailovna asked for assistance, and I promised her that I would do everything in my power to ease Riabchikov's lot.

Soon thereafter, upon being summoned to Stalin on some matter or other, I saw a civilian in his office, standing by the window, examining a folder of papers. While Stalin was talking to me, the stranger, apparently having finished with his papers, came over to us and greeted me. It turned out that this was Avraamii Pavlovich Zaveniagin,[36] the Deputy People's Commissar of Internal Affairs, who had recently returned from Noril'sk where he had directed the construction of a mining and metallurgical combine. I knew from Susanna Mikhailovna that Zaveniagin knew her.

Taking advantage of the opportunity and Stalin's good mood, I decided to tempt fate and began talking to Zaveniagin about Riabchikov. I said that it seemed to me that Evgenii Riabchikov, the *Komsomol'skaia pravda* journalist, an honest young man, an aviation enthusiast and activist in the Central Aeroclub, was being punished on the basis of an absurd accusation. I asked whether it would be possible to reexamine his case. Having listened to this conversation, Stalin said to Zaveniagin:

"Look into it!"

These few words, which did not appear to obligate anyone to do anything, turned out to be sufficient. A week later, Avraamii Pavlovich personally called on the Kremlin phone[37] and said that my request was being taken care of. Shortly thereafter, Zhenia and I were heartily embracing one another in my office in Moscow.

PART II   THE NEW ELITE

Introduction

THE EFFECTS of the Great Purge on the composition of the Soviet political, managerial, and military elite can only be compared to the effects of a revolution. While supreme leadership remained unchanged, the elite that assisted Stalin in governing the country was almost entirely replaced. It was a time when careers were built and broken with dizzying speed, when an obscure director of a textile factory named Kosygin climbed in three short years to the rank of Deputy Prime Minister of the Russian Republic, when a minor engineer in a metallurgical factory named Brezhnev rose in two and a half years to become Party boss of a key industrial province, when a student at a military academy named Paniushkin went in two years as Soviet ambassador to China, when a rank-and-file reporter for a Party newspaper named Mikhailov soared in one year to head the nine million members of the Communist youth organization, and when an ordinary division commander named Zhukov advanced within three years to the position of Chief of the Soviet General Staff.

In some cases, the policy of rapid promotions proved highly successful, as some of these names would indicate. In many more cases, however, the newly advanced officials were "prima ballerinas" for a season, and, failing to display any talent, they disappeared from the scene as suddenly as they

had appeared. In all cases the wholesale turnover of senior executive personnel left the administrative structure a shambles. The new executives, without experience to prepare them for the scope and burdens of their new tasks, had to train on the job at the same time as they bore full responsibility for the everyday business of government. The atmosphere of overwhelming fear generated by the Purge, the knowledge of what repercussions followed from a single misstep resulted in a situation where decision-making in Soviet state institutions—on the highest level as well as in trivial matters—tended to gravitate toward the ultimate center of all power—Stalin. The process of government was increasingly reduced to preparing proposals for Stalin, to asking permission from Stalin, to appealing for help to Stalin, and, above all, to implementing the orders of Stalin. Even if one could assume the ultimate wisdom of all Stalin's decisions, this extremely cumbersome and supercentralized system could not help but produce inefficiency and waste.

The first two excerpts which follow deal with the appointment of two high officials and their experience in their new functions. The author of the first, Admiral N. G. Kuznetsov, moved in less than three years from the obscure post of cruiser commander to Commander in Chief of the Soviet Navy. His memoirs illuminate the method of making ministerial appointments, the atmosphere among senior officers of the Soviet navy, and the role of Stalin in naval affairs. The author of the second excerpt, A. S. Iakovlev, recounts how he was "offered" the post of Deputy People's Commissar of the Aviation Industry in the summer of 1940. His memoirs afford a glimpse into the working of Stalin's mind and the methods used by the Soviet leader to "educate" his new, young ministers.

The third excerpt was written by V. S. Emelianov, distinguished member of the Soviet Academy of Sciences and presently Deputy Chairman of the Soviet Atomic Energy Commission. At the time when his narrative starts in 1939, he headed the department responsible for armored steel production in the People's Commissariat of Defense Industries. He subsequently occupied other important posts in Soviet war industry. His account of a meeting with Stalin deserves special attention, coming as it does from a man whose intellectual capacity, power of observation, and sophistication are clearly superior to those of the authors of the preceding accounts.

Admiral N. G. Kuznetsov
In Charge of the Navy

I WAS FIRST CALLED to Moscow in December 1938 for a meeting of the Supreme Naval Council.[38] The new People's Commissar [of the Navy], M. P. Frinovskii, received me as soon as I arrived.

Frinovskii's appointment took us by surprise. His predecessor, P. A. Smirnov, had no naval education but was at least familiar with the army and navy where he had long carried on political work. Frinovskii, however, had no conception of the navy. He had previously worked in the NKVD, commanding frontier units. It was impossible to understand why he, of all people, had been promoted to People's Commissar just when a large navy was being built. Later I was to realize that Frinovskii was forced to rely entirely on his deputies in deciding various naval questions. . . .[39]

There was much discussion of shipbuilding at the meeting of the Supreme Naval Council. The decision of the Party and government about [building up] the navy opened a new stage in the life of our naval forces. At that time, the international situation was constantly deteriorating. . . .

N. G. Kuznetsov, "Pered voinoi," *Oktiabr'*, 1965, No. 9, pp. 174–82.

It was becoming clear that fascist Germany was our most likely foe and that the time of conflict was not far off.

In such a situation, it seemed risky to make extensive long-range plans for building ships. A large navy means not only ships, but naval bases, docks, shipyards, depots, training centers, and much more. Its creation requires much time and enormous expense. The program would not fit into one Five Year Plan, of course.[40] But at this meeting we fleet commanders were consulted mainly about ships whose construction had been authorized by the government prior to the establishment of the program as a whole. These ships were already being built. In their speeches, the members of the government often emphasized that one or another project had been approved by Stalin personally. By this they indicated that such projects were not open to discussion.

Meetings continued for several evenings. In addition, we tried to resolve our current problems in the Commissariat. At that period it was customary to work until late at night in the government offices in Moscow. A 2:00 a.m. visit to a People's Commissar was considered commonplace. We who came from the Far East found this especially trying. One would sit in a waiting room, barely able to stay awake. After all, day had long since dawned in Vladivostok![41] And when one finally got away, sleep wouldn't come. But there is no evil without its compensation. At that time of night it was especially convenient to talk on the telephone: Moscow slept, the lines were not busy, and in Vladivostok people were up and at work.

Not all the questions troubling us were discussed at meetings of the Supreme Naval Council. Frinovskii hinted to a few people that a meeting with the government was approaching at which important instructions about the future would be given.

At the end of the Council's work, a meeting with Party and governmental leaders took place. A reception was arranged at the Palace of the Facets [in the Kremlin]. It was a solemn occasion. Most of those present, young fleet commanders, were seeing Stalin for the first time. We were praised and told that extraordinary opportunities were opening up for the navy. Toasts were drunk to Stalin, the men of the navy, the fleet commanders. We responded with fervent applause until our hands ached.

This event in the Kremlin raised our spirits, inspired, and deeply impressed us. We remembered that reception long afterward. I left it more determined than ever to devote all my strength to performing whatever was demanded of us. As for the questions we had brought with us to Moscow regarding the large naval construction programs—they somehow faded into the background. . . .

I brought comprehensive plans back to Vladivostok, but I was not to stay there for long. I left for Moscow again at the end of February 1939 for the Eighteenth Party Congress. . . .[42] G. M. Shtern[43] rode with me. We talked over many things on the way. . . . We discussed the arrests of Soviet military leaders. Naturally, the greatest shock was V. K. Bliukher's arrest.[44] We were tormented by doubts but could not force ourselves to express them. Ezhov had been relieved of his post not long before, and some of those arrested had been rehabilitated. But we still had no idea of the true scale of the violations of legality.[45]

. . . .

The Eighteenth Congress of the Communist Party began on March 10, 1939. In a holiday mood, we filed into the Great Kremlin Palace with delegates from all over the country. All anxieties faded away.

Shtern and I were seated in the midst of representatives from the Maritime Territory, but we were not to sit there long. With great surprise, we heard our names when the motion on membership of the Presidium of the Congress was read.[46] We exchanged glances. Had we heard wrong? No—our neighbors already were urging us, saying, "Go on, go on—"

We went forward, without much assurance, and sat in the last row behind the rostrum. We looked upon our having been chosen for the Presidium as an expression of attention to the Far East. What had happened there so recently had, after all, stirred the entire country.[47]

In my free hours, I used to go to the People's Commissariat of the Navy to get the news from the Pacific. There was a strange atmosphere in the Commissariat. M. P. Frinovskii, the People's Commissar of the Navy, was attending the Congress—I noticed him from the Presidium—but he did not visit the Commissariat. Rumors that he would soon be dismissed were already circulating there. All current business was being decided by the First Deputy People's Commissar, P. A. Smirnov-Svetlovskii.

V. M. Molotov[48] came up to me on one of the last working days of the Congress.

"Do you intend to make a speech?" he asked.

I shook my head.

"I'm waiting for my People's Commissar to speak."

"But perhaps he doesn't intend to— I suggest that you think about it."

That evening I told Shtern about this conversation. "The comment was not an idle one," Shtern remarked. "I would prepare a speech just in case."

I immediately began drafting a speech.

The next day, the chairman asked both of us whether we were going to enter our names in the debate. We put in a request and lost all peace of mind from that moment on. It was no light matter to speak from the rostrum of the Congress.

During a recess, Stalin walked past us. Turning to me, he held out a paper he was carrying.

"Read it," he said.

It proved to be a report from M. P. Frinovskii, who asked to be released from his post as People's Commissar "in view of lack of knowledge of naval affairs."[49]

"You understand?" Stalin asked as he passed by us again.

I didn't have a chance to answer. One thing was clear. Frinovskii would not make a speech, and obviously I would be given the floor. I remember the announcement distinctly:

"Sholokhov has the floor; Kuznetsov be ready—"

I walked to the rostrum, trying with all my strength to master my emotion. I spoke of the aggressive schemes of the Japanese military clique and of their provocations on the border. Then I talked about our Pacific Fleet and assured the delegates that the sailors were ready to fulfill to the end their duty to the Homeland.[50]

Prior to the final meeting of the Congress, a proposal was introduced in the Council concerning the new composition of the Central Committee of the Party. Shtern and I were among those mentioned. Again we thought about the importance attached by the Party to the Far East and its armed forces.[51]

After the Congress, I was in a hurry to be off for Vladivostok. There were matters that would not wait. I was unable to leave, however.

"Stay in Moscow a while," P. A. Smirnov-Svetlovskii told me.

He did not explain why I was being detained. But that very night I was roused from bed and told to go to the Kremlin at once. I had to hurry; the car was waiting at the entrance to the hotel.

Stalin received me. When I came into his office, he was standing by a long table. Some papers lay in front of him. He did not speak at once. Without hurrying, he tapped his pipe on the rim of an ashtray, picked up a red pencil that seemed extraordinarily large to me, and wrote something on the top paper. Then he looked at me fixedly.

"Well, sit down."

I went up to the table with little assurance. I was not seeing Stalin for the first time, but I had never spoken with him before or had a chance to look at him carefully close up. Now I studied him intently.

He was almost the same as in his portraits, yet not quite. I had pictured him larger, taller. There was a feeling of great confidence, of knowledge of his own strength in his quiet voice and slow gestures.

He, too, looked at me attentively for some time, and I confess I was intimidated by that gaze. I had spoken with him only in my imagination before. At times, as commander, I was unable to obtain something needed by the fleet or I received orders with which I inwardly disagreed. At those times, I used to think, "If I could just see Stalin, I'd report to him in person and he'd understand and help." Now Stalin was here. However, it was not for me to report. He asked questions and I answered them. They concerned service in the Pacific Ocean, our fleet, and what I thought of the work of the People's Commissariat of the Navy. . . .

"How do you feel about working in Moscow?" he asked at the end of the conversation.

I confessed I had no fixed view on the matter.

"I never worked in the Center, haven't aspired to it, and haven't thought about it—"

"All right, you may go," Stalin said as he dismissed me.

When the car that had taken me to the Kremlin brought me back to the hotel, it was already about 3:00 a.m.

The following day, I was summoned to a special meeting of the Supreme Naval Council. The agenda was not specified. P. A. Smirnov-Svetlovskii opened the meeting and gave the floor to A. A. Zhdanov[52] who announced that there was only one question on the agenda:

"I propose to discuss whether the First Deputy People's Commissar, Smirnov-Svetlovskii, is suitable for his post."

Smirnov, who had sat down in the chairman's place, grew somber and lowered his head. There was no debate. The question was a complete surprise to the members of the Council. A. A. Zhdanov took the floor again.

"There is a feeling in the Central Committee that the leadership of the People's Commissariat should be changed. I propose the appointment of Comrade Kuznetsov as First Deputy People's Commissar in place of Smirnov-Svetlovskii. What is your opinion?"

Zhdanov looked in my direction. Other members of the Council also turned toward me. A few voices seconded the proposal without much assurance.

That same day I was presented with the official red envelope containing the decree appointing me to the new post. I went to see Smirnov-Svetlovskii. He began questioning me about the reasons for his dismissal, but I, of course, knew no more than he. We decided to begin the administrative change-over the following day. The next day, we met as agreed, worked a while, and decided to meet again the following day. I calculated that the transfer of papers would occupy about three days. The following morning Smirnov did not come to the People's Commissariat. I waited for an hour, for two hours— I never saw him again.[53] I was simply presented with the key to the safe.

I became the First Deputy People's Commissar, but there was still no Commissar. Frinovskii was said to be resting at his country house. In the meantime, a huge table in the office was heaped with papers requiring decisions. I went to A. A. Zhdanov for advice.

"You decide and call me on the more important or doubtful questions," he said. "We'll get it done."

This is how my work in Moscow began. . . .

. . . .

To help myself decide how best to begin, I called in Galler, the head of the Supreme Naval Staff,[54] and asked him to acquaint me in detail with the organization of the People's Commissariat, the people working here, and the situation in the fleets. Although such an orientation would take a lot of time, it was extremely desirable. But I did not succeed in carrying out my plan.

A. A. Zhdanov informed me that we were to go to Vladivostok and Khabarovsk to study several important problems. I tried to explain that there was a mountain of unsolved problems in Moscow, but he interrupted me with: "The papers can wait. I advise you not to say a word about them to Comrade Stalin."

The trip was set for March 28, so there was no time to spare. And then Ivan Fedorovich Tevosian[55] phoned to insist upon an immediate meeting. For several weeks no one had ruled upon even the most urgent questions concerning the approval of projects and sea trials.

A half-hour later, Tevosian was in my office. That was our first meeting, and already then I knew that we could work together. The ship building industry was obviously headed by a man of broad vision and tremendous working capacity. He knew his business perfectly.

The longer Tevosian and I discussed the progress of naval construction, the clearer I saw the whole picture of the construction program for a large fleet, whose existence we navy men often spoke of, but whose details had been kept secret. Ships were being built without waiting for approval. The hulks of giant battleships and heavy cruisers grew on the stocks. More and more destroyers and submarines were being put into operation. Some had passed tests at their moorings; others had already gone out to sea for final performance tests. In the Far East and at meetings of the Supreme Naval Council, I had heard only small details of this construction program.

I had no time to go into all the details just then, however. Tevosian and I merely decided the most pressing matters and agreed on how to act further. I had to leave for the Far East.

The trip turned out to be interesting. . . . I had many occasions to speak with Zhdanov. He took a keen interest in our navy people, in our

leaders at the People's Commissariat. That was natural. After all, he was
the Central Committee Secretary in charge of naval affairs.

Zhdanov not only asked questions; he answered all of mine. He gave
a detailed account of our country's foreign policy, much of which I heard
for the first time. A new stage in international relations was beginning.
Hitler was rushing ahead with his plans of aggression. Scarcely had he
finished intervening in Spain than he entered Czechoslovak territory on
March 15 and seized Memel, on the Baltic Sea, on March 22. These
were all recent events. Not to be outdone by Hitler, Mussolini attacked
Albania on April 6, 1939.

In short, clouds were swiftly gathering on the European political
horizon.

"Can this possibly develop into a big war?" I asked Zhdanov.

"The peace-loving countries must join forces to prevent such a fateful turn of events," he replied.

We often returned to this subject. I could not help remembering my
talk with Tevosian. A large shipbuilding program demanded much time.
Would we succeed? This question greatly troubled me, and I decided to
ask Zhdanov, "What will happen to our program if events suddenly take
a dangerous turn?"

"The program will be carried out," he answered.

I don't know whether he was really certain or only said that to reassure the new First Deputy People's Commissar.

What Zhdanov wanted most of all to see in the Far East was the site
where a new commercial port was planned. We sailed into the Bay of
Nakhodka on a destroyer. Then we planned to go to Komsomol'sk, but
on April 15 we were unexpectedly ordered back to Moscow. . . . Zhdanov
and I returned together. We had more time to talk now than on the road
to Vladivostok. . . . We spoke of many fleet commanders during those
hours.

"You know, I never thought Viktorov would turn out to be an enemy
of the people," said Zhdanov.

I heard no doubt in his voice, only surprise. I knew little of M. V.
Viktorov, former fleet commander in the Baltic and Pacific, and later chief
of naval forces. Still other names came up in conversation: V. M. Orlov,
I. K. Kozhanov, E. S. Pantserzhanskii, R. A. Muklevich.[56] We spoke of them
as of men who had passed beyond the grave. The reasons were not discussed. . . .

I did not yet have a clear conception of the situation in all the fleets;
but I knew that henceforth, while we strove to build a large navy, the
problem of handling the new ships would become very critical. New technology cannot be mastered at once. The number of accidents and break-

downs increased as new submarines, destroyers, and other warships were put into service.

The fleets had to be watched over closely; I said that I wanted to visit them all in the coming months. "And wouldn't you also like to take part in the interesting maneuvers and cruises?" I asked Zhdanov.

Much in naval affairs depended on Zhdanov, and I wanted him to know the fleets as well as possible.

"With great pleasure," he answered enthusiastically. "I'd love to go. But it's not always so easy to get away."

He spoke little about himself. Only when we crossed the Kama, near Perm, did he mention that he had seen action in these parts and later was secretary of the provincial [Party] committee in Gor'kii. "In general, I am more of a river-man than a seaman. A fresh-water sailor, as they say," he joked. "But I love ships and enjoy working in naval affairs."

As a member of the Supreme Naval Council, Zhdanov in fact did a great deal for the navy.

.   .   .   .

We returned to Moscow. I went to the Commissariat straight from the station; I had to bring myself up to date. On April 27 I was summoned to the Kremlin. The talk concerned the results of our trip to the Far East. All the members of the Politburo were present. Zhdanov described the impression [the Bay of] Nakhodka made on him.

"That's really a *nakhodka* for us!" [A play of words—"nakhodka" in Russian—"find." Ed.]

The decision was taken at once to build a new commercial port there.

Zhdanov discussed the affairs of the Maritime Territory and the Pacific Fleet. As we were leaving, Stalin said to those present: "Well, shall we decide the naval question?"

Everyone agreed with him. I did not understand what this "naval question" was, but it was awkward to ask.

From the Kremlin, I stopped off at my house. When I returned to work, I saw a red package lying on my desk. It contained a decree by the Presidium of the Supreme Soviet of the USSR appointing me People's Commissar of the Navy.[57]

I read this document with a mixture of joy and anxiety. Too fast an elevation is dangerous for a man. That applies not only to skindivers and pilots. Many dangers also lurk in too fast an elevation up the service ladder. This I understood from my youth. That was why after graduating from the [Naval] Academy, I asked to be appointed senior assistant [to a ship captain], in order to progress in the service step by step. I dreamed of commanding a ship some day—and that was all. But in the past few years my advancement had become quite precipitous. It can only be explained by the wave of forced transfers at that time. Once one accepts a post, however, he must fulfill his duties and not count on any allowances. And I well understood that my new duties were not easy.

That evening I sat in my office a long time, thinking: where to begin, what's most important?

L. M. Galler phoned: "Permit me to report." He stayed two hours. I wanted to seek the advice of this experienced, intelligent man.

"Better make use of the honeymoon," said Galler, stroking his reddish mustache. He glanced at me and added in a confidential way: "At first, they'll look over your proposals quickly. And they'll make quick decisions about them. Later, it will become more difficult—"

I took this advice into account, although I did not realize at once how right it was. A little time passed, and access to Stalin became extremely difficult. But without Stalin no one ventured to decide the large questions concerning the navy. During the first few months, however, I got everything we needed most, without any special delays. Stalin devoted much attention to the shipbuilding program and all other naval affairs.

At that time meetings were held about industrial deliveries for ship construction almost every week. The navy and Tevosian were urgently requested to present for governmental approval projects for ships already under construction, as well as the plans for navy bases, ship-repair installations, docks, depots, and everything else needed by a large navy.

Lieutenant General A. S. Iakovlev
The New Deputy
Minister

ON JANUARY 9, 1940 an event occurred which greatly influenced all my future work, especially during the war.

I was seated in my office at the design bureau, preparing a report on the testing of our fighter plane.[58] The Kremlin telephone rang, and I was told that Stalin would speak with me.

A. S. Iakovlev, *Tsel' zhizni* (Moscow, 1966), pp. 192–202.

"Are you very busy? Would it be possible for you to come here immediately? We need your help in deciding an organizational question."

I called for a car and was at the Kremlin fifteen minutes later.

"They are waiting for you, hurry!" Poskrebyshev[59] said.

In addition to several members of the Politburo there was in [Stalin's] office, a stocky, light-haired man whom I did not know.

Stalin greeted me, invited me to sit down, and said that the Central Committee had decided to relieve M. M. Kaganovich[60] of his position as People's Commissar of the Aviation Industry in view of his failure to cope with his duties. Stalin gave Kaganovich a rather unflattering efficiency rating. Aleksei Ivanovich Shakhurin was being appointed the new People's Commissar. We were introduced to one another.

"And it has been decided to appoint you Comrade Shakhurin's deputy. You will handle the research and experimental development in aviation."

I was astonished. I was prepared for anything but such a proposal. I began refusing. I presented many seemingly convincing arguments. Chiefly, I tried to show that I could not handle such a large administrative job, that I did not have sufficient experience to cope with it.

In answer to this I was told that Shakhurin also lacked such experience; he was Secretary of the Party Committee in Gor'kii province.[61]

"I am an expert designer and not an administrator."

"That is exactly what is needed."

"I am still very young."

"That is an advantage rather than a disadvantage."

Finally, I argued that I could not abandon design work because I could not live without it.

I was answered that no one was forcing me to abandon my design activity. The new People's Commissar would create conditions under which I could combine my duties as Deputy People's Commissar with creative work on the development of aircraft.

I said that I could not bear up under the work regimen, alluding to the fact that they worked until two, three, even four o'clock in the morning at the People's Commissariat every day. The answer to this was that I could establish my own work regimen, the important thing being that the work went well.

There was one other thing that bothered me: I, a designer, occupying the post of Deputy People's Commissar for Research and Development, could become an object of gossip and envy. Designers would accuse me of lacking objectivity and of barring the door to others.

Stalin countered, saying that I, as a person responsible for research and development and occupying the post of Deputy People's Commissar, would be interested in seeing to it that all design groups developed freely and were utilized to the fullest extent, and that if I worked conscientiously, I should make it possible for all our designers to work successfully. In addition, he once more stressed the fact that no one was thinking of depriving me of the possibility of working as a designer. Quite the contrary, they were hoping that I would continue to produce good airplanes.

In a word, not a single one of my arguments was heeded. Nonetheless, I persisted.

"So you don't want to be Deputy People's Commissar?"

"No, I don't, Comrade Stalin."

"Perhaps you want to be the People's Commissar?" he said smiling and then, now very serious, added:

"Are you a communist? Do you acknowledge Party discipline?"

I replied that I did and that if the question were put on such a plane I should have to obey, but that this would be coercion.

Stalin burst out laughing:

"But we are not afraid of coercion. We will not stop short of coercion when it is necessary. Sometimes, coercion is useful. Without coercion, there would have been no revolution. After all, coercion is the midwife of revolution."

Of course, I was proud of the trust that the Party had placed in me. But deep in my heart I was sincerely afraid that I should not be able to justify this trust in an enormous, responsible job which was completely new to me.

On January 11, 1940, a decree of the Council of People's Commissars of the USSR was promulgated, appointing me Deputy People's Commissar of the Aviation Industry for Research and Development.

.   .   .   .

The People's Commissariat began planning the activity of design bureaus and scientific research institutes. . . .

Everything was done so that aircraft designers would not be working on a hit-and-miss basis, but rather on the basis of the very latest scientific research. Conditions for fruitful creative activity were provided for everyone.

Nonetheless, just as I had foreseen—and much earlier than could have been assumed—some designers very readily began to explain their failures by saying that "Iakovlev wasn't giving them a chance." One matter even went as far as the Politburo.

Once, in the summer of 1940, Shakhurin and I were summoned to the Kremlin. We entered Stalin's office where a conference was in progress. Almost all members of the Politburo were seated at the long table. Stalin came to greet us and then picked up some kind of document. He did not invite us to sit down as usual and began to read the document aloud without giving any explanations whatsoever.

The more he read, the worse I felt. It was a letter from a designer who was requesting that he be permitted to implement his design of an aircraft which had very high combat qualities. The designer wrote that he could not count on the support of the People's Commissariat since Iakovlev was in charge of experimental development there and, as a designer, would be afraid of competition and would not approve his design. For this reason he was appealing directly to the Central Committee.

In conclusion, the author of the letter expressed astonishment that such a matter as research and development was headed by a designer who could in no way be objective and who would "squeeze out" others. And he concluded his letter with the promise that if he were given the assignment, he would give the country the very best, the very fastest, and the best-armed fighter.

There was dead silence. All those present were listening attentively.

Stalin finished reading and, without hurrying, arranged the papers neatly.

"Well, what do you have to say?"

I was extremely upset but said:

"This designer did not approach me."

"Well, what if he had?"

"In such a case, we would have examined the design, and, if it turned out to be a good one, we would have proposed to the government that the airplane be built."

"What about the design, is it a good one?"

"It is difficult for me to say since I have not seen it. I don't understand why the author appealed directly to the Central Committee; as I promised, I try to be objective."

Shakhurin had also heard about the design for the first time and was unable to say anything. Then Stalin declared:

"Of course, he should have talked with you first. Without having talked to you, it was wrong to write a complaint about you. I don't know what kind of design it is. Perhaps it will be a good airplane, perhaps a bad one, but the figures are enticing. We'll risk it. Let him build it. By the way, what will such an airplane cost?"

"I would say about nine or ten million."

"We'll have to risk it. The promises are very enticing indeed. Perhaps this will be money down the drain. Well, anyway, I'll assume the responsibility. And I will ask you not to persecute him for this letter but to help him build the airplane."

I gave my word that I would take every step to promote the construction of the airplane. The People's Commissar also made this promise.

When the question had been decided, Stalin said to me:

"You probably find it unpleasant that such letters are written. But

I am glad. By the way, that is not the first letter. It would be a bad thing if no one complained. That would mean that you wanted to live in harmony with everyone at the government's expense. Don't be afraid of quarreling when the matter requires it. This is better than friendship at the government's expense. It is not always the case that the interests of individuals coincide with those of the government. In addition, you are a designer, you have scored great successes, and as long as you work well, you will be envied. The only ones who are not envied are those who have no successes."

I was already in the doorway when I heard [him] calling after me: "Don't persecute the designer for his complaint. Let him build it. We'll risk the millions; the risk will be mine."

It goes without saying that the necessary support was given to the designer. Unfortunately, despite great expenditures, his airplane did not turn out well and crashed during its very first flight. In addition, Nikashin, one of our best military test pilots, died trying to save the aircraft.

Here is yet another, much less tragic episode from the early period of my work at the People's Commissariat.

Once [my] secretary handed me a package together with the morning mail and laughed. Why did she do that? I looked. On the envelope was the letterhead of the newspaper *Izvestiia*.[62] The address was written properly. There was nothing funny.

"Take a look inside."

I took out a sheet of paper with a newspaper clipping attached to it. The well-known journalist and special *Izvestiia* correspondent E. Vilenskii was writing to me.

"Dear Comrade Iakovlev!

"During my stay in Western Belorussia, I found [a copy of] the newspaper *Russkii golos* which announced your 'death.'[63]

"I am sending you a copy of this item. Perhaps it will amuse you. Its date: 1939. Regards, *Izvestiia* special correspondent Vilenskii."

Here is what the newspaper clipping said:

Details on The Murder of Engineer Iakovlev in Moscow

London newspapers are publishing the latest details on the murder in Moscow of Iakovlev, well-known Soviet designer of military airplanes.

According to English newspapers, Iakovlev enjoyed fame as a talented aircraft designer as well as the full confidence of Soviet government leaders. Iakovlev was frequently summoned to Stalin who would discuss various problems connected with aeronautics at great length with him. Iakovlev did most of his work at home where he kept blueprints of various airplane designs.

The other day, Iakovlev was to have gone to a conference at the People's Commissariat of Defense where he was to demonstrate the plans of a military airplane of the latest design. However, Iakovlev did not arrive at that conference. Since he was known for his punctuality, attention was called to this fact. An attempt was made to call his apartment from the People's Commissariat. When there was no answer, this was reported to the People's Commissariat of Internal Affairs, and Beria, accompanied by several other leaders of the People's Commissariat, set out from there for Iakovlev's apartment. The door to Engineer Iakovlev's apartment was broken in, and Iakovlev was found lying dead on the floor of his room. Iakovlev was found to have been wounded with some kind of sharp object, but, in the opinion of the physicians performing the autopsy, death was caused by smothering.

A rather large sum of money in Iakovlev's apartment was untouched. But all the blueprints, including those of the new military airplane that Iakovlev had designed, had disappeared.

In Moscow, there is no doubt but that the murder of Engineer Iakovlev was the work of the counterintelligence service of a foreign government which was interested in stealing the plans for the latest models of Soviet aircraft.

I decided that when I had the opportunity I would show this article to Stalin as a curiosity.

The opportunity soon arose.

Stalin read it through attentively and grinned:

"They're presenting their wishful thinking as reality. This is what they would like."

Then, after a brief silence, he asked:

"By the way, do you have a safe at home?"

"I don't have a safe. I don't need one. I don't work on blueprints and designs at home, and I can do my thinking without a safe."

"That's true. You can't hide thoughts in a safe. And what about the other designers? They don't work at home either?"

"We all have excellent conditions at work, and total secrecy is assured."

"That is good. It is necessary to be very vigilant in these times. For example, we assigned a guard to arms designer Degtiarev;[64] he was taking all his secrets home where he worked on them. We forbade it. But after all you can't assign a guard to everyone, and your work isn't the same thing—an airplane isn't a pistol."

"You can rest assured that state secrets are secure in the design bureaus," I stated.

"But all the same, have a talk with the designers on this subject. I know that there are still some careless people among you. An extra talk won't hurt."

"As you direct, Comrade Stalin. I shall call the designers together and, in your name, talk with them."

"Why in my name? Tell them yourself."

Stalin looked at me angrily:

"There are many who love to hide behind my back. In every detail they refer to me and do not want to take the responsibility on themselves. You are a young man. You are still unspoiled, and you know your business. Don't be afraid to act in your own name; your authority will be greater, and people will respect you."

V. S. Emelianov
Trials of an
Industrial Manager

THERE WAS more than one point of view among military men and specialists in the field of military technology on questions of armor protection for tanks. Some believed that speed constitutes armor protection. It is difficult to hit a tank moving at great speed. Their opponents objected that military operations would take place not on highways, but on broken terrain, where it is impossible to move at great speed. In addition, it would be artillery, not rifles, that would be firing on the tanks. Therefore, it was necessary to develop tank designs with a protection of thick armor, which could withstand not only machine gun fire, but also shelling. The opponents, in turn, contended that firing at tanks with artillery is the same as firing at sparrows with artillery.

There appeared at that time many of the most incredible proposals concerning armor protection, types of armor, methods of manufacturing it, and materials for the production of armor parts. Among them were so many utterly absurd ones that it seemed incredible that their authors could submit them and that those who accepted the proposals dared insist on the necessity of testing them experimentally. One, for example, was based on using the rotary motion of a shell in flight. If the tank hulls were reinforced with approximately the same kind of cutting teeth as on a lathe, it was said, a shell would be turned into steel shavings. In the

V. S. Emelianov, "O vremeni, o tovarishchakh, o sebe," *Novyi mir*, 1967, No. 2, pp. 85–94.

author's drawing of this proposal the tank rather resembled a porcupine. There were ideas for using glass pressed between sheet steel for protection and many others. Some of them were difficult to assess right away. All such papers coming to the Main Administration [of Armor Production] [65] were inscribed: "Strictly secret" and "Special importance." A limited number of persons was allowed to see all these proposals, and it was impossible to have them examined thoroughly by experts. . . .

At that time many inventors were working on screen armor protection for tanks. I first heard about this type of armor from Dmitrii Grigor'evich Pavlov, director of the Armored Vehicle Directorate of the People's Commissariat of Defense. [66] He told me that during the Civil War they had had to protect themselves from rifle and machine gun fire of the Whites, and they used whatever happened to be at hand.

"Once we even piled up bags of flour along the sides of a railroad platform, hid behind them, and fired. Then someone suggested riveting thin sheets of iron together and using them for armor protection. At that time there was no thick sheet iron handy, and the riveted sheets served as our armor. During the war in Spain we used that kind of armor protection—made from two sheets riveted together. But in Spain we had already begun to make different kinds of sheet steel. One sheet, facing the inside of the tank, was made from ordinary boiler plate, and the second, the exterior sheet, which was to absorb the enemy fire, was made from high-grade steel tempered to a very high degree of hardness."

Later engineer Nikolaev improved this type of two-layer armor. He suggested moving the sheets apart and separating the sheet of high-grade steel and the soft sheet of boiler plate by a distance of slightly more than the length of a bullet. He explained his idea this way. A bullet hitting the first sheet would spend a considerable part of its kinetic energy on the destruction of that sheet, and, consequently, the second sheet would be hit with a weaker force. Moreover, the trajectory of the bullet would be changed; the bullet would ricochet and that would also increase the resistibility of the second sheet.

Together with military men and specialists in armor production we discussed Nikolaev's proposal, but it already seemed to me then that it had no practical value. It was the equivalent of putting a patch on old, worn-out trousers. Of course, they could be worn, but is it sensible to build modern military technology on this principle?

"As a matter of fact," I thought, "isn't it really obvious that even the very first round of machine gun fire would knock the thin suit of armor off the tank and the soft boiler plate would be unable to serve as protection. What kind of armor would that be! . . . No," I soothed myself, "they simply will not allow this absurd idea to be accepted. After all,

there are many sensible people among the military men and technicians."
I had forgotten one thing—no one would dare oppose it, once the proposal had already been approved "from above." But what I had supposed would not happen was exactly what did happen. Information
reached me that the idea of manufacturing screen armor had been submitted to the government.

The danger was imminent that factories and research organizations
would be diverted from the real job. It was decided to discuss the idea
of manufacturing tanks with screen armor at a government meeting with
military men and industry officials taking part. We assembled in the
reception room and awaited a summons. At the time, other matters were
being discussed in the meeting room.

Among those invited were D. G. Pavlov, Chief of the Armored Vehicle Directorate, Major General N. N. Alymov, Colonel Puganov, Nikolaev, author of the proposal, and many other military men and civilians
connected with the production of tanks. . . . Colonel Puganov came up
to me. I was on friendly terms with him and respected him deeply. . . .

"Well, what is your attitude toward this armor, professor?" Puganov
asked me.[67]

I cited all my objections and noted in conclusion:

"There are no miracles in this world, Colonel!"

But at that point we were invited into the meeting room. There were
a few people in the circular room where it was held. I discerned L. M.
Kaganovich, V. M. Molotov, K. E. Voroshilov, I. F. Tevosian, Chief of
the General Staff B. M. Shaposhnikov, B. L. Vannikov, and S. A. Akopov,
all seated at the table. I saw Stalin, apart from everyone else, not far
from the long table which was covered with a red cloth. There was nothing on the table except boxes of cigarettes and matches. Stalin was walking around slowly. In one hand he held a notebook and in the other a
pencil. He was smoking the short pipe so familiar to everyone.

When everyone who had been invited had entered and taken seats,
Molotov said that a draft resolution had been submitted to the government on the manufacture of tanks with a new type of armor. It was to
be discussed.

"Who is to report?" asked Stalin, turning to Pavlov. "You told me
that this armor had been further improved. Perhaps we'll hear the author
of the idea right away. Is he here? Was he invited?"

Nikolaev rose from his seat.

"Tell us about your proposal," Stalin said.

Nikolaev went up to the table and began to report. He outlined the
essence of the idea clearly, avoiding specialized terminology, and concluded his account with unusual effectiveness:

"All existing types of armor are passive means of defense. The armor we have proposed is active armor, for in being destroyed, it protects."

I saw that Nikolaev's report was making a very good impression on everyone present. They were listening very attentively. Even though I already knew in all details the idea of armor protection and the proposed method of manufacturing the hulls, I listened to the speaker with interest. He outlined the substance of the idea graphically, concisely, and simply. "Nikolaev is undoubtedly a capable engineer, although this idea of his has no practical value," I thought, while he was making his report.

While Nikolaev was speaking, Stalin smoked his pipe and looked at him intently. Only now and then did he raise the lowered hand holding the notebook and jot something down.

When Nikolaev had said, "in being destroyed, it protects," Stalin removed his pipe and repeated:

"In being destroyed, it protects. Interesting. That's dialectics in action! Well, what do the representatives of industry have to say on this matter, Comrade Nikolaev? What do they think of your proposal?" Stalin asked.

"They object to this type of armor protection," Nikolaev replied quickly.

"Why?"

I saw that Stalin was frowning, and I felt uneasy.

All those seated were following the dialogue intently. I saw Tevosian looking back and forth from Stalin to Nikolaev.

Nikolaev was silent, apparently collecting his thoughts.

"Just what are their objections?" Stalin repeated his question and slowly moved toward Nikolaev.

Finally, Nikolaev, somewhat agitated, replied:

"I have heard no arguments from them on the substance of the proposal. They simply say that there are no miracles in this world."

"Who says it?" And Stalin's eyes bored into him.

Nikolaev hesitated, and it was apparent how agitated he was. Finally, lowering his head, he said hollowly:

"I don't remember who said it, Comrade Stalin."

I gulped, as people do in an airplane when there is a sudden drop in altitude. "But those are my words; I said it." I began to feel sick at heart. "What will happen?"

"You don't remember?"

Nikolaev had probably gotten a grip on himself, and he repeated, more firmly than the first time:

"No, I don't remember, Comrade Stalin."

"That's a mistake. Such people should be remembered!" he said harshly, and, turning around abruptly, he went over to the table. Pulling out his pipe, Stalin tapped it on the table cover and knocked out the ashes.

"Nikolaev," I thought, "is a decent man. After all, as author of the idea he was not only insulted but virtually ridiculed by me before the conference itself. He has made an unfavorable impression on Stalin with his answer 'I don't remember.' His star was only beginning to shine, and he himself has consciously extinguished it." I felt uneasy. "Why was I so abrupt in my opinions? Perhaps I should have talked with him a bit before the idea was submitted to the government? Explained to him the absurdity of producing tanks with that kind of armor. He's not a stupid man, and he would have been able to see his error and drop it. I have more experience; I'm older than Nikolaev. Well, why didn't I do this before, have a friendly talk with him? Now it's too late." All of this went through my mind like a flash, but my eyes were on Stalin.

He was knocking the ashes out of his pipe. He raised it closer to his eyes and peered into it. Then from the box of Herzegovina Flor cigarettes standing on the table, he took two cigarettes at once and broke them. He laid the mouthpieces on the table and began to twirl the tobacco ends of the cigarettes over the pipe, filling it with tobacco. He laid the empty cigarette paper on the table near the cigarette box and pressed the tobacco into the pipe with his thumb. Slowly, he approached the table again, took the matchbox, and struck a match.

I winced.

"You told me," Stalin said, moving closer to Pavlov, after he had removed the lighted pipe from his mouth, "that there was someone who had used this type of armor steel in Spain."

Pavlov rose from his seat and said:

"General Alymov."

"Is he here?"

Alymov rose.

"Perhaps you will tell us what you did there?"

Alymov gave a brief account of how the production of two-layer armor had been set up in Barcelona. The sheets of armor had been riveted together and fastened to the tank hull. Such armor had not been pierced during firing either by ordinary bullets or by armor-piercing bullets. His account was rather like a report.

Pavlov said:

"To us military men the matter is clear. We should begin making such tanks."

"Well then, we can end the discussion here," Molotov said. "Those who were invited for this matter may go."

We left the Kremlin. It was 2:00 a.m. . . .

And so, the decision to develop a tank with the new type of armor protection, which "in being destroyed, protects," was made. What was to be done?

The design bureaus were still intensively developing new types of heavy tanks calculated to withstand artillery shelling. Now all of this work would be slowed down, and perhaps if they were especially zealous in compelling us to make this type of screen armor a reality, all the other work would stop altogether. No, we had to find some means to convince them that they had made the wrong decision. After thinking about it a long time, I came to the conclusion that there was only one real possibility—to manufacture a tank with "active" armor as quickly as possible and to show graphically the absurdity of the design. . . .

At the main firing range, where armor was tested, there were experienced, well-trained specialists. They scrupulously recorded the results of the tests made. Everyone had confidence in their records.

"The tests must be conducted without fail at this firing range," I thought. "It is also very important to set up an authoritative government commission to evaluate the results of the tests."

When the test samples were ready, I spoke to Pavlov.

"A government commission should be formed to test the samples."

"What for? Did you make progress with your armor?"

"Not with ours, with yours," I said, laughing. "The idea of screen armor was yours, you know."

"Did the samples help you?" asked Pavlov.

"Of course. We made exactly the same kind as yours. Now it's time to test them, and after the tests it will be possible to begin production. Whom do you suggest as chairman of the government commission?"

"Who else but you, of course," Pavlov suggested graciously.

"I can't be appointed chairman. I am an interested party. People may say that a person who's not objective was appointed and he was biased in his approach to the preparation of the commission's decisions."

"I trust you," Pavlov said.

"You may trust me, but all doubts as to the correctness of the commission's findings should be removed, you know. I should be on the commission, but the chairman ought to be a person of incontestable authority. It would be better if it were a military man, not a civilian. After all, the military men will be using the tanks, and it is they who ought to assess the new tank armor."

"That's right," said Pavlov. "Well then, Major General Alymov can be appointed. I trust him as I do myself."

When I arrived at the firing range a day before the tests began, I brought five armor plates—four that had been manufactured by our plants and one that I had obtained from Pavlov.[68] All the details of the test had been arranged with the personnel at the firing range, and I awaited the arrival of the remaining members of the commission.

When the whole commission had assembled, General Alymov said:

"Look, he had absolutely no faith in this armor, but now he is more concerned about how the work is done than the author of the proposal."

"I follow the rule," I replied to Alymov, "that before a decision is made, you may debate it and object as much as you please, but once the decision has been made, you carry it out."

"That's the military way," Alymov said approvingly.

"Well then, may we proceed?" I asked Alymov.

"We shall begin from the shortest distance."

After the first round of shots, the firing range official in charge of the tests said:

"All the samples have been pierced."

The distance was doubled. Again all five of the plates had been pierced, the testers reported.

"What five?" Alymov asked. "We're supposed to test four, not five." And he headed for the spot where the armor plates were attached. Going up to the bullet-marked armor samples, Alymov began to shout in great irritation: "Who put up this plate? On whose instruction was this done?"

He recognized the armor sample that Pavlov had sent me.

"It was done at my request," I said quietly to Alymov.

"Why did you do this?"

"You and Pavlov claimed that your 'active' armor offers full protection from armor-piercing bullets at any distance. Now you see for yourself that it's not so. Your armor has been pierced the same as the samples manufactured by our plants."

"I don't understand what happened! Why was it pierced?" Alymov said with bewilderment.

"But I understand," I said, trying to remain calm. "You misled the government. This armor could not have withstood the conditions you reported to the government."

"The tests have to stop," Alymov demanded.

"No, they have to be carried through to the end, and the whole intended program has to be completed."

Alymov waved his hand and withdrew to one side.

The tests were completed. The scorebook was drawn up according to all the firing range regulations, and the commission members, including Alymov, signed the document that had been compiled. I signed for one of the copies and took it with me.

When we returned to Moscow, an infuriated Pavlov literally flew in to see me immediately at the Main Administration.

"What are you trying to do?"

I already knew that the battle had been won, but the winning could only cause me harm. The armor no longer belonged either to the author of the proposal or to Pavlov. But no one would dare report that there had been a mistake and further work should be stopped.

Pavlov would now be on my side, and although he was shouting now, he had no other recourse but to submit a new proposal. He had to be helped with it.

"But you know, Dmitrii Grigor'evich," I began, "isn't it time to abandon altogether a tank armor that offers protection only from bullets, regardless of whether it withstands bullets or not? Antitank artillery has appeared, and we have to create protection against shells, not bullets."

Pavlov became alert. Perhaps this was the way out for him.

"Well, you're right, you know. I've already thought of it myself. Let's talk about it later." And he left, already reassured.

In a talk with Pavlov a few days later, I again raised the question of new tanks with heavy armor that offered protection from shells.

"It's not easy to design such tanks, but if you'll help, we can set to work quickly."

Pavlov grinned and said:

"I'm not an ignoramus, you know." He drew some sheets of paper from a safe and handed them to me. "Here, look."

On a short report entry about the necessity of starting to develop heavy tanks was written: "I am for it. Stalin."

That was the end of "active" armor. I rejoiced inwardly. Now tank production would be developed as it should. Everything was beginning to proceed sensibly. . . .

Three days passed, and suddenly the telephone rang: I was invited to a meeting in the Kremlin. The question of cast tank turrets was to be discussed, this time in the Politburo.[69] We went to the Kremlin. Many people had been invited. There were mainly military men from the Armored Vehicle Directorate in the reception room. There, too, was Tevosian, who was then People's Commissar of Ferrous Metallurgy.

"Well, how are things going?" he asked in greeting. I told him briefly about our work in molding the turrets. It wasn't clear, but why was this question being discussed a second time? No one had objected previously.

Voroshilov was reporting from the draft project. In his hands was the resolution prepared by the Defense Committee. Stalin went up to him and took the sheet. He read it and, turning to Ia. N. Fedorenko, Director of the Armored Vehicle Directorate,[70] asked:

"What tactical and technical advantages does the new turret have?"

Fedorenko began to tell about how it was possible to manufacture the molded turret in foundries, while powerful presses were required for stamping certain parts for the manufacture of turrets of the old type.

"I didn't ask you about that. I asked you what tactical and technical advantages the new turret has, and you tell me about technological advantages. Who in your office handles military technology?"

Fedorenko named General I. A. Lebedev.

"Is he here?"

General Lebedev rose. Stalin repeated the question. Lebedev hesitated and began to repeat essentially what Fedorenko had said.

Stalin frowned and asked angrily:

"Where do you serve—in the army or in industry? I am asking for the third time about the tactical and technical advantages of the new turret, and you tell me about what opportunities are opening up for industry. Perhaps it would be better for you to transfer to work in industry?"

The general was silent. I felt that the decision on changing over to molded turrets might well not be accepted. I raised my hand and asked for the floor. Stalin, seeing my hand raised, turned toward me and said:

"I am asking about the tactical and technical advantages."

"This is what I want to talk about, Iosif Vissarionovich."

"What are you, a military man?" asked Stalin.

"No."

"What do you want to say?" asked Stalin with an unfriendly expression on his face.

I removed from my portfolio the scorecards with results of the armor shelling and went up to Stalin.

"The old turret, which is welded together from individual parts, has vulnerable spots—the welding seams. The new turret is a solid piece; it is uniformly strong. Here are the results of a shelling test of both types at the firing range."

Stalin looked at the scoreboards, returned them to me, and said:

"This is a serious consideration."

He withdrew to the other end of the room.

"Tell me, how will the tank's center of gravity be changed if there is a changeover to the new turret? Is the designer of the machine here?"

The designer rose.

"If there is a change, Comrade Stalin, it will be slight."

"Slight is not an engineering term. Did you make the calculations?"

"No, I did not."

"But why not? That's military technology, you know."

I wanted to express my opinion and, raising my hand, I said loudly:

"Iosif Vissarionovich!"

Stalin looked in my direction, and again I saw that former expression on his face. "Why does he look at me like that?" I thought.

But Stalin turned and went to the opposite corner of the room. I sat down. And suddenly a whisper from the man sitting behind me explained everything:

"Never call him by his name and patronymic. He allows only a very narrow circle of intimates to do that. To all of us he is Stalin. Comrade Stalin." [71]

Suddenly, turning to the designer and without taking his eyes from him, Stalin asked how the load on the front axle of the tank would be changed.

The designer stood up and said quietly:

"Slightly."

"Why do you keep saying 'slightly,' 'slightly,' over and over? Tell me, did you make calculations?"

"No," the designer replied quietly.

"But why not?"

The designer remained silent.

"I suggest that the proposed draft resolution be rejected as inadequately prepared. Instruct the comrades not to submit such drafts to the government. Assign a commission to prepare a new draft; the membership is to include Fedorenko, him"—he pointed at S. A. Akopov, the People's Commissar of the Motor Vehicle and Tractor Industry—"and him." Stalin's finger was pointing at me.

All who had been invited to discuss the question of molded tank turrets quickly rose and headed for the exit.

I. I. Nosenko[72] came over to me.

"You let me down. Send a telegram at once that the production of molded turrets is to stop. Your turrets have not been accepted. Military men will no longer accept them. You have to all intents and purposes halted all production of tanks. Do you know what that can lead to?"

When I was going down the stairs, I felt someone touch my shoulder. I turned. It was General Shcherbakov.

"Don't lose heart," he whispered. "Let's go to Savel'ev. He's a good man, and he'll prompt you on what should be done."

Savel'ev was one of the executives on the Defense Committee, and he already knew that the draft for the molded tank turrets had not been accepted. It was necessary to prepare a new one quickly.

"And the main thing is to prepare memoranda on all the questions that Stalin raised. Put down in the draft that it is authorized to deliver molded turrets along with welded ones," Savel'ev advised.

I drew up the draft resolution and showed it to Savel'ev. Savel'ev made a few corrections and said:

"Now obtain verification from Fedorenko and Akopov and prepare the memoranda quickly, and I'll do the rest. But hurry and keep in mind that the matter is very serious."

Regaining my composure at the People's Commissariat, I retyped the prepared draft and started to phone Fedorenko. No one answered the phone for a long time, and finally the person on duty informed me that Fedorenko would not be at work that day. He had gone out of town.

Akopov was in his office. He signed the draft without discussion and merely asked:

"But what about the memoranda?"

"I'll have them in the morning," I replied wearily.

I returned home at 3:00 a.m. I was shaking all over. I couldn't fall asleep.

In the morning my head was splitting. I went to the Main Administration and again began dialing Fedorenko. The memoranda with calculations of the change in the center of gravity and the load on the front axle lay on my desk. Finally, the familiar voice answered:

"Hello."

"I have the draft resolution ready. Akopov has already verified it. May I see you?"

"Yes, but quickly. I am leaving."

I went immediately to Fedorenko. He read the draft and asked:

"And they won't reject it again?"

"No, I talked with Savel'ev. He assures me that they will accept it."

"Well, Savel'ev knows." And Fedorenko signed his name on the bottom beside Akopov's signature.

Now everything depended on Savel'ev.

Savel'ev read the memoranda, took the draft resolution, put it in his portfolio, and said:

"I shall try to have it signed as quickly as possible."

Savel'ev kept his word. The resolution was signed without corrections.

When the envelope with the resolution was brought to me and I had signed the receipt and opened it, I suddenly felt like sleeping. Never before in my life had I fallen asleep in the daytime or even experienced drowsiness. I asked the secretary to send for a car.

"I'm going home. If anyone asks, say that I took sick."

PART III   THE DEADLY FRIENDS

Introduction

IN STALIN'S OPINION, the "non-interven-
tion" policy of certain European governments in the 1930's revealed

an eagerness . . . to allow all the belligerents
to sink deeply into the mire of war, to encourage them surreptitiously in this; to allow
them to weaken and exhaust one another;
and then, when they have become weak
enough, to appear on the scene with fresh
strength . . . and to dictate conditions to
the enfeebled belligerents.*

What better way to describe what Stalin himself hoped to achieve when he
signed the Nazi-Soviet "Treaty of Nonaggression" in August 1939? The absence
of a clause which released one con-
tracting party from his obligations in
the event of an aggressive act committed
by the other, a usual concomitant of
such treaties in the past, served warning that both Russians and Germans
tacitly acknowledged that the treaty's
value lay precisely in securing German
flanks, thereby removing the last obstacle to Nazi aggression. The attached
secret protocol transformed a declaration of mutual neutrality into an active
partnership in dividing up Eastern
Europe.

While the Nazi-Soviet Pact did not
"cause" the Second World War, it did
enhance Germany's ability to wage the
war.

To Stalin—so it seemed at the beginning—the Pact brought nothing but

advantages; it entailed almost no risks,
and it involved no material concessions of any sort. His advantage lasted
until the successful blitzkrieg in Europe
in the summer of 1940 undermined the
basis of the nonaggression treaty. With
France subjugated and England reduced to a state of desperate defense,
Hitler now had a free hand in the East.
Stalin again faced the old nightmare of
the 1930's—Russia against the mighty
German army. His actions during the
year before the German invasion were
directed toward the parallel but mutually exclusive goals of securing the
most advantageous strategic position
for waging war with Germany on the
one hand and placating Hitler in an
effort to delay the outbreak of war on
the other. While Soviet actions from the
summer of 1940 to the summer of 1941
may have reinforced Hitler's resolve
to destroy the Soviet Union, they did
not inspire it. As Walter Laqueur has
written, Hitler

attacked the Soviet Union not because of
anything the Russians had done after August
1939, but because of what they were—a
strong military power headed by a leader
and a party who remained potential enemies despite all the mutual assurances of
good will and peace.†

The period of the Nazi-Soviet Pact
and particularly the honeymoon which
preceded Nazi victories in the West

---

*I. V. Stalin, *Voprosy Leninizma* (Moscow,
1957), p. 610.

†Walter Laqueur, *Russia and Germany*
(Boston: Little, Brown, and Co., 1965), p. 260.

inconvenience and, indeed, embarrass the Soviet writers of memoirs. Those who touch the subject at all vie with one another in effusive declarations that they personally were repelled by the ideas and practices of their newly found friends. Of the three excerpts which deal with the Pact, by far the most interesting belongs to A. S. Iakovlev, aircraft designer and Deputy People's Commissar of the Aviation Industry. He traveled to Germany twice, in the fall of 1939 and again in March 1940, as part of a delegation sent to purchase German military equipment. He returned in November 1940 with the top-level delegation headed by V. I. Molotov. Iakovlev discusses the attitudes of delegation members and describes his report to Stalin upon his return.

The second excerpt was written by V. M. Berezhkov, an official in the People's Commissariat of Foreign Trade who also accompanied Molotov to Berlin in November 1940. In the capacity of official translator, he attended the meetings with Hitler and Ribbentrop, the Nazi Foreign Minister. His account of the negotiations generally conforms to that expressed in captured documents of the German Foreign Ministry. In all probability, Soviet demands and the aggressiveness with which Molotov pressed them were partly responsible for Hitler's decision to accelerate his planning for the Eastern war. A month after the meeting, on December 18, 1940, top-secret formal orders were issued for Plan Barbarossa; they read in part: "the German Armed Forces must be prepared to crush Soviet Russia in a quick campaign even before the conclusion of the war against England."

The final excerpt has nothing to do with high-level attempts to deal with the Pact. Its author, M. I. Gallai, then a test pilot in the Soviet Air Force, briefly but succinctly recapitulates the feelings of his generation toward "the twenty-two strange and incomprehensible months" when the Pact was in force.

Lieutenant General A. S. Iakovlev
Missions to Germany

THE NONAGGRESSION PACT was followed by the signing of an economic agreement under which the Soviet Union undertook to supply Germany with certain types of raw materials in exchange for German equipment and machines, including aircraft.[73]

A commercial delegation, headed by I. F. Tevosian, was sent to Germany to implement the agreement. The delegation's aviation group included A. I. Gusev (head), I. F. Petrov, N. N. Polikarpov, V. P. Kuznetsov, P. V. Dement'ev, and me, together with several engineers, specialists in various fields.[74] The group was instructed to study German aviation equipment and to select the most worthwhile items. Thus, very shortly before

A. S. Iakovlev, Tsel' zhizni (Moscow, 1966), pp. 208–36.

the war I had a chance to visit Germany. Even though a nonaggression pact had been concluded between our countries, all of us knew that fascism was fascism and that, sooner or later, we would have to fight the fascists. . . .

The Hitlerite officials did their best to behave like genial hosts. In honor of our arrival the Berlin Railroad Station had been decorated with Soviet and German flags. The city and military authorities were there to welcome us. They smiled at us, shook our hands, paid us compliments, and tried to create an atmosphere of friendship and sincerity. We were housed in the "Adlon," the smartest hotel on Unter-den-Linden. . . .

Shortly after we arrived in Berlin we were received by Colonel General Udet, the deputy of Hermann Goering, then Minister of Aviation. . . . Udet was a well-known World War I pilot as well as an engineer-designer. Shortly before our arrival he had set a new world speed record in a Heinkel aircraft. He was a close friend of Heinkel's.[75]

From our very first meeting, Udet made a good impression on me. He was short, thickset, with an open, pleasant face and lively manner. He immediately declared that, at Goering's instructions, he was ready to show us all the airplanes, engines, and equipment used by the German air force.

To begin with, he suggested a demonstration of German matériel on the ground and in the air at the Johannisthal Airfield near Berlin; then a visit to the Junkers, Heinkel, Messerschmitt, Fokke-Wulf, and Dornier aircraft plants; we were to meet with the designers, select our purchases, and then meet again for final talks. The agenda suited us, and the demonstration took place in Johannisthal the next day.

In strict order, as though on parade, a great variety of war matériel was lined up on the airfield markers: twin-engine "Junkers-88" and "Dornier-215" bombers; single-engine "Heinkel-100" and "Messerschmitt-109" fighters, "Fokke-Wulf-187" and "Henschel" reconnaissance airplanes, a twin-engine "Messerschmitt-110" fighter, a "Junkers-87" dive bomber, and other types of aircraft. The crews—pilots and mechanics—stood rigidly at attention by each airplane.

We were welcomed by many officials from the Ministry of Aviation, headed by Udet. To begin with, Udet asked the leader of our delegation, Ivan Fedorovich Tevosian, to take the passenger's seat of a "Storch" ("Stork") liaison airplane, while he himself sat in the pilot's seat. The engine was revved up and, with no taxiing and after a very short run, the plane was airborne. For a few minutes, Udet circled over us at low altitude and then made a splendid landing, stopping exactly where he had started from. Tevosian stepped down and praised the aircraft. Subsequently, Goering presented us with this plane.

Next, we began to look over the various types of aircraft exhibited. We were informed of their flight tactical characteristics, weapons, and equipment. When the inspection was over, one after another, and at one- or two-minute intervals, the airplanes took off, flew over us in formation, and landed in the same order. Everything was impeccably organized and made a rather good impression. Apparently, it was not the first time that such a display had been organized.

We returned to the "Adlon" strongly impressed by what we had seen. Our General Gusev, however, was beset by doubts: how could the Germans show us the true state of their air force equipment? "They probably think us fools and are displaying obsolete, rather than current, airplanes," he said.

I must admit that I too was uneasy at the candidness with which the most secret weaponry data had been revealed to us. Was it possible that we were being led by the nose and humbugged in an attempt to sell us obsolete equipment? After second thoughts, however, we decided not to jump to conclusions but to visit the plants. Things would then become clearer.

Indeed, our trip around the plants did much to disperse our doubts. The assembly line of aircraft and aircraft engines, the type of machinery in the shops, rather convincingly confirmed that what we had seen at Johannistahl was indeed the backbone of the Luftwaffe. All our engineers clearly understood this, but our generals stubbornly held to the opposite. "Obsolete, trash, they are concealing their really modern equipment; there is nothing worth buying," they kept insisting.

Back in Berlin, Udet, as promised, received us cordially once again. His behavior underwent a sharp change however, when our senior, General Gusev, rather tactlessly declared that the aircraft we had seen were obsolete, of no interest to us, and that we were interested in seeing modern matériel. Udet exploded:

"I give you my word as an officer. We've shown you everything; if you don't like what you saw, don't buy. We are not pressuring you—do what you think best."

With that we returned to Moscow.

Reporting to the Central Committee on the trip, I did not hide my initial doubts but said that ultimately, after visiting the plants, I had reached the conclusion that what we saw were the basic armaments of the German air force. Undoubtedly, the Germans had some experimental projects on their drawing boards, but the equipment they displayed was not obsolete. . . .

In March 1940, it was decided to send a second commission to Germany to make the final selection and to purchase German matériel. Again

I. F. Tevosian was appointed head of the commission. Despite the fact that my name was not on the list of delegation members he had submitted, I was appointed head of the aviation group. Thus, entirely unexpectedly, and literally two days before the delegation was to depart, I was informed that I was once again being sent to Berlin.

In the course of this visit to the various German aircraft manufacturers, we once again met and became better acquainted with outstanding representatives of German aviation. . . .

After visiting the plants, I. F. Tevosian was to be received by Goering. It seemed to me that I too should go to Karinhall, Goering's estate near Berlin, since certain questions concerning aviation, including the purchase of aviation matériel, were to be settled there.

For reasons unknown to me, Tevosian did not ask me, the aviation expert, but the artilleryman Savchenko, to accompany him, saying that the Germans had invited Savchenko and not me. That is why I did not come to meet Goering.

After touring the plants and meetings with Messerschmitt, Heinkel and Tank, the members of the aviation commission were very definitely of the opinion that "Messerschmitt-109" and "Heinkel-100" fighter aircraft and "Junkers-88" and "Dornier-215" bombers had to be purchased.

However, the bureaucratic red tape of our commercial mission prevented us from carrying out our assignment rapidly and efficiently, i.e., making a decision on the spot as to the type and number of aircraft to be purchased.

Kormilitsyn, head of the engineering section of our commercial mission, suggested that we follow the standard procedure: submit a request, on behalf of the commercial mission, to *Vneshtorg* [Foreign Trade Commissariat] which would clear it with the air force and the People's Commissariat of the Aviation Industry, i.e., lose a few months in departmental talks, with no guarantee of success.

Realizing the situation, I tried to cable "Ivanov" [Stalin]. The heads of our commercial mission intercepted the telegram and prevented its transmission to Moscow. It was only after I had explained to Tevosian that, foreseeing possible difficulties and considering the importance of the mission, Stalin had given me permission to address myself directly to him in the course of our mission, and that to this effect had given me the coded cable address, "Moscow, Ivanov," did he accede to my request and order that no more difficulties be made.

Literally two days later we received an answer giving us the right to determine on the spot the type and number of aircraft to be purchased, without previous clearance from Moscow. The speed of the reaction to my coded message staggered the commercial mission personnel.

The going became very smooth and our government assignment was carried out successfully. . . .

On the evening of November 8, 1940, I was unexpectedly summoned to the Kremlin. On the occasion of the October Revolution holiday the government offices were closed and the empty corridors of the Council of People's Commissars had a strange air. I was informed that on the next day, at 9:00 p.m., I was to leave for Berlin as a member of the Soviet government delegation headed by V. M. Molotov. I was flabbergasted. "How could this be?" I thought, well familiar with the complex procedure which preceded assignments abroad. "I don't even have a passport." The answer to all my puzzled questions boiled down to one thing: tomorrow, 9:00 p.m., the Belorussian Railroad Station. . . .

In Berlin we were welcomed with honors befitting the diplomatic standing of a government delegation. . . . The Soviet-German talks held in Berlin in November 1940 were brief and, as we know, fruitless.[76] The entire delegation, headed by Molotov, returned to Moscow. I remained behind for another two weeks, with instructions to visit the aviation plants we had missed in the course of previous visits. I had the opportunity to meet with some German aviation specialists and, once again, to visit several plants which were willingly shown to us. At first I wondered: why were the Hitlerites so openly showing their aircraft industry—one of the most secret spheres of armament? They solved the puzzle themselves.

On one occasion we were invited to inspect the Heinkel aviation plant in Oranienburg, near Berlin. It was a fine plant. True, we had never been shown a plant straight off. We always had to give notice of our desire to visit any given factory. We would be taken there but, naturally, would be shown everything in its "prepared" state. Following our tour of Heinkel, the plant director invited me to register my impressions and opinion in the honored guests' book. I was curious to see who else had been there before me. Apparently we were not the first foreigners to visit the plant. Many well-known aviation personalities from all over the world—the USA, Britain, France, and Japan among others—had visited the plant and registered their impressions. I saw that the famous American flier Lindbergh had been there and expressed his enthusiastic reaction.

The plant director pointed out, in particular, the signature of the Commander in Chief of the French Air Force, General Villemin, who had visited the plant shortly before the declaration of war with Germany. The General had written: "This is an outstanding plant, the best in the world, a plant which does credit not only to the builders of the plant but to the German air force as well."

While I was reading, the director kept glancing at me slyly. I asked: "What is so special about this? Your plant well deserves such praise." The director answered:

"The point is that General Villemin visited us about a month and a half or two months before the war. He and his companions looked over our plant and praised German aviation; apparently, however, they failed to draw the proper conclusion since two months later France dared to declare war on us."

It became clear that the French general had been shown this, the best of the German aircraft manufacturing plants, as proof that German air power was immeasurably superior to that of France. They tried to scare the French and the British, they tried to scare the Americans, and they hoped to scare us as well.

It was precisely there at the plant, that I understood something I had wondered about from the very beginning: why the Hitlerites were revealing their secrets to us. It was simply that they were sure of their power and hoped to scare us. We could sense their desire to impress us with their might. They wanted not only to promote respect for German hardware but, principally, to implant in us the seeds of fear of the German military machine, to lay the foundations of something with the help of which they had been able to defeat others, to infect us with a panicky fear of the might of Hitlerite Germany, and to crush our will to resist.[77]

Back in Moscow, I was summoned to the Kremlin practically from the railway station.

Welcoming me in the reception room, Molotov laughed: "Ah, here is the German! Well, now we both will be held responsible."

"For what?"

"Well! Did we dine with Hitler? We did. Did we shake hands with Goebbels? We did. We shall have to repent."

That evening all sorts of problems were discussed, most of which had nothing to do with aviation. Nevertheless, I was not allowed to leave but had to describe everything new I had seen this time in Germany. Stalin was very interested in whether the Germans were hoodwinking us in the sale of aviation equipment.

I reported that now, after this third trip, I had reached the firm conviction that (hard to believe) the Germans had in fact shown us the true level of their aviation technology; and that the samples of the equipment we had purchased, i.e., the "Messerschmitt-109," "Heinkel-100," "Junkers-88," "Dornier-215," and other types of aircraft were representative of the state of modern German aviation weaponry.

In fact, the war subsequently confirmed that in addition to the above-listed aircraft, which we had purchased, only one new fighter plane—the

"Fokke-Wulf-190"—had been produced, and that had fallen short of expectations.

I expressed my firm conviction that the Hitlerites, dazzled by their successes in subjugating Europe, did not even dream that the Russians could compete with them!

Late in the night, before he let us go home, Stalin said:

"See to it that our people study the German planes. Compare them with our new ones. Learn how to beat them."

Exactly one year before the war started, Moscow received five "Messerschmitt-109" fighters, two "Junkers-88" bombers, two "Dornier-215" bombers as well as the latest fighter plane, the "Heinkel-100." By then we already had our own competitive fighters—"Lag's," "Iak's," "Mig's," and "Il" and "Pe-2" attack and bomber aircraft.

V. M. Berezhkov
In Hitler's Chancellery

HITLER was seated at his desk, and in the huge room his slight figure was barely noticeable in his mouse-green field jacket. He stared at us a moment, then rose abruptly and walked to the middle of the room with short, brisk steps. Here he stopped and listlessly, carelessly raised his arm in the fascist salute, turning his palm out in a rather unnatural way. Without having uttered a sound, he walked over and shook hands with everyone.[78] His clammy palm reminded me of the touch of a frog. As he shook hands, he pierced each of us with feverishly burning gimlet eyes. Above his closely shaven mustache jutted a sharp, pimply nose.

After a few words about how glad he was to welcome the Soviet delegation to Berlin, Hitler invited us to sit at a round table in the part of his office that served as his drawing room. Just then, the Minister of Foreign Affairs, Ribbentrop, appeared in the opposite corner of the room from behind some curtains that evidently concealed another entrance. Ribbentrop was followed by Hitler's personal interpreter, Schmidt, and the Counselor of the German Embassy in Moscow, Hilger,[79] who knew Russian well. We all sat down around the table on the multi-colored armchairs and sofa.

V. M. Berezhkov, S diplomaticheskoi missiei v Berlin 1940–1941 (Moscow, 1966), pp. 22–48.

The conference opened with a long monologue by Hitler. One must give him his due—he knew how to talk. He may have had a prepared text, but he did not use it. His speech flowed smoothly, without hesitation. Like a well-rehearsed actor, he delivered phrase after phrase distinctly, with pauses for translation. . . .

The gist of Hitler's speech was that England was already beaten and her final capitulation a matter of the very near future. England would soon be completely destroyed, Hitler claimed. He gave a short survey of the military situation in which he emphasized that the German Empire already controlled all of continental Western Europe. With their Italian allies, German forces were conducting successful operations in Africa, from which the English would soon be uprooted once and for all, Hitler continued. From all this, one could conclude that the victory of the Axis powers was assured. Consequently, the time had come to think about the organization of the world after victory. Thereupon Hitler began to elaborate the following idea: after her inevitable collapse, Britain would leave behind an "uncontrolled legacy," the splinters of the empire scattered throughout the world. This "masterless" property had to be disposed of. The German government had already exchanged views with the governments of Italy and Japan, said Hitler, and now would like to have the opinion of the Soviet government. He was prepared to make more concrete proposals in this connection later.

When Hitler finished his speech, which lasted about an hour, V. M. Molotov took the floor.[80] Without commenting on Hitler's proposition, he observed that more concrete, practical questions had to be discussed. Specifically, would the Reich Chancellor explain what a German military mission was doing in Rumania and why it had been sent there without consultation with the Soviet government? After all, the Soviet-German nonaggression pact of 1939 provided for consultation on important questions touching the interests of both parties. The Soviet government would like to know, too, why German forces had been sent to Finland. And why had this serious step also been taken without consultation with Moscow?[81]

These remarks fell on Hitler like a cold shower. He even seemed to shrivel, and, for a moment, confusion could be seen in his face. But his acting ability still prevailed: dramatically throwing back his head and interlocking his fingers, he fixed his gaze on the ceiling. Then, twisting in his chair, he said rapidly that the German military mission had been sent to Rumania on the request of Antonescu's government to train Rumanian troops. As for Finland, German units were by no means planning to stay there; they were only in transit to Norway.

This explanation, however, failed to satisfy the Soviet delegation. On the basis of reports from its representatives in Finland and Rumania, said Molotov, the Soviet government had formed quite a different impression. The troops which had landed on the south shore of Finland were moving no farther and were evidently preparing for a long stay in that country. In Rumania, too, the matter was not limited to just a military mission. New German military units kept arriving there. There were too many of them for a mission alone. What was the purpose behind these German troop movements? Such measures could not help but arouse concern in Moscow, and the German government should give a clear-cut reply.

Hitler then used a maneuver he resorted to more than once: he pleaded lack of information. Promising to look into the questions raised by the Soviet side, Hitler said he regarded all this a secondary matter. Returning to his opening theme, he said the time had now come to discuss problems brought about by the rapid victory of the Axis powers.

Again Hitler began to elaborate his fantastic scheme for the division of the world. He claimed that in the next few months England would be beaten and occupied by German troops, while the USA would be unable to present a threat to the "New Europe" for many years to come. It was, therefore, time to give thought to the creation of a new order throughout the globe. So far as the German and Italian governments were concerned, they had already marked out their spheres of interest, Hitler said. Europe and Africa entered into these. Japan had expressed an interest in the territories of Southeast Asia. Therefore, Hitler continued, the Soviet Union might declare an interest in the regions south of her borders in the direction of the Indian Ocean. This would open the way to ice-free ports for the Soviet Union. If they could agree on this basis, Hitler added with a broad sweep of the hand, the German government, for its part, was ready to respect the interests of the Soviet Union.

Here the Soviet delegate interrupted Hitler with the remark that he did not see the point of discussing that sort of arrangement. The Soviet government was interested in preserving the peace and security of those regions directly touching Soviet borders.[82]

Hitler, ignoring this remark, again began to develop his plan for the division of the "uncontrolled legacy" of the British. The conference took on a rather strange aspect. The German representatives acted as if they did not hear what the other side said. . . .

The meeting had already lasted two and a half hours. Suddenly Hitler glanced at his watch, and, referring to the probability of an air raid alert, suggested the talk be continued the following day. . . .

The second meeting with Hitler took place the next day. By this time we had already received a message from Moscow. Our report about yesterday's talk had been discussed in the Kremlin, and the delegation received instructions for further negotiations. The Soviet government categorically declined Hitler's attempt to involve us in discussions about the "division of British property." The instructions again stressed that we should press the German government for explanations concerning questions connected with matters of European security and questions which touched directly on the interests of the Soviet Union.[83]

After the exchange of greetings, when everyone had been seated at the round table in the Reich Chancellor's office, Molotov took the floor. He laid down the position of the Soviet government following the instructions received from Moscow and then raised the question of the presence of German troops in Finland. The Soviet government, he said, insisted on being informed of the true aims behind the sending of German troops into a country immediately bordering on such a prominent industrial and cultural center as Leningrad. What was the meaning of this actual occupation of Finland by German troops? According to information in Soviet possession, these troops were not preparing to move into Norway: on the contrary, they were fortifying their position along the Soviet border. Therefore, the Soviet government insisted on the immediate evacuation of German troops from Finland.

Now, twenty-four hours later, Hitler could no longer plead lack of information. He continued to deny that German forces had been stationed in Finland, however, and flatly maintained that it was merely a matter of the transit of troops en route to Norway. Next, resorting to the old adage that the best defense is an offense, Hitler tried to represent the situation as if it were the Soviet Union that threatened Finland.

"A conflict in the Baltic Sea area," he declared, "would complicate German-Russian collaboration—"

"But the Soviet Union positively is not preparing to disrupt the peace in this region and is in no way threatening Finland," objected the Soviet representative. "We are concerned with ensuring peace and genuine security in that region. The German government should take this fact into account if it is interested in the normal development of Soviet-German relations."

Hitler avoided a direct answer and repeated again that the measures were aimed at assuring the security of German troops in Norway and that a conflict in the Baltic region would lead to "far-reaching consequences." His words contained a clear threat which could not have been left unanswered.

"It seems that such a position," the Soviet delegate declared, "introduces a new element into our negotiations which may seriously complicate the situation."

By this Hitler was given to understand that the Soviet Union intended also in the future to press vigorously its demand for the withdrawal of German troops from Finland. . . .

The discussion over German troops stationed in Finland heated the atmosphere to such a degree that Ribbentrop, who had been sitting in silence until then, felt it necessary to try to clear the air.

"There is really no basis for making a problem out of the Finnish question. Obviously there has been some sort of misunderstanding here."

Hitler took advantage of this remark by his Minister of Foreign Affairs and rapidly changed the subject. Once again he tried to draw the Soviet delegation into a discussion of the distribution of spheres of world influence.

"Let us turn instead to the cardinal problems of today," he said in a conciliatory tone. "After England is defeated, the British Empire will be a block of forty million square kilometers in a gigantic auction. Those nations that might be interested in the property of the insolvent debtor should not quarrel with each other over slight, nonessential questions. The problem of the division of the British Empire must be attended to without delay. It is a matter primarily for Germany, Italy, Japan, Russia."

The Soviet representative observed that he had already heard all this the day before and that in the present circumstances it was far more important to discuss matters closer to the problem of European security. Apart from the question of German troops in Finland, on which the Soviet government was still awaiting a reply, we should like to know the plans of the German government with respect to Turkey, Bulgaria, and Rumania. The Soviet government regards the German-Italian guarantees recently granted Rumania as directed against the interests of the Soviet Union. These guarantees should be annulled.

Hitler stated that this demand could not be fulfilled. The Soviet delegate then raised the following question: "What would Germany say if the Soviet Union, taking into consideration its special interest in the security of the region touching its southwestern border, should give Bulgaria a guarantee similar to the guarantees Germany and Italy gave Rumania?"

This, at last, made Hitler lose control. He shouted in a shrill voice "Has Tsar Boris asked Moscow for guarantees, then? I don't know any thing about this. And anyway, I'd have to consult Il Duce about this. Italy is also interested in the affairs of that part of Europe. If Germany needed to look for a motive for friction with Russia, it could find one in another area," Hitler added threateningly.

The Soviet representative calmly remarked that it was the duty of every government to be concerned with the security of its people as well as that of friendly neighboring countries.

The Soviet delegate then turned to other questions. He said that

Moscow was most dissatisfied with the delay in delivery of important German equipment to the Soviet Union. Hitler dodged again. He declared that the German Reich was now waging a struggle with England "not for life, but to the death," and that Germany was mobilizing all its resources for the final engagement with the British.

"But we just heard the English were, in fact, beaten. Which side is waging a struggle to the death and which for life?" Molotov observed sarcastically.[84]

"Yes, it's true that England is beaten," Hitler answered, without perceiving the irony. "But a little still remains to be done." Then Hitler declared that in his opinion the subject of the session had been covered, and that because he had no time that evening the negotiations would be concluded by Ribbentrop. . . .[85]

A meeting was held in Ribbentrop's residence on Wilhelmstrasse the evening of the day the talks with Hitler ended. Ribbentrop's office, substantially smaller than Hitler's, was luxuriously furnished. . . . When everyone was seated, he stated that it would be expedient, in accordance with the Fuehrer's wish, to sum up the results of the talks and agree on something "in principle." He then drew from the breast pocket of his green tunic a paper folded in four, and, slowly opening it, he said: "Some proposals of the German government are jotted down here."

Holding the paper in front of him, Ribbentrop read through the proposals. In essence, they came down to the same boastful argument about the inevitable collapse of England and about how the time had come now to think about the subsequent reordering of the world. The German government proposed in this connection that the Soviet Union join a pact concluded between Germany, Italy, and Japan. All four powers were to decide, with due regard for mutual interests, the question of the final organization of the world. . . .

After hearing this declaration to the end, the Soviet delegate said there was no point in renewing the discussion on this theme. But would it not be possible to have the text that had just been read? Ribbentrop replied that he had only one copy, had not had in mind to give these propositions in written form, and hurriedly hid the paper in his pocket.

At that moment the air raid alarm sounded. We all exchanged glances; there was silence. Somewhere nearby there was a hollow explosion, and the panes of glass began rattling in the high windows of the office.

"It's not safe to stay here," said Ribbentrop. "Let's go downstairs to my bunker. It will be quieter there."

We left the office and walked down a long corridor to a winding staircase that led to the basement. A sentry stood at the entrance to the bunker. He opened the heavy door for us. . . .

When the conversation was resumed, Ribbentrop again began to expatiate on the need to study the matter of the partition of spheres of world influence. There is every gound for considering England already beaten, he added. To this Molotov retorted:

"If England is beaten, why are we sitting in this shelter? And whose bombs are dropping so close we can hear their explosions even here?"[86]

Ribbentrop was embarrassed and fell silent for a moment. Feeling the awkwardness of the situation, he called the adjutant and ordered coffee brought. After the waiter had left, the Soviet delegate expressed a desire to know when an explanation might be expected of the purpose behind the presence of German troops in Rumania and Finland.

Without hiding his irritation, Ribbentrop answered that if the Soviet government continued to be interested in those "nonessential questions," it should discuss them through the usual diplomatic channels. . . .

Again and again the hollow boom of bombs exploding nearby could be heard. Dry wine was served. Ribbentrop began talking of his wineries; he asked about brands of wine made in the Soviet Union. Time dragged on. It was only late at night after the all-clear signal that we were able to return to Bellevue Palace.

The Soviet delegation left Berlin in the morning. The guard of honor was again drawn up on the station platform. But the only high-ranking official present was Ribbentrop.[87]

M. I. Gallai
The Strange
Twenty-two Months

THE TWENTY-TWO MONTHS between the signing of the nonaggression pact with Hitler and the beginning of the war were strange and incomprehensible for our generation. Many things seemed inexplicable, weird, and unnatural. It was not primarily the pact itself which evoked doubts. It was clear to everyone that, under the circumstances, there was no other choice.[88] Most of us took the pact like bitter medicine—unpleasant but necessary. However, later developments were totally incomprehensible. The fascists were no longer called fascists—one could not find any trace

M. I. Gallai, "Pervyi boi my vyigrali," Novyi mir, 1966, No. 9, pp. 24–25.

of this word in the press or in official reports and speeches. Things which we had become accustomed to seeing as hostile, evil, and dangerous from Komsomol and even from Pioneer age had somehow suddenly become virtually neutral. This was not stated directly in words but rather crept into our consciousness from the photograph showing Hitler standing beside Molotov, from reports of Soviet oil and Soviet grain flowing from us to fascist Germany, and even from the introduction of the "Prussian" parade step at that time.

Yes, it was difficult to understand what was what!

In these strange years we were given the opportunity to "touch" German aviation technology with our own hands. This was probably one of the very few positive results which stemmed from our unnatural relations with fascist Germany.

The Germans sold us several of each of their major planes. . . . Of course, this commercial transaction could not evoke any particular misgivings on the part of the Germans: the airplanes had already been taking part in aerial combat for the last several years; many of them had been shot down and had fallen into the hands of Germany's enemies, so that it had long since been unnecessary to treat these aircraft as a state secret. And the senselessness of playing at secrecy when the secret no longer exists, which is apparent to any rational person, was of course understandable to the fascists as well. On the other hand, why not boast to the Russians of their combat might and superiority of their military airplanes, which were triumphantly flying over all of Europe? It was a way of saying: let them know with whom they are dealing! . . .

By the way, the airplanes turned out to be really good.

They contained what comes only from real combat experience and from no other source: simplicity, accessibility to the mass [-trained] pilot of average skill, and ease of operation. These were planes for *soldiers*. . . .

PART IV THE FINNISH LESSON

Introduction

THE NAZI-SOVIET PACT gave the Soviet Union a prize which no alliance with England and France could match—the territories of the old tsarist empire lost by Russia at the time of the revolution. In return for Soviet neutrality the Germans consented to Soviet absorption of eastern Poland. Together with the Baltic States and parts of Rumania annexed in 1940, some twenty million people living in an area from the Black Sea to the Baltic were incorporated into the USSR. The Soviets succeeded in establishing a new frontier with Germany farther to the west without recourse to serious military action. The resistance of the Poles was of no consequence in view of their prior defeat by the Germans. The Baltic States and Rumania, bartered by the Nazis and denied even the hope of help from the West, succumbed without a struggle. Only in one case did a potential victim contest Soviet territorial demands by force of arms.

In the fall of 1939 the Soviet government demanded that Finland cede the approaches to the large northern city of Leningrad and grant facilities for a naval base in the Gulf of Finland. Negotiations collapsed after four fruitless weeks; on November 30, 1939 the Red Army invaded Finland. The establishment of a puppet Finnish government in the Finnish border town of Terijoki served warning that the previous "moderate" demands had been withdrawn in anticipation of a quick military victory. The resilient Finns, however, made of the first Soviet offensive a fiasco. The second offensive in the winter months of 1940 forced the Finns to meet Soviet territorial demands, but its success depended on the wholesale reorganization of the Soviet command and the concentration of new large forces. In March 1940 the fighting came to an end. The Soviets had committed 1.2 million soldiers—five Armies supported by over 1,500 tanks and 3,000 aircraft. A numerically and technically inferior foe had cost them about 200,000 casualties. One Soviet general is said to have commented—"We have won enough ground to bury our dead."

The Finnish war cost the Soviet Union much more than the casualty statistics indicate. It bared to the world the weaknesses of the Red Army. Winston Churchill publicly stated his conclusions about the "military incapacity of the Red Army and Red Air Force." More ominously, however, the course and results of the Finnish campaign buttressed Hitler's subsequent arguments concerning the feasibility of an attack on Russia. The German General Staff evaluated Red Army performance in a document dated December 31, 1939:

> In quantity a gigantic military instrument. . . . Organization, equipment and means of leadership unsatisfactory—principles of leadership good; leadership itself, however, too young and inexperienced. Communication system bad, transportation bad, troops not very uniform; no personalities—simple soldiers, good-natured, quite satisfied with very little. Fighting qualities of the troops in a *heavy* fight, dubious. The Russian "mass" is *no* match for an army with modern equipment and superior leadership.[*]

[*]*Nazi Conspiracy and Aggression* (Washington, 1946), VI, 981–82.

130

The Finnish experience, however, could have benefitted the Soviet leadership by accelerating the process of modernizing the Red Army. To a large extent it did serve this purpose, for a number of reforms were initiated under the leadership of Marshal Timoshenko, who replaced Marshal Voroshilov as People's Commissar of Defense in May 1940. On the other hand, Soviet military and political leaders displayed considerable reluctance to learn from the war; they tended to rationalize and excuse unexpected Russian weaknesses. The four excerpts which appear below exemplify the variety of Soviet reactions to the Finnish campaign.

N. N. Voronov, then Chief of Soviet Artillery, describes his visits to the front shortly before the beginning of hostilities and again at the start of the February offensive. His account provides an amusing contrast between Moscow's expectation in November of an easy victory in less than two weeks and Moscow's disbelief that the February offensive was indeed a success. The second excerpt, by Vice Admiral I. I. Azarov, a senior Political Commissar in the People's Commissariat of the Navy, briefly indicates how political officers were able to explain away both the stamina and determination of Finnish soldiers and the inadequacy of their Soviet counterparts. Admiral N. G. Kuznetsov, People's Commissar of the Navy, then discusses the Moscow conference of military leaders in April 1940 and its failure to treat the question of weakness in the leadership exercised by the Soviet High Command during the Winter War. Finally, Marshal S. S. Biriuzov argues that rather than failing to profit from the lessons of the Finnish war, the Red Army learned them too well, as a consequence of which Soviet troops were prepared for another Mannerheim line and not for mobile combat.

Chief Marshal of Artillery N. N. Voronov
At the Karelian Isthmus

SHORTLY BEFORE the start of military operations, I visited K. A. Meretskov. G. I. Kulik and L. Z. Mekhlis, Deputy People's Commissars of Defense, were with him at the time.[89]

"You have come at the right time!" one of them exclaimed on catching sight of me. "Do you know about the dangerous situation? Have you given any thought to the number of shells that would be needed for possible combat operations on the Karelian Isthmus and to the north of Lake Ladoga? What kind of artillery support is needed? What can we count on?"

N. N. Voronov, *Na sluzhbe voennoi* (Moscow, 1963), pp. 136–37, 153–57.

"In my opinion, everything depends on the situation," I replied. "Are you planning to defend or attack? With what forces and in what sectors? By the way, how much time is being allotted for the operation?"

"Between ten and twelve days."

"I will be happy if everything can be resolved within two or three months."

My words were greeted with derisive gibes. G. I. Kulik ordered me to base all my estimates on the assumption that the operation would last twelve days.

No one knew how much time we had to prepare for the fighting. They said only one thing: the Finns could attack at any moment.

On November 30 fighting provoked by the White Finns broke out.[90] From the very first days, the battles were severe and fierce. On the Karelian Isthmus our forces encountered for the first time deep zones of antitank obstacles, granite posts, antitank ditches, and mighty log barriers. Tanks had difficulty pushing through. Finnish infantry, well adapted to the terrain, showered our troops with a hail of lead: many Finnish soldiers were armed with submachine guns.

Only then did we recall that way back in the beginning of the 1930's, we had acquired a model of the "Suomi" submachine gun which was even tested by a commission of specialists on infantry weapons. The commission decided that it was a police weapon, unsuitable for military combat operations. The design and production of such submachine guns were regarded as superfluous. Acting on his own initiative, the Soviet designer V. G. Federov designed during those years a low-powered submachine gun which used Nagan revolver bullets. After being tested, this submachine gun was also rejected. Now, having encountered the widespread use of submachine guns in the Finnish army, we bitterly regretted these miscalculations.

The underestimation of the submachine gun stemmed from the fact that our combined arms commanders believed blindly in the power of individual rifle fire and feared great expenditure of ammunition. Many were saying that submachine guns should not be given to the soldiers because we could never supply enough ammunition for them. The Mosin rifle with its sliding bolt, which had to be reloaded after each shot, was regarded as ideal. Reliance was placed on light and heavy machine guns which, while they had good ballistic features, weighed a lot.

Now, already in the course of combat operations, the feverish design and production of Soviet submachine guns began. Our first submachine gun, that of G. S. Shpagin (PPSh), was greeted with great satisfaction by the troops. . . .

On February 15 the hurricane of our bombs and shells descended on Summy [Saimaa].[91] I was at a forward observation post. After the artillery had shifted its fire to the required depth, infantry and tanks simultaneously attacked and began to advance successfully. This time the enemy did not hold out. His flanks were in danger of encirclement, and he began to retreat.

The strongpoint fell before my very eyes. Upon returning to the command post of 7th Army, I witnessed a telephone conversation between Meretskov and the People's Commissar of Defense. No one in Moscow would believe that our troops had captured [Saimaa]. Upon seeing me, Meretskov spoke into the telephone:

"Comrade People's Commissar Voronov has just come in. He saw everything with his own eyes."

I gave a detailed report of the course of the battle to the People's Commissar. Nonetheless, he asked me three times if the report that the strongpoint had been taken was true.

Finally, his irritated tone became warm and friendly. The People's Commissar wished the troops a successful completion of the offensive. . . .

At the end of March a Plenary Session of the Central Committee of the Party, which devoted a good deal of attention to examining the lessons of the war, was held. It noted serious shortcomings in the operations of our forces and in the indoctrination and training of our troops. We had still not learned how to make use of the full potential of the new equipment. The slipshod work of the rear services was criticized. The troops were ill-prepared for operations in forests and for coping with freezing weather and impassable roads. The Party demanded that the combat experience accumulated in Khasan, Khalkhin-Gol,[92] and on the Karelian Isthmus be thoroughly taken into account, that armaments be perfected, and that the training of the troops be improved. It became necessary to revise the regulations and manuals in a short time and to make them correspond to the demands of modern warfare. . . .

Artillery matériel was of particular concern. During the freezing weather in Finland, the semiautomatic mechanisms in the guns failed. New types of lubricants had to be developed immediately. When the temperature dropped sharply, the 152mm. howitzer behaved in an erratic manner. Large-scale research work had to be carried out. After some improvements, these guns performed brilliantly in the Great Patriotic War.

Vice-Admiral I. I. Azarov
The Finnish Anomaly

INEXORABLY, the war was drawing closer to us. Practically any conversation in our military circles, whatever it might have begun with or wherever it might have taken place, inevitably turned to a discussion of the situation in Europe, in the Balkans, or in Africa, and revealed our concern for the state of our country's defenses. Sometimes in heart-to-heart talks a few comrades questioned the realism of the categorical assertion that in case of war we would suffer relatively light casualties and would beat the enemy on his own territory. Most of us, however, were astounded to hear such doubts and looked askance at the comrades who expressed them.

It must be admitted that we were reassured by the victories at Khasan and Khalkhin-Gol. When the conversation turned to the Soviet-Finnish war, we explained all its difficulties by the onerous conditions presented by the lakes and forests which hindered freedom of maneuver. We had no doubt that the toiling people of the bourgeois countries when given weapons to fight a war against the first socialist country would consider it time to turn their bayonets against their own imperialists. And this we thought because we denied the enemy the capacity to indoctrinate his soldiers ideologically.

The determination of the Finnish soldiers and their fighting skill we considered an anomaly and to speak openly of such phenomena was considered reprehensible. Scorn for the enemy did not allow the commanding personnel and the political workers, particularly those who had not taken part in war, to reconsider the concept which had become rooted in our circles—that victory would be easy—and to prepare themselves and their troops for a war more difficult and severe than military games, drills, and maneuvers led them to expect.

I. I. Azarov, *Osazhdennaia Odessa* (Moscow, 1962), p. 5.

Admiral N. G. Kuznetsov
The Lesson
That Was Not Learned

ALTHOUGH the campaign dragged out and was a difficult one, there was no organ to coordinate the operations of the army and navy. Major decisions were still made in Stalin's office, where the People's Commissar of Defense and the Chief of the General Staff were usually present. Some executives were also summoned. Apparently, this system dated back to the time when the People's Commissariat of Defense was in charge of all the armed forces, including the navy. Now that the People's Commissariat of the Navy was independent, the navy men found themselves in an awkward position.[93] Very often decisions concerning our fleet were adopted without them.

Somehow, during the Finnish war, Stalin got the idea of sending submarines to the port of Abo,[94] which was situated deep in the reefs. This he decided to do without having first consulted naval specialists. I was obliged to report that this sort of operation is extremely difficult.

"We can send submarines into the Gulf of Bothnia at a calculated risk," I pointed out, "but to go up to the very mouth of Abo through the narrow reef-strewn channel without being seen is almost impossible."

Interrupting me, Stalin immediately called the head of the Supreme Naval Staff, L. M. Galler, and asked him about the possibility of sending submarines to Abo. Lev Mikhailovich was embarrassed at first and reluctant to give a precise answer. However, after hesitating, he nevertheless supported my point of view:

"Getting through to Abo directly is very difficult."

Instructions to the submarines were changed. This and similar examples convinced me that Stalin took the opinions of specialists into account. The men who habitually refrained from opposing and even lavished praise on any proposal he made had a bad influence on him. It was easier to resolve problems with him when he was alone in his office. Unfortunately, that seldom happened.

The hard campaign lasted all winter and ended only in March 1940. It revealed major defects in our combat preparation. We had received a severe lesson. We had to profit by it.[95]

N. G. Kuznetsov, "Pered voinoi," *Oktiabr'*, 1965, No. 9, pp. 188–89.

In April the government decided to hold a broad conference of military leaders to discuss the results of the winter campaign in Finland. Naval questions were not on the agenda, but after the conference we resolved to discuss our own defects which had become visible in the course of fighting and to undertake to remedy them. . . .[96] The lessons of the Finnish campaign were debated vigorously. This was undoubtedly useful and helped to improve considerably the troops' combat preparation. One very important question, however, remained unsolved. This was the question of how the highest authorities were to direct the troops. There were isolated remarks on this subject, too. There were even attempts at criticizing the central apparatus. L. Z. Mekhlis, for example, spoke of mistakes by the People's Commissariat of Defense and by K. E. Voroshilov personally. Mekhlis was sharply rebuked.[97]

After that, criticism of the highest leadership ceased entirely. It was nipped in the bud, so to speak. And yet it was extremely important to discuss these questions either here or in some narrower circle. The Finnish campaign had shown that organization of military leadership at the center left much to be desired. In case of war (large or small) one had to know in advance who would be the Supreme Commander in Chief and what apparatus he would work through: was it to be a specially created organ or the General Staff as it had operated in peacetime? These were by no means secondary questions. Their solution would determine a clear line of responsibility both for prewar preparations and for the conduct of the war itself, once it broke out. One had only to seize this link in peacetime, and a long chain of problems, which had to be decided ahead of time with an eye to any future war, would have been straightened out.

Marshal S. S. Biriuzov
The Lesson Learned Too Well

[AT THE START of the war] we felt the one-sidedness of the Red Army's whole system of combat training, which had become dominant in the

S. S. Biriuzov, *Kogda gremeli pushki* (Moscow, 1961), pp. 31–32.

last year before the war. The fact was that in the period immediately before the war, troop training was undoubtedly influenced by the recent combat operations against Finland. The storming of the "Mannerheim line"[98] was regarded as a model of operational and tactical art. Troops were taught to overcome the enemy's protracted defense by a gradual accumulation of forces and a patient "gnawing through" of breaches in the enemy's fortifications in accordance with all the rules of engineering science. We ceased to deal seriously with mobile combat and with the struggle against highly mobile mechanized units of great striking and firing power. Insufficient attention was paid to questions of cooperation among different branches and services of the armed forces under rapidly changing conditions. We relegated to oblivion the fundamentals of combat-in-depth tactics and of combined arms maneuvers which had been widespread before the Finnish campaign. These tactics had involved large-scale troop concentrations, strikes by tank, cavalry and mechanized units on the "enemy's" rear, and large-scale airborne operations.

The generals and officers who served in the Red Army in the second half of the thirties can well remember the maneuvers in the Ukraine and Belorussia. Military delegations from many capitalist countries were present. Not only that, but on all the screens in our country there appeared a documentary film, "The Fight for Kiev," from which any military man could form a rather clear concept of the ways in which our military art developed. The German General Staff undoubtedly drew definite practical conclusions from this and made wide use of our experience in training its troops, in particular its armored and paratroop units. But we ourselves failed essentially to utilize our rich experience, although we were the first to work out the principles of conducting large-scale combat operations under modern conditions of mechanized war.[99]

The spirit of battles for "the Mannerheim line" continued to hover over our tactics and the combat training of our troops, although by 1940 the Germans had taught everyone a lesson that should not have been ignored. After a few months of the "phony war," the Germans refused to gnaw through the "Maginot line" and sent their armored divisions instead through the unprotected left flank of the French and English armies in Flanders. Their tactics then were exactly the same as those we had to deal with in 1941: massive aerial attacks, tank breakthroughs, pincer movements, and encirclements. And, of course, there was nothing like this on the Karelian Isthmus in the winter of 1939–40.

We had to retrain ourselves under enemy fire, paying a high price for the experience and knowledge without which we could not beat Hitler's army.

PART V   THE LAST WAR GAMES

Introduction

STALIN'S CONTROL over the military establishment was exercised in the years prior to the war not only through the People's Commissariat of Defense and the General Staff, but also through meetings of senior military personnel at which key issues of military policy were discussed by military leaders and then decided by Stalin. In December 1940 and January 1941 the senior Soviet command attended a very important conference followed by war games. It closed with a session in the Kremlin at which Stalin and the members of the Politburo were present. It was the last such gathering prior to the German invasion and significantly influenced the course of Soviet war preparations in the remaining five months. The most visible and direct consequence of the conference was a reshuffling in senior military positions, in particular the appointment of G. K. Zhukov, then General of the Army, to the key post of Chief of the Soviet General Staff in place of General Meretskov.

The purpose of the conference was to examine progress made by the armed forces following the Finnish war and to draw lessons from German victories on the European continent. The role of tank forces provoked serious disagreement. The *enfant terrible* of the Soviet High Command, Marshal Kulik, argued the superiority of the horse over the tank. Although Stalin and his associates defended the tank, it would appear that no executive decision was made at the conference to promote expansion and reorganization of Soviet armor. Indeed, during the remaining few months before the outbreak of war, little was apparently done to repair shortcomings in the mechanization of Soviet forces. In any event, the mere fact that the issue of horse versus tank could divide senior Army officers despite the unequivocal success of German tanks in the blitzkrieg exposes the weakness and apparent regression of professional military thinking on the eve of war in comparison to that which guided the Red Army command before the Great Purge.

The two excerpts which follow were written by participants in the winter conference—Marshal A. I. Eremenko, who was appointed Commander of the 1st Far Eastern Army after the conference, and General of the Army, M. I. Kazakov, at that time Chief of Staff of the Central Asian Military District. The two accounts differ widely in many important details, particularly in their respective descriptions of the Kremlin meeting with Stalin and members of the Politburo. In an effort to avoid duplication, the account of meetings and the war games held prior to the Kremlin session is reproduced from General Kazakov's memoirs. The description of the Kremlin session is given in both variants.

General of the Army M. I. Kazakov
The Government
Draws Conclusions

BEFORE THE WAR it had been something of a tradition to hold annual conferences in the People's Commissariat of Defense to report on results of military and political training. These meetings were usually held in November or December, and the top officers from the military districts always participated.[100]

I first attended this kind of conference in 1938, and I must say that I got much out of it that was useful and applicable to my own work. The same thing happened in 1939 and 1940.

In December of the last year before the war we were summoned to Moscow and, just as on previous occasions, we brought along a report on the results of military and political training. The results of troop training in our district that year were generally satisfactory, and we were in a cheerful and confident mood.

It was only after we arrived in Moscow that we learned that this time the conference was to go far beyond its traditional objectives. In addition to the commanders of military districts, their chiefs of staff, and members of the military district councils, commanders of Armies and several division and corps commanders had also been invited. As to the time schedule, the whole week from December 23 through 29 had been set aside for the conference itself, to be followed by strategic war games played on charts. One could see it was to be a rather unusual conference.

The main speaker on general problems pertaining to the combat training of troops was Chief of the General Staff, K. A. Meretskov. . . .[101] He roundly criticized our shortcomings. He may even have exaggerated them in evaluating the standards of combat training in certain military districts. Nor did he give high marks to the preparedness of the staffs. His statement ran as follows: "The command element of our strategic formations, the Army and Army Group staffs, especially in the air force, do not display an adequate level of operational skill and of military professionalism. We have not devoted enough attention to these problems in the past."

Quite a few interesting ideas were expressed by other speakers. Each was familiar with the state of affairs in his particular specialty and was

M. I. Kazakov, *Nad kartoi bylykh srazhenii* (Moscow, 1965), pp. 56–66.

able to present a series of important problems requiring speedy solution.

In the discussions that followed, commanders of military districts took the floor. . . . But the discussion of problems raised by Meretskov did not end here. It was continued during the discussion over other reports that followed. . . . All these reports made a very favorable impression on us. They outlined the major theoretical views which at that time prevailed among the command element. Close attention was paid to the instruction on combat in depth and the project of the new field regulations. The practical experience gained in the military operations of the Red Army in Khalkhin-Gol and in the war against Finland was also reflected in these reports. The lessons of the attack by fascist armies of Germany on its Western neighbors, especially France, were also carefully considered.

Dozens of the best qualified generals and officers from the district commands participated in the preparation of these reports. The General Staff also had a hand in their preparation. Thus, these reports were the product of joint creative effort, but they were not without certain shortcomings. One was that the rapporteurs were carried away by "pure theory," often to the neglect of practical application. They presented the principal general theses quite well, but shied away from the concrete problems involved in planning actual military operations. Another weakness was that the military operations were analyzed without considering the particular phase of the war during which they were conducted; in particular, the initial stage of the war was not even mentioned. . . .[102]

The Central Committee of the Party showed great interest in our December 1940 conference. From its opening until its conclusion, members of the Politburo were in attendance. A. A. Zhdanov in particular was present almost the whole time.

On New Year's Eve of 1941, the division and corps commanders were given permission to leave Moscow, but the command element of districts and commanders of Armies still had some additional work before them. In the beginning of January 1941 the strategic war games on charts began. These were held in the quarters of the General Staff and were directed personally by the People's Commissar of Defense, Marshal of the Soviet Union S. K. Timoshenko.

Strictly speaking, two games were played on two different strategic sectors, the Western and the Southwestern. The participants alternated in "enacting" various roles. In the first game our Western Army Group (the "East") was under the command of the leaders of the Western Special Military District (D. G. Pavlov and V. E. Klimovskikh). On the opposite side, the armies were headed by General of the Army G. K. Zhukov and Colonel General F. I. Kuznetsov (Commander of the Baltic Military

District). In the next game they exchanged places: G. K. Zhukov commanded the Southwestern Army Group (the "East"), while D. G. Pavlov represented the "Western" adversary.

I myself, at the time of these games, had occasion to act in the capacity of chief of staff of an Army and, subsequently, as a commander of a cavalry-mechanized group made up of two corps of cavalry and one motorized corps.

The game took place in a calm atmosphere. Both adversaries and all participants were given sufficient time to make decisions and to work out the basic operational documents. Everyone was taken with the idea of strikes in depth by the attacking force with the objective of inflicting decisive defeat on the main groupings of the opponent. To none of us was this approach new or unexpected. For a long time we had studied (on charts) the principles of deep penetration tactics. The composition of the troops of the Army Groups was very bulky (50 to 80 divisions in each). Command of the troops was exercised over a large area, from Polesie to East Prussia.[103] The participants in both games were puzzled by how insignificant was the margin of superiority of the attacking forces—only about 10 to 15 divisions. The second peculiarity was that both sides had very unsubstantial second echelons and reserves. . . . The superiority of forces in the axis of the main strike was created by weakening the troop deployment on the so-called passive sectors of the front.

The outcome of the games also seemed to me to be somewhat unusual: for some reason the analysis was not made either by the People's Commissar of Defense or by the General Staff, but by the participants themselves—G. K. Zhukov and D. G. Pavlov.

As soon as the results had been analyzed, the commanders of the military districts prepared to leave, but we, the chiefs of staff, were still detained in the General Staff. However, on January 13, 1941, the whole situation suddenly changed. At 12:00 o'clock everyone was invited to the Kremlin.

There, the Main Military Council[104] was meeting on the results of our conferences. The People's Commissar of Defense was reporting to the Politburo of the Central Committee and to the Soviet government.

Chief of the General Staff K. A. Meretskov related in detail what we had been doing in the preceding three weeks, but it soon became apparent that he had overestimated his capabilities. He spoke from memory, with no prepared text, and as a result he diverged from the truth considerably, making quite a few errors in his conclusions and recommendations.

Subsequently, his views about the draft field service regulations also came in for much criticism. Meretskov said approximately the following: "In preparing the regulations, we proceeded on the assumption that a Soviet division is much stronger than a division of the German fascist army and that there is no question that it can smash a German division in a meeting engagement. In a defensive action, one of our divisions can repel an attack by two or three enemy divisions. In an offensive, one and a half Soviet divisions would be able to overcome the resistance of one enemy division."

One felt especially uneasy when Meretskov started to report on the relative strength of opposing forces in the offensive operation in the Western sector during the war games. It turned out that the "Eastern" side (the "Reds"), comprising 60 to 65 divisions in all, had successfully overcome the resistance of the "Westerners," who were defending themselves with 55 divisions. At this point Stalin posed a question: How could this be possible with such an insignificant superiority in actual fighting strength? General of the Army Meretskov replied somewhat as follows:

"Without having an over-all superiority in the actual fighting force, the commander of the Western Army Group was able to transfer some of the forces from the inactive sectors of the front to the strike grouping. Consequently, he had achieved a local superiority of forces, assuring success of the offensive operation."

At this point Stalin took the floor and emphatically objected to what was being said: In our age of mechanized and motorized armies, local superiority in fighting strength will not insure the success of the attacking force. The enemy on the defensive has similar means of maneuver at his disposal, and at short notice he can regroup his forces, bring reinforcements to the danger area, and thus cancel out the local superiority of the attackers.[105]

After Meretskov reported the ratio of forces in the second game (in the Southwestern sector), another question was put to him:

"Well, who finally won? Was it the 'Reds' again?" Meretskov tried to avoid giving a direct answer and attempted to parry the question with such vague remarks as: Everyone knows that there are no winners and no losers in the war games; the command simply evaluates the correct or incorrect actions of either side. But the dodge did not succeed. Meretskov was reminded:

"The members of the Politburo present at this meeting nevertheless want to know which of the opponents in the war games turned out to be the winner."

Even after that, however, no intelligible answer was forthcoming. At the end of Meretskov's report, Stalin again took the floor. Sharply differing with the speaker, he evaluated the combat readiness and potential of our Rifle Division approximately as follows:

"It may be that for propaganda purposes one should write into the regulations that in a meeting engagement a Soviet division can rout a fascist German division, and that in an attack one and a half of our divisions can break through the defenses of one enemy division, but here among ourselves, in the circle of future commanders of [field] Armies and Army Groups, we have to talk in terms of our real capabilities."

At the end of Meretskov's report, other representatives of the armed forces who had been invited to this meeting were given the opportunity to speak. Particularly active in the ensuing discussion were young air force commanders who had shown good combat qualities in Spain and great courage in saving the crew of the *Cheliuskin*.[106] Participants of the meeting pointed out in a business-like manner deficiencies in the organizational structure of our armed forces and in the training of personnel. But other voices were also heard.

Particularly depressing were the remarks of G. I. Kulik, who at the time was Deputy People's Commissar of Defense.[107] Kulik stubbornly defended the idea of an infantry division of 18,000 men, with horse traction support, opposing in essence the mechanization of the army. He obviously did not understand the nature of the development which had been taking place in the armed forces and underestimated the role of mechanization and tanks in modern warfare. Kulik kept drawing wrong conclusions from the experience of the war in Spain. He knew that in the Spanish mountain region, tanks could be used only in small units (of company, or sometimes of battalion, size) for achieving limited tactical objectives. And there his understanding ended.

Kulik's remarks were often interrupted by Party and government leaders. Finally he was asked a direct question: How many motorized (tank) corps did he believe our armed forces needed? Kulik's level of military professionalism hardly prepared him to answer this question, and he tried to dodge:

"It depends on how many tanks industry can produce," he answered evasively. The chairman's reaction was not overly polite. Kulik was told that it was not his business to think for the government about what industry could or could not do. It was his job as Deputy People's Commissar of Defense to decide simply: how many tanks would be needed by the Army?

Another slippery and vague answer from Kulik was followed by a sharply worded rebuke, this time addressed to Timoshenko. Stalin said:

"Comrade Timoshenko, as long as there is such confusion in the army concerning the question of mechanization and motorization, no mechanization or motorization of the army can take place at all."

Timoshenko answered with dignity that military leaders fully understood the nature of mechanization and motorization and that it was only Kulik who was confused by these problems and could not understand them.

"Well, then let's hear what the district commanders have to say," said Stalin, and he proceeded to ask each in turn his opinion as to the number of mechanized (tank) corps needed for each theater of operations.

The commanders were called on in order of location of districts, beginning with the right flank and moving leftward. All of them knew that under a governmental decision toward the end of 1940, creation of nine mechanized corps had been completed and that, beginning in February 1941, some additional formations would be added, so they had had time to evaluate their requirements. Kirponos (Leningrad Military District) asked for one to two corps, Kuznetsov (Baltic Military District)—two to three corps, Pavlov (Belorussian Special District)—three to four corps, Zhukov (Kiev Special District)—four to five corps, Cherevichenko (Odessa District)—one to two corps, Efremov (Transcaucasian District)—one to two corps, Apanasenko (Central Asian District)—one corps.

These answers did not merely reflect personal opinions of district commanders; they represented the collective opinion of the top officers on the staffs of the military districts. Everybody noticed that the members of the Politburo received these requests with satisfaction. It was then explained to us why the process of equipping our troops with tanks had proceeded at such a slow pace. We were told that in the last few years the Central Committee and the government had literally forced on the leadership of the People's Commissariat of Defense their views that it was necessary to create large mechanized and tank units, but that the People's Commissariat of Defense had allegedly showed a strange timidity about adopting them.[108]

Later Stalin sharply criticized Kulik's erroneous views as to the proper organization and numerical strength of a rifle division. At this time he pointed to an analogy between Kulik's position and that of the opponents of mechanization and collectivization of agriculture. Stalin appraised Kulik's position as follows:

"Kulik supports the concept of a large rifle division of 18,000 troops supported by horse traction and speaks out against mechanization of the army. The government carries out a program of mechanizing the armed forces, introduces the engine into the army, and Kulik comes out against the engine. It is as if he had come out against the tractor and the combine and supported a wooden plow and economic backwardness in the countryside. If the government had taken Kulik's point of view, say, at the time of collectivization, we would still find ourselves with individual peasant farms and wooden plows."

Stalin's criticism of the leadership of the People's Commissariat of Defense was not without persuasiveness, but it boomeranged. Once he saw errors in the way the army was being equipped, why did he not proceed to correct them? We knew that Stalin himself had taken part in the adoption by the Main Military Council of the erroneous decision of November 21, 1939, on the basis of which the tank corps had been dissolved.[109] And, of course, it was with his knowledge that people like Kulik reached high positions in the army.

Toward the end of the session, Stalin summarized the situation as follows:

"Modern warfare will be a war of engines. Engines on land, engines in the air, engines on water and under water. Under these conditions, the winning side will be the one with the greater number and the more powerful engines."

With that the meeting came to an end.

We left with mixed feelings. The prospect of further mechanization and motorization of the army gave us encouragement and hope, but Kulik's speech left a bitter aftertaste. We also felt sorry for the General Staff, which had presented such an unsuccessful report. We felt all the worse because we knew that the data and illustrations for the report had been well prepared by the Operations Department (of the General Staff). Lieutenant General N. F. Vatutin and his closest assistants, Major Generals A. M. Vasilevskii and A. F. Anisov were experienced General Staff officers[110] and could not have committed the sort of blunders Meretskov made in his speech.

Marshal of the Soviet Union B. M. Shaposhnikov, the elder statesman of the Soviet General Staff, took this fiasco very hard.[111] He sat there gloomily, glancing from time to time at the people next to him or toward the members of the Politburo. Only the sad expression in his big intelligent eyes and the faint twitching of his large head betrayed the "old man's" tenseness.

After a conference of this sort, organizational changes had to be expected. They were made the same evening. . . . G. K. Zhukov became Chief of the General Staff. . . . General of the Army K. A. Meretskov was transferred to the position of chief of the Main Directorate of Combat Training, retaining the position of Deputy of the People's Commissar of Defense.[112]

Marshal A. I. Eremenko
The Wrong Conclusions

THE ANALYSIS of the game took place in the Kremlin on January 13, 1941. It was attended by members of the Politburo and of the government. . . . General K. A. Meretskov, Chief of the General Staff, delivered the analysis-report. The report was not a success; it was incoherent. We commanders of military districts took this failure very much to heart; it was distressing that the report of the Chief of the General Staff had created an unfavorable impression on the members of the Politburo. It was said at the time that K. A. Meretskov was removed from his post on the very same day because of this, and G. K. Zhukov was appointed in his place.

K. A. Meretskov was fully equal to the duties of Chief of the General Staff, and, to all appearances, his removal was a mistake. The reason for his poor report consisted of the fact that the meeting was originally to have been held at the General Staff, not in the Kremlin, and it was to have been held one day later. Unexpectedly, Stalin telephoned the People's Commissar [of Defense] and changed the time and place of the meeting. The materials on the game that had just been concluded had not been completely processed, and, therefore, the report based on them was not yet ready. Under such circumstances, no general would have been able to present an exhaustive analysis of the complex game. This is one more example of Stalin's hasty, arbitrary decisions.[113]

The very fact that it had been decided to hold the analysis on the highest level was evidence that special significance was being attached to the matters at hand. This was the first time that I personally attended such a conference. Following Meretskov's report, Zhukov, as the commander of one side [in the game], reported on troop operations. Pavlov and others spoke subsequently.

I should like to dwell on the speech of General Ia. N. Fedorenko who spoke on the use of armored troops in offensive operations. He properly stated that special attention should be given to tanks. Ia. N. Fedorenko said that we still had too few modern tanks and that a number of tanks which were standard equipment in the Red Army were already obsolete. From this, he rightly concluded that no time should be lost in expanding production of the new model T-34 and KV tanks.

A. I. Eremenko, *V nachale voiny* (Moscow, 1965), pp. 45–54.

At the same time he stipulated that if it were not possible to allocate sums to this end in excess of the budgetary sums already earmarked for defense, there should be a redistribution of funds among the branches of the army. In particular, in his opinion, it would be possible to reduce the sums allocated for the production of artillery weapons without harming the common cause. At this point, Fedorenko was interrupted by a sharp rejoinder from Marshal G. I. Kulik: "The artillery will knock out all your tanks. Why produce them?"

To this Fedorenko replied that one should not get excited while discussing the subject. "Tanks," he said, "also have guns and can compete with artillery in fire power as well. In addition, they have an advantage over artillery in mobility and armor protection, and are armed not only with guns but also with machine guns. In mobile warfare they are the most powerful weapon."

G. I. Kulik took the floor immediately after Fedorenko. His speech was of a markedly narrow departmental nature. It was not by chance that someone in the hall remarked in jest: "Every Kulik [Russ. *kulik* = snipe (bird)—Editor.] praises his own swamp." Kulik demanded additional funds for the artillery and indignantly rejected Ia. N. Fedorenko's proposal that the funds be redistributed in favor of the tank troops.

In his address, P. V. Rychagov[114] dwelt on the use of aircraft in modern offensive operations of Army Groups and Armies in the game that had taken place, and, taking advantage of the presence of members of the government, he noted that industry was deficient in mastering [the production of] new models of aircraft and that this was retarding the development of the air force.

Questions relating to the development of military technology and the allocation of funds for equipping the armed forces were not officially on the agenda of the conference in the Kremlin. They apparently arose because they were not being solved satisfactorily. At the same time, the imminence of war was all too clearly felt. The service arms commanders understood their responsibility for equipping the armed forces. Shortcomings and unsolved questions relating to armaments were very numerous, and, therefore, the military leaders used the floor of the Kremlin conference to inform the government of the needs of the troops under their command, and, of course, they were right in doing so.

Following these speeches, Stalin took the floor, apparently for the purpose of reconciling the disputants. He said that our armed forces were developing harmoniously, that certain proportions were observed among the branches, and that at the present time these proportions had reached the desired level. He said that quarrels about funds were idle talk; the

allocations that had been apportioned to the branches for ordering armaments corresponded to these proportions and to the harmonious development of the armed forces. After such a pronouncement by Stalin, no
one spoke further on this question. Stalin's authority was incontestable;
everyone believed in his infallibility.

Now, when one analyzes it retrospectively, it is clear that Stalin was
in error at the time. His idea of the harmonious development of the
armed forces was that all branches should be kept at approximately the
same level.[115] But in fact, the matter should have been approached in
another way. At that time, there existed the relatively old branches, such
as infantry, artillery, and cavalry as well as the new ones—mechanized
troops and aviation. Of course, victory in war depended on the skillful
coordination of all the arms, but the role of each of them was different,
and their condition at the time was also different.

The role of armored troops and aviation had increased considerably.
Where these were weak or totally lacking, victory in a mobile war was
almost impossible. It was clear that their development had to be speeded
up in every possible way since they were the key link in the existing
situation. It should also be borne in mind that artillery, as a relatively
old branch with a glorious history and traditions and a sophisticated
theory of combat deployment and control, had already reached a rather
high level. . . . The green light had to be given to tanks. It was also
necessary to overcome conservatism and to inculcate the military cadres
with the idea that tanks were an independent arm and not an appendage of the infantry. Someone might object, saying that at the moment
I am describing the incorrect attitude toward mechanized troops had
already been eliminated. Unfortunately, the facts speak differently. When,
soon after the conference, I arrived in the Far East and took over the
1st Special Red-Banner Army, the Army had ten tank brigades. There
was not a single tank division, to say nothing of a corps. This is the most
unequivocal proof that not all our command cadres by far had assimilated
the principle of massing tanks as an important prerequisite to success in
war.

Generally speaking, many of us who seriously analyzed the problem
of employing tanks in modern warfare doubted the advisability of organizing tank forces in brigade-size units. The point was that the brigade, being something between a tactical and an operational unit, corresponded neither to the tactical nor the operational tasks with which
tanks are confronted in the course of combat operations. Tactical tasks
required special tank battalions which would be incorporated into rifle
divisions. Operational purposes required a tank division which would be
part of a mechanized corps. Where necessary, mechanized corps could

also be consolidated into Armies. This would be a real concentration of tanks. At the same time, the existence of separate tank battalions would make it possible to provide the infantry with direct tank support. Tactical tank units could operate in infantry battle lines, supporting them with fire and movement and strengthening their morale.

Unfortunately, Stalin did not consider it necessary to go into such "detail," upon which success in war and victory with a minimum of bloodshed truly depend. Stalin was remote from the troops, and he did not wish to listen to the opinions of military leaders. This is eloquently witnessed by the fact that the future Supreme Commander in Chief was not present at the military council where the fundamental questions of our military doctrine were examined and discussed. Only at the last sitting was he present. But even here, he did not wish to heed the advice of experienced generals.[116]

In his speech, Stalin spoke of the impending war and of the possibility of a war on two fronts: in the West with fascist Germany and in the East with imperialist Japan. Therefore, he proposed that our military cadres be distributed accordingly. He did not predict the probable date when war was likely to break out but talked in general about the coming war as a war of maneuver. Such a war required a reexamination of questions relating to the tables of organization of rifle divisions with the aim of streamlining and making them more mobile. He proposed that their numerical strength be reduced and that their rear services be considerably curtailed so as not to burden the troops or hamper their mobility. He spoke at length of the future war as a war of mass armies and of the necessity of achieving a numerical superiority of two to three times over the probable enemy. Stalin emphasized that a modern motorized army, abundantly equipped with automatic weapons and other technical means of warfare, required that exceptional attention be paid to the organization of uninterrupted supply. The rear of the military units and the rear in the broad sense of the term was all the more important since foodstuffs, ammunition, armaments, and equipment had to reach the front in an unbroken flow from all parts of the country. He spoke of the necessity of stockpiling foodstuffs and termed wise the decision of the government of tsarist Russia to stockpile hardtacks. He spoke of hardtacks as a very good product. They are light in weight and can be stored for a long time. "Tea and hardtacks," he said earnestly, "already constitute a meal."

The chairman of the Council of People's Commissars[117] reproached the commanders of military districts for not knowing their missions in the event of war. This was an attempt to shift the blame from himself, however. We did not know our missions because Stalin as the head of the government had not adopted a strategic decision for the eventuality of war, on the basis of which a war plan should have been developed. In accordance with such a plan the commanders could have established the missions for the troops of their districts.[118]

Following the Kremlin conference, there was a major re-shuffling of the higher command personnel. . . . I, having only just assumed the command of the North Caucasus Military District, was designated Commander of the 1st Special Red-Banner Army in the Far East. . . . Other transfers were also effected. This was a matter of re-shuffling the personnel in the event of a war on two fronts. . . .

In the process of the December conference, many shortcomings and sore points in the build-up of our armed forces and their combat readiness were disclosed. . . . Many important questions relating to national defense and the disposition of our troops in the area along the western border were neglected, however. The defense of the border from the Barents Sea to the Black Sea—a total of more than 3,000 km.—rested on the troops of five military districts: Leningrad, Baltic, Western Special, Kiev Special, and Odessa. Some of these consisted of two or three Armies. The Kiev Military District alone had four Armies, but covered a zone 800 km. in length.

The fact that the forces of the border districts covered a wide stretch along our frontiers was quite natural in a country as large as ours; in peacetime, it could not be otherwise. But for the eventuality of war it was necessary to devise another grouping of forces, based on the war plan and the strategic missions which it envisaged. However, such a war plan had not been developed. . . . The plan had to provide for many factors, including the political and strategic aims of the war (if only for the initial period), the determination of the deployment of the troops, and the timetables of their readiness for combat operations.

At one time, Stalin explained the reasons for our failures in the initial period of the war by the fact that delay on the part of peace-loving nations as opposed to aggressive nations in preparing for war is supposedly a natural thing. However, such an explanation has nothing in common with Marxism-Leninism. It would seem that the peace-loving nations are fatally doomed to severe losses and failures at the beginning of a war and that only in the course of it are they able to equal and subsequently to surpass the enemy in strength. Such a thesis would give the aggressors hope for victory and would doom the peace-loving peoples to passivity in the task of preparing to ward off aggression. This assertion directly contradicts the facts because our socialist state possessed all objective conditions for dealing the enemy a crushing defeat from the very beginning. Here, it is not a matter of an objective, "natural" lag of peace-loving nations in military preparedness, but rather the subjective errors of Stalin in this area.

A particularly great error was the fact that our army did not receive a timely decision from the government, on the basis of which it would have been possible to work out a war plan and to prepare the troops. The People's Commissar of Defense and the General Staff are also to blame for the absence of such a plan. They failed to present the government with timely proposals on the basis of which a decision is made and a war plan is then devised. On the order of the Chief of the General Staff, plans for covering, massing, and deploying the Armies were devised in border districts, but this measure also was late in coming. . . .

If two or three years before the war, Stalin, as the actual head of the government, *had* made an efficacious decision concerning preparations for active defense, *had* indicated the timetable for bringing the troops to a state of readiness, *had* outlined the main strategic missions and determined the deployment of the troops for their fulfillment, the situation would have been entirely different at the start of the war. As I have already indicated, we had enough forces not only to stop the offensive of the enemy but also to deal him a crushing defeat by means of counterstrikes and a counteroffensive.

One more thing. Our defense did not take sufficient cognizance of the German methods of warfare in the west. . . . By the end of 1940 one could already conclude that the fascist German command, on the basis of the "blitzkrieg" doctrine, had selected the technique of using mighty tank wedges combined with equally powerful air strikes against the troops and communications of the enemy as its basic method of warfare. The tank wedges were followed by echelons of infantry formations.

If all this had been duly considered, deployments of troops would have been set up somewhat differently at the start of the war; artillery, aviation, and other means of warfare would have been deployed so that they could immediately enter the fighting and withstand the enemy strikes.[119]

PART VI   RUSSIA PREPARES FOR WAR

Introduction

WHILE MANY of the memoir excerpts in Chapters One and Two bear on the modernization of the Red Army, the five fragments below approach the question from a broader perspective and summarize the pre-war situation in different areas of the Soviet armaments program. The first author, B. L. Vannikov, one of the organizers of the Soviet defense industry, occupied the post of People's Commissar (later Minister) of Armaments from 1939 until his death in February 1962 and was chiefly responsible for the production of artillery ordnance. His central place in arms production is underscored by the receipt—no less than three times—of the highest civilian decoration, Hero of Socialist Labor, as well as the Stalin Prize, first class, on two occasions. He was the only Soviet citizen known to be so honored. Stalin ordered his arrest shortly before the German invasion and his transfer from prison to the office of People's

Commissar in the third week of the war. No more competent authority can be found to evaluate the achievements and failures of Soviet preparation for war.

Vannikov's account is supplemented by the memoirs of Chief Marshal of Artillery N. N. Voronov, at that time Chief of Artillery of the Red Army, and Colonel I. T. Starinov, the Army's principal mining expert. Like Vannikov before them, both officers denounce Marshal Kulik, Deputy People's Commissar of Defense, as the main villain in their respective areas of responsibility. The Soviet air force on the eve of the Nazi invasion and the reasons for its poor initial performance are the subject of a comprehensive analysis by A. S. Iakovlev, aircraft designer and Deputy People's Commissar of the Aviation Industry. Finally, N. G. Kuznetsov, People's Commissar of the Navy, evaluates Soviet preparations for warfare at sea.

152

Colonel General B. L. Vannikov
In the People's Commissariat of Armaments

IN THE YEARS following the end of the Civil War and before the beginning of the Great Patriotic War, the artillery weapons of the Soviet army underwent thorough modernization and were perfected on the basis of the latest achievements of science and technology. . . . By the beginning of the Great Patriotic War, the Soviet army was equipped with the very best artillery, which surpassed Western European, including German, artillery in combat and operating qualities.[120] The 76mm. USV-39 gun (in later modification, the ZIS-3), designed by Hero of Socialist Labor V. G. Grabin, may be considered a classic gun of that time in its combat and operating qualities and its technological level and economy of production.

The tank variant of the ZIS gun considerably outclassed the German tank guns in firing range and penetrating ability. The combination of a number of good tactical and technical qualities of the ZIS gun (light weight, small dimensions, convenience in operation, etc.) made it possible to outstrip the Germans and to design the T-34 tank with a 76mm. caliber gun which had a high armor-piercing capability and good accuracy over great distances. Later this tank received a very high evaluation even from the Germans. . . .[121]

Although many artillery weapons newly designed for the Soviet army were distinguished by high qualities, they almost came to a sad end in the last years of the prewar period. Appointed in 1937, the new leadership of the Main Artillery Directorate (GAU), headed by G. I. Kulik, cast doubt on most of the newly designed artillery weapons and characterized the 152mm. caliber ML-20 howitzer (1937 model) as "sabotage." It allegedly did not conform to tactical requirements either as a gun or a howitzer. (In a statement about it, GAU director Kulik said in so many words that it was "neither a gun nor a howitzer.") In spite of the fact

B. L. Vannikov, "Iz zapisok narkoma vooruzheniia," *Voenno-istoricheskii zhurnal*, 1962, No. 2, pp. 78–86.

that this howitzer had successfully passed the entire program of tests, had been accepted as part of the standard armament, had gone into mass production, and was rated the most important in the weapons system, complying with all the new tactical and technical requirements, the GAU directors demanded that it be thoroughly retested.

The retrials corroborated the fine results; moreover, by the end of them a certain sobering of the critics had begun, and the ML-20 was again accorded rightful recognition.

For several months prior to the Great Patriotic War the People's Commissariat of Armaments had to cope with a serious situation, which merits a more detailed treatment. As I remember it, in the beginning of 1941, GAU director G. I. Kulik informed me that, according to intelligence data, the German army was rearming its armored troops at an accelerated pace with tanks that had armor of increased thickness and higher quality, and all our artillery with calibers of 45mm. to 76mm. would be ineffective against them. Moreover, the Germans reportedly would have guns with a caliber of more than 100mm. In connection with this, the question was raised of halting the production of guns with calibers of 45mm. to 76mm. of all variants. It was proposed to employ all free production capacities in the manufacture of guns with a caliber of 107mm., primarily in a tank variant.

G. I. Kulik was noted for his effusiveness, and he easily surrendered to all kinds of rumors; therefore, we did not attach particular importance to the new scheme. However, a few days later G. I. Kulik, having enlisted support from above, suggested that I go with him to Artillery Plant No. 92 in order to discuss on the spot with designer V. G. Grabin and the plant management the possibilities of quickly designing a 107mm. tank gun and organizing its production in place of the 76mm. gun.

I declined to take the trip to the plant, giving as a reason the fact that I did not have instructions from N. A. Voznesenskii (who, as chairman of the defense industry's Economic Council, supervised the People's Commissariat of Armaments).[122] To my question over the telephone, N. A. Voznesenskii replied that he knew nothing about it, but I obtained permission to allow Marshal Kulik to see everything at the plant and to explain anything he was interested in. I gave these instructions to A. S. Elian, the plant director, but at the same time I pointed out to him that he was to assume no obligations without the knowledge of the People's Commissariat of Armaments.

G. I. Kulik also planned a trip to the Kirov Plant in Leningrad with the designer and representatives of Artillery Plant No. 92, so as to continue discussions in which the Kirov tank-makers would participate. Again he insisted that one of the executives of the People's Commissariat of Armaments accompany him. We refused this time, too, supposing that he would investigate the matter for himself and in the end abandon his inopportune and dangerous scheme. But these hopes were not realized.

Several days later, Stalin summoned me. I found him alone. In his hand was G. I. Kulik's memorandum. Pointing to it, he asked: "Have you read Comrade Kulik's memorandum on artillery? What do you have to say about his suggestions to outfit the tanks with the 107mm. gun?"

I did not know what was in the memorandum, and Stalin told me in a few words. Then he asked: "What objections do you have? Comrade Kulik said that you don't agree with him."

I explained the position of the People's Commissariat of Armaments in the following way. Still quite recently, in 1940, we knew that a large part of German tanks were armed with guns of 37mm. and 50mm. caliber and a smaller number of tanks with 75mm. guns. The calibers of the tank and antitank guns, as a rule, correspond to the armor protection of the tanks. Therefore, one might expect that our 45mm. and 76mm. tank and antitank artillery would be sufficiently powerful. It was doubtful that in the short interval (of a year) the Germans could have made the kind of big advance in improving tank technology which the memorandum mentioned. If the necessity arose for increasing the armor-piercing potential of our medium-caliber artillery, then the very first thing to be done would be to increase the muzzle velocity of the 76mm. gun. The shift to a large caliber ought not to begin with a 107mm. gun. It would be more expedient to take the available tipping part of the 85mm. anti-aircraft gun with a large muzzle velocity; it was part of standard equipment and was being manufactured in large quantities. The proposal to remove from production all variants of the 45mm. and 76mm. guns—regimental and divisional—was unconvincing, since they served not only as antitank weapons but were also intended for fighting against many other targets (live forces, various obstacles, etc.) and were highly maneuverable. The 76mm. ZIS gun, which had been designed and put into production only recently, was the best modern gun.

At the end of my explanation, A. A. Zhdanov entered the office. Stalin turned to him and said: "Look here, Vannikov doesn't want to make the 107mm. gun for our Leningrad tanks. But these guns are very good; I know them from the Civil War."

Zhdanov replied: "Vannikov always opposes everything; that's his style of work." Then Stalin said to Zhdanov: "You're the main artillery expert we have;[123] we'll put you in charge of a commission together with Comrades Kulik, Vannikov, Goremykin (then the People's Commissar of Munitions), and anyone else you find necessary, and you look into this matter." And he said again, with emphasis: "And the 107mm. gun is a good gun."

Stalin was talking about a field gun of World War I vintage. Except for the diameter of the bore, it had nothing in common with the gun that had to be designed for modern tanks and modern combat conditions. A remark casually dropped by Stalin usually determined the outcome of a matter, and so it turned out this time, too.

During preparation for the commission's work, directors and designers of the appropriate artillery plants were assembled in the People's Commissariat of Armaments. Once more they examined all the "pros" and "cons" in detail and from all angles and reached the conclusion that the proposal under consideration was not only inexpedient but, at that time, even dangerous.

Present at the meeting of A. A. Zhdanov's commission were: from the military—G. I. Kulik, Major General of Technical Troops M. M. Kaiukov, and others; from the People's Commissariat of Armaments—Vannikov, Mirzakhanov (Deputy People's Commissar), Elian (director of Artillery Plant No. 92), Fradkin (director of the Kalinin Plant), and others; and from the People's Commissariat of Munitions—Goremykin, his deputy, and others.

Right from the beginning, the chairman conducted the meeting incorrectly. He gave the military men the opportunity to state their arguments in detail, but he did not give the same chance to representatives of industry. This manner of conducting the conference impelled us to express disapproval. A. A. Zhdanov replied sharply to this that Vannikov was sabotaging [the work of the commission] and ended with the remark: "The dead hold back the living."

I replied to A. A. Zhdanov: "You are tolerating disarmament in the face of an approaching war." He rose, halted the conference, and declared that he was going to complain about me to Stalin. After this, everyone left, disconcerted by such an end to the commission's work.

I do not know what A. A. Zhdanov reported about all of this; but, shortly afterward, Stalin summoned me and showed me a resolution of the Central Committee and the Council of People's Commissars in the spirit of Kulik's proposals, which he had signed. I tried to object, but Stalin stopped me, saying that he was familiar with my objections and that our unwillingness to shift to a new objective was dictated by departmental interests, to the detriment of statewide interests. Tell the directors, he said, and first of all Elian, that they are to stop production of 45mm. and 76mm. guns immediately and to remove from the shops all equipment that is not needed for the production of the 107mm. gun. It was thereby stressed that there would be no return to a discussion of the question.

So, not long before the attack of fascist Germany on the Soviet Union, it was decided to halt production of 45mm. and 76mm. guns, which were most essential for fighting enemy tanks. Without having fathomed Kulik's completely unsound recommendations, Stalin authorized this decision, which had grave consequences for the army.

From the first days of the war, we became convinced that an inexcusable mistake had been made. The fascist German armies attacked with the most varied and by no means first-class tanks, including captured French Renault tanks and obsolete T-I and T-II German tanks, the use of which the Germans had not foreseen. The information which Kulik had, and which prompted Zhdanov and Stalin to make the erroneous decision to halt production of 45mm. and 76mm. guns, turned out to be without foundation.[124]

The simplest types of artillery weapons—82mm. and 120mm. mortars—can also serve as a case in point. Most regrettably, these inexpensive mortars, extraordinarily simple in production and operation, were not appraised at their true worth in the prewar years, either by military leaders or by managers of the artillery industry. Many artillery experts, designers, and production executives regarded mortars as inferior weapons. The incorrect attitude toward mortars is best illustrated by the fact that the Soviet Union's sole design bureau for mortars, headed by B. I. Shavyrin, had been closed down in 1936 on the pretext that "there was no need for this type of armament." Yet, tremendous combat potentialities were hidden under a simple casing—a pipe and a plate, as mortars were sarcastically called. . . .

Shavyrin's mortars encountered quite a few obstacles on their path to recognition. In 1938–1939, GAU, without any grounds, delayed their final approval and acceptance as standard equipment and demanded that they be tested in comparison with Czechoslovak 81mm. caliber mortars (the Czechoslovak firms could not supply other, larger mortars). The tests took place at an artillery testing range near Leningrad and in spite of the most detailed and, I would say, carping requirements, B. I. Shavyrin's 82mm. mortar performed better on all counts than the Czechoslovak mortars. High standards for arms are indisputably necessary; but in this case there were delays, and much precious time was lost as a result.

Even these tests, however, did not change the basically skeptical attitude toward mortar. These weapons continued to be regarded as second-class. That opinion was still current even at the beginning of 1940.

During the discussion of mortar weapons on the eve of the war, the GAU command cited the experience of the German army. But the information it had was outdated, for at that time the fascist German army, in preparing for war with the USSR, was placing increased emphasis on enlarging the pool of mortars and, particularly, the number of shells per mortar.

After the war with Finland, in our country too, this weapon was appraised at its true worth, and we begin to pay more attention to it. At the beginning of the Great Patriotic War, the Soviet army received excellent models of the 82mm. and 120mm. mortars. They were put into mass production, and on June 1, 1941, there were 14,200 of the 82mm. and 3,800 of the 120mm. mortars. . . .

To characterize the conditions in which the Soviet mortar was created, it is not without interest to cite another very significant episode. Not long before the onset of the war, Beria's henchmen concocted a "case" against B. I. Shavyrin, our only chief mortar designer. He was accused of sabotage, of malicious and premeditated disruption of mortar development.

It must be said that the solution to major scientific and technical problems and design tasks entails large, complex, creative research. Such tasks can be resolved by groups of skilled designers working in close collaboration with many other groups in related branches of science and technology. But because of this, the great importance of talented designers not only does not decline but is enhanced. The arrest of B. I. Shavyrin could have had grave consequences for mortar weapons. Therefore, I spoke out forcefully in his defense. But at the beginning of June 1941, I myself was arrested.

The unjust arrests of a number of highly skilled specialists in industry and the central apparatus, their replacement by insufficiently experienced personnel seriously affected the rearmament of the Soviet Army. The frequent change of personnel engendered a lack of individual responsibility and diffidence; reduced independence; had a negative effect on technical standards; hampered the progress of scientific and technical work; and as a consequence of all this led to a decline in the quality of output.

The painful lessons of the first months of the war taught us to value mortar weapons and their designers. B. I. Shavyrin, who escaped arrest thanks to the outbreak of war, continued to work fruitfully on the development of new models of mortar weapons so essential to our troops at the front. Now he is a Hero of Socialist Labor.

Not even a month had passed from the outbreak of war before prewar mistakes in the area of arms production led to painful consequences. This is the only way I can explain why they turned in the name of Stalin to me, as former People's Commissar of Armaments, with the request to write my views on how to develop armaments, which weapons to produce in which plants under wartime conditions, despite the fact that I was in solitary confinement in a maximum-security prison and had been accused of all grievous crimes.

I worked on this question in prison for several days. I did not know the situation at the front. Isolated from everything and everyone, I could not imagine the situation that had developed at the front and in the country. I could only suppose that we had suffered some small, local defeats. Therefore, I believed that the questions put to me concerned prospects for the future rather than needs of the present. I also assumed that the earlier decisions (before my arrest), with which I had not agreed, had, possibly, not turned out to be gross mistakes. Taking all of this into account, I drew up the requested report. This sad episode in my life ended with my release in July 1941. It speaks of how intolerable was the atmosphere for fruitful work during the period of Stalin's personality cult.[125]

Chief Marshal of Artillery N. N. Voronov
In the Main Artillery Directorate

MY WORK as First Deputy Chief of the Main Artillery Directorate was not easy.[126] It required great attention and care. G. I. Kulik was a poorly organized person who thought a great deal of himself and considered himself infallible. Frequently, it was difficult to understand what it was he wanted. His principal method of work was to keep his subordinates in a state of fear. His favorite saying when assigning missions or giving orders was: "Either prison or a medal." In the morning he would assemble a number of his subordinates, give them extremely vague assignments, and order them to leave his office after having menacingly asked them, "Do you understand?" All those receiving assignments would usually come to me, requesting clarification and instructions.

G. K. Savchenko and V. D. Grendal'[127] worked under equally difficult conditions. We frequently formed a "triumvirate" and attempted to get positive decisions out of our chief.

Only with very great difficulty did we prove the necessity of creating antitank artillery formations. For more than a year, the Hitlerite invaders had demonstrated the massive use of tanks on the fields of Europe. We

N. N. Voronov, *Na sluzhbe voennoi* (Moscow, 1963), pp. 166–68.

had to prepare reliable artillery screens against them. [We] finally succeeded in convincing the command.

A directive forming ten antitank artillery brigades—the first special formations earmarked for combating enemy tanks—was issued. Their formation was carried out at an accelerated pace. Much attention was given to the selection of the command cadres. The best, most capable artillerymen were assigned to command these brigades. . . . Instructions on the combat employment of the new formations were hastily worked out. The brigades received the latest artillery armaments and combat matériel.

Everything seemed to be going well. Then suddenly a new directive appeared—halting the formation of the brigades. I do not know who was the initiator of this harmful measure.

It took much time to secure the repeal of this document. Certain brigades, their organization far from complete, were drawn into battles at the beginning of the Great Patriotic War. Nonetheless, they succeeded in demonstrating their usefulness. The brigades fought heroically.

But misfortune befell me again: an illness resulting from a car accident became worse. After treatment, I was sent to the "Barvikha" sanatorium. . . .

While I was recovering, the regular meeting of district artillery chiefs was held. G. I. Kulik directed it, and, of course, he made a number of mistakes. For example, without any foundation whatsoever, he discredited our new ground artillery firing rules which had been developed by a large group of specialists on the basis of the results of many proving ground tests. Kulik promised at the meeting to issue new firing regulations in the near future. He summoned a minor official in the Artillery Committee of the Main Artillery Directorate and ordered him to rework the rules anew and to present them for approval in the space of two weeks. The officer came to me very distraught, because he had been given an assignment that was clearly beyond him. The misunderstanding was corrected after I had a long private conversation with Kulik. . . .

Work on the draft of the new field service regulations continued. On the eve of the Great Patriotic War, the seventeenth draft version lay on my desk. The work of our commission went slowly. Chairmen of the commission changed frequently; sometimes they would start everything from scratch. Then it would be necessary to return to articles and sections of the Regulations that had already been accepted and to make endless corrections, many of which were not essential. This delayed the publication of this most important document.[128]

At the end of May 1941 I was summoned to the Party Central Committee where it was proposed that I accept appointment to the post of

Chief of the Main Anti-aircraft Defense Directorate. This was completely unexpected. I did not want to leave artillery, to which I had given many years of my life.

They talked to me in a warm and friendly way, emphasizing the great importance of the post that was being assigned to me.

"This is a very serious and long-range task that you will undertake. Generally speaking, the whole matter has already been decided. We are only waiting for your agreement."

"And what if I don't give it?" I asked.

"You will be appointed all the same, Nikolai Nikolaevich."

All that remained to be said was that I agreed.

On June 19, three days before the beginning of the war, I assumed the duties of Chief of the Main Anti-aircraft Defense Directorate.[129]

Colonel I. T. Starinov
In the Main Engineering Directorate

I WAS APPOINTED chief of the obstacle and mine-laying section of the Army-Engineer Training Department in the Main Engineering Directorate [GVIU] of the Red Army. I was both worried and delighted by my new appointment. The experience of the war with the White Guard Finns had shown convincingly that even the most primitive mines, skillfully laid, can inflict tangible losses on advancing troops ana impede the use of communications facilities and of serviceable buildings. Hopefully, this experience should end the underestimation of mine barrages and open up great prospects for our work.

It was with these thoughts that I reported to the chief of the GVIU, Hero of the Soviet Union Major General Arkadii Fedorovich Khrenov, whom I had met many times at the Karelian Isthmus, when his short figure used to bob up in the most dangerous spots.[130]

The General greeted me with a welcoming smile. . . .

[He] immediately set me several specific tasks. All were part of the main job—to eliminate our lag in mine-laying and mine-clearing capabilities as quickly as possible.

I. T. Starinov, *Miny zhdut svoego chasa* (Moscow, 1964), pp. 173–80.

It was easy and pleasant to work with Arkadii Fedorovich. We set to revising the existing rules and instructions and drafting new ones, including "Regulations on the Construction of Operational Obstacles." The approval of this document by the People's Commissar of Defense made it possible to supply the troops fully with mining equipment and also to set up the necessary stores of it.

The work was conducted at a very accelerated pace, but—alas!—time flew even faster. The international situation kept getting more complicated. . . .

One might have expected that all the complications would not have taken us by surprise. But when I familiarized myself with the preparations for defense construction in the border area, I was simply stunned. Even what had been accomplished in this respect in 1926–1933 had in fact been done away with. There were no more stores of ready charges near important guarded bridges and other objectives. Not only were there no brigades prepared to set up our own or dismantle the enemy's mine fields, but there were not even any special battalions. Only small demolition teams and specialized equipment companies remained in the railroad and engineer troops.

Yet back in 1928 a group of commanders of the 4th Railroad Regiment had already suggested the establishment of special units to set up and to surmount mine fields and to disrupt the work of the enemy rear by means of controlled mines! For example, by 1932, the Ukraine had four special battalions stationed at railroad junctions in the border area. There were such battalions in other districts too.

Toward the end of 1937 and the beginning of 1938, the Engineering Directorate had drawn up plans for special mine and demolition battalions. But taking part in the preparation of these plans were officers of the General Staff who, unfortunately, were arrested soon after. The draft plans were buried. The Ul'ianovsk Special Equipment School—the only school that trained highly skilled commanders for units equipped with radio-controlled mines—was reorganized into a communications school.

Between 1934 and 1940, the number and quality of the probable enemy's tanks rose sharply, while our antitank engineering resources remained at the level of the early thirties. A stupid situation developed. In 1939 when we bordered on relatively small capitalist states with weak armies—Poland, Rumania, Estonia, Latvia, and Lithuania—our frontier had indeed been unassailable. But when fascist Germany became our neighbor, the engineer defense fortifications along our former western frontier were abandoned, and even partially dismantled, while construction of fortifications on the new frontier was only just beginning.

Before the war against the White Guard Finns, the leadership of the People's Commissariat of Defense clearly underestimated the engineer troops and the role of the Engineering Directorate of the Red Army. The neglectful attitude toward the engineer troops can be illustrated by the following anecdote: General I. A. Petrov, Chief of the Engineering Directorate, learned about the beginning of the war on the Karelian Isthmus when Colonel A. F. Khrenov, chief of engineers of the 7th Army, telephoned him. True, this instance also testifies to General Petrov's passive attitude and his poor contact with the chiefs of the corresponding departments of the General Staff. But one does not exclude the other.

In 1940, the situation changed somewhat. More attention was paid to engineering aspects of combat and operations and at the same time to engineer troops. The Main Engineering Directorate took advantage of this and in a very short time drew up tactical and technical requirements for mines of various types. The intensive work done by the Scientific Research Institute for Engineering Equipment, by the laboratories and design bureaus, produced positive results: prototypes of up-to-date anti-personnel and antitank mines appeared.

It was different with delayed-action mines.

Instances of new military weapons receiving quick recognition and being introduced into action in large numbers are rare in the history of wars. On the other hand, frequently a new military weapon, even one that has been used successfully in a limited quantity, does not reveal its entire potential, with the result that skeptics and conservatives refuse to believe in it.

This was the case with delayed-action mines. They appeared and were successfully used already in World War I but in very, very small numbers. Clearly, under the circumstances it was impossible to determine the limits of their potential usefulness. And although dedicated Soviet mine designers created extremely "intelligent" delayed-action mines, mass production was not begun.

As it happened, Marshal Kulik and some other leaders in the People's Commissariat of Defense, who controlled allocations and quotas, belonged to the group who interpreted very primitively the clause in Field Regulations which stated that in case of aggression by the imperialists "we shall wage an offensive war by carrying it over to the enemy's territory."

I have already mentioned the serious shortcomings in the engineer preparation of the frontier area for repulsing an enemy attack. In an attempt to remedy the situation, the head of the Main Engineering Directorate suggested that the old frontier fortifications be utilized and obstacle zones established. But his suggestion was rejected. There was no need, they said!

I remember the time I spoke to Colonel M. A. Nagornyi, Chief of

the Army Engineer Training Department of the Main Engineering Directorate. I spoke about taking measures to prepare manifold, deep obstacle
zones along the new frontier.

"Please don't say a word about this to anyone," Mikhail Aleksandrovich said anxiously. "Don't you know that the organization of stores of
explosives and demolition squads along the frontier is associated with the
names of Tukhachevskii, Uborevich, Iakir, and others like them?"

But even after this warning I could not keep silent. I decided to
speak to A. F. Khrenov. Arkadii Fedorovich heard me out attentively
as usual. But as I spoke, his face became more and more anxious. From
that talk I understood that Khrenov shared my anxiety but, unfortunately,
not everything depended on him alone.

In the autumn of 1940, the situation on the Western frontier became
even more alarming. . . . All the indications were that Hitlerite Germany
was preparing to attack our Homeland. Yet the fortified areas on the old
frontiers were being dismantled, while construction on the new frontiers was proceeding at a snail's pace. Because of the shortage of matériel,
the construction of antitank and anti-personnel obstacles was proceeding
just as slowly.

Early in the winter of 1940, I happened to meet G. I. Kulik outside
the building of the People's Commissariat of Defense. He had recently
been made a marshal and was Deputy People's Commissar of Defense.

Kulik recognized me.

"Ah-h-h, sapper! What are you doing here?"

I could not let the opportunity slip by.

"I am working in the Main Engineering Directorate, Comrade Marshal
of the Soviet Union. We're still concerned about mines. I'd like to discuss
it with you."

"Come in."

In the office I reminded the Deputy People's Commissar about the
incident on the mined road in Finland.[131]

"You had to wait impatiently for the mine clearing then, Comrade
Marshal. The mines made a lot of trouble for everybody. And now we
still underestimate them!"

Leaning back in his armchair, Kulik shook his head reproachfully and,
smiling slyly, wagged a finger at me!

"Whoa! Whoa! You are turning the wrong way, sapper! Your mines
are necessary, nobody denies that. But not as many as you and Khrenov
figure."

"But, Comrade Marshal—"

"Wait a minute! I repeat, not as many, and not as complicated as
the ones you propose. All right, the White Guard Finns had complex

mines. That's a fact. But they had simple ones too. Why must we devise something more complicated than the Finnish mines? I tell you straight, sapper: you won't get them. Mines are powerful things, but they are weapons for the weak, for those who are on the defense. We are strong. We don't need mines so much as mine-clearing equipment—"

"But, Comrade Marshal, even the strongest armies in the world cannot advance always and everywhere. And in defense, mines are a powerful weapon! They are also good for covering the flanks of advancing units. And for paratroop drops they are a must. And what about the partisans? In the enemy rear mines are not defensive weapons, they are offensive weapons—"

Kulik actually let out a groan and started gesturing. "Whoa! Whoa! You are lecturing. I see that your job gives you the wrong perspective. Your section was incorrectly named. In accordance with our military doctrine it should have been called the mine-clearing and demolition section. Then you would think differently. But now you keep at it: defense, defense. Enough! Incidentally, I have an idea for a pyrotechnic minesweep, but I have no time to write it up. Take it and think about it. That will do more good than going about complaining."

Frowning, Kulik bent over the desk and started looking at some papers. It was clear that the talk was over.

On General Khrenov's instructions estimates were made of troop requirements for mines of all types. We based our calculations on the principles of Soviet military doctrine as expressed in the 1939 draft Field Regulations. The calculations showed that millions of antitank and antipersonnel mines and hundreds of thousands of other controlled mines would be required.

But the leaders of the People's Commissariat of Defense regarded even the troops' most modest mine requirements as fantastically exaggerated.

Knowing all this and seeing that the Main Engineering Directorate's proposals were not getting any support from the higher military authorities, I decided to appeal to the Central Committee.

I consulted with my colleagues. General Khrenov raised no objections. Neither did my immediate superior, Colonel M. A. Nagornyi. So I sent a letter to the Central Committee in which I pointed out that controlled mines were needed not only in defense but in offensives as well and tried to convey the importance of the special engineer units for setting up and surmounting all types of obstacles.

In the end, A. F. Khrenov's reports, and perhaps my letter too, did start the ball rolling. We were instructed to check the estimates for the quantity of mines required in the first six months of combat.

Marshal Kulik's minute quota (2,500–3,000 antitank and 3,000–4,000 anti-personnel mines per division) was rejected and ours accepted: 14,000–15,000 antitank and 18,000–20,000 anti-personnel mines per division. On this basis, by the beginning of 1941 the entire Red Army was to have had 2,800,000 antitank and 4,000,000 anti-personnel mines, 120,000 delayed-action mines and 350,000 remote-control mines.

But approval of our calculations did not mean that they would be carried out.

On January 1, 1941, the Red Army had only about 1,000,000 antitank mines and no delayed-action or remote-control mines at all. When the war broke out it did not have even half of the minimum number of mines needed for successful combat operations.

Lieutenant General A. S. Iakovlev
Air Preparedness

BY THE TIME of the second Five Year Plan [1934–38] our country's aviation industry was already on a sufficiently firm footing. . . .

Numerous records were set by glider pilots and parachutists.

The entire nation was enraptured by the attainments of the aviators. The newspapers were full of enthusiastic accounts of flights by well-known pilots. Gromov, Chkalov, Vodop'ianov, and Kokkinaki became truly national heroes.[132]

Not only the broad masses of our newspaper readers but many aviation specialists as well were genuinely convinced that we were already flying "higher, farther, and faster than all others." . . .

To be sure, the mid-1930's was a time of aviation triumphs. Never before had aviation occupied such a place in the life of the Soviet nation. The pilots' flights and records were a source of general rejoicing. The winged heroes became the darlings of the people. Anyone directly connected with flying felt particularly proud.

It was at this time that our aviators broke into the arena of international air competitions. The successes of Soviet aviation were based on the creative search on the part of our designers and on our rapidly growing aircraft industry.

A. S. Iakovlev, *Tsel' zhizni* (Moscow, 1966), pp. 173–83.

And as frequently happens in such cases, in addition to evoking a natural feeling of pride, the enormous attainments in the field of aviation also evoked a measure of complacency in some people. There was an air of confidence that both our sports aircraft *and* our military aircraft were the best in the world.

The true state of affairs became known during the events in Spain.

In 1936 civil war broke out in Spain. With the urging of German and Italian fascists, General Franco started a military rebellion against the Republic. When it became clear that General Franco alone could not cope with the Republican forces, Hitler and Mussolini threw their troops and military equipment into the fighting in Spain—guns, tanks, and airplanes. At first, they sent obsolescent Fiat and Heinkel fighters and Junkers-86 bombers. Against an unarmed people, it was possible to fight even with old equipment.

But progressive people from many nations throughout the world— British, French, American, German, and Italian antifascists—came to the aid of the Spanish Republicans. The Soviet people extended a helping hand to Republican Spain. In the fall of 1936, our volunteers with their military equipment set out for Spain to fight in the ranks of the international antifascist forces. . . .[133]

At the beginning, Republican fliers successfully flew I-15 and I-16 fighters (dubbed "snubnoses" by the Spanish) and SB bombers which were given the sentimental nickname "Katiusha." German-Italian aviation suffered heavy losses.

Then the Germans sent their new aircraft, including Messerschmitt fighters, to the aid of Franco.

The Hitlerites openly announced that they regarded Spain as a testing ground for their new arms. The Messerschmitts were substantially superior to the "snubnoses" in combat qualities, particularly in armaments; and this factor, coupled with numerical superiority, gave the Messerschmitts control in the air.

The well-known Soviet journalist Mikhail Kol'tsov, who spent almost the entire war as a *Pravda* correspondent at the front in Spain, told me with great chagrin of the superiority of German airplanes over our own. . . .

More than once, when meeting with Kol'tsov during his brief trips from Spain to Moscow, I heard the puzzling question: "How did it happen that German airplanes turned out to be better than ours?"

Like many other people, he sincerely believed in the invincible might of our aviation and took the failures in Republican Spain very much to heart. "How can it be?" he repeated. " 'Higher, farther, faster than all others' and now this? . . ."

And despite the heroism of the Republican fliers, in the final analysis success was determined by the quality of combat matériel.

In air combat our fighters, despite their good maneuverability, proved inferior to the Germans in speed and especially in the caliber of weapons and the range of fire. The SB bombers could not fly without fighter cover, which our fighters could not provide effectively in view of their inferiority to German fighters.

After all the publicity over our record-breaking feats, this was an unpleasant and, at first glance, an inexplicable surprise. But it was a fact. In the field of aviation, we were clearly lagging behind our potential enemy—Hitlerite fascism. In no way could the sensational, record-breaking aircraft and the giant airplanes substitute for what was required by the conditions of the approaching war.

Urgent, decisive measures were called for to overcome the lag, especially since the international situation was becoming more and more strained. . . .

Stalin reacted very painfully to our failures in Spain. His dissatisfaction and wrath were directed against those who quite recently had been considered heroes and who had been showered with richly deserved honors.

The first to suffer were Smushkevich and Rychagov (both of whom had been awarded the title of Hero of the Soviet Union twice). It subsequently turned out that they were completely innocent.[134]

A group of officials at the Central Aerohydrodynamics Institute, including their chief, Nikolai Mikhailovich Kharlamov, were arrested.

And what were they not accused of!

Shortly before this, most of them, as members of a technical commission headed by Tupolev and Kharlamov, had visited France and the US where, in particular, the license to build the world-famous Douglas passenger plane in the USSR was purchased.

Many failures at that time were explained as sabotage. If a rotten wooden ceiling of an aircraft plant shop caved in, it was sabotage. If the aircraft engine piston rings from some motor plant crumbled, this was sabotage.

The death of Chkalov on December 15, 1938 in a Polikarpov I-180 fighter was sabotage. Beliaikin, Chief of the Main Administration of the Aircraft Industry; the director of the experimental plant where the I-180 was built, Usachev; and the designer Tomashevich, Polikarpov's deputy, paid for this [with their lives].

It was surprising that in a conversation with me in the summer of 1940, Stalin literally said the following:

"Ezhov was a scoundrel. In 1938 he killed many innocent people. We have executed him for this."[135]

I wrote these words down immediately upon returning from the Kremlin.

But what was the situation in reality?

The production facilities of our aircraft plants, created during the first two Five Year Plans, were mass producing airplanes, engines, and instruments. On the whole, the level of the aircraft industry was rather high. The industry provided the army with the necessary quantity of military aircraft. But the thing was that these airplanes were, in part, obsolete and, in part, were not suited to the requirements of war.

If we compare with German counterparts the basic types of Soviet aircraft that were being serially produced at the beginning of World War II, that is in 1939, this comparison will not be in our favor.

At the beginning of the Civil War in Spain in 1936, the I-15 and I-16 met with the Messerschmitts for the first time. These were the first Me-109B fighters with a Junkers JUMO-210 610 hp. engines and a top speed of 470 km/hr.

In terms of speed, our fighters were not inferior to the Messerschmitts—the armaments of both fighters were roughly similar—7.6mm. machine guns, but ours were more maneuverable, and they really gave it to the "Messers."

The leaders of our aviation were very happy with this. An air of placidity developed, and no one was in a hurry to modernize Soviet fighter aircraft. At the same time, the Hitlerites were working feverishly, learning from the results of the first aerial battles in the skies over Spain.

They radically improved their Me-109, installing an 1,100 hp. Daimler-Benz engine which increased the aircraft's flying speed to 570 km/hr. They increased its fire power by mounting a 20mm. cannon on it.

In this form, serial production was begun on the Messerschmitt under the designation Me-109E.

While visiting Messerschmitt plants in Augsburg and Regensburg in the fall of 1939, as a member of a Soviet economic delegation, I saw how widely the serial production of the Me-109E had been developed. In 1939, about 1,500 of them were built.

In August 1938 about twenty Me-109E's were sent to Spain where, under the command of Molders—the best German fighter pilot—they took part in air combat in the final stage of the Spanish tragedy. The superiority of these planes over the I-15 and I-16 was evident.

The Germans had made better use of the lessons of the Spanish testing ground than we.

Only in 1940 did Mig, Iak, and Lag fighters capable of competing with the new "Messers" appear in the form of test models.[136]

Comparison of SB bombers with the JU-88 is also not in our favor.

In terms of speed and bomb load, the Germans were also superior in bomber aircraft.

Just as with the new fighters, the Soviet Pe-2 dive bomber appeared in experimental models only in 1940.

The USSR air fleet had practically no airplanes similar to the German JU-87 dive bomber ["Stuka"] for use in coordinated actions with ground troops.

No need for such a plane was recognized in our country. When in October 1939 we were given the opportunity, not only of becoming acquainted with, but also of purchasing German aircraft, the would-be tacticians categorically refused to purchase the JU-87. "Why throw money down the drain? It's obsolete, slow." Such were the arguments. But in the first days of the war, these "obsolete, slow" machines caused us incalculable calamities.

The fact that the Germans had a large number of JU-87 planes did not attract the attention of our military men to this type of aircraft. [Their] blindness in this case was astonishing.

The Il'iushin Il-2 assault plane, which was far superior to the JU-87 in all respects and which underwent flight tests in 1939, was also received coldly: too little armor, low speed, etc.

This amazing disdain for battlefield aircraft, for planes capable of coordinated action with troops—infantry, tanks, artillery—was clearly demonstrated by the People's Commissar of Defense in his speech to the XVIII Congress of the All-Union Communist Party in March 1939. As if it were an accomplishment, the People's Commissar reported to the Congress that the production of light bombers, assault planes, and reconnaissance aircraft had been cut twofold in favor of heavy bombers.[137]

Flying heavy airplanes, Military Pilot A. B. Iumashev and others had set a number of world records for load-lifting capacity. These records demonstrated that our heavy aircraft had the greatest load capacity, and they created a great impression in the world of aviation. However, the mission of a bomber is not only to lift its bomb load, it must also deliver it to the target—this is the idea [behind bomber aircraft]. But for this our bombers were too slow, and their range was too limited.[138]

In the same way, certain people at that time were carried away by the good maneuverability of our fighters, considering this to be the principal factor. In so doing, they lost sight of the primary mission of a fighter plane, which is to overtake and destroy the enemy. For this, not only maneuverability but, most importantly, speed and powerful armaments are required. But our serially produced fighters in 1937-1938 had neither of these features. . . .

We were very alarmed by the lag of Soviet military aviation by the end of 1938.

According to outward indicators, the level of our aviation was rather high, but its development was one-sided: preference was given to heavy bombers. This preference was to the detriment of other aircraft, especially fighters. After all, in terms of metal and labor expenditures and engines, each heavy four-engine bomber was the equivalent of four fighters. And as we know, superiority in the air is determined by the quantity and quality of fighters.

When our severe lag behind the Germans in fighter planes was discovered, it became clear that they would have air supremacy.

The USSR air force found itself in an extremely difficult position. This is why the government was so alarmed.

In 1939 an emergency crash program was initiated. The Central Committee adopted a number of decisions aimed at strengthening the production base of the aircraft industry considerably and at sharply expanding the number of design organizations and institutes. Fresh forces were channeled into the design collectives, which began to work on the creation of new, up-to-date military planes, chiefly fighters.

Only because the level attained by our aviation science and industry was high by 1939, was it possible to create completely new and up-to-date models of fighter aircraft, bombers, and assault planes and to create a base for their mass production in the short space of two years.

Owing to the measures taken, serial production of all necessary types of combat aircraft was begun. But we had succeeded in producing too few of them by the time war broke out. This was our misfortune.

Admiral N. G. Kuznetsov
Naval Preparedness

I WANT HERE to give a brief outline of the shipbuilding program which we were not destined to complete. Both during the war and after, it aroused some criticism, for which there was good reason; it used up vast amounts of money and metal but failed to increase our naval forces substantially in time. . . .

N. G. Kuznetsov, "Pered voinoi," *Oktiabr'*, 1965, No. 11, pp. 141–44.

In the mid-1930's, the Chief of the Naval Forces held a number of conferences in Moscow. . . . Galler subsequently told me about one of these conferences in late 1936 or early 1937. The fleet commanders were invited to attend a meeting of the cabinet, but they were informed of the subject to be discussed only when they arrived in Stalin's office. The following questions were raised—the types of ships to be built and their armaments and the most likely enemy they would have to contend with in combat operations.

The commanders were unanimous when it came to submarines: all favored their construction. But opinions differed on the surface fleet. Commander of the Pacific Fleet M. V. Viktorov wanted large ships and pleaded the vast expanses of the Far East theater where, he believed, the most powerful fleet had to be based. Commander of the Black Sea Fleet I. K. Kozhanov wanted destroyers, cruisers, and as many torpedo boats as possible.

"You don't seem to know what you want," Stalin is said to have remarked.

However that may be, the first variant of the program was referred to the government by the People's Commissariat of Defense in 1937 and then submitted to Stalin. The amendments he proposed were made, the whole was once again reviewed and approved, and action began on it without waiting for the finishing touches.

The program provided for the construction of hundreds of submarines and torpedo boats, but battleships, heavy cruisers, and other surface ships had pride of place.

Of course now with the benefit of hindsight, it is easier to judge the program than three decades ago, for time has resolved the old doubts and disputes. But even at the time, those who undertook to plan the long-term development of the navy should have grasped the main direction more clearly.

As I have already said, the battleships and heavy cruisers were designated the main strike force. Meanwhile, aircraft carriers had already made their appearance as one of the most important types of surface ships. They were being built by all the major naval powers—the United States, Britain, and Japan. It is true that battleships were still very much in favor, but tests carried out in America in the 1920's proved that planes could sink any ship, no matter what kind of plating it had.[139] Old ideas die hard, however, and tradition was strong in the Western navies.

In the 1930's, we had to take a fresh look at our future navy. Of course, we should have given preference to the most modern types of ships, but perhaps we should not pass too harsh a judgment on those who drew up that program for not giving up the idea of battleships altogether: the time was not yet ripe for that. The unforgivable thing was that the program made no provision at all for aircraft carriers. Just imagine that the program had been completed as planned in the second half of the 1940's. We should have had large squadrons with battleships but without a single aircraft carrier. How far out to sea could they have ventured? . . .

I know that both Isakov and Galler, who took part in working out the program, realized the importance of aircraft carriers. They were unable to defend their viewpoint, however, for their arguments were not always taken into account in the People's Commissariat of Defense (which drafted the first variant of the program), while Stalin, who usually reckoned with the opinion of experts, tended for some unexplained reason to underrate the role of aircraft carriers. I had repeated proof of this during discussions on naval affairs, especially during the approval of the naval construction projects in 1939.

The same thing happened somewhat later during the examination of a project for another program. It included large and small aircraft carriers, but on Stalin's personal instructions the big ships, and then the small ones, were excluded.

I well remember the occasion when Stalin replied to a request for more anti-aircraft facilities on ships in the following words:

"We are not going to fight off America's shores."

I think all this was due to a tendency to underestimate the danger to ships from the air.

The surprising thing is that the view on this matter did not change even after the Great Patriotic War.[140]

Stalin did not change his attitude to the anti-aircraft defenses of the navy either. Very much later we suggested that an anti-aircraft installation should be substituted on some cruisers for one of the main caliber turrets, which would have considerably reinforced the ship's anti-aircraft defenses. But the proposal was firmly rejected.

On the other hand, Stalin had a special and curious passion for heavy cruisers. I got to know this gradually. At a conference in Zhdanov's office I made several critical remarks on the heavy cruiser project. Zhdanov said nothing, as if he had not heard what I said. When we left his office, one of the leading officials of the People's Commissariat for the Shipbuilding Industry, A. M. Redkin, warned me:

"Watch your step, don't insist on your objection to these ships."

He told me in confidence that Stalin had threatened to mete out strict punishment to anyone objecting to heavy cruisers. . . .[141]

I was also aware that Stalin was keen on battleships. One autumn day in 1939, we were at his country house. I remember that K. A. Meretskov and I. S. Isakov had also arrived from Tallinn.[142] At dinner following the official part of our talk we discussed the Baltic theater. I expressed my doubts about battleships, not whether ships of this type were necessary at all, but whether they should be built for such a shallow sea as the Baltic where they would be easy prey to mines.

Stalin got up from the table, paced up and down the room, broke open two cigarettes, and filled his pipe with the tobacco. He lit up and said, deliberately stressing each word and looking severely at me:

"We shall collect kopek by kopek and build them."

I thought that he had his own plans, which he did not consider necessary to share with us. That may well have been so.

The great shipbuilding program started in 1937–1938. The blue-printing and laying of the keels were being carried on at a very fast pace. The scale of the effort was expanded in 1939. Hundreds of ship-yards were working for the People's Commissariat of Shipbuilding, turning out engines and armament. But it took from three to five years to commission a large ship.

When Hitler attacked Poland in September 1939, we should apparently have decided right away what was to be done with the program. The construction of a major fleet could not be continued at the old pace, unless we were sure that the war would not start soon. As we had no such assurance—and we could not have any—this costly program should have been immediately folded up. I must admit that I personally failed to make such a proposal.

Even when war broke out in Europe, however, no changes were made in the program for several months. On the contrary, the pace of it was even increased, and this entailed vast expenditures on the coastal construction of naval bases, docks, shipbuilding yards, etc.

In late 1939 the cruiser *Luetzow* was bought in Germany. I learned about this when I. F. Tevosian called me and said the decision had been made to acquire a partially built cruiser from the Germans. Tevosian was going to Germany to negotiate the deal. This was not the first time that naval questions were decided over the heads of the People's Commissariat of the Navy. I was not in the least surprised. Something else worried me. As Tevosian made clear, there was no cruiser as such: we were merely getting the hull of one with no engines or armament. It would have to be towed to Leningrad and completed there. "What if we don't get everything we need, like ammunition?" I thought. A war was on. Who knew what might happen in Germany. But the decision was already made, and it was too late to argue. The cruiser was purchased, and a German tugboat brought it to Leningrad in the spring of 1940.

The work seemed to go fairly well at first. Then the Germans began holding back deliveries, and, finally, they recalled their engineers. The last engineer left the USSR literally hours before the war began. Later, we remembered this incident with perplexity: "How could one think of buying an unfinished cruiser from a country at war?" . . .[143]

We began to cut back production of large ships in the spring of 1940. But this did not yet mean a radical reassessment of the program. It only reflected the fact that production of all kinds of ground weapons (guns, tanks, etc.) was increasing. There was not enough metal and manpower to go around. That's why we decided temporarily to suspend the production of battleships and heavy cruisers.

The program was radically reviewed in October 1940, after which only submarines and small surface crafts (destroyers, mine trawlers, etc.) were built. The fleets continued to receive them from the shipbuilders and put them into operation right up to the last day of peace. And the battleships remained on the stocks.[144]

CHAPTER TWO

The Disaster

INTRODUCTION

EVEN IN the present age when a formal declaration of war seldom precedes actual fighting and when lightning surprise attacks yield the aggressor immediate high profit and shake the victim by their very unexpectedness, the outbreak of Nazi-Soviet hostilities represents a unique phenomenon.

Unique was the degree of operational and tactical surprise which caught unawares the armed forces of a government that had preached vigilance and had subscribed to a theory of the inevitability of war, that had had sufficient time to observe from afar the pattern of the German blitzkrieg in the West and to draw appropriate conclusions from German military behavior on its own frontiers. Unique was the disparity between the availability of abundant intelligence information, of warnings from friends, neutrals, and even foes and the stubborn refusal of a leadership which boasted of its hard-headedness to face the facts. Here was the spectacle of a leadership which professed belief in historical inevitability, which regarded itself as history's agent trying to escape the inexorable consequences of events, to cheat history, as it were, by pitiful gestures, empty words, and patent self-deception. And unique, finally, was the scale of the initial disaster which surprised even the German generals, if not Hitler himself, and shocked Soviet civilians and military men of all positions and ranks and, at the apex of society, Stalin himself. Shortly after the outbreak of war, the leadership of a government which from its very inception had required stupendous sacrifices of the population in order to build up its defensive capacities faced the virtual destruction of its military establishment.

A limitless gulf separated Soviet prewar prediction of the likely course of war from the actuality; the latter took on the dimensions of a colossal nightmarish fantasy and produced a mental vacuum, a terror of the unexplainable. Even as late as summer 1939, there had appeared in the Soviet Union a novel by N. Shpanov, *The First Strike—The Story of the Future War*. Shpanov's account envisaged no more than a large-scale fascist air attack on the Soviet Union which is repulsed from Soviet air

179

space within twenty-nine minutes from the entrance of the Soviet air force into battle and thirty minutes from the original attack! The author then describes Soviet retaliation against German industry which within five-and-a-half hours of the start of the war results in the destruction or damage of 55 percent of all German Messerschmitt fighter planes, 45 percent of Arado-Udet pursuit planes, and 96.5 percent of all Heinkel bombers. Ten hours after the initial fascist assault, the head of the Soviet air force is reporting to the Supreme Commander in Chief that Soviet aviation has protected the Red Army from German air strikes and is supporting its advance across the borders, and that the military-industrial complex in the Nuremberg region has been destroyed!

The famous Soviet aircraft designer and Deputy Minister of the Aviation Industry, A. S. Iakovlev, had the following to say about Shpanov's novel:

> Shpanov's novel was advertised as "Soviet military science-fiction," but it was a fiction by no means intended for children. The book was published by the Military Publishing House of the People's Commissariat of Defense. Moreover, it was published not as a marginal enterprise but as a part of the training series of the Officers Library! The novel was intended as a popularization of our military aviation doctrine.
>
> Later many of our commanders remembered bitterly this bad "fiction" which unfortunately abounded in our prewar propaganda and sowed the illusion that the war, if it came, would be won quickly, with a low expenditure of our own blood, and on enemy territory.[*]

The disparity between the amount of information available to the Soviet leadership and its persistent refusal to accept intelligence sources as a basis for action has been described in numerous personal accounts by Western and Soviet public figures. Without a doubt Kremlin decision-makers received more and better information on the approaching general danger, even on specific details of date and hour of invasion, than has any other leadership of an attacked country in the history of modern warfare. Winston Churchill's conclusion that "Stalin and his commissars showed themselves to be the most completely outwitted bunglers" would appear to be wholly justified.[†]

As late as a week before the German invasion, in what may have seemed to Soviet military leaders a response to their growing uneasiness, to the flood of secret and not so secret information concerning Nazi concentration on Soviet borders, the Soviet press agency TASS issued an

---

[*] A. S. Iakovlev, *Tsel' zhizni* (Moscow, 1966), p. 254.

[†] Winston S. Churchill, *The Second World War* (6 vols.; London: Cassell and Co., 1950–55), III, 316.

official communiqué which could have originated only with Stalin. It reads in part:

According to the information of the USSR, Germany is observing the terms of the Soviet-German nonaggression pact just as strictly as is the Soviet Union. In view of this, in the opinion of Soviet circles, rumors about Germany's intention to break the pact and to attack the USSR are devoid of all foundation, and the recent dispatch of German troops released from operations in the Balkans to the eastern and northeastern areas of Germany is connected, it must be presumed, with other motives which have nothing to do with Soviet-German relations.*

This communiqué offers additional proof, if any is needed, that the Soviet leadership was well aware of the German concentration on the frontier; the motives, not the fact of concentration are questioned. A timely warning could still have denied the Germans the fruits of tactical surprise; instead the government chose to administer the final tranquilizer to the troops which were facing the mighty invasion force. Those who reflect upon the post-Purge atmosphere prevalent in official Soviet circles at the time will understand that the communiqué abruptly ended discussions of the approaching danger; any commander bent on increasing the combat readiness of his frontier troops ran the risk that colleagues, superiors, and the ubiquitous secret police would call into question his loyalty to the leadership and label him panic-monger and provocateur.

The scale of the disaster wrought by German invaders in the first hours, days, weeks, and months of war can be considered unprecedented in the history of modern warfare. On June 22, 1941 the two greatest forces in the history of warfare stood along a frontier two thousand miles long. The German forces were fully mobilized and equipped; they were led by experienced veterans of numerous conquests; they possessed a detailed plan for the approaching Operation Barbarossa. For the invasion 154 German divisions and 29 divisions and 16 brigades of Hitler's allies had been massed. The invading armies included 19 tank and 13 motorized divisions. The German forces consisted of 3,300,000 men with about 7,200 artillery pieces, 3,350 tanks, and 2,000 airplanes. They were divided into three major groupings: Army Group North, commanded by Field Marshal von Leeb; Army Group Center, commanded by Field Marshal von Bock; Army Group South, commanded by Field Marshal von Rundstedt.

Facing the Germans on the Soviet side of the frontier was about 54 percent of the entire manpower of the Red Army, 170 divisions distributed in five border military districts (Leningrad, Baltic, Western, Kiev, Odessa). The troops of the first echelon comprised 56 divisions and 2 brigades

*Pravda, June 14, 1941.

deployed in depth to 50 km. The troops of the second echelon were grouped in a region 50 to 100 km. from the frontiers, and reserve formations were massed 150 to 400 km. from the frontier.

Soviet military historians assert even today that German forces enjoyed numerical superiority in men and especially in heavy military equipment at the moment of invasion—especially if the contributions of their allies are tallied as well. Their conclusions are disputed by Western studies, however, which attribute to the Red Army approximately the same or even greater strength in infantry and decisive superiority in number of tanks and airplanes. The English scholar John Erickson, for example, estimates on the basis of a comparison of Soviet and German sources that Soviet numerical superiority on the Eastern Front in tanks was at least 7 to 1 and in aircraft 4 or 5 to 1.*

Regardless of the total figures, the point is that German striking groups were clearly stronger in numbers than the first echelon troops on the Soviet side. Even more important, the Germans succeeded in creating decisive superiority along the main axes of their assault. German Panzer groups chose a line of advance against Soviet formations which were in places some five to six times weaker than the powerful German assault units. Numerical comparison is misleading, moreover, when one considers that Soviet tanks and aircraft were to an overwhelming degree obsolete or obsolescent in comparison with the enemy's equipment. Finally, the numerical balance of opposing forces was immediately and drastically upset from the first hours of the campaign, as the element of surprise and the clear German superiority in troop training and officer experience contributed to initial destruction of Red Army manpower and especially of equipment.

Commanders of Soviet military districts had been given warning of the impending invasion a mere 180 minutes prior to the attack. At 30 minutes after midnight on June 22 the People's Commissar of Defense, Marshal S. K. Timoshenko, at last issued a directive ordering troops in border regions to be brought to a state of full combat readiness. The directive informed commanders that a surprise German attack was possible on June 22 or 23. While this directive was indeed a warning, it was a most ambiguous one. In accordance with the basic pattern of all Soviet communications connected with German preparations, commanders of border military districts were ordered to deploy and camouflage their forces, to occupy emplacements in fortified areas at the frontier secretly, to disperse and camouflage aircraft at field air bases, but at the same time

*John Erickson, *The Soviet High Command* (New York: St. Martin's Press, 1962), p. 584.

they were strictly forbidden to undertake other steps without special permission and were told to avoid succumbing to provocations which "may result in serious troubles." The late Minister of Defense of the Soviet Union, Marshal R. Ia. Malinovskii, then a corps commander on the southwest frontier, recalls:

> To our question requesting clarification—"Could we open fire if the enemy invaded our territory?"—the answer followed: "Do not succumb to provocation and do not open fire."[*]

Not only were Soviet commanders sent this ambiguous warning some three hours before the attack; most troops in the field learned of the directive only after combat operations had already begun.

Soviet military historians like to stress that the German armies which assaulted Russia met determined resistance for the first time in their experience; they became entangled in bloody and drawn-out fighting. "The USSR was no Poland or France!" they exclaim. While it should certainly be noted that the Eastern campaign from the very beginning did not repeat the German armies' march through Poland and France, it should also be remembered that Russia was saved in the final analysis by nothing other than immense space, manpower, and resources. If anything, the absolute dimensions of territorial conquest, destruction of matériel, and losses of Soviet troops killed and captured showed the German attack to be even more effective than Hitler's previous campaigns. One month after the beginning of the invasion, German troops controlled Soviet territory more than twice that of France.

While the first phase of the Nazi-Soviet war demonstrated the doggedness and fighting spirit of Red Army units—as memoirs of German generals bear witness—it demonstrated as well the ineptitude of middle and high command levels of the Red Army, particularly of military strategists in Moscow, and of Stalin himself. Soviet war memoirs confirm and reinforce the impression gained from books written after the war by German generals. Decision-makers in Moscow—and in the centralized Soviet command system this means above all Stalin—formed a picture of events on the battlefront which bore little resemblance to reality, and they contributed astonishingly well to German successes by means of unrealistic orders to counterattack when reinforcement of defensive positions should have been the order of the day; by means of their pressure on field commanders to stand fast and yield not an inch of territory when strategic retreat and survival of manpower and equipment were the most desirable objects;

[*] R. Ia. Malinovskii, "Dvadtsatiletie nachala Velikoi Otechestvennoi voiny," *Voenno-istoricheskii zhurnal,* 1961, No. 6, p. 7.

by means of continuously throwing reserves piecemeal into battle after long, tiring approach marches when concentration on secondary defense lines would have had a much greater effect.

All the errors committed in strategic planning, armaments production, and tactical training of troops before the war; all the devastation wrought in the Soviet professional officer corps by the Purge were multiplied by the inexcusable operational and tactical surprise achieved by German armies along the entire line and were compounded by the ineptitude of the Soviet High Command in its direction of the Red Army during the first months of war. The result was an unprecedented military disaster which imprinted a traumatic experience in the memory of every participant and witness. The traumatic character of this experience is clearly discernible in the memoirs of Soviet generals. The reevaluation of the Nazi-Soviet war after Stalin's death and again after Khrushchev's ouster started with just this disaster in June 1941 and the months which followed. For Soviet generals, it retains a compelling fascination.

PART I JUNE 22, 1941 IN MOSCOW AND BERLIN

Introduction

THE RAPID DISINTEGRATION of Soviet defenses after June 22 exposed the inadequacies of the post-Purge military leadership. The Soviet generals, whose professional advancement depended upon steadfast political loyalty and unhesitating acceptance of orders from above, subscribed with their civilian counterparts to the bureaucratic dictum *nachal'stvo luchshe znaet* ("the leaders know best"). Those who directed the futile efforts to blunt the Nazi invasion cannot be charged with sabotaging their leader's instructions. The crime for which many of them were dismissed and some of them shot was neither disobedience nor unwarranted initiative, but rather the failure to reap success from their efforts to execute Stalin's orders to the last letter. Several of the memoirs that follow convey the passive, cautious, and often servile attitudes prevalent in the highest echelons of the military establishment at the start of the war.

The last days of peace and the night of the invasion in the two capitals—Moscow and Berlin—are depicted below by six witnesses. The first of these, General of the Army M. I. Kazakov, Chief of Staff of the Central Asian Military District, arrived at the General Staff shortly before the outbreak of war. He records his amazement in discovering that while a key Staff officer, General Vasilevskii, expected

war in two weeks, the General Staff showed no signs of urgency in formulating measures to meet the danger.

The second account, by the People's Commissar of the Navy, Admiral N. G. Kuznetsov, provides an invaluable chronicle of events through the night of the invasion. The author's place in the official hierarchy, his proximity and access to the center of power, enhance the value of his reminiscences; no other political or military leader of comparable stature has described this fateful day in Moscow in such detail or even attempted to explain the conduct of the leadership during the crisis.

General of the Army I. V. Tiulenev, then Commander of the Moscow Military District, recalls his reactions to the anticipated but nevertheless unexpected invasion. A veteran of both the First World War and the Civil War, the general, like many other officers advanced to high position in the aftermath of the Purge, was a "graduate" of the 1st Cavalry Army. This famous Civil War formation which enjoyed the special patronage of Stalin almost entirely escaped the ravages of the Purge; its leaders—Marshals Voroshilov, Budennyi, and Timoshenko—continued to occupy high positions. (Incidentally, Zhukov, whose attitudes and level of professional expertise differed from those of the

185

Tiulenevs and Voroshilovs, also belonged to the 1st Cavalry Army, a factor which may explain his good fortune during the Purge and may have contributed to his lightning promotion in the two years prior to the war.)

In the fourth account, the Deputy People's Commissar of the Aviation Industry, A. S. Iakovlev, explores the causes of the disaster which shattered the Soviet air force in the first days of the war and assured German monopoly of the skies during the following weeks. The ineffectiveness of this highly prized branch of service was probably one of the most unexpected shocks for Soviet leaders. To the foot soldiers who suffered the relentless and murderous assaults of the Luftwaffe, the air force became an object of scorn. Iakovlev, almost alone among memoirists, placed a major part of the blame on errors and omissions dating back well before the Purge.

The last account from the central military establishment belongs to Colonel General N. N. Voronov, who was appointed Chief of Anti-aircraft Defense two days before the invasion. Voronov and some of his colleagues insist that major disagreements concerning the requirements of the military situation on the eve of the war separated them from their superiors in the People's Commissariat of Defense. Were these superiors to reminisce, one might anticipate a similar effort to dissociate themselves from the views of Stalin and his political associates. A perusal of excerpts from the memoirs of commanders junior to

Voronov, which appear later in the chapter, betrays a comparable zeal in distinguishing their positions from those of their superiors. In the final analysis, blame would logically devolve upon Stalin, but if Stalin is unquestionably responsible owing to his position at the apex of a highly centralized system of decision-making, so also is the very system which prevents the Kuznetsovs from sharing their opinions with close comrades, discourages the Tiulenevs from having any opinions at all, and condemns the Voronovs to regretting the policies of Stalin and the behavior of the Voronovs, Tiulenevs, and Kuznetsovs.

V. I. Berezhkov, First Secretary of the Soviet Embassy in Berlin, describes in the last fragment the final weeks of peace and, in particular, the twenty-four-hour period during which the invasion took place. He offers additional information on the volume and source of warnings available to the Kremlin on the eve of the attack. Of particular value is his eyewitness account of the actual declaration of war which took place in the office of the German Foreign Minister, Joachim von Ribbentrop, after the invasion had already started. The unique Soviet record of the occasion, it differs markedly in its description of Ribbentrop's behavior from the German eyewitness account which appears in the memoirs of Hitler's (and Ribbentrop's) personal translator, Paul Schmidt.°

°Paul Schmidt, *Hitler's Interpreter* (London: Heinemann, 1951).

General of the Army M. I. Kazakov
At the General Staff

WE HELD staff officer training exercises in the beginning of June 1941. Responsible representatives of the General Staff—Major General M. N. Sharokhin, who was then working as sector chief for the Near Eastern theater, and Lieutenant Colonel S. M. Shtemenko—took an active part in directing them. The subject of the exercises was the concentration of a single army in the direction of the state border. Only two weeks remained before the attack by Nazi Germany, but we were busy with routine matters. It appeared that the General Staff representatives were no more concerned than we about the situation on our western borders. Life still rolled along on peaceful rails.

On June 11 a summons came from Moscow. . . . The next day an SB military plane took me from the training exercise area to Tashkent,[1] and the following day I flew to Moscow by passenger plane. A railroad stretched beneath us almost the whole time. A great many trains were moving along it, and it soon became clear to me that these were military trains. They were headed in one direction—northwest. I knew very well that no troops had been dispatched from our military district, and that there were no plans to do so. So these were troops from Eastern Siberia or the Transbaikal. At this point alarming thoughts began to go through my head. Since troops were being sent westward, it followed that serious events were shaping up there. Yes, life was still rolling along on peaceful rails, but now military trains had appeared on those rails as well.

At the General Staff I met M. F. Lukin, who then commanded an Army in the Transbaikal Military District. It turned out that it was his Army that was being transferred by rail. I felt it would be awkward to ask the final destination on the Army's itinerary. A day or two later I saw there a few more Army commanders dressed in field uniforms. It was clear that they were not traveling to maneuvers. I would have known

M. I. Kazakov, *Nad kartoi bylykh srazhenii* (Moscow, 1965), pp. 68–71.

about maneuvers. But there was little time for riddles and guesses. I had to get busy on the matters for which I had come to the General Staff.

Lieutenant General N. F. Vatutin suggested that I clarify certain points in the operations plan of the military district, taking into account recent changes in personnel and in the organizational structure of the troops. Work on the documents took me four or five days. During that time I could not help noticing the increasing activity at the General Staff. Lieutenant General Gerasimenko, who was then commander of the Volga Military District, arrived with his chief of staff. Later, Lieutenant General F. A. Ershakov, commander of the Urals Military District, appeared.

To get my bearings, I decided to investigate the general situation. It was my conviction at the time that of all the generals in the Operations Office of the General Staff, A. M. Vasilevskii was the most objective and thorough in his evaluation of events. I turned to him. He said that Finland's armed forces were mobilizing and Nazi Germany's troops were already concentrated at our frontiers. To my frank question, "When will war with fascist Germany begin?" Aleksandr Mikhailovich replied: "We'll be lucky if it doesn't begin in the next fifteen to twenty days."

When I had finished my work, I had to report the results to the People's Commissar of Defense. During the day of June 18 and the first half of June 19, Lieutenant General N. F. Vatutin and I tried in vain to see him. Finally, after lunch, Vatutin told me that the People's Commissar would see us at 6:00 p.m. I had been looking forward to the possibility of flying to Tashkent on the following day, for the situation urgently required my return to duty as quickly as possible. Several times I reserved a seat on a passenger plane, but then the reservation had to be canceled. Now I remade the reservation for June 20.

Half an hour before the appointed time, N. F. Vatutin and I were in the reception room of the People's Commissar of Defense. . . . Chief of the General Staff G. K. Zhukov passed through into S. K. Timoshenko's office. We continued to wait our turn. How surprised I was when the aide-de-camp, General V. M. Zlobin, suddenly announced:

"The People's Commissar invites you to see a film." I could not but think: Why this "cultural activity" for us? But then a hope glimmered: Perhaps after the showing I could manage to make a report on the documents.

We went. It was a German-made film on the entry of Hitler's troops into the Balkans. The picture was skillfully fabricated. Film extras or traitors who had sold themselves to the Nazis—in small groups, it is true— were "enthusiastically" welcoming the army of the Third Reich. Slavic girls served German officers and soldiers wine and presented them with flowers. We looked and were outraged. Several times Semen Konstantinovich Timoshenko even swore at Goebbels for this swindling forgery.

After the film the People's Commissar asked G. K. Zhukov to dinner. There was nothing for Vatutin and me to do but tuck our fat portfolios under our arms and go "keep watch" in the Operations Office.

S. K. Timoshenko returned from dinner at approximately 10:00 p.m. and was busy with other matters. He did not receive us again. After waiting without results until 1:00 a.m., we put our portfolios away in the safes but continued to inquire in the reception room of the People's Commissar just in case. What are the chiefs doing in there? At 1:30 a.m. we were informed that the People's Commissar had gone to rest, and the Chief of the General Staff also left soon after. In recalling all this, I cannot shake off the thought: Did not the leadership of the People's Commissariat of Defense behave too lightheartedly in the days before the storm? To spend two hours looking at a fascist propaganda film and then go off tranquilly to rest!

On the morning of June 20 I decided at any cost to make a report on my questions at least to the Chief of the General Staff, and I settled down in his reception room. G. K. Zhukov arrived at 11:00 a.m. and immediately asked Vatutin and me to come in. He leafed through our work quite attentively, made me report some of its sections from memory. . . . After this, Zhukov said that the People's Commissar of Defense would evidently be unable to receive me, and authorized me to fly to Tashkent on June 21.

On the evening of June 20 Vatutin and I looked through all the documents once more, sealed the portfolios, put them in safekeeping, and said good-bye to each other for a long time to come.

Admiral N. G. Kuznetsov
At Naval Headquarters

By EARLY 1941 information began to seep through to us on Hitler's far from peaceful intentions. This information was at first very vague but

N. G. Kuznetsov, "Voenno-Morskoi Flot nakanune Velikoi Otechestvennoi voiny," *Voenno-istoricheskii zhurnal*, 1965, No. 9, pp. 73–74; N. G. Kuznetsov, "Pered voinoi," *Oktiabr'*, 1965, No. 11, pp. 146–47, 162–71.

then became much more definite and varied. Despite its efforts, the German command was unable to conceal its preparations for a major offensive on the far-flung front from the Barents Sea to the Bosporus.

The communiqués of the General Staff and the reports from the fleets brought alarming news. The fleet commanders kept asking in personal meetings and telephone conversations how the government viewed Germany's unfriendly acts. I received most calls from the Baltic Fleet commander, V. F. Tributs, for in his area the behavior of the Germans was particularly suspicious. When reporting on current violations of our air space or other incidents, Tributs, an energetic and enterprising man, would always ask: "What are we to make of all this?"

Indeed, what should have been done at the beginning of 1941 was to collate and analyze all these facts and to weigh them against Nazi promises and the nonaggression pact. There was the nonaggression pact with Germany, but there was also Hitler's *Mein Kampf*, in which he elaborated his plans for seizing "Lebensraum" in the East. He never renounced either the book or his plans.

It was in February 1941, I believe, that I informed the government that the Germans were delaying deliveries for the cruiser *Luetzow* more and more frequently. Stalin listened to me attentively and asked me to keep him informed of developments. He remarked that our representatives in Germany were being restricted in their movements.

That same February I had a conversation with Zhdanov, who, as a member of the Supreme Naval Council, often came to the People's Commissariat. One day he stayed behind in my office after a meeting, and we discussed various topics. I then asked him whether he thought Germany's actions near our borders were preparations for war. He said he thought that Germany was incapable of fighting on two fronts. He believed the violations of our air space and the concentration of German forces on our borders were nothing more than precautionary measures on Hitler's part or a means of psychological pressure.

I expressed my doubts:

"If they are only precautionary measures, why should Hitler build up his forces in Finland and Rumania? Why do German reconnaissance planes fly over Hanko and Poliarnyi?[2] After all, these places present no threat to them."

A few months before this talk, I heard Zhdanov make the rather categorical statement that both sides were bogged down in the war in the West and that this gave us the chance to go about our business in peace. On this occasion he did not say as much, but he still believed that a clash with Germany was improbable. He cited the experience of World War I, which showed that Germany was not equal to fighting on two fronts, and he also recalled Bismarck's well-known warning on this score.

Zhdanov may have had doubts in his own mind, or he may have had inside knowledge of some of Stalin's plans which I knew nothing about, and he must have been informed of the vast amount of work that was then being done at great speed to fortify our western frontiers. These efforts made sense mainly in the event of a war with Germany, so it seemed that the possibility of such a war was being taken into account. But it is still a mystery to me why Zhdanov answered as he did and what Stalin was planning. . . .

The last time that I saw Stalin on the eve of the war was June 13 or 14. I reported to him at that time on the latest intelligence from the fleets, on the training exercises conducted in the Black Sea, and on the *de facto* stoppage of deliveries by the Germans for the cruiser *Luetzow*. He did not raise any questions about the readiness of the fleets or issue any instructions in connection with a possible attack by Germany. "Is that all?" he asked me. Everyone present looked in my direction as if to say: Don't hold things up. I left the conference room quickly. I still wanted very much to report that German transports were leaving our ports and to ask whether the traffic of Soviet merchant ships in German waters shouldn't be restricted.[3] But it seemed to me that my continued presence there was obviously unwelcome. The next day I was received by V. M. Molotov. He made decisions concerning several current questions. At the end of the conversation I offered my own unsolicited opinion concerning the suspicious behavior of the Germans, and as the weightiest argument I offered the graph of German merchant ship traffic.[4] He expressed the same point of view on the possibility of war that A. A. Zhdanov had expressed earlier: "Only a fool would attack us."

Today, in pondering the behavior of Stalin and his closest aides, I am inclined to draw the conclusion that right up to the last moment they did not believe in the possibility of an attack by Hitler. Stalin was unnerved and irritated by persistent reports (oral and written) about the deterioration of relations with Germany. He brushed facts and arguments aside more and more abruptly.[5]

While feeling responsibility for the fleets and knowing what fatal consequences might ensue were they caught off guard, I could not express my viewpoint—which was contrary to the official one—even to my close subordinates. Under the pretext of training, we hastened to increase the readiness of the fleets, demanded the acceleration of various measures for strengthening the defense of [naval] bases and at the same time feared a "lowering of the boom" for displaying too much initiative. Being on friendly terms with [the Deputy Chief of Main Naval Headquarters] V. A. Alafuzov, I shared my misgivings with him more openly; but I behaved more officially with [the Chief of Main Naval Headquarters] I. S. Isakov, although I felt that he shared these misgivings. I expressed my opinion to [the Chief of the Main Directorate of Political Propaganda of the Navy] I. V. Rogov more cautiously.[6] I kept in constant but not very close personal contact with Marshal S. K. Timoshenko, People's Commissar of Defense, and with General of the Army G. K. Zhukov, Chief of the General Staff; and I noticed that they, too, were awaiting instructions.

Several days before the outbreak of the war General N. F. Vatutin, Deputy Chief of the General Staff, came to me about some question. He said that he read our operations reports carefully and reported them to his superiors. He promised to notify Main Naval Headquarters immediately should the situation become critical. . . .

Saturday, June 21, passed much the same as the preceding days, full of alarm signals from the fleets. . . .

Silence reigned in the offices of the capital. On normal days it would be dinner time after 6:00 p.m., and the chiefs would go to their homes for about three hours or so, afterward working until late at night. But on Saturday many of them left town. The pressure of business abated.

That evening it was especially quiet somehow. The telephone did not ring at all, as if it had been disconnected. Even such "restless" People's Commissars as V. A. Malyshev and I. I. Nosenko,[7] with whom I was in especially close contact, did not make their presence known with the question that had become habitual of late: "How are things going?"

I sat in my office. The usual city noises could be heard from the street—the rumble of vehicles and occasional loud, carefree youthful laughter. Absent-mindedly I went through my papers, unable to concentrate on them. A very short time before, I had chanced to see a survey of the foreign press and TASS reports. The most diverse newspapers were writing about the approaching war between Russians and Germans. They couldn't all be in collusion![8]

I recalled how wars had begun in the past, in particular, the Russo-Japanese War in 1904. We had frequently been reminded of it at officers' school and at the Naval Academy—perhaps because the first act of this war was played at sea. It began with a surprise torpedo attack which the Japanese destroyers launched against the Russian squadron anchored at the outer roadstead of Port Arthur.[9]

While talking about Port Arthur, Gall', the instructor in tactics at the naval school, . . . emphasized that there was no point in being surprised that the enemy had attacked without a declaration of war; after all, he was the enemy. It would be naive to complain of his perfidy.[10] Rather, one should wonder about our command, which had carelessly placed the fleet in a position where it could be attacked.

School recollections were followed by memories of what I had experienced in Cartagena, where bombs sometimes began exploding before the air raid signal sounded.[11] I recalled the tension that gripped us during the days of the Khasan events when we were expecting Japanese aircraft to strike Vladivostok.

My musings were interrupted by V. A. Alafuzov, Deputy Chief of Main Naval Headquarters. As always, he had come with the evening report. The situation supposedly had not changed: as before, things were very unsettled in the Baltic; on the Black Sea it was more quiet; and in the North [Sea] nothing special was happening.

Alone once more, I called the People's Commissar of Defense.

"The People's Commissar has gone," I was told.

Nor was the Chief of the General Staff at his office.

I decided to contact the fleets. . . . With a certain feeling of relief, I thought to myself: since the commanders are at their posts, if necessary they will be able to get their bearings quickly. But why was there no information whatsoever from above? From our operational reports, the People's Commissar of Defense and the General Staff knew that our fleets had received several days ago the order for operational readiness No. 2.[12] However, the General Staff was not taking similar measures of its own and was not telling us a word.

The time passed slowly. . . .

About 11:00 p.m. the telephone rang, and I heard the voice of Marshal S. K. Timoshenko:

"There is very important news. Come to my office."

Quickly putting into a folder the latest data on the situation in the fleets and calling V. A. Alafuzov, I went with him. Vladimir Antonovich took maps. We were expecting to report about the situation on the seas. . . .

The Marshal was pacing about the room and dictating. It was still very warm. General of the Army Zhukov was writing at a desk, his tunic unbuttoned. Before him lay several sheets from a large pad of radiogram forms covered with writing. It was apparent that the People's Commissar of Defense and the Chief of the General Staff had been working for quite a long time.

Semen Konstantinovich noticed us and stopped. Briefly, without mentioning any sources, he said that an attack by Germany on our country was considered possible.

"The fleets must be ordered to be in combat readiness."

"In the event of attack, are they allowed to open fire?"[13] I asked.

"They are."

Turning to Rear Admiral Alafuzov, he said:

"Run to headquarters and send a telegram to the fleets immediately concerning complete combat readiness. Run!"

7

There was no time to discuss whether it was dignified for an admiral to run down the street. Vladimir Antonovich started running, and I remained for a minute to verify whether I had understood correctly that an attack could be anticipated that very night. Yes, it was true. After midnight on June 22. And it was already past midnight!

As I returned to the People's Commissariat [of the Navy], I was beset by disturbing thoughts: when did the People's Commissar of Defense learn of the possible attack by the Hitlerites? At what hour did he receive the order to bring the forces to a state of full combat readiness? Why was it the People's Commissar of Defense and not the government itself that had given me the order to bring the fleet to a state of combat readiness? And moreover, why was this done in such a semi-official way and so late?

One thing was clear: several hours had already elapsed since the People's Commissar of Defense learned about a possible attack by Hitler. The sheets of paper covered with writing that I had seen on his desk were a confirmation of this. Later I learned that the leaders of the People's Commissariat of Defense—the People's Commissar and the Chief of the General Staff—had been called to Stalin on June 21 at about 5:00 p.m. Consequently, the decision was already made then, under the weight of incontestable proof, to bring the forces to a state of complete combat readiness and, in the event of attack, to repulse it. That means that all this happened approximately ten to eleven hours before the enemy actually invaded our land. . . . It confirms the fact that on the afternoon of June 21, Stalin considered a clash with Germany, if not inevitable, at least highly likely. It is very regrettable that the remaining hours were not used with maximal effectiveness.

Upon arriving at the People's Commissariat, I checked to see that the emergency order had already been issued. It was extremely brief—a prearranged code signal, upon receipt of which all points would know what to do. Still, it takes a certain amount of time for a telegram to reach its destination, and time was precious. I picked up the telephone. The first call was to the Baltic, to V. F. Tributs:[14]

"Without waiting for the telegram that has already been sent to you, bring the fleet to operational preparedness No. 1—combat. I repeat—combat."

Apparently he had been waiting for this. He only asked the same question which I had recently asked Marshal Timoshenko:

"Is it permitted to open fire in case of a clear attack on ships or bases?"

How many times the sailors had been rebuked for "an excess of zeal," and here was the result: Can we fire at the enemy?!

I also reached A. G. Golovko,[15] Commander of the Northern Fleet, at his post. His closest neighbor was Finland. What would she do if Germany attacked us? There were considerable grounds for believing that she would join the fascists. But it was still impossible to tell for certain.

"How should we conduct ourselves with the Finns?" Arsenii Grigor'evich asked. "From their bases, German aircraft are flying to Poliarnyi [Naval Base]."

"On violators of our air space you open fire."

"May I give the order?"

"Yes."

In Sevastopol',[16] Chief of Staff I. D. Eliseev was on the line.

"Have you received the telegram about bringing the fleet to a state of combat readiness?"

It was now one o'clock in the morning. The telegram should have reached the fleets by now.

"I haven't," Ivan Dmitrievich answered.

I repeated to him my order to Tributs and Golovko:

"Act immediately!"

Neither he nor I knew at the time that the first clash of Sevastopol' with the enemy was less than three hours away. . . .

We were still thinking: "Can it really be war?" Somewhere inside us the weak hope continued to glimmer: perhaps it'll all pass? . . .

But it did not pass. This was about to be confirmed. In the meantime, a period of anguished waiting began for me. There was nothing to do. The fleets knew what had to be done. Emergency measures had been carefully defined and worked out. People were working according to plan, and it was better not to disturb them. . . .

In Moscow, dawn broke somewhat earlier than usual. At three o'clock it was already light. I lay down on the couch and tried to imagine what was happening in the fleets. The muffled ring of the telephone brought me to my feet.

"This is the Commander of the Black Sea Fleet reporting."

From the unusually excited voice of Vice Admiral F. S. Oktiabr'skii,[17] I understood that something extraordinary had happened.

"An air raid has been carried out against Sevastopol'. Anti-aircraft artillery is fighting off the attack. Several bombs have fallen on the city—"

I looked at my watch. 3:15 a.m. This is when it started—I no longer had any doubts; this was war!

I immediately picked up the receiver and dialed the number of Stalin's office. The duty officer [Loginev] answered:

"Comrade Stalin is not here, and I don't know where he is."

"I have an exceedingly important message which I must immediately relay to Comrade Stalin personally," I said, attempting to convince the duty officer.

"I can't help you in any way," he answered calmly and hung up.

I did not put the phone down. I called Marshal S. K. Timoshenko. I repeated word for word what Vice Admiral Oktiabr'skii had reported about the air raid that was now in progress over Sevastopol'.

"Do you hear me?"

"Yes, I hear you."

It was no time to brief the People's Commissar on the situation in the fleets and on the state of their preparedness. He had enough of his own business to attend to.

I didn't leave the telephone for several more minutes. I tried again to reach Stalin at various numbers, to talk with him personally, all to no avail. I again telephoned the duty officer:

"I request that you inform Comrade Stalin that German planes are bombing Sevastopol'. This is war!"

"I shall report it to the proper person," the duty officer answered.

A few minutes later the telephone rang, and I heard a dissatisfied, somewhat irritated voice:

"Do you understand what you are reporting?" This was G. M. Malenkov.[18]

"I understand and I report, taking full responsibility, that war has begun—"

G. M. Malenkov hung up. Later I learned that he did not believe me. He called Sevastopol' to verify my report. The talk with Malenkov showed that the hope of avoiding war was alive even at a time when the attack had begun and blood was being spilled over enormous areas of our land. Apparently the orders given to the People's Commissar of Defense the night before, on June 21, had not been very decisive and categorical. Therefore, they had been transmitted without particular haste, and the districts did not receive them before the Hitlerite attack.

Nonetheless, after Malenkov's call, I still hoped that any minute would bring government orders on the initial operation to be carried out now that war had begun. But no orders whatsoever were forthcoming. Then, on my own responsibility, I ordered that the fleets be sent an official message about the outbreak of war and the repulsion of enemy strikes by all means.[19] On the basis of this, the military council of the Baltic Fleet, for example, announced throughout the fleet as early as 5:17 a.m.

on June 22: "Germany has begun an attack on our bases and ports. Repulse all enemy attempts to attack by force of arms."

At that time, of course, the thing to do would have been not only to "repulse attempts to attack" but to inflict counterstrikes against the enemy. But the fleet could not do this alone. Coordinated plans and unified leadership of all the armed forces were required.

It was not difficult to imagine Stalin's state of mind in the face of the dreadful events which, according to his calculations, should have happened much later. He stubbornly denied the possibility of these events happening now, in 1941, right up to the very last days.

His condition communicated itself to those surrounding him, and they were unable to take the reins of command into their hands. They were not accustomed to independent action and could only carry out the will of Stalin, who stood above them. That was the tragedy of those hours. . . .

At about 10:00 a.m. on June 22 I went to the Kremlin. I decided to report on the situation personally. Moscow was resting peacefully. As always on holidays there were few people in the center, and the occasional passers-by looked festive. Only a few cars rushed along, frightening pedestrians with their honking. The capital still did not know that a fire was blazing on the frontiers and that our advance units were engaged in heavy fighting in an attempt to hold back the enemy.

In the Kremlin, everything looked as it did on a normal day off. The sentry at the Borovitskie Gates saluted smartly and, as always, looked into the car. Slowing down slightly, we drove into the Kremlin. I looked around carefully—there was no evidence of anxiety. An oncoming car stopped, as was the custom, and yielded the right of way to us. Everything was silent and deserted.

"Probably the leadership has assembled in some other place," I decided. "But why has there yet been no official announcement of war?"

Finding no one at the Kremlin, I returned to the People's Commissariat.

"Has anyone called?" was my first question.

"No, no one has called."

Main Naval Headquarters had already received more precise data from the fleets. . . . At the end of June 22 the overall picture did not seem gloomy to me, even though the first reports that the Germans were pushing toward Libava had arrived.[20] The enemy did not dare attack the base by sea, and on land I hoped that he would be repulsed by ground units of the Baltic Military District, whose mission it was to defend the city and the base.

It was important that on the first day of war, the enemy did not sink a single ship of ours and that he caused the fleet only insignificant damage.

To be sure, in the future, I would see my errors with my own eyes and would convince myself that in many ways the enemy had forestalled us all the same. This was first apparent in the Baltic Sea. When the war started, the Germans had already succeeded in mining our shores. Their submarines had taken up positions in advance along the probable routes over which our ships would move.

Evidently by the time the war started we should not only have brought the fleets to a high state of preparedness, but we should also have at least partially mobilized and deployed the combat forces. Every step by fascist Germany aimed at preparation for war should have been met with countermeasures. Operation Barbarossa was worked out in detail and implemented gradually. But if Hitler had seen that there would be no element of surprise and that he would meet a fierce and well-prepared resistance, he might have postponed the implementation of this plan and might not have given the order to attack, just as he did not give the order to execute Operation Sea Lion.[21] It is not the passivity of the opposing side but rather its resolution and preparedness to resist that stops and sobers the invader.

Prior to the German attack, headquarters of the Baltic Fleet had received intelligence concerning "suspicious silhouettes" at sea. All we did was report them. And the meaning of these silhouettes was learned only in the first days of war. The cruiser *Maxim Gor'kii* was blown up on mines planted earlier by the Germans. Only the excellent training and the selflessness of the crew saved the ship, and she was soon able to return to duty.

At that time, we discovered many other errors, so we won't write all of them off as "Stalin's incorrect assessment of the situation." He made his errors, we made ours. No matter whose guilt it was, however, the war broke out, and we had to fight the enemy, harnessing all our forces, all our will, and sparing nothing. . . .

.   .   .   .

One thing is apparent to me beyond any doubt: Stalin not only did not exclude the possibility of war with Hitler's Germany; on the contrary, he considered such a war quite probable and even inevitable. He regarded the agreement of 1939 as only a breathing spell, but the breathing spell turned out to be much shorter than he had anticipated. I think his mistake was in miscalculating the date of the conflict. Stalin directed war preparations—extensive and many-sided preparations—on the basis of very distant dates. Hitler disrupted his calculations.

Stalin's suspicions of England and America aggravated the matter. Naturally there was basis enough for thinking that England and America were trying to bring us into conflict with Germany. It was no secret that this was the policy of the Western powers, and Stalin's distrust and hostility toward them was based on it. He received with suspicion or even rejected outright all information about Hitler's actions that came from the English or the Americans. This was his reaction not only to information from casual sources, but even to reports of our official representatives in those countries and to statements made by English and American government officials.

Our embassy people in England reported the transfer of German troops to the Soviet border, naming dates and numbers of divisions. These facts were considered dubious only because they came from English government circles, from Churchill and Cadogan.[22] When such information came from other sources, even from Germany itself, unfortunately it was not taken into account either.

Distrust of Western European political leaders, although well-founded, grew to such proportions that it overshadowed everything. The English were interested in having us fight Germany; therefore everything said about the possibility of war in the near future had been fabricated by them—that is my estimate of Stalin's train of thought.

But despite that, why did he fail to take the simplest precautionary measures? As a man of vast experience, a great statesman, he naturally understood that the only way to sober an aggressor is to be prepared to give him a fitting reply—a blow for a blow. An aggressor can understand a fist; that means you have to show him one. The fist Hitler put up was the divisions he had concentrated on our border. Our fist, therefore, could have been Soviet divisions. But the mere availability of divisions, tanks, planes, and ships was not enough in those circumstances. What was also necessary was a high level of combat preparedness, the full readiness of every military organization and even of the entire country. Everyone—from the People's Commissar of Defense to the common soldier—ought to have known what he was to do immediately in case of war.

I feel that under the weight of irrefutable facts, Stalin began to realize in early 1941 that Hitler might attack. Convinced that his calculations for a war in the more distant future had been wrong and aware that the armed forces and the country as a whole were not ready for war in the coming months, he tried to exploit everything he thought might postpone the conflict.[23] He acted so as to avoid giving Hitler the slightest pretext for an attack in order not to provoke a war. Out of a desire to show that we had no intention of going to war with Germany, he was neurotically sensitive to every retaliation on the part of our armed forces. As a result, when German planes photographed our bases, we were told: Hold your fire! When German air intelligence agents were caught over Soviet fortifications and made to land at out airports, the order was: Release them at once! When the English warned of the possibility of German attack, a declaration was published in answer: We don't believe any rumors; we're keeping faith with the agreement!

General of the Army I. V. Tiulenev
At Moscow District
Headquarters

HOWEVER LONG a June day, it still comes to an end. It was already getting dark when I left the headquarters of the Moscow Military District. Before leaving the office, I turned the page of the desk calendar. Tomorrow was Sunday, June 22. True, in recent months my Sundays had seldom been free. In spite of the existence of the Soviet-German nonaggression pact, war clouds were gathering menacingly over our country, and I, as commander of the military district, was up to my neck in work.

My car, the tires swishing softly over the heated asphalt, merged with the general traffic and then turned off the broad main thoroughfare into quiet Rzhevskii Street, where I lived with my family. . . .

Leaning back in the seat beside the driver, I glanced at, not really read, the Saturday evening paper. Hostilities in Syria—Situation on the Libyan-Egyptian front—British hydroplane crashes—Reuters report: Air Ministry communiqué says small number of German airplanes appeared over England today.

An ordinary, already familiar communiqué from the Western front.

On the right side of the same page was news of the capital: morning at the All-Union Agricultural Exhibit; departure of Young Pioneers for camp; news brief on the forthcoming opening of a water sports stadium in Khimki. . . .

A few more hours would pass and the quiet of night would descend over Moscow. But in the West airplanes with black crosses and spiderlike swastikas were raining bombs on blacked-out European cities. In Berlin, Hitler, surrounded by his field marshals and generals, was bending over a map and drawing new routes for war. Who knew where they

I. V. Tiulenev, *Cherez tri voiny* (Moscow, 1960), pp. 137–42.

would point next, those arrows that indicated the movement of tank armies, drunk on easy victories in Europe, and well-trained, splendidly outfitted SS divisions?

There could be no doubt about it: Hitler was preparing for war against the USSR. Every day, in the line of duty, I studied reports coming to the General Staff from the border military districts. They were not comforting. Violations of our frontiers by fascist airplanes were becoming more frequent. Also, the fact that the trespassing airplanes crossed our border fully armed could not fail to arouse serious thoughts.

In every instance Soviet pilots could have punished the violators, but that was forbidden. It was believed that such incidents were nothing more than provocations by individual officers of the German air force. In the Baltic Military District our fighters forced a flight of fascist airplanes to land. But even after this by no means accidental episode, it was forbidden to open fire on the trespassers.

After only a little thought about this, it was no longer possible to shake off the doubts and the vague sense of alarm that had come over me lately: Was the nonaggression pact signed by the government of fascist Germany really so reliable? Could one trust the word of Hitler, who had crushed Austria, Czechoslovakia, and Poland and had flooded the fields of Europe with blood? On the one hand, there was the nonaggression pact, but on the other, there were more than five hundred violations of USSR air space registered in a short period.

On June 14, 1941 the press published the TASS communiqué.[24] . . . It seemed impossible to disbelieve this quieting statement by our official agency. Still, the facts indicated something else; they were alerting and warning.

The concentration of German troops on our borders had no other purpose but to prepare an attack against the Soviet Union. Suspicion was also aroused by a sudden action of the German government—a widespread wave of arrests of everyone who sympathized with us to any extent began on June 20. History teaches that one of the true portents of war is the isolation within their own country of elements that sympathize with the state against which hostilities are to begin any day.

Of course, on the eve of the fatal day of June 22 we did not know that the government of fascist Germany had decided as early as July 1940 to attack the USSR, and that on December 18 of that same year Hitler had signed Directive No. 1, which subsequently became notorious as Operation Barbarossa.[25]

But neither the TASS communiqué nor the other newspaper articles that unfortunately played a fairly large role in lowering the mobilization readiness of the Red Army and blunting the vigilance of the Soviet people could force us old military men to believe sincerely that fascist Germany had abandoned its delirious idea of "Drang nach Osten," or, to put it another way, a bandit attack on the Soviet Union.

Yes, we, especially the higher military circles, knew that war was not far off, that it was knocking at our gates. But all the same, it must be admitted that misinformation like the TASS communiqué and the insistent propaganda that "if war breaks out tomorrow, if tomorrow there is a campaign, we are ready for it today" led to a certain complacency.[26] The tendency to regard the powerful concentration of German troops on our borders as only a provocation to which, it was said, we should not react oversensitively and to say that Germany was only "playing" on our nerves to some extent cast a spell even on us, commanders of military districts, and on the People's Commissariat of Defense, which had the opportunity to compile an exact forecast of the "war weather" for June, 22, 1941.

Moscow was so beautiful on that last peaceful June evening! . . .

I felt very troubled. All the events of that Saturday and, first and foremost, the telephone call from the Kremlin [at 2:00 p.m.] came involuntarily to mind.

"Comrade Stalin will speak with you."

In the receiver I heard a rather muffled voice:

"Comrade Tiulenev, how do things stand with the anti-aircraft defense of Moscow?"

I reported briefly to the head of government about anti-aircraft defense measures in force for that day, June 21.

In reply I heard:

"Note that the situation is uneasy, and you should bring the troops of Moscow's anti-aircraft defense to 75 percent of combat readiness."

As a result of this brief conversation, I got the impression that Stalin had received new information on the German war plans.

I immediately issued an order to my deputy for anti-aircraft defense, Major General M. S. Gromadin: Do not send the anti-aircraft artillery off to training camp, and put it in full combat readiness.

In the evening I was with the People's Commissar of Defense, Marshal of the Soviet Union Timoshenko, and learned that the alarming symptoms of impending war had been corroborated. There was also a warning in the suspicious activity at the German Embassy—staff members of all ranks were hastily leaving the city.

After leaving the People's Commissar, I looked in at the General Staff. There they informed me:

"According to reports from the headquarters of the military districts, everything appears to be quiet on our western borders, but the commanders have been warned about a possible attack by fascist Germany. These suppositions have been confirmed by our intelligence. The People's Commissar reported the situation to Stalin, but Stalin said that we're creating a panic for no reason."

The answer to my query concerning the Soviet-German balance of forces was:

"As far as we know, the Germans do not have an overall superiority."

So, the actual danger of war emerged quite distinctly.

The commanders of the military districts at the frontier ought to have been given immediately a brief, clear-cut operational plan. This was obvious later on, but, unfortunately, it was not done at the time.

Tired and with troubled thoughts about the impending storm of war, I drove out to my family in the country.

At 3:00 a.m. on June 22, I was awakened by a telephone call. I was summoned to come to the Kremlin at once! Immediately I thought: "War!"

Along the way I dropped in at the General Staff. General G. K. Zhukov was talking over the high-frequency telephone[27] with the headquarters of the border military districts. After finishing, he briefly informed me:

"German aircraft are bombing Kovno, Rovno, Sevastopol', and Odessa. We reported it to Stalin, but he continues to regard it as a provocation by German generals." [28]

I hurried to the Kremlin, where I was met by the commandant [of the Kremlin] and taken immediately to Marshal of the Soviet Union Comrade Voroshilov. Kliment Efremovich asked:

"Where has the command post for the Supreme Command been set up?"

I was rather taken aback at the question.

"Excuse me," I said to Voroshilov, "but no one ever instructed me to prepare a command post for the Supreme Command. The headquarters of the Moscow Military District and the city's anti-aircraft defense have been provided with command posts. If you like, those premises can be transferred to the Supreme Command."

Then I was told that the government had appointed me commander of the Southern Army Group. I was ordered to leave for this destination that very day.

Lieutenant General A. S. Iakovlev
At the People's Commissariat of the Aviation Industry

IT WAS DIFFICULT to believe that war had already broken out. For some reason it seemed that if war came, it would come only when we were completely prepared for it. We both believed and disbelieved the inevitability of approaching war. Now illusions were destroyed. . . .

On the very first day of the war the leadership of the aircraft industry was confronted with the question of plants located in the western and southern regions of the country. While we all counted on stopping the enemy and preventing him from deep penetration into our territory, enterprises located in the zone accessible to enemy aircraft had to be evacuated.

The threat of air attacks also hung over Moscow with its hundreds of plants. While the Moscow anti-aircraft defense system worked well, as future events demonstrated, and anti-aircraft personnel displayed genuine heroism in defending the capital, in the first days many things still had not been well thought through. This was reflected first of all in certain thoroughly awkward attempts at camouflage. For example, in order to camouflage the Moscow Central Airport named after Frunze, the Leningrad Highway—from the Belorusskii station to the race track—was covered with fine slag. Since traffic over this section of the road did not cease, the entire region was enshrouded in billows of ground-up slag. To be sure, they soon had sense enough to remove the slag. Kremlin squares and streets were promptly camouflaged, although it became clear later on that the camouflage did not achieve its purpose. . . .

I will mention one other seemingly insignificant thing concerning camouflage. In contrast to the khaki worn by the rest of the army, our fliers were dressed in blue uniforms, and from the very first days of the war they served as a target for the Hitlerite fliers. Air force personnel dressed in blue uniforms were literally hunted down by the Germans. This oversight, too, had to be corrected in short order. . . .

On the day after the outbreak of war, newspapers carried the first communiqué of the Red Army High Command. In laconic military language it reported that "after fierce fighting, the enemy was repulsed with

A. S. Iakovlev, *Tsel' zhizni* (Moscow, 1966), pp. 243–49, 261–63.

heavy losses. Only in the Grodno and Kristynopol'sk sectors has the enemy managed to achieve insignificant successes and to occupy the towns of Kal'variia, Stoianuv, and Tsekhanovets (the first two within 15, and the other within 10 kilometers of the borders)."

This reassuring news gave rise to the hope that the Hitlerites would not succeed in penetrating deeply. It is well known that all of us at the time had been taught to believe that if there was to be a war, it would be won with "little bloodshed" and "on foreign territory."

Unfortunately, life made serious amendments to this belief. . . . The Soviet Army was in retreat. . . . On June 28 Minsk, the capital of Belorussia, fell. And this on the seventh day of the war! Who could have conceived such a thing! Two days later, L'vov was occupied.[29] This was incomprehensible. It seemed that we were not using our gigantic potential solely because of some kind of fatal misunderstanding.

I was utterly stunned by the announcement of the Soviet Information Bureau that on June 22, 23, and 24 Soviet aviation had lost 374 military aircraft and that these planes had been destroyed by the Hitlerites chiefly on the ground. Subsequently, after the situation had been clarified, the actual figure turned out to be considerably higher. It turned out that the German air force had attacked 66 airfields in our frontier districts. By midday of the first day of the war, we had lost 1,200 aircraft: 300 were lost in air combat, and 900 were destroyed on the ground.[30] All this was evidence of the fact that we had been caught unawares. And somehow you couldn't reconcile yourself to this idea. In general, our airfields in the frontier regions were not prepared at the start of the war. . . .

It was necessary to accelerate the production of new fighter planes in order to put a halt to the unchallenged mastery of the fascist aerial pirates in our skies and to build more assault planes to fight the fascist tanks. After all, ground forces at the front expected aerial defense against the Messerschmitts and Junkers, but we had too few airplanes. No one could understand why we were losing battles, and why the enemy was rapidly advancing onto our territory. There was something inexplicable about this. And we were all greatly alarmed precisely because the events were inexplicable. . . .

What were the sources of the tragedy of the summer months of 1941?

More excruciating than anything else was the thought that the incredible pressure, the overexertion of the workers in the aviation industry, all had been in vain.

With every passing day it became clearer that serious errors and crude miscalculations had been made.

These miscalculations were made not only in assessing the strategic situation on the eve of the war. Several serious errors made in the 1930's had resulted in the difficult situation the country found itself in with respect to aviation in June 1941. Here is how some of these errors look now, twenty-five years after the outbreak of the war.

One of them, the roots of which date back to the end of the 1920's and the early 1930's, was the fascination of some of our tacticians with the Douhet doctrine of the "omnipotence of a strong bomber air fleet," the existence of which would supposedly give the country a decisive military superiority. . . .[31]

The influence of the Douhet doctrine on certain of our aviation leaders in the 1930's was expressed in the overestimation of bomber aircraft and the clear underestimation of other types of aircraft. The airplanes steadily became larger and larger. For a long time, heavy bombers were produced in large series, gladdening the hearts of those who saw in the large machines the basic and decisive striking arm of our air force.

To be sure, the gigantic machines made a great impression at parades and attested to the growing potential of the Soviet aviation industry and the accomplishments of Soviet aviation technology. From the military point of view, however, experience has shown that they were ineffectual. The negative side of the gigantomania and even of the records of that time was that they created an atmosphere of complacency and a false notion that aviation could safeguard the frontiers.

Another error consisted in the fact that up to the end of the 1930's, there were only two major design bureaus in our country—one for bombers and the other for fighters; and each of them monopolized its special field.

To be sure, there were also several small design groups at the time, but most of them had no substantial influence on the development of Soviet aviation. For the entire decade preceding the war it was chiefly the airplanes of A. N. Tupolev and N. N. Polikarpov that were mass produced for the armed forces. Despite all the outstanding merits of these designers, the existence of only two design bureaus for a country like the USSR was a serious miscalculation.

Just what kind of equipment did our air force have at its disposal by 1940?

The basic might of the air force at that time consisted of I-15 and I-16 fighters and TB-3 and SB bombers. These airplanes were obsolete, and, as the experience in Spain had shown, they could not compare with German planes. There is no need to speak of still more antiquated airplanes, a large number of which were still in service.

The rearmament of the air force began for all practical purposes in the first half of 1941. But as we have already stated, our misfortune consisted in the fact that at the time war broke out we still had too few new airplanes, and in the first days of the war our aviation suffered very heavy losses.[32]

But to millions of soldiers at the front—infantrymen, artillerymen, tankmen—and tens of millions of peaceful citizens of Soviet border cities subjected to unchallenged terrorist raids by Hitler's air force, it was incomprehensible—where were our fliers? Where was our air force which during the last five or six prewar years had been so often and so enthusiastically described by our newspapers as the most powerful, largest, and most advanced? Where was this air force? At that time, no one could give a convincing answer.

Our difficulties were aggravated by still another circumstance: the principal aircraft plants were located in the European part of the USSR and almost all of them in the territory between the western frontier and the Volga. Only an insignificant number of plants east of the Volga were beyond the strike range of enemy aircraft. And at a time when the front was pleading for new aircraft, their manufacture had to be virtually halted owing to the necessity of evacuating plants from the European part of the USSR eastward, to Siberia.[33]

This was a difficult time for us—a time of severe trials.

It was more than ten years after the war's end before we fully realized the consequences of the errors that had been made. And those things which we now call errors and miscalculations were then considered the fatal confluence of circumstances—no one thought of them as errors.

Chief Marshal of Artillery N. N. Voronov
At Supreme Headquarters

MY HEART was very troubled. The war was drawing closer with every hour. . . . But at the People's Commissariat of Defense little attention was paid to the danger signals. . . .

In April, May, and June documents of great importance were being compiled in the General Staff. They told of the large-scale operational movements of German troops to our western frontiers and cited the numbers of the corps and the infantry and tank divisions. The authors of these documents did not draw any clear-cut conclusion but merely confined themselves to stating the bare facts. It was clear that the General Staff

N. N. Voronov, *Na sluzhbe voennoi* (Moscow, 1963), pp. 171–75, 178–80.

did not believe that there would be war in 1941. This point of view emanated from Stalin. . . .

Many questions troubled us in those prewar days. It was known, for example, that the troops stationed on our western borders were not moved up to their defense line along the border, for fear of provoking a war. But at the same time, there were large-scale shifts of troops from the interior of our country to the western borders. Units which were not combat ready, which needed more personnel and armaments, were sent there. They were followed by numerous transports with equipment and munitions. This great activity on the railroads could easily have been discovered by the enemy's intelligence service and by his aerial reconnaissance. There was an obvious contradiction here. What was there to fear from moving our troops directly up to the borders and deploying them along these defense lines if at this time we were already making major operational shifts and massing troops in certain regions?

Without any justification whatever, the air force was deployed on a peacetime basis. Why couldn't this air force have been massed at field airbases under the guise of normal exercises, and why couldn't all fighter aviation in the border districts have been aimed at providing air defense for the troops, command points, and important rear objectives?

How could our leadership disarm fortified zones along the former frontier before necessary defensive zones had been built along the new western border of 1939?

The direct orders from above—in no case to provoke the Hitlerites—gave rise to ridiculous blunders. Many of our units in border districts did not even have rifle cartridges before the beginning of the war, to say nothing of live artillery shells. With the knowledge of the General Staff, prime movers were withdrawn from artillery units and used in the construction of fortified regions along the new western border. As a result, the guns were immobilized and could not have been used in the fighting that broke out unexpectedly. . . .

We, the leading officials of the Anti-aircraft Defense Command, were especially alarmed at that time. The broad network of air defense warning posts extensively reported all flights by German reconnaissance aircraft over the territory of our border districts. These data were entered on special maps and immediately reported to the General Staff. Very frequently we would receive the answer: "We already know. Don't worry about it."

We were categorically ordered not to open fire on German planes. Upon encountering German airplanes, our fighters had been ordered not to molest them but to propose that they land at any of our airfields. Of course, the Germans did not accept such proposals and would calmly fly back to their own territory, waving farewell to our fliers as they did so.

At the order of F. I. Kuznetsov, Commander of the Baltic Military District, cities and individual objectives of military importance were blacked out. I immediately reported on this by telephone to G. K. Zhukov, Chief of the General Staff, in an effort to obtain authorization for such blackouts in other border districts as well. My answer was abuse and threats directed at Kuznetsov. Shortly after, the Commander of the Baltic District was ordered to revoke this order.

A few days before the war began, I chanced to meet in Moscow D. G. Pavlov, Commander of the Belorussian Special Military District; I knew him well from joint work in the People's Commissariat of Defense and from the fighting in Spain.

"How are things with you?" I asked him.

"The district's troops are stamping around in various tactical battalion and regimental exercises," Pavlov replied. "Everything is normal with us. And so I decided to take advantage of the calm situation and came to Moscow for one thing and another."

The commander of one of the most important border military districts was in such a placid mood.

On the same day, I was received by G. I. Kulik, Deputy People's Commissar of Defense. Our talk touched on the latest summaries of the General Staff concerning the continuing intensified buildup of German troops, their headquarters, and rear services along our western borders. The data were true—they cited the numbers of the German corps and infantry and tank divisions. On this subject, Kulik said:

"This is big politics. It's not our business!"

And it was the Deputy People's Commissar of Defense who was saying this.

As before, Stalin assumed that war between fascist Germany and the Soviet Union could only result from provocations on the part of fascist military revanchists, and he feared these provocations more than anything. As we know, Stalin liked to decide everything himself. He concerned himself little with the opinion of others. If in these days he had assembled the military leaders and consulted with them, who knows, perhaps this tragic miscalculation would not have happened.

Without question, at that time Stalin committed the most serious error in his assessment of the military-political situation, and it was his fault that our country found itself in mortal danger. This error cost the Soviet people dearly. . . .

If the fascist German invaders who perfidiously attacked us at dawn on June 22, 1941, had met with an organized rebuff from our troops along prepared lines of defense, if our military aviation—having reassembled in good time at field airbases—had delivered strikes against the enemy, and if the entire system for directing the troops had been made to correspond to the situation, we should not have sustained such heavy losses in personnel and combat matériel in the first months of the war. Then the course of the war would have been entirely different. Enormous areas of Soviet soil would not have been given up to the enemy, and the people would not have had to suffer such misery and agony.

.   .   .   .

On the second day of the war the General Headquarters of the High Command of the USSR armed forces was formed, headed by the People's Commissar for Defense, Marshal of the Soviet Union S. K. Timoshenko. On June 30, 1941 the State Defense Committee (GKO) was formed; the entire plenitude of power in the Soviet state was concentrated in its hands. On July 10, 1941, in the interest of improving the leadership of combat troop operations, the State Defense Committee adopted the decision to create three principal strategic sectors: the Northwestern, the Western, and Southwestern. In connection with this, General Headquarters was re-formed as Supreme Headquarters.[34]

I saw Stalin seldom in the first days of the war. He was depressed, nervous, and of an uneven disposition. When he assigned missions, he demanded that they be carried out in unbelievably short periods without taking into account the actual possibility for doing so.

In my estimation, in the first weeks of the war he did not correctly assess either its scope, or the forces and matériel which could really stop the advancing enemy along the extremely long front from sea to sea.

During this very trying time, Supreme Headquarters and the State Defense Committee were quite frequently distracted by trifles, devoted an excessively long time to an evaluation of sniper and automatic rifles, and endlessly discussed whether the infantry should be equipped with infantry- or cavalry-type rifles. Were bayonets necessary? Should they be triangular or knife-type? Should the rifle be eliminated and replaced by the old-model .carbine? Much time was spent on rifle grenades and the spade-mortar.[35] Opinions concerning these types of weapons were solicited from the command element of Army Groups and Armies and the most diverse and contradictory answers received.

At that time, Supreme Headquarters received many reports from the fronts containing patently inflated data on enemy losses. Perhaps this was what caused Stalin to err—he constantly expressed the supposition that the enemy would be defeated in a very short time. Owing to an incorrect assessment of the scale of the war, Stalin did not at first devote sufficient attention to the creation of strong reserves.

During the first days of the war, the General Staff knew little about the situation at the fronts. As a rule, each evening its generals would brief officials of the People's Commissariat [of Defense] on the course of combat operations. These reports were not expressive; they resembled one another and rarely reflected the true picture of the fighting. As a result of this, Marshal of the Soviet Union B. M. Shaposhnikov, who had been appointed Chief of the General Staff, had to experience some bitter moments. Boris Mikhailovich, who was tactful to the highest degree, frequently took upon himself the guilt of his subordinates who were late in reporting. One morning I was present at Supreme Headquarters when a report was being made on the general situation at the fronts. Shaposhnikov said that despite the measures taken, reports had still not been received from two Army Groups.

Stalin asked angrily:

"Have you punished the people who do not wish to inform us about what is happening in their sectors?"

The very kind Boris Mikhailovich replied with dignity that he had reprimanded both chiefs of staff of the Army Groups. Judging by the expression on his face and the tone of his voice, he virtually put this disciplinary action on a level with the highest measure of punishment. Stalin smiled gloomily:

"We give reprimands in every [Party] cell. For a military man that is no punishment."

But Shaposhnikov recalled the old military tradition that if the Chief of the General Staff reprimands the chief of staff of an Army Group, the guilty party must then and there submit a report requesting that he be relieved of his post.

Stalin was apparently satisfied with this answer and merely ordered that all chiefs of staff be warned that Supreme Headquarters would take strict measures against such derelictions. I do not know what measures were subsequently taken, but at the end of June and in July of 1941 our air observation and warning posts continued to be important sources of information about the situation at the front, both on the ground and in the air.

The General Staff was very slow in adjusting its work schedule to wartime conditions. We, the officials of the Directorates, felt this very keenly. Nervousness and confusion frequently hindered the implementation of important decisions. Sometimes we would run afoul of endless bureaucratic obstacles. In peacetime, some chiefs had become accustomed to answering numerous requests with: "There isn't any, and there won't be any!" Now a different answer was required: "There has to be, and as soon as possible!" But they were still riding the old horse—

V. M. Berezhkov
At the Soviet Embassy in Berlin

[FROM THE SPRING of 1941] we at the Soviet Embassy in Berlin witnessed Germany's preparations for military action in the East. Substantiating information reached the Embassy from extremely varied sources; it was furnished us primarily by our friends inside Germany. In the Nazi Reich and within Berlin itself, anti-fascist groups were active deep underground— the so-called Rote Kapelle,[36] Rabb's group, and others. Overcoming unbelievable difficulties, at times risking their lives, German anti-fascists found a way to warn the Soviet Union of the danger hanging over it. They passed on information about the threatening situation building up on the border of the Soviet Union, of the preparations for Hitler's attack on our country.

In the middle of February, a German printer appeared at our Consulate in Berlin. He brought with him one sample of a German-Russian conversation manual printed in a large number of copies. The contents of the manual left no doubt about its purpose. In it you had, for example, sentences in the Russian language printed in Latin letters such as: "Where is the kolkhoz chairman?" "Are you a Communist?" "What is the name of the secretary of the district Party committee?" "Hands up! I'll shoot," "Surrender," and so on. We sent the conversation manual to Moscow at once.

Important intelligence had also been collected at that time by our military attaché, General Tupikov, and by the naval attaché, Admiral Vorontsov. According to their information, echelons of troops and matériel had started to move eastward from the beginning of February 1941. In March and April an already ceaseless stream of trains with tanks, artil-

V. M. Berezhkov, *S diplomaticheskoi missiei v Berlin 1940–1941* (Moscow, 1966), pp. 78–106.

lery, and ammunition moved eastward, and by the end of May, according to all available evidence, the frontier area was fully saturated with manpower and matériel.[37]

At that time the Nazis impudently and more and more openly tested Soviet defenses along the frontiers. German provocations on the Soviet-German border increased especially at the end of May and the beginning of June. Almost every day our Embassy received requests from Moscow to deliver protests in connection with the latest violation of the Soviet frontier area. Not only German border guards but soldiers of the regular army as well systematically intruded into Soviet territory and opened fire on our border troops. . . . Airplanes with the swastika were arrogantly flying over our territory. We communicated all these facts to the German Foreign Office with precise reference to the place and time of their occurrence. But when they received our communications in Wilhelmstrasse they at first promised to initiate an investigation and then assured us that allegedly "your information has not been confirmed."

The following item is also of interest. Not far from the Embassy on Unter den Linden was the luxurious photo studio of Hoffmann, the "court" photographer of Hitler. Eva Braun, who later became the Fuehrer's mistress, once worked in this studio as a model. From the beginning of the war, a large map usually hung under Hitler's official portrait in one of the windows of Hoffmann's studio. It became his custom to display in turn the part of Europe in which military operations were taking place or being contemplated. In the early spring of 1940, it was the region of Holland, Belgium, Denmark, and Norway; then the map of Finland hung there for a rather long time. In April of 1941 passers-by were pausing in front of a map of Yugoslavia and Greece. And suddenly, at the end of May, a huge map of Eastern Europe appeared. It included the Baltic states, Belorussia, and the Ukraine—a whole wide strip of the Soviet Union from the Barents to the Black Sea. Hoffmann was letting it be understood in no uncertain terms where the next events were brewing. It was as if he were saying: "Now it's the Soviet Union's turn!"

From March on, persistent rumors spread through Berlin about Hitler's preparations for an attack on the Soviet Union. Various dates were mentioned in this connection, evidently to put us off the track: April 6, April 20, May 18, and lastly the correct date, June 22—all of them Sundays.[38]

The Embassy regularly reported all these warning signals to Moscow. At the beginning of May a group of our diplomats held a special meeting for the study, processing, and summarizing of information the Embassy had with regard to Hitler's preparations for war on the Eastern Front. . . .

By the end of May we compiled an extensive report. . . . Its main conclusion was that Germany's practical preparations for the invasion of the Soviet Union had been completed, that the scale of these preparations left no doubt that all this concentration of troops and equipment could only mean war. Such a concentration could scarcely be designed for the purpose of exerting some kind of political pressure on our country.[39] Therefore, a German attack on the Soviet Union was to be expected at any moment.

We found ourselves in a rather ambivalent position in those weeks. On the one hand, we had unequivocal information to the effect that war was about to break out. On the other hand, outwardly, it was as if nothing particular were happening. It was decided not to send home the wives and children of employees of Soviet institutions in Germany and German-occupied countries. Moreover, new employees, accompanied by large families and even wives in the last months of pregnancy, arrived almost daily.[40] The delivery of Soviet goods to Germany continued without interruption, although the Germans had almost completely stopped honoring their trade obligations. On June 14 (a week before Germany's attack on the Soviet Union!) the Soviet press published a TASS communiqué which said that . . . "rumors of Germany's intention to break the pact and attack the USSR are devoid of all foundation. . . ."

By this statement, the text of which was handed to the German Ambassador in Moscow, Schulenburg, the previous day, Stalin was trying to probe the intentions of the German government, to influence them. He apparently intended to stave off the German attack on the USSR in this way at the last moment. But Berlin answered the TASS statement of June 14 with an ominous silence. No mention of the communiqué appeared in a single German newspaper.

On June 21, when the hours preceding Germany's attack were numbered, the Embassy received instructions to hand the German government still another note offering to discuss the state of Soviet-German relations. The Soviet government gave the German government to understand that it knew of the concentration of German troops on the Soviet border and that this military adventure could have dangerous consequences. But the substance of the message from Moscow spoke about something else too: in Moscow they still entertained the hope that it would be possible to avoid the conflict, and they were ready to carry out negotiations concerning the situation that had developed.

The weather was lovely in Berlin on Saturday, June 21. Early in the morning it promised to be hot, and many people were getting ready to leave the city in the afternoon for Potsdam Park or Wannsee or Nikolassee, where the bathing season was in full swing. Only a handful of diplomats were obliged to remain in the city. That morning a telegram came from Moscow: the Embassy was to transmit the above-mentioned note to the German government immediately.

I was appointed to contact Wilhelmstrasse—where the Ministry of Foreign Affairs was housed in a pompous palace of Bismarck's time—to arrange a meeting between Embassy representatives and Ribbentrop. The officer on duty in the Ministry replied that Ribbentrop was out ot town. A call to the First Deputy Minister, State Secretary Baron von Weizsaecker, was equally unfruitful. Hour after hour passed, but not a single responsible official could be reached. The director of the political section of the Ministry, Wehrmann, turned up only at midday and merely confirmed that neither Ribbentrop nor Weizsaecker was in the Ministry.

"Apparently the Fuehrer is holding an important meeting of some sort . . ." Wehrmann explained. "If your business is urgent, give it to me, and I'll try to get in touch with the authorities. . . ."

That, I replied, was impossible because the Embassy's instructions were to hand the note only to the Minister in person, and I asked Wehrmann to inform Ribbentrop of this. It was out of the question to entrust to a subordinate the matter on which we were seeking a meeting with the Minister. The Soviet note contained a demand for an explanation by the German government of the concentration of German troops along the Soviet border.

Several times that day Moscow telephoned, pressing us to carry out our instructions. But no matter how many times we contacted the Ministry of Foreign Affairs, the answer was always the same: Ribbentrop was not there, and no one knew when he would be. He was out of reach and allegedly could not even be informed of our request.

At 7:00 p.m. everyone went home. It fell to me to remain in the Embassy and obtain a meeting with Ribbentrop. Putting a clock in front of me, I decided to telephone Wilhelmstrasse every thirty minutes. . . .

It was hard to keep back the thought that the latest Berlin rumor of the date of the possible German attack on the Soviet Union—June 22— might turn out to be the right one this time. It seemed odd that we had been unable to get in touch with either Ribbentrop or his deputy throughout the day, whereas usually, if the Minister was out of town, Weizsaecker was always ready to receive Embassy representatives. And what of this important meeting of Hitler's that Wehrmann said all the leaders were attending?

The next time I telephoned the Ministry of Foreign Affairs, the official who answered politely repeated the stock formula:

"As before, I have been unable to reach the Reich Minister. But I have your request in mind and am taking steps."

When I said I would have to disturb him again because the matter
was urgent, the official replied amiably that that would not trouble him
in the least because he was on duty in the Ministry until morning. Again
and again, long into the night, I telephoned Wilhelmstrasse, but always
without results.[41]

Suddenly, at 3:00 a.m. (5:00 a.m. Moscow time), the telephone rang;
it was now Sunday, June 22. An unfamiliar voice barked that Reich Minister Joachim von Ribbentrop was awaiting the Soviet representatives in
his office in the Ministry of Foreign Affairs on Wilhelmstrasse. There was
something ominous even about the unfamiliar voice and the extremely
official wording itself. But in answering him, I acted as if he were speaking of the meeting with the Minister that the Soviet Embassy had been
seeking.

"I know nothing of your request," he replied. "My instructions are
only to say that Reich Minister Ribbentrop asks the Soviet representatives
to come to his office at once."

I said time was needed to inform the Ambassador and to get our car
ready. To this, he replied:

"The Reich Minister's personal car is already at the entrance of the
Soviet Embassy. The Minister is counting on the immediate arrival of
the Soviet representatives."

As we turned into Wilhelmstrasse, we saw the crowd around the
building of the Ministry of Foreign Affairs from afar. Although dawn was
breaking, the entrance with the latticed marquee was brightly lit by spotlights. Photographers, film cameramen, and journalists bustled about. An
official jumped out of the car first and threw the door open wide. We
got out, blinded by the glare of spotlights and the popping of flashbulbs.
Photographers and film cameramen doggedly accompanied us. Time and
again they ran forward, clicking shutters, while we climbed the thickly
carpeted stairway to the second floor. The long corridor leading to the
Minister's suite was lined with uniformed men at attention. At our appearance, they noisily clicked their heels and raised their arms. At last
we turned to the right and entered the Minister's huge office. . . . Behind
the desk sat Ribbentrop in a greenish-gray everyday ministerial uniform.
Looking around, we saw a group of officials to the right of the entrance.
These men did not move when we crossed the room toward Ribbentrop
and remained where they were throughout the conversation. However,
they were a rather long distance from us and apparently did not hear
what Ribbentrop said.[42]

When we approached the desk, Ribbentrop got up, nodded his head
in silence, offered his hand, and invited us to follow him to the round

table in the opposite corner of the room. His face was puffed and pur-
plish, his eyes were clouded, the eyelids inflamed. He led the way with
his head hanging, swaying a little. "Could he be drunk?" I thought. When
we were seated at the round table and Ribbentrop began to talk,
this suspicion was confirmed. He had obviously had much too much to
drink.

We were unable to present our note, the text of which we had
brought with us. Ribbentrop, raising his voice, said the question at hand
was altogether different. Stumbling over almost every word, he began
explaining in a rather muddled way that the German government had information about the intensified concentration of Russian troops on the
German border. Acting as if completely unaware that throughout the past
weeks the Soviet Embassy had repeatedly called German attention to
flagrant violations of the Soviet border by German soldiers and planes,
Ribbentrop declared that Soviet soldiers had been violating the German
border and encroaching on German territory (although there were actually no facts to support this).

Ribbentrop further said that he would give us in brief the substance
of Hitler's memorandum, the text of which he thereupon handed us. Ribbentrop said the German government regarded the existing situation as a
threat to Germany at a moment when she was waging a war with the
Anglo-Saxons not for life, but to the death. This, Ribbentrop declared,
was taken by the German government and by the Fuehrer personally as
evidence of the Soviet Union's intention to stab the German people in the
back. The Fuehrer's decision was final. An hour ago, German troops had
crossed the border into the Soviet Union.

Next Ribbentrop claimed this German action by no means constituted
an aggression but was merely a defensive measure. Thereupon, he stood up
and drew himself to his full height in an effort to look impressive. His
voice, however, betrayed an obvious lack of firmness and assurance as he
uttered the last words:

"The Fuehrer instructed me to announce these defensive measures to
you officially."

We also stood up. The meeting was over. Now we knew that shells
were exploding on our frontiers. War had been officially announced to us
after the brigands' attack. There was nothing to be done about that now.
Before leaving, the Soviet Ambassador said:[43]

"This is a lie; there was nothing to provoke aggression. You will
regret you attacked the Soviet Union. You will pay dearly for this
yet."

We walked toward the door. And then the unexpected occurred. Ribbentrop trotted hurriedly after us. In a hasty whisper, he claimed that he personally had been against this decision of the Fuehrer's. He had even tried, presumably, to dissuade Hitler from attacking the Soviet Union. Personally he, Ribbentrop, considered this madness. But he had been unable to do anything. The Fuehrer had made the decision; he had refused to listen to anyone.

"Tell Moscow I was against the attack," were the last words we heard from Ribbentrop when we were already in the corridor.[44]

Again the camera shutters clicked, the movie cameras whirred. . . . When we arrived at the Embassy, we saw that the building was heavily guarded. . . . Not a single telephone was working.

At 6:00 a.m. we turned on the radio to hear what Moscow was saying, but all of our stations were broadcasting calisthenics, then the Young Pioneers' reveille, and finally, the latest news, beginning as usual with reports on agriculture and bulletins about the achievements of front-rank workers. Anxious thoughts went through our minds; was it possible they did not know in Moscow that war had begun several hours ago? Were the movements on the border being evaluated as border incidents, even though they were broader in scope than those of the past weeks? . . .[45]

[Later] when I went downstairs, I saw from the window of my office that newspaper vendors were selling special editions. I left the building and bought a few copies of the extras. They already contained the first photos from the front: with a heavy heart we looked at our fighting men—wounded and killed. In the communiqué of the German High Command it was reported that during the night the German air force bombed Mogilev, L'vov, Rovno, Grodno, and other cities. It was clear that the Hitlerite propaganda tried to create an impression that this war would be a short excursion.

Again and again we turned to the radio. As before, it was playing folk music and marches. It was only at twelve o'clock Moscow time that we heard the announcement of the Soviet government:

"Today, at 4:00 a.m., without presenting any claims against the Soviet Union and without a declaration of war, the German Army attacked our country. . . . Our cause is just. The enemy shall be defeated. Victory shall be ours."

"Victory shall be ours." "Our cause is just." These words, coming from our distant homeland, found us in the very lair of the enemy.

PART II   JUNE 22, 1941
ON THE FRONTIER

Introduction

WHILE THE previous memoirs present the start of the invasion from the point of view of men who were thousands of miles removed from the actual fighting, the fragments which follow retell the experience of military commanders who were in the frontier zone on June 22 or shortly thereafter and who survived the first encounter with the Wehrmacht. All these memoirs share some common themes. There is, for example, a paradox, at once unreal and yet credible and human: Almost all commanders testify that they expected an outbreak of hostilities and at the same time were shocked and surprised when it actually took place. Virtually all authors likewise report the initial reactions of disbelief from their superiors in Moscow to reports of what had happened; they report their own feeling that the orders which finally began to come from above bore little relation to combat realities; they report, above all, the feeling that they were confronted with a situation for which their entire past experience had ill prepared them. While they responded automatically as military professionals, they began to realize that perhaps it was not within their power to stop the German steam-roller.

The main thrust of the Nazi attack was directed against the troops of the Western Military District in the cen-tral sector of the German-Soviet frontier. And this is where the devastation wrought by the German army was most telling. Here it was that the first gigantic "pocket" maneuver in which whole armies were encircled—the Belostok-Grodno pocket—was accomplished. Here, finally, in a little more than three weeks the German troops succeeded in advancing to a point 200 miles from the Soviet capital and capturing Smolensk, the largest and the *last* big city directly west of Moscow. The first four memoirs deal with the situation in the Western Military District (renamed Western Army Group after the invasion) before, at the start of, and in the first period after the invasion.

The memoirs of the Red Army's top mining specialist, Colonel I. T. Starinov, vividly recall the June days in the Brest area where he had arrived only two days before the invasion to participate in troop maneuvers as a delegate of the People's Commissariat of Defense. They are followed by the memoirs of General of the Army I. V. Boldin, First Deputy Commander of the Western Military District. He describes the situation within the command of the district shortly before and at the time of the invasion. General Boldin is the only member of the district's top command who survived the June holocaust. Of particular importance is his report on the conversation with Marshal Timoshenko, who relayed Stalin's instructions hours after the war began.

The next fragment is from Marshal A. I. Eremenko who was ordered on the sixth day of the war to take command of the Western Army Group. Shocked by the extent of the initial German success and the inability of troops in the central sector to stop or even to slow down the German advance, Stalin blamed the Army Group leadership for the disaster. The previous commander of the Western Military District, General of the Army D. G. Pavlov, could hardly be considered a talented military leader who met the requirements of this key position. But it was Stalin himself who put an ill-prepared officer in this position. A divisional tank commander, Pavlov became famous as the chief of the Soviet tankmen dispatched to Spain to fight in the Civil War. Returning to Russia in 1937, he was promoted with dizzying speed, advancing in less than a year from commander of tactical tank units to Commander in Chief of Armored Troops and then to commanding officer of this key military district. After being replaced by Eremenko, General Pavlov was arrested, accused of treason, and shot. Executed with him were the chief of staff of the District, General Klimovskikh, the chief of intelligence, and a number of high staff officers.

Colonel Starinov describes as an eyewitness the arrest of Pavlov and its pitiful effects on the officer corps of the Western Army Group which was left to continue the fight. In the last fragment concerning the Western Military District, Marshal S. S. Biriuzov analyzes the factors he believes determined the success of the invading armies and simultaneously exonerates the executed leaders of the Western Military District.

The next two memoir fragments deal with the southern sector of the German-Soviet border. General I. I. Fediuninskii describes the situation up to the invasion and the beginning of hostilities from the point of view of the commander of a rifle corps deployed near the frontier in the Kiev Military District (renamed Southwest Army Group at the start of the war). Marshal I. Kh. Bagramian describes it as chief of operations of the Kiev Military District.

Marshal Bagramian's account is perhaps most notable for the dramatic scene which illustrates the gulf between the military professional and the military politician. The three principal actors in his tale are the Army Group commander, who owed his rapid and ill-prepared advance to the Purge; the Army Group chief of staff, veteran military officer of long standing and high qualification; and the political commissar, illiterate in military matters. Bagramian recounts the respective reactions of these three men to Moscow's order on the evening of the first day of war to surround and destroy the enemy groupings, to launch a counterattack, and to take Lublin, deep in German-held territory, by the end of June 24. The chief of staff responded with deep dismay in view of the Army Group's struggle to maintain even defensive positions. The political commissar admitted the chief of staff's correctness from a military point of view, but not from a political point of view. The Army Group commander, in an effort at reconciliation, proposed to carry out Moscow's order but to hope for the understanding of the People's Commissar when Lublin was not taken. In this case the Army Group commander's attitude caused tragedy only to his troops; but repeated a few months later, it cost him his life.

The reminiscences of Admiral I. I. Azarov and Captain First Rank N. F.

Rybalko supplement the previous account of Admiral Kuznetsov. During
the night of June 22, Captain Rybalko
was the staff officer on duty at Black
Sea Fleet headquarters in Sevastopol'.
He relates step-by-step the last hours
of peace and first hours of war. To

conclude this part of the chapter there
is a brief fragment by air force officer
M. I. Gallai who provides an interesting footnote concerning the reaction
of the younger generation to the coming of war.

Colonel I. T. Starinov
The Frontier Aflame

ON THE EVENING of June 19, 1941 I departed [from Moscow] for Brest[46]
to attend troop exercises in the Western Special Military District. . . .

My traveling companion—stocky, round-faced Lieutenant Colonel
Zakhar Iosifovich Kolesnikov, Deputy Chief of the Army Engineer Training Department of the Main Military Engineering Directorate—kept wip-
ing his bald spot with a handkerchief and drinking *Narzan*[47] without end.

"It's a good thing we're traveling at night," he said, puffing. "In
daytime, we'd roast."

Moscow lay farther behind with every kilometer. The train sped past
silent groves and fragrant meadows with dark shocks of fresh hay. . . .

I thought about the exercises ahead and was eagerly looking forward
to seeing old friends. I was happy that I would again see General Nikolai
Aleksandrovich Klich, chief of district artillery, who had become my
friend in the fighting on the Ebro. It would also be interesting to see
General of the Army D. G. Pavlov, commander of the district. In Spain
he had fought as a tankman. Returning, he made a dazzling career for
himself and now commanded one of the most important military districts. But how would Pavlov receive me? Had he changed much since
I saw him near Belchite, pale and shaken by a tank attack that had
bogged down in the river's sticky floodlands? With these thoughts, I
fell asleep.

I was awakened by the conductor's voice:

I. T. Starinov, *Miny zhdut svoego chasa* (Moscow, 1964), pp. 186–94.

"We're nearing Minsk, Comrade Commanders!" . . .

The first thing we did [when we arrived] at district headquarters was to meet with General P. M. Vasil'ev, chief of the district engineering administration. He was also in an excellent mood. After reporting that everything at the training area was in readiness for the forthcoming exercises, he took us to meet V. E. Klimovskikh, district chief of staff.

Klimovskikh was obviously not in the mood for us. He kept picking up the telephone to listen to reports of some kind. He frowned and grew gloomy before our eyes.

Vasil'ev leaned over my shoulder and said confidentially:

"They are constantly reporting about German spies and planes violating the border. They're stirring up panic."

Klimovskikh excused himself and dismissed us, saying that we would continue our discussion of mines and obstacles at the training area.

As we left his office I asked Vasil'ev whether it might not be possible to meet the commanding officer right then.

"Why not? It can be arranged!"

Pavlov did, in fact, see us shortly thereafter. As we entered his office, he only nodded in greeting, since he was also talking on the telephone.

In an irritated voice, he snapped into the receiver:

"Never mind. More self-control. I know, it has already been reported! More self-control!"

Finally, Pavlov put down the receiver. Then as though suddenly recollecting, he shook hands with us. Hurriedly acquainting himself with the program of exercises, he angrily observed that too much attention was being devoted to the construction of tank obstacles and too little, it seemed to him, to ways of overcoming them.

The telephone rang again.

"I know, it has been reported," he answered firmly. It was obvious, however, that he found it hard to remain calm. "I know, it has already been reported," he repeated. "I know. Those at the top know better than we. That's all!"

He slammed the receiver down violently.

The chief of staff entered. He looked somewhat malevolently at us.

"Please excuse the interruption. This is very important."

"Well, Wolf," said General Pavlov, addressing me by the name he had called me in Spain, "we will meet at the exercises! There things will be freer, and we will talk about everything. . . . But now you will have to excuse me. I'm busy."

With an anxious heart, we left district headquarters. Clearly, things were not as peaceful at the border as it seemed in Moscow in the quiet offices of the People's Commissariat of Defense.

I went to see my old friend, General N. A. Klich.

"Wolf! The devil take you!"

Involuntarily, I became lost in admiration: he was still just as lean, collected, and confident in every movement. In a word, the tireless volunteer of yore, the favorite of the Spanish artillerymen.

"Well, sit down," said Nikolai Aleksandrovich.

No sooner had I sat down than we began discussing the situation at the border.

"What is happening here?" I asked straight out.

"Something bad is happening," answered Klich, just as directly.

"What specifically?"

"Specifically—the Germans are moving troops, tanks, and artillery up to the border. Their airplanes are constantly flying over our territory."

"And what are we doing?"

"We are re-forming and rearming the troops. It is strictly forbidden to shoot down enemy planes. Then there is also the TASS statement of June 14. I don't know how to interpret it. Naturally, it calmed us, but it also lowered the level of our combat readiness."

"What do you think?"

"I think that one must always keep one's powder dry, particularly when one has Germany for a neighbor."

"Then it's up to you."

Nikolai Aleksandrovich looked at me reproachfully. Always reserved, he suddenly became agitated:

"Understand what is bothering me. I have many guns. But the artillerymen are mainly youngsters, and they are inadequately trained. On top of that, the trucks of many artillery regiments have been taken for the construction of fortified areas. They have even dispatched the tractors there. The result is guns without traction power. Do you understand? No traction power!"

"Naturally, you have reported this to Pavlov?"

"And Pavlov reported it and called Moscow, and everywhere we get the same answer: 'Don't panic! Keep calm! The Boss[48] knows about it all.'"

At that time, neither Klich nor I mentioned Stalin's speech at the graduation ceremony for military academy students on May 5, 1941. While this speech was not published, it was heard by many, and individual ideas in it were restated in reports on the international situation. Stalin claimed that the Red Army had been reorganized and substantially rearmed. In reality, the rearming was just beginning. We could not mention this, however, even among ourselves.[49]

A telephone call ended our meeting. Klich was being urgently summoned by the district commander.

On Saturday, June 21, Kolesnikov and I departed for Brest. . . . On the train I met an artillery colonel whom I knew from field exercises. With concern the colonel commented that since the June 14 TASS declaration, the situation on the other side of the border had not changed but that our troops were calmer. He nodded in the direction of soldiers walking along the platform, suitcases in hand.

"Until recently they slept with their boots on. Now they are going on leave. Why? The TASS declaration!"

We stopped at Kobrin, where the 4th Army Headquarters was located. We found the chief of engineers, Colonel A. I. Proshliakov. He offered us the use of his office and promised to send a car for us the next morning so that we could drive to the maneuvers area together. A. I. Proshliakov confirmed the fact that throughout June the Germans had been massing equipment on the Western Bug, installing camouflage shielding in the open sectors, and building observation towers.

The usual Saturday bustle prevailed at the headquarters of the 4th Army, which was covering the Brest sector, on that warm evening of June 21, 1941. We were informed that the exercises had been canceled, and we walked for a long time about the picturesque town. Back at the office of the chief of engineers, we said good night to each other and stretched out comfortably on the sofas.

.   .   .   .

I woke up suddenly. I thought that I had heard an explosion in my sleep. Yet everything seemed quiet. Only the monotonous choking din of airplane engines crept in through the open, brightening windows. I consulted my watch: it was 4:20 a.m. Kolesnikov had also raised up on one elbow and was groping for his watch on the chair next to the sofa.

Not far away, a heavy thud was heard and then an explosion. The house rocked, and the windowpanes jingled mournfully.

"Demolition works, perhaps," I said, thinking out loud.

"More likely a bomb broke away from a plane," Kolesnikov replied, listening intently.

"But what's the matter with those fliers—"

I didn't finish. For a few seconds frequent explosions blended into a deafening roar. Then there was quiet. Again, we could hear the advancing and receding drone of airplane engines.

Suddenly, this strange din reminded me of Spain. The rumble of the Junkers—

Kolesnikov and I raced to the windows. The sky over Kobrin was peacefully turning blue. . . . The sound of boots was heard on the other side of the wall.

"Everyone is to leave the building immediately," resounded in the corridors. There was the muffled ring of telephones in empty offices.

"Zakhar Iosifovich, something has happened!"

Kolesnikov understood this without my telling him.

Hastily pulling our boots on and donning our tunics and leather straps on the run, we dashed into the street.

And just in time.

A squadron of airplanes was heading straight toward headquarters.

"Air attack!" someone shouted.

We ran across the square, jumped a ditch, and flung ourselves into an orchard.

On the run we looked around at the planes and saw thin, seemingly very small bombs detach from the black fuselages.

"Get down, Zakhar Iosifovich!"

The bombs were falling with a piercing shriek. The army headquarters building we had just left was shrouded in smoke and dust. The powerful blasts rent the air and made our ears ring.

Another flight appeared.

The German bombers dived confidently at the defenseless military settlement.

When the raid was over, thick black pillars of smoke billowed up from many places. A newly felled tree lay across the street. Part of the headquarters building was in ruins. Somewhere a high-pitched, hysterical female voice was crying out a desperate, inconsolable "aaaaaa!"

The 4th Army Headquarters was preparing to move to its reserve command post in Bukhovichi. Kolesnikov and I decided to make our way to Brest. There, someone among the representatives of the People's Commissariat of Defense or the General Staff who were gathered for the maneuvers would know what was happening. We got a ride in the first passing vehicle.

Officers were running along the highway in the opposite direction, hurrying to their posts. Along the side of the road a long line of women was moving, carrying hastily dressed, sleepy children, bundles and baskets. They were leaving the military settlement.

The streets of Kobrin, so calm the night before, greeted us with the smell of fires. The rasping of a loudspeaker stopped us in the square. The driver opened the door and leaned out.

The familiar Moscow call signal imperiously invaded the confusion and turmoil of the city which had received the enemy's first bombing strike. Everyone in the square looked up hopefully at the round black loudspeaker mounted on a telephone pole.

"It is 6:00 a.m. Moscow time. We begin our broadcast of the latest news," we heard.

With bated breath, Kobrin waited to hear what Moscow had to say.

Taking turns, the announcers cheerfully reported the labor achievements of the Soviet people, the rich ripening harvest, the fulfillment of the plan by some factory ahead of schedule, celebrations in the Mari Autonomous Republic.

Finally, we heard:

"The German Information Agency reports—"

A girl standing next to us rose on tiptoe.

However, in an official voice, the announcer spoke of sunken British vessels, of German air raids on cities in Scotland; he transmitted a Reuters communiqué on the downing of 17 German bombers over England in a week, mentioned the war in Syria, and fell silent.

The newscast ended with the weather forecast. The girl next to us no longer stood on tiptoe. Morose and perplexed, the people stared at the loudspeaker.

"Let's wait. There may be a special announcement or statement," Kolesnikov said uncertainly.

However, the morning calisthenics began as usual.

The driver spat and slammed the door.

The girl looked around bewildered and, as though remembering something, ran off. The others dispersed hastily.

Trucks loaded with weeping women and children, who were perhaps already orphaned within those few hours, were rumbling eastward through Kobrin. And the cheerful voice of the announcer followed them:

"Stretch your arms out, bend! Livelier! Up, down. Up, down. Livelier! That's it. Very good!"

Enemy airplanes were again approaching the city. Their howl and frightened cries finally drowned out the voice that urged us to jump up and down, to jump as high as possible!

Twenty-three years have passed since that fatal June day, but I cannot forget the square in Kobrin, the black loudspeaker above it, and the unfortunate calisthenics lesson.

Even the German dive bombers made a less shocking impression on the people than the news broadcast at 6:00 a.m. on June 22.

"Strange," said the always calm and restrained Kolesnikov through gritted teeth, "very strange—"

I do not think he was complaining about the radio personnel. . . .

We decided to return to Minsk for instructions. By noon, we reached Pinsk[50] and saw our military airfield, torn to pieces by the enemy air force. It was painful to see the smashed and burning planes. Work was in full swing among the raging fires. Pilots and airfield service personnel, scorning danger, were rescuing what had withstood the enemy bombs and fire.

Yet still we stubbornly thought that it was only here that the enemy had caught our troops unawares and that elsewhere Soviet airplanes were bombing the enemy. After all, there had been so much evidence that an attack was being prepared!

General of the Army I. V. Boldin
At Western Army
Group Headquarters

ON SATURDAY June 21, 1941 I returned home rather late. Although I was extremely tired after a disturbing day, I did not feel like sleeping. Alarming thoughts kept crowding into my mind. Only the day before, intelligence had reported that at about 6:00 p.m. six German planes had crossed our border and had penetrated several kilometers into Soviet territory. Raised by the alarm, our fighters accompanied the trespassers to the border without opening fire. German planes had been systematically invading our air space, but we were under a categorical order: Do not open fire on them.

In the evening Lieutenant General V. I. Kuznetsov, commander of the 3rd Army, reported that toward evening the barbed wire barriers along the border at the Avgustov-Seini road had been removed by the Germans. The roar of many motors had also been distinctly heard from the forest in that same area.

According to the data of the intelligence section of the military district, by June 21 the main part of the German troops was deployed in a zone thirty kilometers from the frontier. In the area of Suvalki and Aris the bringing up of troops and rear services was continuing. German artillery had taken up firing positions. A large number of tanks was concentrated south of Suvalki. Trainloads of pontoon equipment, sectional bridges, and ammunition were arriving at the Biala-Podliaska station.

I. V. Boldin, "Sorok piat' dnei v tylu vraga," *Voenno-istoricheskii zhurnal*, 1961, No. 4, pp. 64–67.

All this attested to the fact that the forces of the German army were concentrated opposite the troops of the Western Special Military District and that they had taken up an attack position.

My heart ached. Was it really war?

I rang up the operations duty officer at headquarters and asked if there was anything new. He replied that there was nothing yet.

Many officers and generals at the district headquarters, including myself as deputy commander of the Western Special Military District, had often visited the border garrisons to become acquainted with the situation on the spot. The facts available indicated that the German command was actively preparing for war against the Soviet Union. I had given detailed reports on the results of my visits to the troops and the frontier to General of the Army D. G. Pavlov, commander of the military district. More than once a report of that nature had drawn rebukes from Pavlov: "Ivan Vasil'evich, believe me, in Moscow they know the military and political situation and our relations with Germany better than you and I do." I recalled that quite recently Major General V. E. Klimovskikh, chief of staff of the military district, had tried in my presence to report to him a plan for measures to increase the combat readiness of the troops. Pavlov had blown up, swept the map away with his hand, and said sharply: "War is possible, but not within the near future. Now we must prepare for autumn maneuvers and take steps to see that no alarmist answers German provocations by opening fire."

I tried to understand what had caused Pavlov to disregard the intelligence reports. . . . He was probably right, and I was exhibiting excessive nervousness. After all, the commander spoke with Moscow every day by direct wire. He was certainly more fully briefed on the situation than I.

But I was still worried. What if these movements of German troops toward the border, which Kuznetsov and the scouts had reported, were not provocations but signalized the beginning of war? As if in answer, the telephone rang shrilly. The operations duty officer transmitted an order for me to appear at headquarters at once. Fifteen minutes later I entered the commander's office and found there Corps Commissar A. Ia. Fominykh, a member of the district military council, and Major General V. E. Klimovskikh, the chief of staff.

"What's happened?" I asked General of the Army Pavlov.

"I can't make it out myself. A few minutes ago I had a call from Kuznetsov. He says that the Germans have crossed the border in the sector from Sopotskin to Avgustov and are bombing Grodno. Wire communications with the units have been broken off. Two radio stations have been demolished. Golubev was on the phone just before you came in. Sandalov also called.[51] The reports are incredible. The Germans are bombing."

Our conversation was interrupted by a telephone call from Moscow. Marshal of the Soviet Union S. K. Timoshenko, the People's Commissar of Defense, was calling Pavlov. The commander reported the situation. A short time later, General Kuznetsov called again: the Germans are continuing to bomb. More and more reports, each one worse than the previous, were flowing into the commander's office from numerous channels. Our intelligence reported that at daybreak on June 22 more than thirty German infantry, five tank, and two motorized divisions had attacked the troops of the Western Army Group.[52]

More and more frequently communications with the Armies were disrupted. After several futile attempts to get through to the headquarters of the 10th Army, Pavlov said to me:

"Golubev called once, and then there were no more reports at all. I'll fly there now, and you stay here in my place."

"In the present situation the commander of the military district should not leave headquarters," I objected.

"You, Comrade Boldin," said the General of the Army, switching to an official tone, "are first deputy commander. I request that you take over for me at headquarters. I see no other solution in the situation that has arisen."

I told Pavlov that it would be better if I flew to Belostok.[53] Pavlov did not agree; he was nervous.

Meanwhile, new reports were coming in. German planes were continuing to bomb our airfields and the cities of Belostok, Grodno, Lida, Tsekhanovets, Volkovysk, Kobrin, Brest, Slonim, and others.[54] Many of our airplanes were destroyed in the very first hours of the war without even getting off the ground. German paratroopers had been reported in some places.

Some time later Marshal Timoshenko called again. Since Pavlov was out of the office at the time, I had to report the situation. I informed him that German planes were continuing to strafe Soviet troops and the civilian population. The enemy had crossed the border in many sectors and was advancing. After hearing me out attentively, Marshal Timoshenko said:

"Bear in mind, Comrade Boldin, no actions are to be started against the Germans without our consent."

"What?" I shouted into the phone. "Our troops are forced to retreat, cities are burning, people are dying—"

"Iosif Vissarionovich [Stalin] thinks that these may possibly be provocations on the part of some German generals."

I was very agitated. I could scarcely find words to describe the situation we were facing.

The conversation with Marshal Timoshenko continued.

"I am issuing an order that aerial reconnaissance be conducted no deeper than 60 km.," said the People's Commissar.

"Comrade Marshal, we must act. Every minute is precious. This is no provocation. The Germans have started a war!"

I urged the immediate use of mechanized and infantry units and artillery, especially anti-aircraft artillery. Otherwise the situation would turn out badly. But after hearing me out, the People's Commissar repeated the previous order.

I obtained his consent to fly to Belostok to 10th Army headquarters, with which there were no communications, in order to clarify the situation and to offer aid.

I repeated to Pavlov the content of the conversation with the People's Commissar of Defense and reported that he had given me permission to fly to Belostok. Before my departure, the command and headquarters took every step to restore the disrupted control of troops.

At about 3:00 p.m. on June 22 two SB planes were ready for flight. I got into one of them with my aide, Lieutenant Kritsyn, and the other was taken by Captain Goriachev of the combat training section and an officer of the operations division of headquarters, whose name, unfortunately, I have forgotten.

We headed for Belostok. Flying over Baranovichi, we saw that the station was on fire. Trains and warehouses were burning. Ahead and to the left of us there were big fires on the horizon. Enemy bombers were continuously streaking through the air. Our pilot turned away from the railroad and flew the plane at the lowest possible altitude. Skirting the populated areas, we neared Belostok. The farther we went, the worse it became. There were more and more enemy planes in the air. It was impossible to continue the flight. Up ahead there was a small airfield with planes burning beside a metal hangar. I made a decision and signaled the pilot to land. At that moment a Messerschmitt caught up with us and, after loosing a few bursts of machine-gun fire, disappeared. Fortunately, everything turned out all right.

We had scarcely managed to get two hundred meters away from the plane after landing, when we heard the roar of motors overhead. Nine Junkers appeared. They came down over the airfield and began bombing. The explosions shook the earth, and planes burned. The planes on which we had just arrived were also ablaze.

Every minute was precious. We had to hurry to General Golubev. There was no car at the airfield, so we took a light truck. There were several soldiers with us, and we headed for Belostok, about 35 km. away.

Gasoline depots and grain warehouses were burning on the outskirts of Belostok. The population was hurriedly leaving the city. We finally reached Army headquarters, but only the chief of rear services was there.

He said that the commander and main personnel of headquarters had left for the field command post. We found out where it was located and headed there.

About twelve kilometers southwest of Belostok we noticed a small wood. At the edge of it was the 10th Army's command post—two tents, with a wooden table and a few stools in each. On one of the tables there was a telephone, and some distance away there was a truck with a radio. This was the entire command post. It was about 7:00 p.m. and getting close to sundown.

I was met by Major General K. D. Golubev and a group of staff officers. I asked why the headquarters of the military district had received almost no reports from him. It turned out that wire communications had been disrupted, and they had not been able to get radio communications started.

"The enemy's air attack caught the Army troops in the camps and barracks," Golubev reported. "Losses are heavy, especially in the 5th Corps, which was overwhelmed by three enemy army corps. Heavy fighting is going on. To keep from being outflanked by the enemy from the south, I deployed the 13th Mechanized Corps on the Nurets River. But the divisions of that corps have very few tanks, and those they do have are obsolete. That's why there was almost no hope that the corps would be able to carry out the mission. . . ." He bent over the map and sighed deeply.

"We have remarkable people—strong-willed, dedicated, and with great fortitude," he said. "But there is very little ammunition, and there were heavy losses of aircraft and anti-aircraft artillery. Fuel is running out."

"Comrade Golubev, I thought you had enough fuel. What's happened to it?"

"In the very first hours of the attack, enemy planes set fire to many fuel dumps at the airfields and in other places. They're still burning. The Germans used incendiary bullets to destroy railroad tank cars filled with fuel."

After a short pause Golubev continued:

"The situation is grave, Ivan Vasil'evich, very grave. . . ."

The communications officer interrupted our conversation.

"Comrade General Boldin, we have established communications. Minsk is calling you."

I went over to the set and heard a distant voice:

"Pavlov speaking. Have you found out what the situation is?"

After reporting, I said I believed the situation in the 10th Army sector to be very grave. . . .

"Here is the order," said Pavlov. "You are to organize an attack force made up of the 6th and 11th Mechanized Corps and the 36th Cavalry Division. Destroy the enemy on the left bank of the Neman with a counterthrust, and do not allow the German units to break through into the area of Volkovysk. After that, the whole force will be transferred to the command of General Kuznetsov. This is your immediate assignment, and you are personally responsible for carrying it out.

"Tell Golubev that he is to occupy Osovets, Vizna, Bel'sk, and Kleshchele. All of this is to be done tonight, with organization and dispatch."[55]

I tried to tell him that it was impossible to carry out the assignment in the present situation.

Pavlov was silent for a fraction of a minute, then ended with:

"That's all I have to say. Get started on the assignment."

With that, our first and last conversation ended. I thought how far removed from reality Pavlov was. We already had too little strength to strike a counterblow at the enemy. A large part of the Army was engaged in fierce fighting with the advancing enemy and was yielding one position after another.[56]

Marshal A. I. Eremenko
Change of Command

ON SUNDAY June 22, the day of my departure for Moscow, I received a telephone call from Lieutenant General I. V. Smorodinov, Chief of Staff of the Far Eastern Army Group.[57] In the Far East it was already afternoon, while in the European part of the country, dawn was only breaking. Skipping the usual greeting, Smorodinov said excitedly: "A report has just come from the General Staff. At 4:00 a.m. Moscow time the Germans crossed the border and began bombing our cities. War has begun!"

I must admit that I was not able to answer Smorodinov immediately, but when I came to my senses, I asked him:

"Why did Army Group headquarters keep secret from the commanders of the Armies the General Staff's communications on the approach of war?"

"Because there weren't any communications."

My forehead broke out in a cold sweat: that meant that the strike had caught us by surprise.

The probability of war with fascist Germany, which had become the

A. I. Eremenko, V nachale voiny (Moscow, 1965), pp. 61–65, 78–80.

striking arm of imperialism, had been apparent to me, as a person who had devoted himself to the military profession, and probably to all servicemen and to the majority of the Soviet people. But I could not conceive that I would receive news of the war only after it had begun. Knowing nothing of the reasons underlying this tragic turn of events, I attributed it to the poor organization of our intelligence on the western frontiers. . . .

A long trip lay ahead of me on the train which I boarded several hours after my talk with Smorodinov. . . . The whole time it seemed that the train was going too slowly; I wanted to be where the fate of the Homeland was being decided as soon as possible. And as if in fulfillment of this passionate desire of mine, when the train arrived in Novosibirsk, the Chief of Military Communications of the Siberian Military District relayed to me the People's Commissar's order to leave the train and to fly to Moscow. And so from Novosibirsk, I continued my trip by air.

On June 28, I went directly from the airfield to the People's Commissariat of Defense and reported to Marshal S. K. Timoshenko.

"We have been waiting for you," he said and immediately got down to business.

From the brief account of the People's Commissar, I realized that the situation at the front was even more serious than I had imagined. The People's Commissar linked the cause of our failures chiefly to the fact that the command of the border districts had not been up to the mark. There was, of course, a certain amount of truth to that. When S. K. Timoshenko described the situation briefly and showed me on the map the territory we had already lost, I literally did not believe my eyes. The People's Commissar criticized the activity of General of the Army D. G. Pavlov, Commander of the Western Army Group, and expressed great concern for the fate of his troops.

"Well, Comrade Eremenko," he said to me in conclusion, "now the picture is clear to you."

"Yes, it's a sad picture," I replied.

After a brief pause, Timoshenko continued:

"General of the Army Pavlov and his chief of staff have been relieved of their posts. By decision of the government you are appointed commander of the Western Army Group, and Lieutenant General G. K. Malandin has been named its chief of staff. Both of you are to depart for the front immediately."

"What is the Army Group's mission?" I asked.

"To stop the enemy advance," the People's Commissar replied.

Then and there, S. K. Timoshenko handed me an order appointing me commander of the Western Army Group, and on the evening of June 28, Malandin and I set out for a point in the forest near Mogilev,[58] where Army Group headquarters were located. . . .

We arrived at the command post of the Western Army Group early in the morning. At the time, the commander was having breakfast in a small tent which stood off by itself. I entered the tent, and General Malandin went in search of the chief of staff of the Army Group. As was his custom, General Pavlov greeted me rather loudly, showering me with a multitude of questions and exclamations.

"How long it has been! What fate brings you to us? Are you staying long?"

Instead of answering, I handed him the order. After scanning the document, Pavlov, without concealing his bewilderment and concern, asked:

"And just where am I going?"

"The People's Commissar has ordered you to Moscow," I replied.

Pavlov invited me to the table. I declined breakfast and said to him:

"We have to analyze the Army Group's situation as soon as possible. We must ascertain the state of our troops and discover the enemy's intentions."

After a brief pause, Pavlov started to talk:

"What is there to say about the situation that has developed? The stupefying strikes of the enemy caught our troops unawares. We were not prepared for battle. We were living peacefully, training in camps and on ranges. Therefore, we sustained heavy losses, primarily in aircraft, artillery, tanks, and in personnel as well. The enemy has penetrated far into our territory; Bobruisk and Minsk have been taken."

Pavlov also referred to the tardy receipt of the order to put the troops on combat alert. As we now know, it is true that had that order been received a little earlier, and had the military district command in its turn taken measures to increase combat readiness, the troops would not have sustained such losses, and the enemy would have received the rebuff he deserved.

The delay in ordering the combat alert was due to the fact that Stalin, as head of the government, put his trust in the pact with Germany. He did not pay due heed to reports reaching him about fascist preparations to attack our country and considered them provocations. Stalin believed that Hitler would not dare to attack the USSR. Therefore, when there was still time, he did not execute urgent and resolute defensive measures, fearing that this would give the Hitlerites a pretext for attacking our country. As head of the government, Stalin bears the principal burden of responsibility for our defeats.

But the highest military authorities also bear a definite share of responsibility for the fact that the enemy strike was a surprise to our troops, and also for the subsequent dramatic events of the fighting on the frontier. They should have seen to it that more was known about the probable enemy, his plans and designs, and the concentration of his forces along our western borders. If the government had been presented comprehensively analyzed and sufficiently reliable data concerning the situation on the western frontier, I do not think it could have ignored them. But even if the government committed a flagrant error by not taking the necessary measures, the People's Commissariat of Defense and the General Staff could have taken steps within their own spheres of competence, steps which would not have conflicted with the orders of the government. By this I mean increasing the combat readiness of the troops and the vigilance of the command element and of all personnel. It would have been entirely possible, for example, to take part of the forces out of winter quarters and training camps and to transfer them to prepared areas near the border, ostensibly for training. This also applies to artillery, which, in the decisive moment, was too far away at its summer training areas, and to the air force, which could have been transferred little by little from stationary to field air bases.

Even these partial measures would not only have increased the combat readiness of the cover troops, but would also have placed them in more favorable conditions than those they found themselves in at the moment the fascist army struck. We would have preserved the combat capability of a part of our air force, and we could have fought the enemy with all kinds of modern weapons. Moreover, if the People's Commissariat and the General Staff had known the true designs of the enemy and his plans for the first days of the war, and had also correctly assessed the data they possessed on the forces and matériel of his strike groupings, they could have directed the troops more confidently and successfully in the first weeks and months of war.

At the end of the talk with Pavlov, it was decided to call together the leadership of the Army Group. Before the generals and officers arrived, I went to present myself to Marshals K. E. Voroshilov and B. M. Shaposhnikov, who had recently arrived at Army Group headquarters. The aim of their trip was to make an assessment of the situation on the spot and to assist the Army Group command.

K. E. Voroshilov said to me:

"Things are very bad. We haven't yet reestablished a continuous front. There are individual points where our units are staunchly beating off fierce attacks by superior enemy forces. Communications between them and Army Group headquarters are weak. Pavlov's command of the troops is very poor. Reserves and second echelons must be brought up immediately in order to close up the gaps that have developed and to halt the enemy advance; troop control must be properly organized."

Boris Mikhailovich Shaposhnikov was more specific. He told me in which directions it was necessary to deploy the reserves without delay.

After this talk, I had another with P. K. Ponomarenko, Secretary of the Central Committee of the Communist Party of Belorussia, and member of the military council of the Army Group. He, like the marshals, criticized the work of the Army Group's command and headquarters in directing the troops.[59]

Colonel I. T. Starinov
The First Scapegoat

GENERAL OF THE ARMY PAVLOV was not long to remain in command of the Army Group or, indeed, among the living. On July 1, 1941 the State Defense Committee decreed the dismissal of the Western Army Group command. Major General G. K. Malandin was appointed in place of Klimovskikh [Chief of Staff], and Lieutenant General A. I. Eremenko assumed temporary command of the troops.

I saw Pavlov at the moment of his arrest. It seemed that this extremely exhausted and, one suspects, even broken man experienced a feeling of long-awaited relief. At last he was released from responsibility for the troops of an entire Army Group, which was beyond his ability to command. Let's be frank about this. No commander who had known Pavlov for a long time considered him well equipped to occupy the high posts assigned to him in the last two or three years. But he tried to serve as best he could. And he unswervingly executed the last instructions from above—"not to succumb to any provocations."

And now he was being removed. Apparently, in his naiveté, the Army Group commander supposed that Stalin's punishing hand would stop with his dismissal. Dmitrii Georgievich did not suspect that both he and his closest associates would be immediately sacrificed in order to preserve the prestige of the "greatest and wisest sage" who had made a fool of himself. Pavlov was immediately arrested and then shot. He shared his bitter fate with the Chief of Staff of the Army Group, Major General Klimovskikh; the commander of the Army Group's artillery, Lieutenant General Klich; and several others, without doubt commanders of great merit.

I was especially struck by the arrest of N. A. Klich. I was convinced

I. T. Starinov, *Miny zhdut svoego chasa* (Moscow, 1964), pp. 210–12.

of his honesty and innocence. Wasn't it from Klich that I heard some two weeks before about the complacency of those at the top and about the fact that the country and the army were threatened by mortal danger and that careerists and blind men did not wish to recognize this? Klich was doing everything to raise the combat preparedness of the military district's artillery. But his tractors were being taken away from him; his personnel was being employed on defensive construction; his old guns with ammunition were being replaced by new guns without ammunition. What could Klich do about this? Protest? He did protest, but he was snubbed by those who stupidly and repetitiously asserted that "Comrade Stalin knows all and takes care of everything." Could Klich refuse to carry out these orders? No, this he could not do. He was duty bound to carry them out.

At Western Army Group headquarters one could again sense confusion and despondency. The arrests pulled the carpet out from under the commanders' feet. Nobody was certain what would happen tomorrow. All remembered 1937 too well. The reprisal against the command element of the Western Army Group had a deleterious effect on the troops as well. An attempt was made to convince all of us that Pavlov was a traitor, and soldiers began to look with suspicion on other generals. The explosive situation is best described by the following tragicomic episode.

On the day Pavlov and other commanders were arrested, I was unable for a long time to report to anybody on the progress of my work in preparing the mine fields. Finally, I succeeded in reaching the new chief of staff of the Army Group, Major General Malandin. But he was busy with other problems and directed me to one of the staff commanders. This commander was engaged in conversation with a major whom I did not know.

"May I enter?" I asked.

The commander lifted his head and paled; his chin started to shake in a nervous tic. The major with him jumped up and stood at attention. In bewilderment I stepped forward to report the matter about which I had come. And then the commander to whom I came to report suddenly started to mumble some pitiful excuses.

"I was with the troops, and I did everything—I am not guilty of anything—"

He was looking over my shoulder, and, involuntarily, I looked back. Suddenly the truth struck me like a thunderbolt. Behind my back, with their eyes goggling, stood my two companions, officers of the [NKVD] border guard troops. Because of an unpleasant incident at the bridge near Viaz'ma, I had gone nowhere for a long time now without border guard officers to help me smooth relations with the guard of military objectives. From habit, I had taken them with me to make my report. And it was they who created the entire commotion. The energetic, experienced commander, who would not normally lose his composure in the most difficult combat conditions, lost his self-control when men in green caps [of the NKVD] entered his office. I understood his reaction too well.

Marshal S. S. Biriuzov
The Fatal Miscalculation

TWENTY YEARS LATER, now that we have access to authentic documents about the balance of forces along the enemy's main lines of attack, it is easy to see why our army was forced to retreat. But in the summer of 1941, the retreat was baffling. Naturally, not one of us senior commanders accepted the sensational announcement of treason by the leadership of the Western Special Military District.

From my experience in the Khar'kov Military District, I knew that our commanders and political officers incessantly impressed upon the personnel of their units the need to be prepared at all times and to keep their powder dry. There was no reason to doubt that the same activity was being carried out in the border districts as well. It was not by accident that one of the most popular songs of the time, "If War Comes Tomorrow," was imbued with the spirit of combat readiness. Nevertheless, even in the immediate border zone most of the units planned to spend June 22 just like any other day off, although signs of the approaching storm were already at hand.

I dare say that the main reason behind all this, leading to such painful consequences, was . . . our exaggerated faith in the nonaggression pact with Germany. On the other hand, it must be conceded that our concepts of the nature of combat readiness did not fully correspond to the demands of the time. We tried to measure the conversion from a peace to a war footing by an obsolete standard based on classical examples from World War I.

But 1941 was not a repetition of 1914. At the moment of its treacherous attack on our country, Hitler's Germany already had a fully mo-

S. S. Biriuzov, *Kogda gremeli pushki* (Moscow, 1961), pp. 10–13.

bilized regular invasion army poised on the borders of the Soviet Union. German militarists based all their calculations on a surprise attack, an unexpected "lightning" strike, that would immediately incapacitate Red Army units and, first and foremost, our air force and navy.

Under these circumstances, the measures taken by the People's Commissariat of Defense to increase the combat readiness of troops in border districts proved belated and clearly inadequate, as experience has shown. When World War II was in full blast and its flames were roaring in close proximity to Soviet borders, different measures were needed to prepare troops for the repulsion of an enemy invasion. It should have been taken into account that aviation had developed to such a level that a sudden and massive air attack by an aggressor gave him considerable advantage, particularly in the initial period of the war.

In my opinion, it is now indisputable that in the prewar period our military theorists were not exactly up to the mark. The predatory techniques by which fascist Germany invaded other European countries were not sufficiently studied by us and, above all, were not translated into meaningful practical conclusions which could and should have found a tangible reflection in army and navy field manuals and in all other military regulations.

I happen to know that even before fascist Germany's treacherous attack on our country, Marshal B. M. Shaposhnikov, then Chief of the General Staff, made very valuable suggestions about the deployment of troops in the western border districts. He proposed that the main forces of these districts be deployed within the old state frontier behind the already strongly fortified line and that only a covering force, sufficient to secure the deployment of the main forces in case of a surprise attack, be left in the newly liberated territories of Western Belorussia, the Western Ukraine, and the Baltic region. However, this sensible opinion of an experienced military leader was ignored at the time. Right on the new border were units that were still in the process of formation and not even provided with their full complement of personnel and equipment.

At the very beginning of the war we already realized that this was a fatal error, an obvious oversight by a number of military leaders, and, therefore, we were not convinced by the charge of treason. The decree that branded the former commander of the Western Special Military District, General of the Army D. G. Pavlov, and his closest associates traitors to their country made the most painful impression on me personally. It was difficult to imagine that a combat general, who had selflessly fought the German fascists in the Spanish Civil War, would switch to their cause. . . .

The tragedy of the Western Special Military District was that, in the very first moment, it was suddenly hit by the worst blows of fascist Germany's air and armored units. The misfortune, and not the fault, of Pavlov was that he was strictly executing the orders of the People's Commissar of Defense—orders written at Stalin's personal directive—and he did not order the troops to combat readiness until the last minute, although he was aware of the concentration of German divisions at our borders.

A much greater share of the fault for failing to take decisive steps to increase the combat readiness of our troops in border districts must be laid to the General Staff. The new Chief of the General Staff, G. K. Zhukov, who had replaced B. M. Shaposhnikov shortly before the war, failed to appreciate the significance of his predecessor's proposals, and, knowing Stalin's negative attitude to them, he evidently did not press for their fulfillment. He deliberately reinforced the confidence of the head of the government in the correctness of proposals and calculations which history proved clearly erroneous. At that time all aspects of our life, including the military, were too strongly influenced by the spirit of the personality cult, which fettered people's initiative, stifled their will, and led to irresponsibility in some and to immobility in others.[60]

General of the Army I. I. Fediuninskii
With the 15th Rifle Corps on the Frontier

It was April 1941. Upon completing my studies in Moscow, I went to the Western Ukraine and assumed command of the 15th Rifle Corps of the Special Kiev Military District [located in Kovel']. . . . I arrived in Kovel' when the situation on our western frontier was becoming more and more tense. . . . At that time, however, relations between the Soviet Union and Germany were judged to be normal and to be proceeding in accordance with the nonaggression pact. Any reports about the aggressive designs of the Hitlerites were considered provocations.

Quite understandably, we, the military, had the impression that for the time being no direct threat of imminent war existed. We still did not know then that Stalin, by refusing to believe the data provided by the intelligence and the reports of the commanders of the western frontier

I. I. Fediuninskii, *Podniatye po trevoge* (2nd rev. ed.; Moscow, 1964), pp. 5–15.

districts, committed a serious mistake in appraising the international situation and, above all, in establishing the probable date of fascist German aggression against our country. . . .

Meanwhile, we at the western frontier sensed with each passing day that the smell of gunpowder was getting stronger. Ominous rumors of an inevitable and imminent war were persistently circulating in Kovel'. Of course many of them were spread for provocative purposes. It became clear later, however, that in several cases these rumors had a factual basis. It was almost openly said to the wives of our officers in Kovel', L'vov, and Lutsk: "You just wait; the war will begin soon. The Germans will show you!"[61] . . .

While I was inspecting the units and subunits of the corps, the tension at the frontier mounted. The border troops were reporting the growing insolence of the Hitlerites: "Earlier, when our officers appeared at the border, the German sentries would stand at attention and salute. But now, see for yourself—" It was easy to see that they were right; at the sight of us, fascist soldiers would deliberately turn their backs. The officers would say pensively: "It looks as though relations with our 'good' neighbors are beginning to deteriorate. . . ."

On the evening of June 18 the commander of a border detachment called me: "Comrade Colonel," he said excitedly, "a German soldier just crossed over to our side. He is giving us very important information. I don't know whether he can be believed, but what he says is very, very important—"

"Wait for me," I answered, and immediately left for the border troops. Upon entering the office of the detachment commander, I asked that the German be brought in. He entered and, coming to attention, froze in the doorway. I looked him over for a minute. He was the first Hitlerite soldier I had seen so close up and the first with whom I had occasion to talk. He was a young, tall, rather ungainly fellow. . . . The German looked at me intently and waited. His big, red hands trembled perceptibly. I allowed him to sit down. He sank onto a stool in the middle of the room and again stared at me expectantly with his colorless eyes.

I turned to the translator. "Ask him why he came over to us," I said.

The German had been waiting for this question and readily answered. While drunk he had struck an officer. They had threatened to shoot him; so he decided to flee across the border. He had always sympathized with the Russians, and his father was a communist. The German gave particular emphasis to the latter.

"Will my life be spared?" he asked.

"Certainly. But why should you have any doubts about that?"

"War is going to start soon, and the German army will be the enemy of the Russian." The sergeant repeated to me what he had already told the border detachment commander: at 4:00 a.m. on June 22, Hitler's troops would launch an offensive along the entire length of the Soviet-German border.

"Don't worry. We don't shoot prisoners, especially those who come to us voluntarily," I reassured the German.

The information was extraordinary, yet I had doubts. "Can he be trusted?" I thought, just as the border detachment commander had thought an hour ago. The Hitlerite soldier's information appeared quite incredible, and his personality did not inspire any particular trust. Yet, what if he was telling the truth? Besides, why should he lie, naming the exact day and even hour of the start of the war?

Noticing that I mistrusted his information, the German rose and declared with conviction and a certain solemnity:

"Colonel, sir, at 5:00 a.m. on June 22 you can have me shot, should it turn out that I have lied to you."

Back at corps headquarters I rang up the commander of the 5th Army, Major General of the tank forces M. I. Potapov, and reported the information.

"We should not believe provocations!" the general's calm and assured basso droned over the wire. "A German fearing for his skin could babble anything."

True, all this looked like a provocation, yet I felt uneasy. I reported to General Potapov that in my view some measures should be taken all the same. I requested permission to move from encampments to the forests closer to the frontier two rifle regiments each from the 45th and the 62nd Divisions which were not occupied with building fortifications and to summon the artillery regiments from the firing range.

General Potapov answered angrily:

"You are sounding the alarm without reason."

In support of my request, I referred to the possibility of using these regiments for work in the security zone and thus reducing the time required to complete the construction of defense installations.

"There is no reason to fear that this could evoke German displeasure," I said. "The troops will be located eight kilometers from the border, in a thick forest."

The Army commander thought about it and agreed.

On June 20, I was visited by the commander of the mechanized corps, General K. K. Rokossovskii, who was on his way from the training area. We had a frank talk. Rokossovskii shared my fears. He, too, was worried by the situation and by our excessive fear of provoking [the

Germans], a fear which impaired the combat readiness of troops located along the frontier.

I invited the general to remain overnight, but, thanking me, he refused:

"At such times, it is better to be closer to one's units."

On Saturday, June 21, I went to bed rather late but could not fall asleep for a long time. I tossed and turned. . . . "Was the German lying or not?" The thought gave me no peace. . . . My musings were interrupted by the telephone. General Potapov was on the line.

"Where are you, Ivan Ivanovich?" asked the Army commander.

"In my apartment—"

"Go to headquarters immediately and stand by the high frequency telephone." I could hear alarm in the general's voice.

Without waiting for the car, I threw a leather coat over my shoulders and started walking. The distance was short.

Three men, whom I did not know, were standing at the end of the block. Their cigarettes were red dots flickering in the dark. They were talking quietly about something, but when I approached they became silent.

The high frequency telephone communication was broken. I had to call the Army commander by ordinary telephone. General Potapov tersely ordered me to alert the divisions to prepare ammunition for the troops, but not to issue it yet and not to yield to provocations.

I felt that Army headquarters too was not yet finally convinced that the Hitlerites intended to start extensive combat operations.

While issuing the necessary orders to units, I heard several pistol shots resound in the quiet night. Shortly afterward, the staff duty officer reported that the car which he had sent for me had been fired at on its way back to headquarters and that the driver had been wounded.

I immediately remembered the three men in the alley. They probably had not recognized me in the darkness. But they saw the car approach my house, heard the driver knock at the door, and, when the car had scarcely turned around, they opened fire, assuming that the corps commander was inside. The very same thing happened to the chief of staff, Major General Rogoznyi. He too, following the telephone call from the duty officer, left for headquarters on foot, and the car sent for him had also been fired upon. Clearly, fascist agents had been given the task of liquidating the corps command in the first hour of the war.

Soon after, communications with the Army broke down completely. German planes appeared over the city. The heavy rumble of an artillery cannonade could be heard from the direction of the border.

Marshal I. Kh. Bagramian
At Southwestern Army Group Headquarters

IN THE BEGINNING of June the intelligence section of our military district received so much alarming information that its chief, Colonel G. I. Bondarev, became the most frequent caller on the commanding officer. After each of his visits, M. P. Kirponos became gloomier and gloomier.[62] On June 10 he called a meeting of the military council at which the intelligence chief reported everything he knew. . . .

General Purkaev[63] was unusually taciturn at this conference. He knitted his thick beetle brows and from time to time nodded in approval of one suggestion or another. But when Kirponos stopped talking, Purkaev said suddenly that it would not be a bad idea to tell Moscow about the necessity of bringing the transport facilities of the divisions and corps of the second echelon up to full complement.

"After all, if something should happen now," he reasoned, "the corps would be unable to move out a considerable part of the artillery. There are no tractors; many divisions are not fully equipped with transport; there is nothing on which to deliver ammunition; and there is also a shortage of manpower."

Everyone looked at Kirponos questioningly.

"This is a matter of state policy," he replied. "You and I ought to understand that the Party and government leaders and Comrade Stalin personally, while taking every possible step to strengthen the country's defense capacity, are preoccupied with one thought: Not to allow an outbreak of war with Germany, which the British and French [sic!] governments so obstinately wish to provoke. To build up the manpower of our divisions and corps to full strength and to supply them with the tractors and trucks they lack and with other resources would require partial mobilization. It would be almost impossible to hide it from German intelligence. Our leaders can scarcely resort to such steps."

"You are right. That makes sense," Vashugin [the commissar][64] said

---

I. Kh. Bagramian, "Zapiski nachal'nika operativnogo otdela," *Voenno-istoricheskii zhurnal,* 1967, No. 3, pp. 52–68.

heartily in support. "In such a serious matter we need to exercise caution and more caution. We must strictly observe the pact with Germany and refrain from taking any steps which might provoke Germany to break it." . . .

Not even twenty-four hours had passed since the military council's discussion of new steps to increase the troops' combat readiness when a telegram arrived at the military district. In it General of the Army G. K. Zhukov, Chief of the General Staff, stated:

> The chief of border troops of the People's Commissariat of Internal Affairs [NKVD] of the Ukrainian Republic has reported that the chiefs of fortified areas have received instructions to occupy the forward zone. Report to the People's Commissar of Defense on what grounds the units of fortified areas in the Kiev Special Military District received the order to occupy the forward zone. Such actions can immediately provoke the Germans to armed conflict and are fraught with all kinds of consequences. Cancel the order immediately and report who, specifically, issued that arbitrary order.

We had scarcely succeeded in transmitting an order to the troops to leave the forward zone and to pull back those units which had been moved up closer to the frontier guards when alarming new reports began to pour in from the Armies. . . .

In the middle of June, I remember, the commander of the 17th Rifle Corps of the 12th Army during a report on events which were taking place on the other side of the border said outright that the fascists were definitely preparing for an attack. In connection with this he pointed out with great alarm that the 17th Rifle Corps (which was stationed right at the frontier) would be completely unprepared to parry an attack if its forces were not gathered and prepared positions were not occupied in advance. About half of the corps' forces had been dispersed in company-size units over a vast area. They were building pillboxes, the completion of which was planned for September. Also, the disposition of the divisions, unfortunately, did not ensure the corps' combat readiness.

At the same time, the chief of intelligence reported new information on the situation to the [district] commander. It had been learned that about six new German divisions had arrived in the area of Chelm, Bilgoraj, Iuzefuv, Janow, and Tarnogrod alone. A large group of enemy troops from Yugoslavia had been dispatched toward Tomaszow from the direction of Krakow. Divisions from France were continuing to unload in the Tomaszow area. . . .

A growing stream of alarming reports, queries, and requests related to the situation on the frontier continued to come in from the Armies on June 19. In my opinion, the most typical was a telegram from General

P. G. Ponedelin, Commander of the 12th Army. He asked the commander
in what cases anti-aircraft artillery might open fire were German airplanes to invade our air space. General Kirponos ordered the chief of staff
to give the following reply:

You may open fire:

(a) if special instructions of the district military council are issued;

(b) if mobilization is declared;

(c) if the cover plan is put into operation and if at the same time there is
no special prohibition.

(d) The 12th Army military council knows that we do not fire at German
planes in peacetime.

It was the only possible answer the command of the military district
could give.

On the same day, General Purkaev called me in. He informed me that
he had received instructions to our military district from the People's
Commissar of Defense S. K. Timoshenko to the effect that the field command of the Southwestern Army Group should be selected and should
depart for the field command post in Tarnopol'. He ordered me to prepare corresponding instructions on preparations for relocation to the new
station immediately.[65]

I was greatly agitated by this unusual instruction. What did it mean?
Was it a simple precaution or had Moscow learned that danger was
imminent?

"But what about the troops?" I could not resist asking.

"I can add nothing to what I have already said," replied Purkaev.
"For the time being, only the instruction regarding the military district's
command element has come in. The main command element of the military district, the commander, the military council member, all the chiefs
of the Army branches and services, and I will go to Tarnopol' by car on
the morning of June 21. Don't waste any time; prepare all documents of
the plan we worked out for deployment of the military district's troops
and send it to the General Staff by train with the proper escort. On the
night of June 22 you follow us, also by car, with your own section. You
are responsible for the organized, prompt arrival of the operations section in Tarnopol'."

I expressed surprise that the command of the military district was
moving to the command post without the operations section. After all,
if anything happened, it would not be able to command the troops if it
did not have at hand either operations officers or code clerks (code clerks
had been incorporated in the operations section not long before the war).
For some reason, Purkaev did not approve my suggestion to leave two or

three officers with me and to send the rest with my deputy to Tarnopol' along with the military council. He said there was no need for that, since by the morning of June 22 the operations section would already be in Tarnopol' and that was quite sufficient.

On the morning of June 21 we bade good-bye to the men driving to Tarnopol'. No one seemed particularly alarmed. Some were convinced that this was a planned exercise and that they would return to Kiev no later than the following Saturday.

On that same day, after we had dispatched all urgent documents to Moscow, we also began to prepare for the trip. It was still quite light when our column crossed the city with its lively Saturday air and reached the Zhitomir highway. In the car at the head of the column, I looked hastily through the newspapers I had not had time to read during the day. There was nothing alarming in the papers. . . . The column had to stop a few times during the night for car repairs. The unforeseen stops disrupted the schedule for the march. It was possible that I would be unable to get my motor column to Tarnopol' by 7:00 a.m. as Purkaev had ordered me to do.

During one of the stops I passed along the column, and when I returned and was on the verge of giving the signal to move on, I suddenly heard the powerful drone of airplane motors in the air over Brody. Everyone stopped to listen. We heard booming explosions in the area of the Brody airfield, where fighter and assault planes were based. The ground under our feet shook. One of the officers shouted:

"Look! Look! Fire!"

Pitch-black clouds of smoke rose beyond Brody. Keen eyes detected that the fuel dump was on fire. Everyone sank into an uneasy silence. It was not difficult to guess what thought was gnawing at the mind of each man: "Can it be war?"

Yes, it was war! It had come to our land. From the town of Brody we turned southeast in the direction of Tarnopol'. Along the remaining 60 km. stretch of road our column was bombed twice by small groups of fascist planes, but, fortunately, they caused no serious damage. We arrived in the area of the new location of military district headquarters even earlier than scheduled—somewhere between 6:00 and 7:00 a.m.; henceforth, according to the plan, it became the headquarters of the Southwestern Army Group. At the sound of the arriving cars, General Purkaev darted out of the headquarters building. His usually austere face bore an expression of impatience and annoyance. It seemed as though he were about to shout: "What hole did you fall into?" But he kept quiet. Apparently, he had not forgotten our conversation just before the departure from Kiev. Scarcely listening to my report about our arrival, the general waved his hand impatiently.

"Unload as quickly as you can and get to work! Inform the commanding officers of the second echelon corps immediately, through all channels of communication, that the plan of operation is now in force. Get confirmation from them that they have received this instruction. When they have received it, report to me." . . .

On the last Saturday evening before the war and in the early morning hours on Sunday, events at the border had developed in the following sequence. The commanders of Armies, corps, and divisions in the border zone, who had received no orders to bring their troops to combat readiness and to deploy them for immediate occupation of the lines prepared at the frontier, anxiously watched the suspicious activity of the Germans on the other side of the border.

On June 21, with the onset of darkness, the border guards and army intelligence noticed a great stir along the other side of the border; quite clearly one could hear the rumble of tanks and the noise of tractors. It was not hard for experienced fighting men to guess what such activity might mean! In addition to everything else, at about midnight a German soldier in the 222nd Infantry Regiment, 74th Infantry Division, deserted to our side in the zone of the 5th Army west of Vladimir-Volynskii. When he had learned that the attack on the Soviet Union was to begin at 4:00 a.m., he slipped quietly into the water and swam across the border river at the risk of being shot by German security forces or Soviet border guards. . . . The deserter reported that everything was ready for an attack which was to begin at 4:00 a.m. The chief of the border outpost reported it through channels. The message was so important that General Khomenko, chief of border troops of the Ukraine, was routed out of bed. He immediately reported to his superiors in Moscow and informed the commander of the military district. Everyone's first reaction to the message was, "But isn't this a provocation?" Naturally, the district military council did not dare without Moscow's sanction to issue an order to put into operation the plan for covering the state border. Only General M. I. Potapov, Commander of the 5th Army, who had also learned about the deserter, decided not long before the attack to put his corps on the alert.[66] Therefore, they had at their disposal somewhat more time to prepare to meet the enemy. At their own risk, the commanding officers of the 41st and 87th Rifle Divisions, stationed right at the border, also brought their units to combat readiness.

At 2:30 a.m. the communications center in Tarnopol' began receiving a telegram, in which the People's Commissar and the Chief of the General Staff warned that "a surprise attack by the Germans may possibly take place on June 22–23, 1941." The task of our troops was not to yield to any provocation. It was categorically demanded that commanders of border military districts hold their troops "in complete combat readiness to meet a possible surprise attack by the Germans and their allies." The telegram also outlined measures for bringing the troops to combat readiness, and the commanders of military districts were instructed to carry the measures out. But at 3:45 a.m. the war had already begun. The moment it became known that Hitler's hordes had treacherously invaded our territory, Kirponos, with the approval of the military council member and the chief of staff, ordered the following telegram sent to the Armies: "Put Kiev Special Military District Plan No. 41 into operation. Open the sealed special orders."

If only this command had been issued twenty-four hours earlier! It is not difficult to imagine that then the Hitlerite hordes which attacked our country would have run up against an organized and firm defense by the cover troops right at the border. If the aggressor's troops had managed to break through our defense in any direction, in a short time they would have come under an organized counterattack by second echelon troops from our interior. If the war had begun this way, the German troops would hardly have been able to push so swiftly and deeply into our territory. Unfortunately, the war began differently.[67]

The first German air attacks were unleashed on Kiev and other large cities in the Ukraine and on the most important airfields in our military district. The military council immediately reported to Moscow what had happened and what steps had been taken.

The commander and the chief of staff started to put order into troop control, trying as quickly as possible to impart a more organized character to the combat actions of the Army Group's cover troops and air force. After receiving the order to push the invading German units back over the state boundary line, divisions of first echelon cover troops headed for the state border under relentless enemy bombing.

While sealed orders were being opened at headquarters of the Armies and orders were being issued to the troops about putting into operation the plan for covering the border, the German air force was making a second series of attacks, this time on the troops and airfields closest to the border. These attacks, which caught the majority of the units still at their permanent stations, led to the first serious losses among troops located in the border zone.

The fact that German planes had gained supremacy in the air from the very start of the invasion was particularly alarming. The military district air force lost 180 airplanes in the first German air strikes. Our troops, which had started advancing toward the frontiers, did not have adequate cover against air attacks. Only small isolated groups of fighter planes broke through the German air umbrella to support them.

When the Army Group chief of staff reported the situation, M. P. Kirponos immediately summoned General E. S. Ptukhin, commander of the air force, and demanded that he concentrate the air force's major effort on resolving three main tasks—covering the troops moving toward the border, destroying the enemy's motorized and tank groups, and attacking the closest German airfields.

Ptukhin left and General Purkaev laid on the table a directive from the People's Commissar of Defense that had just been sent from the operations section. Headquarters received it only at 9:00 a.m. Turning to Vashugin, Kirponos read it aloud, slowly and distinctly. It stated that at 4:00 a.m. on June 22, 1941, German aircraft had made raids on our airfields and cities along the border and had bombed them without provocation. Simultaneously, German troops had opened artillery fire and crossed our frontier in different places. In connection with this, the People's Commissar of Defense ordered that enemy troops be attacked with all forces and weapons and destroyed in the areas where they had crossed the Soviet frontier. Our ground troops were not to cross the frontier until they had received special instructions. Bombers were to destroy enemy planes on their airfields and were to bomb the principal enemy concentrations of ground troops. Air strikes were to be made against enemy territory to a depth of 100 to 150 km. We transmitted the directive from the People's Commissar to the troops without any change.[68]

We had to send our own first report to Moscow at 3:00 p.m. I sat down to draw up the document. It was perhaps the most difficult report in my entire career as a staff officer. In essence, the situation remained unclear. What the true position of the Armies was, where the enemy was striking the main blow, how the enemy was grouped, and what his plan of action was—could only be guessed. Therefore, our first combat report to Moscow, to our sincere distress, was full of generalities and vague statements.

In the evening on the first day of the war, we received a second directive from the People's Commissar of Defense. In the directive, the People's Commissar and the Chief of the General Staff gave a highly optimistic assessment of events on the first day of the war. Believing that the Germans had had only negligible success, they categorically demanded of the Southwestern Army Group command the following: "While maintaining a solid hold on the state boundary adjoining Hungary, concentrate attacks by the forces of the 5th and 6th Armies in the general direction of Lublin, and with at least five mechanized corps and all the Army Group's air force surround and destroy the enemy group attacking on the Vladimir-

Volynskii–Krystynopol' line. Capture Lublin by the end of the day on June 24. Protect yourself well from the direction of Krakow."[69]

This directive right on the first day of the war caused obvious bewilderment. Now, when one can quietly and soberly analyze everything, the directive is explicable only by the fact that the Red Army [High] Command did not have sufficiently complete information from the Army Groups and could not properly size up the whole complexity of the situation in the Southwestern Army Group's sector. The situation was the direct consequence of the extraordinarily unfavorable conditions under which our troops had entered the war. When I read this directive to the chief of staff, he reached for it in disbelief. He reread it intently once, twice. Then we exchanged opinions briefly and established that we had the same point of view on the situation and on the content of the directive we had received.

Purkaev took my situation map, and, holding the directive that had so astonished him, he silently motioned me to follow him to the commander.

"What are we to do, Mikhail Petrovich?" he began as soon as he reached the commander's door. "Would to God we could stop the enemy and disorganize him in defensive battle, but they are demanding that we take Lublin the day after tomorrow!"

General Kirponos, as usual, did not rush to make conclusions. He silently reached for the document that had so upset the usually imperturbable chief of staff. The commander read the directive carefully and did not give so much as an inkling of what he felt about it. After thinking for a while, he picked up the telephone receiver and called Vashugin.

"Nikolai Nikolaevich, come to see me, please. A new directive has been received."

The military council member appeared. His whole external appearance was one of cheerfulness, vigor, and nervous excitement.

"What has happened?"

The commander silently held out the directive. Running his eyes over it quickly, Vashugin leaned on the back of a chair and gave a puzzled look at those present.

"Well, comrades, what surprises you? The order has been received, and it has to be carried out. And as quickly as possible, while they still haven't pushed very far into our territory. The fascists have to be routed. Do you really think differently?"

"That's true, Nikolai Nikolaevich," responded Purkaev, "but we're not ready now to smash the enemy with a determined assault. For the time being we have to think about defense, not attack."

Reading a growing expression of anger on Vashugin's face, he raised his hand placatingly and continued even more forcefully:

"Let's take a sober look at the present situation. In the direction of Lutsk alone, in the zone between Luboml and Sokal, just today in the first enemy echelon we identified about ten infantry and tank divisions against our less than four divisions of the 5th Army. . . . It is quite obvious that the chief enemy grouping is concentrated on the Lutsk axis. Tomorrow we shall have there, at best, the 135th Rifle Division and two divisions of the 22nd Mechanized Corps. As unfortunate as it may be, Potapov does not know right now where the 41st Tank Division of this corps is. Just before the attack it was stationed at the border in the area of Vladimir-Volynskii, exactly in line of the Germans' main attack. . . . So tomorrow we shall have less than seven divisions against ten enemy divisions. How can we talk about an immediate offensive? And think of another thing. All the reserve corps heading for the frontier are at different distances from it. If we assign them the mission of shifting to a counter-offensive against the main enemy striking force, then only the very closest mechanized corps will be able to start doing so, and not for one or two days at that. The corps will be drawn into battle by units, since they will encounter on the march the German troops which are now pushing eastward. There will be a meeting engagement under the most unfavorable conditions for our troops. What this holds in store for us we can't fully imagine now, but our situation will undoubtedly be grave."

Purkaev cleared his throat, took a breath, and declared firmly:

"Comrade Commander, all we can do is report this situation to Moscow and urgently request that the frontier cover troops engaging in stiff defensive fighting be allowed to offer maximum resistance to the advance of German fascist troops into our interior. Request that under their cover the forces of the rifle and mechanized corps forming the second echelon of the Army Group be allowed to set up a firm defense deep inside the Army Group's zone of action—on the line of Korosten', Novograd-Volynskii, Shepetovka, Starokonstantinov, and Proskurov fortified areas°— and to give the enemy a decisive battle there. After the cover troops have pulled back behind the line of the fortified areas, they can then be used as reserves. This is exactly the solution I see in the present situation."

There was general silence for a minute. General Kirponos remained sunk in deep thought. The corps commissar [Vashugin] was the first to speak.

"Everything you say, Maksim Alekseevich, may be correct from the military viewpoint, but, in my opinion, it is absolutely wrong politically! You are thinking purely as a military specialist—disposition of forces, etc.

°General Purkaev had in mind the fortified areas along the old state boundary that had been dismantled and closed before the war.

But are you considering the moral factor? No, you are not! And have you thought of what moral harm it will do if we, who have trained the Red Army in a high offensive spirit, shift to a passive defense in the first days of the war and, unresisting, leave initiative in the hands of the aggressor! And you are even proposing to let the fascists go deep into Soviet territory!"

Then the military council member added more quietly, almost gently:

"You know, Maksim Alekseevich, my comrade-in-arms, if I didn't know you as a tried and true Bolshevik, I would think you were beginning to panic." Noticing that the muscles in Purkaev's wide-cheeked face had begun to tighten, Vashugin added softly:

"Forgive me. I didn't mean to offend you. I'm simply unable to hide what I'm thinking. In my opinion, one thing is clear. We must begin our combat action with one idea—how best to carry out the combat order of the People's Commissar and how to avoid injecting confusion into the overall strategic plan of the Supreme Command with our own proposals."

Purkaev wanted to object, but the debate was interrupted by the commander.

"I think you are both right. I have no objections to the operational expediency of your proposals, Maksim Alekseevich, but they do have one vulnerable aspect. The old fortified areas are not ready to receive troops and to provide them with favorable conditions for a successful defense."

"The second echelon troops, aided by combat engineer units, can begin to bring these fortified areas to combat readiness immediately," Purkaev objected.

Without answering the chief of staff's rejoinder, Kirponos continued in his calm tone:

"But as for Nikolai Nikolaevich's arguments, they're not illogical either. An order is an order. It has to be carried out. And if every commander, instead of strictly carrying out a combat order when he receives it, were to make his own counterproposals, no good would come of it. Of course, we're hardly in a position to take Lublin by the end of the day on June 24, but we must try to strike a powerful counterblow at the invading enemy forces. To do this, we can immediately bring in up to four mechanized corps. It's true that only two of them are more or less equipped with new tanks and can be considered fit for combat. But still, I think altogether these corps constitute a fairly large force; therefore, we can hope for the total defeat of the fascist troops which have crossed the frontier. That's how we'll carry out the order of the People's Commissar. And he'll understand if we don't take Lublin. That task is obviously not within our power.

"On the basis of these considerations," the commander continued, "I believe that our main task now is to ensure a rapid concentration of the mechanized corps in the battlefield zone and organize their immediate employment in a powerful counterattack. Maksim Alekseevich, we have to get the appropriate combat instructions to the mechanized corps immediately and see that they are carried out. Particular attention should be paid to giving the mechanized corps a reliable air cover when they are advancing into the concentration areas and when they are moving into battle. Along with this Potapov should be given the following assignment: All forces and weapons of the 5th Army, in coordination with the right-flank troops of the 6th Army and supported by the main forces of the Army Group's air force, are to keep the invading fascist troops from advancing any deeper into our territory."

"This is talk that makes sense," Vashugin said in support. "I heartily approve such a decision."[70]

In accordance with these instructions from the commander, we began to prepare combat orders for the troops. . . .

The Army Group command's planned counterattack by forces of the mechanized corps began on June 24. A major tank battle lasted five days in the northwestern areas of the Ukraine, in the Vladimir–Volynskii–Radziekhow–Dubno triangle where Soviet tank troops displayed exceptional courage and fearlessness. More than 1,500 tanks were gradually drawn into this battle from both sides. General Kleist's tank armada was kept in the frontier area for more than a week despite the extremely unfavorable conditions in which tank units of the Southwestern Army Group found themselves (their formation was incomplete; they were committed to battle at different times, directly from the march, and even then without all forces at once). During this desperate fighting Kleist's armada suffered its first serious loss of men and tanks.[71]

Thus, surmounting immense difficulties in the combat situation, the soldiers, officers, and political workers of the Southwestern Army Group entered the selfless struggle against the enemy.

Captain First Rank N. F. Rybalko
At the Black Sea
Fleet Headquarters

On the evening of June 21 I came on duty at 6:00 or 7:00 p.m. The Chief of Staff of the Black Sea Fleet, Rear Admiral I. D. Eliseev, was working in his office at Fleet headquarters. I and Captain Second Rank Nikitin, from whom I was taking over, reported the changing of duty officers to the rear admiral.

That day things were calm in the Black Sea theater. The ships were replenishing supplies used during exercises. The personnel of ships and units were being given a rest following their intensive efforts. Furlough procedures were as usual. Even though the lights of the ships were blacked out, as was required by the high operational readiness, the city was brightly lit, and the boulevards, parks, and streets were crowded with strolling people. Exercises at sea were not planned for June 22; air flights had been scheduled for daytime only and were very few in number; no night flights were envisaged.

In a word, there was nothing unusual to elicit any alarm this peaceful summer evening. Everyone was resting, and, it seemed to me, I could expect an uneventful tour of duty. One thing was somewhat disturbing, however. Those days there were three German transport ships plying the Black Sea. They made regular trips between our ports and those of Rumania and Bulgaria, and, as a rule, they were either in passage or loading in the various ports. This time all the German transports were in Rumanian and Bulgarian ports. Nikitin, whom I was replacing, said in response to my inquiry that this unusual circumstance was worrying him too and that he had reported the location of the transports to the fleet command.

A tug pulling a refuse barge sailed out to sea between 10:00 and 11:00 p.m. By my order, to ensure its safe exit and re-entry, the Inker-

N. F. Rybalko, "V pervyi den' voiny na Chernom more," *Voenno-istoricheskii zhurnal*, 1963, No. 6, pp. 63–66.

man range beacons and the Kherson lighthouses were switched on. Telephone communications with the lighthouses were in order.

At 1:00 a.m. on June 22, I was relieved by my assistant and went to rest. I had hardly shut my eyes, however, when I was called in by I. D. Eliseev, who showed me a telegram from People's Commissar of the Navy N. G. Kuznetsov. I remember it verbatim and am uncertain only about the order in which the fleets and the flotillas were listed: "The Northern, Baltic, and Black Sea Fleets and the Pinsk and Danube Flotillas are to assume operational readiness No. 1 immediately."

I. D. Eliseev ordered me to open an envelope containing documents which specified the actions to be taken with the assumption by the fleet of the highest state of operational preparedness.

In accordance with these documents the entire operational service of the fleet was to execute the order of the People's Commissar of the Navy. The fleet communications duty officer instructed all naval bases and fleet formations urgently to bring their forces up to a state of full combat preparedness. The order was immediately communicated to the commander of the Black Sea Fleet, Vice Admiral F. S. Oktiabr'skii. At 1:55 a.m. the general alarm signal was sounded at the main fleet base. The sleeping city echoed with the sound of sirens, signal shots from battery guns, and loud announcements on the city radio relay system. From all parts of the city, navy personnel hurried to ships and units.

In accordance with the documents, ships and units began to load ammunition, fuel, and supplies and to build up their crews to prescribed strength. The fleet rear services provided the vessels with all necessary combat supplies. . . . The transition of the fleet to the highest state of preparedness had been well planned and took place without any substantial departures from the plan.

A few minutes after the general alarm signal, the city was plunged into darkness. The beacons in the area of the main base, however, remained lit. In our efforts to transmit the order to turn off the beacon lights, we discovered that the connection with all of them had been broken. We had to turn to the garrison commander, Major General P. A. Morgunov, who ordered motorcycle runners sent to the lighthouses from the nearest batteries or military units.

The beacon lights were extinguished before the beginning of the enemy air raid except for that of the Upper Inkerman Lighthouse, which the motorcyclist had been unable to reach in time. The light remained on during the enemy air raid. This beacon alone, however, could not provide a reliable reference point for the enemy aircraft to hit the important main base targets or fleet ships. Soon after the enemy air raid, communications with the lighthouses were restored. I cannot prove that this break in communications was an act of sabotage. It probably was, however, since contact had been broken simultaneously with all lighthouses, whereas prior to that point I cannot recall a single instance of a communications break with even one of them.

Shortly after we received the telegram of the People's Commissar, Fleet Commander Vice Admiral F. S. Oktiabr'skii and Divisional Commissar N. M. Kulakov, a member of the fleet's military council, arrived at fleet headquarters. The staff officers of the fleet began to gather after the "general alarm" signal had been given. The overwhelming majority of them were puzzled by the unexpected summons. They soon went about their business, however, and started obtaining gas masks, weapons, etc. Some formation commanders asked to be informed about the situation. To this I and my assistant answered only that ships and units must be brought to a state of immediate readiness; we could tell them nothing more.

Soon after the "general Alarm" signal was given, the chief of staff, I. D. Eliseev, the chief of operations, Captain Second Rank O. S. Zhukovskii, the chief of intelligence, Colonel D. B. Namgaladze, and many other leading staff officers of the fleet gathered in the room of the operations duty officer.

At approximately 3:00 a.m. reports started to arrive from the bases and formations of the fleet, from the coastal defense, from the antiaircraft and air force units that operational preparedness No. 1 had been put into effect. The Danube Flotilla also assumed operational preparedness No. 1.

At about 3:00 a.m. I began to receive reports from posts of observation and air warning in the area of Evpatoriia and Cape Sarych to the effect that the sound of aircraft engines on a course toward Sevastopol' could be heard. Immediately afterward Colonel I. S. Zhilin, Chief of the Fleet Anti-aircraft Defense, rang me up. He had also received the reports of the air warning service and was asking whether he should open fire on the unidentified aircraft. I reported this to I. D. Eliseev. The latter ordered me to report to the fleet commander. Using the direct telephone line, I rang up Fleet Commander F. S. Oktiabr'skii, whose office was across from mine. The chief of staff stood by my side and heard not only my report to the fleet commander, but also some of his answers.

Having heard my report concerning the appearance of unidentified aircraft, the fleet commander asked: "Are some of our planes airborne?" I answered: "We have no planes in the air!" I then repeated my question: "What about opening fire?" After a brief pause the fleet commander answered: "Act according to instructions."

The chief of staff who had heard my conversation with the fleet commander said: "Give the order to Colonel Zhilin to open fire." I immediately rang up Colonel Zhilin and transmitted the order: "Open fire." Colonel Zhilin answered: "Keep in mind that you bear full responsibility for this order. I am entering it in the combat operations log." I repeated the order to Comrade Zhilin and said: "Enter it wherever you wish. I realize my responsibility. But open fire on the airplanes." On this our conversation ended.

Shortly afterward, when enemy aircraft approached the base, anti-aircraft units turned on their searchlights; anti-aircraft batteries opened fire, and so did anti-aircraft guns on the ships. This took place at 3:13 a.m. on June 22.

The enemy airplanes were flying at a low altitude. As we learned later, they carried only parachute proximity mines against which, at that time, we had no effective counter-weapons. Their task was to blockade the ships of the Black Sea Fleet in Sevastopol'.

The enemy's attempt to catch the fleet unprepared to repulse its air strike did not succeed. The enemy airplanes, encountering unexpected anti-aircraft fire, were unable to carry out their mission in full. Two parachute mines fell on shore within the city limits, a few fell in the shallow waters of the entrance to Sevastopol' (Northern) Bay and beyond the city limits, and only two or three mines fell in the channel. We learned all this somewhat later. At the time of the raid and shortly afterward, the situation remained unclear. . . .

It must be said that until the air raid many servicemen, including commanding officers, not to speak of the civilian population, had assumed that all the events of that fateful night were nothing but exercises. Later I heard many officers say that they had admired the fire of our anti-aircraft artillery. "How well organized this unexpected anti-aircraft fire is," they said, "and right after the fleet maneuvers, so as to test our vigilance." . . .

Following the repulsion of the enemy air raid and the clarification of its full results, the room of the operations duty officer emptied. The fleet chief of staff and other commanding staff officers went to their positions to take charge of fleet combat operations. . . . The dispersion of the fleet's ships began in the morning. Toward evening it was completed. . . .

The enemy attempt to catch the Black Sea Fleet unawares failed. The fleet suffered no losses whatsoever from the enemy air raid and maintained its freedom to maneuver. This was due to the superior combat training and readiness of the ships, units, and formations of the fleet. The element of surprise in the attack on the Black Sea Fleet did not yield the results that the enemy expected.

Admiral I. I. Azarov
Is the War
Really On?

VICE ADMIRAL OKTIABR'SKII was talking to Moscow on the high frequency telephone.

"Whose planes are they?" I asked Kulakov.

"German probably," he answered, handing me a cable to the military council from the People's Commissar. It read:

On June 22 and 23 a sudden attack by the Germans is possible. The German attack can begin with provocations. Our task is not to yield to any provocations which could give rise to complications. . . .

"As you can see," Kulakov said, "we are already being bombed. This is no provocation. This is real war."

Drawing the blinds, we looked out over the balcony. Tracer bullets raced through skies, splitting the searchlights. Again and again we saw white bursts of exploding shells—anti-aircraft coastal and ship batteries were firing at the enemy.

"That was a good welcome!" Kulakov said. In his voice you could hear his pride in the navy.

The phone conversation of the fleet commander drew our attention. With unusual sharpness Oktiabr'skii was saying:

"Yes, yes, we are being bombed—"

A strong explosion rattled the windowpanes.

"There, a bomb fell just now, not far from headquarters," Oktiabr'skii went on excitedly.

We looked at one another.

"Moscow does not believe that Sevastopol' is being bombed," Kulakov said quietly.

I. I. Azarov, *Osazhdennaia Odessa* (Moscow, 1962), pp. 16–17.

M. I. Gallai
A *View* *from Below*

AND HERE it was—war!

There is no need to describe the way it was received by my comrades and myself or the thoughts and feelings it evoked. In all probability, they were identical to those of all our fellow citizens. I have never seen such a precise correspondence of thoughts and strivings as during the war years. Misery brings people together, and here we were confronted by a major disaster which threatened not only individuals or more or less large groups of people but the entire nation. . . . Somehow we had to digest the numerous surprises brought about by the war in order to maintain our emotional balance.

And the war brought a far greater number of surprises than we should have liked!

I shall not speak of the generally known surprises—with or without quotation marks—beginning with the very circumstances in which the war fell upon us. . . . For many years we had all expected war *in a general way*, but very few among us (including, unfortunately, persons occupying the highest posts in the army and the nation) were prepared for it *in a specific way*. The youth of our generation had been reminded of the danger of an attack against the USSR for so long and with such regularity—regardless of the degree to which the danger was real at any particular moment—that it had gradually become used to it and, therefore, no longer responded emotionally. It turned out that repetition is not always the mother of learning. And talk of the future war, despite all its objective foundation, came to be considered not as evidence of real danger but rather as an ordinary and in itself not especially troublesome background of our everyday lives. Even the most meaningful words lose their significance when used to excess, as we subsequently learned on numerous occasions.

M. I. Gallai, "Pervyi boi my vyigrali," *Novyi mir*, 1966, No. 9, pp. 9–11.

In addition to this, as we know, at the moment when the threat of war was greatest—when the Hitlerite armies were already in attack positions for their invasion of the USSR—it was almost as though we were reassured on purpose. We were told: Don't worry, everything's all right. Germany is strictly observing [the terms of the nonaggression pact]—I doubt that anyone of our generation has forgotten the sadly memorable TASS communiqué published exactly a week before June 22!

Yes, the war descended upon most of us as a complete surprise. It started with this great surprise, and the subsequent surprises—almost all of them bad—followed one after another.

It was well known that the Germans possessed powerful bomber aviation and that it was their practice actively to bomb important centers in their enemies' interior. Two years of war in Europe, beginning with the long and difficult air battle for Britain, which inflicted heavy losses on both sides, attested to this with utter certainty.

But the thought that the Hitlerites would, of course, attempt to bomb Moscow in the event of war did not enter the heads of persons whose immediate duty it was to think about it. At any rate, the sole air force formation assigned to defend Moscow—the 6th Air Corps—was literally created in days or, more accurately, hours before the start of the war. The order appointing Colonel (at the time of writing, Major General of the Air Force) I. D. Klimov commander of the corps was dated June 21, 1941. Prior to this the existing fighter aviation of Moscow's anti-aircraft defense was composed of separate, uncoordinated regiments and divisions. Klimov and his closest aides . . . had to create virtually from scratch a unified air defense system controlled from a single center, while simultaneously carrying out combat missions.

It turned out—and this was one of the series of surprises—that units of the 6th Air Corps were equipped for the most part with obsolete airplanes—the same I-16's and Chaikas that had performed brilliantly in Spain and satisfactorily at Khalkhin. Now, however, at the onset of a major war, they had clearly to be replaced. And they were being replaced—the re-equipping of our air force had already begun . . . but, unfortunately, it had only just begun.

In those days there was a vexingly large number of things that we had *almost* managed to do—at least in aviation. I do not know which is sadder—omission, pure and simple, the carelessness which was suddenly revealed to everyone at the start of the war, or correct decisions, the implementation of which had already begun—but was not completed in time!

If one thinks about it, there is really nothing extraordinary in the very fact of cyclical fluctuations in the level of combat matériel. It is quite normal that, after having replaced obsolete airplanes, tanks, and guns with new ones, any country will reap the fruits of this replacement for a certain time—it will possess the most up-to-date technical matériel for its army. But it is impossible to undertake such replacements very frequently: even the wealthiest power does not have the resources for that. As a result, after a certain period of time, excellent equipment becomes only good and, subsequently, merely satisfactory. Of course, the periods of peaks and dips in this complex periodic curve do not coincide in different countries. And it must be said that in attacking us, the Hitlerites in addition to everything else, naturally considered the fact that with respect to the quality of combat matériel, our army (and in particular, our air force) had scarcely emerged from the latest low point [in the curve] and was just beginning to rise.

This was felt everywhere. It was also felt in the fighter aviation units of the Moscow anti-aircraft defense zone. There were still very few new airplanes; a few regiments had received them, but even in those that had, by no means all pilots had mastered even daylight flying in these machines, let alone the considerably more complex night flying. And, *inter alia*, it was precisely at night that enemy raids could be anticipated. This, too, had been self-evident but apparently—like many other things—only *in a general way*.

CHAPTER THREE

Moscow

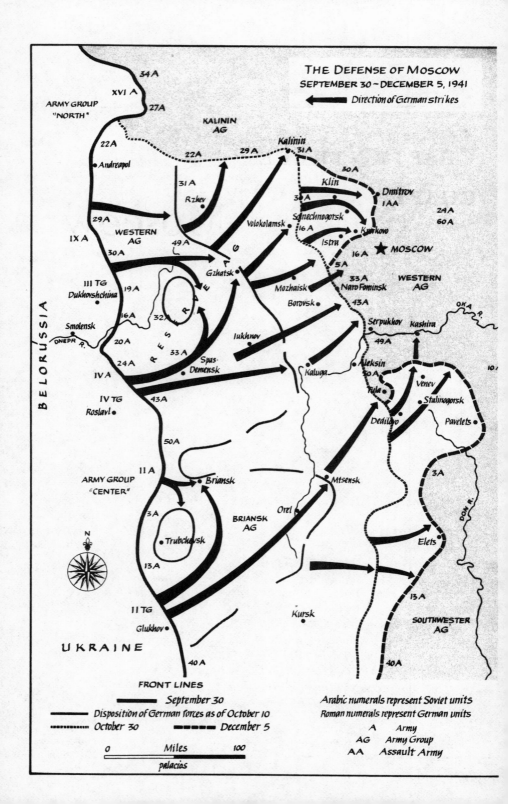

THE DEFENSE OF MOSCOW
SEPTEMBER 30 – DECEMBER 5, 1941

← Direction of German strikes

ARMY GROUP "NORTH"

34 A
XVI A
27 A

22 A
Andreapol

KALININ AG

22 A   29 A   Kalinin   31 A
30 A   Klin   Dmitrov
1 AA   24 A   60 A

31 A
Rzhev

29 A
IX A
WESTERN AG
30 A   49 A
Volokolamsk   Solnechnogorsk   16 A   Kryukovo
16 A   Istra   16 A   ★ MOSCOW

III TG
Dukhovshchina
19 A
16 A   32 A   Gzhatsk   5 A
Mozhaisk   33 A   Naro Fominsk   WESTERN AG
Borovsk   43 A

Smolensk
DNEPR R.
20 A
24 A
IV A
33 A   Iukhnov
Spas-Demensk

IV TG   43 A
Roslavl

50 A

11 A
ARMY GROUP "CENTER"   Briansk

3 A
Trubchevsk
13 A

11 TG
Glukhov

UKRAINE

40 A

BELORUSSIA

R E S E R V E

Kaluga   Aleksin   50 A   Tula   Dedilovo   Venev   Stalinogorsk   Pavelets
Serpukhov   49 A   Kashira   OKA R.
33 A   43 A
101

Mtsensk
Orel
BRIANSK AG

Kursk

Elets
3 A
DON R.
13 A
SOUTHWESTER AG
40 A

N

FRONT LINES

――――― September 30
――――― Disposition of German forces as of October 10
············· October 30   ▬▬▬▬▬ December 5

0   Miles   100
palacios

Arabic numerals represent Soviet units
Roman numerals represent German units

A   Army
AG   Army Group
AA   Assault Army

INTRODUCTION

MILITARY HISTORIANS do not always agree which of the major battles in the Soviet-German theater of operations during the period between the German attack in June 1941 and the Soviet summer offensive of 1943 (the start of the final expulsion of the German army from Soviet territory) should be considered the decisive battle, the turning point in the struggle of the two gigantic war machines. The three battles that are most commonly mentioned in this regard are the Battle of Moscow, in the fall and winter of 1941; the Battle of Stalingrad, in the fall and winter of 1942; and the Battle of Kursk-Orel, in the summer of 1943. Each of these gigantic battles was in its own way a turning point in the Soviet-German war, and each had in its own way an extremely important influence on the outcome of the war. The division of opinion among military historians hinges less on an analysis of the battles themselves than on each historian's opinion as to what constitutes a turning point in the course of a war. Depending on the definition of turning point, each of these three battles may qualify for such a distinction.

Stalingrad symbolized the high-water mark of German territorial conquest in the East. The encirclement of the German 6th Army numbering half a million men, the traumatic experience of its destruction despite all the German efforts to break the encirclement, the humiliation of the surrender of a German field marshal for the first time in German history made the Soviet victory at Stalingrad the most celebrated symbol of the beginning of the end of the invincible German army.

The Kursk-Orel battle marked the last attempt by the Germans to develop a broad-scale offensive on the Eastern Front. The greatest tank battle in military history, the Kursk-Orel encounter was at the same time the first major Soviet victory in a summer campaign. The German military-industrial machine was unable to replenish the matériel lost during this battle. From that moment on, the offensive initiative passed completely and irrevocably to the Soviet armed forces.

If territorial conquest is considered the basis for determining the turning point in the Soviet-German war, therefore, the distinction belongs to Stalingrad. If the final loss of offensive initiative is regarded as such a basis, the Kursk-Orel battle qualifies as the turning point. It seems, however, that if one considers as the basis for the turning point the breakdown of the German High Command's general strategic plan for war against the

Soviet Union, this distinction belongs rightly to the Battle of Moscow.
The prominent American military analyst, Hanson Baldwin, has characterized the over-all significance of the battle for Moscow as follows:

> The military turning point of the Eastern Front—and, indeed, of the war—
> was the Battle of Moscow (and prior to that the Battle of Britain), and the
> operations immediately preceding and following the Battle of Moscow. For
> Germany's attempt to achieve a rapid victory over Russia failed at the gates of
> Moscow, and a war of *blitzkrieg,* which Hitler might well have won, turned into
> a war of attrition, which he could not possibly win.°

It is interesting to note that all three key Soviet victories in the first
half of the Soviet-German war started with a German offensive and ended
with a Soviet counteroffensive which was mounted almost immediately
after the German attack had bogged down. This sudden and dramatic
turning of the tables was nowhere more pronounced than in the battle
for Moscow, and in no other case did Soviet fortunes shift more miraculously from near disaster to victory.

After the shock of German superiority in the first months of war had
subsided somewhat, the Soviet High Command expected to be able to
stabilize the front and to gain time to utilize its enormous human and
natural resources for a buildup of its armed forces through the introduction into battle of reserves which would make the enemy pay dearly for
his territorial gains. It was the classic strategy of trading blood and space
for time. By the end of September 1941, however, with the start of the
German assault in the central sector, known as Operation Typhoon, the
Soviet leadership came to realize that its territorial losses were approaching the critical point where failure to stabilize the front would jeopardize
Moscow itself. When what developed as the battle of Moscow had already
begun, the Soviet High Command found itself with poorly prepared defense lines on both the far and immediate approaches to the capital. It
had been misguided by earlier hopes of stopping the enemy and by the
refusal to believe that Hitler would launch an offensive so close to the
winter season. Despite the desperate efforts of the Soviet High Command
to bring up reserves to the Moscow sector and despite the frantic orders
to the defending troops that any further retreat would be tantamount to
treason, some forward German units were as close as 5 to 20 miles
from the city limits of Moscow by the end of the German assault.
The fall of the Soviet capital seemed imminent. Informed Western observers in Moscow at that time expressed an almost unanimous opinion
that the Soviet capital as well as the 1941 campaign, if not the war, was
lost beyond rescue.

°Hanson Baldwin, *Battles Lost and Won* (New York: Harper and Row, 1966), p. 443.

That doubts about the possibility of stopping the Germans—not to speak of launching a counteroffensive—were shared not only by Westerners but also by Soviet leaders may be seen clearly from the conversation with Stalin recounted by Marshal Zhukov in his memoirs (p. 291). But the strength of the German assault was exhausted at the moment it was closest to reaching its goal. On December 5, 1941, the Red Army started its counterblow. Within one month, under the onslaught of newly arrived Soviet reserves, the German lines were pushed back from 100 to 200 miles west of Moscow. The German army had suffered its first major defeat in land warfare since the beginning of the war in September 1939.

On the Soviet side, the battle for Moscow was fought primarily by three Army Groups (Briansk [later Southwestern], Kalinin, and Western). At the outset of the battle over 40 percent of all Soviet ground forces deployed on the 2,000-mile front from the polar region to the Black Sea, over 35 percent of all tanks and airplanes, and over 40 percent of all artillery were concentrated in this sector. Hitler's attacking Army Group Center included about 38 percent of all German infantry and 64 percent of all tank and motorized forces deployed on the Eastern Front. The importance of the Moscow battle for the Soviet side went far beyond its immediate military significance. In the eyes of the Russians as well as of the whole world, enemies as well as allies, Moscow was the symbol of the centralized Soviet state and of the authority of its leader, Stalin; the psychological repercussions of its fall might have led to a fatal weakening of the entire Soviet war effort.

Why the Germans failed to capture Moscow and why they suffered a painful defeat at the hands of an enemy which they had beaten in battle after battle for over five months is a question open to various interpretations. These interpretations differ less in their enumeration of the factors contributing to the outcome of the battle for Moscow than in the assignment of different weights to particular key factors. And here the differences between the prevailing Soviet and German interpretations are considerable.

In German explanations of the reasons for their defeat at Moscow, Hitler's major strategic errors in planning the whole Russian campaign are usually stressed as the decisive factor. Particular weight is given to Hitler's decision of July 1941 to change the immediate strategic objective of the campaign from the decisive defeat of the main concentration of Russian armies in front of Moscow and the capture of the Soviet capital to the conquest of the rich agricultural and industrial region of the Ukraine and the destruction of a large Soviet troop concentration around Kiev.

On July 16 Field Marshal von Bock's Army Group Center reached Smolensk, 200 miles west of Moscow, and there it halted for over two months, weakened by transfer of several infantry divisions to Army Groups South and North and denied its offensive fist with the removal of Guderian's Panzer Group. Only in September was the decision to capture Moscow restated by Hitler; German troops gradually returned to the central sector; and on September 30, dangerously close to the autumn rains and winter frost, Operation Typhoon was launched.

This fateful decision led inevitably to what most German interpretations consider the second major reason for their defeat—the Russian mud and the hard winter that followed. These two factors—Hitler's strategic errors, in which he stubbornly persisted despite advice to the contrary from his generals, and the Russian General Frost—are credited by German accounts with a lion's share of responsibility for their defeat.

Not surprisingly, the Soviet interpretation views the Moscow victory somewhat differently. The official Soviet history of World War II does not even acknowledge that the July–September pause in the German drive in the central sector resulted from a change in Hitler's strategic priorities and led to the subsequent weakening of Army Group Center.

> In the summer of 1941 the Red Army broke up the first German attempt to break through to Moscow. As a result the Soviet people won precious time for a more thorough organization of the defense of Moscow and fortification of its approaches.
>
> The failure of the adventurous scheme to force the way to Moscow from the march brought the Hitlerites to their senses somewhat. In any case, they understood that a new offensive against Moscow required considerable forces and careful preparation. That is why the German High Command ordered Army Group Center in the western sector to revert to the defensive and began a detailed elaboration of the operational plan for capturing Moscow. This operation received the bombastic code name Typhoon. For its preparation the German command required about one month.*

In the military memoirs about the battle of Moscow, scant notice is taken of this aspect of German strategic plans. Marshal Zhukov disputes the German generals' charge that Hitler made the fatal mistake of delaying Army Group Center's assault:

> As far as the decision to halt the offensive on Moscow temporarily and to redirect a part of the forces to the Ukraine is concerned, one may say that by not carrying out the Ukrainian operation, the situation of the central grouping of the German troops might have been worse. One has to consider that the reserves of Soviet Supreme Headquarters, which during September were utilized

*Istoriia Velikoi Otechestvennoi voiny Sovetskogo Soiuza, 1941–1945 (Moscow, 1963), II, p. 233.

to fill up the operational gaps in the southwestern sector, could have been used for a strike against the flanks and the rear of Army Group Center during its offensive against Moscow.*

German explanations which denounce the harsh Russian weather conditions fare no better in Soviet military memoirs. The "weather argument," however, is confronted head on. With considerable justification, Soviet generals place the blame where it belongs—not on the winter itself, but on the overconfident Nazi military leaders' bad planning and ill-preparation for combat in winter conditions.

The picture which emerges from Soviet memoirs on the Moscow battle is that of the doggedness of Red Army troops and of the Soviet High Command's harsh determination to defend Moscow at any price. It was this determination that made it possible to utilize in the crucial winter of 1941 the superior Soviet potential of manpower and resources and to throw it on the scale of the Moscow battle. It is also a picture of the strength and tenacity of the command of the Moscow sector, and especially of Marshal Zhukov, which prevented the deployment of strategic reserves piecemeal during the critical moments of defensive fighting and thus made possible a strategic counteroffensive. One of the major actors of the Moscow battle, Marshal Rokossovskii, characterizes as follows this important factor in the Soviet victory near Moscow, a factor which differed so radically from "normal" Soviet military behavior during the first months of the war (and which, incidentally, was absent in the Soviet offensive of January–March 1942):

Notwithstanding all the enemy's efforts, he was unable to break the front of our defense. We all understood that the enemy was approaching the point of exhaustion, that we had to hold out for a little longer, and that we were obliged to hold out. By decision of Supreme Headquarters, reserves were moving toward Moscow and the endangered districts. The command of the Western Army Group also did everything possible to reinforce to some extent at least the weakened units, but at the same time to preserve intact for the decisive moment the strategic reserves which were arriving. This required a sense of rigid timing and extraordinary self-restraint.†

In Soviet accounts of the battle its two principal actors emerge in bold relief: Stalin, whose power of decision affects not only all major questions of strategy but such minor matters as the distribution of a few dozen machine guns to front line units; and Zhukov, who assumes greater power than any of Stalin's generals before (or after). The interaction and clash of these two personalities form the compelling leitmotif of a battle in which nearly three million soldiers engaged in mortal combat, the outcome of which might have changed world history.

*Proval gitlerovskogo nastupleniia na Moskvu (Moscow, 1966), p. 41.
†Voenno-istoricheskii zhurnal, 1966, No. 12, p. 57.

PART I THE DEFENSE

Introduction

DURING THE MONTHS of October and November Soviet troops fought a desperate defensive battle on the approaches to Moscow. The epic story of these months as told in the memoirs of Soviet military leaders begins with a short account by Marshal I. S. Konev, who commanded the central grouping of Soviet forces covering Moscow when the German assault started. In his account of the situation during the last days before the battle began, he evinces an unmistakable desire to answer such critics as Marshal Zhukov who censure the Army Group command for its inability to withstand the enemy's initial onslaught.

The author of the second account, Lieutenant General K. F. Telegin, a political commissar in the Red Army, was appointed in July 1941 head of the Political Administration of the Moscow Military District and a member of the military council of the Moscow District and later of the Moscow Defense Zone. Telegin's vivid eyewitness version of the incredulous reaction to the unexpected breakthrough of German tanks at the start of the Nazi offensive in the first days of October is extremely interesting both as an illustration of the breakdown of communications between Supreme Headquarters in Moscow and front line formations and as evidence of the gross miscalculation of Stalin despite his experience

with German capabilities during the first months of war.

The third fragment presents part one of Marshal Zhukov's own authoritative description, which appeared in the Soviet Union in the fall of 1966 on the twenty-fifth anniversary of the battle. It presents the first extensive analysis of this battle by the commander of the combined Soviet forces which defended Moscow and then routed the German armies in an unexpected counteroffensive. At the time when writing war memoirs became a respectable occupation for leading Soviet generals, Marshal Zhukov was already a "nonperson." He had been dismissed from all his posts in November 1957 and publicly disgraced as a power seeker. Only after Khrushchev's ouster in the fall of 1964 did his name reappear in print, and not until twenty-five years after the Moscow battle did his side of the story become available. Early in September 1941, owing to the rapidly deteriorating and extremely perilous situation in the Leningrad sector, Zhukov was appointed commander of the Leningrad Army Group. His memoirs begin with the early days of October when the center of gravity in the Soviet-German struggle shifted from Leningrad in the north and from the Ukraine in the south to the central sector at the very approaches to Moscow.

270

Marshal I. S. Konev
September Warnings

ON SEPTEMBER 12, 1941, I was appointed commander of the Western Army Group.[1] . . . At Army Group headquarters . . . we could not fail to notice that the enemy was preparing to resume his offensive. . . . I, as newly appointed Army Group commander, had to become thoroughly familiar with all aspects of the situation before making the correct choice on the organization of our defenses. . . . By September 23 Army Group headquarters had arrived at the firm conviction, on the basis of intelligence data, that the enemy was preparing to launch an offensive and was massing large numbers of troops against the Western and Reserve Army Groups for it. On September 25 the Army Group command reported to Stalin that enemy aviation was regrouping. . . .

On September 26 the Army Group command once again dispatched a report to the Supreme Commander in Chief and the Chief of General Staff Marshal Shaposhnikov about the enemy's preparations for an offensive.°[2] . . .

A Supreme Headquarters directive received on September 27 was the answer to our reports and requests. It ordered us to prepare for sustained defense and to take emergency measures to strengthen our defense lines.

° "To the Supreme Commander in Chief, Comrade Stalin. To the Chief of the General Staff, Comrade Shaposhnikov. September 26, 1941, 3:30 p.m. Data from various intelligence sources and the interrogation of a captured fighter pilot, a first sergeant, have provided us with the following information:

"1. The enemy is continuously bringing up reserves from the rear on the Minsk-Smolensk-Kardymovo railroad and the Minsk-Smolensk-Iartsevo-Bobruisk-Roslavl' highway.

"2. The enemy is creating the following groupings: against the Western Army Group, opposite the 19th, 16th, and 20th field armies in the Dukhovshchina, Iartsevo, Solov'evskaia crossing, Kardymovo railroad station, and Smolensk area, and facing the Reserve Army Group in the Roslavl' area, in the direction of Spas-Demensk.

"3. According to evidence of the captured flier, the enemy is preparing an offensive against Moscow. The main grouping will follow the Viaz'ma-Moscow highway. The enemy has already brought up as many as 1,000 tanks, some 500 of which are in the Smolensk

I. S. Konev, "Nachalo Moskovskoi bitvy," *Voenno-istoricheskii zhurnal*, 1966, No. 10, pp. 56–58.

The directive was obviously late, yet it confirmed the measures already begun by the Army Group for the purpose of strengthening its defenses. ... The Army Group command submitted daily reports to Supreme Headquarters on preparations made by the enemy for its offensive, on the measures we had taken, and on our plans for defensive operations. ...

On September 28 the Army Group command also submitted its considerations to Marshal Shaposhnikov. Our requests to Supreme Headquarters were quite modest, despite the fact that circumstances were becoming quite complex and that, according to all available information, we had reason to believe that the enemy grouping which was preparing to attack was quite strong. We realized, however, that at this time Supreme Headquarters did not have the necessary reserves. Therefore, essentially, the Army Group received no reinforcements whatsoever.

Lieutenant General K. F. Telegin
German
Breakthrough

THE DIFFICULT MONTH of September was coming to an end. ... The Party and Supreme Headquarters continued to strengthen the three Army Groups covering Moscow with manpower and matériel, allowing us to hope that the enemy would advance no farther. Our mood of hope was also supported by the fact that in September the 1st Moscow Motorized Infantry Guards Division and the 312th Infantry Division had left Mo-

K. F. Telegin, "Moskva—frontovoi gorod," *Voprosy istorii KPSS*, 1966, No. 9, pp. 101–104.

and Pochinki area. According to the deposition of the captured flier, up to 100 divisions from all arms will be brought up by the enemy for this offensive.

"4. The offensive will be launched on October 1. Keitel and Goering, who are expected in Smolensk any day now, will be in charge of the Moscow operation. The air power necessary for this operation is being brought here from Leningrad and Kiev. Troops are being transferred from Germany and from Kiev (deposition of captured flier).

"5. Our front reserves are lined up in the Iartsevo-Viaz'ma direction, the Dorogobuzh railroad station area and north of it. We are building antitank defenses. Army Group reserves are limited: four rifle divisions and three tank brigades only. Request information on whether the front will be given additional reserves, in what number and when.

"Konev, Lestev, Sokolovskii."

zhaisk for the Southwestern Army Group and Volkhov; the 32nd Far Eastern and 316th Central Asian divisions, which had been assigned to defend Moscow, had been sent to Volkhov[3] as well. Moscow lived tensely on a war footing but faced the future calmly and confidently thanks to the reliable shield which protected it on the west.

In the second half of September, however, intelligence reports and operational briefings of the General Staff began to note with persistence the regrouping of enemy forces in the central sector of the Soviet-German front, the advancement of reserves from the rear, and the intensive massing of tanks and artillery. Increased flights over key industrial installations east of Moscow as well as over Moscow itself, and increased air strikes against railroad stations and junctions alerted us and forced us to plan for any unexpected contingency with which a treacherous enemy might confront us. The bitter experience of the past war months had already taught us a great deal. . . .

In an effort to forestall any eventuality, the air force was ordered to fly daily reconnaissance missions east of the Reserve Army Group's lines of deployment and to report any significant troop movements to the military council. Furthermore, all aerial observation posts behind the Mozhaisk defense line were ordered to report immediately any changes in the situation in their area.[4]

The first alarm concerning the start of the German offensive against the forces of the Briansk Army Group was received on the night of September 30. On October 2 the district commander went to Tula to organize the defense lines and to put the reserve brigade and the garrison units in a state of readiness. On October 3 the enemy burst into Orel. Encircled units of the Briansk Army Group were engaged in heavy combat; Tula was seriously threatened. . . .[5]

Until October 5 the full attention of the Party Central Committee, the Supreme Command, and the [Moscow] district military council was focused on the drastically deteriorating situation at Tula. On October 4 Political Administration personnel provided us with a translation of Hitler's radio speech. The Fuehrer declared that the "final decisive offensive" had begun on the Eastern Front and that the Red Army "was beaten and would never again regain its strength."[6] It was not clear which "decisive offensive" and "defeat" of the Red Army Hitler was speaking about. The General Staff was receiving no such reports from the Western and Reserve Army Groups, while the offensive in the sector of the Briansk Army Group was somehow not deemed serious yet, even though it was very dangerous. Nevertheless, the night of October 5 passed in a state of great concern. Telephone communications with the Western Army Group had been broken, and our liaison officer could report nothing.

At about 9:00 a.m., the commanding officer of the Maloiaroslavets fortified region[7] reported that he was holding some soldiers of the Reserve Army Group's rear services. On October 2, according to them, the enemy had broken through the defenses of the 43rd and 24th Armies, parts of which had been surrounded and were engaged in heavy fighting. Since the General Staff could not confirm this, it was believed that these soldiers were spreading panic. Yet before noon fliers of the 120th Fighter Regiment on a reconnaissance mission reported a column of enemy tanks and motorized infantry some 25 km. long moving along the highway from Spas-Demensk toward Iukhnov.[8] They said that they had not seen any of our troops in front of it.

The news was hard to believe but impossible to ignore. The general situation at the front as well as Hitler's worldwide radio broadcast called for extreme circumspection. Doubt could only be dispelled by the General Staff through the use of its vast and varied communication links with the Army Groups. I used my "kremlin" telephone to reach Marshal B. M. Shaposhnikov. The general on duty said that as yet there were no changes reported in the Western Army Group sector. I reached B. M. Shaposhnikov, and he said the same thing. I then called Colonel N. A. Sbytov, air force commander of the military district, and told him that our fliers had apparently erred. I requested a second flight immediately in order to try to identify the column from the lowest possible altitude. Sbytov's assurances that the fliers were reliable and trustworthy made it necessary to alert the military schools and to bring the garrison units, the anti-aircraft crews west of Moscow, and all available air force units to a state of combat readiness. There were no field troops in or near Moscow, and only rear units, military schools and academies were available to block the enemy advance.

The second group of aircraft returned from its reconnaissance mission. The commanding officer of the 120th Air Force Fighter Regiment reported by telephone that the enemy was indeed advancing on Iukhnov, that his planes had been fired upon by anti-aircraft guns, and that there had been some hits. It was necessary to inform the General Staff. Still there remained a hope that the fliers had somehow been deceived and that perhaps one of our own units had fired on them in the belief that they were enemy reconnaissance, since the enemy had frequently utilized captured Soviet aircraft. Moreover, it seemed impossible that the General Staff could be unaware of such a deep enemy penetration beyond our lines—almost 100–120 km.—and I was hesitant to sound the alarm. We decided to report the situation to the General Staff once again. The same procedure was followed and the same response came back: no alarming news had been received from the Western or the Reserve Army Groups.

The entire affair was peculiar. Sbytov was most agitated, insisting that his fliers had not been mistaken but had reported the bitter truth. I believed him but could not conceive of how the General Staff could be unaware of the situation. We decided to send out our best pilots on a third mission. They were under orders to fly as low as necessary, even at the risk of their lives, and to identify exactly what kind of column was moving toward Iukhnov.

Owing to the tense situation, the assistant commanding officer of the military district in charge of higher military schools, Brigade Commander Eliseev, left immediately for Podol'sk to prepare the infantry and artillery schools for combat as soon as possible and to deploy the students along the perimeter of the Maloiaroslavets fortified area with orders to stop the enemy at all costs. Orders declaring a state of combat alert were also issued to the Military School named after the Supreme Soviet of the RSFSR, the Lenin Military-Political School, the Lenin Military-Political Academy, and units of the 33rd Reserve Infantry Brigade in encampments around Moscow.

Squadron commander S. A. Pestov and combat fliers Druzhkov and Serov made the third flight. They fully confirmed the previous data. They reported that enemy tanks had entered Iukhnov. There was no further room for doubt. All the same, however, Marshal Shaposhnikov was once again asked about the situation of the Western Army Group. When Boris Mikhailovich expressed displeasure at having been disturbed repeatedly for the last two and a half hours, he had to be told of the fliers' report.

At first the news was received with puzzlement and mistrust.[9] We had to insist that the information had been checked and rechecked and that the fliers' reports could not be doubted. Then the conversation ended abruptly. Two or three minutes later Stalin called back. He asked about the source of the information and its reliability. After listening to the answer and a brief report on steps taken by the district, Stalin said: "Very well. Act decisively and energetically. The district military council is ordered to mobilize every available resource to hold the enemy at the Mozhaisk line at all costs for five to seven days until we can bring up the Supreme Headquarters reserves. Every development in that area must be reported to me directly or through Shaposhnikov. Locate Artem'ev[10] and tell him to return to Moscow immediately."

Following Stalin, other members of the State Defense Committee and officials of the People's Commissariat of Defense began to call, as did Beria, People's Commissar of Internal Affairs. His reaction was quite different. Beria stated categorically that this was a provocation. Our people at the front, he said, meaning the NKVD officials and officers of the special sections, had always informed the center promptly about the situation, but they had reported nothing about this German breakthrough. We repeated to him that the information left no room for doubt and that the district command accepted the fliers' reports completely. "Very well," was his only answer.

I paid little attention to his tone of voice then and only felt its import two hours later, when N. A. Sbytov literally hurled himself into my office. He was pale and trembling. Something unusual had affected this energetic and strong-willed man. What had happened was that following Beria's telephone call, Sbytov was ordered to report immediately at the NKVD to Chief of Army Counterintelligence Abakumov, who proceeded to abuse him and to accuse him of spreading panic.[11] He threatened Sbytov and the fliers with field court-martial for cowardice, for creating panic, and for disorganizing the work of the central establishments. Hearing Sbytov out, I immediately asked the Central Committee to protect us in future from such attacks which hampered our work at such a difficult and dangerous time. We were not bothered on this score any further.[12]

Between October 6 and 12 the Podol'sk Infantry and Artillery Schools, supported by the 17th Tank Brigade, artillery, and reserve units, held back the enemy on the approaches to the Mozhaisk defense line in heroic fashion. The blood and lives of hundreds of the best sons of the people, future commanders and political officers, were sacrificed to gain those valuable five to seven days, in the course of which Supreme Headquarters brought five infantry divisions, three tank brigades, five guards mortar battalions,[13] about ten artillery regiments, and many other units up to the line, thus making it possible to reestablish the defenses of the Western Army Group and to frustrate the enemy's plan for the lightning capture of Moscow.

On October 7 General of the Army G. K. Zhukov arrived at the Mozhaisk defense lines. . . . On October 10 he was appointed commander of the Western Army Group. . . . From that moment military leadership of the defense of the distant approaches to the capital was concentrated in the hands of one man. This could not help but improve the situation.

Marshal G. K. Zhukov
Battle

EARLY IN October 1941 I was in Leningrad commanding the troops of the Leningrad Army Group. . . . Despite the fact that we were extremely busy, we naturally could not fail to be interested in the situation in other sectors of the vast Soviet-German front. As a member of Supreme Headquarters, I received information from the General Staff which allowed me to judge the seriousness of the danger hovering over the homeland. . . .

In October the enemy launched an offensive which, according to his plans, should have led to the capture of our capital. At the start of the German offensive directed toward Moscow, resistance on the far approaches to Moscow was being offered by three of our Army Groups—Western, Reserve, and Briansk. The mission of the Western Army Group, which consisted of six reinforced Armies, was to prevent an enemy breakthrough to Moscow. The Reserve Army Group established defensive positions behind the lines of the Western Army Group. Its four main Armies were designated to repulse enemy strikes in case he penetrated through the defensive deployments of the Western Army Group. The mission of the Briansk Army Group, which consisted of three Armies and one operational group,[14] was to prevent the enemy from breaking through in the direction of Briansk-Orel.

By the end of September the combat formations of the three Army Groups consisted of about 800,000 fighting men, 770 tanks, and 9,150 artillery pieces. The largest forces and the bulk of the matériel were in the Western Army Group.[15] The German Army Group Center, as we now know, consisted of over one million men, 1,700 tanks and assault guns, along with over 19,000 artillery pieces and mortars. Its operations were supported by the powerful Second Air Fleet which was commanded by Field Marshal Kesselring. In his directive of September 16 Hitler assigned

G. K. Zhukov, "Vospominaniia komanduiushchego frontom," *Bitva za Moskvu* (Moscow, 1966), pp. 55–77.

the following mission to Army Group Center: penetration of Soviet defenses; encirclement and destruction of the main forces of the Western, Reserve, and Briansk Army Groups; pursuit of the remnants of the forces; and occupation of Moscow by enveloping it from the south and north.[16]

On September 30, 1941 the enemy launched his offensive against the forces of the Briansk Army Group. On October 2 he directed heavy strikes at the forces of the Western and Reserve Army Groups. Particularly heavy blows came from zones north of Dukhovshchina and east of Roslavl'. These blows were directed at the 30th and 19th Armies of the Western Army Group and also at the 43rd Army of the Reserve Army Group. The fascist German forces succeeded in penetrating our defenses. The main attack forces of the enemy advanced rapidly and enveloped the Viaz'ma troop groupings of the Western and Reserve Army Groups.

An extremely grave situation developed on the Briansk sector as well where the 3rd and 13th Armies were threatened with encirclement. Without encountering any special resistance, part of Guderian's army headed toward Orel. The area around Orel did not contain forces which could repulse the enemy. On October 3 the enemy occupied Orel. The Briansk Army Group was now cut in two. Its forces, sustaining losses, were retreating to the east and southeast, as a result of which a threatening situation developed along the Tula axis of advance.

On orders of the commander of the Western Army Group, Colonel General I. S. Konev, the operational group of Lieutenant General I. V. Boldin mounted a counterattack against the northern enemy grouping which was executing an envelopment maneuver. The counterattack was unsuccessful, and by October 6 most of the forces of the Western Army Group and of the Reserve Army Group were encircled in an area west of Viaz'ma.

On the evening of October 6, Supreme Commander in Chief Stalin telephoned me to ask how matters stood in the Leningrad sector. I reported that the enemy had ceased attacking. . . . Our air reconnaissance confirmed a large movement of mechanized columns, including tanks, from the Leningrad region to the south. It was obvious that the fascist German command was transferring its troops in the direction of Moscow.

Stalin listened to the report, was silent for a moment, and then said that the situation, particularly of the Western Army Group on the Moscow front, had become very complicated.

"Leave the Chief of Staff, General Khozin, in temporary charge of the troops of the Leningrad Army Group, and you fly to Moscow," Stalin ordered.

After I transmitted the Supreme Commander in Chief's order to M. S. Khozin, I said good-bye to the members of the military council and flew to Moscow. At dusk on October 7, our plane landed at the Central Airport, and I went directly to the Kremlin.

Stalin was in his living quarters, sick with the grippe. He greeted me with a nod of the head, pointed to the map, and said:

"Here, look, a very difficult situation has arisen, but I haven't been able to obtain a detailed report on the actual state of affairs in the Western Army Group." He suggested that I leave immediately for Army Group headquarters and the troops, that I investigate the situation thoroughly and call him back at any time of the night.

"I will wait." He ended the conversation.

In fifteen minutes, I was at the office of the Chief of the General Staff to get the operations map and to familiarize myself at least generally with the situation. Marshal of the Soviet Union B. M. Shaposhnikov looked exhausted. As he greeted me, he said that he had already been called by the Supreme Commander in Chief who had ordered him to give me the map of the western sector. . . .[17]

Having told me about the difficult situation at the front, he added that the building of the defensive boundary on the Mozhaisk line of defense and on the nearest approaches to Moscow had still not been completed and that there were hardly any troops there. . . . On the night of October 7, formations and units from the reserve of Supreme Headquarters and of the neighboring Army Groups began the transfer to the Mozhaisk line. . . .[18]

After obtaining the map, I immediately left for the headquarters of the Western Army Group. On the way, with the help of a weak flashlight, I continued to study the situation and the troop movements. In order to overcome drowsiness we stopped the car periodically to take runs of 200 to 300 meters. We arrived at Army Group headquarters at night. The officer on duty reported that all the top officers were with the Army Group commander. The room in which the Army Group commander [I. S. Konev], the member of the military council [N. A. Bulganin], the chief of staff [V. D. Sokolovskii], and the chief of the operations section [G. K. Malandin] were assembled was lit by candles and was almost dark. Even in this light it was quite apparent that all those seated at the table were exhausted. I said that I had come on the instructions of the Supreme Commander in Chief to investigate the situation and to report to him by telephone.

"I talked with Comrade Stalin only a few moments ago," said Bulganin, "but I was unable to report anything specific to him, because we ourselves do not know what is going on with the troops encircled west of Viaz'ma."

What General Malandin was able to tell me in answer to my questions to some degree added detail and accuracy to my information on the events which had occurred in the period of October 2–7. . . . The defense of our Army Groups could not withstand the massed attacks. By October 7, the western sector no longer had a continuous defense line. There were large gaps in our lines, and we had nothing to fill them with, since the command had no reserves left.

At 2:30 a.m. on October 8, I called Stalin. He was still working. Having reported the situation of the Western Army Group, I said:

"The main danger now is that the routes to Moscow are virtually undefended. Weak rear detachments, positioned on the Mozhaisk line, cannot protect Moscow from a breakthrough of German armored troops. It is necessary to draw troops to the Mozhaisk line of defense as quickly as possible from wherever possible."

Stalin asked: "Where are the 16th, 19th, and 20th Armies of the Western Army Group and the 24th and the 32nd Armies of the Reserve Army Group now?"

"They are encircled west and northwest of Viaz'ma."

"What do you intend to do?"

"I will go to [Marshal] Budennyi. . . ."

"And do you know where his headquarters are now?"

"No, I do not know. I will look for him somewhere in the region of Maloiaroslavets."

"Very well, go to Budennyi, and call me from there." . . .

At daybreak on October 8 we approached the Obninskoe juncture (105 km. from Moscow). . . . In ten minutes I was in the office of Army Commissar First Rank L. Z. Mekhlis who was with the Chief of Staff of the [Reserve] Army Group, Major General A. F. Anisov. Mekhlis was harshly upbraiding someone on the telephone. Hanging up, he inquired about my presence here. I explained that I had come as a member of Supreme Headquarters on the instructions of the Supreme Commander in Chief to learn the true situation, and I asked him about the whereabouts of Budennyi. Mekhlis explained that the day before, in the afternoon, the Army Group commander had been with the 43rd Army, but his present whereabouts were unknown, and there was anxiety at headquarters that something might have happened to Semen Mikhailovich. The liaison officers who had been sent in search of him had not yet returned. Mekhlis and Anisov were not able to say anything concrete about the troop positions of the Reserve Army Group or the enemy. . . .

We had to proceed farther in the direction of Iukhnov, through Maloiaroslavets and Medyn', hoping to be able to assess the situation more quickly that way. Passing through Protva and Obninskoe, I unwittingly recalled my childhood and youth. From here my mother had sent me, then a twelve-year-old boy, to relatives in Moscow to learn the fur trade. Four years later, already a craftsman, I had traveled frequently from Moscow to my parents' village. I knew the whole countryside of Maloiaroslavets well, for in my youth I had walked far and wide over the area. Ten kilometers from Obninskoe, where the headquarters of the Reserve Army Group was currently located, stood the village of Strelkovka of the Ugodsko-Zavodskoi district. There I was born and lived during my childhood, and there my mother and sister with her four children lived even now. I could not suppress the thought: What would happen to them if the fascists came here? What if they found out that here were the mother, sister, nephews, and nieces of General Zhukov? Three days later my aide brought them from the village to my apartment in Moscow.

When we reached Maloiaroslavets, there wasn't a living soul even in its very center. The city was completely deserted. But near the building of the district soviet[19] stood two light cross-country vehicles. A driver slept at the steering wheel. When I woke him up, he said that the car belonged to Semen Mikhailovich Budennyi who had arrived here about three hours ago.

Entering the district soviet, I saw S. M. Budennyi. We exchanged warm greetings. It was obvious that he had lived through a great deal during these tragic days.[20] Having learned about my journey to Western Army Group headquarters, Budennyi explained that he himself had had no communication with Konev for more than two days. While he was in the 43rd Army, the headquarters of his own Army Group had been moved, and he did not know its new location.

I informed Semen Milhailovich that his headquarters was now 105 km. from Moscow behind the railroad bridge on the river Protva, and that he was expected there. I also told him that the situation in the Western Army Group was desperate. A large part of its forces had been surrounded.

"Our situation is no better," Budennyi replied. "The 24th and 32nd Armies have been cut off, and there is no defensive front. Yesterday I myself almost fell into the hands of the enemy between Iukhnov and Viaz'ma," he related. . . .

"Who holds Iukhnov?"

"I do not know now. Two infantry regiments and another small detachment were stationed at the river Ugra, but they had no artillery. I think that Iukhnov is in enemy hands."

"And who is protecting the road from Iukhnov to Maloiaroslavets?"

"When I was on my way here," said Semen Mikhailovich, "I saw no one except three policemen in Medyn'."

We agreed that Semen Mikhailovich would leave immediately for the Western Army Group headquarters and would report the state of affairs from there to the Supreme Command, while I was to head toward Iukhnov and then on to Kaluga. . . .

On October 9 an officer from Reserve Army Group headquarters found me and handed me a telephone message from the Chief of the General Staff, B. M. Shaposhnikov. It read: "The Supreme Commander in Chief orders you to come to Western Army Group headquarters. You have been appointed its commander." . . .

Early on the morning of October 10, I arrived in the region three to four kilometers northwest of Mozhaisk where Western Army Group headquarters was located. I found at work there a special commission of the State Defense Committee, composed of K. E. Voroshilov, G. N. Malenkov, V. M. Molotov, and others. I don't know how or what the commission reported to Moscow, but from the very fact of their sudden hurried arrival at the front and from my conversations with the members of the commission it was not difficult to conclude that the Supreme Commander in Chief was extremely worried about the very precarious situation in the vicinity of Moscow.

In the first ten days of October, the troops of our Western, Reserve, and Briansk Army Groups suffered serious reverses.[21] The command of the Army Groups had obviously made serious miscalculations. The troops of the Western Army Group and the Reserve Group had been stationed in defensive positions for nearly a month and a half, and they had had enough time to prepare for the enemy attack. The necessary measures, however, had apparently not been taken. They failed to determine correctly with the help of their own intelligence the extent of the enemy force or the direction from which it was preparing the thrust, even though they had received a warning from Supreme Headquarters of very heavy fascist German troop concentrations against them. Consequently, despite the fact that the enemy lacked the advantage of surprise for the attack against our troops, he caught them unprepared. They had not built defenses in depth, and, moreover, our backbone—the antitank defenses—were not ready in time. Neither were the Army Group reserves brought up to help offset the attack. Artillery and air force counter-preparations against enemy concentrations in their initial attack positions were not organized. And when our defenses were penetrated in the region of Viaz'ma, the command failed to organize the withdrawal of troops, which resulted in the complete encirclement of the 16th, 19th, 20th, 24th, and 32nd Armies.

[Marshal Konev explains:[22] Considerable forces of the Western and Reserve Army Groups had been encircled by the beginning of October 1941. How and under what circumstances had this occurred? What were the reasons? I should like to express, briefly, my opinion on this subject.

First of all, at that time the strategic initiative along the entire Soviet-German front belonged to the enemy. The enemy benefited from overwhelming superiority in forces and matériel, particularly in tanks and aviation, which ceaselessly bombed the retreating troops. This was made particularly clear in the report dated October 7, 1941, submitted by Commander of the 32nd Army S. V. Vishnevskii. It stated that the principal reason for failures was the incessant withering bombing of our troops by enemy aviation and our lack of anti-aircraft facilities. A similar situation existed in other Armies.

Secondly, the enemy was far superior in terms of mobility; he was able to engage in extensive maneuvering. We lacked adequate air and antitank forces to strike the enemy columns on the march and to resist their advance on the main roads.

Thirdly, the Western Army Group was inadequately supplied with weapons, ammunition, and combat matériel. Our artillery and tank density per 1 km. was quite low: tanks—1.6; guns—7; antitank artillery—1.5. At the beginning of the enemy offensive the stock of ammunition of some units and formations totaled about half of a unit of fire and, in very few units, no more than two units of fire. The Western Army Group was too spread out. The defending troops were very undermanned, and the Army Group lacked sufficiently powerful reserves in depth.

Fourthly, we could still localize a breakthrough toward Viaz'ma from the north by regrouping our troops. But the breakthrough of the fascist German forces through Spas-Demensk allowed the enemy formations to penetrate from the south deep into the rear of the Western Army Group. And the Reserve Army Group had almost no forces in that direction. . . .

. By October 10 it had become quite clear that the forces of the Western and Reserve Army Groups had to be merged into a single Group, under a single command. Gathered at the command post of the Western Army Group in Krasnovidovo, Molotov, Voroshilov, Vasilevskii, member of the military council Bulganin (Chief of Staff V. D. Sokolovskii was in Rzhev at the time), and I, after discussing the situation, reached the conclusion that the Army Groups had to be integrated without delay. We recommended that General of the Army G. K. Zhukov, Commander of the Reserve Army Group as of October 8, be appointed commander. We submitted the following suggestions to Supreme Headquarters:

"Moscow, to Comrade Stalin.

"We request Supreme Headquarters to adopt the following decision:

"1. Integrate the Western and Reserve Army Groups into the Western Army Group for purposes of unifying the command of troops west of Moscow.

"2. Appoint Comrade Zhukov Commander of the Western Army Group.

"3. Appoint Comrade Konev First Deputy Commander of the Western Army Group.

"4. Appoint Comrades Bulganin, Khokhlov, and Kruglov members of the military council of the Western Army Group.

"5. Comrade Zhukov to assume command of the Western Army Group at 6:00 p.m. on October 11.

"Molotov, Voroshilov, Konev, Bulganin, Vasilevskii.

"Received by teletype at 3:45 p.m., October 10, 1941."

Supreme Headquarters agreed to these suggestions, and its order to merge the Army Groups followed immediately.

The night of October 12 we informed Supreme Headquarters that I had relinquished command of the Western Army Group and that Zhukov had accepted it.]

During my conversation with members of the commission [on October 10], I received a message directing me to telephone the Supreme Commander in Chief. I proceeded to the communications room and called Stalin, who told me himself of his decision to appoint me commander of the Western Army Group and asked me whether I had any objections to the decision. I had no reason to object. I gathered from the ensuing conversation, however, that Stalin's intention was to replace the entire former leadership of the Western Army Group. In my opinion, this was not the best solution in the extremely complicated circumstances. Stalin agreed with my reasons for leaving I. S. Konev as my deputy commander, and he also agreed that it would be very useful to entrust to Konev, as deputy commander of the Western Army Group, leadership of the troops in the Kalinin sector.[23] These troops were too far removed from headquarters and were obviously in need of additional supervision. I was also informed that the remaining troops of the Reserve Army Group, the units on the Mozhaisk line, and the reserves of Supreme Headquarters which were moving toward the front were all to be united under my command of the Western Army Group.

"Organize the Western Army Group quickly and act!" were Stalin's parting words to me.

Having discussed the situation with I. S. Konev and V. D. Sokolovskii, we decided to move Army Group headquarters to Alabino. Konev, with . . . a group of officers, set out to coordinate the operations in the Kalinin sector; I drove out to Mozhaisk with Bulganin, member of the Army Group's military council, to see Colonel S. I. Bogdanov, the commander of the Mozhaisk Fortified Region, in order to determine the situation on the spot.

The headquarters of the Mozhaisk Fortified Region, where we arrived on the afternoon of October 10, was in the city's House of Culture. The artillery fire and the explosions of aerial bombs could be heard distinctly. Colonel Bogdanov reported that the 32nd Infantry Division, reinforced with artillery and a tank brigade, was waging a battle against the enemy's forward mechanized and tank units on the approaches to Borodino. Its commander, Colonel V. I. Polosukhin, was a highly experienced officer. Having given S. I. Bogdanov instructions to hold the line at all costs, we returned to Army Group headquarters in Alabino. Here extensive organizational and operational work was already under way. Its goal was to establish firm defenses along the line Volokolamsk-Mozhaisk-Maloiaroslavets-Kaluga as quickly as possible, to develop this defense in depth, and to create reserves for the Army Group.

The Mozhaisk line of defense had a number of clear advantages from the operational-tactical point of view. At its forward edge flowed the Lama, Moskva, Kolocha, Luzha, and Sukhodrev rivers. The high bluffs of these rivers constituted a serious obstacle for tanks. At the rear of the Mozhaisk line there was a developed system of roads and railways which provided maneuverability for troops in all directions. Here it was possible to establish a multiple-line defense system that would offer increasing resistance the deeper the enemy penetrated.

The trouble was, however, that by October 10 there were very few of our troops along the Mozhaisk line, which stretched for a distance of 220 km. . . . To cover it we had a total of 45 battalions instead of the minimum of 150 required for any successful defensive action. . . . This left the road to Moscow virtually unprotected.

Supreme Headquarters took drastic measures in order to avert the threat hanging over the capital. . . . It dispatched five newly formed machine-gun battalions, ten antitank artillery regiments,[24] and five tank brigades to this area. . . . On this defensive perimeter the retreating units of the Western and Reserve Army Groups were concentrating; they were being joined by units transferred urgently from the right wing of the Western Army Group, by units from the Northwestern Army Group, by troops from the Southwest sector, as well as by reserves from the interior of the country. . . .

By 11 o'clock on the night of October 12, in accordance with the directive of Supreme Headquarters, all troop units and components of the Moscow Reserve Army Group merged into the newly formed Western Army Group. Meanwhile, the situation grew progressively more complex. . . . By the middle of October the newly formed 5th, 16th, 43rd, and 49th Armies contained only 90,000 men. These forces were far from adequate for a continuous line of defense, so we decided to cover the main routes first of all—Volokolamsk, Istrin, Mozhaisk, Maloiaroslavets, Podol'sk-Kaluga. The basic artillery and antitank resources were also being concentrated along these approaches. . . . Extensive field-engineering work was under way to the rear of the first echelon troops in order to develop the defense in depth. Antitank obstacles were placed along all axes of advance threatened by tanks. Reserves were being pulled up to the main approaches. Army Group headquarters moved from Alabino to Perkhushkovo and was connected by telephone and telegraph to ground and air units and to the General Staff and Supreme Headquarters. Matériel and technical supplies were urgently brought in; medical and other rear-guard services were expanded. In this way a new Western Army Group, which was to repulse the attack on Moscow by the fascist German troops, was born.

. . . .

In the middle of October it was most important for us to gain time in order to prepare our defense. From this standpoint, due credit must be given to units of the 19th, 16th, 20th, 24th, and 32nd Armies and the Boldin group, encircled west of Viaz'ma, for their heroic fight. They did not lay down their arms when they found themselves in the enemy rear but continued to fight valiantly and to make attempts to break out and join up with Red Army units. . . . Thanks to their persistence and staunchness the enemy's main forces were detained in the days most critical for us. We gained precious time to organize the defense on the Mozhaisk line. The bloodshed and the sacrifices made by the encircled troops had not been in vain. . . .[25]

On October 13 our troops withdrew from Kaluga under the enemy onslaught. Fierce fighting broke out in all principal directions. The enemy threw large forces of mobile troops into battle on October 13 along all the axes of approach to Moscow. On October 15, according to Army Group intelligence, as many as 50 tanks reached the regions of Turginovo and Borovsk; 100 reached Makarovo, Karagatovo, and Lotoshino; and 40 tanks reached the region of Borodino.[26]

In view of the mounting threat to Moscow, the Central Committee of the Party and the State Defense Committee decided upon the urgent evacuation from Moscow to Kuibyshev[27] of some Central Committee and government offices and the entire diplomatic corps as well as the removal of especially important state valuables—just in case. Evacuation began on the night of October 16. The people of Moscow responded with full understanding to all the steps taken. However, as the saying goes, there are black sheep even in the best of families. There were some cowards, alarmists, and self-seekers, who bolted from Moscow in all directions, spreading panicky rumors that Moscow was going to be surrendered for certain. In order to mobilize the troops and the capital's population for resistance to the enemy and also to put a stop to the instances of panic that occurred in Moscow on October 16 and for which subversive elements were responsible, the State Defense Committee issued a decree on October 19 introducing a state of siege in Moscow and adjoining areas.

The forces holding the Volokolamsk-Mozhaisk-Maloiaroslavets-Serpukhov defense were still weak, and the enemy had already captured some places along the line. To prevent a breakthrough to Moscow the

Army Group council decided to establish the main line of defense through
Novo-Zavidovskii, Klin, the Istra Reservoir, Zhavoronki, Krasnaia Pakhra,
Serpukhov, and Aleksin. . . .[28]

Although the retreat from the Mozhaisk line had been approved by
Supreme Headquarters, we knew that troops were fighting fiercely as they
withdrew. They were doing their best to hold back the enemy as long as
possible and to gain maximum time for the deployment of formations
coming up from Supreme Headquarters reserve and for the fortification of
the rear defense line. The military council of the Western Army Group
at that time issued an appeal to the troops which said:

"Comrades! In this grim hour of danger to our state every soldier's
life belongs to the Fatherland. The Homeland demands of each one of
us. the greatest exertion, courage, heroism, and staunchness. The Homeland calls upon us to become an insurmountable wall and to bar the
path of the fascist hordes to our beloved Moscow. Now as never before
we must have vigilance, iron discipline, good organization, determined
action, inflexible will to victory, and readiness for self-sacrifice." . . .

The result of the October defense battles near Moscow is well known.
In a month of fierce and bloody battles the fascist German troops succeeded in advancing 230-250 km. all told. But the plan of the Hitlerite
command to capture Moscow was defeated; the enemy's forces were
seriously drained; his assault groups became extended. The German offensive was losing impetus with each day; it was stopped at the end of October on the line of Turginovo–Volokolamsk–Dorokhovo–Naro Fominsk–
west of Serpukhovo-Aleksin. By that time the Kalinin Army Group defense had become stabilized.° The Briansk Army Group, whose troops
had withdrawn by October 30 to the Aleksin-Tula-Efremov-Tim line,
had defeated the enemy's plans to capture Tula and blocked the approaches to Elets and Voronezh. . . .

Much has been said in postwar years about the frequent complaints
of Hitler's generals and bourgeois historians concerning the impassability
of the Russian roads, the mud, Russia's frosts. . . . Did the Hitlerite generals planning their Eastern campaign expect to roll along smooth, well-
traveled roads straight into Moscow and farther? Well, if they did, all
the worse for the fascist German troops that were stopped at the approaches
to Moscow [allegedly] by mud. In those days I saw with my own eyes

°Owing to the great extension of the Western Army Group and also the difficulties
in controlling the troops of the Army Group, Supreme Headquarters decided on October
17 to unite the 22nd, 29th, and 30th Armies under the command of the re-formed Kalinin
Army Group. Colonel General I. S. Konev was appointed commander of the Kalinin Army
Group; Corps Commissar D. S. Leonov was appointed member of the military council;
Major General I. I. Ivanov was appointed chief of staff. [Author's note.]

how thousands upon thousands of Moscow women—city dwellers who were completely unaccustomed to heavy digging—left their city apartments in light dress, dug antitank ditches and trenches, set up obstacles, built barricades and tank barriers, dragged sacks of sand through the same mud and along the same impassable roads. The mud stuck to their feet, too, and to the wheels of the wheelbarrows in which they carted the dirt. It increased immeasurably the weight of shovels which were awkward enough for women's hands as it was. I do not think there is any need to pursue the comparison. I may add for those who are inclined to use mud to camouflage the real reasons for their defeat at Moscow that in October 1941 the period of impassable roads was comparatively short.[29] At the beginning of November the temperature fell; it snowed, and the terrain and roads became passable everywhere. During the November "general offensive" of Hitler's troops the temperature in the battle area on the Moscow axis was 13°–20° Fahrenheit and at that temperature, as everyone knows, there isn't any mud.

Yet in the frost, too, Moscovites continued to work selflessly to build defense fortifications. The construction of the outer ring around Moscow within the limits of the Moscow defense zone was completed by November 25. And I knew that more than 100,000 Moscovites, mostly women, worked on it. On that line they built 1,428 artillery and machine-gun pillboxes of reinforced concrete and earth-and-timber, 165 km. of antitank ditches, 111 km. of triple-rowed barbed wire barriers, and a large quantity of other obstructions. Yet this is not the entire extent of their contribution to victory over the enemy. The selflessness of the working people in defense of their capital had a tremendous effect on the troops' morale. It multiplied the men's strength and increased their will to fight the enemy. . . .[30]

The Soviet High Command continued in the first half of November to take every precaution possible under the circumstances to thwart once and for all the anticipated new enemy offensive against Moscow. The troops of the Western Army Group continued to fortify their defense positions and regrouped frequently. By decision of Supreme Headquarters the 50th Army and the defense of Tula were transferred to the Western Army Group on November 10 at 6 p.m., and the Briansk Army Group was dissolved. This transfer extended considerably the defense line of the Army Group, while the [50th] Army was greatly weakened. However, fresh units, army equipment, arms, ammunition, communication supplies, and technical matériel kept arriving from Supreme Headquarters reserve. Short sheepskin coats, felt boots, warm underwear, quilted jackets, and hats with earmuffs arrived at the warehouses. In the middle of November our men were dressed warmly and felt much more comfortable than fascist German soldiers, who wrapped themselves in warm clothes taken from the civilian population. In those days many Hitlerite soldiers began to wear huge straw "overshoes" which severely hampered movement. Nevertheless, all data indicated that the enemy had nearly completed the regrouping of his troops; a resumption of the offensive was to be expected soon.

We concentrated the infantry and tank troop reinforcements from Supreme Headquarters reserve in the most dangerous sectors, principally in the Volokolamsk-Klin and Istra sectors, where we expected the main thrust of the enemy tank groups. . . . It should be noted that although the Western Army Group had received considerable reinforcements and by the middle of November was composed of six Armies, it did not have enough troops in depth, especially in the center, because the front line was more than 600 km. long. We tried, therefore, to use the reinforcements primarily in order to increase the security of the most threatened directions on the flanks; and, when possible, we put some in the Army Group reserve so we might use them to maneuver with if necessary. On November 13, however, an order from the Supreme Commander in Chief altered our plans considerably. Stalin telephoned.

"How is the enemy behaving?" he asked.

"He has nearly completed the preparation of his strike groups and will probably launch an offensive soon," I replied.

"Where do you expect the main thrust?"

"We expect the stronger thrust from the area of Volokolamsk and Novo-Petrovskoe in the directions of Klin and Istra. Guderian's Army will probably by-pass Tula and strike at Venev and Kashira."[31]

"Shaposhnikov and I think we should thwart the enemy's attack by counterattacking first," Stalin said. "We could launch one counterblow from the north, by-passing Volokolamsk, and another from the Serpukhov area against the flank of the Germans' 4th Army. Large forces are obviously gathering in these areas to strike against Moscow."

"What forces are we to use for counterattacks?" I asked. "We don't have any available troops in the Army Group. We have merely enough to hold the lines we are now occupying."

"Use formations of Rokossovskii's Army, the 58th Tank Division, some cavalry divisions, and Dovator's cavalry corps in the Volokolamsk area. Use Belov's cavalry corps, Getman's tank division, and part of the troops of the 49th Army in the Serpukhov area," Stalin proposed.

"We cannot do that now," I answered. "We cannot send the Army Group's last reserves into uncertain counterattacks. We won't have reinforcements for our Armies when the enemy throws his strike groups into the offensive."

"You have six Armies in your Group. Isn't that enough?"

I replied that the defense line of the Western Army Group was very extended; that with twists and turns it was now more than 600 km. long; that we had very few reserves in depth, especially in the center.

"Consider the question of the counterattacks settled. Report your plan tonight." Those were the last words I heard from Stalin on that occasion. I made another attempt to convince him that there was no point in counterattacking with the only reserves we had. This time I argued that the terrain was unsuitable north of Volokolamsk. But I heard the receiver click.

This conversation made a very painful impression on me—not, of course, because the Commander in Chief had not taken my opinion into account, but because Moscow, which the men had vowed to defend to the last drop of blood, was in mortal danger, and now we had been ordered to throw our last reserves into extremely dubious counterattacks. If we expended them, we would not be able to reinforce the weak sectors of the defense.

About fifteen minutes later Bulganin came to me. It turned out that immediately after the Supreme Commander in Chief had talked with me, he telephoned Bulganin and said: "You and Zhukov there have been giving yourselves airs. But we'll find a way to deal with you." Stalin demanded that the military council member and the Army Group commander organize the counterattacks at once.

Within two hours Army Group headquarters had issued the order for counterattacks to the commanders of the 16th and 49th Armies and of other formations; Supreme Headquarters was informed. The counterattacks took place, but immediately afterward, on November 15, the fascist German command renewed its offensive against Moscow. . . .[32]

As is known, northwest of Moscow the enemy struck simultaneously at the left flank of the Kalinin Army Group's 39th Army, which had very weak defenses south of the Moscow Sea, and at the right flank and center of the Western Army Group's 16th Army. The enemy sent more than 300 tanks against these Armies, while our combat formations here had only 56 tanks, and light ones at that.

On the morning of November 16, having pierced the 30th Army's defense line, the enemy swiftly developed the attack in the general direction of Klin. We had no reserves in this section. That same day the enemy struck a powerful blow in the Istra direction from the Volokolamsk area. He sent in 400 medium and heavy tanks, while our troops had barely 150 light and medium tanks.

On November 17 at 11:00 p.m. Supreme Headquarters transferred the 30th Army from the Kalinin Army Group to ours. As a result, the Western Army Group's defense line was extended even farther northward, right up to the Moscow Sea.[33] After a fierce battle the enemy captured Klin toward the end of the day on November 23 and headed for the Dmitrovo area; some of the tanks turned toward Solnechnogorsk. On November 25 the 16th Army withdrew from Solnechnogorsk. The Army Group military council sent there to General K. K. Rokossovskii everything it could spare from other sectors, including platoon-size units and groups of soldiers with antitank rifles, tanks, artillery batteries, and antiaircraft artillery batteries taken from Moscow's Anti-aircraft Defense Command. The situation was becoming critical. Our defense line bent; at points it became very weak. The irremediable seemed about to happen. But no! Soviet soldiers fought with tremendous courage and held out until the arrival in the Solnechnogorsk area of the 7th Division from the Serpukhov area, two tank brigades, and two artillery antitank regiments from Supreme Headquarters reserves.[34] When reinforcements arrived, our troops again formed an insuperable defense front. In early December it became evident from the nature of the action and the force of the fascist German attacks that the enemy was becoming exhausted and no longer had the strength or the means to conduct serious offensive operations in this direction. . . .

Despite losses the enemy stopped for nothing; his tank wedges tried to break through to Moscow at any cost. But our deeply echeloned artillery and antitank defense withstood the savage onslaught thanks to well-organized interaction among formations and units of all branches and services of our armed forces. The Hitlerites covered the battlefield with many thousands of dead, but they did not succeed in breaking through to Moscow at any point. In the course of the battle Soviet troops would withdraw in good order to previously prepared positions held by the artillery and would continue to fight stubbornly, repulsing the furious attacks.

The State Defense Committee, part of the leadership of the Central Committee, and the Council of People's Commissars continued to work in Moscow. The working people labored indefatigably twelve to eighteen hours a day, providing the defending troops with arms, equipment, ammunition, and other materiel. . . .

I don't remember the exact date that Stalin telephoned, but it was soon after the Germans' greatest tactical breakthrough in the sector of the 30th Army and on the right flank of General Rokossovskii's Army—November 19, I think. He asked:

"Are you certain we can hold Moscow? I ask you this with pain in my heart. Speak the truth, like a communist."

"We'll hold Moscow without doubt. But we've got to have at least two more Armies and no fewer than 200 tanks."

"It's encouraging that you are so certain," Stalin said. "Call up

Shaposhnikov and arrange with him where to concentrate the two reserve Armies that you request. They'll be ready by the end of November, but for the time being we don't have any tanks."

Half an hour later Boris Mikhailovich [Shaposhnikov] and I arranged that the 1st Assault Army, which was being formed, would be concentrated in the Iakhroma area and the 10th in the Riazan' area.

By December 5 the fascist German troops were exhausted, and in the face of attacks by our troops began reverting to defensive positions in all sectors of the Western Army Group. In effect, this signified the collapse of Hitler's plan for a "blitzkrieg." Failure to complete any of the strategic operations on the Soviet-German front [35] had an adverse effect on the morale of the fascist German troops and sowed the first seeds of doubt about the successful outcome of the war. The fascist military-political leadership was compromised in the eyes of world public opinion. . . .

I have been asked many times since the end of the war how it was that Soviet troops managed to withstand the onslaught of the extremely strong fascist German groupings against Moscow. Much has been written about the course of the battle for Moscow, and most of it is correct. As the former commander of the Western Army Group, however, I should like to give my opinion.

In planning a large-scale, complex strategic operation like Typhoon, Hitler's High Command seriously underestimated the strength, condition, and potential of the Soviet Army in the struggle for Moscow and greatly overestimated the potential of the troops it had concentrated for the purpose of piercing our defense line and capturing the capital of the Soviet Union.

Serious miscalculations were also made in the formation of assault groups in connection with the second stage of Operation Typhoon. The flank assault groups of the enemy, especially those operating in the Tula area, were weak; they did not have a sufficient number of combined arms formations. Experience demonstrated the error of exclusive reliance upon armored formations in the given conditions. The tank units were exhausted; they suffered heavy losses and spent their breakthrough capacity.

The German command did not succeed in organizing a timely attack aimed at pinning down the center of our front, although it had sufficient forces to do so. In the absence of such an attack we were able freely to shift our reserves—including the divisional reserves—from the central sectors to the flanks where they opposed the enemy assault groups. Great losses, unpreparedness for combat in winter conditions, and the fierceness of Soviet resistance affected the enemy's combat capacity.

By November 15 our reconnaissance had succeeded in discovering concentrations of enemy assault groups on the flanks of our defense line and had correctly predicted the direction of the main thrusts. A deep echeloned defense with comparatively good antitank and engineering support was counterposed in good time to the enemy's assault groups. All the main tank units were also concentrated here. Our soldiers had a deep sense of personal responsibility for the fate of Moscow, for the fate of the Homeland; they were resolved to die rather than let the enemy pass.

An important role was played by the well-known State Defense Committee decree of October 19 which introduced a state of siege in Moscow and adjoining districts and proclaimed a vigorous struggle for the strictest discipline and establishment of proper order among the troops defending Moscow.

We sharply improved control over the troops at all command and staff levels, a factor which contributed to the efficient fulfillment of their combat objectives.

The Operations Office of the General Staff and the Deputy Chief of the General Staff, Lieutenant General A. M. Vasilevskii, worked hard and well to organize the defensive actions of the troops of the Western strategic sector. General Vasilevskii's correct evaluation of the situation in the Western sector in the period October 2–9 and his concrete proposals formed the basis of the measures adopted by Supreme Headquarters. Day and night the indefatigable officers of the General Staff . . . watched the enemy's every move and made creative suggestions of ways to eliminate dangerous situations.

The enemy did not succeed in piercing our defense line; he did not succeed in encircling a single division or in firing a single artillery shell at Moscow. By early December he was exhausted and without reserves, while at the same time the Western Army Group received from Supreme Headquarters two newly formed Armies and a number of formations from which a third Army, the 20th, was organized. This made it possible for the Soviet command to organize a counteroffensive. . . .[36]

PART II   THE COMMANDER

Introduction

WHEN Marshal Zhukov was virtually exiled to a relatively obscure military post in 1946, the accepted—and realistic—explanation of his misfortune focused on the fact that he was the most famous and popular Soviet military leader. Stalin, some said, was jealous of Zhukov's reputation as the foremost Soviet strategist; and, added others, Stalin owed him too much to feel comfortable in his presence. Stalin's greatest debt to Zhukov was no doubt incurred during the course of the battle for Moscow.

The two excerpts which follow point to still another possible source of the Marshal's later misfortune. At the time when Stalin needed him badly, Zhukov not only exercised real authority over military operations; he also evidently let Stalin know that he appreciated his own significance. While Zhukov's memoirs themselves betray relatively little of this aspect of his relationship with the Supreme Commander in Chief, the first of the two memoirs which follow makes this point with scant equivocation.

The author of the first memoir, Colonel General P. A. Belov, was transferred together with the 2nd Cavalry Corps which he commanded to Zhukov's Western Army Group early in November 1941. On November 9 he was summoned to Zhukov's head-quarters and ordered to prepare in the very next hours a plan to counter-attack in the Serpukhov sector within a few days. For this purpose a special assault group composed of the 2nd Cavalry Corps, 415th Rifle Division, 112th Tank Division, two tank brigades, and 15th Rocket Mortar Regiment was formed under his command. Belov's story begins on the evening of November 9 when he presented his plan to Zhukov.

It is interesting to note that according to Zhukov himself the whole idea of the counterattack originated with Stalin over Zhukov's opposition. It is, therefore, even more intriguing to record Belov's impressions of the relationship between Stalin and Zhukov during the crucial days of the battle for Moscow.

The second excerpt by Marshal K. K. Rokossovskii, who knew Zhukov through most of his military career, contains indirect confirmation of General Belov's impressions. At the time of the Moscow battle Marshal Rokossovskii was in command of the 16th Army on one of the main axes of the German advance. While Rokossovskii criticizes Zhukov for countermanding one of his orders, he goes to some length to make explicit that this order had in fact been approved by Stalin himself.

Colonel General P. A. Belov
With Zhukov in the Kremlin

ZHUKOV looked over my plan and approved it.

"Tomorrow we'll go see Comrade Stalin in Moscow. Be ready," he warned, as he left.

At 3:45 p.m. I drove to the agreed spot on Frunze Street. The cold and gloomy day was drawing to an end. The early autumn twilight was descending. Zhukov's car soon arrived, and I got in.

We entered the Kremlin by the Borovitskie Gates. Part of the way was on foot. We walked silently and quickly. Only in one place did the commander slow down a bit. He pointed to a round hole.

"Aerial bomb."

The crater was big. I judged at a glance that it must have been made by a half-ton bomb.

Not far from the crater was the entrance to the underground headquarters. We went down some steps into a long corridor. To the right was a row of doors, as in a railroad sleeping car. There was a heavy security guard.

Zhukov left me in one of the "sleeping compartments." I took off my cap and overcoat. Naturally, I felt a certain excitement and nervousness before my first meeting with the Supreme Commander in Chief. I looked myself over. My clothes were not quite right for such a meeting: a field tunic and hunting boots with turn-down tops. "If I'm asked why I'm not in regulation uniform, I'll say the uniform wore out," I reassured myself. "And you can't do much fighting now in fine leather boots anyway." Scarcely had I thought of this, when Stalin's secretary appeared, greeted me, and led me out.

At the very end of the corridor, a door opened into a spacious, brightly lit room. In its far left corner stood a large desk. There were several telephones. Zhukov presented me to Stalin, who stood in the middle of it.

Recalling the past now, I can't help but remember petty, seemingly insignificant details, which at that time surprised and perplexed me.

P. A. Belov, *Za nami Moskva* (Moscow, 1963), pp. 42–45.

In those years much was written of Stalin in the newspapers. He was called firm, perspicacious, brilliant—in short, the adjectives were not spared.

I hadn't seen him since 1933. He was greatly changed since that time. Before me stood a short man with a tired, haggard face. In eight years he seemed to have aged twenty. His eyes had lost their old steadiness; his voice lacked assurance. But I was even more surprised by Zhukov's behavior. He spoke in a sharp, commanding tone. It looked as if Zhukov were really the superior officer here. And Stalin accepted this as proper. At times a kind of bafflement even crossed his face.

When the Commander in Chief learned the plan of counterattack, he approved it. He assigned three air divisions for the operation. Next, a timetable was set up.

The Supreme Commander in Chief ordered the attack delayed by one day. It so happened that General K. K. Rokossovskii's Army, far to the right of us, was also preparing to participate. The operation was to begin simultaneously in both sectors in order to interfere with the enemy's freedom to move his reserves.

I asked that the cavalry corps be provided with automatic weapons, on the grounds that in battle the German infantry had a clear firing advantage over the dismounted cavalrymen. The Germans had many automatic weapons, while we were armed with rifles. . . . The meeting ended with my being promised 1,500 automatic weapons and two batteries of the newest 76mm. guns. The guns were also very welcome, because a substantial part of the corps' artillery had worn out. . . .

When I came out of the underground shelter the street was in deep night darkness. There was no light to be seen. I groped my way out of the Kremlin and found my car.

Marshal K. K. Rokossovskii
Under Zhukov's Command

ON OCTOBER 10, 1941, Supreme Headquarters appointed General of the Army G. K. Zhukov to command the Western Army Group. On that

K. K. Rokossovskii, "Na volokolamskom napravlenii," *Voenno-istoricheskii zhurnal,* 1966, No. 11, pp. 46–47, 52–54.

very day, I was present at the command post of the Western Army Group where K. E. Voroshilov presented the new commander to us.

I had known Georgii Konstantinovich for many years prior to this. More than once before, military fate had brought us together and then separated us for long periods of time; our positions in the service with respect to one another changed. In the mid-1920's we were completing our training at the Higher Cavalry School in Leningrad together with other cavalry commanders. At the beginning of the 1930's, I commanded a cavalry division, while G. K. Zhukov was the commander of one of its regiments and later of a cavalry brigade. But in 1940, when I was commanding the 5th Cavalry Corps, the now General of the Army Zhukov, as commander of the Kiev Special Military District, was my superior.[37]

In my mind, G. K. Zhukov will always remain a man of strong will and resolution, brilliant and gifted, exacting, persistent, and purposeful. Unquestionably, all these qualities are essential in a major military leader, and G. K. Zhukov possessed them. To be sure, at times his severity exceeded permissible limits. Running a little ahead of my story, I shall note that in the heat of the combat operations near Moscow, in my opinion our Army Group commander was occasionally unjustifiably harsh. . . .

In the course of three days of fighting, the fascists had realized that they would not succeed in penetrating our defenses in the Volokolamsk sector.[38] Accordingly, while continuing to make strike after strike in this sector and slowly pressing back our units 2–3 km. a day, they began preparations for a breakthrough south of the Volga Reservoir. . . .

Considering the rapid buildup of enemy forces in the Klin sector and the aggravation of the threat from the north as well as the unceasing pressure on our left flank, where all our reserves were already in action, it was necessary to think of measures which would make it possible to improve the position of the 16th Army and to halt the enemy's advance. At that time, the fighting in the center and on the left flank was raging along the line of defense 10–12 km. west of the Istra Reservoir.

The reservoir *per se*, the Istra River, and the adjacent terrain were very good natural defense lines. If these lines were occupied by our troops in good time, it seemed to me that it would be possible to organize a firm defense with small forces, to transfer certain units to the Army's second echelon—and in so doing, to create a defense in depth—and, in addition, to save a certain number of troops for strengthening the defenses in the Klin sector.

After thinking everything over from all angles and having painstakingly discussed the situation with my aides, I reported our plan to the commander of the Army Group. I requested him to authorize a withdrawal to the Istra line of defense, without waiting for the enemy to hurl back the defending troops to that point by force and in close pursuit of our retreating units to force both the river and the reservoir. . . . General of the Army G. K. Zhukov, having heard our proposal and request, categorically disagreed with us and ordered us to stand to the death without retreating a step.

It hardly need be said that in war, in combat, situations frequently arise when the commander's order to stand to the death is the only possible decision. This is unquestionably justified when an important goal can be attained in this way: that of saving the majority from destruction; or when this creates the prerequisites for changing a difficult situation or for ensuring success in general. In such cases, the destruction of those who must stand to the death can be justified. But in the given instance, the enemy was many times stronger in numbers, and there were no troops behind the 16th Army that could withstand the enemy onslaught.

I considered the question of withdrawing to the Istra line of defense so serious that I could not agree with the decision of the Army Group commander. I appealed to Marshal of the Soviet Union B. M. Shaposhnikov, Chief of the General Staff, on this matter and substantiated my proposal in detail.[39] A few hours later, we received an answer from him. We were told that the proposal was correct and that he, the Chief of the General Staff, sanctioned it.

Knowing Boris Mikhailovich Shaposhnikov from service in peacetime, I was confident that this answer had undoubtedly been agreed upon with the Supreme Commander in Chief, or that, in any case, he knew of it.[40] Having received the authorization of the Chief of the General Staff, we immediately prepared an order to withdraw the main forces to the Istra Reservoir line of defense at night. . . . Now, we thought, the enemy will smash his teeth on the Istra line of defense. His basic force—tanks—will bog down in an impassable obstacle, and his motorized units will be unable to make use of their mobility.

But these calculations were not destined to come true. No sooner had the forces of the Army received our order when a short telegram arrived, this time from the commander of the Western Army Group. The telegram read as follows:

> The troops of the Army Group are under *my* command! I revoke the order withdrawing forces to the Istra Reservoir and order that the defense be maintained on the present line without retreating a step backward. General of the Army Zhukov.*

An order is an order, and we as soldiers obeyed it. Thus, our plan remained unimplemented.[41]

PART III THE CAPITAL

Introduction

THE BATTLE for Moscow has been viewed in the foregoing memoirs mainly from the vantage point of commanders on the front line. In the following four excerpts leaders in Moscow itself tell their story.

The first fragment by Deputy People's Commissar of the Aviation Industry A. S. Iakovlev recalls an episode in Stalin's Supreme Headquarters when the front line was still far from Moscow, although the range of enemy bombers was coming inexorably closer. The author of the second account, Chief Marshal of Artillery N. N. Voronov, was closely connected with the organization of the capital's defense and with the battle itself. The author of the third excerpt, Lieutenant General K. F. Telegin, political commissar of the Moscow Defense Zone, recalls how a state of siege was declared by the Soviet leadership in an effort to cope with the "Moscow panic," the disorganized flight of officials and citizens from the city at the height of the German attack.

General Telegin's superior, Colonel General P. A. Artem'ev, the commander of the Moscow Military District and the Moscow Defense Zone, as well as Lieutenant General K. R. Sinilov, the military commandant of the capital, provide fascinating, and sometimes amusing details of the planning and execution of the military parade held in Moscow's Red Square on November 7, 1941. An annual event to commemorate the anniversary of the Bolshevik Revolution of 1917, the parade was reviewed by Stalin himself while German armor stood poised at the near approaches of the city and German aircraft hovered in the skies close to the capital. Stalin's daring gesture of defiance had tremendous political and psychological importance for the city and nation, especially in view of Hitler's boast a few days earlier that on the anniversary of the formation of Soviet power, German troops would march through Red Square. This part of the chapter concludes with excerpts from a Soviet journalist's interview with Generals Artem'ev and Sinilov.

°The editors of *Voenno-istoricheskii zhurnal* asked Marshal of the Soviet Union G. K. Zhukov, former commander of the Western Army Group, to explain why the withdrawal of the 16th Army to the Istra River had been forbidden. He answered that the question of the withdrawal of the 16th Army had to be decided not only in terms of the Army's own interests but in terms of the situation of the entire Army Group. The withdrawal of this Army to the Istra would have denuded the right flank of the 5th Army, and the area in the direction of Perkhushkovo, where the Army Group command post was located, would have been left without cover.

Lieutenant General A. S. Iakovlev
Moscow
Prepares

As a result of the fact that the front lines and, consequently, the enemy's airfields were drawing nearer, the danger of attack by enemy aircraft on the capital became real. A war game was staged at Supreme Headquarters—in order to check the [efficacy of] anti-aircraft defense machinery in warding off an aerial attack on Moscow. The war game was held in a small building near our People's Commissariat which housed Supreme Headquarters in the first days of war before the Kremlin bomb shelter had been completed. People's Commissar Shakhurin, Deputy People's Commissar Dement'ev, and I were among those invited to attend this exercise.

Sketches of different variants of possible attack on Moscow, maps showing the distribution of anti-aircraft batteries around the city and locations of the airfields of anti-aircraft defense fighter aviation hung on the walls of the small hall. Chairs supported a large plywood board on which a map of the Moscow anti-aircraft defense zone was mounted. In the center of the plane-table was a map of Moscow encircled by rings of various colors which denoted the system of short-range and long-range anti-aircraft defense. The plan of the city also indicated the location of anti-aircraft batteries and blimps. P. F. Zhigarev, Commander in Chief of the Air Force; I. F. Petrov, his deputy; and several generals, whose names I unfortunately did not note down at the time and whom I do not remember, were also present at the exercise.[42]

Reports were delivered by Major General Gromadin, Commander of Anti-aircraft Defense, and Colonel Klimov, Commander of Anti-aircraft Defense Fighter Aviation. Several variants of an air raid on Moscow, i.e., day and night attacks from various directions at different altitudes, were worked out, and the corresponding methods for repulsing these attacks

A. S. Iakovlev, *Tsel' zhizni* (Moscow, 1966), pp. 264–65.

by various arms of the anti-aircraft defense system were demonstrated.

Throughout the entire exercise, Stalin observed and listened to everything attentively but did not say a word. When the game ended, and, as was to be expected, the attacks of the imaginary enemy airplanes had been repulsed, he silently walked around the plane-table. One had the impression that the variants played during the game convinced him of nothing at all and that he regarded the whole affair somehow with mistrust. Finally, lighting up his pipe, he muttered through his teeth:

"I don't know, perhaps that's the way it should be."

Then he walked silently into his office, after having invited Shakhurin, Dement'ev, Zhigarev, Petrov, and me to join him.

This war game made on him, just as on us, the impression of a child's game; it was somehow schematic and artificial. There was no confidence that Moscow's defense from the air was secure. Everyone was concerned about the fate of Moscow.[43]

In his office Stalin said again:

"Perhaps that's the way it should be. Who knows?"

And a little later he repeated several times:

"There aren't the people on whom one can rely— There aren't enough people—"

When Stalin started to talk about people, Dement'ev whispered to me:

"Let's ask about Balandin."

I nodded to him, and we made use of the pause in the conversation:

"Comrade Stalin, it's already been more than a month since Balandin, our Deputy People's Commissar in charge of aircraft engines, was arrested. We don't know what he was arrested for, but we can't conceive that he was an enemy. He is needed in the People's Commissariat— the management of engine production has deteriorated significantly. We ask you to examine this case. We have no doubts about him."

"Yes, he has already been in prison for about forty days but has acknowledged nothing whatever. Perhaps he isn't guilty of anything— It is very possible— It can happen that way too—" Stalin answered.

The next day, Vasilii Petrovich Balandin, with hollow cheeks and shaven head, already occupied his office in the People's Commissariat and continued to work as though nothing had happened.[44]

Marshal N. N. Voronov
Moscow Endangered

Moscow was experiencing anxious days. Once [in October] I chanced to see Stalin standing at his desk, talking excitedly with someone on the telephone.

"Parachutists? How many? A company? And who saw them? Did you see them? And where did they land? You are insane. It cannot be. I don't believe it. I tell you I don't believe it. The next thing you'll be telling me is that they have already landed on your office!"

The Supreme [Commander in Chief] slammed down the receiver in irritation and said to me:

"For several hours now, they have been tormenting me with wails about German parachutists. They won't let me work. They all allude to rumors, but they themselves have not seen [the parachutists] and do not really know. Blabbermouths and panic-mongers!" . . .

During our talk, telephone calls concerning supposed enemy parachutists continued to come in. Stalin did not want to listen to these reports any longer and, before slamming down the receiver, would answer:

"Lies! These malicious panic-mongers should be court-martialed!"

In the face of such a tense situation, the report I had come with turned out to be timely. I proposed the formation of new antitank artillery battalions for the purpose of strengthening Moscow's defenses and suggested that they be armed with 76mm. guns which had been accumulated in our reserve. At that time, we did not have guns of other calibers on hand.

"Have they even started hiding guns from me?"[45] the Supreme [Commander in Chief] said. "How many battalions can you form?"

"Ten battalions, each of which will have sixteen guns."

"That is, of course, not very many. If only there could be twice as many."

N. N. Voronov, *Na sluzhbe voennoi* (Moscow, 1963), pp. 197–202.

He reflected. "Listen, what if we were to call those battalions regiments?"

I began to protest. What kind of regiment would it be with only sixteen guns?

"No, no, think about it. What is a battalion? In our understanding it is a very small unit. The battalion commander will be subordinate to some relatively low-ranking commander, and no one will pay any attention to him; as a result, the artillery will not be used properly. But let us call the new units regiments. Commander of an Artillery Regiment—that has a ring to it! Not only a division commander but even a corps commander will have to reckon with him! So there are too few guns in the regiment. So what? As things are now, it happens that a division has fewer people than a normal regiment. But, nonetheless, a division commander remains a division commander. So we'll have artillery regiments. Later we shall increase their number of batteries just as soon as our industry is better able to supply us."

It is a simple thing to call an artillery battalion a regiment, but how should the actual reorganization be carried out? A regiment would require a larger command element and more personnel, and in those arduous autumn days they were nowhere to be found. Moreover, in combat all combined-arms commanders without exception would immediately realize with whom and with what they were dealing. But what could one do? The order had to be obeyed. We were given ten days in which to form the new regiments. . . .

Once A. A. Blagonravov,[46] who was temporarily performing the duties of chief of the Artillery Academy, came to me and told me how difficult it had become to train artillery cadres in the present situation. The Academy was pestered continuously. Once the Moscow city commandant had summoned Blagonravov and directed him to draw sizable quantities of explosives from the [ammunition] dumps.

"Why, what for?" Blagonravov asked in surprise.

"To destroy enemy tanks in the streets of Moscow."

"How?"

"Academy personnel must spread explosives over the city streets. The enemy tanks will roll over them and explode."

A. A. Blagonravov and I laughed heartily over the esteemed commandant's military ignorance. . . .

Exactly within the deadline, I reported to Supreme Headquarters on the preparedness of the new antitank artillery regiments. Moreover, I reported that there were not ten, but twelve. I requested permission to ask the General Staff for a directive concerning where and when to dispatch these units. The Supreme [Commander in Chief] looked at me in amazement:

"And who there [on the General Staff] could make such a decision now? Let us make the decision here and now and dispatch the regiments to the front immediately. And you must see to it that they reach the precise destinations to which they are directed by Supreme Headquarters."

A map was immediately spread out, and Stalin entered on it the points to which the new units were to be sent.

Lieutenant General K. F. Telegin
Moscow Besieged

BY THE END of October, the fascist German troops had reached a point only 80–100 km. from the capital. The Party Central Committee and the government decided to evacuate industrial enterprises,[47] central establishments, and some of the population and to create a Moscow defense zone.

It was under these complex and extremely threatening circumstances that the State Defense Committee decided to declare a state of siege in and around Moscow. The critical situation at the front was aggravated by the spontaneous flight of disorganized people and some official institutions. Those were difficult times for the front's immediate rear. The military council needed to adopt decisive measures to localize the outburst of unauthorized evacuation, but it obviously lacked the power to do so.[48] At about 10:00 or 11:00 p.m. on October 19 the commander of the military district and I were urgently requested to attend a meeting of the State Defense Committee.

The meeting took place in Stalin's office. Almost all the members of the State Defense Committee were seated at a long table covered with a green cloth. A. S. Shcherbakov[49] was there as well. Stalin, smoking the inevitable pipe, paced up and down the narrow carpet. There was a tense silence in the office. The faces of those present revealed that a stormy discussion had just taken place and that feeling was still running high.

We stopped at the door and reported our arrival. Turning to us without a greeting, Stalin asked:

K. F. Telegin, "Moskva—frontovoi gorod," *Voprosy istorii KPSS*, 1966, No. 9, pp. 104–107.

"What is the situation in Moscow?"

The district commander reported that it remained alarming. Measures had been taken to ensure order, but they were inadequate.

"What do you suggest?" Stalin asked.

"The military council requests that a state of siege be declared in the city," Artem'ev replied.

Stalin thought for a few seconds. "Correct!" he said. He asked Malenkov to draft a decree of the State Defense Committee.[50]

The draft turned out to be quite verbose and was obviously not to Stalin's liking. He continued to pace the room and became more and more somber and irritated as Malenkov read the draft. Malenkov had scarcely finished reading when Stalin rushed to him, spoke sharply, and literally snatched the sheets of paper from him. Then he asked Shcherbakov to take down what he said and began to talk. The text of the document Stalin dictated was approved by all those present. It was then given to the secretariat with orders that it be published in the newspapers, posted in the streets of Moscow and the suburbs, and broadcast on the radio. Such was the origin of the State Defense Committee decree which was to play such a tremendous role in normalizing the life and the defense of the capital.[51]

Generals P. A. Artem'ev and K. R. Sinilov
Moscow Defiant

(An Interview by Z. Khiren)

LEAFING THROUGH my notes on the war years, I [Z. Khiren] came across one entry based on the words of General Kuz'ma Romanovich Sinilov, who had just been appointed military commandant of the capital. . . . It was recorded after the military parade of November 7, 1941. Almost all through October, the prisoners of war, who were then quite insolent and cocky, insisted repeatedly that the war would end on November 7 with the entry of the German army into Moscow. Noting this fact at the beginning of

Z. Khiren, "Parad sorok pervogo," *Ogonek*, 1966, No. 45, pp. 3-6.

our talk, Sinilov added that the Germans had even celebrated the capture of Moscow in the occupied areas around the city. . . .

It was under these circumstances that Sinilov was informed of the forthcoming November 7 parade.[52] The plan seemed almost incredible. There were not many troops in the city, and even these were scheduled to depart for the front at any minute. Air raids, which previously occurred only at night, had become more frequent during the day. Usually, preparations for military parades began one and a half or two months in advance. In this case, only three days were allowed; and, moreover, a warning was issued to the effect that it must all be kept secret. But how was this possible when those who were to march in Red Square had never seen Moscow before and were entirely unfamiliar with the city! Sinilov was allowed to inform the unit commanders only at 2:00 a.m. on November 7. The parade was scheduled for 8:00 a.m.[53]

In describing all this, Sinilov did not conceal that he had experienced then a certain bewilderment. It was precisely during those days that troops units and Home Guards were being intensively trained for service at the front, but now attention had to be focused on a parade.

The weather on the eve, on November 6, while somewhat cloudy, was still flying weather. This could not but worry the commandant and all other military commanders responsible for safeguarding the skies over Moscow. On the evening of the 6th, however, thick wet snow began to fall, and a snowstorm developed toward morning. While inspecting the troops, Sinilov kept glancing at the sky and rejoicing. In addition to regular army units, more than 20 battalions of Home Guards were to take part in the parade. Many of them had not yet been issued uniforms or weapons; they were carrying meager knapsacks instead.[54] They provided a strange contrast to the cadets from the military schools. The heavy military equipment had been dispersed: tanks and guns were located on Manezh Square, on Gor'kii Street, on the Mokhovaia, on Herzen Street, on Pushkin Street, and in Sverdlov Square, for the weather could improve at any time, at which point an enemy air raid was not excluded.[55] The troops marched in solemn parade step. It was somehow unbelievable: when had they learned to march so well? The snowstorm, which was saving us from air attack, at the same time created highly unfavorable conditions for maneuvering the tanks and artillery. All the sloping approaches to Red Square were sanded before the parade. But the infantry carried off the sand on their boots. Furthermore, severe winds blew away what sand remained and covered the streets with snow. It was feared that the machines would skid. In fact, in some places the artillery crews literally had to carry their guns. The snowstorm was followed by icing. In a word, there was no shortage of obstacles.

Tanks and guns rolled along Red Square. Then something entirely unexpected occurred. In front of the Mausoleum itself, a KV tank turned and started off in the opposite direction. It was followed by another tank. We must remember that these tanks were fully armed with combat ammunition. Sinilov was ordered to investigate the incident immediately and to punish the culprit severely. He caught up with the tanks, and a young helmeted tank commander emerged from the tower of the first and quite calmly began to explain what had happened. He, it appeared, had received a signal that a comrade in command of another tank was in trouble. This meant that he had to hurry to help him. After all, this is what he had been taught to do in the training camp outside Moscow. That was all that was behind the incident in Red Square. But Sinilov, of course, could not be satisfied with this explanation. He immediately went to the second tank which had followed after the first. And here the general heard approximately the same version of the story. He then looked for the tank which had given the trouble signal, but by then a mass of equipment had jammed the approaches to Red Square, and it was impossible to locate it.

Sinilov returned to the Mausoleum and made his report, laying stress on their reference to aid in combat. On hearing the story, the members of the State Defense Committee laughed approvingly, and the question of punishment was forgotten.

At that time I was unable to see and to talk to Sinilov again. And now twenty-five years later, when I leafed through my notes and wanted to talk to him again, I learned he was dead. I then turned to Colonel General Pavel Artem'evich Artem'ev under whose command K. R. Sinilov had served in October 1941. . . . I visited the general on October 20, 1966.

"Indeed," said Artem'ev quietly, "who would think today that the GUM department store,[56] which is now crowded with people on a holiday buying spree, caused me nothing but trouble twenty-five years ago." The general waved his hand and went on: "When it was decided to hold the parade, I received the assignment of providing for a dreadful contingency: bombs could fall on the parade participants. So medical units with their stretchers, bandages—in a word, with every first-aid requirement—were stationed on the premises of what is now GUM. The night before, the parade ambulances were stationed in the side streets adjoining Red Square and in near-by courtyards. Special emergency wards were set up at the military hospital in Lefortovo. Furthermore, evacuation procedures were arranged to get casualties to hospitals in Moscow and in the suburbs."

The conversation turned to Sinilov. I mentioned my notes to Artem'ev. He remarked:

"You have noted there that Sinilov learned of the parade three days

ahead. That's not so. He did not know about it, and here is why: By
order of the Supreme Commander in Chief no one except [Marshal]
Budennyi, who was to review the parade, knew until the evening of
November 6 just when the parade was to take place. When I asked Stalin
what time to schedule the parade, he answered: 'See to it that no one
knows, not even I, until the last hour, when the parade will start.'
'But when will we announce it?' I insisted. 'There will be a solemn meeting on the 6th to commemorate the 24th anniversary of the October
Revolution,' Stalin answered. 'Tell me there, after the meeting.' "

"But what was the sense in Sinilov's saying he knew three days in
advance?" I asked.

"You forget what it was like when you got the interview." Artem'ev
looked at me sternly, attentively. "This was the situation. I learned of the
forthcoming parade on October 30th. But, as I have already told you, I
was forbidden to mention it to anyone. What then could I do? Three
days before the parade I told Sinilov that the leaders of the Moscow
Party organization wanted to review those who would depart imminently
for the defense line of the capital. Then some sort of drill exercises began
in the Krymskii Bridge area. Apparently, it was this drill that Sinilov had
in mind when he mentioned the three days."

"Can you tell me how the idea of the parade originated?"

"Today everyone clearly appreciates the tremendous military and
political significance of the November 7, 1941 parade in Red Square. Then,
however, in those difficult circumstances, to me, an officer carrying out
orders, such a parade seemed—but how shall I say it—somehow unnatural.
In those days I was concerned with the defense of the nearest approaches
to Moscow and with training the reserves. Even the thought of such a
parade would not have entered my head. Each day I reported to Supreme
Headquarters on progress in building defense lines and supplying them
with truops. Yet, on October 30, after listening to my regular report,
Stalin somewhat casually asked me to report on the preparations of Moscow garrison troops for a parade to celebrate the 24th anniversary of the
October Revolution. I answered that our situation both on the ground
and in the air did not permit any parade this year. I said that the troops
of the garrison were not being drilled for a parade. Stalin said nothing.
Then I added that at the very most only the infantry could take part in
such a parade. The artillery was in firing positions, in combat, and the
garrison had no tanks at its disposal. One of the members of the State
Defense Committee tried to support me, but Stalin put an end to it
and ordered:

" 'A parade will be held on November 7. With the help of Colonel
General Iakovlev, artillery will be found. Tanks will arrive near Moscow

two to three days before the parade. I will see to it personally. No one must know of the preparations for the parade except Budennyi, who will review it. You will command the parade, Artem'ev. It is up to you to determine the hour it will start.'

"I could only acknowledge the order. I repeat, the situation was exceptionally difficult. We were anticipating another attack on Moscow by fascist German troops. Shortly before this conversation I had received orders to hasten the completion of Moscow's defense system. In this connection my report on measures to accelerate the tempo of constructing the defense lines was heard at a conference in the office of A. S. Shcherbakov, on the afternoon of October 28. This conference will never be forgotten by any of those present. The meeting was in full swing when a heavy bomb fell on the premises of the Party Central Committee where it was taking place. Many officials of the Central Committee and of the Moscow Party Committee were among the casualties; some were killed in the anteroom of the office where we were gathered." . . .

Pavel Artem'evich recalled what happened to him at the parade. For the first time in his life he had to command a military parade in Red Square. A long time had passed since he last rode a horse. The night before the parade he chose a calm bay for himself. He took as his horse-holder a 56-year-old experienced cavalryman and pinned all hopes on him. Naturally, Artem'ev, like everyone else connected with the parade, had no time to practice. Until that very morning he had been tied to the telephones, and it was only in the early morning hours that his sheepskin cap and sword were brought to his office and he rushed to the Kremlin. Waiting for him there, seated on a beautiful mount, was Semen Mikhailovich Budennyi. Budennyi started to issue instructions: Artem'ev should not lag behind; he should maintain the proper distance; and when he, Budennyi, emerged from the Spasskie Gates and Artem'ev from the Nikol'skie Gates, they should try to meet exactly in front of the Mausoleum. Everything would have gone well had Artem'ev's horse not misbehaved from the very first. Despite every effort, the horse pulled constantly to the right. It later turned out that Artem'ev's horse was blind in one eye.

PART IV THE COUNTEROFFENSIVE

Introduction

On December 5, 1941 the respective roles of the two adversaries at Moscow were decisively reversed; the Soviet winter offensive began. The ability of the Soviet High Command to concentrate substantial reserves in the Moscow sector and to preserve them intact despite the fact that the German push against the capital had not yet subsided was decisive in enabling the Soviet side to pass rapidly from a desperate defense to a counterattack and then to a strategic offensive. Some of these strategic reserves were composed of active combat units transferred from other sectors of the Soviet-German front; some were composed of well-trained and well-equipped regular troops which, until then, had been deployed on the far eastern frontiers of the Soviet Union as a security guard against possible sudden attack by Japan. These were the troops which are most often credited by German generals and Western military historians with turning the tide in the Moscow battle.

As a matter of fact, however, by far the largest part of the Soviet strategic reserves was composed of newly formed units, hastily assembled, inferiorly armed, and with almost no combat training.

In the following reminiscences Marshal F. I. Golikov, then a Lieutenant

General, tells of the days when an army of 100,000 men was being formed under his leadership deep in the Soviet rear for participation in the Moscow counteroffensive. Golikov's memoirs convey vividly the sense of urgency in the formation of the 10th Reserve Army and describe in detail the difficulties encountered in completing this task in the unprecedented time of one month.

Marshal G. K. Zhukov, chief architect of this first Soviet victory, provides his own description of the counteroffensive, which differs from the official Soviet history in some particulars, as for example his explanation concerning preparations for the start of the Soviet counteroffensive and in his stress on its largely unplanned evolution. Most importantly, however, Marshal Zhukov offers personal insight into the way Soviet leaders arrived at crucial decisions during the battle for the Soviet capital—both the right and the wrong ones.

Of great interest is Zhukov's story of Stalin's insistence that the Moscow counteroffensive be followed by an all-out strategic offensive. It illuminates how erratic was Stalin's evaluation of the Nazi-Soviet balance of armed power. Stalin's initial underestimation of German offensive capacities on the eve of the battle gave way to his doubts of the Soviet capacity to defend the capital and then reverted to a depreciation of German defensive capabilities after the Soviet counteroffensive proved successful.

General Rudolf Hofmann, Chief of Staff of the German 9th Army, writes that

The final result of the battle for Moscow was to bring both sides temporarily to the end of their strength. Neither side succeeded in attaining its objectives. The Germans did not capture Moscow, though for a while it looked almost within their grasp, and the Russians did not succeed in disintegrating and destroying Army Group Center.*

*Rudolf Hofmann, "The Battle for Moscow 1941," in *Decisive Battles of World War II: The German View*, eds. H. A. Jacobsen and J. Rohwer (New York: G. P. Putnam's Sons, 1965), p. 178.

General Hofmann's conclusion does not do full justice to the significance of the Soviet victory at Moscow. While the German army did not achieve either its immediate goal (the capture of Moscow) or its long-range goal (the final defeat of Russia), the Soviet army did succeed in its immediate aim to stop the German drive and push the front line away from the close approaches to the capital. Marshal Zhukov's account suggests that perhaps even the more far-reaching Soviet hope to destroy the German Army Group Center could have been attained, had a concentrated effort been made in the central sector of the front rather than a general offensive launched according to Stalin's plan, an offensive which resulted in the dissipation of Soviet forces.

Marshal F. I. Golikov
To Moscow's Rescue

ON OCTOBER 21, 1941 I was summoned to Supreme Headquarters.[57] I arrived at noon, as I remember. The Supreme Commander in Chief, Stalin, received me at once. B. M. Shaposhnikov, Chief of the General Staff, was with him. A pause followed our brief exchange of greetings. Stalin was silent a minute, pacing about his office. Then he came up close to me and said slowly, softly, and very seriously:

"We know you want to go to the front. Is that correct?"

"Yes, Comrade Stalin."

F. I. Golikov, "Rezervnaia armiia gotovitsia k zashchite stolitsy," *Voenno-istoricheskii zhurnal*, 1966, No. 5, pp. 65–76.

"It is our intention to appoint you commander of an Army. What do you think about that?"

"I accept— Thank you for your confidence."

"Then the matter is clear. Consider it settled. Address any further questions to Comrade Shaposhnikov."

B. M. Shaposhnikov and I drove off at once for the General Staff. . . . In the General Staff, where we continued the conversation started at Supreme Headquarters, I learned that the 10th Reserve Army, which I was to command, did not yet exist and still had to be formed. The nine divisions which would constitute the Army were moving toward the Penza sector from various towns in the Moscow, Orel, Siberia, and Turkestan military districts. Their condition varied greatly. As yet, the Army had neither a staff nor a field headquarters. We had to select personnel for the key positions at once and to leave for Kuznetsk in Penza province[58] where Army headquarters was to be formed. . . .

Time was pressing. Meanwhile, the concentration of our divisions (in the Army formation sector) proceeded slowly. Despite the 10th Army command's keen desire to see its divisions assembled as soon as possible, it nevertheless took twelve to thirteen days. It was only finished on November 8. . . .

In our efforts to put together our units and to prepare them for combat, we had to take into account the backgrounds of our soldiers, commanders, and leading personnel.

The bulk of our middle command and political personnel came from the reserves; less than a third were regular army officers. The divisional commanders had undergone satisfactory military training, had sufficient command experience in lower posts, and were quite well acquainted with the latest models of Soviet military equipment. They were all deeply devoted to their duty; military service was their profession. The divisional chiefs of staff were regular staff officers.

Almost all the regimental commanders were just recently promoted. Only isolated individuals had been graduated from military academies. The majority had merely completed an ordinary advanced training school for officers. Unfortunately, many of them were simply lacking in general education. As a rule, they were capable, firm, and decisive officers. Some of them had already taken part in combat. . . . A few commanders were assigned regiments directly from military school, where they had served as instructors in tactics. . . . Nearly all the regiments in the cavalry divisions were commanded by reserve officers. In the 75th Cavalry Division, only one regiment was headed by a regular army officer.

The majority of infantry and even artillery battalions were also commanded by reserve officers. Only a handful among them had had combat experience. The reserves likewise provided the staff officers of divisions, regiments, and battalions. Only the heads of the basic sections of divisional headquarters and the chiefs of regimental staffs were regular army officers, and even they, with rare exceptions, had almost no experience at their jobs. In artillery units, however, the majority of command positions were occupied by regular army officers. Some of them had had combat experience from the first months of World War II and had come to us after being released from hospitals. The political sections of the Army and its formations had but a few professional political officers—only 15 percent.[59]

By ethnic composition, the Army consisted almost 90 percent of Russians. About 4 percent were Ukrainians. A large part of the 326th Infantry Division consisted of Mordvinians—3,246 men.[60]

Numerically, the communists in the Army were not strong: only 5,387 men, i.e., slightly more than 5 percent. The Komsomol representation was even smaller: 3,718. Of the total number of communists, about one-third were still candidate members of the Party [61] The small number of Komsomol members is chiefly accounted for by the age composition of the troops; there was little youth in the 10th Army. The Party membership in infantry divisions was 4–4.5 percent. Only in the 322nd Division did it approach 8 percent. Yet Supreme Headquarters had ordered that the Party and Komsomol stratum in newly formed divisions should account for no less than 15 percent.

We asked Supreme Headquarters and the Political Administration [of the Red Army] to increase the number of communists and Komsomol members in the 10th Army. Our request was answered. Early in November, 700 communists and several teams of activists came to us. They were experienced soldiers and officers who had just come out of hospitals. These comrades played a large role in our companies and battalions, both militarily and politically.[62]

Thus, the composition of the 10th Army was marked by a large percentage of those with no previous military service; by the advanced age of its enlisted men and noncommissioned officers; by the overwhelming preponderance of reserve officers in its combat subunits, staffs, and political sections; by the great heterogeneity of its units; and by the varied level of their organization, combat training and readiness.

To give an idea of the troops' combat preparation at the time of the Army's formation it is sufficient to mention the 328th Rifle Division, which was considered one of the best. Before joining the 10th Army, this division had undergone one and a half months of combat training in the sector of its own formation. The men were taught how the individual soldier acts in defense and offense; they had rifle target practice at 100–

200 meters and individual combat firing practice with machine guns. Only 60 to 85 percent of the troops went through those firing exercises. It was very difficult to improve firing skill in such a short time because the platoon and company commanders themselves were not trained in marksmanship. Only one-fourth of the division had any practice in throwing hand grenades.

After three weeks with the 10th Army, the division raised the combat coordination of its subunits somewhat, but there were still serious shortcomings in the individual training of enlisted men, noncommissioned personnel, and junior officers. The men acted slowly and inefficiently, especially the artillery, mortar, and machine-gun crews. Physical training and drill were also at a low level.

Many shortcomings were evident in the level of preparation of the 326th Division. But even weaker were the 324th and 325th Divisions, most of whose soldiers had no previous army service and absolutely no conception of army life.

In November the Army units received tactical training on the company level. . . . In a number of units, we had to begin with platoon level tactical exercises. Basic attention in training was paid to questions of offensive combat. With a number of formations the Army command managed to carry out a few tactical exercises on a division level. . . .

In mid-November, the commander of the 323rd Division sent me the following telegram: "In connection with the onset of heavy frosts, I request your permission to postpone the division drills for a few days, in view of the fact that the men are in summer uniform, garrison caps, and without gloves. During the November 12 drills, the division had incidents of first degree freezing of the extremities."

Winter was indeed making itself felt, especially since many soldiers were in summer clothes. We did all we could to improve conditions for soldiers in combat training. But it was impossible to stop training for a day or even an hour. To grant such a request would mean to take the path of least resistance, to side-step difficulties, and consequently to find ourselves in an even more difficult position in the near future, but this time face to face with the enemy. We made no concessions, and I think we were right. . . .

Among other things, the Army's military council, at its first meeting in Kuznetsk, raised the question of mass agitation among the troops. . . . The troops had to be brought to a state of high combat readiness in order to overcome the hardships of field life in low temperatures with summer uniforms and certain food shortages. . . . Political indoctrination was carried on constantly, permeating the whole life of formations, units, and subunits. The war slogans of the Party—"Death to the German invaders!"

and "All for the front, all for victory!"—became the slogans of our troops. All Party political work in regiments, battalions, and companies had but one aim: to strengthen and increase the ranks of brave, resilient, skillful fighting men in the Red Army.

I wish to note parenthetically that now, a quarter of a century after World War II began, you can often see certain comrades sneer as they say: "But those are generalities!" "We've heard all that already!" . . .

But for us in those days, they were not "generalities." I am convinced that they are not generalities even now.

During the brief period of formation, the political sections of the Army and of the divisions did much to organize Party cells in units and subunits. . . . The Army newspaper—*Beat the enemy*—played no small role in educating soldiers and commanders, especially since there was a great demand for the printed word at that time. We had too few newspapers, especially from the center. In November, the whole 322nd division received 120 copies of *Pravda*, 160 of *Izvestiia*, 5 of *Komosomol'skaia pravda*, 15 of *Krasnaia zvezda*, and 50 of the Penza provincial newspaper.[63] The 326th and 328th Divisions received no central newspapers at all. . . .

Reports to the Army command from commanders, political officers, and supply officers as well as our personal acquaintance with the units showed that an extremely poor situation existed with regard to the supply of matériel to the troops. . . . How poor the situation was may be seen from the following telegram dated November 1 which I sent to the Quartermaster General:

> So far there have been no instructions or even answers from your directorate to three telegrams sent by me and Bogatyrev [Quartermaster of the 10th Army] about acutely urgent problems of food supply. You put us in an extremely abnormal position. I repeat: there have been no requisition authorizations for food and forage. We have no sugar, fats, fish, vegetables, hay, tobacco, and no monetary allowances. All the divisions are continually getting larger. Golikov.

We wrote to the chief of the Main Political Administration. . . . That same day we had to send a telegram to Stalin, to members of the State Defense Committee, and to the Chief of the General Staff. . . . A few days later came a new order to "organize supply of the units from local food resources, as found by the Army's commissary sections." This order corresponded far better to reality.

We were greatly worried by the lack of winter uniforms. The 323rd, 325th, and 328th Divisions had no padded jackets and trousers, warm foot-cloths,[64] caps with earmuffs, or gloves, until mid-November. The 322nd and 330th Rifle Divisions had only 30–50 percent of their quota of warm clothing. The lack of overcoats and underwear was especially bad in the 324th Rifle Division.

An even more serious obstacle in bringing the troops to a minimum of combat readiness was the shortage of arms and equipment. At that time, our country was having the greatest difficulties producing and supplying the armed forces with arms, ammunition, and technical equipment. Chiefly for that reason, communication was also bad in all divisions. There was a great shortage of men and matériel in the Army Signal Regiment. Not only airplanes but even the most ordinary means of liaison —automobiles and motorcycles—were missing. . . . The Army Signal Regiment had only one long-range and two short-range radios. Three infantry and two cavalry divisions had no radios at all.

The transportation of food and matériel from central military depots caused more difficulties, largely because of the railroad situation. . . . We had very little of the auto transport to which we were entitled. The divisions and Army Signal Regiment had only 12–15 percent of the required auto transport.

Appointment to vacancies in field headquarters and Army staff proceeded very slowly. The chief of the Main Directorate of Formation was ordered by Supreme Headquarters to form an Army headquarters with maintenance units and to turn them over to the 10th Army by October 26. But the order took a long time to execute. . . .

On November 10 our military council reported to the Deputy People's Commissar of Defense that "the 10th Army's field headquarters is only 65 percent staffed; its operations section—20 percent; intelligence—22 percent; engineering—20 percent; and rear control—50 percent."

The Army operations section had only one officer for the first two weeks—Captain Dmitriev. Only at the beginning of November did section chief Colonel L. B. Sosedov and his deputy F. F. Shishov arrive. Sosedov had served until then as senior aide to the operations section chief in the headquarters of the Commander in Chief of the Southwestern sector. Shishov had been graduated from the Academy of the General Staff ahead of schedule. Several days later a topographer also joined the operations section. But he immediately left for the topographic service depot to find maps of the district where the Army was being formed and of the sector of its probable combat activities. The importance of his mission may be judged by the fact that the entire field headquarters had only two copies of the map—one with me, the other with the chief of staff; and Comrade Sosedov also had a military map drawn to a 1:420,000 scale.[65] . . .

All the officers who joined the staff and Army field headquarters were sufficiently well-prepared, especially those in the operations and intelligence sections. Two intelligence officers were academy graduates; three had completed all but the last semester in the Frunze Military Academy; and two officers had completed intermediate military studies.

The staff and the field headquarters of the Army were not concerned merely with organizing themselves. They had at the same time to receive, organize, teach, provide for, and prepare the troops; to keep in mind questions of the Army's immediate combat future. . . .[66] We did not manage to carry out a single exercise with Army headquarters as a whole—let alone with the entire field headquarters—either in the field or in the classroom. . . .

. . . .

I have related what we had to deal with in preparing the 10th Reserve Army in order to show what difficult circumstances surrounded its formation. . . . I should point out that other reserve units were created under similar circumstances. The front had a great need for reserves, without which a breakthrough in the military situation would have been impossible.

I believe that in those complicated circumstances, the military council, commanders, political officers, and all the troops of the 10th Army did everything possible and sometimes perhaps even more. In an extraordinarily short time, an Army was created numbering about 100,000 (including two divisions, shifted to it later, in the Riazan' district—the 239th Rifle and the 41st Cavalry Divisions).* Its soldiers had 65,632 rifles, 2,000 light and heavy machine guns, 1,209 submachine guns, 249 pieces of regiment and division artillery, 237 battalion and 18 regiment mortars, 27 anti-aircraft guns of 20–37mm. caliber, and 69 antitank guns (45mm.). Of course, we received far less than we were supposed to. For example, we did not then receive a single one of the 1,000 antitank rifles assigned to us. It is easy to see from the above figures that the Army lacked the necessary amount of artillery—especially antitank artillery, mortars, antitank rifles, submachine guns, and heavy machine guns.

However, when we speak of all these shortages and defects, we must not forget that the Army's difficulties with supply and recruitment were inevitably conditioned by the limitations of our country's material resources at that time. Moreover, our transport system was under a colossal strain. And then, we were forming several reserve armies at the same time, and they all needed at least a minimal amount of arms, rations, uniforms, etc.[67] The situation was made still more critical by the fact that in mid-October 1941 many People's Commissariats, including that of Defense, and almost the entire General Staff were evacuated from Moscow

---

*Each rifle division numbered 11,447 men; each cavalry division, 3,500 men. . . .

to Kuibyshev and other towns. This complicated the resolution of a number of organizational and supply problems. Many things were supplied to the 10th Army only on the road to the front or even during combat—winter uniforms, equipment, arms, and a minimum of ammunition. . . .

Events at the front did not permit further delays. On the afternoon of November 24, I received a call by high frequency telephone from Chief of the General Staff B. M. Shaposhnikov. He said: "Filipp Ivanovich, consider the Army's stay in the Kuznetsk sector finished. Be ready to move out by rail!"

"So soon?!" I could not help exclaiming.

I confess that though each of us understood that the situation at the front required our Supreme Command to cut to the minimum the time required for the formation and training of reserve armies, I still had not expected this deadline to come so soon. Counting from the arrival of our command in Kuznetsk—October 27—less than a month had passed. And if one takes into account the first day all our divisions were mustered—November 9—then we had had only fifteen days.

B. M. Shaposhnikov, laconic and friendly as usual, told me the relocation point—the Riazan' district. He also said the Army should be ready for action in the Zaraisk and Venev region.[68] Transfer of the troops had to start immediately; the commanding officer and Army headquarters would leave with the first echelon. After wishing us success, he finished by saying that in the evening we would receive a directive from Supreme Headquarters which would clarify everything.

And so, on November 24 we got ready to leave for the front.

Marshal G. K. Zhukov
First
Victory

In DISCUSSING the passage of the troops near Moscow from defense to offense, it is necessary to bear in mind the peculiarity of the situation which obtained in the Western strategic sector at the end of November

G. K. Zhukov, "Vospominaniia komanduiushchego frontom," Bitva za Moskvu (Moscow, 1966), pp. 77–89.

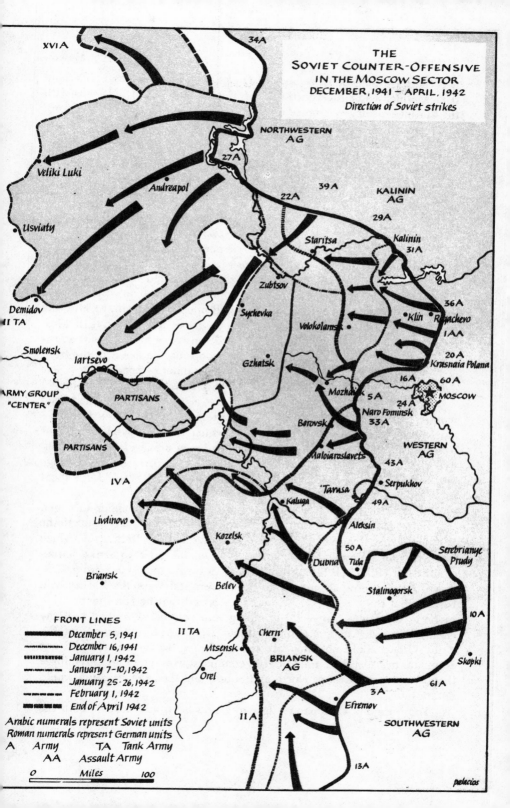

THE
SOVIET COUNTER-OFFENSIVE
IN THE MOSCOW SECTOR
DECEMBER, 1941 – APRIL, 1942
Direction of Soviet strikes

XVI A

34 A

NORTHWESTERN
AG

27 A

Veliki Luki

Andreapol

22 A

39 A

KALININ
AG

29 A

Staritsa

Kalinin

31 A

Usviaty

Zubtsov

36 A

Klin

Rogachevo

Demidov

II TA

Syckevka

Volokolamsk

1 AA

20 A

Krasnaia Polana

Smolensk

Iartsevo

PARTISANS

Gzhatsk

Mozhaisk

5 A

16 A

60 A

MOSCOW

ARMY GROUP
"CENTER"

24 A

Naro Fominsk

33 A

PARTISANS

Borovsk

WESTERN
AG

IV A

Maloiaroslavets

43 A

Tarusa

Serpukhov

Livdinovo

Kaluga

49 A

Aleksin

Kozelsk

50 A

Serebrianye
Prudy

Briansk

Dubna

Tula

Belev

Stalinogorsk

10 A

FRONT LINES

—————— *December 5, 1941*
·················· *December 16, 1941*
▪▪▪▪▪▪▪▪▪ *January 1, 1942*
– – – – – *January 7-10, 1942*
——————— *January 25-26, 1942*
––––––––– *February 1, 1942*
▬▬▬▬▬ *End of April 1942*

Arabic numerals represent Soviet units
Roman numerals represent German units

A Army   **TA** Tank Army
   AA Assault Army

II TA

Chern'

Mtsensk

BRIANSK
AG

Skopki

Orel

61 A

3 A

Efremov

SOUTHWESTERN
AG

II A

0 Miles 100

13 A

palacios

and the beginning of December 1941. By that time the fascist German troops, which had struck northwest of Moscow and in the Tula area with the aim of crushing resistance on the flanks of the Western Army Group and capturing Moscow in a pincer movement, were physically and morally exhausted and extended all along the front. Lacking both operational and tactical reserves, the enemy could no longer count on the successful outcome of his offensive, although, by force of inertia, he continued to gnaw at our defense positions. In his rear, the partisan movement was becoming increasingly active.[69]

Nonetheless, the situation for the defending side was still extremely tense and critical. Soviet troops, which also sustained heavy losses, still had not stopped the foe completely. The enemy had approached the very threshold of the capital, and in some sectors the distance between the capital and our forward defense line did not exceed thirty kilometers. Consequently, the Soviet command could not regard the defensive mission completed. The enemy had to be stopped once and for all, at all costs.

In view of this special situation, the Soviet counteroffensive at Moscow developed in the very course of the defensive fighting; it was an extension of the counterblow begun by our troops on the flanks of the front in late November and early December. The manner of conducting it was determined and refined in the process of delivering the counterblows.

Up to the end of November no plan for a counteroffensive had been worked out either by Supreme Headquarters or by the Army Groups—particularly the Western Army Group, which was deployed directly in front of Moscow. At that time, all plans and measures were aimed exclusively at stopping the main enemy groupings that had driven a deep wedge into our defense lines and at dealing them a blow which would force them to abandon the offensive.

On November 29, I telephoned the Supreme Commander in Chief. Having reported the situation, I requested him to order the transfer to the Western Army Group of the 1st Assault Army and the 10th Army, which were in the Supreme Headquarters reserve, in order to strike harder against the Hitlerites, to stop them, and to throw them back from Moscow. After listening attentively to the report, Stalin asked: "But are you certain that the enemy has reached a crisis and that he is no longer able to bring some new, powerful grouping into action?" I replied that the enemy was exhausted, but that without fresh forces the troops of the Army Group could not liquidate the menacing wedges. If we did not eliminate these wedges, the Hitlerite command would be able to reinforce them from Army Groups North and South, and then the situation would deteriorate.

The Supreme Commander in Chief said he would consult with the

General Staff. At my behest, V. D. Sokolovskii, the Army Group's chief of staff, who also believed it was time to put the basic forces of the 1st Assault and the 10th Armies into action, telephoned the General Staff and explained the expediency of transferring these Armies to the Western Army Group as rapidly as possible. Late in the evening of November 29 we were informed of the decision of Supreme Headquarters to transfer the 1st Assault, the 10th and the 20th Armies to the Western Army Group. At the same time, we were ordered to present a plan concerning their deployment.

Before dawn on November 30 Stalin called to ask the opinion of the military council about staging a counteroffensive by the troops of the entire Army Group. I replied that we did not yet have either the manpower or the matériel for such a counteroffensive. Perhaps it might be carried off by expanding our counterblows on the flanks of the front.

On November 30 the Army Group command worked out a plan for the counteroffensive which provided for the utilization of the Armies transferred to us. The essence of our decision was as follows: Taking into consideration the time required for unloading and concentrating the 1st Assault Army, the 20th and 10th Armies, the Army Group could begin the counteroffensive on December 3–4.* The immediate task was to crush the main enemy grouping on the right flank by means of strikes against Klin, Solnechnogorsk, and the Istra sector and to rout the enemy on the left flank of the front by means of strikes against Uzlovaia and Bogoroditsk in the flank and in the rear of the Guderian group. The Armies in the center were to begin the offensive on December 4–5 with a limited aim—to pin down the opposing forces and to prevent the enemy from transferring his troops.

Prior to beginning the counteroffensive, our aim was to stop the forward movement of the foe to the northwest of Moscow and along the Kashira axis, using for this the forces situated there as well as the forward formations of the Armies transferred to us from Supreme Headquarters reserve.

On November 30 our decision concerning the counteroffensive was reported to Supreme Headquarters together with an explanatory memorandum; it was confirmed without changes by the Supreme Commander in Chief. . . .[70]

Our immediate aim amounted to elimination of the direct threat to Moscow. It was decided to assign further tasks to the Armies on the

---

*In view of the fact that we had to expend substantial efforts in order to liquidate an enemy breakthrough in the Naro-Fominsk region in the early days of December, the beginning of the counteroffensive was moved to December 6.

basis of the developing situation. At that time we did not have the forces to immediately assign more far-reaching and decisive goals to the troops of the Army Group. Despite the fact that our Group had been assigned three new Armies (1st Assault, 10th, and 20th), we still did not have numerical superiority over the enemy (except for aircraft). Moreover, in terms of tanks and artillery, he was superior to us. This circumstance is characteristic of the situation near Moscow at that time.[71]

I am not quite certain, but I think it was on the morning of December 2 that Stalin asked me on the telephone: "How does the Army Group estimate the enemy and his capabilities?" I replied that the enemy had reached the limits of his endurance. Apparently, he had no possibility of reinforcing his shock groups with reserves, and without reserves the Hitlerite forces could not sustain an offensive. Stalin said: "Fine. I'll call you back." I realized that Supreme Headquarters was pondering the further actions of our forces.

In about an hour Stalin called again and asked what our plans were for the next few days. I reported on the preparation of the troops of the Army Group for the counteroffensive in accordance with the approved plan.

In those days, Supreme Headquarters and the General Staff were considering how to organize the activities of other Army Groups—the Kalinin Army Group and the right wing of the Southwestern Army Group—in order to provide potential support for the Western Army Group and to achieve a greater effect from the limited forces available. On December 1 Lieutenant General A. M. Vasilevskii, Deputy Chief of the General Staff, expressed this idea in a talk with Colonel General I. S. Konev, commander of the Kalinin Army Group. "We must have decisive actions and a definite goal in order to frustrate the German attack on Moscow," he said, "and in so doing not only to save Moscow, but also to make a real start toward crushing the enemy. If we don't act in the next few days, it will be too late.[72] The Kalinin Army Group, which occupies an exceptionally advantageous operational position for this purpose, must participate."

In a telephone conversation on December 2 Stalin said that the Kalinin Army Group and the right wing of the Southwestern Army Group had been ordered to support our strikes, which should be made simultaneously with those of the neighboring Army Groups.[73]

Late in the evening of December 4 the Supreme [Commander in Chief] called me by direct line and asked: "What help does the Army Group need in addition to what has already been given?"

It was clear that one could not ask for much in view of the extremely limited resources available at that time. Therefore, I deemed it important to obtain the support of aviation from Supreme Headquarters reserve and from the Anti-aircraft Defense Command. Of course, the rapid development of a strike would have urgently required at least 200 tanks and crews since the Army Group had only a very limited number of these. "There are no tanks. We can't give them to you," Stalin replied. "We'll give you aircraft. I will call the General Staff immediately. Bear in mind that on December 5 the Kalinin Army Group assumes the offensive, and on December 6 the operational group of the right flank of the Southwestern Army Group will start an offensive from the Elets region." . . .

In the last days of November and the early days of December when we organized resistance to the enemy and then assumed a more active form of defense by delivering counterblows, there was still no clear-cut notion in our minds that we were starting a counteroffensive which would turn out to be as grandiose as it did. The first formulation on November 30 of our tasks with respect to the counteroffensive pursued an aim which, while important, was for the time being limited. The aim was to hurl back those enemy forces which posed the gravest threat of breakthrough toward Moscow. The depth of the strikes was to be up to 60 km. in the north and about 100 km. in the south. But already in the course of the counterblows in early December, it became apparent that the enemy was so exhausted by previous fighting and had grown so weak that not only could he not continue his offensive, but he was also unable to organize a firm defense. And when the enemy began to retreat on the right and especially on the left flank of our front, the Army Group command ordered a step-up in the strength of blows both along the front and in depth. On December 5–6, the counteroffensive became a reality. As far as I recall, no special order or directive for the counteroffensive was issued. Both immediate and subsequent combat missions were assigned by Army Group headquarters one after another in separate directives.

Thus, the Moscow counteroffensive did not have such a markedly pronounced beginning as, for example, the Stalingrad counteroffensive. It was the result of the development of counterblows. Air strikes were stepped up; additional large formations were brought in; etc. It was prepared by the whole course of preceding events. On the one hand, the troops of the central sector had exhausted the enemy and had denied him the possibility of completing the operation he had begun. On the other hand, we had a concentration of forces near Moscow at the decisive moment. By putting them into action, we were able at the beginning to hurl back the most dangerous enemy groupings and then to organize their destruction.

Index of approximate temperatures (Fahrenheit) in the Moscow Region *(Savelov raion)* at 7:00 a.m. from November 15 to December 15, 1941.

November		December	
15 : 20°		1 : 18°	
16 : 22		2 : 12	
17 : 18		3 : 19	
18 : 13		4 : 0	
19 : 16		5 :-13	
20 : 20		6 :-15	
21 : 26		7 :-20	
22 : 24		8 : 5	
23 : 25		9 : 24	
24 : 16		10 : 32	
25 : 13		11 : 22	
26 : 16		12 : 28	
27 : 18		13 : -7	
28 : 22		14 : -2	
29 : 30		15 :-17	
30 : 30			

During those days, as we can see from the table above, severe frosts had set in in the central region of the USSR. The deep snow and cold seriously hampered the concentration, regrouping, and dispatch of troops to the attack positions. Nonetheless, our heroic soldiers and officers overcame incredible difficulties and were ready to carry out their combat mission at the appointed time. . . .

On December 6 following concentrated air strikes and artillery preparation, troops of the Western Army Group launched the counteroffensive to the north and south of Moscow. In the battle which developed, initiative turned out to be completely on the side of the Soviet forces. By this time, formations of the Kalinin Army Group, which had begun their attack a day earlier, had driven a wedge into the enemy's defense to the south of Kalinin.

On December 13 the 1st Assault Army together with elements of the 30th Army reached Klin. Surrounding the city from all sides, our troops entered, and, after fierce fighting on the night of December 15, cleared it of the enemy.

The 20th and 16th Armies successfully developed their attacks. By the end of December 9 the 20th Army had reached Solnechnogorsk while the 16th Army, after having liberated Kriukovo on December 8, developed its strike along the axis of the Istra Reservoir. On December 12 the 20th Army drove the enemy out of Solnechnogorsk. The advance of the troops of the right wing of the 5th Army contributed much to the success of the

16th Army. The combat operations of the right wing of the Western Army Group proceeded without interruption.

Beginning on December 3 troops of the 50th Army on the left wing in the area of Tula supported the strike of the reinforced cavalry corps of General P. A. Belov and jointly prepared to rout the Tank Army of Guderian. The 3rd Tank, 17th Tank, and 29th Motorized Divisions of this Army hastily began to fall back to Venev, leaving 70 tanks on the battlefield. The success of our attack was greatly facilitated by the fact that at the moment our left flank grouping struck the enemy, his 2nd Tank Army, which was striving to seize Tula from the rear, was exceedingly strung out and had no reserves whatever. On December 6, our 10th Army also joined the fighting in the region of Mikhailov where the Hitlerites were attempting to maintain a defensive position while covering the flank of the retreating 2nd Tank Army of Guderian.

The strike by formations of the 50th Army, which followed on December 8 from the Tula area, threatened the retreat routes of fascist German forces from Venev and Mikhailov. Deeply flanked and without the forces to parry the thrusts of the Western Army Group and the operational group of the Southwestern Army Group, Guderian began a hasty withdrawal in the general direction of Uzlovaia, Bogoroditsk, and Sukhinichi. In panic, the Hitlerites left heavy artillery, trucks, prime movers, and tanks in the wake of their retreat. In the course of ten days of fighting troops of the left wing of the Western Army Group inflicted a serious defeat on the enemy's 2nd Tank Army and advanced 130 km. . . .

The operational design for further actions by the troops of the Army Group was reflected in directives of the Group's command and headquarters in the period from December 13 to 24. It provided for the rapid advance of the right wing to the Zubtsov-Kozel'sk line. Meanwhile, the troops of the center deployed farther to the rear along the Mozhaisk-Maloiaroslavets line. In other words, the plan was to effect a situation in which our advanced groupings in the right and left wings of the Army Group would create the prerequisites for encircling the main forces of the fascist German Army Group Center.

I am sometimes asked why the central Armies of the Western Army Group (33rd, 43rd, 49th) did not participate in the counterblows and why they advanced so slowly in the subsequent counteroffensive. The point is that in the course of the defensive fighting it was necessary to reinforce the Armies of the right and left wings in order to perform the main task which was to be carried out by the flanks of the Army Group. We had to transfer to the wings literally everything possible from the Armies of the center. And, moreover, with the beginning of the counteroffensive these Armies were not given a single soldier, gun, or machine gun.

Deprived of the capability to make any concentrated strikes, they awaited the development of events, so to speak. And when the enemy flanks were broken up and the enemy began to retreat hurriedly to the Ruza and Lama rivers and also to flee under the blows of the 10th and 50th Armies and the Belov group, it became possible, by means of certain regroupings, to set the 33rd, 43rd, and 49th Armies in motion. Their slow advance, which yielded few results, can be explained still further by the lack of tanks and sufficient artillery. All efforts of the Army Group were concentrated precisely on the flanks in order to smash the enemy's main forces and to advance the flanks forward more rapidly, and in so doing, to endanger the forces of the enemy center.

The Army Group's air force, the nation's Anti-aircraft Defense Command, and the Strategic Aviation Command contributed a great deal to the success of our December counteroffensive at Moscow. The fliers were courageous and skillful. Thanks to the common effort of our aviation, the enemy lost the initiative in the air for the first time in the Great Patriotic War. . . .[74]

Noting the fact that the headquarters and command post of the Army Group were located in Perkhushkovo [2–3 miles from the forward line], I should like to answer a question which I am often asked: "How do you explain such close proximity to the front line of the Army Group and Army headquarters, especially at the end of November and the beginning of December?"

It is true that all headquarters—of the Army Group, the Armies, divisions, and smaller units—were located extremely close to the front line, a situation which is not consonant with accepted norms of safety for command and staff personnel. Again the explanation rests with the singular, exceptional situation. In this connection I recall one episode. On December 2 there was a breakthrough at the juncture of the 5th and 33rd Armies. A rather large enemy group—apparently a reinforced regiment—broke through to Army Group headquarters; a battle broke out in the birch forest where we were located. The security regiment and staff officers took part in it. The Germans were beaten and hurled back. . . . But all the same—even in the most critical moment of the defensive fighting—the thought of moving the Army Group headquarters farther to the rear never entered our minds. Why? Because the move would have become known immediately to lower level headquarters and to the troops. What kind of impression would it have made on them? The command and Army Group headquarters were unreservedly and harshly making seemingly impossible demands on the troops and ordering them to stand to the death. Hundreds and thousands of political officers, propagandists, and communists were explaining to the troops that behind us was Moscow and that there was nowhere to retreat. Our soldiers were doing everything humanly possible and even more to execute the order of the Homeland to stop the enemy and then to smash and destroy him. And at such a time, Army Group headquarters should suddenly pick up and move to a new location? Of course, its place is not at the forward line. But this was required for our cause, for the firm leadership of the troops. In this particular case, customary norms were inapplicable.

Moreover, the military council took into consideration the fact that the enemy was not making his principal strike in this direction. It also kept in mind that communications were excellently organized in Perkhushkovo. I have already spoken of this, but I should like to return to it inasmuch as this circumstance also affected the method of directing troops.

The proximity of the capital and the utilization of all lines in the governmental and civilian communications network enabled us to maintain reliable telephone and telegraph communications with Supreme Headquarters, the General Staff, and all Armies comprising the Group—thanks to the untiring efforts of Army Group communications chief N. D. Psurtsev and his subordinates. Emergency means of communication had been prepared to meet all possible contingencies. Where necessary, headquarters or the command post of the Army Group could even contact a given division directly.

It must be said that the war demonstrated the absolute necessity and usefulness of commanders' work with their troops prior to the start of a battle or operation. It is necessary so that the troops will have a thorough understanding of the situation and be able to organize the forthcoming operations efficiently. But at the start and during these operations, commanders must be at their headquarters or command posts, from which they direct the troops.

We were guided by these considerations in directing the troops during the Battle of Moscow. In the period of defensive fighting, the great length of the front (over 600 km.) and the complex and tense situation did not allow the Army Group commander to leave his headquarters, where all the data on the actions of the enemy, his own forces, and neighboring Army Groups were concentrated and where constant communication was maintained with Supreme Headquarters and the General Staff. But all the same, I once had to leave headquarters and visit one of the divisions of the 16th Army even during the period of defensive fighting. Here is what happened.

Somehow the Supreme Commander in Chief received information that our troops had abandoned the town of Dedovsk to the northwest of Nakhabino. This town is very close to Moscow, and, naturally, he was very disturbed by such an unexpected report.[75] After all, on November 28–29 the 9th Guards Rifle Division, commanded by Major General Beloborodov, had still been repulsing continuous, fierce enemy attacks in the region of Istra with some degree of success. But not twenty-four hours had passed and it appeared that Dedovsk was in the hands of the Hitlerites.

I was summoned to the telephone by Stalin.

"Are you aware that Dedovsk has been taken?"

"No, Comrade Stalin, I am not."

The Supreme [Commander in Chief] lost no time in having his say on the matter, and he noted with irritation: "A commander should know what is happening on his front." And he ordered me to go there immediately, "to organize the counterattack personally, and to recapture Dedovsk." I tried to object that it would hardly be circumspect to leave Army Group headquarters in such a tense situation.

"Never mind. We'll manage somehow. Put Sokolovskii in your place while you're gone."

After hanging up, I immediately contacted K. K. Rokossovskii and demanded an explanation for the failure to notify Army Group headquarters of the loss of Dedovsk. It immediately became clear that the village of Dedovo was probably at issue since the town of Dedovsk had not been taken by the enemy. . . . Clearly there had been a mistake. I decided to call Supreme Headquarters and explain that there had been a misunderstanding. But it was like running up against a brick wall. Stalin lost his temper and ordered me to go to Rokossovskii immediately and to see to it that this ill-fated settlement was taken back from the enemy without fail. Moreover, he ordered me to take along 5th Army Commander L. A. Govorov: "He's an artilleryman. Let him help Rokossovskii organize artillery fire. . . ."

In such a situation there was no point in objecting. When I summoned General Govorov and put the assignment before him, he quite sensibly said he saw no point in the trip. The 16th Army had its own chief of artillery, Major General Kazakov, and the commander himself knew what to do and how to do it. Why should he, Govorov, forsake his own Army in such a tense time? In order to stop further discussion of the matter, I told the general that this was Stalin's order.

We stopped for K. K. Rokossovoskii and drove with him to A. P. Beloborodov's division. The division commander was scarcely pleased with our appearance in the midst of his units. At the time he was up to his neck in problems, and here he had to make explanations about a few houses occupied by the enemy in the village of Dedovo on the other side of the ravine. In reporting on the situation, Afanasii Pavlant'evich explained quite convincingly that it was not tactically expedient to take back these houses which were located on the other side of a steep ravine. Unfortunately, I could not tell him that in this case I had to operate according to considerations far removed from tactics. Accordingly, I ordered Beloborodov to dispatch a rifle company and two tanks to drive off the platoon of Germans that had moved into these houses. This was done, as I recall, at dawn on December 1.

In the meantime, it turned out that I was being sought everywhere by telephone. Since the communications with the 16th Army had been disrupted for a time, a signal officer was sent to Beloborodov's division with this news. Soon I was able to make contact with General Sokolovskii, chief of staff of the Army Group. He reported that Stalin had phoned Army Group headquarters three times already, asking: "Where is Zhukov? Why did he leave?" It turned out that on the morning of December 1 the enemy had gone over to the offensive in the sector of the 33rd Army where, up to then, things had been relatively quiet. Having agreed with V. D. Sokolovskii on immediate measures to eliminate the threat that had developed, I started telephoning Supreme Headquarters. I got through to A. M. Vasilevskii who relayed Stalin's order: return immediately to Army Group headquarters, and in the meantime Supreme Headquarters would decide on which reserves to give us in order to liquidate the enemy breakthrough along the Aprelevka axis.

Upon my return to headquarters, I immediately telephoned Moscow, and this time was connected directly with the Supreme Commander in Chief. I reported that I had familiarized myself with the situation and described the measures we had taken to destroy the Hitlerite units which had broken through in the center of the front. Stalin no longer touched on my and Govorov's trip to the 16th Army nor on the reason he ordered us there. Only at the very end did he ask me casually: "Well, and what about Dedovsk?" I replied that a rifle company supported by two tanks had routed a platoon of the enemy from the village of Dedovo. So ended one of my absences from Army Group headquarters during the defensive fighting near Moscow.

But during the counteroffensive, visits to troops in the field were necessary. I had to spend some time in K. K. Rokossovskii's 16th Army, L. A. Govorov's 5th Army, K. D. Golubev's 43rd Army, and I. G. Zakharkin's 49th Army. The purpose was principally to help the Army commanders coordinate their operations with their neighbors, to warn them against conducting frontal attacks, to force the troops to be more daring in by-passing enemy strong points, and to pursue the enemy more energetically. . . . In a number of cases, the Armies' assault groups became involved in bloody, drawn-out frontal attacks. In the area of Klin, for example, the advance of the 30th and 1st Assault Armies was delayed for this reason. In those days an extraordinary burst of offensive spirit, an exceptional rise in morale and political esprit could be observed among our troops everywhere: Soviet soldiers at last saw the fascist German army reel under their blows. But at the same time we cannot forget that we had not yet acquired sufficient combat experience and that many commanders lacked skill, especially in the conduct of offensive operations. Even during the offensive, some of them still had not gained enough confidence in their forces and occasionally feared that they might somehow be encircled. This explains why sometimes units and formations were not resolutely introduced into gaps which had formed in the front line. The art of conquering a powerful and experienced enemy was not learned easily. Moreover, at that time we acutely felt the lack of mobile armored formations which could, after breaking through the defense, advance rapidly into operational maneuvering space. . . .

In the first days of January . . . we considered that the first stage of the Soviet counteroffensive near Moscow was essentially over. It appeared to us that as the next stage Army Groups in the western sector (Western, Kalinin, Briansk), after having received suitable reinforcements in manpower and matériel, should pursue the counteroffensive to its very completion, i.e., to the restoration of positions occupied by these Army Groups prior to the start of the German offensive operation known under the code name Typhoon. Had we succeeded in obtaining as reinforcements from Supreme Headquarters even four Armies (one each for the Kalinin and Briansk Army Groups and two for the Western Army Group), we should have had a real chance to inflict new defeats on the enemy, to throw him still farther back from Moscow, and to reach the Vitebsk-Smolensk-Briansk line. In any case, opinion was unanimous among the members of the military council and at Army Group headquarters that in order to continue the counteroffensive all available forces had to be used in the western strategic sector so as to inflict the heaviest losses on the enemy. I think that this view was a correct reflection of the concrete situation in the field.

Without a doubt, the December counteroffensive in the central strategic sector had been a very considerable success. The assault groups of German Army Group Center had suffered a severe defeat and were retreating. But on the whole the enemy was still strong, not only in the western but in other sectors as well. In the central sector of the front the enemy was offering fierce resistance; our successfully begun offensive operations near Rostov [in the south] and Tikhvin [in the north] had failed of completion and had assumed a protracted character. But the Supreme Commander in Chief, under the influence of our successes in the counteroffensive, was optimistic. He believed that in other sectors of the front as well, the Germans, being unprepared for winter fighting, would not survive the strikes of the Soviet army. Hence he conceived the idea to begin an offensive as soon as possible along the entire front from Lake Ladoga to the Black Sea.

In those days, member of the Army Group military council N. A. Bulganin and I often came to Supreme Headquarters. Stalin frequently summoned us, explaining that he wanted to confer with us personally about the state of affairs in the Army Group and about our assessment of the situation for the near future.

On the evening of January 5, 1942, as a member of Supreme Headquarters,[76] I was called to Moscow to discuss plans for future operations. Present at this meeting were members of the State Defense Committee, Chief of the General Staff B. M. Shaposhnikov, and, if my memory does not deceive me, his deputy A. M. Vasilevskii; N. A. Voznesenskii had also been invited. Shaposhnikov delivered a short briefing on the situation at the fronts and presented in rough outline the plan of our operations. It turned out that the Supreme Commander in Chief, in addition to the counteroffensive of the Soviet Army Groups in the Western sector, intended to launch an offensive by Soviet forces in all other sectors as well, with the aim of crushing the enemy near Leningrad, to the west of Moscow, and in the south of the country. Thus, the counteroffensive in the central sector was supposed to expand into a general offensive along the entire front.

The main strike was to be directed against [Hitler's] Army Group Center. The defeat of the Group was to be accomplished by forces of the Western and Kalinin Army Groups and by the left wing of the Northwestern and Briansk Army Groups. Troops of the Leningrad Army Group, of the right wing of the Northwestern Army Group, and of the Baltic fleet were assigned the task of routing Army Group North and lifting the Leningrad blockade. Troops of the Southwestern and Southern Army Groups were to defeat Army Group South and to liberate the Donbass. The Caucasus Army Group and the Black Sea Fleet were to liberate the Crimea. It was planned to go over to a general offensive in a very short time.

Summarizing Shaposhnikov's talk, Stalin said:

"The Germans are now in a state of confusion after their defeat at Moscow, and they are badly prepared for winter. This is the most suitable time for launching a general offensive."

The plan for the general offensive was vast, but at that time we had neither the men nor the matériel to carry it out.

"Who wishes to speak?" Stalin asked after the Chief of the General Staff had explained the entire plan.

I took the floor and reported that the Army Groups had to continue the offensive in the western strategic sector where the most favorable conditions had been created and where the enemy had not as yet succeeded in returning the units to combat readiness. But for this, we needed reinforcements in the form of personnel, combat matériel, reserves—in particular tank units, without which it would be difficult to carry out the planned missions. With regard to an offensive by our forces near Leningrad and in the southwestern sector, there they would have to break through heavy defenses and would be unable to do so without heavy artillery support; hence they would only exhaust themselves and would sustain heavy, unjustifiable losses. Therefore, the Army Groups of the western sector should be reinforced, and a more powerful offensive waged in this sector; for the time being, we should refrain from offensives in other sectors.

From the remarks thrown out by Stalin in the course of my talk, I realized that the decision had already been made and would not be reviewed. Nonetheless, N. A. Voznesenskii, who took the floor after me, also spoke out against a general offensive. He argued that we did not possess sufficient matériel to support a simultaneous offensive on all fronts. After allowing him to finish, Stalin said:

"I have talked with Timoshenko. He is for the offensive. We must grind up the Germans more quickly so that they will not be able to attack in the spring."

Malenkov and Beria supported Stalin, saying that Voznesenskii always found unforeseen difficulties which could be overcome. No one else asked to speak. The Supreme Commander in Chief ended the discussion:

"On that, if you will, we shall conclude the meeting."

I had the impression that Stalin had called us to Supreme Headquarters not for the purpose of discussing the advisability of a general offensive but to "shake up the military" as he was fond of saying. When we left Stalin's office, B. M. Shaposhnikov said:

"You argued in vain. This issue had been decided beforehand by the Supreme [Commander in Chief]. Directives have already been given to almost all Army Groups, and they will begin the offensive in the next few days."

"Then why was our opinion solicited?"

"I don't know, dear fellow, I don't know," Boris Mikhailovich answered with a deep sigh.

From what Boris Mikhailovich said in his report and from his remarks cited above, it became clear to me that the General Staff did not initiate the plan for the general offensive.

Army Group Headquarters received the directive concerning the offensive on the evening of January 7. . . .[77]

On January 10, following an hour and a half artillery barrage, the offensive was launched by the 20th Army, part of the 1st Assault Army, the 2nd Cavalry Corps of I. A. Pliev, the 22nd Tank Brigade, and five ski battalions. The aim was to break through in the area of Volokolamsk. As a result of two days of stubborn fighting, the defense was penetrated. The cavalry corps of Major General I. A. Pliev with the ski battalions and the 22nd Tank Brigade was sent through the gap in the direction of Shakhovskaia. On January 16 and 17 troops of the Army Group's right wing, assisted by partisan detachments, occupied Lotoshino and Shakhovskaia and cut across the Moscow-Rzhev railroad line. It would seem that this would have been the place to augment the forces in order to develop the success of the operation. But it turned out differently. On January 19 the order came: transfer the 1st Assault Army from the front line to Supreme Headquarters reserve.

Both Comrade Sokolovskii and I kept telephoning the General Staff and asking them to let us keep the 1st Assault Army. There was only one answer: this was the order of the Supreme [Commander in Chief]. I called Stalin and heard him say: "Transfer it without any backtalk!" In response to my statement that the departure of that Army would weaken the assault group, he replied: "You have many troops. Count how many Armies you have." I said that our front was very broad and that there was fierce fighting in all sectors which precluded the possibility of a regrouping. I requested that the 1st Assault Army not be taken from the right wing of the Western Army Group until the completion of the offensive under way, since this would weaken our pressure on the enemy in this sector. Instead of answering, Stalin hung up. This meant: the conversation was at an end.

The strength of the right wing of the Western Army Group was seriously weakened by the transfer of the 30th Army to the Kalinin Army Group, which took place by order of Supreme Headquarters on December 16, and now by the transfer of the 1st Assault Army to Supreme Headquarters reserve. It was necessary to extend the 20th Army across a wide front. The weakened forces of the right wing were stopped by the enemy at Gzhatsk and could push no farther. . . .

In making a critical examination now of these events in the winter of 1941–42, I must emphasize that we made a mistake at that time in our appraisal of the operational situation in the Viaz'ma area. We underestimated the capacity of the opponent; the "nut" turned out to be harder to crack than we had thought.[78]

During the month of March Supreme Headquarters demanded the intensification of offensive action in the western sector; but at that time the Army Groups' manpower and matériel were exhausted.

The resources of our country at the time were strained to the utmost. The needs of the troops could not be satisfied in a way consonant with the requirements of the missions and of the situation. Things reached a point where every time we were summoned to Supreme Headquarters we literally wheedled out of the Supreme Commander in Chief some 10–15 antitank rifles, 50–100 submachine guns, 10–15 antitank cannons, and the necessary minimum of artillery and mortar shells. Everything we were able to procure in this way was immediately loaded onto trucks and dispatched to the Armies in greatest need. The ammunition situation was particularly bad. Thus, of the munitions planned for delivery to the Army Group in the first ten days of January we received 1 percent of the 82mm. mortar shells and 20–30 percent of the artillery shells. For all of January we received 2.7 percent of 50mm. mortar shells, 36 percent of the 120mm. shells, 55 percent of the 82mm. shells, and 44 percent of the artillery shells. The February plan was not fulfilled at all. We did not receive a single one of 316 boxcars planned for the first ten days. Owing to the lack of ammunition for rocket-launching artillery, part of it had to be moved to the rear. It is probably difficult to believe, but we had to establish a norm of 1–2 rounds per gun per day. And this, please note, was during the offensive! . . .

At the end of February and the beginning of March 1942, Supreme Headquarters reached a decision to reinforce the Army Groups operating in the western sector with men and matériel. But the enemy, alarmed by the development of events, also extensively reinforced his Viaz'ma grouping. And then he began active operations against the troops of the Western and Kalinin Army Groups from previously fortified positions. With great difficulty, the 29th Army of the Kalinin Army Group, consisting of 6,000 men, was brought out of encirclement on February 28, without its heavy weapons.[79]

It was becoming harder and harder for the exhausted and extremely weakened troops to overcome enemy resistance. The frequent reports and requests of the Army Group command and its military council concerning the need to stop and to consolidate achieved positions were ignored. Stalin demanded the attack. "If you don't have results today, you will tomorrow. Even though you achieve nothing by your attack but the pinning down of the enemy, the result will be felt in other sectors of the front." However, neither the Kalinin nor Southwestern Army Groups made any advance at all. The Leningrad Army Group and the right wing of the Northwestern Army Group were engaged in drawn-out fighting. The same held true for the south. Despite heavy costs and failure to achieve a strategic result Supreme Headquarters again demanded in a directive dated March 20 that the previously assigned mission be carried out with greater vigor. But even counting the insignificant increment of reinforcements, the forces of the Army Groups of the western sector were clearly inadequate. In late March and early April, the Army Groups of the Western sector made one more attempt to carry out the directive of March 20, which demanded the destruction of the Rzhev-Oleninsk-Viaz'ma grouping. Again, unsuccessfully. The spring season, with its bad roads, complicated troop operations and troop supply still further. Supreme Headquarters was forced to order a reversion to defensive positions. . . .

During the offensive in January–March 1942, the troops of the Western Army Group had advanced 70–100km. in some sectors and had improved somewhat the general operational-strategic situation. But our troops in the western sector could unquestionably have achieved significantly greater results if we had concentrated as many forces here as possible in order to profit from the success of the December counteroffensive.

As is known, the winter offensive operations of the troops of the Leningrad, Volkhov, and Northwestern Army Groups were far from successful. Here, too, the basic reason was the lack of men and matériel needed to break the enemy's resistance. The offensive of the Southern and Southwestern Army Groups also began to bog down quickly, since they lacked superiority in men and matériel and encountered stubborn resistance.

What I am now saying stresses our unrealized opportunities and relates to the area of strategic planning and utilization of reserves. This, however, can in no way minimize the importance of the great victory which Soviet troops won in the battle of Moscow. The Hitlerites lost on the battlefields of Moscow a grand total of over half a million men, 1,300 tanks, 2,500 guns, over 15,000 vehicles, and much other matériel.[80] The fascist German troops were thrown back 150–300 km. from Moscow toward the west. . . .

The winter counteroffensive of 1941–42 was conducted under complicated conditions of a snowy and severe winter and, most importantly, without a numerical superiority over the enemy. We had more Armies than the enemy, but each of them in terms of men and matériel was barely equal to a German army corps. In addition to this, the Army Groups had neither tank nor mechanized formations. And without them, as wartime experience showed, it is impossible to conduct modern large-scale offensive operations with decisive aims. Only with mighty tank and mechanized formations is it possible to outmaneuver the enemy, to go around his flanks quickly, to harass his rear, and to surround and cut up his groupings.

I am often asked: "Where was Stalin during the battle for Moscow?"

Stalin was in Moscow, organizing men and matériel for the destruction of the enemy at the capital. He must be given his due. Relying on the State Defense Committee, on the members of Supreme Headquarters, and on the creative collective of the leadership in the People's Commissariats, he performed an enormous task in organizing the strategic reserves and the material and technical means needed for armed struggle. By means of his harsh exactitude he continued to achieve, one can say, the well-nigh impossible. During the battle for Moscow, he was very attentive to advice; but, unfortunately, he sometimes made decisions which did not correspond to the situation, as for example the transfer of the 1st Assault Army into the reserve and the launching of an offensive on all fronts.

. . . .

In the battle for Moscow, the Red Army for the first time in six months of war dealt a mighty strategic defeat to the main grouping of the Hitlerite forces. Until the fighting in the Moscow area, there had been some quite successful actions by Soviet troops in other sectors of the Soviet-German front, but, in terms of scale, they cannot compare with the results of the great battle at Moscow where the organized and steadfast defense against Hitler's superior forces and the rapid passage to the counteroffensive enriched Soviet military art and demonstrated the growing operational and tactical maturity of Soviet military leaders. . . .

When I am asked what I remember most of all from the last war, I always answer: *the battle for Moscow*. A quarter of a century has passed, but these historic events and battles have remained in my memory. In the severe, at times catastrophically complex and difficult conditions our troops became hardened, matured, experienced; and, receiving the minimum of the necessary technical means, they were transformed from a retreating, defensive force into a mighty, offensive force. Grateful descendants will never forget the heroic feats of labor by the Soviet people during that period and the military feats of the fighting men of the Soviet armed forces. The battle for Moscow laid a firm foundation for the subsequent defeat of fascist Germany.

CHAPTER FOUR

Leadership

INTRODUCTION

A NUMBER of military writers admit that prior to the outbreak of hostilities there was no clear decision as to how the Soviet High Command would be organized and how it would function in the event of war. The conversation between Marshal Voroshilov and General Tiulenev on the day of the Nazi invasion reveals that even facilities to house High Command headquarters had not been prepared (see p. 203). It would appear that preparations for the transfer of field commands to a wartime footing were somewhat more advanced; frontier military districts automatically became Army Groups responsible for strategic sectors of the front. The command and staff personnel of military districts moved to previously designated and prepared field headquarters from where troops in the area of Army Group responsibility were directed.

After initial uncertainties of organization, the basic structure of the Soviet High Command assumed a form which remained essentially unchanged for the remainder of the war. Four key institutions directed the Soviet war effort from Moscow: Headquarters of the Supreme Commander in Chief (*Stavka*—Supreme Headquarters); the General Staff of Soviet Armed Forces; the People's Commissariat of Defense; and the State Defense Committee. While neither the divisions of responsibility between these institutions nor the details of their respective organization are always clear, the general outline is known, and Soviet war memoirs help to supplement our knowledge.

Supreme Headquarters was the office of the Supreme Commander in Chief, Joseph Stalin; it bore overall responsibility for military decisions. Here were decided questions of strategic planning, deployment of forces, distribution of matériel, formation and utilization of reserves, and from here special emissaries empowered to supervise and control the implementation of these decisions were sent to the Armies in the field. Supreme Headquarters was not a large organization with numerous personnel. It would appear to have included a few close associates of Stalin and no more than one or two dozen key senior officers. Whatever the number of members, however, Supreme Headquarters never operated as a collective body; its decisions were ultimately those of Stalin himself. An authoritative Soviet source acknowledges that "The high military leadership was completely concentrated in Stalin's hands."

For the direction of military operations, Supreme Headquarters relied on its "working organs," to use General Shtemenko's phrase—the General Staff and the People's Commissariat of Defense. Shortly after the start of war, the General Staff was transformed from its subordinate position in the People's Commissariat of Defense into the independent central institution of the Soviet armed forces, charged with the control of combat deployment and operation and responsible directly to Supreme Headquarters. It unified and directed the activities of the main staffs of all arms branches and services and constituted the basic information source and the planning and control arm of Supreme Headquarters.

The People's Commissariat of Defense concentrated on questions of mobilizing military manpower, forming new reserve units, and organizing replacements for units in the field. It issued directives concerning combat training, prepared field regulations and manuals, organized the supply of war matériel, and maintained the records of military personnel. Under its aegis operated the Main Directorates of arms branches and services and their subordinate organizations (with the exception of the naval command which formed a separate People's Commissariat).

The State Defense Committee exercised general control over the total Soviet war effort. Its authority reigned supreme over all military, police, economic, administrative, and Party organizations and hierarchies. Both the Secretariat of the Central Committee of the Party and the Council of People's Commissars served as its executive arms. The Committee's decisions—some 10,000 were promulgated during the war—carried the full force of law in all its wartime harshness. Their implementation was controlled by Committee representatives who were assigned to every ministry and governmental department connected in any way with the war effort, to every province and territory of the Soviet Union, and even to the most important industrial enterprises and construction projects. In cities near the battle zone, local Defense Committees, responsible directly to the Committee in Moscow, exercised unlimited power over local authorities and citizens. The State Defense Committee was small; it consisted initially of five and later of eight members. It assembled irregularly. Its decisions, from which there was no recourse, were often made by the chairman alone or by individual members alone. Its rights and powers were nowhere clearly defined and thus, in fact, were limitless.

Formally, the organizational structure of Soviet power during the war lacked the ambiguities and duplications between state and Party organs or civilian and military authorities which characterized it in peacetime. Unified direction of the total war effort, however, resulted less from simplified and rational organizational arrangements than from concentration of all channels of decision-making and control in one single office and in one single man—Stalin. Shortly before the war, Stalin had already assumed the two primary Party and governmental offices; he was General Secretary of the Party, and on May 6, 1941 he became Chairman of the Council of People's Commissars (Prime Minister). From the second month of war, Stalin became, in addition, People's Commissar of Defense, Supreme Commander in Chief of the Soviet armed forces (and thus head of Supreme Headquarters), and Chairman of the State Defense Committee.

Prior to the war, the business of government was conducted in such a way that input channels of information and output channels of decision and control tended increasingly to converge—at Stalin's office. The war accelerated this tendency until a point was reached where the limits of concentration were solely physical and where power exercised by even key military and civilian officials was delegated power. Soviet military memoirs leave no doubt that all information on military operations and internal affairs flowed into Stalin's office in the Kremlin "corner" or the air-raid shelter at Supreme Headquarters, and all decisions on both military and civilian matters of even secondary and tertiary importance flowed from there. The superimposition of the prejudices, errors of judgment, and fallacies of a single man on his subordinates, the stifling of their initiative, and the delays in deciding secondary questions could only affect adversely the political, economic, and military conduct of the war, but the concentration of authority nevertheless assured single-minded direction of the Soviet war effort and swift resolution of primary questions. Unhesitating acceptance of Stalin's personal authority together with concentration of the five highest military and civilian positions which lent to the powers of the wartime dictator a stamp of formal legitimacy was decisive in cutting through the labyrinth created by personal conflicts among powerful associates, interdepartmental squabbling, enmity between civilians and the military, and differences within the military establishment itself.

Stalin's key role in directing the Soviet war effort should in no way minimize the importance of considering the quality of the civilian and military leadership group, Stalin's associates and senior subordinates. Just because the range of Stalin's decisions was so all-encompassing and his verdict final, the quality and effectiveness of his own leadership depended to a crucial extent on the human and professional quality of men who surrounded him. Even those memoirs most critical of Stalin's behavior testify that the Supreme Commander relied heavily on the judgment of subordinates, especially after the first year of war. The depth and accuracy of his information, the range of alternative decisions, the methods of supervising their implementation depended significantly on the knowledge, level of professional expertise, and, last but not least, the courage of those people with whom he dealt on a daily basis.

A comparison of the composition of the State Defense Committee, the highest authority in the conduct of the overall war effort, and Supreme Headquarters, the highest military authority, reveals a major difference which became accentuated with the progress of the war. The latter was, if not originally, then gradually and more pronouncedly over the course of the war, a military body. The former was, first and foremost, a civilian body. It reflected clearly the effort to preserve the superiority of political over military authority at a time when the potential danger of encroachment by the military into the preserves of politicians was very great.

The State Defense Committee was chaired by Stalin with Molotov as his deputy. Other members included Malenkov, the senior Party secretary; Beria, chief of the secret police; and Marshal Voroshilov, former head of the military and Civil War crony of Stalin, a man primarily "political" in his orientation. The Committee was later enlarged to include other members of Stalin's prewar Politburo, such as Kaganovich, head of railways, and Mikoyan, head of trade and supply organizations. The principal newcomer was Voznesenskii, the chief economic planner. Not only was the State Defense Committee recruited overwhelmingly from Stalin's closest associates of the prewar Politburo, but neither in the initial stage of war nor in the later stage was there even one professional military leader in this body. Only one man, Stalin himself, could speak there for the military and speak from a position of military authority. (Marshal Voroshilov must be discounted, for his authority virtually disappeared after the first months of war.)

During the first three weeks of war, Supreme Headquarters was purely a military establishment headed by the most professional of Stalin's Civil War generals, Marshal Timoshenko. In July, when it was re-formed into the Headquarters of the Supreme Commander in Chief, it was enlarged to include under Stalin's chairmanship his closest political associate, Molotov, and his two most faithful and best-known political marshals, Voroshilov and Budennyi, in addition to professional military leaders. Thus Supreme Headquarters was a mixed military-political body. While little is known about changes in membership during the war, not the slightest doubt exists, even assuming the composition remained unchanged, that the weight and visibility of the military as compared to the political or political-military component increased tremendously and indeed predominated from the fall of 1942. In the first months of war Voroshilov, Timoshenko, and Budennyi assumed direction of combat operations along the entire German-Soviet front as commanders of the northern, central, and southern sectors, respectively. By 1943, however, all three had been removed from major positions of military authority—Voroshilov after October 1941, Budennyi in the fall of 1942, and Timoshenko a year later.

Marshals Shaposhnikov, Zhukov, Vasilevskii, Voronov, and, later, General of the Army Antonov constituted the core of Stalin's military braintrust. The first had completed the Academy of the General Staff in tsarist times; the others had been merely colonels and majors three years before the outbreak of war. Shaposhnikov, Vasilevskii, and Antonov were very similar in the type of professionalism they represented, in the role they played in Stalin's entourage, and even in personal temperament. They were first and foremost senior staff officers, military planners, and teachers, with the thoroughness, attention to detail, military culture, patience, and self-restraint required for this type of activity. Shaposhnikov, Chief of the General Staff from the first month of war until June 1942 when he retired from operations work owing to ill health, and Antonov, Acting Chief of Staff from winter 1943 until the war's end, were confined almost entirely to staff work in Moscow itself. Vasilevskii, Chief of Operations from the fall of 1941 and Chief of the General Staff from June 1942, combined his staff duties in Moscow where he participated in planning large operations with on the spot supervision and coordination of field armies. The three men, and especially Shaposhnikov, were distinguished not only for their military talents which engendered respect, but also for their readiness to defer to Stalin.

Zhukov's role in the military establishment was unique. A knowledgeable and talented strategist, a man of immense willpower, self-confidence, decisiveness, and toughness toward self and subordinates, he thrived less on staff work in Moscow than on direct supervision of military operations in the field. He began the war as Chief of the General Staff, but after a few weeks he assumed the more congenial role of Stalin's personal emissary to key sectors of the front, that is, to places where in the first phase of war a crucial Soviet defeat was in the making and where in the later phase of war a crucial Soviet victory was in the making. (His formal title from August 1942 was First Deputy Supreme Commander in Chief.) He not only participated in the planning of all major strategic operations of the war, but he bore general or particular responsibility for such operations as the Soviet counteroffensive along the El'nia salient in the Smolensk sector (August 1941), the defense of Leningrad in the period of greatest danger (September 1941), the defense of Moscow, the Battle of Stalingrad, the Kursk-Orel operation; he commanded the Voronezh sector in the campaign of spring 1944, the central sector in the Belorussian offensive (summer 1944), the central sector in the winter offensive of 1945, and finally, the main direction in the Battle of Berlin. More than any other single man during and after the war, Zhukov epitomized the new professionalism achieved by the post-Purge military high command in the trials of war.

The last of the five principal commanders, Voronov, was in charge of Soviet artillery, the main breakthrough force of Soviet armies. A military professional whom Stalin personally trusted, he was used continuously for the same kind of missions to field armies as those entrusted to Vasilevskii and Zhukov, although his missions were of less importance.

The ascendancy of new military professionals in Stalin's entourage reflects not only the dismal failure of old "personal" generals and the talent of the newcomers, but also Stalin's growing appreciation of his own misconceptions about war and the ways to conduct it. Stalin entrusted enormous responsibilities to men like Budennyi not because he did not know the man but rather because he did not know the business of war; he shared with his Civil War cavalry hero the basic attitudes and views on military leadership and concepts. While it would be foolish to compare the ability, strength of character, human experience, and mental range of Stalin and Budennyi, they may be likened, at least in the first months of war, with regard to military experience and level of professionalism. Stalin learned quickly, as Budennyi may perhaps never have learned. But then Stalin was given time to learn and did not have to pay personally for his ignorance. The full price of Stalin's education and mistakes was paid by his people and his soldiers and to some extent by his appointees in top military posts who became victims of their military ineffectiveness. It was the good fortune of Soviet Russia that Stalin came to realize the need for able, efficient, and professional soldiers around him; this was a crucial step in his military education. The aphorism "War is too serious a business to be left to generals" is valid only so long as military operations are conducted *with* the generals.

PART I   THE HIGH COMMAND

Introduction

THE ORGANIZATION of the Soviet High Command, its schedule of work, its style, atmosphere, and personalities concern the authors of all but the last two memoirs in this part. Particular attention is focused on Stalin's daily routine and on the evaluation of the Supreme Commander in Chief as taskmaster by his closest subordinates. What emerges most vividly from these accounts is Stalin's personal involvement both in key strategic planning and in trivial details of actual operations, of supply, and even of protocol. Colonel General Shtemenko, for example, relates Stalin's preoccupation with procedures for celebrating the victories of Soviet troops. Like his superior, he evinces no surprise either in the fact that the Supreme Commander in Chief personally directs Operation Gun Salute or in the fact that the Chief of Operations of the General Staff takes full charge of its correct execution. Shtemenko complains merely of Stalin's ill-tempered reaction to the clerical errors committed by his highest ranking military experts!

Characteristic of Stalin's work habits is his insistence on receiving exhaustive information from his subordinates, which in the case of operational reports of the General Staff represents an accounting down to the level of the regiment. Stalin displays what amounts to constitutional inability to yield to his associates the right to make any decision of consequence. In most cases, it would seem, Stalin simply approved the proposals advanced by his associates. Thus, while Stalin made all the decisions, the decisions did not have to be made by Stalin. Ingrained suspicion of the motives and trustworthiness of subordinates characterizes Stalin's relations with his associates. The very fact that his personal approval was required for all decisions may perhaps have been considered by Stalin a sufficient stimulant to subordinates who were expected to prepare thoroughly and to incorporate in their work the point of view of the Supreme Commander. Moreover, one may suspect that this arrangement satisfied some inner need to feel indispensable even with regard to the smallest details and to reassure himself constantly that his control was total. The memoirs indicate that while the satisfaction of Stalin's inner need conflicted with rules of effective organization, it nevertheless became reconciled with the substance of expert advice preferred by professional military associates.

As the memoirs demonstrate, the organs of the Soviet High Command functioned smoothly, efficiently, and professionally in the second half of the war, a noteworthy achievement in view of the extent of its shortcomings prior to the Battle of Stalingrad. The responsible leaders of these organs, however, paid a high price in mental and physical exhaustion as a result of the iron regimen, the continuous pressure, and the constant fear of daily "examinations" by Stalin. The burden was particularly difficult in the case of those officers like General Antonov or, in part, General Shtemenko whose duties did not often permit occasional escape from deadly routine to the freedom and exhilaration of inspection tours in the field.

In the first excerpt which follows, Admiral N. G. Kuznetsov, Chief of the Navy, criticizes the failure to prepare in peacetime for the High Command's function of leadership in war. He traces the gradual and painful process of adaptation to new conditions on the part of both the High Command and its supreme leader. In the second excerpt, Marshal A. M. Vasilevskii offers a brief description of his duties as Chief of the General Staff and, in particular, of his relationship with Stalin.

The memoirs of Colonel General S. M. Shtemenko, Chief of Operations of the General Staff, are divided into three parts: the first describes the normal working day of top Staff officers; the second introduces General of the Army A. I. Antonov, who served from 1943 formally as First Deputy Chief of the General Staff and in fact as Acting Chief of Staff, and characterizes the style and habits of work at the General Staff and at Supreme Headquarters; the third captures the atmosphere in the Soviet High Command as the elaborate ritual is devised to celebrate the increasingly frequent victories of Soviet arms. A valuable picture emerges from the writings of Stalin's close military expert of the Supreme Commander's daily work habits and conduct.

Chief Marshal of Artillery N. N. Voronov demonstrates the absurdities of extreme centralization at the apex of the command hierarchy; the Chief of Rear Services of the Red Army, General A. V. Khrulev, relates how what was perhaps the most neglected and underestimated peacetime military service gradually evolved during the war to secure the flow of supply to the front line units; Deputy People's Commissar of the Aviation Industry, A. S. Iakovlev, describes how problems of war production were treated in Stalin's office.

The last two excerpts in this part deal with the operational planning and leadership of the High Command. In the course of the war the operational leadership of the Soviet High Command experienced a profound improvement in quality and in capacity to master problems of increasing complexity. Virtually up to the Battle of Stalingrad, operational planning at Supreme Headquarters consisted largely of short-range response to enemy moves; from Stalingrad, when initiative passed into Soviet hands, to the spring of 1944, it focused on the planning of individual major operations; in the final war year it concentrated on the coordination of several large-scale operations which were being conducted simultaneously.

The operations directed by Supreme Headquarters in the first period of the war were characterized by errors in strategic judgment, by retention of patently unsuitable principles of planning. The outcome of these early operations was afflicted by the discrepancy between strategic goals and the magnitude of means and forces mobilized to achieve them; by the rigid and frequently costly attachment to the principle of linear defense to the last man even under the most unfavorable conditions; by haste in organizing counterattacks together with procrastination in ordering timely withdrawal; by uneconomical use of available reserves; and by failure to discern the intentions and to estimate the capabilities of the enemy. While Stalin and the Soviet High Command continued to direct resistance despite the initial shock of unexpected defeats, while they never flinched from the application of the most extreme emergency measures, while they demonstrated what was the crucial ability to mobilize numerically superior reserves and to organize in the zone of the interior round-the-clock production of war equipment, they only gradually and slowly began to comprehend the nature of war from the strategic and operational point of view.

The first significant steps in perfecting the procedures and quality of planning and leadership took place at the time of the Battle for Moscow. They have been described in the previous chapter by both members of the High Command and field commanders. Chapter Five will describe the planning and implementation of the Red Army's final campaign in Europe. The memoirs which are presented here serve to supplement these accounts by describing certain operations prior and subsequent to the Battle for Moscow. In the first excerpt Marshal I. Kh. Bagramian, then Chief of Operations at the headquarters of the Southwestern Army Group, recounts the single most devastating defeat suffered by Soviet forces, the encirclement at Kiev; the ineptitude and poor judgment of Supreme Headquarters may be considered a decisive factor in the outcome of this battle. In the one remaining excerpt, Marshal A. I. Vasilevskii attributes to Supreme Headquarters and the General Staff a major share of responsibility in permitting German armies to regain initiative after the Battle of Moscow and to push on as far as Stalingrad in 1942. His opinion gains weight and importance when one recalls that by virtue of his position as Deputy Chief and then Chief of the Soviet General Staff he bears some measure of guilt for erroneous evaluations and unwarranted strategical and operational decisions which created the grave situation.

Admiral N. G. Kuznetsov
Command in Transition

I SHOULD LIKE to linger, if only briefly, on the question of how armed forces leadership was organized before the war. Military organization should be scrupulously tested and perfected in times of peace. It will be

N. G. Kuznetsov, "Voenno-morskoi flot nakanune Velikoi Otechestvennoi voiny," *Voenno-istoricheskii zhurnal*, 1966, No. 9, pp. 65–67.

subjected to a real test only during war. But then it will be very difficult
to correct old mistakes.

In the late 1930's, although the People's Commissariat of Defense
was considered subordinate to the Council of People's Commissars and
its chairman, military questions were, in reality, decided by Stalin. When
I was appointed People's Commissar of the Navy, in my ignorance I at
first attempted to bring all questions to V. M. Molotov, Chairman of the
Council of People's Commissars. But it was very difficult. Minor, daily
affairs still moved, but important ones got stuck. Whenever I was persistent, it was suggested that I turn to Stalin. And this was not easy at
all. At first he treated me indulgently, since I was a new People's Commissar; but soon he became stern, official, and rarely accessible. He often
left our written reports unanswered. One had to wait for the opportunity
to bring up the same questions again in personal conversation. But when
would such an opportunity arise?

In 1940, when Stalin assumed the post of Chairman of the Council of
People's Commissars, the system of leadership did not, in effect, change.[1]
In any event, I cannot say that it became better. Stalin himself supervised the People's Commissariat of Defense, without delegating any of
his authority. The People's Commissar of the Navy found himself in a
still more complicated situation. Molotov, as Stalin's deputy, and A. A.
Zhdanov, as secretary of the Central Committee, handled naval affairs.
But naval affairs were connected, as a rule, with general military questions, which these men were in no position to decide. . . .

Before the war, neither military institutions nor high defense officials
had clearly defined rights and obligations. Experience has shown that in
questions of supreme importance, the smallest ambiguity is intolerable.
Each official should know his place and the limits of his responsibility.
The war caught us without a properly prepared organization of the highest military leadership. Only with the start of war was it hastily organized. Undoubtedly this should have been done long before, in peacetime. On June 23, 1941 General Headquarters was created, with People's
Commissar of Defense, S. K. Timoshenko, as its head. Stalin was listed
as only one of the members of this General Headquarters. On July 10
Supreme Headquarters was established. On July 19, almost a month after
war had begun, Stalin was named People's Commissar of Defense, and
only on August 8 was the Supreme Headquarters of the Armed Forces
reorganized into Supreme Headquarters of the [Supreme] Commander
in Chief. From that date also, Stalin occupied the post of Supreme Commander in Chief of the Armed Forces. However, not many people knew
about that yet. It was only after victories at the front that Stalin began
to be called Supreme Commander in Chief in the communiqués published
in the press.

After his radio speech on July 3 [1941] Stalin began to appear in the office of the People's Commissar of Defense.[2] Why he was absent until then, I cannot say. He gradually assumed leadership of the war and tried to become familiar with the situation. In those days, as events unfolded with incredible speed and the enemy swiftly tore along toward Moscow and Leningrad, G. K. Zhukov, then Chief of the General Staff, was sent to the front. B. M. Shaposhnikov again became Chief of the General Staff. The necessity for changing people in such an important post at such a difficult moment was also the result of a superficial approach to military leadership and personnel selection. . . .[3]

Supreme Headquarters and the State Committee of Defense, which was created on June 30, continued for a long time to experience organizational malfunctions, inevitable in the shake-down period. With time, organization improved. In a year or two Supreme Headquarters or, more correctly, Stalin, developed closer ties with field commanders. Stalin listened more to their opinions. All major operations, such as those at Stalingrad, Kursk, etc., were already planned with the full participation of Army Group commanders. Several times I was to observe how Army Group commanders summoned to Stalin did not agree with his opinion. Each time he proposed that everything be weighed again in order to reach the proper decision—and he often agreed with the opinion of the commanders. I suspect he even liked people who had their own point of view and were not afraid to stand up for it. In cases where opinions differed, certain of his closest associates exerted a negative influence. Less knowledgeable about military matters than either the field commanders or Stalin, they usually advised the former not to oppose but to agree with Stalin.[4] Later I became firmly convinced that it was best to make decisions when Stalin was alone. He then listened calmly and drew objective conclusions. Unfortunately, this was very rare. During all my years of work in Moscow I had only two or three such opportunities.

The central defense establishment underwent many changes in the course of the war and finally became more flexible, thereby serving the Army Groups and fleets better. But its improvement took a great deal of time, which is so precious during a war. We paid long and heavily for our poor organizational preparation. If the organization of military leadership at the center was a cause for worry, the situation in the field in this respect was no less so. In peacetime we already knew that combat operations in a future war would develop rapidly, and decisive battles would begin in the very first hours. This was shown by the experience of both World War I and the war in Spain. We had also seen how rapidly events unfolded in Poland and then in France in 1939–40, when the "phony war" ended.

For military men it has long been a truism that powerful air strikes can be expected in the first hours or even minutes of war. As a consequence, communications can be broken. The local command must be able to act independently, without waiting for instructions from above. All possible instructions must be given ahead of time, in peacetime. Much has been said about this in many documents. But because the organization at the center was not clear, it was equally impossible to decide many questions in the field. This state of affairs weighed especially on the navy because of its subordinate position both at the center and in the field. We were perplexed by the questions: To which Army Group would one fleet or another be subordinate in time of war? How would their coordination be arranged? At every naval base the naval personnel was supposed to act together with ground troops, usually in a position of subordination. Hence, for us navy men, a clear delineation of rights and responsibilities was an important practical problem.

Marshal A. M. Vasilevskii
Chief of the
General Staff

As CHIEF OF THE GENERAL STAFF, my primary function was to keep the Supreme Commander in Chief up-to-date on all major events at the front. In reporting changes in the situation, I also had to inform Stalin about actual steps taken by Army Group commanders in response to these changes, about their decisions and their requests to Supreme Headquarters. At the same time I reported the General Staff's point of view on each question.

In every twenty-four-hour period the Chief of the General Staff had to give the Supreme Commander in Chief two oral reports on the situation at the front: one at twelve noon about events which had taken place during the night, and one at 9:00 or 10:00 p.m. about changes which had taken place during the day. The General Staff was obligated to report to Stalin immediately all serious developments or major events. Before giving my own report, I in turn listened to reports of the chiefs of operations

A. M. Vasilevskii, "Nezabyvaemye dni," *Voenno-istoricheskii zhurnal*, 1966, No. 3, p. 27.

of each Army Group headquarters in the presence of the officer or general from the Office of Operations [of the General Staff] who was responsible for the given Army Group. For all questions requiring clarification, I immediately contacted the chief of staff or the commanding officer of the Army Group, as well as senior officials of the People's Commissariat of Defense in charge of the given problem. When I was in the field, acting as Supreme Headquarters' representative, I usually confined my reports to those Army Groups, for the coordination of whose actions I was responsible. A day seldom passed, however, when I did not touch in my talks with Stalin upon questions regarding other Army Groups as well as questions concerning the formation and utilization of Supreme Headquarters reserves.

When I was with the field armies, I maintained even closer contact with Army Group commanders, and not only was I always fully up-to-date on their decisions, but, as a rule, I took direct part in making them. Thus, all proposals about operational questions which I took to Supreme Headquarters represented not merely my personal ideas, but ideas worked out together with the command and staff element of the Army Groups as well as with senior personnel of the General Staff and of the People's Commissariat of Defense.

Colonel General S. M. Shtemenko
Stalin,
the Taskmaster

ACTIVITY at Supreme Headquarters and the General Staff then and always was very intense; it was not confined within the walls of conference rooms. By this time [1944] extensive experience had already been accumulated from the work of representatives of Supreme Headquarters in the most important front sectors, where the representatives, together with the local command, solved problems connected with the preparation and conduct of very important operations. It is true that after the war certain Army Group commanders expressed the view that constant utilization of

S. M. Shtemenko, "Pered udarom v Belorussii," *Voenno-istoricheskii zhurnal,* 1965, No. 9, pp. 44–46.

the Chief of the General Staff, Marshal A. M. Vasilevskii, and of the First
Deputy Supreme Commander in Chief, Marshal G. K. Zhukov, as representatives of Supreme Headquarters in Army Groups had a deleterious
effect on leadership of front-line formations.[5]

In some measure this was indeed so. But it seems to me that, in the
last analysis, despite this (in the main postwar) criticism, the activity of
Supreme Headquarters' representatives was justified under existing conditions. The situation required the presence in the Army Groups of persons
whose experience and authority would enable them to make quick decisions together with the Army Group command concerning the most important questions of combat operations. G. K. Zhukov's missions to key
front sectors were the result, *inter alia,* of his position as First Deputy
Supreme Commander in Chief. A. M. Vasilevskii, of course, should have
spent more time in the General Staff itself. But the Supreme Commander
in Chief did not consult with anyone in this regard. He apparently considered such a situation normal; every time they returned from the armies
in the field, he asked when they thought they would go back again. . . .

Service on the General Staff was never easy, all the more so in that
difficult war period. Collection of data and assessment of the current situation in all Army Group sectors, the working out of practicable solutions
and preparation of orders that were dictated by this situation, the preparation of designs and plans for forthcoming operations, plans for supplying
armies in the field with armament and munition, the build-up of reserves,
and other important questions, naturally, occupied the chief place in the
activity of the General Staff. All these questions were very complex,
and it was not always possible to solve them in the way one would have
liked.

The General Staff was closely linked with Supreme Headquarters
as its working organ, particularly with the head of the State Defense
Committee and Supreme Commander in Chief Stalin, who personally
established the General Staff's round-the-clock work schedule. For
example, A. I. Antonov[6] was assigned rest time from 5:00 or 6:00 a.m.
until 12 noon, while I, as Chief of Operations, was allowed to rest from
2:00 p.m. until 6:00 or 7:00 p.m. The work and rest hours of all other
leaders were regulated in the same way.

Reports to the Supreme Commander in Chief were made three times
in every twenty-four-hour period by telephone and in person. The first
report was usually made between 10:00 and 11:00 a.m. by telephone. This
task fell to me. At 4:00 or 5:00 p.m. Antonov made his report. At night,
as a rule, Antonov and I drove to Supreme Headquarters together to
present a summary report on the preceding twenty-four hours.[7] For this
report, maps to the scale of 1:200,000 were prepared for each Army

Group separately; they showed the troop's position down to a division and, in some cases, even down to a regiment.

After a summons by telephone, we would set off by car through deserted Moscow for Supreme Headquarters or Stalin's "nearby" country house.[8] We would drive through the Borovitskie Gates into the Kremlin; and, circling the building of the Supreme Soviet of the USSR through Ivanovskaia Square, we would swing into the so-called "little corner" in which Stalin's apartment and office were located. We entered the small room of the chief of the personal guard through Poskrebyshev's office and from there went into the Supreme Commander in Chief's suite.

On the left-hand side of the office, not far from the wall, stood a long, rectangular table. We used to roll out the maps on it and use them to make a report on each Army Group in detail, starting with the one where major action was taking place at that given moment. No notes were made in advance, for we knew the situation by heart, and it was marked out on the maps. At the end of the table, in the corner, there was a large globe on the floor. I must say that in the hundreds of times I visited this office, I never once saw the globe used during a discussion of operational questions.[9]

In addition to the Supreme Commander in Chief, as a rule, members of the Politburo and members of Supreme Headquarters were present at these briefing sessions. N. N. Voronov, Commander of Artillery; Ia. N. Fedorenko, Commander of Armored and Mechanized Troops; N. D. Iakovlev, head of the Main Artillery Directorate; A. V. Khrulev, Chief of Red Army Rear Services; A. A. Novikov, Commander of the Air Force, and others were summoned when necessary to make reports and to give information on specialized matters under their jurisdictions. Usually, all civilians present sat along the table against the wall facing us, the military, and the huge portraits of Suvorov and Kutuzov which hung on the opposite wall of the office. Stalin used to pace up and down along the table on our side as he listened. From time to time, he would go over to his desk, which stood far back on the right, take two cigarettes, tear them open, and stuff his pipe with the tobacco.

The report usually began with an outline of our own troops' action during the previous twenty-four hours. The Army Groups, the Armies, and the tank and mechanized corps were referred to by the names of their commanders, and the divisions, by numbers. That was the way Stalin had organized it. Afterward, we became used to it and introduced the same procedure in the General Staff.

After briefings on the situations in the various front sectors, proposed directives to be issued by Supreme Headquarters or in its name were reported. Supreme Headquarters' documents were signed by the Supreme

12

Commander in Chief and by the Chief of the General Staff, or, when he was not there, by A. I. Antonov. Frequently orders were written directly in Supreme Headquarters. Usually I wrote while Stalin dictated. Stalin then had the text read aloud and corrected it during the reading. The corrected documents, as a rule, were not typed but usually, when urgent, were immediately transmitted to the front from a communications room close by.

Next we turned to requests from the Army Groups. For the most part these concerned reinforcements, the delivery of armaments, equipment, and fuel supplies. Naturally, these requests had been previously examined by the General Staff with commanders of the service branches involved.

We returned to our offices at 3:00 or 4:00 a.m. and issued the necessary orders. Only after this did Aleksei Innokent'evich [Antonov] take a rest. Sometimes we made two visits to Supreme Headquarters in twenty-four hours. In the intervals between briefings and trips to Supreme Headquarters, we compiled information on the situation in the Army Groups, analyzed it, prepared suggestions, and took care of the usual staff work. That was the way the working day went.

The rigid work schedule that Stalin had established and no one could change, its excessive volume and urgency, made service on the General Staff extremely exhausting and difficult; it demanded enormous physical and moral resources. It meant work to the point of exhaustion, which not every man could take, the more so because, as a rule, men were dismissed from the General Staff for the slightest mistake, with all the ensuing consequences. It was not by chance, therefore, that a number of officers and generals of the General Staff suffered nervous exhaustion and prolonged heart trouble, and many of them went into the reserve immediately after the war without having served to their retirement age.

Colonel General S. M. Shtemenko
Profile of a Staff Officer

IN JUNE 1942 Marshal of the Soviet Union B. M. Shaposhnikov was forced to retire as Chief of the General Staff owing to serious illness and to assume the less demanding post of Chief of the Higher Military Academy. General A. M. Vasilevskii, previously Chief of Operations of the General Staff, was appointed in his place.

The departure of General Vasilevskii had an extremely deleterious effect on the Office of Operations. There began a period in which one chief succeeded another. In the space of some six months this post was held by General A. I. Bodin, twice by General A. N. Bogoliubov, and by General V. D. Ivanov. Between their appointments the post was occupied on a temporary basis by Generals P. G. Tikhomirov, P. P. Vechnyi, and Sh. N. Geniatulin. A. I. Bodin was killed on a trip to the Transcaucasian front, and the others, as the saying goes, did not fill the bill.[10]

The situation was complicated by the fact that conditions of work at Supreme Headquarters required A. M. Vasilevskii to spend the greater part of his time at the front, while the duties of Chief of the General Staff in these cases of necessity devolved upon Major General F. E. Bokov, Commissar of the General Staff—a wonderful person and a good Party leader but a man who was unprepared for purely operational functions.[11]

The long absence of the Chief of the General Staff and the frequent turnover in chiefs of the Office of Operations gave rise to a nervous atmosphere at work and disrupted its rhythm and precision. Comrades who found themselves at the head of the Office and of the General Staff and who were frequently replaced did not have time to understand what was going on, to work into the situation; and, accordingly, they did not feel confident when they went to Supreme Headquarters to make a report. They had to surround themselves with chiefs of sectors in the event that some question suddenly came up and a reference was needed.[12] The "bath house locker room," as we called the reception room [of the Chief of Operations], was always full of people. Some of them would be writing something while they waited to be called, but the majority lounged on the sofas simply wasting their time. A call would come from Supreme Headquarters, and one of the people waiting would answer a request for some kind of information. Sometimes the sector chiefs would be sum-

S. M. Shtemenko, "Vydaiushchiisia sovetskii voenachal'nik," *Voenno-istoricheskii zhurnal*, 1966, No. 8, pp. 42–46.

moned to Supreme Headquarters to give a more detailed report. Such were the conditions under which the General Staff worked in the summer and fall of 1942.

In the early part of December we learned that Lieutenant General A. I. Antonov, former chief of staff of the Transcaucasian Army Group, had been appointed Chief of Operations and Deputy Chief of the General Staff. Many people knew him and commented favorably on his appointment. Others, the skeptics, said that they would judge after he had made two or three trips to Supreme Headquarters and after they had seen how he managed there. They phrased it this way because Antonov's predecessors in this post were usually discharged after several trips to Supreme Headquarters.

A. I. Antonov arrived in Moscow in December 1942. I met him in my capacity as head of the southern sector at that time. From his very first days at work there was a feeling in the Office [of Operations] that a remarkable person had come, someone who knew staff work very well, that things would now go well. Antonov began by becoming closely acquainted with his people; he began a painstaking study of the situation in all sectors of the front. He did not hurry to report to Supreme Headquarters as his predecessors had done but rather went there about six days after his arrival when he already knew well the situation in all sectors of the front. Everyone was particularly pleased by this. We realized that the new Chief of Operations understood precisely what the General Staff needed. This opinion was reinforced still more after Antonov's first visits to Supreme Headquarters, when not only did everything go well, but the constant, unnecessary "vigil" in the reception room ceased. Antonov aided the Supreme Commander in Chief in establishing a difficult and severe but, on the whole, necessary and acceptable regimen for General Staff work, one that was preserved in all subsequent years. At the same time, A. I. Antonov bore equally with us the burden of everyday work. . . .[13]

Inasmuch as the Supreme Commander in Chief frequently sent A. M. Vasilevskii to the forces in the field, A. I. Antonov was appointed First Deputy Chief of the General Staff five months after he had been named Chief of Operations. In the absence of A. M. Vasilevskii, the entire indescribable range of problems that confront the Chief of the General Staff in wartime descended on his shoulders. During all this time, of course, he maintained the closest contact with Aleksandr Mikhailovich [Vasilevskii], briefed him by telephone on everything that happened at the General Staff, and always received corresponding instructions, counsel, and support from him.

It can be said without exaggeration that Aleksei Innokent'evich was an exceptional person. His chief distinguishing traits were first and foremost outstanding erudition as well as general and especially military knowledge. These traits were manifested in the breadth and depth of his approach to all questions of work, in his speech, conduct, and relations with people. In the space of six years of joint work at the General Staff, never once did I see him lose control of himself, flare up, or scold anyone. While he was remarkably even-tempered, he was by no means spineless. Antonov's even temper and sincerity were combined with a rare firmness and resoluteness, and, I would say, even with a certain aridity in official matters. He would not tolerate superficiality, haste, imperfections, and formalism. He was sparing with his praise. The only people to win it were those who used their heads and who displayed initiative, precision, and flawlessness in their work. He valued time very much and planned it painstakingly. Evidently, it was for this reason that his speech was distinguished by brevity and clarity of thought. An enemy of long and frequent conferences, he held them only in exceptional cases, and then they were always brief. Somebody even called him pedantic in official matters and conduct. But this was a rash judgment. It was a matter of something else, and we who worked with him understood it very well and were thankful to A. I. Antonov for the consistent, highly principled, demanding attitude which is absolutely necessary in military service, all the more so during days of a difficult war. . . .

Antonov had to visit Supreme Headquarters daily, and sometimes even twice a day. Even though Aleksei Innokent'evich knew the situation at the front thoroughly, all the same before every visit to Supreme Headquarters he would carefully prepare himself for two or three hours. He would contact the commanders of the Army Groups; he would clarify certain questions relating to the situation, the planning, or the course of operations; he would consult with them and through them verify the correctness of his assumptions; and then on this basis he would prepare his proposals to the Supreme Commander in Chief. Then, together with the Chief of Operations, he would examine the Army Groups' requests and requisitions; and in the final hour before departing for Supreme Headquarters he would examine and edit the draft directives and orders that were to be prepared for signature. . . . As a rule, his report to Supreme Headquarters went smoothly and did not call forth any special questions. Before departing for Supreme Headquarters we would sort in advance materials requiring the decision of the Supreme Commander in Chief and place them in three differently colored folders. In the red folder we placed documents of primary importance, those which would have to be reported without delay—chiefly orders, directives, dispositions, plans for the distribution of armaments among field troops and reserves. In the blue folder we placed papers relating to questions of second priority—various kinds of requests. Finally, in the third, green, folder we placed promotions and awards lists, documents relating to transfers and appointments to the command element, which went through General Staff, and other documents.

The documents in the red folder were always reported in their entirety. Aleksei Innokent'evich was unusually persistent and would not leave the Supreme Commander in Chief until all the documents had either been cleared or signed. The blue folder was reported on to the extent possible, but as a rule on a daily basis. The green folder was reported only if the occasion permitted. Sometimes we would not open it for two or three days, and other times the documents in it would be reported on the very first trip. Aleksei Innokent'evich was a master at assessing the situation correctly and judging when to raise a particular question; he almost never erred in telling me, "Give me the green folder." To be sure, Stalin soon saw through this simple device. Sometimes he would say, as if in warning, "Today we shall examine only the important documents," and another time he would turn to Antonov with the words: "Well, now, let us look at your 'green' folder."

Aleksei Innokent'evich enjoyed the great respect of the Supreme Commander in Chief for his knowledge and for his courage in submitting straightforward, truthful, and unembellished reports. No matter how bitter it was, everything corresponded to fact. It was apparent that Antonov enjoyed this respect also because he dared, when necessary, to take issue with Stalin and in any case to express his own opinion.

Listening to the reports of the Army Group commanders, the Supreme Commander in Chief, as a rule, would ask us: "What is the opinion of the General Staff? Has the General Staff examined this question?" and "the General Staff" in the person of Antonov would always present its point of view, which in many cases did not differ from the views of the Army Group commanders. But once these views had been solicited, they were presented.

The Supreme Commander in Chief did not tolerate the slightest falsehood or embellishment of real facts. He severely punished those who were caught doing so. For example, in November 1943, the chief of staff of the 1st Ukrainian Army Group was removed from his post because he had not reported that the enemy had taken one populated point from which our troops had been driven out.[14] One could recall other instances of a similar nature. Naturally, during the reports, we were careful about their wording. We ourselves made it a rule never to report on unverified or doubtful facts. And they were numerous. In the reports one would frequently encounter the phrases: "The troops have penetrated point N," "Our troops have occupied (or are holding) the outskirts of point X," and similar imprecise phrases. In such cases, Antonov would report: "Our troops are fighting for point N (or X)," since experience had more than once proved that this was the most precise way of describing the actual situation at the front. . . .

Aleksei Innokent'evich almost never traveled to the Army Groups, for the situation did not permit him to do so. Nonetheless, he was in constant contact with them and had daily telephone conversations with their commanders and chiefs of staff. . . . In addition, officers of the General Staff were appointed permanent General Staff representatives to the armies in the field. All this made it possible for him to know not only the true situation in the Army Groups and their requirements and demands, but also, so to speak, to feel the pulse beat of every Army Group. . . .

From December 1942 to the war's end, there was not a single significant operation in the Great Patriotic War in whose planning and preparation A. I. Antonov did not participate. He himself was the originator of plans and ideas for several operations. . . .[15] The Order of Victory which Antonov was awarded for his role in developing the decisive operations of the war symbolized the high valuation placed on his labors by the Homeland. This order has been awarded to only eleven Soviet military leaders, and among these was Aleksei Innokent'evich.[16]

Antonov was a member of the Soviet delegation to the Yalta and Potsdam conferences in 1944 and 1945. He worked on military questions and conducted negotiations in various commissions there and in meetings with Allied military representatives. Stalin knew whom to choose. At that time Aleksei Innokent'evich was probably the military leader best prepared for that mission. He was well informed on events in all Army Groups; he knew the plans of the Soviet command and, to the extent that it was possible, the intentions of the Allies and all questions relating to combined actions with them. In addition, as we have already said, Antonov was a very precise man; he expressed his ideas well both orally and in written form; he had the gift of saying less and listening more, a great virtue in all negotiations. All in all, he was the best possible choice for this assignment.

Aleksei Innokent'evich would prepare long and scrupulously before each of these trips. He would work out several variants for one or another situation that might arise at a conference. He studied the possibilities and was abundantly supplied with data. As far as I know, the head of the delegation was satisfied with his work.[17]

On February 17, 1945, in connection with A. M. Vasilevskii's appointment as commander of the 3rd Belorussian Army Group, Aleksei Innokent'evich was appointed Chief of the General Staff. He occupied this post until March 25, 1946. When A. M. Vasilevskii returned to his former post, that of Chief of the General Staff, A. I. Antonov again became his first deputy until November 6, 1948. He thus worked about six years in the General Staff.[18]

Colonel General S. M. Shtemenko
Rituals
of Victory

DAYS PASSED. The war continued. Battles proceeded with varying success. On July 5, 1943 the defensive stage of the famous Battle of Kursk began with an enemy attack. Day and night, our troops beat back massive attacks of tanks, planes, and infantry, waging extremely bitter and bloody fights. The enemy's mountains of steel forged ahead, but after eighteen days of bitter fighting against our well-prepared defenses, they only dented the Orel-Kursk sector and drove a wedge into the defense in the Belgorod-Kursk sector. As the day of July 23 was ending, our defending Army Groups in conjunction with the Western and Briansk Army Groups, which had already begun a counteroffensive, threw back Hitler's soldiers to their initial lines and fully reestablished their original position.[19]

Prior to the next regular report to Supreme Headquarters we evaluated the situation at the front as usual in the office of the Chief of the General Staff, A. I. Antonov. Our conclusion was as follows: the defensive tasks of Soviet troops had been successfully carried out, and the attack by the main forces of the fascist German troops in the Orel-Kursk sector had completely collapsed. The enemy's plan for the whole summer campaign was buried with it. . . . On the night of July 24, these conclusions went into a report to Supreme Headquarters concerning the situation at the front. The next morning Stalin phoned the General Staff and ordered A. I. Antonov to prepare a congratulatory message to the troops in honor of their victory in the Battle of Kursk. . . .

S. M. Shtemenko, "Pobediteliam i geroiam," *Voenno-istoricheskii zhurnal*, 1966, No. 7, pp. 18–25.

On July 24, about 4:00 p.m., General Antonov and I were summoned to Supreme Headquarters. Stalin was in a joyously jubilant mood. He did not want to hear my report on the situation, which he had known since last night, but asked that the draft of the order be read aloud.

The first lines emphasized the extremely important strategical advantage won by the Red Army and were followed by a brief statement about the enemy's plan and strength:

Yesterday, on July 23,. the successful actions of our troops completely liquidated the Germans' July offensive against Kursk from the sectors south of Orel and north of Belgorod.

On the morning of July 5, large forces of fascist German tanks and infantry, heavily supported by aircraft, started an offensive in the Orel-Kursk and Belgorod-Kursk sectors. The Germans threw into the attack against our troops their *main* forces, which they had concentrated in the Orel and Belgorod sectors.

So far, the text elicited no adverse comment. The reading continued:

It has now become clear that in the Battle in the Orel-Kursk sector the German command threw in seven tank, two motorized, and eleven rifle divisions; and ten tank, one motorized, and seven rifle divisions in the Belgorod-Kursk sector.

In all, the enemy used seventeen tank, three motorized, and eighteen rifle divisions. Having concentrated these forces in narrow sectors of the front, the German command planned to break through our defense by means of concentric blows from the north and south in the general direction of Kursk, to surround and destroy our troops positioned along the arc of the Kursk salient.

This new German offensive did not catch our forces by surprise. They were prepared not only to repulse the German attack but to deliver powerful counterblows. At the cost of tremendous losses of life and equipment, the enemy managed to drive a wedge 9 km. deep into our defense on the Orel-Kursk line, and 15–35 km. deep on the Belgorod-Kursk line. In furious battles, we exhausted the Germans' crack divisions, and in subsequent decisive counterblows we not only threw back the enemy and fully restored the pre-July 5th situation, but we also broke through the enemy's defense and moved 15–25 km. in the direction of Orel. . . .

Stalin stopped us after we read the conclusion: "Thus, the German plan for the summer offensive should be considered a total failure—"

After a moment's thought he dictated the following addition: "Thereby the legend that Germans are always successful in a summer attack, while Soviet troops are allegedly forced only to retreat, is exposed."

"That must be mentioned," he explained. "Goebbels and all the Germans have been maintaining that legend ever since the winter defeat at Moscow."

Then followed a listing of the troops who had distinguished themselves and the names of the commanders of the Armies. Then the enemy's losses were specially mentioned. This time the ending of the message differed from previous ones. We could not neglect to mention those who had stopped the enemy with their own bodies and won victory at the cost of their lives. They were numerous. A brief word in honor of the fallen heroes was to follow the congratulations of the victors. The message concluded:

"I congratulate you and your troops on the successful liquidation of the German summer offensive.

"I express my gratitude to all the soldiers, commanders, and political workers of your troops for their excellent combat performance.

"Eternal glory to the heroes who fell on the battlefield in the struggle for the liberty and honor of our Homeland!"

The message was signed at once and announced over the radio. Supreme Headquarters found the message to its liking. It ordered that this form be preserved in the future: Address the official message to the Army Group commanders, mention the names of commanders of Armies and other units whose troops had distinguished themselves, and briefly summarize the results of the battle on the occasion of which the order was being issued. The ending in honor of the fallen heroes also was to be kept. It was improved editorially from time to time and finally received the form: "Eternal glory to the heroes who fell in the struggle for the freedom and independence of our Homeland. Death to the German invaders!" Except for the last words, this ending was also included in the official message on the victorious conclusion of the war, as a memorial to those who did not return from the fields of past battles.

Twelve days later on August 5, when Orel and Belgorod were taken, Supreme Headquarters conceived another idea. As soon as the Army Group commanders reported to Stalin on the capture of these cities (for they always hastened to report to him immediately whenever they won victories), General Antonov and I were summoned to Supreme Headquarters. We set out at once, taking our maps, reference notes, and documents, as usual. The members of Supreme Headquarters were all there.

"Do you read military history?" Stalin asked us, just as we walked in. We were confused, not knowing how to answer. The question seemed strange. We had no time for history.

"If you had read, you would know that in ancient times, when troops won victories, all the bells would be rung in honor of the commanders and their troops. It wouldn't be a bad idea for us, either, to signify victories more impressively, not just with messages of congratulation. We"— he nodded in the direction of the members of Supreme Headquarters seated around the table—"we're thinking of giving artillery salutes and arranging some kind of fireworks in honor of the troops who distinguished themselves and the commanders who led them."

Naturally, we agreed. It was decided to proclaim victories of our troops by solemn artillery salvos in Moscow, to accompany every salvo with multicolored fireworks, and to precede the salute by reading Stalin's official message over every radio station in the Soviet Union. The General Staff was charged with the implementation and organization of this procedure. On that same day, August 5, a congratulatory message was issued, and the first salute was given in honor of the liberation of Orel and Belgorod. The 5th, 129th, and 380th Rifle Divisions were surnamed "Orel Division," the 89th and 305th, the "Belgorod Divisions." [20]

The first salute consisted of twelve salvos from 124 guns. [21] We figured it would also be that way in the future. But on August 23, Khar'kov, the second capital of the Ukraine, [22] was taken, and we saw at once that one shouldn't treat all victories in an identical way. Khar'kov had very great significance, and it was decided to give twenty salvos from 224 guns in honor of its liberation.

Subsequent developments showed that we acted correctly. The fact was that the salutes and messages were received with great enthusiasm, not only by the civilian population but by the troops as well. We had no respite from the phone calls of Army Group commanders, who demanded salutes for almost every inhabited point that was taken. Some kind of gradation had to be introduced to indicate the great distinction, for example, between Kiev and Berdichev, Riga and Shiauliai, Minsk and Dukhovshchina. [23] But the liberation of all these cities was honored by a salute.

Three categories of salutes were worked out by the General Staff and approved by Stalin: 1) 24 salvos from 324 guns; 2) 20 salvos from 224 guns; 3) 12 salvos from 124 guns. Only Stalin could grant permission to fire a salute. With rare exceptions, the salute was given the day that the objective was taken. The units and commanders to be honored in the message that accompanied the salute were proposed by the Army Group commanders. The congratulatory message was prepared by the Office of Operations [of the General Staff], while the introduction, i.e., a description of the actions for which the troops were being honored, or, as we called it, the "cap," had to be reported to Stalin, usually by telephone. At the same time the category to which the salute belonged had also to be confirmed.

The entire text of the messages, except for the first ones, was not reported to Stalin. The "caps" were usually written by Lieutenant General A. A. Gryzlov or myself. Gryzlov displayed an especially masterful hand at this. As a rule, the "caps" were only rarely amended and then, if one may say so, usually on historical grounds. For example, in a message of January 27, 1945, given in connection with a breakthrough in the Masurian Lakes sector, Stalin added the following insertion—"considered by the Germans since World War I to be an impregnable defense system" —which strongly underlined the significance of that victory.

Naturally, the organization and carrying out of salutes is a pleasant duty, since it is directly connected with the victories of our armed forces. However, although this extra duty occupied only a secondary place in the great mass of work at the Office of Operations, it demanded quite a bit of time and attention. In preparing the official message, one had to check carefully the numbering of all the forces and units and the names of the commanders, not to mix up or omit anything. And all we had was one or two hours for this. Cities were usually taken toward evening, when the actions of the day had produced their most palpable effects. The salutes, on the other hand, could not be given before darkness, or the fireworks would lose their effect, but they could not be given later than 11:00 p.m. As you can imagine, there were quite a few days when salutes came one after the other. We were saved from a difficult situation only because our officers and generals had excellent knowledge of the situation, of the troops' numbering, of the commanders' names, and were able to work quickly and accurately. The messages were usually drafted in the office of the chief of operations and by the time the "caps" were reported [to Stalin], the rest was usually almost ready.

Up until November 30, 1944, the messages were only addressed to the commanders of Army Groups. But on that day, a message to the troops of the 2nd Ukrainian Army Group was being prepared. As usual, the details were checked with the Army Group chief of staff, Colonel General M. V. Zakharov.[24] He criticized the General Staff for underestimating the role of the Army Group staffs: Everyone was mentioned in the messages but the chiefs of staff. We took this into consideration and reported it to Stalin. He said: "Zakharov is right. The role of the staffs is great. In the future, address the message to two people: the commander and the chief of staff."[25] So it was done. The first such message went that very day, November 30, 1944, to the 2nd Ukrainian Army Group. The chiefs of staff of all the Army Groups were very pleased.

All the salutes did not always go smoothly. There were quarrels about who took this or that objective. There was discontent if the General Staff refused to give a salute. Many commanders telephoned Stalin personally to report on the capture of an important point, and he himself gave orders to the General Staff to prepare the salute and the official message. Some commanders, especially those of Army Groups active in sparsely settled areas, asked that the salute be given for what the General

Staff considered insignificant objectives. If the General Staff did not agree, they would appeal directly to Stalin, and he sometimes overruled us. Thus, for example, a salute was given for the capture of Dukhovshchina and a few other such settlements. If the General Staff managed to get its way, the salutes were not given, but the messages were issued nonetheless.

Great pains were taken with the messages. Stalin himself looked after this. He ordered the old names of cities, if there were any, to be written in brackets—e.g., Tartu [Iur'ev, Dorpat].[26] We had to appoint a special officer to look after this. When Polish land was liberated, both the Polish and German names of cities were written. If maritime cities were liberated and the navy took part in the operation, the navy ships were also saluted.

Units received honorary titles after the names of the cities they liberated. But time showed that the same units participated in the liberation of several cities. What was to be done? After all, one couldn't give them five or ten honorary titles. It was decided to give only double ones, e.g., "the 291st 'Voronezh-Kiev' Air Assault Division." Troops which distinguished themselves repeatedly received medals, and, finally, divisions and Armies received "Guards" status.[27]

Occasionally there were snags in connection with the messages. . . . Once during my report at Supreme Headquarters, I. S. Konev called to report the capture of some large city. It was already around 10:00 p.m. Stalin ordered the salute to be given at 11:00 p.m. There was hardly time to prepare the message. I immediately wrote the "cap," which was approved, and then I telephoned Gryzlov from the adjoining room to give me the troops' numbers and the commanders' names. Next I called Comrade Puzin[28] about transmitting the message on the radio, and, finally, I phoned the commandant of the Kremlin about the salute. Then I gave the "cap" to the typists and sat down to draft the message according to the map and my list of commanders. About half an hour later, Gryzlov and I collated our data, and I went to dictate the message to the typists' pool. When everything was done and the message sent out, I returned to Stalin's office, where A. I. Antonov was still giving his report, and I announced that everything was ready, and the salute would be given at 11:00 p.m.

"Let's listen to it," said Stalin, and turned on the simple, round speaker on his desk. I should point out that the message was timed to be read on the radio not more than one minute before the salute roared out.

As always, Iu. B. Levitan[29] began to read the message in his solemn, inimitable voice: "To the commanding officer of the 1st Ukrainian Army Group! The troops of the 1st Ukrainian Army Group, as a result—" etc.

Suddenly Stalin shouted loudly: "Why did Levitan omit Konev's name?!

Let me see that message!" Konev's name was missing from the text. It happened that when I prepared the "cap," I abbreviated the heading, forgetting that it was not going to be typed at the General Staff, where the typists themselves expanded the necessary headings.

Stalin was dreadfully angry.

"Why did they omit the commander's name? What kind of anonymous message is this?!" he yelled. And turning to me, he said sarcastically: "What have you got on your shoulders?!"

I kept silent.

"Stop that broadcast and read everything over again!" he ordered.

I rushed to the telephone and warned the command post not to fire any salvos after the end of the message. Then I called the radio station, where Levitan had already finished reading. I asked that he repeat the message, this time mentioning Konev's name.

Without losing time, Levitan began reading the message again, and I again called the command post and ordered it to ready the salute. All this took place under Stalin's eyes. "You may go," he said then.

I gathered my maps from the desk and waited for A. I. Antonov outside.

"It's a bad business," said Antonov, coming out of the office. "He swore but said nothing about dismissal."

Since five chiefs of the Office of Operations had already been re-placed before me, I knew which way the wind was blowing. To tell the truth, I felt saddened and yet almost glad at the same time. If relieved of my duties, I could leave the General Staff and go to the front. There were many who wanted to do that because service here was unreward-ing and, as a result of constant nervous tension, very difficult. Besides, a desire to go to the front was natural to all of us at that time.

No one either in the General Staff or in the Army Group noticed our wretched mistake. There were only questions as to why the message was read twice. After this incident, everyone was ordered not to make any abbreviations and to write rough drafts out in full. I did not go to Supreme Headquarters for two days, and Stalin did not phone me in the mornings, as he usually did; he waited for Antonov's arrival.

On the third day, General Antonov again went to report to Supreme Headquarters alone. But in his absence, news arrived of the capture by the 2nd Ukrainian Army Group of a large objective. As usual, we hastily prepared a "cap" of the message for the salute, and I asked through Sta-lin's secretariat that it be reported to Antonov. Antonov's call soon came: "Bring the message yourself," he said. A few minutes later I entered Stalin's study.

"Read it," Stalin told me. "You didn't leave out the name?"

I read it and received permission to pass it on.

Antonov finished his report, and we left together. On that, the unpleasantness came to a relatively happy ending.

The salute messages involved a lot of fuss. Levitan read them continuously. Sometimes it happened that the message did not reach the
radio studio in its entirety. The time for the salute would arrive, but the
message would still not be ready. Levitan might read the second page,
for example, but the third would still be missing. But somehow we always
found a way out, and everything went well except for isolated misfires.[30]

Chief Marshal of Artillery N. N. Voronov
The Vexations
of Centralization

WHEN I RETURNED to Moscow from the front in January 1944, I keenly
sensed the general animation and a certain special lift in spirits among
the officers of Supreme Headquarters, the General Staff, and the Main
Directorates of Artillery and Anti-aircraft Defense. Everyone was busy
with preparations for major offensive operations. . . .

This was a time of the greatest centralization. Not one important
decision or order, no single major document could go to Supreme Headquarters or to the General Staff without my signature. If my signature
was lacking on a document, Stalin invariably asked: "Has this been
cleared with Voronov?" It was, of course, not a question of me personally.
Stalin demanded the very same procedure from all other branches and
services of the armed forces. The excessive centralization was extremely
vexing. It not only robbed one of a great deal of time and prevented one
from concentrating on the main thing, but it fettered the initiative of
subordinates, slowed things down, and lowered efficiency. Sometimes,
absolutely urgent decisions were made only when long overdue.

Did Stalin understand this? Evidently he did not. He could not
tolerate the decision of even secondary matters without his knowledge.
But people were often afraid to report to him. For that reason, many
innovations in every possible area were artificially delayed. This caused
a great deal of harm.

N. N. Voronov, "Podvig sovetskogo naroda," *Istoriia SSSR*, 1965, No. 4, pp. 3–5.

It was likewise difficult for my deputies and the artillery staff to do any work when I was at the front. While I was with the Western Army Group, N. D. Iakovlev became swamped with the most serious matters, which could not be resolved without me. I could not return to Moscow then, and Iakovlev could not possibly go to the Western Army Group, since he was in charge of supplying all Army Groups with arms and equipment. What was to be done? We found the solution by meeting at a halfway point, in the town of Iukhnov. There we spent several hours conferring and making a series of very important decisions. . . .

It was with some agitation that I walked through the Kremlin corridors when I was summoned to Supreme Headquarters for the first time after a long absence. That day, the progress of preparations for the forthcoming operations was discussed in the Kremlin. . . . I listened attentively to the reports of General Staff members and watched Stalin closely. It was striking how much more calmly and confidently the work of Supreme Headquarters was proceeding. Stalin was more balanced, far more even-tempered than before.

The plans of forthcoming operations were worked out in an interesting manner. Every detail of the missions in each operation was provided for, and everyone was sure that they would be executed. Each operation complemented the ones that preceded and succeeded it. A blow in one sector followed a blow in another, so that the enemy had no chance to transfer his forces from one sector to another. Still more attention was paid to the combination of massive blows with swift maneuvering. We now remembered bitterly the lessons of our failures at Leningrad, in the Western Army Group, and in other sectors where there was no opportunity for broad maneuvering. So now the closest possible coordination between Army Groups had been worked out at last!

General of the Army A. V. Khrulev
Quartermaster at Work

IN THE YEARS preceding the war there were various conflicting viewpoints in the People's Commissariat of Defense concerning which agency should be in charge of supplying the troops during a war. When Marshal A. I.

A. V. Khrulev, "Stanovlenie strategicheskogo tyla v Velikoi Otechestvennoi voine," *Voenno-istoricheskii zhurnal*, 1961, No. 6, pp. 64–80.

Egorov was Chief of the General Staff (1931–1937), he strove to retain for the General Staff only the function of issuing directives concerning the accumulation of supplies and that of control over the quartermaster agencies. He feared, with justification, that if the General Staff were charged with yet another organizational role in military supply, then the General Staff itself, as well as the staffs of the Army Groups and Armies, might be overwhelmed by such a major and independent job and that this would adversely affect their ability to command the troops.

General of the Army G. K. Zhukov, who became Chief of the General Staff in February 1941, had a different viewpoint. He supported those on the General Staff who believed that a general outline sufficed as a basis for directing the supply of the army in the field: the General Staff would calculate needs and issue a directive; the quartermaster services subordinate to it would dispatch everything requested from them; and the commandant's offices of the General Staff's Military Transportation Service, to which motor vehicle, rail, water, and air transport were subordinate, would deliver to the troops all types of authorized supply. In theory this scheme looked smooth and harmonious. . . .

But the war began, and from the very first days this system of administration did not withstand the test. The rear service agencies were immediately faced with very complex tasks. It was necessary to supply matériel for the deployment and concentration of troops and for the retreating units; rear service establishments and material resources had to be evacuated while under attack, and the necessary level of supplies to the troops engaged in defensive operations had to be maintained. . . .

The staffs of formations and units, overloaded with their own immediate work, were unable to untie the knots of the many-faceted logistical work that arose in the complex operational situation during the initial period of the war.

The situation at the front was becoming more and more tense and confused. Because of the forced retreat of our troops from the western regions, more than 1,300 major industrial enterprises were hastily evacuated to the east. A great deal of collective and state farm property, livestock, grain, as well as equipment and supplies for mobilization and reserves of matériel were being evacuated.[31] Two gigantic train flows were moving in opposite directions with incredible difficulty under constant air attack by the enemy. In July 1941 alone there were 1,470 enemy air raids on railroad targets, i.e., an average of fifty objectives were attacked every day.

In the very first month of the war serious miscalculations were discovered with respect to the location of hospital facilities. There were clearly not enough facilities to handle the wounded. Large quantities of military stores in the Ukraine and Belorussia were in danger of being captured by the enemy. Back in 1940 the government had considered the problem of where to concentrate equipment and supplies for mobilization. Army officials had suggested they be located beyond the Volga. L. Z. Mekhlis, People's Commissar of State Control, resisted this. He insisted that they be accumulated in border areas, even in close proximity to the probable enemy. Mekhlis regarded any objection to this as sabotage.

"But at least leave the sheepskin coats, felt boots, and other winter clothing beyond the Volga," military men said.

"How do you know when the war will begin?" Mekhlis asked them. "Suppose it begins in the winter?"

Stalin yielded to Mekhlis' arguments and accepted his viewpoint. Subsequently, we had to pay very dearly for this. A great deal of matériel was either destroyed by our troops when they retreated or was captured by the enemy.[32]

The deployment period required superhuman effort and sleepless nights from officials at all command levels. The General Staff, completely taken up by operational problems, was unable to deal with logistical tasks. The quartermaster services were, in fact, left without guidance. There was a crying need for radical improvement in the entire work of supplying the troops with matériel and equipment.

The areas of responsibility were divided among the members of the State Defense Committee, which was created as an emergency agency of supreme authority for the duration of the war. A. I. Mikoyan, Deputy Chairman of the Council of People's Commissars and a member of the State Defense Committee, was in charge of army supply matters from the beginning to the end of the war. In the first six weeks of the war A. A. Andreev, Secretary of the Party Central Committee, handled military transport.

In actuality, the State Defense Committee worked through the apparatus of the Central Committee of the Party, the Council of People's Commissars, and the People's Commissariats. The Committee issued all instructions for waging the war and resolved all questions of coordination between the armed forces and the national economy. Members of the Committee who reported on prepared draft resolutions, each in his own field of activity, always had free access to Stalin. Military leaders, People's Commissars, and other responsible persons constantly went to the committee, not only in response to summons but also on their own initiative if they had an important and urgent problem. There were no meetings of the Committee in the ordinary sense, that is, with a definite agenda, secretaries, and minutes. The procedure for coordinating with the State Planning Committee, the People's Commissariats, and the state organizations the questions of supply for the armed forces, including the organization of new types of production, was simplified to the utmost, thanks to the desire of economic leaders to service the front and rout the enemy as quickly as possible, regardless of the effort required.

Of course, this does not mean that questions were always decided smoothly in the Committee. I remember an acute situation that once arose when we discussed the output of artillery shells and other ammunition. N. A. Voznesenskii, Chairman of the State Planning Commission and a member of the State Defense Committee, was in charge of this branch of production. On the basis of his report, the Committee approved a plan for the production of 1,000,000 shells in July 1941. Actually, 800,000 were produced. Without allowing for the fact that a certain number of enterprises producing ammunition were located in the combat area and that many factories were in the process of evacuation to the east, N. A. Voznesenskii had planned an output of 2,000,000 shells for August and 3,000,000 for September. But only 600,000 shells were produced in August, and the September plan also was not fulfilled.

At the Committee meeting, the People's Commissars who dealt with the production of ammunition reported that they were receiving plans known in advance to be unrealistic. The situation was aggravated by the fact that the vast production capacities of Leningrad's defense industry were being utilized less and less: the city was already under blockade in September, and no more metal was being shipped there.

The Committee relieved N. A. Voznesenskii of direct leadership of the war industry.[33] In order to make up for lost time as quickly as possible and to satisfy the increasing needs of the front, the Committee drew many enterprises with metalworking equipment into the production of artillery shells, mines, and other ammunition, as well as of various types of arms. Factories of the People's Commissariats of Transportation, the Meat and Dairy Industry, the Food Industry, the Textile Industry, Light Industry, Agriculture, and even the workshops of producers' cooperatives became suppliers of ammunitions and arms. The results came quickly. The output of shells, mines, hand grenades, mortars, and other combat matériel increased sharply. . . .[34]

The success of Party and government agencies in placing the national economy on a war footing created rapidly developing sources of war consignments for the armed forces. But the actual system for supplying the front was imperfect. Without interrupting its operations, it had to be reorganized immediately so that the military agencies could distribute war supplies economically and effectively. When I, as Chief Quartermaster of the Red Army, did not receive any instructions from the General Staff concerning what supply resources were needed and which Army Groups had priority, I went to G. K. Zhukov, Chief of the General Staff at the beginning of July 1941. I was accompanied by General N. D. Iakovlev, head of the Main Artillery Directorate. Zhukov was sitting in his office, tired and red-eyed from sleepless nights. When I asked how matters stood with regard to supplying the troops, Zhukov waved his hand in disgust and said:

"I can't tell you a thing. I can't make sense of a lot of things myself yet. And as for what the troops need now, I don't know."

This conversation reinforced my conviction that the General Staff, which was completely engrossed in the operational leadership of the troops, was unable to organize successfully supply for the front. . . . Soon after my conversation with G. K. Zhukov, I informed A. I. Mikoyan of my ideas on improving the supply work as quickly as possible, establishing a reliable structure for the Soviet Army's rear services, and overcoming the impotence of the existing organization of the quartermaster services. At the same time I gave him the 1914 Regulations [on the Field Command of Troops in Wartime] to read.[35]

The next day Comrade Mikoyan called me up:

"Comrade Khrulev," he said, "the Supreme Commander has charged you with drafting a State Defense Committee decision on the organization of the Red Army rear in wartime." . . .

The draft decree of the State Defense Committee was ready at the end of July. Leading Committee members met in Stalin's office. The Supreme Commander in Chief read the document and silently handed it to the Chief of the General Staff, G. K. Zhukov. Zhukov read the draft quickly and declared peremptorily:

"I do not agree. The authors of the draft want the rear services to undercut the General Staff."

Casting an expressive glance at G. K. Zhukov, the Supreme Commander in Chief took the draft back and signed it right then and there. The Main Directorate of the Red Army Rear was formed by order of the People's Commissar of Defense on August 1, 1941. It combined the staffs of the Chief of the Rear, of the Military Transportation Directorate, the Highway Administration, the Chief Quartermaster Directorate, the Fuel Supply Directorate, the Military Medical Directorate, and the Veterinary Directorate. The services for supply of combat and technical equipment remained subordinate to the commanders of the respective branches of the armed forces. Delivery of this equipment to the army in the field was planned and executed by the rear service agencies, which had charge of all transportation facilities.

As Deputy People's Commissar of Defense, I was appointed Chief of the Red Army Rear. . . . In addition, the post of Chief of the Army Group Rear was introduced. He was a deputy of the Army Group commander and simultaneously subordinate to the Chief of the Red Army Rear. A similar structure was also adopted in the Armies. . . .

By August 3 the commanders of the Army Groups and the Armies were to establish the headquarters of the chiefs of the rear. Eminent officers with considerable service experience in command posts were selected as chiefs of the rear of the Army Groups. On July 30 all those selected gathered in Stalin's office. . . . The Supreme Commander in Chief acquainted those present with the situation at the front and emphasized the exceptional difficulties in supplying the troops with matériel and evacuating the wounded.

"The war requires an iron-clad procedure for supplying the troops," he said. "This procedure must be carried out by the firm hand of the chiefs of the rear of the Army Groups and Armies. You must be dictators in the rear zone of your Army Groups, and each one of you must understand this well."

The Supreme Commander in Chief regarded the supply of the armed forces with everything necessary as more than a simple supply function; he regarded it as operational work, organically linked to the combat operations of the troops. . . .

The cumbersome rear services inherited at the beginning of the war were a great burden for the troops. They were not in keeping with the mobile nature of combat operations in conditions of a rapidly changing operational situation. There were too many depots, bases, medical and other offices in the Army Groups. For example, in August 1941, the Southwestern Army Group had more than 100 depots. And what about the rear services of the divisions? To transport a rifle division by rail, 33 trains were needed, of which 14 were used to carry rear units and subdivisions. . . .

[Following various organizational changes] the rear services began to function more flexibly and with greater maneuverability. The rear service agencies, however, still remained cumbersome. Many clothing, food, medical, veterinary, artillery, and other supply subdivisions and offices had been formed in the haste of the first days of the war by independent decisions of the military councils of the Army Groups, Armies, and military districts without confirmation by the central authorities. In these supply subdivisions a very large proportion of personnel was fit for active service. . . . There was one way out: to eliminate all superfluous rear-service subdivisions and offices created by the Army Groups in the summer of 1941. The staffs and offices of service and rear units had to be cut. Wherever possible, men were to be replaced by women. All this was carried out by order of the People's Commissar of Defense. . . .

During the battle for Moscow many officers in the Rear Services Directorate concluded, after having visited the Volkhov, Kalinin, and Western Army Groups, that extensive emergency measures had to be

taken to combat losses, waste, and sometimes even theft of freight that
was on its way to the troops in the field. Clearly, the troops did not
economize sufficiently.

The resolution of the State Defense Committee "On Safeguarding the
Military Property of the Red Army in Wartime," which was conveyed
to all the troops, pointed out that a large quantity of food, fuel, and war
supplies was being wasted, lost, and spoiled as a result of bad management. Military freight was carelessly handled in transit, at the destination stations, at temporary field depots, and at transfer points. Even the
simplest storehouses, shelters, or enclosures were not constructed. Military
property was poorly guarded during transport and evacuation in field conditions. Many truck and wagon drivers and their escorts did not carry
documents indicating the nature and quantity of freight they were carrying,
their destination, and the name of the consignee.

All this often happened right under the eyes of the commanders, political
officers, and service chiefs. . . . This resolution introduced a compulsory
procedure: an "open sheet," which described the freight and consignee,
was issued for every train, truck, and wagon hauling freight. It was strictly
forbidden to deliver or to receive freight without an "open sheet." Persons
in positions of responsibility who violated this procedure for shipping freight
were to be put on trial under wartime laws. The same liability applied
to those who delivered the freight and were found to have unjustified
shortages. The introduction of this and a number of other measures for
the protection of state property played a tremendous role in helping to
establish order. . . .

In the autumn of 1941, and especially during the first winter of the
war, we had many heartaches owing to our inadequate network of dirt
roads. Before the war we had not clearly realized how important they were
in a country like ours. Take the Kalinin Army Group, for example. The
lack of dirt roads there sometimes placed our troops literally in a disastrous position, as was the case with the units of the 1st Guards Rifle Corps,
the 39th Army, and several other units.[36] Alarming telegrams about the
disruption of supply came not only from the Kalinin Army Group, but also
the Leningrad, Volkhov, Western, and other Army Groups. Near Kursk
and Orel, motor transport literally sank in the impassable mud after it
rained. Yet the troops required regular deliveries daily.

Could air transport have changed the situation? No, of course not.
We did not have enough aircraft, and also we had far too few landing
strips.

The solution was obvious—the organization of horse-drawn wagon
trains. Officials of the rear services did not doubt for a minute that in
these conditions it was the only way out. But to do this it was neces-

sary to have a resolution of the State Defense Committee! What would they think of such a suggestion? How many poisonous remarks would greet such a project! This is exactly what happened.

When I reported to Stalin on the proposal, he said sarcastically: "There's news for you: It's the age of technology, and suddenly—a sack of oats, wagon drivers, sleighs!"

But even he was unable to find any other way. The proposal was adopted.

Nevertheless, some commanders greeted the directive concerning animal-drawn transport battalions with skepticism. But on December 24, 1941, the first 76 animal-drawn transport battalions were distributed among the Army Groups. (Each battalion consisted of 250 wagons or sleighs, each drawn by a pair of horses.) The Western Army Group received the most (twelve battalions). Nineteen battalions remained in Supreme Headquarters reserve. Before long we were literally overwhelmed with requests for horse-drawn wagons. It turned out that everyone needed them very badly. The very first sleigh train had brought more supplies to the 39th Army than air transport had in the course of many days.

The transport battalions, which had seemed archaic to some at the beginning, helped us immensely to solve the problem of uninterrupted delivery of supplies to the troops during that difficult period. It should be pointed out that after the horse-drawn trains made their appearance, reindeer-drawn trains appeared in the north and camel-drawn trains in the Caspian steppes. In the mountains of the Caucasus, pack-mule caravans came in very handy. Subsequently, the animal-drawn transport battalions did so well that the government allotted another 4,000 horses to the Red Army rear services. This facilitated the formation of the animal-drawn transport units that were used to haul vegetables of the 1943 harvest and to establish centralized reserves to supply the needs of the army in the field. Thus, the shortage of motor vehicles and the difficult road conditions compelled us to resort to this economical improvisation. . . .[37]

On November 20, 1941, the People's Commissar of Defense issued an order on improving the management of logistics and on prompt supply of food and other items due the soldiers. . . . Back in September 1941, A. I. Mikoyan and I had prepared a report to the State Defense Committee which proposed the establishment of differentiated food-supply norms for the troops during wartime. This was a necessary measure, as it was clear that we would not be able to feed all servicemen in accordance with the high norms established for peacetime. Four categories of rations were established for the land forces. The highest norm was set for the troops of the forward echelon; it was even a bit higher than the peacetime norm. The lowest (fourth) category applied to all military personnel in rear-service offices and units that were not part of the army in the field. Fliers and engineering personnel had special norms.[38] The norms we proposed were accepted by the State Defense Committee and were maintained for the duration of the war. . . .

The organization of victualing soldiers is indeed of paramount importance. A great deal of energy was put into this work! The State Defense Committee often handled questions of victualing. How much effort Party and government leaders put into it! Nevertheless, there were officers and quartermaster personnel who slighted this matter of state importance. In May 1943, serious breakdowns were uncovered in the organization of the food supply to troops of the Kalinin Army Group. Interruptions occurred even at a time when the Army Group and all its formations were fully supplied with foodstuffs. In response to this situation, on May 31, a special resolution of the State Defense Committee and an order of the People's Commissar of Defense were published; they had widespread repercussions in the army.

The order enumerated instances where provisions were unevenly distributed among the separate divisions and regiments, as a result of which some divisions had more of some products than they needed, while others did not have enough or any at all. This situation came about because the Army Group military council did not pay proper attention to victualing the soldiers. Army Group and Army agencies of the provisions service concerned themselves only with the distribution of supplies; they did not supervise the preparation of food in the field kitchens. There were some "wise men" who formally adhered to the "substitution table," but for no reason at all substituted powdered eggs for meat or put into the pot flour for thickening instead of vegetables.[39]

The order was drafted in strong terms. . . . The People's Commissar of Defense emphasized:

> Our commanders have evidently forgotten the finest traditions of the Russian Army, when such great generals as Suvorov and Kutuzov themselves, from whom the generals of all Europe learned and from whom Red Army officers should learn, displayed paternal solicitude for the everyday life and nourishment of the soldiers and strictly required the same from their subordinates. Yet, as is evident from the above-mentioned instances, there are officers in the Red Army who do not regard solicitude for the soldiers' everyday life and nourishment as their sacred duty and who thereby display an uncomradely and intolerable attitude toward the fighting men.

The culprits were reprimanded severely, and some were even tried by a military tribunal. Command personnel who permitted stoppages in feeding the soldiers or shortchanging them in foodstuffs were to be sent to penal battalions and companies by decision of the military council of the Army Group.[40]

But the point was not merely to punish. This order further increased the significance of quartermaster work. In order to strengthen the leadership of military supply work, all first members of the Army Groups' military councils were made personally responsible for dealing with all questions pertaining to the organization of the rear services of the Army Group. And it should be remembered that among them were such outstanding leaders as Politburo members N. S. Khrushchev and A. A. Zhdanov.[41]

This alone indicates what immense attention the Party paid to the work of organizing the rear services. This is the way it was all through the war.

Lieutenant General A. S. Iakovlev
Production
for War

IN THOSE DAYS [1943] we, the directors of branches of defense industry, were called to the Kremlin very often to discuss questions relating to the production and delivery of all types of weapons. The Politburo of the Central Committee of the Party, the Council of Ministers, the State Defense Committee, and Supreme Headquarters were daily occupied with these questions. The decrees, decisions, and orders of these organs came out of Stalin's plain Kremlin office with its arched ceiling. The office was decorated with bright oak paneling to the height of a man. Portraits of Suvorov and Kutuzov hung in golden frames on the wall, and there was a plaster of paris death mask of Lenin in a glass case. . . . At that time everyone was in a jaunty and fighting mood. Stalingrad, Kursk, Krasnodar, Rostov on the Don, and Voroshilovgrad had been liberated. Officials of the People's Commissariat of the Aviation Industry attributed a share of our troops' success to their own work. After crushing German aviation near Stalingrad, our fliers began their quest for air supremacy. But in order to secure this, it was necessary to give the front still more fighters, assault planes, and bombers.

A. S. Iakovlev, *Tsel' zhizni* (Moscow, 1966), pp. 317–32.

Frequent summons to the Kremlin had always been connected with questions of quantity, but most recently an interest was also expressed in improving the quality of airplanes. And we who were continuously taking all possible measures to increase the production of airplanes and engines also undertook to improve the flight characteristics of our aircraft.

In order to give an idea of how problems were resolved in the war industry at that time, I shall describe several episodes from the first half of 1943.

On the evening of February 11, 1943, People's Commissar A. I. Shakhurin and I were called to the Kremlin concerning the question of fighter escort for IL-4 bombers and IL-2 assault planes. Of the combat planes that had seen action, the IL-4 had reached the most venerable age; it had been created in 1936. Between 1937 and 1943, a total of roughly 6,500 IL-4 planes were built. The IL-4 became the basic long-range bomber of the USSR air force during the Patriotic War. But its top speed—450 km. per hour—was not sufficient to permit it to fly daylight combat missions without great risk in the absence of fighter escort. In the first period of the war, therefore, at a time when we still had few fighters and could not provide escorts, the IL-4 was used primarily at night. . . .

When we arrived, certain members of the Politburo, Marshals of Aviation Novikov and Golovanov, and several high-ranking tank commanders were already seated at the long table in Stalin's office. Apparently, they had been discussing something with the tankmen before our arrival. Just as soon as we entered, the conversation with the tankmen was interrupted, and Stalin raised the question of the possibility of daylight bombing, using the IL-4's.

"It is no longer 1941 when we didn't have enough fighters and when the IL-4's suffered heavy losses while making daylight flights without protection," he said. "We now have enough fighters to provide escorts for the Il'iushin bombers. We're not satisfied that the IL-4's work solely at night and that we lack daylight bombers. The IL-4 must be used for daylight bombing."[42]

Then he started talking about assault planes, about the need for their more energetic and daring employment over the battlefield.

"They must have more reliable fighter cover in order to decrease the loss of assault planes due to enemy fighter aircraft. The pilots of assault planes must be able to work with greater daring, without fear of enemy fighters!"

Marshal Novikov gave his point of view and expressed the wish that fighter escort be in the ratio 1:1.5, i.e., three fighters to two assault planes. Shakhurin immediately protested against Novikov's proposal, saying that if the 1:1.5 ratio were adopted, and the number of planes needed to cover daylight IL-4 flights added to that, we should not have enough fighters.

A heated exchange broke out between Novikov and Shakhurin. After letting them sound off for a while, Stalin interrupted the argument, saying: "Apparently, the matter is not clear. We must determine more precisely the balance of fighters, assault planes, and bombers for the near future, and after that we'll make a decision." . . .

On the evening of February 16, 1943, we were again called to the Kremlin. We did not have to wait. We were immediately invited into the office. Molotov, Mikoyan, and Shcherbakov were already there. We entered at the moment when Stalin, standing, was reading the [draft] communiqué of the Soviet Information Bureau concerning the taking of Khar'kov. He was editing the text of the announcement, reading it aloud, and making corrections with a thick blue pencil. Finally, when all the corrections had been made, he read it through again and said: "Well, that will be all right!" And he handed the final text to Shcherbakov, who took it away to be typed and broadcast over the radio.

After this, Stalin read aloud a letter from designer N. N. Polikarpov which reported on a new high-speed fighter that had undergone factory tests and had demonstrated high speeds. He asked: "What do you know about this machine?"

I replied: "It's a good machine. Its speed really is high."

Stalin immediately said:

"Forget your corporate loyalty. You don't want to offend the designer, and you comment on it favorably. How do you view it, impartially?"

Shakhurin and I tried to give an objective assessment of the aircraft and to describe it as exhaustively as possible. But since the plane had only gone through part of the factory flight tests, it was impossible to draw a final conclusion.

Among other things, Stalin was interested in the fighter's range, noting that speed without the necessary range meant little. We named the range.

"Has it been verified in flight?"

"No, its range has still not been tested in flight. These are estimated data."

"I don't believe words. Check its range in flight first, and then we'll decide what to do with the plane. It's too early to decide now."

And he put Polikarpov's letter aside.

Then Shakhurin was asked about the M-82 engine—a powerful aircooled engine of Shvetsov design. Previously, Stalin had said more than once that more of these engines should be produced, and now he asked Shakhurin what was holding up their serial production. The plant that was supposed to be serially producing the M-82 was indeed having great difficulty with it, and production had been greatly delayed.

The People's Commissar began citing various reasons to explain the delays.

Stalin flared up:

"Why don't you report about your difficulties in time? If you yourself can't eliminate them or solve them, you should report it. We will not refuse to help. But you must report these difficulties if you yourself can't cope with them."

Then Shakhurin raised the question of the possibility of serially producing the Tupolev Tu-2 frontline dive bomber which had undergone government testing successfully.

"To begin serial production of a new plane now, in wartime, would be a risky gamble," Stalin said. "For a certain time we'll build up the number of other airplanes, and then we'll return to this question."

Shakhurin and I continued to insist on the necessity of manufacturing the Tu-2, since in terms of combat qualities, it was superior to the Pe-2 and the IL-4. But Stalin was immovable.

"In principle, I am for it, but for the time being we'll wait."

(Indeed, after our military situation improved, the question of producing the Tu-2 was resumed, and at the end of 1944 the first Tu-2 planes began reaching the front.) . . .

The flight range of fighters—the La-5 and Iak-9 in particular—became the subject of conversation in discussing any aviation question in the Central Committee. No matter what was under discussion, ultimately the topic would be shifted to range. This is explained by the fact that the Supreme High Command had planned a major offensive in the summer of 1943, and it was necessary to provide fighter air cover for the rapid advance of ground troops. We could not build airfields immediately behind land forces which were pressing the enemy and hurling him back. Therefore, to increase fighter aircraft range became the number one problem.

On a March day in 1943 we were called to the Kremlin concerning the Klimov VK-107 engine, and once again the conversation turned to the flying range of fighters. We reported that designer Lavochkin had produced a new modification of the La-5 airplane with an M-71 engine—the powerful air-cooled engine of designer Shvetsov—and that this airplane had demonstrated good flight characteristics.

Stalin was pleased and started asking us all about this machine. But then he noted:

"Tell Lavochkin that the range of his airplane is too short. We require that it be not less than a thousand kilometers."

Then he started comparing our fighters to the English Spitfire and the American Air Cobra. In so doing, he said that the performance data issued by foreign producers were exaggerated. When he cited the data on the Spitfire, I assumed that he was talking about the reconnaissance Spitfire with a range of over 2,000 km. I said that this airplane was not armed, that it was a reconnaissance plane and not a fighter.

To this, Stalin retorted: "What kind of nonsense are you talking? Am I a child? I am talking about a fighter and not about a reconnaissance plane. The Spitfire has a greater range than our fighters, and we must of necessity improve in this respect."[43]

I promised to take all possible measures, in particular to increase to 1,200 km. the range of fighters armed with heavy cannon. I have cited these episodes to show the atmosphere in which the preparation of our aviation for the summer offensive of 1943 was carried out. . . .

At the beginning of June 1943, we quite unexpectedly landed in trouble. At the last moment, when our troops were preparing to ward off the new enemy offensive, it developed that the Iak's which the front had received from factories in the east and which comprised the majority of fighter aircraft in the Kursk sector were unfit for combat.

On June 3, 1943, P. V. Dement'ev, Deputy People's Commissar in charge of production, and I were summoned to Supreme Headquarters. In addition to Stalin, Marshals Vasilevskii and Voronov were in the office. We immediately noticed some pieces of cracked wing-covering fabric on the table and understood what was up. An unpleasant talk lay ahead.

The point was that the wing covering of Iak-9 fighters produced at one of the eastern plants was cracking and coming off.[44] There had been several cases in which the fabric was torn from the airplane's wings in flight. This was caused by the poor quality of nitro dyes delivered by one of the Ural chemical enterprises where hastily tested substitutes were employed. The paint was not durable and was quickly affected by atmospheric conditions. It would crack, and the fabric gluing of the wing would come loose from the plywood. We already knew of this defect and were trying in every way to eliminate it.

Stalin pointed to the pieces of defective covering lying on the table and asked: "Do you know anything about this?" He began to read the report which had been sent together with specimens of the defective covering from the air Army deployed in the Kursk region.

We said that we knew of cases where the covering had ripped off. He interrupted us: "What do you mean 'cases'? All the fighter aviation is unfit for combat. There have been as many as ten cases in which the covering ripped off in the air. The pilots are afraid to fly. How did this happen?"

Stalin picked up a piece of fabric on which the coat of paint and varnish had completely cracked and broken into pieces. He showed it to us and asked: "What is this?"

Dement'ev explained the reason for it and said that we knew of the defect and that we were taking steps to stop the production of defective planes and to repair those already manufactured. He promised to remedy this error in the shortest possible time and to ensure the combat fitness of all airplanes recently produced.

Stalin turned to us in indignation: "Do you know that this is wrecking an important operation which cannot be carried out without fighter participation?"

Yes, we knew that preparations were being made for serious fighting in the Orel-Kursk area, and we felt terrible at that moment.

"Why did this happen?" Stalin continued, losing his composure more and more. "Why were several hundred airplanes produced with defective coverings? After all, you know that fighters at this point are as vital to us as the air we breathe! How could you permit such a thing? Why weren't counter-measures taken sooner?"

We explained that it would have been impossible to discover this defect at the time the airplanes were produced. It was discovered only in the course of time when the airplanes were not under a hangar roof but at frontline air bases under open skies, exposed to rain, sun, and other atmospheric elements. It was also difficult to discover defects at the plant itself since the planes were immediately dispatched to the front from the shop.

I had never seen Stalin in such a rage.

"That means this was not known at the plant?"

"No, it was not known."

"That means that this became apparent at the front only in the face of the enemy?"

"Yes, that is so."

"Do you know that only the most cunning enemy could do such a thing?! This is exactly what he would do: turn out airplanes in such a way that they would seem good at the plant and no good at the front. The enemy himself could do us no greater harm. He could have devised nothing worse. This is working for Hitler!" Several times he repeated that the most cunning enemy could not have done greater harm.

"Do you know that you have put fighter aviation out of commission? Do you know what a service you have rendered Hitler?! You Hitlerites!"

It is difficult to imagine our condition at that moment. I felt that I was shivering. And Dement'ev stood there, completely flushed, nervously twirling a piece of the ill-fated covering in his fingers.

Several minutes passed in tomb-like silence. Finally Stalin, who had been pacing back and forth in contemplation, calmed down somewhat and asked in a businesslike way:

"What are we going to do?"

Dement'ev replied that we would immediately repair all airplanes. "What does immediately mean? How soon?"

Dement'ev thought for an instant, exchanged glances with me, and said:

"In two weeks."

"You aren't deceiving me?"

"No, Comrade Stalin, we'll do it."

I didn't believe my ears. It seemed to me that at least a couple of months would be required for that work.

Stalin simply did not expect that the planes could be repaired so quickly. Frankly, I was also surprised and thought to myself: Dement'ev's promise has temporarily diverted the storm, but what will happen later?

The deadline was accepted. Nonetheless, Stalin ordered the military prosecutor's office to make an immediate investigation of the matter and to find out how defective nitro dyes and glues had reached the aircraft plant and why the lacquers had not been sufficiently tested under laboratory conditions.

Then and there, the order was given to dispatch two investigating commissions—one to the Ural paint and varnish plant and another to the plant that was serially producing the Iak's.

After this, Stalin turned to me:

"Isn't your self-esteem suffering? How do you feel? They are scoffing at you. They are burying your plane, and what are you doing about it?"

"Comrade Stalin, I feel terrible because I understand very well what a blow to the cause this ill-fated happening has been. But, together with Dement'ev, I promise that we will take the most energetic measures, and this defect will be eliminated in the shortest possible time."

When we had left Stalin's office, I heaved a sigh of relief, but at the same time I could not but say to Dement'ev:

"Listen, how can such a job be accomplished in two weeks?"

"We'll think about it, but it has to be done," Dement'ev replied.

The burden of eliminating the consequences of the defective wing gluing lay on Dement'ev, and he must be given his due. He showed unbelievable energy and initiative.[45]

Marshal I. Kh. Bagramian
Debacle in Kiev

On September 10 the fascist command succeeded in driving a mighty tank wedge from the north deep into the rear of the Southwestern Army Group.[46] In response to the Army Group command's request for help, Marshal S. M. Budennyi [Commander in Chief of the Southwestern Strategic Sector] was forced to reply: "I have no reserves and therefore cannot help you with troops."

After assessing the situation thoroughly and realizing that troops of the Army Group had exhausted all their potential for holding the line, General Tupikov, together with my deputy, Colonel N. D. Zakhvataev, went to see General Kirponos. Seated in his office were the greatly agitated members of the Army Group military council—M. A. Burmistenko and E. P. Rykov. Tupikov silently unfolded the latest situation map that had been brought in and looked inquiringly at the commander. General Kirponos wearily stood up from the table, bent over the map, and asked softly:

"What do you have to say?"

General Tupikov tapped a pencil on the point of the wedge of Guderian's tank troops and declared:

"The aim of the Hitlerite command to catch us in a trap has become unmistakably clear and evident. For precisely this reason it diverted from the Moscow sector an entire field army and its best tank group headed by Guderian—the Wehrmacht tank commander best known in the West. Both these armies are now insistently tearing into the rear of the Kiev grouping. Guderian's tanks have already reached the rear communication lines of the troops of our Army Group."

Sighing heavily, the chief of staff stated emphatically:

"This fact is in itself sufficient cause for alarm. And if you recall the latest reports of our scouts to the effect that the Kleist tank group is being brought up to the Kremenchug region to reinforce the German 17th Army, there is more than enough cause for alarm.

"Just imagine," he continued with great anxiety, "if the Kleist tank group reaches the bridgehead in the Kremenchug area.° In such a case, not only will there be no hope of liquidating this bridgehead, but the troops of the

---

I. Kh. Bagramian, *Gorod-voin na Dnepre* (Moscow, 1965), pp. 120–56.
°The chief of staff did not know then that the Kleist divisions were already massing on the bridgehead northwest of Kremenchug.

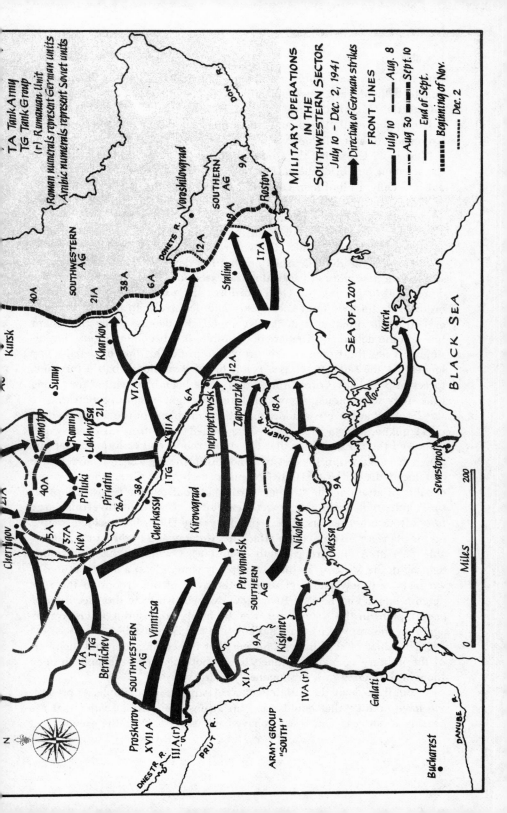

MILITARY OPERATIONS
IN THE
SOUTHWESTERN SECTOR
July 10 – Dec. 2, 1941

➤ Direction of German strikes

FRONT LINES

━━━ July 10
━━━ Aug. 8
━ ━ ━ Aug 30
▬▬▬ Sept. 10
━━━ End of Sept.
▬▬▬▬ Beginning of Nov.
······· Dec. 2

TA Tank Army
TG Tank Group
(r) Rumanian Unit
Roman numerals represent German units
Arabic numerals represent Soviet units

Kursk

Sumy
Konotop
Romny
Lokhvitsa
Priluki
Piriatin
Cherkassy
Kirovograd

Chernigov
Kiev
Berdichev
Vinnitsa
Proskurov
Pervomaisk

Kharkov
Lokhvitsa

Dnepropetrovsk
Zaporozhe
Nikolaev
Odessa

Voroshilovgrad
Rostov
Stalino

Kerch

Sevastopol

Galati
Kishinev
Bucharest

SOUTHWESTERN AG
SOUTHERN AG
ARMY GROUP "SOUTH"

DON R.
DONETS R.
DNEPR R.
DNESTR R.
PRUT R.
DANUBE R.

SEA OF AZOV
BLACK SEA

40 A
21 A
38 A
6 A
12 A
18 A
9 A
I TA
VI A
XVII A
VII A
V TA
I TG
26 A
40 A
5 A
37 A
XI A
9 A
IV A (r)
III A (r)
VI A

N

Miles
0   200

38th Army—who are holding a defense line 200 km. long—will surely be unable to hold back this tank group, which will inevitably push north toward the Guderian forces."[47]

Bending over the map and measuring the distance from Romny to Kremenchug, he exclaimed:

"Just look! Even now the Guderian forces are only 150 km. away from the Kremenchug bridgehead. For tank troops this means two days at the outside. Only a blind man could fail to see what this is leading to."

M. A. Burmistenko, who had been listening to the chief of staff very attentively, could not restrain himself:

"And what can the Army Group military council do in such a situation?"

Trying to speak calmly, Tupikov replied without hesitation:

"Despite the difficult situation that has developed on our flanks, we still have a possibility of frustrating the execution of the fascist command's design and of placing the Guderian forces in a difficult position. But in order to do this, we must act quickly and decisively. In light of the general strategic situation that has developed, the defense along the Dnepr line and the defense of Kiev are not feasible. It is becoming utterly impossible to keep the troops of the Army Group on this line of defense any longer. At the same time, as a result of the two-month battle for Kiev, forces of [German] Army Group South have been bled white. For a long time, they were pinned down and forced to fight exhausting battles."

Looking at the commander and at the members of the military council, Tupikov, after a moment's pause, added with stress on every word:

"And the main thing is that the stubbornness and endurance that our troops have shown in the last two months in the Kiev sector have finally convinced the Hitlerite High Command that Army Group South is not capable of attaining the strategic goals that confront the fascist troops on the southern flank of the Soviet-German front without diverting large forces from other sectors. This is precisely why Hitler has decided to give up his plans for an immediate attack on Moscow and to direct a considerable part of Army Group South against us. Owing to this, our troops fighting in the Moscow sector have already won at least a month's time. If we make a timely and organized withdrawal of our troops to the rear defense line along the Psel River now, we will frustrate the execution of enemy plans in the Kiev sector, too, by firmly confronting fascist troops again on the approaches to Khar'kov and the Donbass."

The chief of staff paused. Seeing that the commander and members of the military council continued to say nothing and were sunk in deep thought, he added in a pronouncedly sharp voice:

"But if we delay the withdrawal, a catastrophe is inevitable. At present, we have nothing that could stand up against the fascist armies that are tearing at our rear. Our reserves have been used up. With the exception of

General Kostenko's Army, all our Armies are already engaged in fierce battles with the superior enemy forces that are attacking them. At present it is impossible to take a single division away from them. Only the 26th Army remains. It has five divisions which are covering 150 km. of defense line. Even if part of General Kostenko's forces were taken from him, they would not save the situation. This is like trying to stop a breach in the Dnepr Dam with a spade."

Having finished his report, the chief of staff sat down wearily. There was a long silence.

The silence was interrupted by the quiet voice of the Army Group commander.

"Everything that you have reported, Vasilii Ivanovich, is right. I can raise no objection to your proposals. The unfortunate thing is, however, that it is unlikely that we will get permission to carry them out. Supreme Headquarters will not allow a withdrawal. You can just imagine how Marshal Shaposhnikov will report the latest situation in our sector to Comrade Stalin. Like an academician, he will carefully weigh everything 'for' and 'against,' and, in conclusion, without making a concrete proposal which would correspond to the situation that has developed, he will ask: 'What is your command, Comrade Stalin? Shall they be permitted to withdraw?' Without question, Stalin's answer will be: 'We shouldn't be thinking about withdrawal. Rather, we should be thinking about how to hold Kiev and the Dnepr line.'"

Continuing his thought, Kirponos added: "It must not be forgotten that Supreme Headquarters still believes the Briansk Army Group is capable of crushing Guderian."[48]

Pausing for an instant, he exclaimed in genuine distress:

"It is sad but true that the commander in chief of the strategic sector cannot decide a single important question without Stalin's permission.[49] If the decision to withdraw rested with him, the question could be considered solved. He sees with his own eyes the impossible situation our troops are in. Therefore, in order to hasten the solution of the problem, we shall present our request to Supreme Headquarters and Comrade Budennyi simultaneously. I shall try to talk with Comrades Shaposhnikov and Budennyi this very day."

"The Supreme Commander in Chief should be informed of this personally. Let Comrade Stalin know that the Army Group military council unanimously supports the request to withdraw the troops to a rear line!" Rykov exclaimed, looking inquisitively at the first member of the military council.

M. A. Burmistenko frowned with displeasure and, lowering his head, did not answer Rykov. The heart of this fervent Kiev patriot could not be reconciled even to the thought that abandonment of the city was inevitable. In a moment of genuine agony, he said: "It is better to die on the streets of Kiev than to abandon it and remain alive." Crushed by the logic of events that attested to the inexorably approaching catastrophe for the troops fighting in the Kiev sector, he gloomily remained silent, without making the decision to support the proposal to withdraw the troops.

"Yes, of course it would be better to inform Comrade Stalin personally, but that is not so simple," Kirponos objected thoughtfully.

Having ordered General D. M. Dobykin to arrange talks with Supreme Headquarters and the commander in chief [of the strategic sector], Kirponos proceeded to current affairs.

"Mikhail Petrovich," Rykov interrupted suddenly. "If we are not permitted to withdraw our troops to the rear line, then at least we should be permitted to take the troops out of the Kiev fortified area and with their help to strengthen the right flank of our Army Group and to create at least a small reserve."

"I think this is what we should ask for," the commander agreed. "If they do not allow us to withdraw to the rear line, then let them allow us to free the troops that are occupying the Kiev fortified area. . . .

"Of course," he continued, "right now it would be possible to take almost all the rifle formations out of the Kiev fortified area, since the fascists, having received a real rebuff there, are now afraid to ask for trouble. Moreover, frontal attacks on Kiev have now lost their meaning. Nonetheless, the Supreme Commander in Chief has categorically forbidden us to remove troops from there even though he at the same time refused to supply us with reserves from the center. And only yesterday, as we all know, Supreme Headquarters decided to take the Borisov cavalry group from our right flank and transfer it to the Briansk Army Group. I find it difficult to explain what Supreme Headquarters hopes for in this already critical situation by condemning us virtually to wait passively until our lines of communication are seized by the enemy. This is clearly not the time for half-measures, such as the transfer of one or two divisions from one sector to another."

Having listened to the commander thoughtfully, General Tupikov remarked:

"Apparently, Stalin has developed the deep conviction that the situation on the right flank of our Army Group is not so hopeless. He probably believes that Guderian will be crushed any day now. After all, he ordered the commander of the Briansk Army Group to do this, and the latter up to this very time has not, apparently, ventured to admit that his troops are not in a position to carry out the order."

"What's that? Are you guessing?" Burmistenko asked with unconcealed interest, slowly nearing the map beside which Tupikov stood.

The chief of staff glanced quickly at Burmistenko and, meeting his intent, inquiring gaze, retorted: "No, not at all. I already reported to you concerning the order that Stalin gave to the commander of the Briansk Army Group."

Pausing, he continued with barely perceptible irony:

"The other day I learned the pre-history of that order from an authoritative and very well-informed comrade. While talking with him, I expressed concern for our right flank, against which the field army and the tank group of [German] Army Group Center are pushing. In an attempt to reassure me, he literally said the following: Everything will be all right, Vasilii Ivanovich. Comrade Stalin is working on this personally. Already on August 19, General of the Army G. K. Zhukov reported to Comrade Stalin that the wedge made by troops of Army Group Center in the Gomel-Starodub sector had created conditions for launching a strike at the rear of the Southwestern Army Group. At that time Comrade Stalin answered that he had foreseen such a contingency and, to avert it, had created the Briansk Army Group with General Eremenko at its head. As you see, our Supreme Commander in Chief has long since penetrated the fascist High Command's design. No sooner had Guderian turned to the rear of the Southwestern Army Group than Comrade Stalin reinforced the Briansk Army Group by merging it with the Central Army Group. And now, Comrade Stalin has charged this Army Group with the mission of striking from the east against the flank and the rear of the Guderian tank group and crushing it at all costs.

"As you see," the chief of staff summed it up, sighing, "the events of the last days confirm that this was actually the case. And right now Guderian is already in Romny, i.e., deep in the rear of our troops, and, as before, Comrade Stalin expects the Briansk Army Group to crush him. It will be a long time before the people at Supreme Headquarters will venture to report to the Supreme Commander in Chief on the unreality of this mission." [50]

Having listened to his chief of staff attentively, General Kirponos gloomily knit his eyebrows and said softly:

"The worst of it all is that the Chief of the General Staff, who should understand the situation better than anyone else, cannot muster the courage to tell Comrade Stalin the whole truth. Nor can I believe that this very competent old General Staff officer does not see the mortal danger that threatens the troops of our Army Group."

Approximately one hour later, the chief of the Army Group's signal service reported to General Kirponos that he could talk with the Chief of the General Staff. After informing Kirponos that the Supreme Commander in Chief was busy, Marshal B. M. Shaposhnikov asked the Army Group commander to report on the situation and to present the request that he wanted to discuss with the Supreme Commander in Chief. When the conversation was over, the Chief of the General Staff promised to report all this to Stalin "at the first opportunity."

Further events unfolded in exactly the way that General Kirponos had predicted. During the night, General Tupikov rushed in to see the commander and, in a voice that trembled with anger, reported:

"Comrade Commander, you are a real prophet. General Shtromberg [Deputy Chief of Staff for the Southwestern Strategic Sector] just reported that Marshal Shaposhnikov has replied in Stalin's name: 'Supreme Headquarters considers for the time being that withdrawal of troops of the Southwestern Army Group eastward is premature.' As a 'rescue' measure, the Chief of the General Staff 'advises' (not orders) that two divisions be taken from the 26th Army and deployed against Guderian in the Romny area." . . .

The next day a more cheerful Army Group chief of staff reported to Kirponos:

"There is good news! In the name of the strategic sector's military council, Comrade Budennyi has dispatched this telegram to Comrade Stalin."

Without speaking, Kirponos put on his glasses and, picking up the proffered sheet of paper, began to read:

The military council of the Southwestern Army Group considers that in view of the situation that has developed it is necessary to permit the Army Group to make a general withdrawal to the rear line.

Replying to this proposal in the name of Supreme Headquarters, Marshal Shaposhnikov, Chief of the General Staff, ordered that two rifle divisions be taken from the 26th Army and used to liquidate the enemy that had broken through in the Bakhmach-Konotop area. At the same time, Comrade Shaposhnikov indicated that Supreme Headquarters considered the withdrawal of troops of the Southwestern Army Group eastward to be premature for the time being.

I personally think that the enemy plan to envelop and surround the Southwestern Army Group from the Novgorod-Severskii and Kremenchug sectors is now fully evident. A powerful group is needed to counter this plan, but the Southwestern Army Group is not in a position to do this.

If, in turn, Supreme Headquarters cannot mass such a powerful group at the present time, then withdrawal of the Southwestern Army Group is entirely warranted. The transfer of the two divisions from the 26th Army, which the military council of the Army Group must execute, may be considered only a supporting measure. In addition, the 26th Army will be depleted to the extreme: only three rifle divisions will be left for a defense line of 150 km.

Delay in withdrawal of the Southwestern Army Group can result in the loss of troops and an enormous amount of matériel.

Having read the text, General Kirponos was silent for a long time, lost in deep contemplation. Then, waving his hand with regret, he said: "If Supreme Headquarters has already made up its mind about something, neither the combat experience of Semen Mikhailovich [Budennyi] nor the authority of the sector's entire military council is to any avail." . . .[51]

The rest of the day was spent on attempts to stop up innumerable breaches that had developed along the entire defense line and to free individual formations of the 5th and the 21st Armies from the encirclement into which they had fallen.

The next day, the first news—news that greatly disturbed the Army Group command—was the report that Supreme Headquarters had relieved Marshal S. M. Budennyi as commander in chief of the Southwestern Strategic Sector and had appointed Marshal S. K. Timoshenko in his place. This news meant that Supreme Headquarters was not going to permit the command of the Southwestern Army Group to bring its troops out from under the clear threat of encirclement. There was no doubt that the assessment of the situation which was formulated by the military council of the Southwestern Strategic Sector with full objectivity and frankness, and which clearly contradicted the opinion of Supreme Headquarters, had been the deciding factor in the removal of S. M. Budennyi from his post.

But on September 12, i.e., on the very day that Marshal S. K. Timoshenko was to have arrived to assume command, there was a turn of events in our Army Group sector which confirmed once and for all the correctness of the evaluation of the situation given by the commander of the Southwestern Army Group and the commander in chief of the Southwestern Strategic Sector, and their well-founded urgent requests that the troops be withdrawn. . . . The Kleist tank group had secretly crossed the Dnepr in the Kremenchug area. . . . It was not difficult to guess the direction of the offensive: Kleist was pushing on to link up with Guderian, who by that time was already far to the south of Romny. . . . Neither the Army Group command nor the command of the Southwestern Strategic Sector had anything to put up against the tank armies of Guderian and Kleist. . . .[52]

Such was the extremely difficult situation that greeted the new commander in chief who arrived to replace S. M. Budennyi. Fortunately, Marshal S. K. Timoshenko quickly understood the situation and was able to realize the fatal consequences of further delays in withdrawing troops of the Southwestern Army Group from the as yet incomplete ring of encirclement. From the very first day he supported the position of the Southwestern Strategic Sector's military council, and worked in close contact

with S. M. Budennyi. Immediately after his arrival, he and S. M. Budennyi
telephoned General M. P. Kirponos and M. A. Burmistenko. The greeting
was followed by:

"Report on the latest situation and your plans."

After describing the situation briefly, the Army Group commander
reported his plans. . . .

[The marshals] could not agree on the most important question for
the Army Group—the question relating to the use of troops from the Kiev
fortified area in the threatened sectors—referring to the fact that only
Stalin could make this decision. In conclusion, they cautioned General
Kirponos not to be hasty in relocating his command point. They emphasized that in order not to lose control, it was necessary to stay put as
long as possible and, in any case, to move—not to the east but to the
west, nearer to the Army Group's main forces. This was for the time
being all that the two marshals could suggest to the Army Group command. . . .

By the end of September 13 the Army Group's situation had wors-
ened considerably. Only the troops of the 37th Army's left flank that were
defending the Kiev area and the 26th Army, which was engaged in defensive action along the Dnepr to the south of the 37th Army, continued
to hold firmly the lines they occupied. In the zones of the 21st and 5th
Armies and the right-flank divisions of the 37th Army, however, the troops,
with no reserves whatsoever, were slowly retreating under the onslaught
of superior force. A continuous solid line of defense existed no more.
Gaps between Armies expanded, and enemy formations and units rushed
into them like water into cracks that have formed in a dam. . . .

By this time the enemy had established considerable over-all superiority
in infantry and absolute superiority in tanks. For the first time in the war,
two out of the four German tank Armies deployed on the entire Soviet-
German front were aimed at a single Army Group alone. . . . Only a
few dozen kilometers separated the attacking tank groups of Guderian
and Kleist which were moving toward one another. The ring of enemy
forces could close at any moment.

The over-all length of the front of combat operations had increased
to 600 km. and there was simply no place to take reserves from in order
to stabilize such an enormous front, even though it was urgently required
that a new line of defense be set up east of Bakhmach, Priluki, and Piriatin. Units of two rifle divisions taken from the 26th Army began moving
out to this almost 150-km.-long defense line.

In this situation Tupikov decided on a desperate step for which he
was defamed, without any foundation, as a coward. At the end of the
day he called in my deputy, Colonel N. D. Zakhvataev, and ordered him
to prepare a report to the Chief of the General Staff on the latest situa-

tion at the front. Twenty minutes later Colonel Zakhvataev placed before the chief of staff the text of the report which summarized again in brief the reasons why the troops of the Army Group should be withdrawn to the rear line immediately. After reading the report, General Tupikov added a few lines of his own. He very frankly and sharply emphasized that further delay in withdrawing the troops from the threat of total encirclement would inevitably lead to a catastrophe, the responsibility for which would rest completely on the conscience of the Supreme Command.

After reading the prepared text of the telegram, General Kirponos refused to sign it, declaring it to be a useless undertaking. Then the chief of staff sent the telegram under his own signature.

Tupikov's telegram was reported to the Chief of the General Staff. It is now difficult to say whether or not he reported its contents to Stalin. Judging by the answer, one thing only is clear: Tupikov's resolute phrasing of the question was not to Supreme Headquarters' liking. Colonel General Kirponos summoned his chief of staff and silently handed him a telegram which he had received from Marshal Shaposhnikov, in which the Marshal, contrary to his usual restraint, called Tupikov a panic-monger. He stated that, on the contrary, the situation demanded from commanders at all levels exceptional coolheadedness and endurance. There was to be no yielding to panic, and all measures had to be taken to hold presently occupied positions, especially to hold the flanks firmly. Kuznetsov and Potapov (commanders of the 21st and 5th Armies) should be made to stop their retreat. The entire Army Group had to be inculcated with the necessity for fighting stubbornly, *without looking over the shoulder.* It was imperative to carry out to the letter Comrade Stalin's orders of September 11.

Having read the telegram, the chief of staff exclaimed angrily:

"We're talking to him about one thing, and he is talking to us about another. In the report I clearly indicated that one can only marvel at the fact that the troops of Kuznetsov and Potapov still manage to hold back superior enemy forces, fighting as they are almost constantly in partial or even complete encirclement. Under these conditions, what more can be asked of Kuznetsov and Potapov? The troops *are* fighting without looking over the shoulder." . . .

The next day, small mobile enemy detachments began to appear near Priluki. Information reached us that the advance units of Guderian and Kleist had linked up. The ring of enemy troops had closed.

Having reported to the commander in chief that the troops of the Army Group were now fighting in encirclement, General Kirponos requested permission to move his command point to Kiev. When on the evening of September 14 we in Reshetilovka received the news that the Army Group command point was being moved to Kiev, my heart sank: the possibility of my rejoining headquarters had become still more remote.

On the morning of the following day, however, I at last received a summons to appear before the commander in chief of the Southwestern Sector which gladdened me no end. The hope of returning to Army Group headquarters was rekindled in my heart. Without waiting for General Vol'skii who had departed for the tank brigades, I quickly drove with my assistant to the headquarters of the commander in chief, which was located near Poltava.

I found Marshal S. K. Timoshenko, new commander in chief of the Southwestern Sector, together with N. S. Khrushchev, member of the sector's military council. They were listening to the report of General A. P. Pokrovskii, their chief of staff. I waited until the Marshal was free and asked the adjutant to announce me. I was immediately invited into the office.

"Well, are you still as anxious as ever to get back to your comrades?" Marshal Timoshenko greeted me with a question.

I had already nurtured the hope of finding myself back with my comrades-at-arms for so many days that I answered the commander in chief's question without a shadow of hesitation:

"Yes indeed, Comrade Commander in Chief!" . . .

Looking at me with evident approval, the commander in chief began to talk about the situation in the Kiev sector. He informed me that the operational situation of the troops was growing worse from hour to hour. The day before, the enemy had been literally 20 km. away from Army Group headquarters. At any moment, control of the troops of the Army Group could collapse.

Slowly rubbing his temples with his fingers, as if soothing a pain, he said:

"All attempts to convince Comrade Stalin of the necessity to pull back the troops of the Southwestern Army Group immediately have been to no avail. Now we are doing everything we can to help the Army Group: we are pulling together all the forces we can gather into the Romny and Lubny sectors. . . . With these forces, we shall try to break the encirclement of the troops of the Army Group.

"We realize," the commander in chief continued, "that all these measures will not suffice to liquidate the two fascist tank armies which have broken through into the Army Group's rear, but the creation of breaches in enemy lines will help the Army Group's main forces to break out of encirclement. This is the only thing that makes the strikes by the forces we have assembled meaningful; otherwise, they will hang in midair. This is why we have decided to issue an order to organize a breakout from the encirclement in the expectation that in this situation the Supreme Commander in Chief will ultimately permit the Southwestern Army Group to fall back to the Psel River. We are convinced that Comrade Stalin will finally realize that there can be no further delay. As it is, we are already inexcusably late in pulling the troops back. And every extra day of delay will only increase the dimensions of the catastrophe.

"This very day," he continued, "we are once again going to try to talk to Stalin personally. I hope that we'll succeed in convincing him of the necessity to pull back the troops. And while we are negotiating, Kirponos can organize the withdrawal of his main forces from encirclement, taking advantage of the fact that as yet the enemy has not succeeded in creating a continuous front of encirclement in the Army Group's rear." . . .

Timoshenko, whose face involuntarily brightened at the very thought that it might be possible to save the troops of the Army Group, finished in a severe, commanding tone:

"Comrade Bagramian, report to General Kirponos that in the situation that has developed, the military council of the Southwestern Sector, which does not have at its disposal the necessary reserves, considers that the only expedient solution for the troops of the Southwestern Army Group is an organized withdrawal by all forces to the rear line along the Psel River. Communicate my verbal order to the Army Group commander: the Army Group's main forces are to begin an immediate withdrawal to the rear defense line along the Psel River, abandoning the Kiev fortified area and leaving a small covering force along the Dnepr River. The principal mission of the Army Group's forces, with the support of our reserves, is to crush the enemy who gained the Army Group's rear and, subsequently, to take up defensive positions along the rear line."

Having heard this decision—the only proper one in the situation—I breathed a sigh of relief and felt happy. "There is still a chance to save the Army Group!" There was only one thing that bothered me: the important authority which the military council of the sector vested in me was not backed up by any kind of document. Of course, it was necessary to consider the possibility that the airplane in which I would be flying might be shot down while over enemy-held territory.

After giving a number of instructions for the Army Group command with regard to procedure for troop withdrawal and organization of troop control during the break out of encirclement, the commander in chief extended his hand and exclaimed:

"Hurry, Comrade Bagramian, and see that Kirponos loses no time! Your flight from Poltava to the Piriatin area will be arranged by General Falaleev." . . .

After long trials, we finally succeeded in crossing the front line in a bomber during the latter half of the day on September 16. . . . With no little difficulty, I finally found headquarters, which was located a little to the north of Piriatin in the village of Verkhoiarovka. Losing no time, I went to the chief of staff.

Upon seeing me, General Tupikov firmly embraced me and joyfully exclaimed:

"You made it back to us after all! That's very good. Well, what did you bring us?"

When I reported to Tupikov about the new order of the commander in chief, he immediately said:

"We are going to the commander. We have to hurry. The ring of encirclement has been complete for two days now. If we delay any further, it will become so tight that to break it will be very difficult."

The Army Group military council was located in a farmstead about 7–8 km. from headquarters. We went there in a car. On the way, General Tupikov told me in detail why their attempts to break through to Kiev had been to no avail. It had developed that powerful German forces penetrated the point of junction between the 5th and 37th Armies in the Kobyzhech area and seized the roads leading to Kiev. Some of the forward detachments of a signal regiment ran into the Germans, and it was necessary to turn toward Piriatin.

We found M. A. Burmistenko and E. P. Rykov with General Kirponos. The Army Group commander ordered that I report on the decision of the commander in chief. Upon hearing the long-awaited news, both members of the Army Group military council automatically shifted their gaze to the commander. General Kirponos silently looked at me, as if waiting for something. Tupikov looked at him impatiently and said:

"Comrade Commander, the order we have received is so in keeping with the situation that there is no need to discuss it. Will you permit me to prepare the order for the troops?"

Without answering his chief of staff, General Kirponos sternly asked me:

"Did you bring a written order authorizing the withdrawal?"

"No, I reported what Marshal S. K. Timoshenko, the commander in chief, ordered me to transmit verbally."

General Kirponos knit his bushy eyebrows, thought a while, and then anxiously declared:

"There's something wrong here. Comrade Stalin has personally forbidden us to retreat. He ordered us to hold Kiev at all costs. We can violate that clear order only in the event that we receive a written order from the commander in chief of the Southwestern Sector or a new order from Comrade Stalin."

The commander could not be moved by any amount of arguing and

pleading by his comrades-in-arms, Rykov and Tupikov, concerning the
necessity for immediate execution of the order that had been received.
It appeared that M. A. Burmistenko was also wavering. In any case, he
did not attempt to convince the commander of the necessity to order the
troop withdrawal. He was silent for a long time, and then, calling me
over, he asked softly:

"Is Comrade Khrushchev aware of this order of the commander in
chief?" Upon hearing my affirmative answer, he walked away in silence.

After agonized contemplation, the commander of the Army Group
summoned the chief of staff and said firmly:

"Vasilii Ivanovich, prepare a radiogram to Comrade Stalin. Inform
him of the receipt of the commander in chief's order to withdraw the
troops and ask him what to do."

And the following telegram was dispatched to the Supreme Commander in Chief:

Commander in Chief Timoshenko has transmitted a verbal order through the
Army Group's deputy chief of staff to the effect that our primary mission is to
withdraw our Armies back to the Psel River and to crush the mobile enemy
groups in the Romny and Lubny sectors. A minimum force is to be left to cover
the Dnepr and Kiev.

The commander in chief's written directives give absolutely no orders concerning a withdrawal to the Psel River and permit us to remove only part of
the forces from the Kiev fortified area. There is a patent contradiction here.
What should be carried out? I consider the withdrawal of the Army Group to
the Psel River to be correct, and, in such a case, it would be necessary to
abandon Kiur, Kiev, and the Dnepr River entirely. We urgently request your
orders.

Having transmitted the radiogram to Supreme Headquarters with no
little difficulty, General Tupikov and I, in gloomy concentration, bent
over the map on which the latest data on the situation were entered.
To me, as an operations officer of considerable experience, the map presented a sad picture. There was no solid front line. Along the entire cir-
cumference stretching from north to south where our troops were fighting,
there were enormous holes like gaping wounds in a living body; these
holes were evidence that there was no one to oppose the foe any more.
And the red line which indicated that our troops were still in position—
what was going on there? The latest battle reports indicated that a fight
to the death was in progress there.

Deeply grieved by the picture that unfolded on the map before him,
Tupikov said gloomily:

"The fate of our Army Group was being decided, essentially, during
the last ten days. And the thing which exasperates me most of all is that

we ourselves have put our troops in such a catastrophic situation. We ourselves are involuntarily helping the enemy carry out his rather simple
plan. They called me a coward merely because I dared to tell the truth
to the Chief of the General Staff. All these days I have had the feeling
that I have been tied hand and foot and beaten without being given the
possibility of defending myself.

"Didn't we see the approaching danger?" he continued bitterly.
"Couldn't we have avoided it? We saw it clearly, and we could have
avoided it. But this would have required the ability to assess the situation
soberly, and this they could not do at Supreme Headquarters. If Supreme
Headquarters had given the order just a week ago to pull back the troops
to the rear line, the design of the fascist command which was as clear as
day would have been an idle exercise. Even yesterday or today we could
still hope for an organized withdrawal. We could have assigned the Armies
appropriate missions and given direction to their desperate resistance.
And tomorrow, perhaps, will already be too late."

Recalling these indescribably sad words of General Tupikov now, I
must say that in fact the fascist German command in those days feared
most of all that the Soviet command would pull the troops of the Southwestern Army Group back to the Psel River. This would have been a
terrible blow to the fascists; then, after all, everything that Hitler had
prepared for so long would collapse, and the time lost in diverting two
Armies from the Moscow sector would have been in vain. One can imagine
with what rejoicing the German command in those days heard the report
that the Russians had no intention of withdrawing. . . .[53]

I completely shared the genuine indignation of General Tupikov. And
not only because I respected him for his high principles and resolve but
also because he understood the full depth of the abyss into which inexorable time and the hesitancy of Supreme Headquarters were plunging the
troops of our Army Group. Every hour of waiting for the Army Group's
fate to be decided was a source of unbearable pain. It seemed absurd:
everyone saw the earth slipping away from under the building which
stood over an abyss and knew that it would fall into the abyss at any
moment; yet not a single dweller in the building dared lift a finger to
save himself.

Now, time was working for the enemy. Every hour we delayed
brought his triumph closer. The troops of the Army Group, cut off from
the rear, were not even receiving ammunition, which could only be delivered by air; the last of their strength was ebbing.

And it was only late at night on September 17 that Supreme Head-
quarters, in the person of the Chief of the General Staff, finally responded.
The radiogram from Marshal Shaposhnikov stated laconically: Supreme
Headquarters authorizes the abandonment of the Kiev fortified area and

authorizes the troops of the 37th Army to cross over to the left bank of the Dnepr. Again there was no word about withdrawal of the Army Group's main forces to the rear line.

Having read the contents of this radiogram in a loud voice to the commander, the chief of staff raised his hands in confusion and exclaimed with characteristic candor:

"That's a real Solomon-like decision: to abandon Kiev, but under no condition pull out from encirclement. You can see, Mikhail Petrovich, what is happening. We can abandon the Kiev fortified area, but we are not permitted to fight our way out of encirclement. What then is the sense of withdrawing the Army from the Kiev fortified region right into the embraces of the fascists who have enveloped Kiev from the east? If we have to remain in encirclement, then we should continue to remain in the fortified area as long as we have any strength left."

"Yes, it is an illogical decision," the usually restrained and "correct" M. A. Burmistenko said. "Having said 'a,' they do not want to say 'b.' I think that in this situation, God himself would favor the execution of the commander in chief's [Timoshenko's] orders."

General Kirponos, who had asked me for the map showing the latest data on the situation of the troops, sat hunched over it for a long time in agonized contemplation. . . . He had never had to solve an operations problem with so many unknowns. Upon consulting with Tupikov, Burmistenko, and Rykov, he decided to begin the withdrawal of troops immediately. . . .

Even under such unbelievably difficult conditions very many brave, ingenious officers and commanders at the head of forces of considerable size fought their way across several rivers and also succeeded in breaking through the deep line of fascist troops to link up with their own forces. Among these were the glorious commander of the 26th Army, Lieutenant General F. Ia. Kostenko, who broke out at the head of what was left of his Army; Brigade Commander A. B. Borisov, who broke out of the ring of fascist troops at the head of several thousand of his cavalrymen; corps commanders—Major Generals K. S. Moskalenko and N. V. Kalinin; Brigade Commander F. F. Zhmachenko; and many other prominent military leaders at the head of sizable detachments of their forces. A large number of Red Army soldiers, commanders, and political officers broke through the encirclement in small groups of 30–50 men.[54]

Nor was there any necessity for the Army Group military council and headquarters to remain in Piriatin in this situation. After a brief exchange of opinions, it was decided to withdraw that very night to the northeast and to break through the encirclement near Lokhvitsa.

Unfortunately, the fascists were apparently successful in discovering the direction in which the group of the military council and Army Group headquarters was moving. At dawn on September 20, a mere 15 km. southwest of Lokhvitsa, the group was surrounded by large German forces. The column of the military council and Army Group headquarters—which had been joined by the headquarters of the 5th Army—numbered over 1,000 men, of whom 800 were officers, chiefly officers of the headquarters of the Army Group and of the 5th Army. Among this group were Colonel General M. P. Kirponos; members of the military council M. A. Burmistenko and Divisional Commissar E. P. Rykov; Major Generals V. I. Tupikov, A. I. Danilov, and D. M. Dobykin; General Astakhov, commander of the Army Group's air force and his chief of staff, General Ia. S. Shkurin; Major General M. I. Potapov, commander of the 5th Army; members of that Army's military council, Divisional Commissar M. S. Nikishin and Brigade Commissar E. M. Kal'chenko; Major General D. S. Pisarevskii, Army chief of staff; and a number of other military leaders.

Pressed from all sides by the powerful Hitlerite forces, the column of the Army Group's military council took up a circular defensive position in the Shumeikovo grove next to the Driukovshchino farmstead. The fascists immediately attacked from all sides hoping to make short shrift of the Red Army commanders, a considerable number of whom were armed only with pistols and grenades. The battle immediately became so fierce, however, that the fascists' hopes for an easy victory were dashed. The fascists succeeded in penetrating the clearing to the grove, but the fierce counterattack of those encircled threw them back. In the course of the counterattack, Colonel General Kirponos was wounded. Major General Potapov was wounded and received a severe concussion, while his chief of staff, Major General Pisarevskii, died the death of the brave in that battle. Toward evening, Army Group commander M. P. Kirponos was killed by a shrapnel fragment. M. A. Burmistenko, member of the Army Group military council, was also killed.[55]

When it became dark, the encircled, headed by the chief of staff, attempted to break through the ring of enemy troops. In the course of the night breakthrough, General V. I. Tupikov died, but many were nonetheless able to get through, and they stubbornly continued their difficult way.

Despairing of the possibility of crushing the resistance of the encircled Soviet soldiers, the fascists on the next day, speaking through an amplifier, attempted to persuade them to surrender, promising them "life and liberty." But those who were surrounded categorically refused to enter into negotiations, and their only answer to the enemy proposals was fire. In the succeeding days they continued to fight with the same persistence. As long as the encircled had bullets, the fascists could not penetrate the grove. Only on September 24, when a deadly silence descended on the Shumeikovo grove, did collective farm workers from nearby homesteads steal down there. They were confronted by a tragic sight: the entire clearing was sown with the corpses of Red Army officers who died with their weapons in their hands. Eyewitnesses subsequently reported that they did not find a single unexpended round of ammunition on any of the dead. The Germans succeeded in capturing only those commanders and political officers who were severely wounded. Among these were E. P. Rykov, member of the military council. He was subjected to inhuman torture and executed. Wounded and suffering from concussion, Major General M. I. Potapov, commander of the 5th Army, fell into the hands of the fascists; imprisonment in ·the Hamelsburg concentration camp awaited him.[56]

Those who succeeded in breaking out of encirclement in groups stubbornly pushed their way through the disposition of fascist troops. By the end of September, they could again enter the ranks of the defenders of the Homeland. Among them was the author of this account.

All those who broke out of encirclement were assigned to the newly created Southwestern Army Group which, after having consolidated along the Belopol'e-Lebedin-Shishaki perimeter, barred the advance of Hitlerite troops to the east. Marshal S. K. Timoshenko assumed command of the forces of the Southwestern Army Group. As part of this Army Group, the defenders of Kiev who had broken out from enemy encirclement continued to fight the enemy with the same persistence as before. And many of them had the good fortune to march victoriously through the streets of Kiev in November 1943.

Marshal A. M. Vasilevskii
Between Moscow and Stalingrad

IN MARCH 1942 our winter offensive died. The reasons—insufficient personnel and matériel to continue it.[57] In order to conduct active operations—if only in individual sectors—reserves, armaments, ammunition, etc., were needed, but time was required for their manufacture and stockpiling. One could not speak of active operations by our troops in the spring of 1942, not even in some sectors. The troops had been compelled to revert to the defensive.

A. M. Vasilevskii, "Nekotorye voprosy rukovodstva vooruzhennoi bor'boi letom 1942 goda," *Voenno-istoricheskii zhurnal*, 1965, No. 8, pp. 3–10.

At that time, the leadership of the country's armed forces was confronted with the question of planning military operations for the summer of 1942. There was no doubt that the enemy would again undertake serious active operations on our front no later than the beginning of summer in order to wrest the initiative from our hands anew and to inflict a decisive defeat upon us. The absence of the second front was conducive to this: it permitted the fascist command to transfer with confidence large additional forces from occupied countries and Germany for use on our front.

Supreme Headquarters, the General Staff, and the entire command element of the armed forces were faced with the problem of penetrating the enemy's designs for the spring and summer of 1942 in good time and of making a more precise determination of those strategic directions in which the key events were destined to take place. In the course of this, everyone realized perfectly well that the outcome of military events in the approaching summer campaign would greatly affect the further course of the world war, e.g., the possible entry of Japan, Turkey, etc. into the war against the USSR, and could also, perhaps, greatly affect the outcome of the war for us in general.

In the summer and autumn of 1941, the most powerful enemy grouping was operating in the Moscow strategic sector where fierce battles had developed. The memories of these tragic events were still fresh. Despite the fact that Soviet forces in the winter campaign of 1941–42 had hurled the enemy back from Moscow, he continued to threaten our capital. Up to the end of April 1942, the most powerful enemy grouping, as before, was in the central sector of the Soviet-German front. Taking this into account, Supreme Headquarters and the General Staff arrived at the erroneous conclusion that with the beginning of summer the principal military events would again unfold around Moscow and that precisely here, in the central sector, the enemy would once more attempt to make a decisive strike against us. I know that the command element of the majority of the Army Groups shared this view.[58]

At the end of the winter campaign of 1941–42, at a time when our armed forces were still considerably inferior to the enemy in numbers and especially in weapons and equipment and at a time when we did not have ready reserves and matériel, the General Staff became firmly convinced that the primary immediate mission of the troops of our Army Groups for the spring and the beginning of summer 1942 must be temporary strategic defense. Its aim was to engage in defensive fighting along lines of defense well prepared in advance and, in the process of the defensive action, to launch powerful counterblows against the assault groupings of the enemy. In so doing, the aim was not only to frustrate the blow pre-

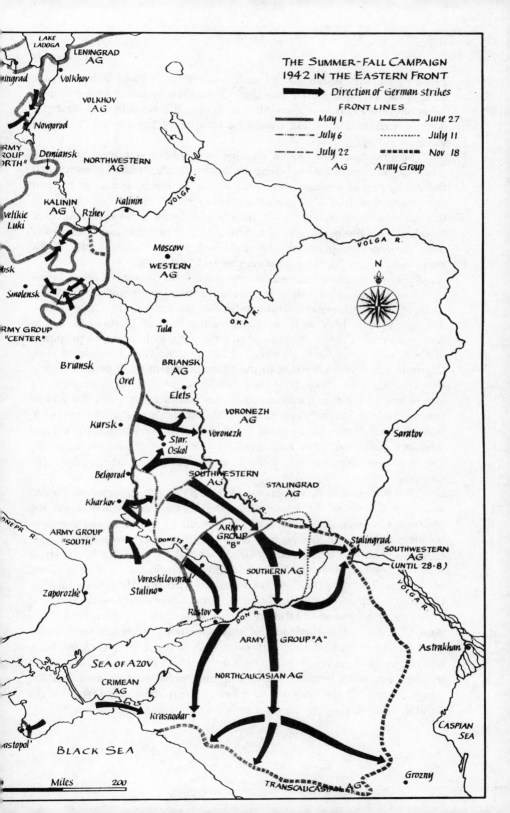

pared by the enemy but also to undermine his forces and thus to create conditions favorable to our launching a decisive offensive with minimal losses. Moreover, it was thought that during the transition to strategic defense, principal attention should be focused on the central [Moscow] sector.

The principal task of the country as a whole was seen to be the creation (no later than May–June 1942) of mighty, trained reserves and the stockpiling of weapons, ammunition, tanks, planes, and other combat equipment as well as all necessary matériel with which to supply troops in the subsequent offensive. In the middle of March, these considerations, together with the necessary substantiations and calculations, were in my presence reported personally by the Chief of the General Staff, B. M. Shaposhnikov, to Supreme Commander in Chief Stalin.

Supreme Headquarters was involved with this question a second time at the end of March when it examined the plan, presented by the command of the Southwestern Strategic Sector, for conducting a large offensive operation in May with the forces of the Briansk, Southwestern, and Southern Army Groups. Stalin agreed with the conclusions and proposals of the Chief of the General Staff, but at the same time he ordered that, simultaneously with reversion to the strategic defensive, individual offensive operations be carried out in a number of sectors: in some with the aim of improving the operational position and in others with the aim of forestalling the enemy's launching of his offensive operations. As a result of these instructions, plans were made for conducting individual offensive operations near Leningrad, in the region of Demiansk, in the Smolensk and L'gov-Kursk sectors, in the Khar'kov area, and in the Crimea.[59]

The preconceived, erroneous idea that in the summer the main enemy strike would be launched in the central sector *dominated* the Supreme Commander in Chief all the way up to July. This is attested to by his refusal to conduct an individual offensive operation in the Kursk-L'gov sector of the Briansk Army Group—initially planned in May—which was to have helped troops of the Southwestern Sector in their conduct of the Khar'kov operation. As is known, on April 24, 1942, General F. I. Golikov, commander of the Briansk Army Group, met with Stalin at Supreme Headquarters. After hearing a report on the plan which the Army Group had worked out for this operation, Stalin countermanded it and ordered instead that a broader operation be prepared for June, but in the Orel rather than in the Kursk sector. This is also attested to by the persistent demands which Supreme Headquarters made on the Army Group all the way up to July—to keep the main forces of the Briansk Army Group in the Orel rather than in the Kursk sector.[60]

Many who are not informed about the difficult conditions under which the General Staff had to work during the last war may justly charge its leadership with failure to prove to Stalin the negative consequences of the decision to defend and attack simultaneously. In the face of the very acutely felt shortage of trained reserves and matériel, the conduct of individual offensive operations resulted in an intolerable expenditure of forces. The events which unfolded in the summer of 1942 clearly showed that had there been only the reversion to temporary strategic defense along the entire Soviet-German front and had the conduct of offensive operations (e.g., the Khar'kov operation)[61] been rejected, the country and its armed forces would have been spared serious defeats, and we could have resumed active offensive operations much sooner and could have again taken the initiative into our hands. . . .

The miscalculations of Supreme Headquarters and the General Staff in planning military operations for the summer of 1942 were taken into account in the future, especially in the summer of 1943, when a decision on the nature of combat operations in the Kursk salient was made. Supreme Headquarters, together with the General Staff and the commanders of the Army Groups, having the necessary and ready forces with which to deliver a powerful blow against the enemy in this area and knowing precisely that the enemy himself was simultaneously preparing his basic blow here, made the proper decision: first to wear the enemy out in defensive battles and then launch a counteroffensive, completely crushing the main grouping of his forces, massed in the area of the Kursk salient. Everyone knows the outcome of this decision.[62]

PART II THE HIGH COMMAND AND FIELD COMMANDERS

Introduction

THE QUALITY of field command in large operational units improved radically over the course of the war. According to both German and Western sources, it was excellent for the most part during the second half of the war. The majority of Red Army officers who remained in active service with general's rank at the end of the war (12 marshals of the Soviet Union, 2 admirals of the fleet, 3 chief marshals, and 11 marshals of arms branches, 13 generals of the army, and 5,586 generals and admirals of lower rank) owed the possibility of achieving their rank, if not the achievement itself, to their survival of the Great Purge. The achievement of their rank they owed to success in demonstrating their ability as soldiers in the ultimate test of combat. With few exceptions the command element of Army Groups in the last phase of war had occupied staff or line positions in tactical units of corps, divisions, or even of lower levels in June 1941.

During the first half of the war Supreme Headquarters tolerated scant initiative on the part of field commanders. Not only were these commanders severely circumscribed in

their adjustment of orders to unforeseen circumstances, but participation in the actual planning of major operations and the general process of decision-making at Supreme Headquarters was denied to field commanders who in most cases learned of decisions only after their formal adoption. During this period Supreme Headquarters exercised its control in the field through emergency measures, that is by temporary assignment of members of the High Command to key field commands or by the dispatch of high ranking ad hoc delegations of political and military leaders to crucial front sectors. In addition, Supreme Headquarters from summer 1941 to summer 1942 relied upon an intermediary element in the form of Strategic Sector Commanders, each of whom supervised several Army Groups. Since Supreme Headquarters communicated directly with the Army Groups, this intermediary element introduced only duplication in the chain of command and scarcely improved operational leadership.

In the second half of the war, from the victory at Stalingrad, relations between the Soviet High Command

and Army Group commands were characterized by a well-integrated procedure designed to derive advantages from centralized leadership on the one hand and from utilization of local expertise on the other. Strategic and operational planning and decision-making were highly centralized, even for operations of marginal importance; the preparation and conduct of all operations (with the sole exception of the 1945 campaign) were strictly and closely supervised on the spot by emissaries from Moscow. At the same time senior field commanders participated in the planning of these operations and in the preparation of Supreme Headquarters' directives for their execution.

The first group of memoir excerpts treats the institution of Supreme Headquarters' representatives, the major means through which Supreme Headquarters controlled and supervised the field commands in the preparation and execution of major operations. Colonel General S. M. Shtemenko describes the functions, duties, and style of work of these representatives on the basis of his experience as representative of the Soviet High Command with the 1st Belorussian Army Group during the Belorussian operation of summer 1944. Chief Marshal of Artillery N. N. Voronov offers insight into the relationship between the emissary and the Army Group commander, in this case between himself and Marshal A. I. Eremenko, commander of the Kalinin Army Group.

The next two accounts, those of Generals of the Army P. I. Batov, commander of the famous 65th Army, and M. I. Kazakov, chief of staff of the Voronezh Army Group, record the ease with which Supreme Headquarters through its representatives punishes even high-ranking officers for alleged inadequacies of leadership, a subject which occupies an important place in the memoirs of field

commanders and one to which they are especially sensitive. At the beginning of the war several high-ranking Soviet generals were executed for failure to prevent the destruction of their troops and combat equipment (e.g., D. G. Pavlov, commander of the Western Army Group; V. E. Klimovskikh, his chief of staff; A. A. Korobkov, commander of the 4th Army; P. N. Rychagov, air force commander of the Northwestern Army Group). Their failure was represented as "an act of treason." No further cases of execution of high-ranking commanders have been reported for later stages in the war, including the disastrous retreat of summer 1942. Severe sanctions, however, and in particular peremptory dismissal greeted errors and failures regardless of their circumstances even in the period of successful advance. While punishments in the summers of 1941 and 1942 may demonstrate an attempt to deflect blame for failure from the Supreme Command and Stalin personally, the harsh treatment of field commanders in the later period points to more ominous sources: Stalin's suspiciousness which equated errors of judgment, real or alleged, with lack of faith; the assumption that orders from Supreme Headquarters were infallible regardless of their applicability to real conditions; the general system of civil discipline in which it was assumed that unconventional behavior and unsuccessful action had deep social causes, in which "guilt" and "accountability" were inseparable and the authority of superiors was little checked by countervailing social controls.

Another point of contention between field commanders and Supreme Headquarters pertains to the frequent reorganization of field commands, which was not always justifiable from a military point of view. This subject concerns the author of the next excerpt, General of the Army L. M. Sandalov, who at this time served as an Army Group chief of staff.

The next group of excerpts focuses on one critical period, the fall of 1941, when Soviet northern defenses disintegrated and the German troops of Fieldmarshal von Leeb raced to the gates of Leningrad. Admiral N. G. Kuznetsov, who went to the city as a member of a delegation from Supreme Headquarters, relates how Stalin assessed the extreme gravity of the situation. The further development of events is described by Colonel General I. I. Fediuninskii who accompanied the new commander of Leningrad defenses, Marshal Zhukov, and by Lieutenant General B. V. Bychevskii, chief of engineers of the Leningrad Army Group. Both generals provide a vivid account of the moment when Voroshilov relinquished his command of Leningrad to Zhukov, and they outline Zhukov's methods for stabilizing the city's defenses.

The final excerpt in this chapter consists of a brief and, to our knowledge, unique eyewitness account of Stalin's only visit to the front in four years of war. The event took place during the summer of 1943 in the cen-

tral sector. While Stalin still lived, the visit was described by Politburo member N. A. Bulganin who was, at the time, Defense Minister.

To assess on the spot the readiness of our troops for a specific operation, Stalin himself visited the front. Before the Smolensk operation was launched, he came to the sector of the Western Army Group. Upon his arrival at Army Group headquarters, he verified the preparedness of the Army Group commander and his troops for the forthcoming operation; he gave exhaustive and infinitely clear instructions concerning the deployment of forces and saw to it that they were supplied with aircraft, tanks, artillery, and all other support and materiel. He directed the commander's attention to the individual stages of the operation and pointed out the different phases of its development. As a result of this, the commander achieved a better understanding of the importance of the forthcoming operations, and, as we know, the operation was conducted with great success in full conformity with the plan approved by Supreme Headquarters.[*]

Marshal Voronov's account of this visit offers an amusing and credible contrast to Bulganin's enthusiastic paean.

[*]*Bol'shevik*, No. 24, December 1949, p. 69.

Colonel General S. M. Shtemenko
The Inspector General—I

COMPLETION OF WORK on plans for the operation in Belorussia was carried on at the same time as preparation of the troops in the field.[63] Representatives of Supreme Headquarters, whose duty it was to solve a number of problems defined in the light of their experience in previous operations, were sent to the front. First and foremost, the representatives had to make certain that the instructions of Supreme Headquarters were understood correctly, that missions were clear, and that Army Groups and Armies had no other interpretations. Then, together with Army Group commands and staffs, they had to work out the best ways and means of executing the given missions, and later they had to control their ultimate implementation. Moreover, they inspected troop and staff preparations for the offensive on the spot and helped the Army Groups to organize the supply of necessary matériel. Supreme Headquarters' representatives reported to the Supreme Commander in Chief on the progress of preparations for the operation, on all difficulties that arose, and on other important matters as well. Their duties also included such matters as observation of field commanders and preparation of suggestions for their most expedient employment.

We also had to do all that on this occasion. But this time the crucial operations of the summer campaign were at stake. Therefore, Supreme Headquarters' representatives were given especially broad powers; they had to know every detail of preparation in each Army Group operation and in the campaign as a whole. Moreover, we had to insure as far as possible a certain collegiality in the making of major decisions concerning the forthcoming operations.

G. K. Zhukov was charged with coordinating the commands of the 1st and 2nd Belorussian Army Groups. A. M. Vasilevskii was sent to the 1st Baltic and 3rd Belorussian Army Groups.[64] Their commanders did not yet have sufficient experience in organizing and conducting Army

S. M. Shtemenko, "Pered udarom v Belorussii," *Voenno-istoricheskii zhurnal*, 1966, No. 2, pp. 57–64.

Group operations on such a large scale. Cherniakhovskii at that time had no such experience at all.[65] Therefore, A. M. Vasilevskii, talented both as a major military commander and as a teacher, was exactly right for this role. . . .

The 2nd Belorussian Army Group was sent, in addition, a group of General Staff officers headed by the Chief of Operations [the author of these memoirs—Ed.] whose position was defined in a somewhat peculiar fashion. On the one hand, he was subordinate to G. K. Zhukov in all operational questions, insofar as the operations of the 2nd Belorussian Army Group were closely connected with those of the right flank of the 1st Belorussian Army Group. On the other hand, as the group's senior officer he had the right to report directly to the Chief of the General Staff about the progress of preparations for the offensive and all other questions.

We were also charged with orienting the 2nd Belorussian Army Group's new commander (who replaced I. E. Petrov)—Colonel General G. F. Zakharov, formerly commander of the 2nd Guards Army—and we had to help him in his work, at least in the beginning. Besides myself, Colonel General Ia. T. Cherevichenko and several General Staff officers composed the group which was sent to the front. The representatives of Supreme Headquarters left for the front with the knowledge that historically significant events were approaching.

Supreme Headquarters' representatives checked on the spot, first of all, that the Army Group commanders had a correct understanding of the missions assigned by the Supreme Commander in Chief. In the 1st and 3rd Belorussian Army Groups no difficulties were met, since the commanders themselves had offered suggestions ahead of time about the use of their troops. Therefore, A. M. Vasilevskii, who arrived in Cherniakhovskii's sector as early as 4:00 p.m. on June 4, and G. K. Zhukov, who flew in to Rokossovskii's sector at 5:00 a.m. on June 5, could proceed to define the best means of action without losing time. But those of us who went to the 2nd Belorussian Army Group found ourselves in a different situation, because, as I said before, the previous commander had been replaced, and the new one had not taken part in planning the forthcoming operation.

I. E. Petrov, who had quite recently been given the 2nd Belorussian Army Group, was replaced on Stalin's personal command. One day, when Antonov and I were making our regular report at Supreme Headquarters, Stalin told us that Mekhlis, military council member of the 2nd Belorussian Army Group, had sent him a letter accusing I. E. Petrov of being spineless and unable to insure the success of the operation. Mekhlis said, moreover, that Petrov was ill and devoted a lot of time to doctors.

He poured a bucket of other unpleasant and essentially untrue accusations on Petrov's head. They were totally unexpected for us. We all knew Ivan Efimovich Petrov as a brave and sensible combat commander and a fine man totally devoted to his work. . . . But thanks to Mekhlis, Petrov was removed after commanding the Army Group only a month and a half. The injustice of this soon became apparent. Exactly two months later, on August 5, 1944, he was again appointed commander of an Army Group (the 4th Ukrainian), and on October 26 of the same year he received the rank of General of the Army.[66]

Stalin appointed as commander of the 2nd Belorussian Army Group Colonel General G. F. Zakharov, an extremely hotheaded man, very eccentric in his actions and deeds.[67] It fell to me to make the change of command as painless as possible. I must confess that such a mission was profoundly unpleasant to me. I was afraid that the new commander would start to interpret in his own way the plan of operations already approved by Supreme Headquarters and that serious conflicts might arise first with Mekhlis and then with the Army Group chief of staff, Lieutenant General A. N. Bogoliubov, an experienced but likewise eccentric and very hotheaded man.

A few hours after Zakharov's arrival at the Army Group's command point we reviewed the situation in our sector. First, Petrov reported the situation, and then we examined the plan of the forthcoming operations. . . . During his report, Petrov could have been expected to exaggerate the difficulties confronting the Army Group and to paint the situation in gloomy colors. It was important not to create a bad first impression and a feeling of insecurity in the new commander. But everything went smoothly. Petrov did not exaggerate. It was clear that the common interest was more important to him than his personal wrong. . . . After Petrov's report, we listened to the chief of staff and the commanders of the various arms branches and services. Then the former commander left.

The next morning, in the presence of the commander of the 49th Army, Lieutenant General I. T. Grishin, the new commander inspected, in their battle zone positions, one regiment each from the 290th and 95th Rifle Divisions of the 49th Army. Zakharov wanted, first of all, to see at least a small part of the troops and the terrain on which they were deployed. Both regiments were fully manned, with troops of good potential and adequate training. They made a favorable impression. The shortcomings observed could easily be corrected. But it was an unpleasant surprise to find that some enlisted men, noncommissioned officers, and platoon, company, and battalion commanders who had been fighting since the first day of war, who had displayed heroism in combat and had been wounded several times, had not yet been decorated with any order or medal. Decorations were rare in combat units but rather plentiful among the personnel in the rear zone. This situation was soon corrected.

That same day, as we had expected, Zakharov (like certain other commanders, unfortunately) lost no time in announcing that until his arrival everything had been bad, and now he was going to have to make up for other people's sins. First, he tried to protest the direction of the main thrust as defined by Supreme Headquarters. . . . Only after all the considerations regarding terrain and fire had been explained to Zakharov and he had been told that a decision approved by Supreme Headquarters could not be changed without its knowledge did he give in reluctantly. Thereafter, he made no more attempts to diverge from Supreme Headquarters' instructions about the plan of operation. . . .

We, the representatives of Supreme Headquarters, gave our main attention to organizing a breakthrough of the enemy's defense and securing its rapid success. I must confess that not everything was clear—or clear immediately—concerning the best methods of action during a breakthrough. The methods were not always worked out smoothly. The following incident occurred in the 2nd Belorussian Army Group on June 7. That morning, the commanding officer and I visited I. T. Grishin's 49th Army in order to hold a briefing with the corps and division commanders. We intended to hear reports on the situation in certain sectors, to set tasks concerning the troops' combat training, and to let them know what we expected of them. The briefing had a clearly defined guidance aim. It was held in a large hospital-like tent, and the new commanding officer's remarks were awaited with impatience.

Zakharov gave a detailed autobiography, especially of his combat life, and then proceeded to explain the difference between an ordinary meeting and a combat briefing, underlining the word "combat" several times. "The difference between a briefing and a meeting," he continued, "consists in the fact that at this briefing I shall speak and you shall listen and write down my instructions."

Such behavior put everyone on the alert.

He then gave a detailed explanation of the importance of secrecy and demanded that all present hold up their field notebooks to show him. Many hands with sheets of paper, ragged pads, or nothing at all rose in the air. The regulation field notebooks of divisional commanders, of course, were simply nonexistent. Seeing this, Zakharov ordered the distribution to those present of notebooks prepared ahead of time. Everyone got ready to write, but there were no instructions. Instead, Zakharov proceeded to call on commanders and ask them questions, not only about the situation in their sectors, but about regulations and tactics in general.

Many became confused and answered incorrectly.

Zakharov got worked up and permitted himself to be rude, especially to those who answered incorrectly. He raised his voice sharply. One could feel the atmosphere heating up, and it became necessary to do something. Since the meeting had already lasted quite long, I insisted upon a short break.

While the officers were out of the room, smoking and carrying on strained conversations, Zakharov and I had a short, but heated exchange of views on the "examination." Zakharov at first held his ground but soon agreed that he ought not continue in that spirit and tone. After the intermission he spoke of how to organize a breakthrough of the enemy's defense. He spoke to the point, sensibly expounding the essence of the field regulations on breaking through an entrenched defense.

It soon became apparent that, despite the sharpness of the first half of the briefing, Zakharov was establishing a rapport with his audience. The officers calmed down and listened attentively. But when he chose as the ideal guide to follow the "Instructions on Breaking Through a Defense," a booklet which applied to the Crimea, everyone became agitated. Their agitation was understandable. The situation in the Crimea was entirely different. There, you had a typical steppe terrain, as flat as a table; the forward battle lines of the adversaries in the 2nd Guards Army sector were almost touching each other; the neutral zone was very narrow. Therefore, the "instructions" recommended covering the distance to the enemy trenches in a single rapid push, after the transfer of artillery fire. But in Belorussia, our front line faced a low floodland from the Pronia River almost two kilometers wide, and only beyond that did the enemy lines begin. Such a distance cannot be covered in one push. The terrain beyond the floodland was broken by forests. Troop action had to be different here than in the Tauride.

The agitation of those present did not pass without notice. Zakharov made the necessary reservations and warnings that when selecting ways of action, one must approach the situation creatively and from all angles. The "Instructions," large bundles of which had been brought by him from the Crimea, remained undistributed, and the briefing ended without further incident. In the future, Zakharov took great pains to see that the methods of attack in Belorussia corresponded to local conditions, and he always demanded strict attention to the peculiarities of the given situation.[68]

Chief Marshal of Artillery N. N. Voronov
The Inspector
General—II

[ON AUGUST 30, 1943] I received a call from Supreme Headquarters and was ordered to depart immediately for the Kalinin Army Group and to check on troop preparedness for the forthcoming offensive.[69]

General A. I. Eremenko, commander of the Army Group, and General D. S. Leonov, member of the military council, were waiting for me at the command post of the Kalinin Army Group.

The Army Group commander finished his brief report with the words: "We shall begin the offensive on the appointed day and at precisely the appointed hour. We are ready for it."

"And how are you fixed for fuel and ammunition?" I asked.

"Well, not everything has been brought up; much is still on the way. But we won't postpone the launching of the operation."

I insisted that the commanders of arms branches and the chief of rear services be summoned. The generals reported major deficiencies in supplies. Fighter aircraft, for example, had only enough fuel for one day of combat. Artillery supplies for a number of calibers were so inadequate as to make the launching of an offensive operation risky.

Of course, I understood the importance of launching an offensive by the Kalinin Army Group without delay. Nonetheless, all estimates showed that the supply situation could not change for the better in less than six or seven days. Therefore, the launching time for the operation should be postponed.

Three people remained in the dugout—Eremenko, Leonov, and myself. I advised A. I. Eremenko to call Moscow and request permission to postpone the beginning of the operation. Eremenko categorically refused. I then proposed that the member of the military council do so, but Leonov also refused. For my part, I very much objected to speaking out again at Supreme Headquarters in the capacity of petitioner on behalf of others,

N. N. Voronov, *Na sluzhbe voennoi* (Moscow, 1963), pp. 391–97.

especially concerning such a ticklish question. On such occasions in the past I had had more than once to listen to many unpleasant and abusive words.[70]

But what could a representative of Supreme Headquarters do in such a case?

I had to call Moscow.

Stalin came to the phone. I briefly told him that the Kalinin Army Group was still not ready to begin the operation at the appointed time and requested permission to change the time for beginning the operation by plus six days.

"What do you mean 'plus six days'?"

I did not want to name the date for the beginning of the offensive over the telephone, but when asked a second time I named the date— September 14.

The answer was:

"The change of date is approved, but remember—not a minute later!"

With this, the conversation ended. I hung up and looked expectantly at those present. They were anxiously awaiting the answer. When I announced the decision of the Supreme Commander in Chief, Eremenko was overjoyed. He decided to say nothing about the new date but simply to postpone the offensive from day to day. He considered this advisable so as not to "unwind the subordinates." I spoke firmly against this. Finally, Andrei Ivanovich agreed with me.

All commanders of Armies and formations, together with their artillery chiefs, were immediately summoned to the Army Group command point. Everyone greeted the change of date for the offensive joyfully. . . .

On September 14—the day of the offensive—Andrei Ivanovich [Eremenko] and I hurried to the advance observation point.

The road to the observation point turned out to be in poor condition, and we were jolted and shaken along the way. I was again overcome by an attack of my illness. With difficulty I suffered through to the beginning of the artillery preparation, and then I made my way to the nearest shelter in order to lie down. . . . By the time the artillery preparation was over, I was already able to get up. . . .

Our troops advanced resolutely. The fighting became more stubborn as our advancing infantry and tanks began to penetrate the enemy's line of defense deeper and deeper. It was clearly apparent that the Hitlerites *had* known about our preparations for an offensive and had taken steps to reinforce their defensive positions in this sector.

It was decided to continue the fighting at night so as not to permit the enemy to collect himself.

At day's end I set out for the Army Group command point with the intention of calling Supreme Headquarters and reporting on the initial results of the offensive. When I arrived, I was informed that Supreme Headquarters had already called several times.

Disturbed by such nervousness in Moscow, I decided to consult first with General A. I. Antonov. He expressed utter amazement that the Kalinin Army Group was marking time, not carrying out the assigned mission, etc.

"Where did you get that idea?" I asked.

A. I. Antonov replied that starting at noon, Supreme Headquarters had been calling Army Group headquarters and had been getting the same stereotyped answer—that the fighting was still in the first line of the enemy trenches. I made a rather detailed report on the considerable successes of the first day of the offensive. At this point, our conversation was interrupted. Excusing himself, the general started talking on another telephone. I could hear individual words. The conversation was about the Kalinin Army Group. Antonov was reporting what he had just heard from me. Then he again picked up the receiver and relayed the order that I call Supreme Headquarters immediately.

Before putting in a new call to Moscow, I inquired at Army Group headquarters who had reported the false information to Supreme Headquarters. It turned out that in the morning, prior to setting out for the observation post, the Army Group commander had ordered that all questions from Moscow be answered with "The fighting goes on in the first trenches."

"When I return," the commander explained to his subordinates, "I will personally report to Supreme Headquarters on our results."

A few minutes later, I was connected with Moscow. By the stern exclamation, "Report what's going on out there," I could guess the extreme irritation of the Supreme Commander in Chief. I calmly outlined the situation and reported on our initial successes—breakthrough of 16 km. into the defense lines of the enemy and up to 7–11 km. in depth.

"How do you assess the work of the chief of staff of the Army Group and the headquarters as a whole? Why don't they help the commander and why don't they participate in the war?"

I gave a favorable description of the chief of staff and the entire headquarters' personnel and said:

"They should not be blamed. They were carrying out the direct orders of the Army Group commander."

"How do you know this?"

Upon hearing my answer, the Supreme Commander in Chief, mollified, said:

"Have Eremenko call me as soon as he reaches the command point."

When A. I. Eremenko arrived, I reproached him for the ill-advised order to his headquarters.

"And now call Moscow!"

I considered it awkward to witness this conversation which in all probability would not be very pleasant. I went to my quarters.

General of the Army P. I. Batov
The Inspected General

AT THE BEGINNING of June [1944] K. K. Rokossovskii and G. K. Zhukov, accompanied by a large group of generals, unexpectedly visited the Army's command post (in the forest not far from Prosvet village) at dawn.[71]

The first question asked by the representative of Supreme Headquarters [Zhukov] was:

"When was the last time you were with the troops?"

"Last night."

"Where?"

"Ivanov's corps, in the sector of the 69th Division."

"Show me on the map."

"Here, see this swamp—"

"Is passage possible?"

"I don't recommend it. It's an exposed terrain, under artillery fire. A night trip would be better."

"We are going now!"

Naturally, one did not ask what was the hurry. Yet, traveling in daytime was dangerous. Furthermore, I feared that we might alert the Germans to [possible action in] this sector if they noticed the reconnaissance.

"If we have to go, Comrade Marshal, let only very few go. There should be a two to three minute interval between the vehicles."

We left the edge of the woods on foot and soon reached the connecting trenches. The sun was just rising over the horizon. It was chilly in the swamp. The guests were wearing black leather overcoats. That

P. I. Batov, *V pokhodakh i boiakh* (Moscow, 1962), pp. 274-91.

was quite a garment for the forward lines! Worriedly, I walked ahead of the party. Fortunately, the enemy was quiet. From time to time there was a burst of machine-gun fire. The reports of the commanders of the forward sub-units were followed by the curt order:

"As you were, carry on."

From the forward trench Zhukov and Rokossovskii looked through their binoculars, appraising the terrain and the tactical depth of enemy defenses. A happy thought flashed through my mind: "They are looking for the direction of the main strike. Perhaps our plans coincide!"[72]

"At least remove your cap," I implored the representative of Supreme Headquarters, when he stood up, almost waist-high above the trench. "I scarcely need your solicitude!" Yet, the cap came off.

They were late in warning General Ivanov about the departure of superior officers to the forward defense line. He was unable to meet us and arrived when the reconnaissance in the sector of the 69th Division was already over. Zhukov did not want to listen to the explanation of the corps commander; he abused him and ordered me to lead him, Zhukov, to the sector held by the 44th Guards Division. . . .

Trouble never comes in small doses. The division was under the command of Colonel P. G. Petrov, a skillful and competent officer but a man with a difficult past. At the beginning of the war, as a division commander, he had suffered a series of failures and had been removed from his post. It was then that someone began to take an interest in him, and he was sent back from the front line to study at a military academy. After his training, he asked for an assignment with the 65th Army. His feeling of insecurity had disappeared; he was regaining his past firmness and questioning mind. Yet now, in the presence of the Marshal, Petrov lost his aplomb somewhat. His report on the situation was confused. It was very difficult to approach the division's observation post in daylight. The enemy was firing with mortars, even at individual soldiers. In his concern for protecting the lives of his superiors, the division commander led us to the reserve observation point, which was not yet completed. An officer-observer was sitting on a plank platform at the top of a pine tree. Zhukov tried to climb up hastily nailed laths; he reached the middle of the tree and came down, enraged. It was pitiful to watch Petrov. We went to another sector. . . .

The cars followed the forest tracks, jumping as they rolled over the roots of trees. Zhukov was sitting next to the driver. Without turning to me, he ordered:

"The corps commander is to be removed. The commander of the 44th [Division] is to be sent to the penal company."

His words sounded to me like thunder from a clear sky. There was a definite line of conduct followed in our Army: One does not dismiss a commander indiscriminately for an error; one tries to improve him. This line was firmly followed by the Army commander and members of the military council. This line also prevailed in the corps. How should I defend the commanders?

"Why are you silent?"

"I am listening, Comrade Marshal. I'm not used to interrupting. I am writing this down."

"There is nothing left for you to say. There is slackness in your Army!"

"I admit it. The first to be punished should be the Army commander. With your permission I should like to report my opinion on those officers."

I described everything I knew about Petrov and the corps commander. These were dedicated and experienced people. We worked a lot on Petrov, helping him to regain his balance, and he undoubtedly was improving. General Ivanov was a hero of the Dnepr crossing—

"What is your suggestion? Be specific."

"A reprimand will suffice. I have faith in these two comrades. I have known them personally in combat and in the course of long prewar service."

"There we are, nepotism! Prepare a draft order."

From this day on, the operations group of the Supreme Headquarters' representative settled down in the area of the 65th Army's command post. We provided them with twenty-nine of our dugout shelters. My draft order was rejected by Zhukov. Finally, at Rokossovskii's insistence, he agreed to lower the punishment: I. I. Ivanov was sharply reprimanded, and the division commander was relieved of his duties. P. G. Petrov left us on the following day. In the Belorussian operation, as deputy division commander in the 3rd Army, he participated in forcing the river Drut' with the first echelon, bravely and skillfully guided the battle, and at the bridgehead was mortally wounded. His exploit was acknowledged by the Fatherland. Pavel Grigor'evich Petrov was posthumously awarded the title Hero of the Soviet Union. . . .

Slutsk was liberated. Nesvezh was captured. While the 48th Army was cutting off the communication lines of the Minsk enemy grouping and was blocking its retreat in the direction of Baranovichi, our Army was to capture this major railroad junction and thus make our contribution to the encirclement of the 4th German Army.[73]

Throughout that time, the operations group of the Army commander remained among the troops in an effort to increase the tempo of the operation. . . . Radetskii and I managed to break loose for the Army command post at Vel'ka hamlet which was finally reached by the entire Army headquarters headed by Bobkov. For the first time in several days we were able to take care of our personal appearance. We had just managed to shave and clean our shoes when some cars screeched to a stop in front of our hut. Radetskii looked through the window. Zhukov! We rushed to the porch. I was hoping to please the representative of Supreme Headquarters [with the news of the imminent capture of Baranovichi], but things turned out differently.

"You are shaving? Using cologne water? Why haven't you taken Baranovichi?"

Somehow, we managed to bring Zhukov into the hut. There he kept dressing us down. In my long army service I had never experienced such humiliation. Radetskii kept a stone face. Finally, we were able to report that the units were advancing successfully and that the town would be captured any time now. The response was no better than the opening.

"The commanding officer has reported the truth, Comrade Marshal," Radetskii said. Zhukov paid no attention.

"The commanding officer has reported the truth," repeated the member of the military council. The abuse was switched to him. This intolerable scene ended with Zhukov ordering Radetskii to go into Baranovichi and not to come back until the town was captured. Kicking the stool out of his way, Zhukov left, slamming the door behind him.

A heavy silence reigned.

"Relax, Pavel Ivanovich," Radetskii said. "Whom are we serving— Zhukov or the Soviet Union? Let's have supper. All this is rubbish. I wonder, however, what is it that got him mad?"

To tell the truth, I did not feel like analyzing it. Radetskii continued:

"Vasilevskii is nearing Vil'nius. And here is Zhukov competing to be the first to report a victory to Supreme Headquarters. Well, I must go as ordered."

I was left alone. The troops did not worry me. Combat operations were proceeding normally. I couldn't find peace of mind, though. Was this the type of leadership that we army commanders expected from a major military leader?

Radetskii rang me up the next morning:

"Everything is going all right."

"Where are you calling from?"

"From Baranovichi. Alekseev and I have toured the entire city. I am sitting at Grebennik's observation post at the cemetery. The battle is proceeding with success about one-and-a-half kilometers west of us."

In the hut where Zhukov was resting, a general, a briefcase on his knees, was dozing on a stool by the door. The Marshal was sleeping. I woke him up and reported the capture of Baranovichi.

"Any news on Vil'nius? No? Well, then, let me sleep some more."

General of the Army M. I. Kazakov
Hasty
Penalties

I RECALL with a feeling of regret that in 1942 we were in the habit of drawing hasty conclusions and meting out severe penalties to our military leaders. The battle of Voronezh[74] was not yet over when a search for the "guilty" ones had already begun. The first person to "get it" was F. I. Golikov—he was removed from his post of Army Group commander. This happened on July 7, only five days after his arrival in the Voronezh sector to take over direct command of military operations in the area.

After listening on the high frequency telephone to Golikov's report concerning the situation in Voronezh, Stalin asked:

"Can you guarantee that Voronezh will hold out?"

Filipp Ivanovich answered honestly that, evaluating things realistically, he could not give such a guarantee. Literally within a few minutes Lieutenant General N. F. Vatutin, who at the time represented the General Staff at the Army Group's command post, was called to the phone. His report was more optimistic. His estimate of the situation in the sector was that the town of Voronezh could hold out against the enemy. The security head of the Army Group's rear zone added still more fuel to the fire. As representative of the People's Commissariat of Internal Affairs, he reported to Moscow through his own channels and insisted that, allegedly, there were no Soviet troops in the Voronezh area with the exception of two NKVD regiments subordinated to him personally. But this simply was not true. As a matter of fact, the NKVD regiments had been withdrawn from the city, while units of the 40th Army stubbornly continued to fight the enemy in the city itself.

Supreme Headquarters reacted instantly. There followed an order ap-

M. I. Kazakov, *Nad kartoi bylykh srazhenii* (Moscow, 1965), pp. 130–33.

pointing N. F. Vatutin commander of the Voronezh Army Group. F. I. Golikov was left as his deputy. In the meantime, the enemy gained almost complete control of Voronezh.

A few days later we read another equally severe order concerning Major General I. Kh. Bagramian, chief of staff of the Southwestern Army Group. He was accused of poor troop management during the May offensive in the Khar'kov region.[75] He also was relieved of his position, and we, Bagramian's old friends, took this patent injustice very hard. Obviously, one can always find some fault in the work of an Army Group's chief of staff, but in this case these faults were hardly responsible for the Khar'kov setbacks.

It is known that as early as March 1942 the military council of the Southwestern Army Group had approached Supreme Headquarters with the suggestion to carry out an offensive operation to achieve important strategic objectives. Three Army Groups—Briansk, Southwestern, and Southern—would participate. This plan anticipated the destruction of a strong German force and the advance of our troops to the rivers Sozh, Dnepr, and the Southern Bug. As it happened, Supreme Headquarters did not accept the plan at that time. Instead, the Southwestern Army Group command was ordered to prepare and carry out an offensive operation with the limited objective of defeating the enemy in the Khar'kov region and liberating the city. We encountered many difficulties and complications in this operation. Troops of the Southwestern Army Group started the operation in isolation from other Army Groups. As a result, the flanks of their main force were strongly counterattacked by the Germans; they suffered significant losses and did not achieve their objective.[76] It was simply incomprehensible why the entire responsibility for this failure should rest with the Army Group's chief of staff. One should add, however, that shortly afterward S. K. Timoshenko, commander of the Army Group, was also relieved of his post.

At the time of all this confusion I was still with the Briansk Army Group. Its commander at the time was Lieutenant General K. K. Rokossovskii. I worked under Konstantin Konstantinovich for a very short time, but I remember those eight or ten days during which I had the opportunity to be close to him. What particularly and greatly impressed the generals and officers of Army Group headquarters was the attention he paid to views of his subordinates. A highly civilized man, he knew how to listen patiently to everyone. He recognized instantly the essential point of ideas expressed by others and utilized the knowledge and experience of the collective as a whole in the common cause. It can truly be said that in a very short period Rokossovskii was able to win over all his new fellow officers. We liked his calm efficiency very much.[77]

Colonel General L. M. Sandalov
Musical
Chairs

IN THE REGION of Briansk, the autumn of 1943 was dry and clear. . . . I was returning in a jeep from the 50th Army's command post to my temporary home—a miraculously preserved log cabin, where I intended to shave, wash up, clean my tunic and boots, and in general to get ready for a meeting of the military council.[78] There was quite enough time for this, so I was in no particular hurry. . . . But hardly had I set up the mirror on the windowsill and lathered my face, when there was a knock at the door, and in walked the orderly of the Army Group commanding officer. He reported that General of the Army M. M. Popov urgently requested my presence.

I wiped off the lather and got into the car. I tried to guess why the commander could want to see me so urgently. There were still three hours left before the meeting of the military council. So it must be something else, something special. This guess was confirmed when I entered the familiar wooden conference-house and saw Popov pacing gloomily back and forth.

"Read that!" Popov jabbed a piece of paper lying on the broad table.

It was a telegram from Supreme Headquarters. I ran through it hastily and could not believe my eyes. It ordered us to transfer nearly all our troops to the Central Army Group, and it ordered the immediate relocation of our Army Group headquarters together with the 11th Guards and 15th Air Armies, the artillery corps and special units to the region north of Velikie Luki.[79]

"How do you like that?" asked Popov.

"I don't understand."

"Imagine that! Neither do I. Why should such a decision be taken now, just when we're making a successful advance?"

L. M. Sandalov, *Trudnye rubezhi* (Moscow, 1965), pp. 3–10.

The liquidation of the Briansk Army Group struck me as ill-advised and extremely ill-timed. After the Orel operation and the resounding defeat of a strong enemy grouping in the Briansk forests, our troops had emerged into operational space; and, taking advantage of the dry weather, they had driven the Germans to the Dnepr.

The commander had already been considering how best to take Rogachev, and now, without a by-your-leave, the troops were to be transferred to Velikie Luki.

"Well, an order is an order. We'll carry it out," said Popov, upset.

Then and later, I vainly tried to discover the reasons for such a strange decision. Some of the officers of the General Staff explained it by saying that our Army Group had been formed two years ago solely for action in the Briansk sector. And now that it had fulfilled its mission, there was no further need for it. Others explained it by saying that the Western, Briansk, and Central Army Groups had simply crowded one another.

None of these arguments seemed sufficiently convincing. Were not all our Armies transferred to Rokossovskii's command continuing to advance in their previous operational formation?

I then telephoned A. I. Antonov, Deputy Chief of the General Staff: "Aleksei Innokent'evich, Rokossovskii now has ten Armies. Half of them are advancing in Belorussia, the rest in the Ukraine. It's very difficult to command such a mass of troops. We'll have to form one more Army Group anyway. So why did you disband our Army Group?"

Antonov remained silent.

"Very well," I continued. "If you people think that Briansk Army Group's present command is incapable of directing the activities of troops in the central sector competently, why not replace the command alone? Why transfer with us the whole bulky apparatus of the Army Group staff and, in addition, even a part of the troops?"

Antonov again avoided a direct answer.

But another high official of Supreme Headquarters gave me this edifying answer: "You should know by now, Leonid Mikhailovich, that the reasons for such shuffles should not always be looked for in operational expediency."

The military council, headed by M. M. Popov, and nearly the entire Army Group staff were the first to take the road to the north. Only I and the chief of staff of the rear, Major General I. I. Levushkin, stayed behind with a group of officers to direct the dispatch of troops and matériel.

One after another, long trains pulled away from the loading platforms—freight cars carrying the infantry; passenger cars with the staff officers; flatcars carrying tanks and artillery. Truck columns moved along the highways and dirt roads. Bomber and fighter squadrons took off from the airfields and vanished into the blue. Moving such a mass of people and military matériel over 500 km. was no joking matter, especially when you consider that our routes led through the rear areas of the Western and Kalinin Army Groups. It cost us considerable effort to move personnel and equipment without getting in the way of anyone else.

When this operation was finished, I took off for the new command post by plane. From high up, I looked for the last time on the dark-red sea of forests, slightly misted with blue smoke. . . .

. . . .

From October 1 to 20, 1943, our newly established Army Group was called the Baltic, and on October 20 it became the "2nd" Baltic.

Our troops extended from Lake Il'men' to Velikie Luki. The Northwestern Army Group and some units of the Kalinin Army Group which were occupying this line of defense were transferred to us.

Our mission was to prepare operations for the liberation of the Baltic region.[80]

In mid-November, Lieutenant General I. Kh. Bagramian, commander of the 11th Guards Army, left us. He was appointed to command the 1st Baltic Army Group (as the former Kalinin Army Group had now come to be called). The Army which Bagramian had commanded was transferred with him. And we were given the 10th Guards Army, which was then concentrated northwest of Nevel'.

A. I. Antonov immediately advised me: "You'll very soon have use for the 10th. The Leningrad and Volkhov Army Groups will attempt to break the blockade [of Leningrad]. Your mission is to engage the forces of the German 16th Army and to prevent its transfer to the north. You'll have to make a thrust at Idritsa. You'll start action two days before the Volkhov Army Group."

So on November 22, the 10th Guards Army, in cooperation with its neighbors, assumed the offensive. At first it advanced 8–10 km. a day. But at the approaches to Novosokol'niki, the tempo fell off sharply. The Germans were able to bring considerable reinforcements into this area, and our troops had to wage furious battles for every mile. We tied up the enemy, but that was all. The Supreme Commander in Chief expressed dissatisfaction with our Army Group's command and ordered the leadership of the 10th Guards Army changed. Popov appointed his own deputy, Lieutenant General M. I. Kazakov, to replace Lieutenant General A. V. Sukhomlin; and he appointed my deputy, Major General Sidel'nikov, to the post of Army chief of staff.

. . . .

I don't remember exactly, but I believe it was on February 14, 1944, that I received a phone call from my old friend Lieutenant General F. P. Ozerov, chief of staff of the Volkhov Army Group:

"Leonid, our Army Group sends you greetings!"

Two days later, I was talking on the phone with the former commander of the Northwestern Army Group, Colonel General P. A. Kurochkin. For the time being, he remained in our rear zone, along with the Army Group staff, which had been withdrawn to Supreme Headquarters reserve. Kurochkin dismayed me with yet another piece of news:

"I'm calling you from here for the last time. The Army Group's staff is being transferred to the region south of Poles'e, and there it will take charge of the Armies in the Belorussian Army Group's left flank. I thought they were all under your control before, weren't they?"

"So it's come full circle," I thought with bitterness.

Early in the spring of 1944 our troops continued to push westward—very slowly, it is true. We were separated from the Gulf of Riga by dense forests, bogs, rivers, and streams, many of which didn't even have names. Lakes were obstructing our path even more frequently. A spring thaw took us by surprise. The roads turned to mush; water filled hollows and ditches. The infantry could barely pull their boots out of the mud. Trucks and guns got stuck. Units straggled and fell behind.

On one such day, Major General S. I. Teteshkin, recently sent by the General Staff to replace Sidel'nikov, came to see me.

After discussing official business, he added as a kind of aside: "A new Army Group, the 3rd Baltic, is being formed in the Pskov sector."

"But the Armies of the Leningrad Army Group are there!"

"Precisely, so three of them will form the nucleus of the new Army Group."

"But why?" I wondered. "The leadership of the Leningrad Army Group is managing quite well!"

"At Supreme Headquarters they consider it advisable to have a separate Army Group for each Baltic republic."

"So why not utilize the Volkhov Army Group staff to head the 3rd Baltic Army Group? That would be much simpler than breaking up one Army Group and forming another from scratch."

Teteshkin shrugged his shoulders.

.   .   .   .

The so-called "Eastern Wall," which the Germans advertised as unconquerable, followed the line Pskov-Novorzhev-Vitebsk. Our task was to break through its northern sector. The defense there was powerful and deep. Some 40–50 km. behind the first line was a second, and behind the second—three more intermediary lines.

The enemy defended the approaches to the Baltic region by means of the operational group "Narva" and the 16th, 18th, and part of the 3rd Tank Armies. The Baltic region had great strategic importance for fascist Germany. Its retention made it possible to continue the blockade of our fleet in the Gulf of Finland, to protect Eastern Prussia, and to hit Soviet troops from the flanks, should they start an offensive in Belorussia.

We had our work cut out for us.

And suddenly, the transfers began again. Late in April [1944] I received a call from the Deputy Chief of the General Staff, Colonel General Shtemenko, who said that Supreme Headquarters had decided to change our commander and the member of our Army Group's military council before the start of the summer offensive.[81]

"Whom do you intend to send in their place?" I inquired.

"General of the Army Eremenko and Lieutenant General Bogatkin."

I was well acquainted with Andrei Ivanovich Eremenko even before the war, when he commanded the Special Red-Banner Far Eastern Army. He was a thickset, broad-shouldered man who had traveled a hard road from private to commander and had tremendous military experience behind him. I had already fought under him in 1941 in the Briansk sector. In a difficult situation, Eremenko acted calmly and with confidence. But it was not easy to work with him. Eremenko had a stern character and seldom agreed with the opinions of his subordinates. He listened to their suggestions but decided as he thought best.

The new commander had still another trait to which I could never accustom myself. He never told anybody when and where he was going. Apparently he was afraid that one of us might forewarn, out of friendship, unit commanders to whom he was going.

"Where can you be reached in case of need?" I would ask.

"I'll call you myself from where I'll be," answered Eremenko.

Lieutenant General V. N. Bogatkin was a man of another type. Most of all, I liked his calm, worldly wisdom and genuine Party integrity. Erudite and modest himself, Bogatkin could not tolerate ignorant and arrogant people. He was demanding toward others, very demanding toward himself, and did not show favoritism even toward his son, who was a front line officer in the 10th Guards Army. . . .

But perhaps Bogatkin is best characterized by the following incident. In 1938 he was appointed a member of the military council of the Siberian Military District. Scarcely had he assumed his post, when one evening he had a visit from two officers of the NKVD, with a warrant for the arrest of the commander of the military district.

Bogatkin scanned the warrant several times and returned it, saying that he knew the commander to be an honest and dedicated communist.

"If you go on like this, the next thing you'll even be calling me an enemy of the people," said Bogatkin.

The following day he flew to Moscow. He went to the very highest authorities and obtained a nullification of the unjust decision. One scarcely need say what civic courage was required to do this at that time. Such a man was the new member of our military council.

Admiral N. G. Kuznetsov
Leningrad in Danger

I WAS DELAYED by naval affairs and flew from Leningrad to Moscow [on September 12, 1941] one day later than the other representatives of Supreme Headquarters. . . .[82] I had not had a chance to familiarize myself with the situation in the People's Commissariat of the Navy when I was summoned to the Kremlin. It was about noon, and in those days summons usually came in the evening. In the evening and at night Supreme Headquarters was located in a separate building near an air raid shelter, but during the day, when there were few air raid alerts, everyone went to his usual office. Stalin also was in his own office that day. When I entered, he was talking to someone on the telephone. He was alone. I made an attempt to explain the Baltic Fleet situation, but he quickly interrupted me and asked whether I knew that G. K. Zhukov had been assigned to Leningrad in place of K. E. Voroshilov. When I answered that I did not know it, he said tersely, literally in a few words, that the decision had been made only yesterday and that G. K. Zhukov was apparently already at his new post. Pacing the office and then sitting down on the couch against the wall, he asked me several questions: What ships did we have in the Baltic, where were they stationed now, and were they taking part in the defense of Leningrad, which he referred to as "Peter."[83] I unrolled some naval maps on which the Baltic situation had been plotted. Among the territories in our hands were the islands of Sarema and Khiuma, the peninsula of Hangö to the west, and the islands of Hogland, Lavansaari,

N. G. Kuznetsov, "Osazhdennyi Leningrad i Baltiiskii flot," Voprosy istorii, 1965, No. 8, pp. 114–16.

and others in the eastern part of the Gulf of Finland; both shores and the entire expanse of water were in the hands of the adversary. I again tried to steer the conversation to the situation in the Baltic Sea, but Stalin went up to a small-scale land map on which the front line was drawn in the direct vicinity of Leningrad and proceeded to the matter for which I had been so urgently summoned.

He considered Leningrad's situation exceptionally serious. "Perhaps it will be necessary to abandon it," he said. Then he again posed a series of questions about the composition of the Baltic Fleet. "Not one single warship must be allowed to fall into enemy hands," he continued. Asking if I understood what he was talking about, he emphasized that if the order to sink the ships was not carried out, the guilty would be severely punished. I realized this was no time for any further discussion of the matter and awaited subsequent orders.

"Write a telegram to the [fleet] commander and give orders for everything to be ready in the event that the destruction of the fleet becomes necessary."

"I cannot sign such a telegram."

The words escaped me unexpectedly somehow, and Stalin, who had obviously not anticipated a reply of this kind, stopped dead and looked at me in astonishment.

"Why not?"

I pointed out that the fleet was operationally under the jurisdiction of the commander of the Leningrad Army Group and that a directive of this kind could be issued only under his, Stalin's, signature. After a brief silence, I added that special authority was necessary to execute an assignment of such grave responsibility, and an order from the People's Commissar of the Navy was not enough in itself. It is hard for me to say why Stalin did not want to sign this directive, but I was later convinced that I had been right not to sign it by myself. (Approximately a year later, when Leningrad's situation had improved somewhat and the question of destroying the fleet had been dropped, State Security organs sent Stalin a report in which someone accused the fleet commander, V. F. Tributs, of panic-mongering and of premature preparation to blow up his own ships in 1941. A copy of this report also came into my hands. I had to issue an urgent reminder of how matters had stood and to clear the fleet commander.) After brief reflection, Stalin ordered me to go see Marshal B. M. Shaposhnikov, Chief of the General Staff, and to write the telegram under two signatures, that of Marshal Shaposhnikov and my own, as People's Commissar of the Navy. I made no objection to this. My conversation with Boris Mikhailovich went just as I had anticipated.

"What are you thinking of, my dear fellow!" he replied when I passed on Stalin's instructions. "This is purely a naval matter, and I won't put my signature to it."

"But these are Stalin's orders," I rejoined, and at last he changed his tone, although he maintained his position.

After exchanging views, we decided to write the telegram and to go to Stalin and insist on his signature. Stalin agreed. Instead of signing the directive at once, however, he kept it. Now, as I write these lines, I ask myself: Did Stalin reckon with the possibility of abandoning Leningrad? Undoubtedly, he did. Otherwise such a serious decision would never have been made. True, this does not in any way mean that the situation was thought so hopeless; it simply shows that Stalin was worried about the possibility that the enemy might seize the fleet.[84]

General of the Army I. I. Fediuninskii
With Zhukov
to Leningrad

ON THE MORNING of September 13, an Li-2 airplane took off from Vnukovo Airport and, protected by a flight of fighters, set its course for Leningrad. The airplane carried General of the Army G. K. Zhukov, who had been appointed commander of the Leningrad Army Group, as well as Generals M. S. Khozin, P. I. Kokorev, and myself.

Zhukov spoke about my new appointment in a way that was not entirely clear:

"For the time being you'll be my deputy, and later we'll see."

We arrived in Leningrad safely and drove immediately from the airport to Smol'nyi, where Army Group headquarters was located. . . .

A. A. Zhdanov and A. A. Kuznetsov—members of the military council—were at headquarters.[85] They briefed us in detail on the situation that had developed near Leningrad. And at that time it was very serious, even menacing.

The 700,000-man enemy Army Group North which was active along the Leningrad strategic axis, consisted of 32 divisions (including 4 tank

I. I. Fediuninskii, *Podniatye po trevoge* (2nd rev. ed.; Moscow, 1964), pp. 41–47.

and 5 motorized divisions), with about 1,500 tanks, 1,200 aircraft, and 12,000 guns and mortars. . . . In beginning the campaign, its commander, Field Marshal von Leeb, counted on capturing the Baltic states by means of a strike from East Prussia and, in conjunction with the Finnish army, on seizing Leningrad. It appeared at the outset that his plans were being realized. Troops of Army Group North succeeded in penetrating far into our territory. After the enemy breakthrough in the Luga defense zone and the withdrawal of our troops from the cities of Kingisepp and Chudovo, bloody fighting developed on the close approaches to Leningrad.

The fortified area that had been created in the Krasnogvardeisk sector presented a serious obstacle to the further advance of the Hitlerite armies. All enemy attacks in this direction were repulsed. Then to the west of Krasnogvardeisk von Leeb formed a grouping which consisted of 8 divisions for a thrust along the Krasnoe Selo–Uritsk–Leningrad axis. Simultaneously, three divisions launched a secondary strike from the area to the south of Kolpino along the Moscow Highway.

On September 12 the enemy occupied Krasnoe Selo and Pushkino, penetrated the Krasnogvardeisk rear and, having seized part of Petergof, emerged at Strel'na on the Gulf of Finland. By that time fascist German troops attacking from the Tosno area had occupied the Mga railroad station and Shlissel'burg. Leningrad was blockaded from land. . . .[86]

In the afternoon of September 15 I was summoned to the Army Group military council and ordered to depart immediately for the Pulkovo heights to make a detailed assessment of the situation there. The danger of a breakthrough from Pulkovo heights was imminent. In that area, the front line had advanced to the very outskirts of Leningrad. The enemy had massed his main forces in this sector and was preparing to deliver the last, as he saw it, strike.[87] Formations of the 42nd Army had been severely depleted in many days of fighting and were barely holding the defensive line.

Headquarters of the 42nd Army was located in reinforced concrete pillboxes in the Pulkovo fortified area. The distance from there to the forward line was so slight that I could hear the familiar, angry whine of bullets overhead as I walked through the trenches to the Army commander's dugout shelter. Lieutenant General F. S. Ivanov, commander of the Army, sat in the shelter, supporting his head with both hands.

Before the war, Ivanov and I had attended courses together at the General Staff Academy. At that time we were in the same study group. Subsequently, he became deputy commander of the Kiev Special Military District. I had known General Ivanov as a person distinguished by an enviable buoyancy, as a very energetic, efficient, and resolute man. But now he sat before me, tired, his face unshaven and sunken, depressed, and in low spirits. Ivanov expressed no surprise whatsoever upon seeing me, just as if only several days had passed since we last met. He only asked me and, by the way, without special interest, simply out of politeness:

"How did you get here? I seem to recall that you were commanding a corps in the Southwest Army Group."

I replied that I had come as deputy Army Group commander in order to acquaint myself with the situation. I asked Ivanov to indicate on the map the disposition of the Army's troops.

"I don't know," Ivanov said irritably. "I don't know anything."

"Are you in communication with your formations?"

"There isn't any communication, either. The fighting was heavy today. In some places we had to retreat. Communications were disrupted." Ivanov did not even attempt to make excuses.

It was necessary to summon the chief of staff, Major General Larionov, and the chief of the operations section in order to get a general picture of the situation. And the more I became acquainted with it, the more I realized that the defensive positions in the zone of the 42nd Army were literally being held by a miracle. During the day there was fierce fighting along the entire front line from Uritsk to the outskirts of Pulkovo. The enemy occupied Novoe and Staroe Panovo and had infiltrated Uritsk in individual groups. It was a good thing that apparently the enemy had also become exhausted and had stopped the attacks by nightfall. But at any moment, the onslaught could begin anew and then— Then it would be readily apparent that the gates of Leningrad were not tightly closed at this point.

What was to be done? I was already formulating certain priority measures in my mind when I was urgently summoned back to Smol'nyi. Accompanied by Ivanov, I left the dugout shelter. On the forward line, directly before the Army's command post, machine-gun fire had become more intense. From time to time, flares would fly up into the dark sky, remain suspended for an instant, and then swiftly fall downward, throwing off glittering sparks.

"I guess we'll have to move the command post again," Ivanov said. "It's too close from here to the forward line."

"No, there can be no withdrawal," I objected. "As deputy Army Group commander, I forbid moving the command post."

"Well, all right, we'll try to hold out," said Ivanov, accepting with a sigh.

At Smol'nyi, I was immediately taken to Zhukov. Also present were comrades A. A. Zhdanov and A. A. Kuznetsov. I was preparing to make my report when the commander interrupted:

"A report isn't necessary. I know everything already. While you were on your way here, Ivanov moved the command post to the basement of a school opposite the Kirov Plant."[88]

The commander was silent for a minute and then said firmly:

"Take over the 42nd Army, immediately."

Despite the seriousness of the situation I could not resist a smile. Zhukov noticed it and asked, "Why are you smiling?"

"It seems to me that the commander has not expressed himself with complete precision," I replied. "How can one take over an Army in such a situation? I can only assume its command."

"All right, assume command then," the commander said. "You have to . . . put the Army in order. Select the officers you need from among the people at Army Group headquarters and go to work."

Then and there, A. A. Kuznetsov took a pencil and wrote out an order appointing me commander of the 42nd Army. Comrades G. K. Zhukov and A. A. Zhdanov signed it. Accompanied by Major General L. S. Bere-zinskii, who had been appointed chief of staff of the Army, and several staff officers, I again set out to see Ivanov and on the way thought how best to begin.

Not far from the Kirov Plant, our path was blocked by a tank column. Their treads rumbling over the asphalt, they were crossing the square. I instructed my adjutant to find out where these tanks came from and to find the column commander. A few minutes later, a broad-shouldered tankman with helmet straps undone, in tightly belted coveralls, came up to me. This was the commander of a tank regiment which was part of the 42nd Army. At the order of Army headquarters, the regiment was withdrawing to the outskirts of Leningrad. I ordered the commander to return the tanks to the previous deployment area and instructed him to come with me.

In the school where Army headquarters was housed, a stormy meeting of the military council was in progress. The room was cloudy with cigarette smoke, and the ashtrays were filled with butts. Lieutenant General Ivanov and the members of the military council, Solov'ev and Klement'ev, were discussing the situation and were unable to agree. Since, as before, there was no communication with the troops, the argument was purely theoretical. No matter what decision the military council reached, it would be impossible to implement it.

I entered when the argument was in full swing. The point of it seemed to be whether to withdraw the artillery or to leave it for the time being in its present firing positions.

"I have been appointed commander of the Army," I said by way of greeting, and, in order to put an immediate end to the fruitless argument, I declared: "I order the meeting of the military council closed. You, Comrade Ivanov, are summoned to Smol'nyi."[89]

Lieutenant General of Engineers
B. V. Bychevskii
Zhukov
in Command

AND JUST at this tense moment, the Army Group's command was changed again. K. E. Voroshilov was called back to Moscow. General of the Army G. K. Zhukov arrived to replace him. Lieutenant General M. S. Khozin became chief of staff.

The formalities of the reception and transfer of the Army Group command did not take much time. P. P. Evstigneev and I. N. Kovalev said that after the reconnaissance and operations maps were signed over, Voroshilov and Zhukov went to the telegraph room. The conversation with Supreme Headquarters was brief. General A. M. Vasilevskii received the message in Moscow. Zhukov wired: "I have taken command. Tell the Supreme Commander in Chief that I propose to be more active than my predecessor."

Voroshilov did not wish to converse with Moscow and left the office without a word.

He soon called in the heads of the [various] services to take leave of them. He saw Generals A. A. Novikov, V. P. Sviridov, N. Z. Bolotnikov, P. P. Evstigneev, I. N. Kovalev, and myself. Voroshilov shook hands with us gloomily.

"Good-bye, comrades! Supreme Headquarters has called me back." He was silent a moment, then added, "That's what an old man like me deserves! This is not the Civil War. Now we have to fight differently. . . . But don't doubt for a minute that we'll smash the fascist scum! They're swarming toward the city with their tongues hanging out and choke on their own blood already. . . ."

That same night, Voroshilov and most of his staff flew back to Mos-

B. V. Bychevskii, *Gorod-front* (Moscow, 1963), pp. 92–95, 98–100.

cow. The next day, G. K. Zhukov summoned me. My first meeting with the new commander bore rather a strange character. After hearing me present myself in the usual way, he looked me over for several seconds with cold, suspicious eyes. Then he asked abruptly: "Who are you, anyway?"

I didn't understand the question and reported again: "Chief of Engineers for the Northwestern Army Group, Lieutenant Colonel Bychevskii."

"I'm asking *who* you are. Where did you come from?"

His voice had a note of exasperation. Zhukov's heavy chin moved forward. His short but thickset figure rose up from the table.

Is he asking for a biography? I wondered, not understanding that the commander had expected to see somebody else in my post. Who needs a biography now? I hesitantly proceeded to report that I had been chief of engineers for eighteen months, first for the district and then for the Army Group, and that during the Soviet-Finnish War I was chief of engineers with the 13th Army on the Karelian Isthmus.

"So you replaced Khrenov, then? That's what you should have said! And where's General Nazarov? I summoned him."

"General Nazarov worked on Voroshilov's staff and coordinated the engineering operations of both Army Groups,"[90] I explained. "He flew back last night with the Marshal."

"He coordinated—he flew back—" muttered Zhukov. "Well, the hell with him! Report what you have there."

I spread out the maps and showed what had been done up until the breakthrough at Krasnoe Selo, Krasnogvardeisk, and Kolpino; what the situation was at the Pulkovo position; what was being done in the city, on the Neva, on the Karelian Isthmus; and where minelayers and pontooniers were working.

Zhukov listened without asking questions. Then, whether accidentally or not, his hand moved the maps so brusquely that some sheets fell to the floor. He turned his back on them and without a word began to examine a large map of the city's defense plan tacked to the wall.

"What tanks are these in the Petroslavianka district?" he suddenly asked, turning to me again and watching me put away the maps that had fallen on the floor. "What are you hiding? Give it to me! What kind of nonsense—"

"These are dummy tanks, Comrade Commander," I said, pointing to the symbol of a decoy tank force that had caught his eye. "The Mariinskii Theater workshop made fifty of them. The Germans have bombed them twice."

"Twice!" laughed Zhukov. "And have you kept those toys there long?"

"Two days."

"You're looking for fools. The next thing you know, the Germans will also start to drop wood on them. Remove them tonight! Make another hundred and put them in two spots outside Sredniaia Rogatka tomorrow morning. Here and here," he pointed a pencil.

"The theater craftsmen can't make 100 dummies in one night," I said without thinking.

Zhukov raised his head and looked me up and down. "If they can't, you'll be court-martialed. Who is your commissar?"

"Regimental Commissar Mukha."

"Mukha? Go and tell this *mukha* [fly—Ed.] of yours that you'll both go before the tribunal if you don't carry out my order. I'll see for myself tomorrow."

Zhukov's threatening, staccato phrases were like cracks of a whip. He seemed to be deliberately testing my patience.

"I'll go to the Pulkovo position tomorrow to see what you've 'accomplished' over there. What were you thinking with? Why did you start to fortify it so late?" And then, without waiting for an answer, he said abruptly: "You may go."

The new commander treated the other senior officers of the [Northwestern] Army Group no better. He threatened nearly all of them with the tribunal.

The chief of operations, Colonel Korkodin, left for Moscow after his very first brief conversation with Zhukov. The next day Zhukov replaced the 42nd Army command. And a week later he relieved Major General V. I. Shcherbakov and Divisional Commissar I. F. Chukhov, a member of the military council, of their command posts in the 8th Army.

As for the purely operational decisions and orders of the new Army Group commander, they were not essentially different, and, indeed, could not be different, from what we had had until then. As before, the primary need was for "a continuous counterattack," in order to take back from the enemy whatever settlement, station, or position was yielded yesterday or today. The situation itself required this. . . .[91]

. . . .

It was 4:00 a.m., when Zhukov's aide came looking for me.

"Your orders are to go to the Smol'nyi Institute at once."

In the waiting room I met the 42nd Army's new commander, Major General I. I. Fediuninskii, and Corps Commissar N. N. Klement'ev, a member of that same Army's military council. Judging by their faces, a trying conversation with Zhukov had just taken place here.

When I, wet and muddy, entered the office, G. K. Zhukov and A. A. Zhdanov stood bending over a map. Zhukov looked in my direction:

"So you came, finally. Where do you hang out that we have to spend all night looking for you? You must have been snoring."

This beginning did not augur anything good.

"I was carrying out your orders to inspect the defense boundary along the Belt Railway," I replied.[92]

"Well? Is it ready?"

"Seventy firing positions of antitank artillery are ready. The trenches are dug. The placing of obstacles and mines is finished."

"Does the 42nd Army commander know about this line?"

"This afternoon I gave a sketch of the line to the Army chief of staff, General Berezinskii. General Fediuninskii himself was going out to the troops."

A fist hitting the table was the answer to what I thought was an accurate report.

"We're not asking you what clerks you gave the sketch to. We're interested in something else: Does or does not the Army commander know about this line? You do understand the Russian language?" To these last words, Zhukov added a strong expression.

And at that moment, the devil must have possessed me to answer naively: "General Fediuninskii is here in the waiting room, Comrade Commander."

A new outburst of rage followed. "Are you thinking about what you're saying? I know without you that he's here. Don't you understand that if Antonov's division doesn't occupy the defense line on the Belt Railway, the Germans will break into the city? And then I'll have you shot in front of the Smol'nyi Institute as a traitor."

A. A. Zhdanov frowned. He clearly disapproved of the commander's tone. Zhdanov himself did not know how to swear—it just didn't come off with him. Now, wishing to smooth over Zhukov's rudeness, he said: "Comrade Bychevskii, how is it that you didn't think of finding Fediuninskii himself! Don't forget, he took command of the Army just recently. And Antonov's division, which is supposed to occupy the new line, was literally formed just the other day. That division will be bombed if it goes out there in daylight. Do you understand the situation now?"

I really must have been in a state of stupor, for only now did I realize why I'd been summoned. At once, before dawn, we had to secure the transfer of [Antonov's] 6th Division of Home Guards to the new defense line that we had prepared.[93] I did not dare report that until now I hadn't known about today's order from Zhukov to merge this 6th Division into the 42nd Army and quickly occupy a line in the rear of the Pulkovo position under cover of night. Instead, I said:

"Comrade Commander, permit me to leave with the Army commander [Fediuninskii] at once, and we will take the division out to the prepared line."

"You've seen the light—" Zhukov cursed again. "Go at once and remember: If the division is not in place by 9:00 a.m., I'll have you shot."

When I went out to the waiting room, Ivan Ivanovich Fediuninskii, a swarthy, dark-haired general with the star of a Hero of the Soviet Union on his chest, smiled slyly. "Did you catch it, engineer?"

At that time I did not yet know this good-natured man well. His question seemed inappropriate and spiteful, and I answered rather curtly:

"A mere trifle, Comrade General. The commander promised to have me shot if the 6th Division is not on the Belt by morning. Let's go. Obviously there was no one on your staff who would arrange such a petty affair as escorting a division to the line. But the Army has the diagram!"

"Don't get angry, engineer!" said the Army commander, smiling broadly, as if he knew Zhukov's character. "You had it easy. Georgii Konstantinovich promised to have me and the member of the military council hanged for the very same thing. We were about to leave when you came. So we decided to wait, knowing that the commander wouldn't detain you long."

Fediuninskii's grin made things seem more cheerful. As soon as we left the Smol'nyi Institute, we were plunged into the darkness of the autumn night.

By morning, the 6th Division of Home Guards had successfully occupied the last defense line outside the city.

Chief Marshal of Artillery N. N. Voronov
Stalin at the "Front"

ON AUGUST 3 [1943], out of the blue, we were summoned to Iukhnov. This was rather far from the front lines, and we had to travel a considerable time even though we drove our vehicles for all they were worth.[94] Finally, we came to a beautiful grove where small wooden

N. N. Voronov, *Na sluzhbe voennoi* (Moscow, 1963), pp. 384–85.

structures nestled among the trees. We were met by a general who led us to a small house. We entered the room and saw Stalin.

It was as though they had deliberately selected the most unsightly house. In the center of the hut stood a wretched wooden table that had been hastily dashed together. Instead of legs, the table was supported by two cross-pieces reinforced by a cross-beam. Beside it were two equally crude benches. On the windowsill stood a telephone and the telephone wire ran through the casement window to the street.

General Kamera whispered to me:

"Well, this is some situation!"

The thought flashed through my mind: "It's intentional—to resemble the front more closely."

First of all, Stalin asked whether it was far from there to the Army Group's command point. Then he ordered a briefing on the situation. We spread out the maps and began reporting on the enemy and on our troops. Sokolovskii was about to describe the design and missions of the forthcoming offensive operation, but Stalin interrupted him:

"We will not go into detail. By spring 1944, the Western Army Group must reach Smolensk, prepare thoroughly, collect its strength, and take the city." This sentence was repeated twice.

Essentially, the conversation ended on this.

The comrades attempted to protest that the Western Army Group had not received sufficient reserves and combat equipment.

"We'll give everything we can," came the answer, "and if we cannot give you any more, you'll have to get along with what you have."

We started back. Many of us were surprised by the secret visit of the Supreme Commander in Chief to Iukhnov. Why had it been necessary to travel so many kilometers over a road that was rutted by tanks and tractors and was impassable in places, and to stop in a little town so far removed from the forward lines? He could see nothing from there, and he saw no one besides us. It was much more difficult to contact the Army Groups from there than from Moscow. It was a strange, unnecessary trip—[95]

PART III PROFESSIONAL SOLDIERS VERSUS POLITICAL LEADERS

Introduction

A MAJOR ISSUE in all modern armies has been the relationship between professional soldiers and political leaders. The problem has been especially acute in the Red Army from its very inception; still today it preoccupies both Party authorities and military leaders. In the Soviet case the question of the relationship between political and military authority is not confined to the basic issue of subordinating strategic and operational plans to a war's overall objectives, the definition of which is usually considered the sole domain of civilian authority. It concerns, in addition, the perpetuation of a system of political control *within* the army through numerous devices, the chief of which is the institution of political officers or commissars. Throughout the war, but especially in the 1941–43 period, one crucial issue was never resolved to the satisfaction of the new breed of Red Army professional soldier: how the imperative of maintaining tight political control over military commanders and troops with the attendant diminution of the professional soldier's authority and freedom of action was to be reconciled with the equally strong imperative of developing an efficient professional war machine.

As a result of the Winter War in 1940, unitary command was introduced into the Red Army in an effort to strengthen its professional élan. The newly created deputies for political affairs who were attached to each commander enjoyed far fewer rights than their predecessors, the commissars. In the fourth week of war, however, the institution of military commissars was again restored and with it the dual command system. Behind this measure was the attempt to strengthen the resolve of the Red Army during this period of chaotic retreat. The commissars shared with the commander full responsibility for the combat performance of troops; they were empowered with equal rights in combat leadership. The commissars served as direct representatives of the Party and government in the army. Their duties included, according to the Decree of July 16, 1941, "warning the High Command and Government against officers and political functionaries who are unworthy of their position . . . [and] conducting an unceasing struggle against cowards, panic-mongers, and deserters." Commissars served in military units below the Army level. In Armies, Army Groups, and Fleets there existed military councils composed of the commander as official chairman, the chief of staff, and a political functionary who was simply called the member of the military council. Later in the war when, as a rule, more than one political functionary participated in the council, the senior political man was called first member of the military council.

Soviet sources state that the military council combined the principles of collegiality and unitary command, a notion scarcely distinguished by clarity. Decisions concerning all matters, including those of operations, were to be made by the council collectively, but the authority of the commander, his duty and right to direct troops were not to be infringed. One has the impression that while the relationship between the commissar and commander on lower army levels was well institutionalized, the relations of members of the military council with the commanders of Armies and Army Groups were more flexible. The exercise of their rights and real influence apparently depended to a considerable extent on who they both were.

Senior members of the military councils of Armies and Army Groups were of two types. The first type consisted of individuals who spent most of their life in political work within the Red Army, in other words, the "professional" military commissars. During long years of service they acquired through special education and experience some knowledge of military affairs. While their primary identification remained with the Party whose functionaries they were, at the same time they shared to some degree the professional's *esprit de corps*. In this category one may include Lieutenant General K. F. Telegin, member of the military council of Marshal Zhukov's 1st Belorussian Army Group in the 1945 campaign; Colonel General A. S. Zheltov, member of the military council with Marshal Malinovskii's 3rd Ukrainian Army Group; Lieutenant General N. K.

Popel', member of the military council of General Katukov's 1st Guards Tank Army. The second type of senior military council member, and by far the more numerous, consisted of civilian political leaders assigned to the Red Army for the duration of the war or for a single campaign or operation. Almost immediately after the start of war, over 40 percent of the total membership of the Central Committee of the Party, that is, 54 members and alternate members, were assigned to military work. In all, the Party sent to the army 120 secretaries of territorial, provincial, and republican Party Committees—in other words a quarter of those key Party officials employed outside Moscow. Stalin himself assigned some of his close associates to top political positions in the armed forces, including members of the Politburo; perhaps the most advertised of these in the post-Stalin period was N. S. Khrushchev.

In October 1942 the institution of military commissars was again abolished, and the system of Deputy Commanders for Political Affairs was reinstated. This change, together with such measures as the reintroduction of epaulettes, reflected Stalin's recognition both of the new competence acquired by line commanders and of the necessity to strengthen their authority and enhance their status in the interest of better combat leadership and higher discipline. The status of political functionaries at higher command levels did not change as a consequence of the October 1942 decree; the military councils were retained in their previous form. One may suggest, however, that as the professional stature, achievements, and fame of top Red Army commanders grew with the continuation of the war, the role, influence, and visibility of political leaders diminished. Stalin returned some political leaders to civilian duties and sent his close political associates less often from Moscow to inspect, supervise, and interfere with the actual conduct of military operations.

The authors of the memoirs which follow are all professional soldiers who relate their own experiences with political functionaries and leaders. Some episodes concern political leaders who served as members of military councils in the field (Lieutenant General N. I. Strakhov and Major General I. T. Zamertsev). Other accounts recall the conduct of political leaders who visit the front line units as representatives of Moscow (General of the Army I. V. Tiulenev, Colonel General S. A. Kalinin, Major General S. D. Luganskii). The remainder describe encounters with political leaders at Moscow headquarters, sometimes in the presence of Stalin (Colonel I. T. Starinov and Chief Marshal of Artillery N. N. Voronov). This last group concludes with the dramatic clash of Marshal K. K. Rokossovskii and Stalin at Supreme Headquarters.

Five major villains emerge from these accounts: L. P. Beria, Chief of the Secret Police; G. M. Malenkov, Secretary of the Central Committee of the Party; L. M. Kaganovich, Politburo member and chief of the Soviet transportation system; V. M. Molotov, Stalin's most trusted associate; and L. Z. Mekhlis, the *bête noire* of the Soviet military, head of the Main Political Administration until June 1942 and thus the Chief Political Commissar of the Red Army. The criticism expressed in these memoirs is directed against political leaders who were purged in the post-Stalin period. (The sole exception was Mekhlis who died at almost the same time as Stalin.) It seems hardly likely that only those political leaders who were officially denounced by the Party behaved in the manner described in these memoirs. Other political leaders no doubt escaped censure thanks either to death without disgrace or to political survival in Kremlin halls.

Lieutenant General N. I. Strakhov
Kaganovich

IN THE BEGINNING of August [1942], as soon as I arrived at Army Group headquarters in Georgievskoe (north of Tuapse), I presented myself to the commander, Marshal S. M. Budennyi.[96]

His first question was:

"Colonel, aren't you ashamed of running away from the Germans

N. I. Strakhov, "Na voenno-avtomobil'nykh dorogakh," *Voenno-istoricheskii zhurnal*, 1964, No. 11, pp. 68–71.

like that?" Even at such a time, the Marshal had retained his dash and
sense of irony. With a heavy heart, I answered:
  "I'm terribly ashamed, but what could I do?"
  That night a meeting of the Army Group military council took place
at which my report on road conditions was heard. Although by that
time we were beginning to get the highway service under control, the
situation was still far from satisfactory. The stopping of a single vehicle
on a narrow stretch would immediately cause a bottleneck. Horse-drawn
transports, evacuees with their vehicles, cattle herds, tractors, and even
self-propelled combines would squeeze into the motorized columns and
completely prevent us from moving. Therefore, even Army Group headquarters could move only with great delays. . . .
  When L. M. Kaganovich, who was a member of the Army Group
military council, arrived, he immediately snapped at me:
  "When will you have the roads in shape? It's impossible to get
through; everything is clogged with cattle, tractors, refugees. It's an
outrage!"
  L. P. Korniets[97] tried to explain to him that in the Southern Army
Group sector traffic was under control despite difficult conditions, but
that we had only been here a few days, and previously the highway service troops had been under a different command. But Kaganovich, refusing to listen to anything or anybody, went on spouting threats. . . .
  I began to report my plan for putting the roads into proper shape.
This required a complete ban on daylight movement of cavalry, pack
animals, tractors, and cattle; at points of merging traffic and on narrow
stretches, traffic toward the front was to have priority; positively no transports were to be allowed to stop in the middle of a road; narrow stretches
had to be widened immediately, single-lane stretches eliminated, and
areas for stopping, waiting for transports, etc. to be established.
  These suggestions were approved. The Army Group commander directed me to submit to him for signature the corresponding order to the
Army Group troops and to ensure its strict observance.
  I still remember vividly that meeting of the military council. It went
on till morning; enemy aircraft bombed Georgievskoe at regular intervals; fires blazed all around. As soon as each consecutive air raid started,
Colonel P. P. Zelenskii, the Marshal's aide, would come in to close the
windows (afterward they were opened again, for it was a very stuffy
night) and would say coaxingly:
  "Comrade Marshal of the Soviet Union! The German planes are
coming again, you really must go into the shelter!"
  But Semen Mikhailovich would merely twist his mustaches and
answer in his high-pitched voice:

"Never mind, let them bomb"; and the meeting would go on.

It was decided that night to take the engines off the disabled combines and push the combines themselves off the roads, since they were the main cause of traffic tie-ups.

On the following day, intensive road work was started, first to provide sidings, then to eliminate single-lane stretches on the key roads of the front. The road network was divided into sectors. The recently issued order on traffic control was difficult to enforce in the first few days; all officers of the auto highway service were on the road, but after the second or third day, clashes became rarer; there was no more shouting, cursing, or warning shots by traffic control personnel because the order was being enforced uniformly.

In addition to measures stipulated in the order, we set up a vehicle repair service, not only at all road command posts, but in the form of a mobile repair squad. The repair patrol vehicles tried to repair disabled vehicles on the spot whenever possible, or else they swiftly towed them away. Traffic now flowed unimpeded. . . .

The chief of staff did not have a single occasion to reprove the highway service, whose efforts were aimed at helping our Armies carry out their operations. It should be noted, however, that especially in the initial period, the transportation of troops along the Black Sea coast was not entirely smooth. We had few vehicles. After the battering they had suffered during the summer retreat and in view of the state of mountain roads, they often broke down, and we did not have sufficient repair equipment.[98]

But that was only half the trouble. A great deal of precious time was wasted in the very organization of the transports. I remember when I received my first assignment to form a truck column and when with the help of the Headquarters Operations Department I quickly drafted a plan for moving a division, this plan was approved without any delay by the chief of staff of the Army Group, Lieutenant General A. I. Antonov. I had already asked for permission to issue all executive orders, but General Antonov said that in addition the plan had to be submitted to the Army Group's military council member, L. M. Kaganovich. We had to wait several hours in Kaganovich's anteroom: when he was not resting, he was busy with something. It was getting late, and the transport was to be finished by midnight of the following day. A few precious hours of darkness had already elapsed, and I felt as though I were sitting on hot coals. At last, at about two in the morning, Kaganovich received the chief of staff and myself, went over the plan, and wrote his decision: "Transport to be over by 8:00 p.m." I started arguing that in the three or four hours of remaining darkness it would be impossible to make a 200-km. trip, but in reply I heard only rude threats and the order: "Report personally at 8:00 p.m. on the execution of the order, or else—" Of course, I did my best, but by 8:00 p.m. only the lead cars with the division commander and myself had reached their destination, while the whole division was still on the move and completed the journey only six hours later. However, at 8:00 p.m. I reported by telephone that the assignment had been completed, and that the division commander and I had reached our destination. Literally it was true, but in substance, of course, it was a lie. But I was obliged to do it.

The same thing happened again a few days later. Kaganovich, as usual fingering amber beads or a key-chain, received us only in the morning hours to hear a report, and nevertheless ordered us to complete a transport by 7:00 p.m. of that very day. It was almost dawn, but he was adamant: "You are not thinking like a colonel, but haggling like a 'tramot' manager [in the early days of the Revolution, local soviets had transportation departments called "tramots"—Ed.]. Last time you also said you couldn't transport the division in the scheduled time, and then you did! Just keep that in mind—etc." Fortunately, the transport was a fairly small one, and it was a rainy day. We were able to break it into small motorized columns that we dispatched by daylight.

I had learned my lesson, and thereafter I started the transports as soon as the plan had been approved by the chief of staff, since Kaganovich never changed anything but the deadline anyway. After giving all necessary orders to the men in charge, I calmly waited for official confirmation in Kaganovich's anteroom. Sometimes I even managed to take a nap while sitting in the well-furnished anteroom or to read the papers while the transport was already on its way, and not once did anything go wrong. Maybe that is why Kaganovich was relatively pleasant with me, whereas many other commanders complained that he was often rude, menacing, and arbitrary.

For instance, this is what happened to Army Engineer second rank A. I. Kolkunov. . . . As a routine promotion he was appointed chief of the 56th Army's highway department. The military highway of Dzhubga–Khadyzhensk–Goriachii Kliuch included a single-lane stretch of about 20 km. that at one point passed near Army headquarters. Traffic on that stretch followed the rule of 2:1, i.e., two hours toward the front to one hour in the opposite direction. On the fifth day after Kolkunov had taken charge, he learned that a high ranking superior was expected at Army headquarters. He decided to drive out to meet him and to advise the control posts on the way of his expected arrival. At the control post just before the start of the single-lane stretch, Kolkunov was told that a short while earlier, a column of about twenty trucks coming from the front had gone through; it was led by a captain with special authorization from Army headquarters to pick up some projectiles for rocket launchers. After instructing the control post not to let anybody through in that direction for the time being, Kolkunov set out to catch up with the column. Two or three kilometers farther on, he saw trucks at a standstill which impeded the passage of a few cars coming from the opposite direction. Seeing Kaganovich with a group of commanders, Kolkunov went up to introduce himself He tried to report that he was immediately going to order the trucks to back out to the siding area to make way for the cars. But Kaganovich would not listen to a word he said and screamed instead: "Demote! Arrest! Court-martial! Shoot!"

Kolkunov was arrested, questioned that same night, and it was only on the following day that Kaganovich consented to listen to the arguments of the Army commander concerning the fact that Kolkunov had been with this Army for only four days. Kaganovich then agreed merely to dismiss him from his post. . . .

When Colonel General Ia. T. Cherevichenko took over the command of the Black Sea Army Group, the situation at headquarters became very unhealthy.[99] Intrigues and squabbles began. Kaganovich started fancying himself a great strategist, making decisions and issuing orders all on his own.

In early autumn, Kaganovich demanded a plan on winter maintenance of military highways. He found fault with all aspects of the plan I had submitted and gave me a long lecture on the methods of coping with snow drifts and the management of railways in wintertime. He offered me the help of one of the railway managers whom he kept on his staff in reserve, but I decided to work out a plan by myself. I put one of my technicians and a draftsman to work and within a week was able to hand Kaganovich a plan. It consisted of an album with a separate page including a color diagram and explanatory note for each incline, bridge, and turn. Kaganovich was studying the album with evident satisfaction and getting ready to approve it when Ia. T. Cherevichenko came in. After greeting me, he asked:

"What are these little pictures you brought, Strakhov?"

After listening to my explanation, he declared:

"There's no snow around here, and if any falls it's all melted an hour later. I know this region quite well!"

Kaganovich angrily slammed my album shut and said: "You may leave."

With the obvious approval of "Lazarus" (that's what we called him among ourselves), Kaganovich's own arrant cult of personality quickly developed.[100] The suite of officers of his personal bodyguard and "consultants" from Moscow encouraged the appearance of toadies, wranglers, and intriguers. Kaganovich "favored" some of the staff officers from among his "rapporteurs" and could not bear others, who were treated with scorn or simply removed. The former atmosphere at Army Group headquarters of friendly cooperation, comradely trust, and mutual help gave way to scheming, suspicion, and distrust. People's intimate problems were aired in public and usually turned out to be nothing but gossip spread by the unhealthy-minded. Fortunately, "Lazarus" did not stay with us too long. Everybody heaved a sigh of relief when he left, and Colonel General I. E. Petrov took over the command of the Black Sea Army Group. Headquarters and all service branches again returned to a businesslike, matter-of-fact leadership.[101]

Major General I. T. Zamertsev
Mekhlis

SOVIET TROOPS, advancing rapidly, freed the towns and villages of the Western Ukraine one after the other in the autumn of 1944. . . . Abandoning their heavy weapons, Hitler's troops rolled on to the Carpathians. They hoped to consolidate their positions in the mountains or to retreat farther, to Hungary.[102]

The 11th Rifle Corps, which I then commanded, was in the Army Group's left flank. We received orders to advance parallel to the Carpathians in order to cut off the enemy's roads of retreat. . . . But then something unexpected happened. The 4th Ukrainian Army Group under Colonel General I. E. Petrov joined the offensive. Our 1st Guards Army under Colonel General A. A. Grechko was transferred to this Army Group.[103]

The mission confronting the Guards Army was altered. The 11th Rifle Corps received new orders. We began a new maneuver, and our forces were spread out more than 30 km. in depth. The corps advanced toward the L'vov-Uzhgorod road, an extremely important highway along which a huge German grouping was retreating in an effort to reach the Carpathians at any cost.

I. T. Zamertsev, *Cherez gody i rasstoianiia* (Moscow, 1965), pp. 3–8.

Following our orders, we continued to move west in a broad column, while the Hitlerites were moving in on us from behind. The situation became critical, and I sounded the alarm: I sent several coded messages to the Army commander and also sent a personal radiogram to military council member of the 4th Ukrainian Army Group L. Z. Mekhlis.

To help cut off the enemy's line of retreat more effectively, the 101st Guards Rifle Corps was brought into battle to our right. But the enemy struck suddenly on its flank and pushed it back 12 km. As a result, the flank and rear of our 271st Rifle Division became exposed. The fascists attempted a breach on the L'vov-Mukachev road, but there they encountered stiff resistance from the 24th Guards Rifle Division. . . . An experienced officer, Major General F. A. Prokhorov, commanded this formation. His troops managed to repel the enemy's pressure. Seeing that it was too difficult to reach the Carpathians by the shortest route, the Germans turned off the road, and the entire enemy avalanche came down upon the rear of the 271st Rifle Division, which continued to advance to the west. The Germans cut this division off from the corps' main forces, and for four days we did not know what had happened to them. . . .

Colonel Ia. S. Shashko had been appointed commander of the encircled division just before our advance began. Earlier he had been deputy commander of this same division and had distinguished himself. During the war the former miner Shashko often got into tight spots and always acquitted himself well. He was known for his integrity, energy, and courage. He knew his officers and men well, and they respected him deeply for his fairness and understanding.

Shashko did not let us down this time either. After four days his 271st Rifle Division rejoined our corps' main forces. It had killed many fascist soldiers and destroyed a considerable amount of enemy equipment. Furthermore, it had managed to preserve 90 percent of its men. . . . True, the fascist tanks had managed to destroy part of the artillery and cause damage to the division's rear, but, in general, losses were not very great.

The commander, the officers, and the soldiers had displayed their best qualities. They had fought several days without food or rest. I immediately ordered mobile kitchens from other divisions sent out to Shashko. But his troops were too tired to eat.

There was nothing left but to thank Shashko and all the men for their skillful actions in difficult circumstances. But it so happened that I was unable either to see the colonel or to hear his report.

Shashko left the encirclement with his last sub-units. The minute he reached our lines, he was put into a car and taken to the Army Group commander. He was not even permitted to change clothes. He appeared before Colonel General I. E. Petrov dirty, tattered, with bloodshot eyes.

Shashko later told me that Petrov greeted him cordially, asked for all the details of the operation, the decisions he took, the mood of the men and officers. Shashko reported that his regiments destroyed many sub-units covering the enemy's flank and rear, that the 271st Division had destroyed dozens of enemy trains since the advance began and had captured about 100 guns and up to 5,000 prisoners.

"Well, well," said the Army Group commander. "You fought pretty well, but the minute you slipped up, you got your comeuppance. That was an expensive lesson! You'll be smarter next time!"

General Petrov assigned 20 guns and some trucks to reinforce the division and allowed three days rest. After asking Shashko to convey his gratitude to the men, Petrov advised him to drop in at once on Mekhlis, the member of the military council.

"What kind of hoodlum has turned up?" was the way Mekhlis greeted Shashko, without even letting him present himself or explain why he was at Army Group headquarters in such an unpresentable state. As it was, Mekhlis knew very well why. The scouts who "nabbed" Shashko at the front line said later that they had acted on Mekhlis' personal orders.

Shashko felt outraged by such a greeting. He was one of those who display courage not only in battle.

"In the first place, I'm not a hoodlum, but a colonel of the Soviet Army and commander of the 271st Rifle Division," Shashko answered sharply. "And in the second place, I must ask you not to yell at me!"

Mekhlis jumped up but stopped short. Evidently, the expression on the face of the man standing calmly before him gave him pause.

"Get out of here! You'll be court-martialed!"

When Shashko returned to the corps, he came straight to me. I calmed him by saying that Mekhlis had simply lost his temper and that there was nothing to court-martial Shashko for. However, he had earned a severe reprimand for rudeness to a superior.

"I should have kept quiet," said Shashko bitterly. "But I couldn't take it when he called me a hoodlum for no reason. And who called me that? Someone who was appointed to see to it that justice is being done."

It was clear to me that the whole incident was all Mekhlis' fault. I had told him about the 271st Division's critical position in time, but he took no countermeasures at all. And now he wanted to recover face at Shashko's expense. How much time and energy these "dressings down" took! And what did they ever do but harm?

Shashko returned to his division. He was in no mood for rest! Neither was I. The military prosecutor demanded evidence against Colonel Shashko

15

from me. It turned out that Mekhlis had decided to try him for treason. Needless to say, I didn't have any "evidence." Furthermore, I was convinced that Shashko had fought honestly and courageously, as becomes a Soviet officer. The accusation was simply ridiculous. Would a traitor lead his division out of encirclement? So I announced that I considered the order illegal and could not fulfill it. The prosecutor left without even saying good-bye.

I was in a grim mood, to put it mildly. I understood very well what sort of unpleasantness lay ahead, but I could not throw a perfectly innocent man and a good commander "to the lions." I could not allow him to be put to a hasty and unjust trial!

"We're advancing," I thought. "Our situation is fairly quiet. Everything can be explained objectively. And then, even such a hot-tempered man as Mekhlis must remember the interests of our cause. He's not the most important judge here, anyway!"

These meditations were interrupted by the telephone. I was ordered to go immediately to the office of the prosecutor of the 4th Ukrainian Army Group. As soon as I arrived, the prosecutor's assistant announced that I would be tried for malicious refusal to carry out an order of the member of the military council. He asked whether I acknowledged my guilt. Naturally, I answered in the negative, on the grounds that the order to bring Colonel Shashko to trial contradicted the spirit and letter of Soviet law. I was sure I was right and stood firm. After working on me for twenty minutes without success, the military jurists left. Evidently, they went to consult Mekhlis.

I had heard a great deal about the arbitrariness and wild caprices of Mekhlis. Those who were with him during the unsuccessful Crimean campaign spoke especially ill of him.[104] Now I myself could realize that I was dealing with an unprincipled individual whose morbid vanity overshadowed everything else.

At last the "rulers of my destiny" came back into the room. I was advised to return to my corps and await further orders. It was clear there would be no trial. "So even Mekhlis, for all his high position, can't break Soviet laws with impunity," I thought.

Yes, there was no trial, but at corps headquarters I was given a radiogram, which said: "For loss of control of the 271st Rifle Division and for loss of communication with it for a period of three days, Major General Zamertsev is to be relieved of his corps command and appointed deputy commander of the 30th Rifle Corps."

Heads he wins, tails I lose!

The officer who took the radiogram said that there had already been two calls from Mekhlis' office demanding that I leave for my new post at once. This haste convinced me once again that Mekhlis was wrong and was now trying to hush things up. But I had no desire to suffer for nothing. I ordered a diagram made of the situation during the advance of our corps and of the 271st Rifle Division, the latter's struggle behind enemy lines, and its breakout from encirclement. I wrote a brief explanation and sent the whole thing off to Moscow, to Marshal of the Soviet Union G. K. Zhukov, with a plea for protection against unfounded attacks.

I was soon summoned to the Army commander, Colonel General A. A. Grechko. He asked me not to complain to anyone, since the Army Group commander understood everything and had his own plan: I would get the corps back. But it was too late. And I did not feel like accepting such a suggestion, anyway. For in that case, I would appear to admit, however indirectly, my nonexistent guilt.

Anyhow, two weeks later, I was in Moscow. The investigation of my "delinquency" lasted another twenty days. A colonel from the General Staff came out to the Army Group especially for this, on orders of Supreme Headquarters. A little later, I was placed under the command of Marshal R. Ia. Malinovskii, commander of the 2nd Ukrainian Army Group. I was completely satisfied with this appointment. I had served under Malinovskii before. He received me well and for a start appointed me deputy commander of the 25th Guards Rifle Corps, with a promise to return me soon to the post of corps commander.[105]

General of the Army I. V. Tiulenev
Beria

IN RECALLING the defense in the foothills of the Caucasus, I cannot pass over in silence the base role of the villainous enemy of the people, Beria. He arrived at the Transcaucasian front on August 22, 1942, as the representative of Supreme Headquarters, and stayed two weeks. Along with Beria came a large group of his "henchmen"—Kabulov, Mamulov, Piiashev, Tsanava, and others.[106] Beria issued all his orders in the name of Supreme Headquarters and demanded that they be carried out without fail. On

I. V. Tiulenev, *Cherez tri voiny* (Moscow, 1960), pp. 196–97.

any grounds, and even without grounds, he and his closest aide, Kabulov, exceeded their authority and discredited generals of the Soviet army.

R. Ia. Malinovskii, thanks to his straightforwardness, was the object of special hostility on their part. They heaped all kinds of slander upon him and even threatened him with arrest.

When a particularly serious situation developed at the front, I posed before Beria the question of placing fifteen to twenty thousand NKVD troops at our disposal. In reply to this, he burst into foul abuse and threatened to break my back if I even tried to mention it again.

There were often instances when Beria and Kabulov issued instructions over the head of the Army Group's command, thereby disorganizing the work of headquarters. Taking advantage of his unlimited powers, Beria set up at Transcaucasian Army Group headquarters a parallel group for the defense of the chief Caucasus range and placed at its head his NKVD favorites, who were ignoramuses on military questions.[107]

To ensure the successful defense of the Caucasus, Supreme Headquarters had planned to send us several units and formations of regular troops from its own reserve. But Beria spoiled that, too. Instead of the reserves of Supreme Headquarters, there arrived in the Caucasus new units of the NKVD, which could not be utilized in active combat.

When I was in Moscow on November 15, 1942, I again raised the question of subordinating to our command at least some units of NKVD troops stationed in the Transcaucasian zone. Stalin approved my suggestion, but Beria, who was present, objected sharply and, moreover, coarsely abused the Army Group command. He agreed to place a certain number of troops at the disposal of the Army Group only after Stalin insisted.

All during his brief stay at the front, Beria did not once display a serious interest in the defense system worked out by the Army Group military council and approved by Supreme Headquarters. Although saboteurs and spies were frequently dropped by parachute, Beria and his retainers Rukhadze and Kabulov did not take effective steps to catch and destroy them.

Beria's trips to the defense lines in the area of Makhachkala, Groznyi, Vladikavkaz, and Sukhumi boiled down to showiness and noise, to the creation of a semblance of concern about the organization and consolidation of defense. As a matter of fact, by his criminal attitude and conduct he only disorganized, hindered, and essentially disrupted our work.[108]

Lieutenant General S. A. Kalinin
Beria

ON THE EVENING of July 14 [1941], I received a phone call from General of the Army G. K. Zhukov, who was at that time Chief of the General Staff. He had received news to the effect that the Germans had dropped a sizable paratroop detachment in the vicinity of the town of Belyi. I told General Zhukov that we at Army headquarters knew nothing about this, and I added that I would look into the matter at once and report the situation in the Belyi region within a few minutes.[109]

"What kind of commanding officer are you, if you don't know what's going on under your nose?" I heard in reply.

"Major General A. D. Berezin's division is in the Belyi region. He is an experienced commander, and he would have told me about the paratroop drops," I tried to explain, but no one was listening any longer.

The next morning, Major General K. I. Rakutin arrived at Semlevo where our headquarters was then located. He had orders to relieve me of the command of the 24th Army. Although the rumors about German paratroopers had already been proved false the night before, I paid dearly for their consequences.

Several days later I met General Ia. N. Fedorenko, who had been with General N. N. Voronov in Zhukov's office while Zhukov was talking to me. Fedorenko told me how the question of my dismissal from the 24th Army command had been decided.

Beria had come to see General Zhukov. It was he, in fact, who started the whole conversation about the enemy paratroopers who had allegedly landed in the Belyi region. He then asked whether there were any Red Army units in the town.

"The town of Belyi is the right flank of the 24th Army," Zhukov replied. "Lieutenant General Kalinin commands it."

"And what sort of man is Kalinin?"

"I hardly know him."

S. A. Kalinin, *Razmyshliaia o minuvshem* (Moscow, 1963), pp. 136–37.

"If you hardly know him, why did you agree to his appointment as commander?" asked Beria in a menacing voice. He walked out without waiting for an answer.

The transfer of the Army command did not take much time.

Major General S. D. Luganskii
Malenkov

AT ARMY GROUP HEADQUARTERS we were invited to a spacious, well-outfitted dugout shelter.[110] The furnishings, the calm atmosphere, and the businesslike air in this shelter contrasted sharply with everything we had seen en route. They were hurrying us. We groomed ourselves as we walked, dusting off our tunics and slapping our forage caps on our knees. We entered the large room discreetly. The several protective layers overhead created an impression of complete peace and security. Aides bustled about in a businesslike way, paying no attention to us whatever. Next to a table heaped high with maps, I noticed a large group of military men with insignias of the highest ranks. This room contained the brain of the Army Group; here were the commanders and the representatives of Supreme Headquarters. Having overcome my excitement, I began to recognize the faces of military men familiar to me from pictures: A. M. Vasilevskii, G. K. Zhukov, and A. I. Eremenko. Major General T. T. Khriukin, commander of our 8th Air Army, was also here. There were several persons in mufti.

It turned out that, in addition to us, representatives of all aviation regiments had been called to Army Group headquarters. Now it became clear that all this had nothing to do with any awards. The fliers lined up along the wall.

Only then did I notice among the generals a short man with a soft, puffy face who was wearing a tunic—it was G. M. Malenkov. It was he who was preparing to "read off" the fliers.

"Who was engaged in the fighting on such-and-such a day in—?" he asked in a soft voice and named a region in the suburbs of Stalingrad.

Major General T. T. Khriukin provided the information.

Looking at a piece of paper, Malenkov asked the names of the com-

S. D. Luganskii, *Na glubokikh virazhakh* (Alma-Ata, 1966), pp. 83–85.

manders of aviation regiments, the airplanes of which, according to his data, had not been sufficiently active in the fighting on such-and-such a date. The majority of the "guilty" were present here. As before, without raising his voice, Malenkov gave brief orders: This one is to be court-martialed, this one demoted, etc.

"Some awards," I thought to myself.

"Major Stalin!" Malenkov called out drily, looking at the large group of fliers lined up at the wall. A short flier with his hair smoothly combed back stepped forward. There were two bars on his collar tabs.[111]

"Major Stalin, the combat performance of your fliers is revolting. In the last battle not one of your twenty-four fighters shot down a single German. What is it? Did you forget how to fight? How are we to understand this?"

The short major's face flushed. We knew that Vasilii Stalin collected the most spirited fliers in his regiment. But if Malenkov was giving *him* a scolding, what could *we* expect? All this flashed through my head in an instant. And Malenkov, as if confirming our fears, descended upon us—or, more precisely, on Major General T. T. Khriukin, commander of our air army.

"And now you, general in a skullcap," he said, addressing with derision the commander who wore a regulation forage cap. "Did you intend to fight or simply play around?"

General Khriukin, a man of great personal bravery and endurance, reddened. It was embarrassing for all of us. Of course, a reprimand is a reprimand, but why should it be delivered in such an insulting form? And Malenkov continued to "pick apart" poor Khriukin. It was as though he gave us to understand that if he could give Stalin's son a proper scolding, there was no reason to stand on ceremony with a run-of-the-mill general.

In conclusion, G. K. Zhukov spoke. He was a stocky general with an angular, resolute face, the representative of Supreme Headquarters. His orders were brief and weighty: Within forty minutes the engineers were to organize a crossing of the Volga; General A. I. Rodimtsev was to bring the regiments of his 13th Guards Division across to the right bank; Captain Luganskii was to cover the crossing in such a way that not a single enemy bomb would fall. Failure to carry out the order meant court-martial. I was so stunned by all I had seen and heard that it was not until I was in the car that I could draw a free breath.

Colonel I. T. Starinov
Mekhlis

WHEN I ARRIVED in Moscow, I gave Nikita Sergeevich's [Khrushchev] letter to the Central Committee.[112] I was told that it would be read and that I should be ready to appear in the Kremlin at any time. I was given a telephone number to call in case I left Moscow.

Late in November [1941] I was summoned to the Central Committee and told to be in Stalin's waiting room at 10:00 p.m. As I prepared for the meeting, I thought only of how to express my ideas as briefly and persuasively as possible, without forgetting anything. I was certain that an immediate decision would be made on the question of the [production of] mines and the formation of special demolition brigades to be used at the front and in the enemy's rear.

At 9:30 p.m., combed and pressed, I was at the Kremlin entrance. My identification papers were inspected; I was searched for weapons; then the inspection was repeated over and over.[113] At 9:50 I was in the waiting room. Two others were already waiting in the cozy room. Each of them had a file of papers in front of him. I sat in a large soft armchair and began to plan the forthcoming conversation once again. Gradually, the room filled up. Some of those entering greeted the waiting room employees like old acquaintances, and then sat down in silence. One of the arrivals, a solid, painstakingly combed and shaved man with a file of papers in his carefully tended hands, sat near me. He was clearly agitated; he tried to read newspapers, opened his file, leafed through the papers, closed it again, and looked at his watch several times.

Time passed. I noticed that those who were acquainted with the waiting room employees and hence not here for the first time, were considerably more perturbed than those who, in all probability, were here for the first time. But now a slight noise passed through the room. My neighbor suddenly turned pale. No one said anything, but it was clear to everyone that "the boss" had arrived. My neighbor wiped drops of sweat from his brow and dried his hands on a handkerchief. In a few minutes, people began to be called in. Soon my neighbor also rose. When

I. T. Starinov, "Eto bylo tainoi," *Voenno-istoricheskii zhurnal*, 1964, No. 4, pp. 90–91.

the receptionist finally called him by name, he went livid, wiped his trembling hands on his handkerchief, picked up his file of papers, and went with hesitant steps. I remembered General Kotliar's parting words to me: "Don't get excited. Don't think about disagreeing with anything. Comrade Stalin knows everything." [114]

But I was not called in. After waiting two hours, I was told I would not be received and was sent to Mekhlis. Mekhlis received me at once. Comrade Khrushchev's letter and our report to the military council of the Southwestern Army Group lay on his table. Without hearing me out, Mekhlis himself spoke first. He proceeded to unfold a plan for the building of obstructions outside Moscow, or rather of destructions, such that I gasped in horror. The essence of his "obstructions" was to "drive the Germans into the cold." This required the destruction of all settled points in the German-occupied zone and the burning down of all forests. The all-encompassing mining plan that he envisaged really would have created difficulties for enemy troops, but it would have created even greater difficulties for the Red Army.

I don't know whose ideas Mekhlis was expressing, but it seems to me that he would scarcely have bothered to do so if they hadn't had support from above. I ventured to remark that the forests were guerrilla bases, and where could the population go, since we couldn't evacuate it into our rear. And later, when we began to advance, we would have to conquer a desert that we ourselves had created. But Mekhlis paid no attention to my reply. Fortunately, his plan was not implemented. I did not succeed in deciding with Mekhlis any of the questions raised in our report. I left him with a heavy heart.

Chief Marshal of Artillery N. N. Voronov
Beria and
Malenkov

THE LEADERSHIP of the Main Artillery Directorate took energetic measures to ensure that new equipment quickly reached the points where new

N. N. Voronov, "Podvig sovetskogo naroda," *Istoriia SSSR*, 1965, No. 4, pp. 21–22; N. N. Voronov, *Na sluzhbe voennoi* (Moscow, 1963), pp. 194–95.

artillery formations and units of Supreme Headquarters reserve were being formed.[115] Each artillery formation was a complex organism. In addition to a variety of artillery ordnance, it had also to be supplied with diverse engineering equipment, communications equipment, prime movers, automotive transportation, and much else. We were given effective help by the People's Commissariat of Defense. The most complicated matter was to obtain auto transport. Here we were confronted by many unexpected obstacles.

One day Stalin ordered a fully equipped artillery corps to be transferred immediately to one of the Army Groups.

"The corps is ready, but it cannot be sent. We have no auto transportation," I replied.

Stalin frowned. "How many trucks do you need?" he asked.

I answered that 900 trucks were required, according to the schedule. . . .

Stalin turned to Malenkov and Beria. "Go and find out where to get them. And you stay," he told me. "Report on the progress of the new formations."

He was satisfied with my report.

When I left, I was met by Malenkov and Beria. "Take 400 trucks, and let's hear no more about it!" said Beria gruffly.

"Nine hundred trucks are needed for an artillery corps. That is the minimum," I replied.

The conversation became increasingly sharp. I was advised to limit myself to 450 trucks, then to 500—

"I shall go back and report to the Supreme Commander in Chief that I cannot send the corps," I finally answered firmly.

"Where should the trucks be sent?" Malenkov then asked in quite a different tone.

I named the formation points. The next day, 900 trucks were there. Supreme Headquarters' urgent request was carried out. Such, at times, were the difficulties which accompanied the creation of new formations. . . .

As a rule, once a month, N. D. Iakovlev and I (and when I was away, he alone) would report a draft concerning the distribution of armaments and munitions for the next month of war to Supreme Headquarters.[116]

Once in the process of approving this list, Stalin's eye fell on the figures: "50,000 rifles for the NKVD." He showered us with questions: Who, specifically, had made this request; why did the NKVD need so many rifles? We said that we too were surprised but that Beria insisted on it. Beria was immediately summoned. The latter attempted to give an explanation in Georgian. Stalin interrupted him irritably and ordered him to answer in Russian: Why and for what purpose did he need so many rifles?

"They are needed to arm newly formed NKVD divisions," Beria said. "Half—25,000—will be enough."

Beria began to insist stubbornly. Stalin made two attempts to reason with him. Beria did not want to listen.

Then, irritated to the limit, Stalin said to us:

"Cross out what is written there and write in 10,000 rifles."

He then approved the list.

When we left Stalin's office, Beria overtook us and said malevolently: "Just wait, we'll fix your guts!"

He hurled this phrase at N. D. Iakovlev and me more than once when he was dissatisfied with our reports or actions. At that time, we did not attach the proper significance to these words, considering this to be some kind of Oriental joke. Only later did we learn that this monster and traitor usually carried out his threats.

A short time later, we were again reporting a draft concerning the distribution of artillery armaments and munitions for the coming month. Iakovlev whispered to me that it was time to report on the reserves we had stockpiled. We were afraid that the Supreme Commander in Chief would lose his temper because we had kept quiet about reserves in such a difficult time. Everyone knew about his quick temper. But these fears were unfounded. He was very glad to learn that he had about a million 76mm. shells in his reserve. He praised us and then and there increased the allocations of shells to certain Army Groups. Thus, a constant reserve was established, a reserve from which it would be possible to satisfy unexpected requirements of the Army Groups.

Marshal K. K. Rokossovskii
Stalin, Molotov, Malenkov

(As reported by K. Nepomniashchii)

AT A MEETING in Moscow in May 1944 at a time when the big offensive in Belorussia was being planned, the commander of the 1st Belorussian

K. Nepomniashchii, "Bobruiskii 'kotel,' " *Polki idut na zapad* (Moscow, 1964), pp. 238–41.

Army Group [Rokossovskii] insisted that a double blow must be struck against the enemy's Bobruisk grouping. Stalin proposed striking a single blow. Rokossovskii understood better than anyone else that Stalin's proposal, if accepted, would lead to huge, senseless sacrifices.[117]

The following picture of the events preceding our offensive in Belorussia emerges from the report of Rokossovskii and several other participants at the meeting in the headquarters of the Supreme Commander in Chief.

Reporting his plan for the offensive at the meeting, Rokossovskii proposed to break through the enemy's defense not only from the Dnepr bridgehead, but in one additional sector.

"The defense must be breached in one place," Stalin interrupted him.

"If we breach the defense in two places, Comrade Stalin, we shall gain many advantages."

"What advantages?"

"If we breach the defense in two sectors, we can bring more forces into the attack," Rokossovskii explained, "whereupon we deny the enemy the possibility of transferring reinforcements from one sector to another. In addition, Comrade Stalin, a success achieved even in one of these sectors will place the enemy in a difficult position, while guaranteeing to our Army Group a successful development of the operation."

"And that's what you call advantages?" asked Stalin contemptuously. "Go out and think it over again." The voice of the Supreme Commander in Chief had a threatening overtone.

General Rokossovskii went into the next room. No one was there. An old-fashioned clock on the mantelpiece said 10:20 p.m. Solid furniture, closely drawn curtains, silence. Voices from Stalin's office did not penetrate here. Konstantin Konstantinovich liked to be alone, but right now this solitude and this silence were oppressive and unpleasant. He sat down, but instantly jumped up again and began to pace the room. What would he tell Stalin? Should he agree to strike one main blow from the Dnepr bridgehead? No, no! He could not, must not agree. They must strike two blows from different sectors. Simultaneously. Yes, but doesn't this contradict the established view that an attack requires striking one main blow, with a concentration of the main forces and resources in one place? Yes. Perhaps. But in this particular case, the state of the enemy's defense and the complex terrain dictate two blows, two! One would be a crude error, and it might cost the lives of many soldiers.

The door opened. He did not notice who called his name and hurriedly entered the conference room. All eyes were riveted on him, and few doubted that Rokossovskii would now proceed to demonstrate the advantages of the single blow.

"Have you thought it through, General?"

"Yes sir, Comrade Stalin."

"Well, then, that means we'll strike a single blow?" he asked, squinting, and pushed a marker along the map toward Rogachev.

It was very quiet in the office when Rokossovskii, who had followed the marker with his eyes, said: "Two blows are more advisable, Comrade Stalin—"

"Will we not thereby dissipate our forces from the very beginning?"

"A certain dissipation of forces will occur, Comrade Stalin. But we do this, while taking into account the forested and swampy terrain of Belorussia and the disposition of enemy troops."

Silence ensued.

Without taking his eyes off the map, Stalin said: "Go out and think it over again. Don't be stubborn, Rokossovskii."

So now he was alone again. . . .

His reflections were interrupted.

Someone stood over him. Rokossovskii raised his head. Seeing Molotov and Malenkov, he got up.

"Don't forget where you are and with whom you're talking, General," said Malenkov harshly. "You are disagreeing with Comrade Stalin," he added after a pause.

"You'll have to agree, Rokossovskii," said Molotov. "Agree—that's all there is to it!"

The door opened, and the general quickly went through it.

"So what is better: two weak blows or one strong blow?" asked Stalin.

"Two strong blows are better than one strong blow," answered Rokossovskii.

"But which of them should be primary, in your opinion?"

"They should both be primary."

At these words, that ominous silence set in which in this office usually preceded terrible outbursts of rage.

"Can it be that two blows are really better?" said Stalin after a lengthy pause. He finally agreed with Rokossovskii's plan, although he still did not believe in the soundness of two blows.

The Army Group commander had held his ground, and this seemed to augur success.[118]

CHAPTER FIVE

Epilogue

INTRODUCTION

SOVIET STRATEGISTS have always shared with Clausewitz the view that war was a continuation of politics by different means. While the Soviet Union fought for its very existence in the 1941–42 period, however, or even while it conducted operations to expel German armies in the 1943–44 period, it maintained the primacy of military over political considerations in the formulation of war plans. Only during the last year of war did broader political aims begin increasingly to press and to overshadow purely military aims. From the moment that Soviet forces crossed their own frontier and from the moment that the Western Allies commenced a massive land war against Germany, political aims were the dominant theme of discussions if not in the Soviet General Staff, then certainly in Stalin's Supreme Headquarters.

Following the great battles of spring and summer 1944, when ten consecutive blows by the Red Army cleared Soviet territory of German troops (except in the Baltic region), the central sector of the Nazi-Soviet front came to a standstill. In mid-August 1944 Soviet Armies in the central sector halted on the line of the Vistula and San Rivers in the middle of Poland. There they remained, after securing some bridgeheads on the southern flank of the front, until mid-January 1945. Only bridgehead fighting, skirmishes, and local engagements agitated the central sector during these five months.

What explains this protracted halt? To be sure, Soviet groupings in the central sector had been weakened considerably by the long and almost continuous advance of 600 km. They were plagued by logistical difficulties, and clearly a respite alone would provide adequate conditions in which to redeploy and resupply the troops. Such military considerations, however, scarcely explain the long standstill. In the south, at the gates to the Balkans, where the Soviet advance in 1944 had been no less rapid than in the center and where problems of logistics were no less difficult, the autumn and early winter of 1944 witnessed the start of a large offensive operation.

It is to long-range political considerations that we must look for the principal explanation of this basic shift in the center of gravity from the central sector to the Balkans (and in part also to the northern sector). On the one hand, Anglo-American penetration of "Fortress Europe" in the West had not yet assumed proportions which could menace Soviet claims in central Europe. Moreover, the protracted fighting in the West with each passing day and week facilitated the prospective Soviet invasion of Germany. On the other hand, the shift of emphasis to the south, the conquest of the Balkans removed the possibility that the fate of this area would be decided after the German capitulation. To decide this crucial question by force of arms was incomparably more effective, in Stalin's judgment, than any recourse to the conference table.

On January 12, 1945 the central sector of the Nazi-Soviet front was reactivated. The long expected Soviet offensive finally started; the center of gravity in the whole eastern theater of operations again shifted to the principal axis of advance, where the distance between the Soviet army and the German capital was shortest.

Official Soviet history and memoirs treat the decision to start the January offensive as a very special case of demonstrated Soviet loyalty to the Allied cause. Indeed, the official version suggests, Western leaders incurred an extraordinary debt to the Soviet Union even at this late stage in the war. The argument which threads endlessly through Soviet accounts may be summarized as follows: The German offensive in the Ardennes (the Battle of the Bulge) placed American and British armies in a precarious position. All the world knows that Churchill, on behalf of the Allies, asked Stalin to cushion that blow by activating the Eastern Front. The Soviet army, the argument continues, true to its obligations, launched a great offensive from the Vistula ahead of schedule despite unfavorable weather conditions. This offensive compelled Hitler to engage his best troops, including those from the Ardennes, on the Nazi-Soviet front. The Allies were saved!

While certain elements of this account are undoubtedly true—the Allied armies were indeed in a precarious position, and Churchill did indeed solicit Stalin's cooperation—the last part of the Soviet argument may be termed true only in part, for it omits several pertinent factors. First, the German offensive in the Ardennes could have been launched only on the assumption that the Soviets would not start an offensive; in this calculation Hitler was proved correct. Second, the start of the offensive in mid-January was no less advantageous to Stalin than to his Allies; the Ardennes offensive had already proved a strategic fiasco, and Allied countermeasures were already turning the tide. With German forces in the central sector of the Eastern Front dangerously weakened, the fate of the Balkans all but sealed, the time had come to invade Germany itself. Given these factors one could even reverse the Soviet position in order to argue that it was the Western Allies through their efforts in the Ardennes who facilitated Russia's great victory in the winter 1945 offensive. The Battle of the Bulge siphoned off from the East large quantities of German heavy armor and a number of freshly equipped German divisions; pitifully small reserves were left to defend the elongated central sector of the front against the Soviet onslaught.

Three Army Groups bore principal responsibility for the January offensive—the 2nd Belorussian in the north, the 1st Belorussian in the center, and the 1st Ukrainian in the south. As if to underscore the decisive importance of the offensive, the most popular and famous Soviet marshals were in command of the Army Groups—Rokossovskii in the north, Konev in the south, and Zhukov in the crucial center.

The northern Soviet flank commanded by Rokossovskii played a secondary though essential role in the January offensive and in the subsequent battle for Berlin. Its major task was to pin down the German concentration in the north and thus to secure the extended right flank of Zhukov's armies against German countermeasures as Zhukov thrust toward Berlin. The perimeter of the two Army Groups commanded by Zhukov and Konev measured about 310 miles. Together these two Army Groups in center and south amassed 31.5 percent of all Soviet combined-arms formations active along the entire Nazi-Soviet front and 43.2 percent of all tank and mechanized formations. Zhukov and Konev commanded 2.2 million men (163 divisions) with over 32,000 guns and mortars, 6,460 tanks and self-propelled guns, and almost 4,800 airplanes. The armies of Zhukov and Konev were opposed by German Army Group A, which at the start of the operation was commanded by Colonel General Harpe. According to official Soviet sources, the ratio of Red Army superiority over the enemy was 5.5:1 in manpower, 7.8:1 in artillery, 5.7:1 in armor, and 17.6:1 in aircraft. On the main axis of the assault, Soviet superiority reached 9:1 in manpower and 10:1 in armor and artillery.

Three weeks after the start of the January offensive, the great Soviet advance measured about 200 miles in the southern sector (Konev) to over 300 miles in the central sector (Zhukov), that is, from the Polish river Vistula to the banks of the German rivers Oder and Neisse. Soviet troops stood about 30 miles from Berlin at their closest point (Loetzen). By February 2, 1945, the force of the Soviet offensive was spent; the central sector came to a standstill which lasted until the start of the Battle for Berlin on April 16. The final battle for the German capital was marked by two weeks of fighting on the approaches to the city and in the streets of the city itself. Then all resistance ceased. On May 2, 1945, the official

Epilogue

surrender of the Berlin garrison was signed. Six days later, Allied military leaders accepted the formal unconditional surrender from representatives of the Third Reich.

The magnitude of the Soviet effort, the length of time it took to achieve final victory, and the extent of Soviet casualties impel Soviet military authors to dwell on the strength and ferocity of German resistance during the last battle for Berlin and to impugn the motives of those Western authors who appear to minimize it. Marshal Chuikov, for example, addressed a protest to Cornelius Ryan, author of *The Last Battle;* his letter was published in the Soviet press under the headline "This Work Is Dirty":

> Mr. Ryan's attempt to belittle the Soviet Army's contribution to the final defeat of Hitlerism is a blasphemous outrage against the memory of the many Soviet soldiers who sleep forever in the soil of Berlin and whose ashes are honored with deep gratitude by all the world.[*]

Still another Soviet critic attacked Ryan in the authoritative Party daily *Pravda:*

> Ryan [asserts] that there were no obstacles except natural ones on the path of the Soviet Army from the Oder to Berlin—no antitank ditches, no permanent weapons emplacements, no tank traps, and no other barriers. He says that Berlin was only called a "fortress," but that actually it was an open city. . . . Ryan repeats the nonsense told him by the defeated Hitlerite General [Heinrici].[†]

If Soviet memoirs tend to exaggerate the strength of German forces defending Berlin and the difficulties of the battle, their purpose may be deemed political—to emphasize the decisive role of the Red Army in crushing Hitler and to demonstrate Soviet superiority over the Western Allies, who allegedly desired to seize Berlin but lacked the capacity to do so. At the same time, however, their viewpoint apparently reflects personal experience in planning and executing the battle.

In actuality, Soviet strength in manpower and matériel was so overwhelming at Berlin that the outcome of the battle was a foregone conclusion. The Army Groups of Zhukov and Konev together with Rokossovskii's support Armies in the northern sector started the operation with 2.5 million men, 41,600 guns and mortars, 6,250 tanks and self-propelled guns, and 7,500 war planes. According to Soviet estimates, this massive concentration assured Soviet superiority at the ratio of only 2.5:1 in manpower, 4:1 in artillery and tanks, and 2.3:1 in aircraft. Again according to official Soviet sources, from April 16 to May 8, 1945, that is, from the

[*]*Literaturnaia gazeta,* August 2, 1966.
[†]D. Kraminov in *Pravda,* July 10, 1966.

beginning of the Berlin operation to the German capitulation, the casualties in the 1st and 2nd Belorussian and 1st Ukrainian Army Groups totaled 305,000 men killed, wounded, and missing. Losses in equipment were said to include 2,156 tanks and self-propelled guns, 1,220 guns and mortars, and 527 aircraft.

The Germans place their defending forces at Berlin well below the Soviet figures. Even if the garrison manning the inner perimeter of Berlin's defenses approached the Soviet estimate of 200,000, it was in large part composed of "Hitler-jugend" and of "Volkssturm," not unlike the detachments of Home Guards mobilized for Moscow's defense in the fall of 1941; it could scarcely have presented Soviet commanders with any difficulties comparable to those of earlier key battles. In explaining defeat, the Germans concentrate less on the size of their defending forces and more on the critical lack of transport, the desperate shortage of artillery shells, the almost complete absence of fuel, and the sorely disrupted communications. They might well add the factor of chaotic and often unprofessional leadership which gave further stimulus to a useless slaughter during the last weeks and days of the war.

Neither the Western writers who stress the superior Soviet ratio of forces nor the Soviet writers who exaggerate the size and quality of opposing German armies can be dismissed as insincere or dishonest purveyors of a particular political viewpoint. The former depend for their source material primarily on German documents and accounts which focus on German weaknesses, and, moreover, they as outsiders do not yield to the natural tendency of participating commanders—Western no less that Soviet—to attribute their victories more to the fighting qualities of victorious troops and the military talent of their leaders than to the failings of the foe. On the other hand, Soviet writers—many of them participants in the battle—recall vividly the difficulties of planning, preparing, and executing the final operation and minimize the disarray in the German camp about which most of them learned only later. Their accounts reflect the very same overestimation of the scale and quality of enemy forces which was characteristic at the time of these events by the Soviet High Command and, one must assume, field commanders as well. One need look no farther for an explanation of this overestimation than to deep respect for the fighting ability of the opponent and the unshakable belief that the Russians were facing the finest combat-ready units shifted by the Nazi command from all other war theaters.

Still another factor which accounts for the Soviet bias may be found in the uneconomical employment of those numerically superior Russian forces. The Soviet plan of battle emphasized speed in forcing the capitulation of the German capital. When Stalin addressed to Marshals Zhukov and Konev the question—"So, comrades, who will capture Berlin, we or the Allies?"—he perhaps intended to spur his commanders to greater effort. Yet one cannot exclude the possibility that he and his commanders may still have feared a deliberate German collapse on the Western Front which would tempt the Allies to race for Berlin regardless of the delineation of occupation zones agreed upon at Yalta. The haste and recklessness which multiplied the human cost of the final battle can be attributed not only to the energetic execution of battle orders from Supreme Headquarters, but also to the rivalry of Zhukov and Konev, who disputed the Berlin prize, the zeal of subordinate field commanders who seized their last chance to earn glory in combat, and, last but not least, the psychology of both commanders and troops whose emotional commitment and excitement led them to despise caution and risk death in order to realize their heroic victory sooner.

The fall of Berlin ended a war which Stalin in 1939 had predicted would transform the efforts and sacrifices of the belligerents into profit for the Soviet Union. His miscalculations had brought the Soviet Union close to disaster. Among the Allies, his people paid the highest price for victory and, indeed, a higher price for victory than the Germans paid for defeat. In terms of an increment of national power, however, the outcome of the war far exceeded Stalin's initial hopes; and in terms of an increment of personal power, Stalin stood at his apogee on May 8, 1945, when the Allies received the act of final surrender in the city captured by the Red Army. To his soldiers, to the peoples of the Soviet Union, to the Allies, to the entire world, Stalin was the leader whose genius, strong will, and unrelenting perseverance had brought the Red Army to unprecedented victory.

PART I   TO GERMANY'S FRONTIER

Introduction

THE TWO EXCERPTS which follow focus on the initial stage of the Soviet invasion of Germany, the offensive of January–February 1945 which carried the Red Army from the Vistula to the approaches to Berlin. In the first, Colonel General S. M. Shtemenko relates how the operation was planned by the Soviet General Staff in which he then occupied the key post of Chief of Operations. In the second, Marshal I. S. Konev, commander of one of the two Army Groups which played the decisive role in this offensive, recounts the activities of his troops from the preparatory stage of the assault to its final completion.

Of considerable interest is Konev's account of his difficult decision to refrain from issuing the order to encircle and destroy large German forces in Silesia. It confirms and amplifies the official Soviet explanation that the Soviet command deliberately permitted German armor to escape encirclement because "to have liquidated them in this mining area would have risked serious damage to the welfare and economy of our Polish allies."[°]

The official Soviet explanation has been questioned by the author of one

important book on the Russo-German conflict. Alan Clark writes:

But [economic] considerations of this kind had not affected the Soviet commanders when fighting in their own territory—as for example, the Donetz basin—and it is unlikely that they would have paid much heed to them on foreign soil had they disposed of the means and the ability to destroy the enemy on the spot.[†]

Konev's stress on the primacy of economic over narrowly military factors in reaching the decision appears more convincing than Clark's suggestion of inadequate means. It should be remembered, first of all, that Silesia cannot unequivocally be declared "foreign" as compared to the Donetz basin. The overwhelming bulk of Silesian mining and factory equipment was eventually assigned to the Soviet Union as war reparations, a prospective prize which could not have been overlooked by Soviet leaders. That Soviet strategic planners were fully cognizant of the need to save the Silesian basin, the most important industrial area within the Soviet zone of influence in Europe, may be indicated by Stalin's pithy and pointed characterization of this area in his conversation with Konev—"Gold."

[°]*Istoriia Velikoi Otechestvennoi voiny Sovetskogo Soiuza, 1941–1945,* (Moscow: Voenizdat, 1963), V, 81.

[†]Alan Clark, *Barbarossa: The Russian-German Conflict, 1941–45* (New York: William Morrow Co., Inc., 1964), p. 428.

It should be remembered also that the battle for Silesia was fought in the last stage of the war. While it is true, as Alan Clark writes, that highest priority in previous Soviet operations had been given to the destruction of enemy forces "on the spot," at this stage of the war it may well have yielded place to goals of freeing major Soviet forces for further advance into Germany and of occupying as much German territory as possible as quickly as possible.

The winter 1945 offensive in the central sector of the Soviet-German front was the most rapid Soviet offensive of World War II. Enjoying a tremendous superiority in forces, the Red Army moved along the axis of its main thrust at the rate of over thirty miles a day. In the west, Allied armies had overcome the last German bid to halt their advance at the Battle of the Bulge and were starting to move rapidly into Germany. The defeat of the Third Reich was at hand.

Colonel General S. M. Shtemenko
In the General Staff

ON THE BASIS of available documents and personal recollections I should like to describe how the General Staff planned and Supreme Headquarters decided the course of operations at the final stage of the war.

. Let us begin with the General Staff's estimate of the situation in the autumn of 1944 and the planning of the initial operations of the 1945 campaign. Planning of the concluding stage of the armed struggle on the Soviet-German front had already begun during the summer-autumn campaign of 1944. The General Staff and Supreme Headquarters did not assess the strategic situation and draw their conclusions hastily or as a result of a single meeting; rather they made their assessment gradually in the course of day-to-day work, as they studied the totality of facts and anticipated the development of combat operations at the front.

The results of the unprecedented advance of the Soviet army in all sectors were more than encouraging. . . . By the end of October 1944, Soviet forces were at the Finnish border and were successfully advancing in northern Norway. They had cleared the Baltic territory with the exception of the Syrve Peninsula and Courland where 34 enemy divisions had

S. M. Shtemenko, "Kak planirovalas' posledniaia kampaniia po razgromu gitlerovskoi Germanii," *Voenno-istoricheskii zhurnal*, 1965, No. 5, pp. 56–64.

been isolated. They had penetrated East Prussia. South of East Prussia, the Narev and Vistula rivers had been forced in many sectors, and important bridgeheads had been taken. The troops were pointed in the strategic direction of Berlin. Significant successes had been achieved in the eastern part of Hungary where the 2nd Ukrainian Army Group was advancing toward Budapest. In the zone [of advance] of the 3rd Ukrainian Army Group, Belgrade, the capital of Yugoslavia, had been liberated on October 2. . . .

Our victories did not come easily, however. The ranks of the divisions were thinning. The pace of the Soviet advance, which had lasted several months with no operational halts, slackened noticeably. By removing troops from some sectors of the front in Western Europe and by using their reserves, the Hitlerites had been able to shift part of their forces to the East and to form a solid, continuous front in this area, the breaching of which required extensive preparations.[1]

In evaluating the situation, the General Staff realized how difficult it would be to develop the success still further. The conditions and prospects for an advance were not identical at all points. The enemy defenses in Courland were exceptionally strong. The breaching of these defenses all the way to the total destruction of the enemy troops that were dug in there could cost us a great deal.

The situation in East Prussia seemed more favorable. The troops of the 3rd Belorussian Army Group had a certain superiority of forces. On this basis, in the last third of October 1944, the General Staff considered that a major strike could be made, cutting through all of East Prussia as far as the mouth of the Vistula to a depth of 220–250 km., if the Army Group were reinforced to some extent from the Supreme Headquarters reserve. Further analysis of the situation showed, however, that at least for the time being we should have to confine ourselves to more modest objectives.

Particularly strong resistance was expected in the directions of Warsaw, Poznan', Lodz, Kalish, and also Silesia where the fate of Berlin was essentially being decided. This, as we believed at that time, would not permit us, even with the maximum exertion of our forces, to engage the 1st Belorussian and the 1st Ukrainian Army Groups in offensive operations to a depth greater than 140–150 km.

In the zones of the 4th, 2nd, and 3rd Ukrainian Army Groups [in the south], on the other hand, the General Staff hoped for considerable successes, essentially on the basis of political considerations. There were prospects for a headlong drive to the Moravska Ostrava-Brno line and to the approaches to Vienna, for the capture of Budapest, and for forcing the Danube. A considerable part of the enemy infantry in this area was made up of Hungarian divisions whose stability, in our estimation, might well be fundamentally undermined by the growing anti-war feeling and the atrocities committed by fascists in their efforts to keep Hungary on the side of Hitler's Reich. The fall of the Szalasi regime would have taken the country out of the war and placed the German troops in a difficult situation. Unfortunately, these calculations proved to be wrong. The fascist dictatorship, with German support, was able to keep Hungary tied to Germany's war chariot for a while longer.[2] By the end of October extremely heavy and bloody fighting had broken out in the direction of Budapest. According to our estimates at the time, 39 formations were opposing the 2nd Ukrainian Army Group. The nucleus of this large grouping was formed by seven tank divisions (five German and two Hungarian). Our troops were advancing slowly. The bad weather created control and supply problems. The enemy, supported by a diversified system of well-prepared fortifications, was offering fierce resistance. Even though the Hungarian capital was blockaded, it was not captured until February 13, 1945.[3] This was the situation when the General Staff in October 1944 was working out the design and plan for the final campaign in Europe.

The very limited successes we had attained in October indicated that we had to reinforce the troops advancing to the south, to give some rest to the divisions which had not been relieved for a long time, to re-deploy, to strengthen our logistics, and to stockpile the matériel we needed for the breakthrough and the subsequent development of operations. Finally, after having evaluated the situation, we had to choose the most favorable directions and draft the necessary plans for the most rapid and final defeat of German fascism in the approaching year, 1945. All this called for time and the preparation of necessary means.

At the very beginning of November 1944, Supreme Headquarters thoroughly reviewed the existing situation in the zones of advance of the 2nd and 1st Belorussian and the 1st Ukrainian Army Groups. Faced with the bulk of the enemy Army Groups Center and A—the main strategic enemy grouping—our Army Groups at that time lacked the superiority of forces required for an offensive.[4] From this it followed that it was not advisable to continue the offensive in the Berlin direction and that it appeared necessary to revert temporarily to the defensive.

In a report to the Supreme Commander in Chief, General of the Army A. I. Antonov, First Deputy Chief of the General Staff, placed particular emphasis on the necessity to revert to defensive positions along the western sector, and he requested permission to draft the necessary directives. We obtained Stalin's permission, and orders to take up defensive positions were issued on the night of November 4, 1944 to the 3rd and 2nd

Belorussian Army Groups. Similar orders were issued to the troops of the right flank of the 1st Belorussian Army Group a few days later.

At the same time, the General Staff continued work on the design of the forthcoming operations. From the very beginning it was assumed that the objective of crushing Hitlerite Germany would be accomplished by means of two consecutive thrusts, which later comprised the two stages of the final campaign. In the first stage, active operations were to continue chiefly in the old (if one can use the expression) direction, on the southern flank of the Soviet-German front, in the Budapest area. Here a breakthrough was to be achieved by concentrating the main forces of the 3rd Ukrainian Army Group at the confluence of the Tisza and the Danube in the area south of Kecskemet where they could assist the forces of the 2nd Ukrainian Army Group by striking in a northwesterly and westerly direction. It was conceivable that the forces of these two Army Groups would be able to advance rapidly and to reach the Banska Bystrica–Komarno–Nad'kanizha line by November 30 and to gain the approaches to Vienna by December 30.[5]

Undoubtedly, the threat of having its southern flank defeated would force the German command to move additional forces into this area from the western sector [of the Soviet-German front], which in turn would create favorable circumstances for the advance toward Berlin of our main forces, the Army Groups deployed north of the Carpathians. The General Staff assumed that at the beginning of 1945 the Soviet forces would gain a line from the lower reaches of the Vistula, as far as Bydgoszcz; they would take Poznan' and seize the Breslau-Pardubice-Jihlava-Vienna line; i.e., they would advance in all these directions to a distance of 120–350 km. from their positions of October 28. The defeat of the main enemy forces and the attainment of this line would prepare the ground for the second stage of the campaign, as a result of which Germany would be forced to surrender.

Thus, at the end of October 1944, the initial outline of the design merely indicated the general content of the final campaign of the war and its division into two stages. The direction of the main thrust had not as yet been determined, and the idea of splitting the strategic defense of the enemy and fragmenting his eastern groupings had not yet been expressed.

With a view to working out a more precise plan of operations for 1945, the General Staff at the beginning of November summed up the main results of the phase of war operations already concluded and made a concise evaluation of the strategic position of the opposing sides. Briefly, it was as follows. The Soviet army had won victories which were deciding the outcome of the war. The outcome of the struggle on the Soviet-

German front was now all but decided in our favor, and the hour of the enemy's final defeat was approaching. At the present time we were superior to the enemy not only in terms of numerical strength but also in military skill and weapons. Our material needs were fully assured by the well-organized effort of our rear, which supported the front to an ever increasing degree.

The strategic position of Soviet troops and those of other members of the anti-Hitlerite coalition was such that we considered the encirclement of Germany imminent. The strikes by our forces were well coordinated with the operations of our Allies in Western Europe. The Soviet army and the Anglo-American forces had taken up their attack positions for the decisive advance against the vital centers of Germany. There now remained a final headlong thrust and the complete defeat of the enemy within a short period of time. All in all, we were on the eve of total victory. . . .

As a rule, the following officers participated in the preliminary discussions of operational plans with General A. I. Antonov: the Chief of Operations; his deputies, A. A. Gryzlov and N. A. Lomov; and the chiefs of the [strategic] sectors involved. Working from A. I. Antonov's map, the Office of Operations clarified the details and calculated [the strength and distribution of] forces, matériel, and all other elements of the operation. Finally, the plan of operation with all its estimates and premises was graphically plotted on a special map at which time once again, carefully— even captiously—it was discussed by General Antonov and the operations officers. As in previous years, the initial operations were planned in the greatest detail. The further missions of the Army Groups were projected in their general aspects only.

In the course of this creative search, an overall major idea was born and developed, an idea which concerned the prerequisites for the success of our operations in the main sector. The idea was to draw the enemy forces away from the central sector by means of active operations on the flanks of his strategic front. It was proposed to achieve this not only [by active operations] in Hungary and Austria, which were farther away from the main direction of our future offensive, but in East Prussia as well. This called for an energetic development of the offensive in the Budapest area and the carrying out of offensive operations in the Koenigsberg area.

We knew that the enemy was displaying an increased sensitivity about [the fate of] East Prussia and Hungary. This meant that upon being subjected to great pressure, he would inevitably shift his reserves and troops to this area from front sectors in areas that were not subjected to attack. As a result, the enemy's western [central] sector, which was of great importance for the Soviet army's attainment of a decisive success, would be seriously weakened.

Our expectations were fulfilled. As a result of the offensive operations of our troops in East Prussia and the Budapest area in November–December, the enemy concentrated, according to our estimates, 26 divisions in East Prussia (7 of them tank) and 55 divisions in the area of the Hungarian capital (including 9 tank divisions). As we later learned, however, Hitler believed anyway that the Soviet army would strike its main blow in 1945 not in the central sector, but through Hungary and Czechoslovakia. He focused the attention of the German High Command in that area, therefore, and concentrated his forces there.[6] Once again, as in 1944, the Hitlerites made a flagrant strategic miscalculation and kept only 49 divisions in what for us was the main sector of the front. Only five of these were tank divisions.[7] Thus, the calculations of the General Staff turned out to be correct.

The fact that the enemy's front line had taken on a peculiar shape which was dangerous to him, with strong defensive groupings on the flanks and a weak center unsupported by strong reserves, led us to consider the most expedient ways of operating in the main sector. Was it not preferable, in this case, to abandon the idea of a uniform advance along the entire front—which would have required pushing the enemy out—and instead to break through this weak center with a direct strike, to split the German strategic front, and, without losing time, to develop the attack directly against Berlin? In this case, the divided enemy forces could be destroyed far more easily, and the achievement of our goal to end the war would be considerably facilitated. The General Staff adopted the second idea, which subsequently turned out to be the correct one.

Thus, from the time the General Staff began to plan the final campaign, it considered that the strike against Berlin should be launched and pursued as soon as possible and with no pauses. Consequently, those comrades are wrong who claim that the General Staff was postponing for an indefinite period the question of taking Berlin. To be sure, circumstance brought about some amendments to this plan.

Evaluation of the operational position, probable missions, and methods of operation of each of the Army Groups presented specific difficulties. This was particularly true of the 3rd Belorussian Army Group. The German grouping in East Prussia was very strong and was deployed in depth. It was supported by powerful permanent fortifications, natural obstacles, and populated points prepared for defense and reinforced by engineering installations and obstructions. It could strike at the flank of our forces advancing directly toward Berlin. Such flank attacks were all the more dangerous because the strength of the German forces in this area was increasing considerably. Consequently, the East Prussia grouping had not only to be contained but also to be isolated from the remaining sectors of the strategic front, and, if possible, to be split up in order to prevent the German command from utilizing all its forces in a concentrated way in one sector.

Such a multi-faceted operational task—contain, isolate, and split—meant that the offensive in East Prussia called for the use of at least two Army Groups—one to strike against Koenigsberg from the east and the other to separate the East Prussian forces from Army Group A and from the [German] rear by enveloping it from the south and the southwest. This Army Group would moreover secure the advance of our troops along the Warsaw-Poznan'-Berlin axis. By virtue of the disposition of the Army Groups, which resulted from the 1944 operations, East Prussia could be struck from the east by the 3rd Belorussian Army Group, while the 2nd Belorussian Army Group could envelop the enemy forces.

The 1st Belorussian and 1st Ukrainian Army Groups could be used for the main operation—to breach the strategic front of the enemy and to start a headlong advance to the west—since they were already in this sector and had established bridgeheads on the Vistula. . . .

In the last three days of October and the beginning of November 1944 General Antonov and the operations officers of the General Staff worked out the operational aspect of the forthcoming offensive. At this stage of work the minimal time required for the final defeat of Germany had been estimated approximately. It was conjectured that defeat could be achieved in 45 days of offensive operations, to a depth of 600–700 km. by means of two consecutive efforts (stages) with no operational halt between them. The objective of the first stage, [an advance] to a depth of 250–300 km., consisted in routing enemy forces and reaching the Bydgoszcz-Poznan'-Breslau-Vienna line. It was to take 15 days. The second stage—the final defeat of Germany and the capture of Berlin—was to take 30 days. The pace was not fast, since fierce resistance was expected in the final fighting to destroy the main forces of fascist Germany. In actuality, heroic Soviet troops fulfilled all these plans ahead of schedule. . . .[8]

As to the directions of the strikes, it was now definitely established that the 2nd Belorussian Army Group would attack toward Marienburg in order to cut off the East Prussian forces from Germany and from other [German] troops and toward Allenstein in order to split up these forces. It was planned that part of the 1st Belorussian Army Group's forces would envelop Warsaw and strike in the direction of the advancing 1st Ukrainian Army Group in order to crush the Kielce-Radom German troop concentration. Finally, the zone of operations of the adjoining groupings of the 1st and 4th Ukrainian Army Groups (the Krakow area) was charted. During the first stage of the campaign Vienna remained the final objective of the offensive of the two southern Army Groups—the 2nd and the 3rd Ukrainian.

In our daily reports to Supreme Headquarters we kept raising to a greater or lesser extent questions relating to the operations of the Soviet armed forces in the final campaign. For this reason, many of the operations had already been cleared with the Supreme Commander in Chief even before they were extensively discussed with the Army Group commanders. During November many clarifications were made in the plan. This reflected the already firmly established procedure of operational planning in which the initial considerations of the General Staff were no more than the point of departure for working out the future plan of operations for the Army Groups.

While drafting the plan for the 1945 campaign, Supreme Headquarters did not call the commanding officers to a special conference as it had done in the past, e.g., in the case of Operation Bagration, which concerned the summer offensive in Belorussia.[9] This time the commanding officers were called individually by the General Staff in order to discuss all aspects related to the operations of their respective Army Groups; then the already coordinated ideas were submitted to Supreme Headquarters.

Up to November 7 and during the holidays connected with the [anniversary of the] October Revolution, Army Group commanders—Marshals F. I. Tolbukhin, K. K. Rokossovskii, I. S. Konev, and General of the Army I. D. Cherniakhovskii—and the representatives of Supreme Headquarters to the various Army Groups worked in the General Staff.[10] The General Staff painstakingly reviewed a variant of the general plan of the 1945 combat operations against Germany. Then the Army Group commanders, A. I. Antonov, and I went to Supreme Headquarters where, after Antonov had submitted a brief report, an extensive discussion of the draft plan was held. No major corrections were made in it. The beginning of the offensive in the main sector was planned for January 20, 1945. For the time being, however, plans for the operation had not been given final approval, and directives were not issued to the Army Groups.

A few days after Supreme Headquarters had discussed the draft plan for the initial 1945 operations, the Supreme Commander in Chief decided that the forces which were to capture Berlin would be headed by his first deputy, Marshal G. K. Zhukov, and on November 16, 1944 Zhukov was appointed commander of the 1st Belorussian Army Group. Marshal K. K. Rokossovskii replaced General G. F. Zakharov, commander of the 2nd Belorussian Army Group. Stalin personally telephoned this order to the officers involved.[11]

The job of coordinating activities of the four Army Groups in the Berlin operation during this final campaign of the war was undertaken by Stalin himself. This rendered superfluous the task of the Chief of the General Staff, A. M. Vasilevskii, with the 3rd Belorussian Army Group. As a representative of Supreme Headquarters he was left in charge of operations of the 1st and 2nd Baltic Army Groups; on February 20, 1945, following the death of General of the Army I. D. Cherniakhovskii, he assumed command of the 3rd Belorussian Army Group.[12]

Thus, according to the plan of the General Staff—drafted jointly with the Army Group commanders—the 1945 campaign was to begin with powerful simultaneous strikes by the Army Groups located in the strategic direction of Berlin. The purpose of the strikes was to break through the enemy defense line and to split it into parts, to disrupt enemy communications, to disorganize the coordinated activity of the enemy groupings, and already during the initial stage of the campaign, to destroy the basic forces of the German troops facing us. The operations during the first stage of the campaign were thus to create conditions favorable to the termination of the war. . . .[13]

The entire planning of the operation by Supreme Headquarters and the Army Groups took about two and a half months. Naturally, preparation of the operations throughout this period went at full speed. Work was done to concentrate reserves and matériel needed by the various Army Groups. When the basic features of future operations had been concerted with the commanders of the Army Groups, the stockpiling of necessary supplies in the field began. Thus, by November 1944, the picture of the Soviet army's forthcoming winter offensive was fully drawn, even though Supreme Headquarters did not confirm the plan of operations until the end of December. Subsequently, no more than partial amendments were made to the plan of the campaign and of the initial operations.

Marshal I. S. Konev
From the Vistula
to the Oder

AT THE END of November 1944, I had been summoned to Moscow. I had brought with me the plan of the operation as worked out by the Army Group command and was giving a personal report on it to Stalin in the presence of members of the State Defense Committee at Supreme Headquarters.

I. S. Konev, *Sorok piatyi* (Moscow, 1966), pp. 3–51.

I well remember that Stalin made a detailed examination of the plan of the operation and directed particular attention to the Silesian industrial area, which stood out in relief on the map. According to our plan, the attacking troops were to by-pass the area, enveloping it to the north and south, because the area was studded with industrial installations which were built, as a rule, of reinforced concrete next to pits which had powerful equipment at the pithead. All in all, troops maneuvering in any frontal attack against this industrial area would encounter very great obstacles.

Even on the map the scale of the Silesian area and its might were quite strikingly shown. I well understood the significance of Stalin's drawing my attention to this fact. He pointed to the map, made a circle with his finger around the area, and said: "Gold."

This was said in such a way as to require no further comment.[14]

Even without that, however, it had been clear to me, as commander of the Army Group, that the question of liberating the Dabrowa-Silesian industrial area required a special solution; steps had to be taken to preserve its industrial potential in every possible way, especially in view of the fact that after liberation these ancient Polish lands were to be returned to Poland. But I must say that when Stalin deliberately moved his finger over the area and said "Gold," I was moved to give even more careful and deep thought as to how to preserve and not merely to liberate the area. . . .

Our plan met with no objections from Supreme Headquarters and was approved entirely. With the approval of the plan I did not lose much time in returning to the front, where we began our preparations. . . .

By that time the Army Group consisted of the following forces in terms of weapons and matériel: 3,240 tanks and self-propelled guns, more than 17,000 guns and mortars, and 2,580 planes. This was a great force; and with it the Army Group was capable of solving its major strategic task. . . .[15]

We were to advance from the Vistula to the Oder, where the enemy had thrown up beforehand seven defense zones to a depth of up to 500 km. Most of these zones ran along the banks of the rivers Nida, Pilica, Warta, and Oder, which themselves presented additional obstacles. Three of the zones were manned by enemy troops. Behind them was Berlin, and they had no choice. To retreat was to sign their own death warrant. . . .

On January 9 I had a call from General A. I. Antonov, Acting Chief of the General Staff, who informed me that in view of the grave situation which had taken shape in the Ardennes on the western front, the Allies had asked us to start our offensive as soon as possible. Antonov said that, following the Allied request, Supreme Headquarters had reviewed the opening date of the offensive. The 1st Ukrainian Army Group was to start its offensive on January 12 instead of 20.

Antonov was speaking on behalf of Stalin. Since the operation had already been approved by Supreme Headquarters and fully planned, no changes except the date and no other basic questions were raised in the conversation. I informed Antonov that the Army Group would be ready for the offensive on the new date set by Supreme Headquarters.[16]

With the benefit of hindsight I have no intention either to minimize or to exaggerate the difficulties this created for us. On the whole we were quite ready, and that is why I did not hesitate to tell Antonov that we would be ready for the new date. But the more than eight days of which we had now been deprived had, of course, to be compensated for by the most intense effort squeezed into the remaining two and a half days. All the echelons of command had to make a supreme exertion in order to complete the preparations on time. . . .

Apart from everything else, we were not happy about the earlier date of the offensive because of the weather forecasts. For the original date of the start of the offensive, the forecast had been relatively more favorable than for the next few days. In preparing to start the offensive on January 12, owing to bad weather we had to reckon on the certainty, not the possibility, that German defenses would have to be suppressed by artillery alone, without the aid of air strikes. . . .

Apart from other final preparations, we were engaged at the time in executing a large-scale camouflage measure designed to mislead the enemy. We advertised a false concentration of a large tank grouping on our left flank. That was where we sent all the dummy tanks, self-propelled guns, and artillery pieces. They were all concentrated in the sector of General Kurochkin's army, on the eastern bank of the Vistula, from which the Germans could expect an attack on Krakow. . . .

In spite of wretched weather conditions, the enemy's reconnaissance planes made a rather large number of sorties in the area of the false concentration. In the last two days before the offensive, the Germans carried out more than 220 artillery attacks on the areas where our dummy guns were installed. In the German rear there was evidence of some regrouping of the forces of the 17th Army—some of its units were pulled away to the south. Let me say beforehand, that even in the course of the offensive the Germans did not venture to move part of the 17th Army from the south to the north, because they still allowed for the possibility of a secondary attack from the direction where we had made a show of concentrating our forces.

Finally January 12, 1945 arrived. . . . I arrived at the observation post with Generals Krainiukov and Kalchenko, members of the military council, and General Sokolovskii, chief of staff of the Army Group. At 5:00 a.m. sharp, after a powerful artillery barrage, the forward battalions attacked and swiftly captured the enemy's first defense trench. It was clear from the very first reports that the enemy had not pulled back at all and that he was right there in the zone of all the artillery strikes we had planned.

The artillery barrage, for all its brevity, was so powerful that it gave the enemy the impression that it was the start of a general artillery preparation. They mistook the activities of our forward battalions for a general offensive by our troops, and they tried to stop it with all the fire power at their disposal. But that was just what we had counted on. The forward battalions occupied the first trench and hit the dirt between the first and the second. The artillery preparation began at precisely that moment. It lasted for one hour and forty-seven minutes and was so powerful, judging from a number of captured documents, that it seemed to the enemy to have lasted for at least five hours.[17]

After starting our artillery preparation, we did not follow the usual practice of pulling back the forward battalions which had occupied the first enemy trench. Each battery had been assigned a specific sector from the general grid reference so that we were planning, as they say, to try to hit a mosquito in the eye. All artillery observers and battery commanders had maps giving the exact location of the first trench, which had already been captured by our troops, and the position of the second, which was still held by German troops. Only one thing was required of the artillerymen—precision work. Not once did they make a mistake. At any rate, this time no one anywhere along the line of attacking troops issued the alert: "Stop! You are firing on your own troops."

The weather forecasts proved to be correct, with a vengeance. Visibility was virtually down to zero, not only in the dark when the shelling began but even later, at daybreak. The air was thick with falling snow, as if nature were especially concerned about providing us with additional camouflage. A few hours later, when Rybalko's tank army went past my observation post to join the breakthrough, his tanks were so covered with snow that they could be distinguished only because they moved.

Of course, that kind of weather has its drawbacks. What is good for camouflage is bad for observation. But everything had been so thoroughly prepared and coordinated in advance that there was no confusion either during the artillery preparation or the breakthrough, or when the tank armies joined the breakthrough. All our plans went like clockwork that day—something, I must add, that is not often achieved in warfare. That is why I recall the day of the breakthrough with particular satisfaction.

During our artillery preparation the enemy troops—including part of the reserves which were deployed in the tactical defense zone or, to put it simply, those which had been drawn up too close to the front line—came under such heavy artillery fire that they were demoralized and rendered incapable of carrying out their assignments. Fascist German unit commanders captured in the first hours of our breakthrough testified that their officers and men had lost all self-control. They abandoned their positions without permission (something, let me say, that is not typical of Germans). The German soldier, as a rule—and this rule was confirmed throughout the war—stayed where he was ordered to stay until given permission to leave. But that day, January 12, the fire was so relentless that those who survived it could no longer control themselves.

Control and communications in enemy units and formations were completely disrupted. That was no accident, but something we had planned because we had pinpointed all the enemy observation and command posts. We particularly struck out at the entire system of control and communications, and in the very first minutes of the artillery fire and air strikes we made direct hits on them, including the command post of the German 4th Tank Army, which was deployed opposite us in the breakthrough sector.

In analyzing this operation, military historians of the Federal German Republic are inclined, as they are in a number of other instances, to blame Hitler alone for the defeat in this particular operation. They accuse him of having ordered the reserves, including the 24th Tank Corps, to be deployed in the immediate proximity of the front line. As a result, these reserves are supposed to have come under our powerful shelling and suffered heavy losses.

I think in this instance the military historians are partly right. Since the 4th Tank Army was holding the defenses in a key sector covering the distant approaches to Berlin, I do not exclude the possibility that Hitler, according to his own notions of how stability of the troops should be assured, had ordered the reserves moved right up to the front line. At any rate, it was not my wartime impression that the German generals were in the habit of deploying strategic reserves in that clumsy way. From the standpoint of the elementary rules of the art of warfare, it was pure sacrilege.[18]

Though Hitler was partly to blame, we take the blame for all the rest of it. The German reserves were deployed, after all, not on the front line but in the rear. They would not have suffered such disastrous losses in the very first hours had not our artillery preparation been conducted with such density and to such a depth. . . .

An hour or two after the artillery preparation, when our infantry and accompanying tanks rushed into the breach, I inspected the sector of the breakthrough. The whole place was literally plowed up, especially in the direction of the main attack by the armies of Zhadov, Koroteev, and Pukhov. Everything was one tangled mass, covered with debris. As a matter of fact, disregarding small-caliber guns and mortars, we had struck at the enemy with 250–280 and, in some cases, 300 guns per kilometer of front—a "slugger," as the soldiers call it.[19]

Part of Gordov's 3rd Guards Army, Pukhov's 13th Army, Koroteev's 52nd and Zhadov's 5th Guards Armies on the first day of the fighting advanced to a depth of fifteen to twenty kilometers, and after breaking through the main German defense line, widened the breach to the left and right from forty to sixty kilometers.

This allowed me to send the tank armies of Rybalko and Leliushenko into the breach by midday. The enemy could not be allowed to organize a counterattack with the two tank and two motorized divisions he had in reserve. These divisions had been partly hit by our long-range artillery fire, but they were still a formidable force. . . .

Over-all the situation in the sector of our Army Group at the end of January 17—that is, five and a half days after the start of the operation—was as follows. The German defenses had been breached on a 250-km. front to a depth of 120–140 km. Our Army Group had routed the main force of the 4th Tank Army and of the 24th Reserve Tank Corps, and had inflicted a telling defeat on the 17th German Field Army, which was a part of Army Group A under General Harpe. Our success created favorable conditions both for an extension of the offensive in the main Breslau direction and for a thrust against the flank and rear of the Krakow-Silesia enemy grouping.

The Germans had been trying to make use of everything they could lay their hands on, both the remnants of the retreating units and the reserves that were brought up from the rear, so as to prevent our main grouping from advancing any farther toward the Oder. Simultaneously, they continued their stubborn defense of Krakow, and it appeared that despite their critical position to the north they were prepared to put up a fierce fight in the Silesian industrial area. It would have been strange, indeed, if they had decided not to fight there. In output, the Silesian area was only second to the Ruhr, which, incidentally, had by that time also been confronted by a direct threat from our Allies. The Germans were apparently hoping to contain us by leaning on the strongly fortified Krakow defense area, and then, at the first opportunity, to strike northward, at the flank and rear of our main grouping, thereby breaking up our offensive and retaining the whole of the Silesian industrial area.

I think this is the right place to say a few words about the strength of the German resistance in this operation as a whole. By the start of the operation, the German divisions (especially those deployed against the Sandomierz bridgehead) had been brought up to strength and had up to 12,000 officers and men each. In other words, one enemy infantry division was numerically equal to roughly two of our rifle divisions. Their forces were impressive, and all along we had expected the Germans to fight fiercely, especially in view of the prospect that our operations would be carried into the territory of the Third Reich.

By no means all Germans yet realized that the Third Reich was coming to an end, and the grave situation in the meanwhile had had almost no effect on the conduct of the German soldier on the field of battle. He continued to fight as he had fought before, distinguishing himself, especially in defense, with a steadfastness that bordered at times on fanaticism. German army organization was on a high level; the divisions were up to strength and were supplied with all or nearly all the prescribed equipment.

In the circumstances it was too early to speak of the breakdown of German army morale. Add to this such important factors as, on the one hand, Goebbels' propaganda, which scared the soldiers by telling them that we would raze Germany to the ground and drive the whole population to Siberia and, on the other hand, the harsh repression applied against those same soldiers, which intensified toward the end of the war.

Morale in the German army rose noticeably as a result of the Ardennes offensive. Judging from the testimony of prisoners, there was a rather widespread belief among German officers and men at the time that once the Allies were defeated in the Ardennes and forced to sign a separate agreement, the German command would throw its forces from all fronts against the Soviet Union. These rumors were circulating even when the German offensive in the Ardennes had finally come to nothing. . . .[20]

The nearer our troops approached the Oder, the more sure we became that the enemy would try to retain the Silesian industrial area at all costs. . . . We were faced with three tasks which eventually merged into one: to crush the enemy's Silesia grouping without suffering great losses; to do this swiftly; and, if possible, to preserve undestroyed the industry of Silesia. We decided to use tank forces for a wide envelopment of the area and then in cooperation with the [combined-arms] Armies advancing on Silesia from the north, east, and south, to force the Germans out into the open under threat of encirclement, and to rout them there.

With that aim in view, Rybalko's 3rd Guards Tank Army was instructed by the Army Group command on January 20 to change the direction of its advance. Earlier, Rybalko's troops were headed toward Breslau, but in view of the situation shaping up in Silesia his Army had to make a sharp turn from north to south along the Oder. For Rybalko the task was not only unexpected but also highly complicated. It was not easy for an entire tank Army which was on the march and headed in one direction to execute a sharp turn. Corresponding orders were issued to the other Armies. . . .

On the night of January 23, our intelligence reported the composition of the enemy group defending the Silesian industrial area. It consisted of nine infantry divisions, two tank divisions, several so-called combat groups, two separate brigades, six separate regiments, twenty-two separate battalions, including several machine gun training battalions and an officers' penal battalion. According to an assessment of the situation, the arrival of two or three infantry divisions and one tank division could be expected in the near future. . . .[21] Thus, the enemy grouping in the Silesian industrial area, although consisting mainly of battered troops, was still a solid force.

Rybalko's 3rd Tank Army, having made a right-angle turn by January 27, reached its designated area with its forward units threatening the enemy's Silesia grouping [from the north]. . . . Meanwhile, the 21st and the 59th Armies had already reached the immediate vicinity of the Silesian industrial area. They were already at Bytom and were fighting for Katowice. The 60th Army, advancing southward, had captured Oswiecim [Auschwitz].

On the second day after the liberation of that horrible camp, which has now become the symbol of fascist barbarism throughout the world, I was rather close to it. I had already been given the first report of what kind of camp it was. It was not that I did not want to see the death camp with my own eyes; I deliberately did not allow myself to do so. The fighting was at its peak, and my duties were so taxing that I did not believe I had the right to give any time or energy to my personal emotions. There, in wartime, I did not belong to myself.

On my way to the front lines I thought of the decisions that had to be made. The advance of the 60th Army from the south and the 3rd Tank Army from the north had already formed a pair of pincers around the enemy, which had only to be snapped shut to complete the encirclement of the German grouping in the Silesian industrial area. There was every possibility of doing this. But I asked myself: ought we to do it? I realized that if we encircled and started to fight the German grouping, which numbered ten to twelve divisions apart from the reinforcements, its resistance could be prolonged for a very long period, especially in view of the area where the fighting would take place. That was the whole point. . . . But to refuse to trap the enemy was not an easy decision to make. I must admit I hesitated, and the position was complicated by the fact that a few days before, at the start of the operation, when we had yet to reach the Silesian area and to realize the losses and destruction which long fighting in this area would entail, I had issued the order for encirclement.

As I was driving toward Rybalko's Army, which was approaching from the north, I became more and more convinced that we had to take the area intact, which meant we had to let the Germans out of the trap and rout them later, when they were out in the open. But on the other hand, encirclement was the highest form of strategic art, the crowning achievement. Were we to give up the chance? As a career soldier, trained in the notion that the enemy was to be surrounded on all possible occasions, his communications cut, and his troops destroyed in the trap, it was very hard for me to suddenly break all precedents and act counter to the established views, to which I myself fully subscribed.

My mental agitation was compounded by the fact that Rybalko's Army would have to be turned around once again should I decide not to encircle the enemy. This Army was advancing with a determination to surround the enemy, to close the circle around him, not to let him out. I was faced with the prospect of upsetting all their justified expectations and reorienting the Army and its commander toward another task.

On my way I tried to take a cold look at all the advantages and drawbacks. Suppose we did encircle the Germans in the Silesian industrial area. They were about 100,000 strong. Half of them would be killed in the fighting and the rest taken prisoner. Those, you might say, were all the advantages. That was a great deal, but that was all. What about the drawbacks? Once we had closed the circle, we would have to devastate the whole area, inflicting tremendous damage on a major industrial complex which was to become a part of Poland. In addition, our troops would suffer heavy losses because the fighting there would mean storming one plant after another, mine after mine, building after building. Even if one has superiority in weapons, house-to-house combat exacts a stiff price, a life for a life. We had already lost enough men in the four years of the war. Victory was well in sight. Wherever possible, the men had to be spared, so that we could go on together, alive, to victory.

My responsibility was great in this instance, and although I was never one to hesitate, in that particular case I admit I took a long time to analyze the problem from every angle. As a result of weighing all the pros and cons I finally decided not to encircle the Germans, to leave them a corridor to escape from the Silesian area, and then to finish them off when they emerged. My decision was borne out by subsequent events.

To implement this plan, I had to issue a two-fold order. On one hand, I had to turn back the units of Rybalko's tank army which were about to cut the corridor and, on the other, to step up the operations of the troops that were advancing directly on the Silesian industrial area. It was not enough to leave the Germans a corridor. They had to be made to see it was the only avenue for escape. That called for a show of force and determination to drive them out of the area by attacking and pushing them southwest in the direction of the escape vent.

With officers of my operational group I sent instructions to Korovnikov and Kurochkin, 59th and 60th Army commanders, and on my way to Rybalko I personally called on Gusev, the commander of the 21st Army. Under the initial plan, Gusev's Army, while conducting a frontal assault, was also to envelop Silesia from the northwest. He was now instructed to mount a head-on attack as swiftly as possible, constantly pressing and pushing the enemy out. Let me say in advance that the 21st Army fulfilled its task in a most commendable manner both on that day and on the days that followed. . . .

I was now faced with the prospect of seeing Rybalko. In making my decision, I had some qualms as to how it would be viewed "up there," in Supreme Headquarters. But that was not my only worry. I was also thinking how it would be taken by my subordinates, notably Rybalko, who within a few days had executed a most complex maneuver precisely for the purpose of closing the ring around the enemy grouping in Silesia. . . .

It is not easy to recall conversations that took place twenty years ago, but this conversation with Rybalko was one of those that stick in your mind. If I can trust my memory, here is what we said to each other:

HE: Comrade Marshal, to fulfill your order I must turn the Army once again.

I: But, Pavel Semenovich, you are used to that sort of thing. Your Army has just executed a brilliant maneuver. Let it execute another half-turn. Incidentally, you have a full corps which is not yet deployed and is advancing in the second echelon. Let's send it straight in the Ratibor direction and stop the other two, since your radio communications with all corps, as far as I am aware, are excellent.

HE (making a wry face and, I felt, still inwardly resisting): Yes, that could perhaps be done.

I: Your communications work fine, am I right? Are you in contact with all forces?

HE: Yes, we are in contact with all of them. The radio has been working without a hitch.

I: Well, radio an order immediately to these two corps to stop, and to the other corps to advance on Ratibor.

The radio cars were right there, both mine and Rybalko's, and he lost no time in radioing his order. . . .

When you recall the battles of the past you want to give the reader a visual picture of certain moments. I shall try, to the best of my abilities, to show the reader what I have seen with my own eyes. What was this advanced observation post of the 3rd Tank Army, where this conversation took place? It was neither a house nor a dugout, but merely a small hill that commanded a good view of the terrain. It was there that the Army commander stood, and I by his side. We had a view that was really panoramic. Before us lay the field of battle, and both of us saw it and the movement of Rybalko's tank formations on it, as if we were at an exercise. His brigades maneuvered before us under enemy fire as they moved on toward the Silesian industrial area. In the distance we saw the industrial area itself, with the smoking stacks of the plants. To the left of us, where Gusev's 21st Army was fighting, we heard the incessant roar of artillery and saw the advance of the infantry. Deep back in the rear new masses of tanks were moving up—it was the corps Rybalko was turning toward Ratibor.

Modern warfare involves great distances. The actions of large masses of troops do not usually fit into your field of vision even when you are at an observation post. Usually they are visible only on a map. The greater was my satisfaction when I was able to watch the swift advance of the battle formations of the tank brigades, which was bold and energetic despite the enemy's fire and resistance. I could see the tank-borne infantry and the motorized troops, some of the men playing accordions.

Incidentally, many tanks in this operation were camouflaged with curtain lace. At first sight, the lace and tanks do not seem to go together, but there was logic in the combination. It was winter, the fields were covered with a light layer of snow, and the tank troops had the night before captured the warehouse of some textile mill. The camouflage turned out to be pretty good.

I can still visualize this picture with all its contrasts: Silesia's smoking chimneys, the artillery shelling, the clang of the tank treads, the curtain lace on the tanks, and the accordion-playing tank-borne infantry, whose melodies did not reach us. . . .

Our decision not to complete the encirclement of the enemy's Silesia grouping produced positive results. Under the strong frontal assault and fearing the deep flanking maneuver, the Germans had to fall back rapidly through the gateway we had left them. By January 29 the whole of the Silesian industrial area was cleared of the enemy and captured intact. When we broke into the area, many plants were running at full capacity and continued to run and turn out goods.

The Germans suffered serious losses when they tried to break away from us and escape from the industrial area through the corridor we left them. But their main losses came after they emerged into the open, where they were under concentrated attack by Rybalko's tank troops and Kurochkin's 60th Army. Judging by the data we had, after the series of blows inflicted on the enemy in the open, the German grouping in Silesia was reduced to something like 25,000 or 30,000 men from various scattered and uncoordinated units. That was all that came out of the contemplated encirclement, the idea of which we had abandoned at the last moment.

We had apparently let some German generals escape whom we could have taken prisoner in the encirclement. But I was not sorry because we had gained so much more.

All this while I have been describing the operations primarily of the southern flank of the Army Group. However important the operation of capturing the Silesian industrial area was, our actions were not confined to it. It was about 500 km. from the left flank of the Army Group, where we were next to the 4th Ukrainian Army Group, to the right flank, where we bordered on the 1st Belorussian Army Group; and fighting was in progress in that whole vast area. . . .

As for the Vistula-Oder operation as a whole, during the twenty-three days of the offensive the troops of the 1st Belorussian and the 1st Ukrainian Army Groups, with the active support of the 2nd Belorussian and the 4th Ukrainian Army Groups advanced to a depth of 600 km., widened the breakthrough to 1,000 km., and swept across the Oder where they established a number of bridgeheads. The 1st Belorussian Army Group, having taken the Kuestrin bridgehead, was within 60 km. of Berlin.[22]

In the course of the operation, the troops of the 1st Ukrainian Army Group drove the enemy out of southern Poland and its ancient capital Krakow, captured the Silesian industrial area, and, having set up operational bridgeheads on the western bank of the Oder, created favorable conditions for dealing subsequent blows at the enemy, both in the Berlin and the Dresden directions. . . .

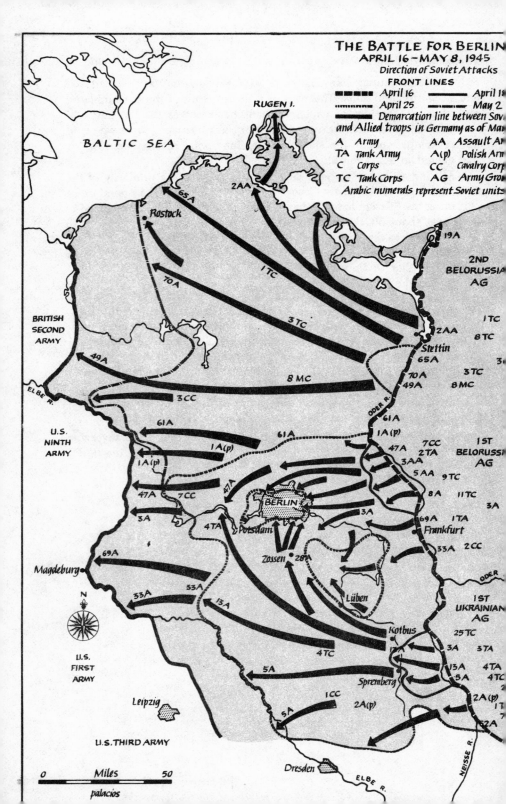

THE BATTLE FOR BERLIN
APRIL 16 – MAY 8, 1945
Direction of Soviet Attacks
FRONT LINES

▬▬▬ April 16	▬▬▬ April 18
······· April 25	▬▬▬ May 2

▬▬▬ Demarcation line between Sov
and Allied troops in Germany as of Ma

A	Army	AA	Assault Ar
TA	Tank Army	A(p)	Polish Arm
C	Corps	CC	Cavalry Corp
TC	Tank Corps	AG	Army Grou

Arabic numerals represent Soviet units

BALTIC SEA

RUGEN I.

2 AA

65 A

Rostock

70 A

1 TC

3 TC

19 A

2ND
BELORUSSIA
AG

1 TC

2 AA

8 TC

Stettin

65 A

3

70 A

3 TC

8 MC

49 A

8 MC

ELBE R.

3 CC

BRITISH
SECOND
ARMY

49 A

61 A

ODER R.

61 A

1 A(p)

U.S.
NINTH
ARMY

61 A

1 A(p)

7 CC

2 TA

1 ST
BELORUSSI
AG

1 A(p)

47 A

3 AA

5 AA

9 TC

47 A

7 CC

BERLIN

47 A

8 A

11 TC

3 A

3 A

Potsdam

3 A

69 A

1 TA

4 TA

Zossen • 28 A

Frankfurt

33 A

2 CC

Magdeburg

69 A

33 A

33 A

13 A

Lüben

1 ST
UKRAINIAN
AG

Kotbus

25 TC

3 A

3 TA

U.S.
FIRST
ARMY

4 TC

5 A

13 A

4 TA

5 A

4 TC

Spremberg

2 A(p)

1 T

Leipzig

1 CC

2 A(p)

5 A

52 A

N

U.S. THIRD ARMY

NEISSE R.

Dresden

ELBE R.

0   Miles   50

palacios

PART II THE BATTLE OF BERLIN

Introduction

WARS ALMOST ALWAYS start suddenly but usually end slowly. Even when the outcome is no longer in question, men continue to die. The period of particularly senseless dying in the generally senseless business of war was especially prolonged in World War II on the European continent. The Allied policy of unconditional surrender on the one hand and the German fear of retribution, the ruthless and effective control over the population by the Nazi leadership on the other hand served to perpetuate German resistance until virtually every square mile of German soil was controlled by foreign troops, until the supreme leader was dead, and until the capital city, Berlin, yielded to its conquerors.

The five excerpts below retell the story of this final encounter, the Battle for Berlin. The authors speak with authority: Colonel General S. M. Shtemenko served as Chief of Operations of the Soviet General Staff; Marshals G. K. Zhukov and I. S. Konev commanded the two Army Groups which launched this final assault of the European war; and Marshal V. I. Chuikov commanded the 8th Guards Army which stood on the axis of the main thrust against Berlin and personally accepted the surrender of the Berlin garrison.

The two principal actors on the Soviet side were Marshal Zhukov, commander of the 1st Belorussian Army Group, and Marshal Konev, commander of the 1st Ukrainian Army Group. Fate and Stalin's design pitted against one another in the most dramatic circumstances during the last days and hours of the war the most famous Soviet soldier, G. K. Zhukov, and his most distinguished rival, I. S. Konev. For Zhukov, whose armies were directly pointed at Berlin, the capture of the German capital would represent the logical crowning of his extraordinary war record. Indeed, if history proceeded according to logic, what could have been more fitting and just than to award this final trophy and honor to the defender of Leningrad, the savior of Moscow, and the organizer of the Stalingrad and Kursk victories? For Konev, the Battle for Berlin would represent the last chance to prove at least once the superiority of his military command over the always "lucky" Zhukov.

As the memoirs indicate, Stalin well understood the rivalry between his two principal commanders; he used it skillfully in the planning and implementation of the Berlin operation. By deliberately leaving open the question of precise zones of operation for the troops of both Zhukov and Konev in the vicinity of Berlin, he offered the latter the prospect of victory. This time fate favored the underdog. The man who had the misfortune of watching his troops destroyed by the Germans and his command pass into Zhukov's hand at the battle for the Soviet capital in 1941 now shared at least a part of Zhukov's glory in seizing the German capital.

The memoirs disclose an important controversy among Soviet commanders concerning the necessity and advisability of pausing some ten weeks (from February 3 to April 16, 1945) after the attainment of the Oder line and prior to the start of the last assault on Berlin. The Soviet controversy finds its counterpart among Western commanders and political leaders who at the last stage of the European war asked the question: Should we try to take Berlin? and after the war asked: Should we have tried to take Berlin? and Could we have succeeded? One Soviet commander, Marshal Chuikov, asked the question: Could we have captured Berlin in February 1945 instead of May? To his resounding affirmative, Marshal Zhukov with the implicit support of both Marshal Konev and General Shtemenko returned a resounding negative.

Marshal Chuikov wrote in an article several months after the publication of his memoirs where he first raised the question:

When I publicly stated my opinion that continuing our advance on Berlin in February 1945 was both possible and advisable, I was opposed by some of my comrades. Characteristically, the opposition did not come from active participants in the Vistula-Oder Operation, but either from men who had been connected with formulating the orders of Supreme Headquarters and the Army Group to stop the advance on Berlin and carry out the Eastern Pomeranian Operation or from authors of various historical works.[*]

At the time Chuikov published his memoirs and his article, the most "active participant in the Vistula-Oder Operation," Marshal Zhukov, was still a non-figure. A scant one month later, on the occasion of the twentieth anniversary of the Battle for Berlin, Zhukov was permitted to speak. His reminiscences were published, and there he bitterly and bitingly disputed both Chuikov's facts and his logic. In the light of present knowledge concerning the state of Berlin's defenses (thanks to the testimony of leading German participants) and with the benefit of hindsight, Chuikov's arguments are persuasive as far as the possibility, albeit the risky possibility, of seizing Berlin in February. They seem to exaggerate, however, the extent of the increase in Germany's capacity to resist which, Chuikov charges, took place in the weeks after the Red Army halted on the Oder River.

[*]*Novaia i noveishaia istoriia*, 1965, No. 2, p. 7.

Colonel General S. M. Shtemenko
In the General Staff

THE ADVANCE of Soviet troops in East Prussia, on the Vistula, and in Silesia was so decisive and swift that, two weeks after starting, the forces of the 1st Belorussian and the 1st Ukrainian Army Groups had accomplished their mission of reaching the Poznan'-Breslau line. Having attained the goal of the first stage of the campaign, it was necessary to determine without delay how to move farther, inasmuch as the strike against Berlin was the order of the day and was now, so to say, the most immediate goal.

On January 26, 1945 the General Staff was informed of the decision of the 1st Belorussian Army Group commander to continue his essentially uninterrupted advance until the capture of the German capital itself. In the space of four days he proposed to move up the troops—especially the artillery—and the rear services; to replenish his supplies; to put matériel for mechanized units in order; to place the 3rd Assault Army and the 1st Polish Army into the forward echelon; and, on February 1–2, to continue the advance with all forces of his Army Group. His first objective was to force the Oder from the march. This was to be followed by a swift strike at Berlin, focusing his main effort on the envelopment of the German capital from the northeast, north, and northwest. The 2nd Guards Tank Army would envelop Berlin from the northwest and the 1st Guards Tank Army from the northeast.

The following day the General Staff received the decision of the 1st Ukrainian Army Group commander, according to which his Army Group would also act without any appreciable interruption. It was to begin its offensive on February 5–6 and to reach the Elbe on February 25–28, while its right flank, in coordinated action with the 1st Belorussian Army Group, was to take Berlin.

Thus, both Army Groups aimed at capturing Berlin without any stop whatsoever. Yet, if this was the case, how could we square Marshal Konev's decision with Stalin's instructions that Berlin was to be taken only by the 1st Belorussian Army Group? After heated discussions in General Antonov's

S. M. Shtemenko, "Kak planirovalas' posledniaia kampaniia po razgromu gitlerovskoi Germanii," *Voenno-istoricheskii zhurnal,* 1965, No. 5, pp. 65–72.

office, the General Staff suggested that both decisions be approved. Supreme Headquarters agreed to this suggestion. The demarcation line between the Army Groups, however, was the one recommended by Marshal Zhukov: The previous line was to remain in effect up to Smiegel; beyond that, the line was to be Unrustadt–Obra River–Oder River–Ratsdorf–Friedland–Gross Keris–Miechendorf. This demarcation line actually pushed the forces of the 1st Ukrainian Army Group back to the south of Berlin, leaving them no opening whatsoever for a direct strike from the south or the southwest and forcing them to advance toward Guben and Brandenburg.[23]

The General Staff was aware that it was absurd on the one hand to approve Marshal Konev's decision to advance on Berlin with his right flank while establishing on the other hand a demarcation line which made this impossible. The situation had somehow to be resolved. We believed that either the situation itself would introduce necessary revisions or that we should somehow be able, in the course of the operation, to correct this absurdity, the more so since it was still a long way to Berlin. But as further events indicated, the offensive against Berlin could not be completed in the short time planned for it.

By the end of January we discovered that the enemy was setting up a strong grouping in Pomerania. The General Staff judged this to be a threat to the right flank and rear of the forces advancing on Berlin. Furthermore, a gap of over 100 km. had developed between the 1st and 2nd Belorussian Army Groups; the gap was secured solely by cavalry. At the same time, the troops were experiencing an acute shortage of ammunition and fuel, since their supplies had remained on the Vistula.[24] This situation forced Supreme Headquarters and the General Staff to review their initial decision. We could not make a dash for Berlin, ignoring the strong enemy forces on our flank and neglecting rear and supply problems. Now, twenty years later, when all the cards are on the table and nobody has to bear responsibility for the decision, some comrades draw profound conclusions in their memoirs about the possibility of taking Berlin in February 1945.[25]

By mid-February, the enemy grouping in Pomerania had launched an offensive. The fight was dogged, but the Soviet command had no doubt that the Germans would be unable to overrun our advancing forces. Yet, without crushing this grouping, there could be no thought of an uninterrupted advance toward Berlin by all the forces of the 1st Belorussian Army Group. Most of these forces had to be hurled against this Pomeranian annoyance. Later, when the main forces of the 2nd Belorussian Army Group had been turned against Pomerania, the rear of the 1st Belorussian Army Group could be considered secure.

A more favorable situation prevailed in the zone of the 1st Ukrainian

Army Group. Its right flank was approaching the Neisse River (which it reached on February 24). It then successfully crushed the enemy in Upper Silesia (in the Oppeln area). Yet this Army Group, too, would still have required considerable time for the complete defeat of the enemy.

An encouraging situation was developing in sectors held by the 4th, 2nd, and 3rd Ukrainian Army Groups. Hitlerite resistance in Budapest was finally crushed on February 13. This, in the opinion of the General Staff, opened up prospects favorable to the development of an offensive in the direction of Olomoutz–Prague and Vienna–Pilsen—the very underbelly of fascist Germany—and made it possible to draw the greatest possible number of enemy forces to this area, including those from the most important central sector. We did not know then that the enemy saw in these [southern] directions of our attack the principal threat to him and that he aimed his crack troops at this sector in the hope of changing the situation here in his favor.

The General Staff continued to work on the plan of operations in Austria and Czechoslovakia, proposing to capture the Pardubice-Brno-Vienna line in a 15–20 day offensive and to force the river Vltava and liberate Prague on the 40–45th day. The Soviet advance in those directions would deprive fascist Germany simultaneously of its major coal mining areas (Moravska Ostrava), oil fields (western Hungary), and iron ore fields (Linz), which, together with the loss of the Silesian industrial area and the agricultural areas of East Prussia, would undermine considerably the economic foundations of the enemy's military potential.

With regard to the further course of the war, estimates were based on the most unfavorable circumstances possible, i.e., on the eventuality that the Allies would not be able to overcome German troop defenses. It was considered possible, in such a case, that the enemy would resort to a withdrawal of considerable numbers of troops from the Western Front and would transfer them to the East to defend the capital of the fascist state. . . .

The General Staff's work in planning the final strikes was complicated to the extreme by the subjective and categorical decision made by Stalin as to the special role of the 1st Belôrussian Army Group. This made it particularly difficult for General of the Army A. I. Antonov, who had assumed the arduous and responsible position of Chief of the General Staff on February 19.

It was extremely difficult to capture a city as large as Berlin, which was intensely prepared to defend itself, with a single Army Group, even one as strong as the 1st Belorussian. The situation urgently required that at least the 1st Belorussian and 1st Ukrainian Army Groups be aimed against Berlin. At the same time, of course, it was necessary to avoid somehow a frontal assault of scant effect by the main forces. Therefore, the January idea of the General Staff and the Army Group commanders— to take Berlin by means of an enveloping strike of the 1st Belorussian Army Group from the north and northwest and a double enveloping strike of the 1st Ukrainian Army Group from the southwest and the west—was charted on General Antonov's map. The troops of the Army Groups were to link up in the Brandenburg-Potsdam area. In this way Berlin would not only be encircled by an interior ring but by an exterior one as well, which would permit the repulsion of any possible counter-activities by German troops from the west and southwest. Should the Hitlerites succeed for some reason in restoring their defensive line west of Berlin, we would naturally have to continue our advance until their final defeat.

Subsequent events eliminated the question with regard to the actions of our allies. Slowly and cautiously, they moved ahead. During February and March 1945, Allied armies pushed the enemy back beyond the Rhine, and in some places they established bridgeheads on the Rhine and began their preparations for operations east of this river.

On the Soviet-German front, the battle's fierceness did not abate but, on the contrary, increased. Many important events took place in February and March. In eastern Pomerania, the forces of the 2nd and part of the 1st Belorussian Army Groups routed the enemy and eliminated the threat of a flank strike from the north into the rear of the armies which were aimed at Berlin.[26] At the same time, a bloody battle was successfully waged by us to extend the bridgehead on the Oder, west of Kuestrin. Soviet troops were 60 km. away from the German capital.

Armies of the 1st Ukrainian Army Group's right wing surrounded and destroyed over five German divisions in Upper Silesia and, forcing the others back into the Sudetenland, took up a position favorable to launching strikes against Dresden and Prague. Notable successes were also achieved by the forces of the 4th Ukrainian Army Group in the Carpathian Mountains.

Combat operations in western Hungary, in the direction of Vienna, had exceptionally important consequences. Despite generally unfavorable conditions, the enemy tried in this sector to effect a radical change of the situation in his favor. To this end, he concentrated all possible re-serves here and launched a counteroffensive against the 3rd Ukrainian Army Group in the area of Lake Balaton. The extremely fierce Battle of Balaton lasted ten days. The enemy attempt to capture the initiative failed. Literally the day after the battle in the area of Lake Balaton ended, our offensive against Vienna was launched.[27] Supreme Headquarters had warned the commander of the 3rd Ukrainian Army Group in advance that the 9th Guards Army had to be kept free from defensive operations, since it was earmarked for the offensive against the Austrian capital. This made it possible for the troops of both the 2nd and the 3rd Ukrainian Army Groups to push forward immediately. On April 13, Vienna was liberated, and our troops moved farther to the west.

Our Allies used the final days of March to force the Rhine and to develop their offensive simultaneously into the central part of Germany and Bavaria. Subsequent plans called for linking up with the Soviet army and splitting up the German forces. On March 28, the Soviet Supreme Command was informed of this plan by General Eisenhower, Commander in Chief of the combined Anglo-American forces. The plan grew out of decisions adopted at the Crimean Conference of the heads of state of the three principal Allied powers.[28]

The Allies were now moving ahead faster than before. In the Ruhr they surrounded a large German grouping which was then split up and which soon thereafter ceased to resist. The main Anglo-American forces, encountering weak opposition, moved east toward the Elbe and toward the Baltic coast in the Luebeck area. There remained no doubt whatsoever that the Allies intended to capture Berlin before us, even though, according to the Yalta Agreements, the city fell within the zone designated for occupation by Soviet troops. As we learned from the memoirs of the late Churchill, he in every way urged Roosevelt and Eisenhower to seize the German capital. . . .[29]

At the end of March all fundamental considerations with regard to the Berlin operation were worked out. . . . Therefore, as soon as it became clear that the Allies were striving to be the first to capture Berlin, the commanders of the 1st Belorussian and 1st Ukrainian Army Groups were immediately summoned to Moscow.

On March 31 the General Staff considered a plan of operations for the Army Groups together with their commanders, and an agreement was reached on all its details. Marshal Konev became very agitated concerning the demarcation line with his neighbor on the right, for it did not give him the possibility to strike at Berlin. No one in the General Staff, however, could remove this obstacle.

On the following day, April 1, 1945, the plan for the Berlin operation was reviewed at Supreme Headquarters. The situation on the front and the operations of the Allies and their plans were reported in detail. During the conference at Supreme Headquarters, Stalin concluded that it was necessary to take Berlin in the shortest possible time; and, therefore, the time remaining to prepare the operation was extremely curtailed. It was necessary to begin not later than April 16 and to finish everything in not more than 12 to 15 days.

The Army Group commanders agreed with these conclusions, and they assured Supreme Headquarters that the troops would be ready in time. After this the plan of the offensive, coordinated with the Army Group commanders, was discussed. The Chief of the General Staff, in reporting the plan, remarked that the demarcation line between Army Groups precluded direct participation by the troops of the 1st Ukrainian Army Group in the battle for the city, a factor which might adversely affect the time required to accomplish the mission. Marshal Konev spoke against such a demarcation line and emphasized the advisability of directing part of the forces of the 1st Ukrainian Army Group, particularly its tank armies, toward the southwest outskirts of Berlin. Apparently, Stalin understood that the grounds on which the demarcation line was drawn between the Army Groups were insufficient, and, wishing to take Berlin as quickly as possible, he solved the problem in his own way—he neither repudiated his earlier idea entirely, nor did he agree with the General Staff and the commander of the 1st Ukrainian Army Group. Without saying a word, he brought the demarcation line on the map of the plan up to the settlement of Luebben, 60 km. southeast of the city; and, stopping there, he crossed out that part of the line which cut off the 1st Ukrainian Army Group from Berlin. "Whoever reaches Berlin first—let him take it," he announced to us later.[30]

Such was the origin of the specific demarcation line between the 1st Belorussian and 1st Ukrainian Army Groups in the Berlin operation. This line did not continue into the full depth of the offensive but came to an end at the southeast approaches to the city. The General Staff was satisfied with such a turn of events, since that accursed line had not given us any peace of mind for more than two months. Marshal Konev raised no objection either, for this also suited him. Events developed in such a way that both Army Groups took Berlin.

Marshal V. I. Chuikov
The Costly Delay

IN EIGHTEEN DAYS of continuous fighting, we [Zhukov's 1st Belorussian Army Group] advanced more than 500 km. and made a strategic thrust that was enormous in scope and remarkable for its swiftness. And if Supreme Headquarters and the headquarters of the Army Groups had orga-

V. I. Chuikov, "Konets tret'ego reikha," *Oktiabr'*, 1964, No. 4, pp. 128–32.

nized supply as they should have and had succeeded in bringing the necessary quantities of ammunition, fuel, and food up to the Oder; and if our aviation had succeeded in moving up to airfields near the Oder; and if the pontoon-bridge building units had provided crossings for the troops across the Oder, then our four Armies—the 5th Assault, the 8th Guards, and 1st and 2d Tank—could have developed the offensive against Berlin further in the beginning of February. They could have gone another 80–100 km. and completed this gigantic operation by taking the German capital from the march.

The situation favored us. Naturally, the Hitlerite divisions that were tied down by the offensive operations of our troops in Courland, in East Prussia, and in the Budapest area could not quickly come to the aid of the Berlin garrison. The divisions that Hitler had transferred from the Ardennes Forest, on the other hand, were still not ready for active operations. I am certain that the 1st Belorussian and 1st Ukrainian Army Groups could have assigned an additional three to four Armies each, which could have joined us in a resolute advance on the main military and political center of fascism—Berlin. And the capture of Berlin determined the outcome of the war. Of course, this would have been fraught with great risk. But what military operation is without risk? In the given circumstances success depended chiefly on the timely and adequate supply of ammunition and fuel. . .

Of course, during the organization of the operation on the Vistula, it was not only difficult but, in my estimation, simply impossible to foresee the development of events at the front. Nonetheless, military leaders and headquarters should be able to assess the situation rapidly and to take the overall political and strategic situation into account in order to make correct decisions in the course of the actual operation. The basic prerequisite for this is close contact between the General Staff and headquarters of the Army Groups and possibly even of the Armies. Staff officers must constantly keep a finger on the "pulse" of the fighting and request an evaluation of the situation from lower-echelon commanders in good time. It is apparent that we did not have this kind of reciprocal communications at the time. Everyone waited for Stalin to say what should be done next.

In the course of an operation as extensive and deep as the Vistula-Oder operation, it was of course very difficult to prepare what was in essence an additional new operation—the offensive against Berlin, i.e., to allocate and to bring large forces up to the Oder after supplying them with everything necessary. But all the same, I believe that it would have been possible to organize such a new operation against Berlin. After all, the 1st Belorussian Army Group succeeded in allocating two tank and three combined-arms Armies with large support elements for the Pomeranian operation in February 1945.[31]

Was not our Supreme High Command being overly cautious in its fear that the Hitlerite troops of Army Group Vistula would strike from Pomerania to the south? I think that it would have been more correct to throw five Armies from the 1st Belorussian Army Group against Berlin, instead of sending them to the north. And to reinforce them by three or four Armies which the 1st Ukrainian Army Group could doubtless have allocated. And then the fate of Berlin—and of all fascist Germany with it—could have been decided as early as February.

All these considerations make it possible for me to assert:

that we had enough forces to continue the Vistula-Oder operation all the way up to the storming of Berlin;

that the fears for the right flank of the 1st Belorussian Army Group were superfluous, since the enemy did not have sufficient reserves with which to launch a serious counterblow (this is acknowledged, incidentally, by Guderian himself);[32]

that the planned enemy strike from the Stettin area could not have been carried off earlier than February 15, and even then with insignificant forces;

that a resolute offensive against Berlin in the first half of February with the strength of seven or eight Armies, including two or three tank Armies, could have frustrated the enemy thrust from the Stettin area and continued the movement to the west:

that in the beginning of February Hitler had neither sufficient forces and matériel to defend the capital of Germany nor prepared fortified lines of defense. Consequently, the road to Berlin was essentially open.

It was indeed difficult to supply the matériel for the Berlin operation. Nonetheless, the offensive against Pomerania with the turn to the east, to Gdynia, required no fewer forces and no less matériel.

I repeat that the capture of Berlin in February 1945 would have meant the end of the war. And the losses could have been considerably fewer than those we sustained in April.

The reader would be justified in asking why we, the generals to whom command of the Armies was entrusted, did not ourselves move ahead and, in so doing, carry along with us the higher command.

On February 2, 1945 headquarters of the 1st Belorussian Army Group issued an order in which—referring to the instructions of Supreme Headquarters—it directed that two zones of defense be set up within the framework of the Armies' operations in order to secure the territory occupied by the troops of the Army Group. Thus, Supreme Headquarters was orienting the troops toward the defense of occupied territory. In the face of the decision by Supreme Headquarters and the order of the Army Group command to revert to the defensive, an advance against Berlin by any of us would have been regarded as failure to obey an order.

Two days later, on February 4, Marshal Zhukov, commander of the 1st Belorussian Army Group, indicated the forthcoming actions in an operational directive: "It is the mission of the Army Group in the next six days to consolidate achieved successes through active operations, to move up all lagging units, to lay in supplies for two refuelings and two combat munitions units, and to take Berlin with a lightning thrust on February 15–16, 1945."

These two documents, which contradicted each other on the key question, served to disorient the troops. Marshal Zhukov's instructions of February 4 would have been preferable. We were unable to stockpile two combat munitions units and two refuelings in the space of six days, however. It was impossible to bring up such a quantity of goods from Army Group depots which were located along the Vistula. During the last week we did not receive a single shell or a single ounce of fuel from the Army Group depots. To state it simply, the Army Group command was very late in arriving at a decision on the necessity to launch a rapid assault. Such a decision should already have been taken during the course of the operation when our troops had crushed the enemy on the Vistula or, at the latest, when the Armies of the two Army Groups reached the Schneidemuehl-Poznan'-Breslau line.[33]

Guderian writes about this period as follows: "On the same day (this was January 27, 1945—V. Ch.) the transfer of Sixth Panzer Army to the East began. . . . I now proposed to Hitler that all available forces be assembled in two groups east of Berlin, one in the Glogau-Cottbus area, the other in Pomerania, east of the Oder. . . . But Hitler clung to his original plan, which was not to use these forces to defend Germany and, in particular, the German capital, but to employ them in an offensive in Hungary."

Guderian's statements attest to the extent to which the main—Berlin—direction was weakly covered at the end of January and beginning of February 1945. Of course, our command did not know of the disorder and vacillation in Hitler's General Headquarters; nonetheless, the course of events and the situation in other sectors of the front indicated that delay in the launching by our troops of an offensive against Berlin would be fraught with very unpleasant consequences for us.

Already from the Lodz line or, at the very latest, from the Poznan' line, Supreme Headquarters should have thought the situation through and assessed it properly. It could have had at its disposal five to six fully equipped Armies supplied with fuel and ammunition, which it could have hurled against Berlin without delay on February 3–5 from the Oder River base of operations. There was no reason to doubt the success of this—in about ten days Berlin would have been taken.

Miscalculations in the planning of the Vistula-Oder operation were made from the very beginning. According to the plan of Supreme Head-quarters, the troops were to reach the Lodz-Kutno line on the tenth or twelfth day of the operation. In fact, the troops reached this line on the seventh day. This was very indicative and dictated the need for re-examination and correction of previous estimates. An analysis of the situa-tion would have made it possible to define the speed of the advance and the troops' missions more precisely.

The Vistula-Oder operation is called a "cleaving" operation. This is only partly true. We could have brought this cleavage right up to Ber-lin. The lag of the 2nd Belorussian Army Group, which was hammering the enemy's East Prussia grouping and could not simultaneously develop the offensive against Pomerania, gave the impression that the right flank of the 1st Belorussian Army Group was open. It was this that prompted Supreme Headquarters to order the 1st Belorussian Army Group to re-vert to the defensive in the beginning of February. Instead of the 1st and 2nd Tank Armies moving on Berlin, in February they had to make their way from the Kuestrin region northward toward Kolberg and Cammin and then to the east—to Gdynia and the mouth of the Vistula. It was, so to speak, "an offensive with a turn to the rear."

For the sake of objectivity it must be said that Marshal G. K. Zhukov, commander of the 1st Belorussian Army Group, had properly assessed the situation in instructing his troops to consolidate the successes they had won and then to "take Berlin on February 15–16, 1945 with a light-ning thrust."

On February 4, he arrived at the headquarters of the 69th Army and called all Army commanders to a conference. Berzarin, Kolpakchi, Katukov, Bogdanov, and this author arrived. We sat down at a table, unfolded maps, and began discussing the offensive against Berlin. I was seated next to Zhukov, close to the telephones. In the heat of the dis-cussion, the telephone rang. It was Stalin calling Zhukov. I became an involuntary party to this conversation. I shall relate it from memory:

STALIN: "Where are you? What are you doing?"

ZHUKOV: "I am at Kolpakchi's headquarters. All commanders of the Group's Armies have gathered here. We are planning the opera-tion against Berlin."

STALIN: "You are wasting your time. After first consolidating on the Oder, you must turn as many forces as possible to the north, to Pomerania and crush the enemy's Army Group Vistula together with Rokossovskii."

Further, Zhukov was instructed to present his views on this score as soon as possible.

Georgii Konstantinovich hung up the receiver, rose from the table, and, saying good-bye to us, went to his headquarters. We understood that the offensive against Berlin was being postponed for an indefinite period.

From that moment on, transports with ammunition and fuel were turned from the central—Berlin—direction to the north, to Pomerania. The support units of the Armies, 70 km. away from Berlin, also went north and then eastward to the mouth of the Vistula.

To this very day I do not understand why Marshal Zhukov, as First Deputy Supreme Commander in Chief and as someone who knew the situation perfectly, did not attempt to convince Stalin of the necessity of waging the offensive against Berlin instead of Pomerania. All the more so since Zhukov was not alone in his view; he was well aware of the mood of the officers and the troops. Why then did he agree with Stalin without a murmur?

Marshal G. K. Zhukov
On the Berlin Axis

SUPREME HEADQUARTERS thought that future operations of the troops of the 1st Belorussian Army Group after reaching the Bydgoszcz-Poznan' line could be decided later, depending on how the situation was developing at the time. The troops of the 1st Belorussian Army Group, however, required much less time to carry out their mission than was foreseen by Supreme Headquarters. By as early as January 23, the right flank had seized Bydgoszcz and had developed the offensive to the northwest toward Schneidemuehl and Deutsch-Krone. On January 25 the center of the Army Group surrounded a large grouping of enemy forces in Poznan', and the left flank, acting in close coordination with the 1st Ukrainian Army Group, reached the area around Iarotsin.

Stalin telephoned me in the middle of the day on January 25. After listening to an estimate of the situation, he asked me what I intended

G. K. Zhukov, "Na berlinskom napravlenii," *Voenno-istoricheskii zhurnal*, 1965, No. 6, pp. 12–22.

to do. I answered that since the enemy was demoralized and no longer able to offer serious resistance, it had been decided to continue the offensive with the aim of reaching the Oder. The main axis of advance was to be toward Kuestrin where we would try to seize a bridgehead. The right flank of the Army Group was to deploy to the north and northwest against the enemy's East Pomerania grouping, which did not present any great immediate danger.

Stalin said: "When you reach the Oder, you will have separated yourself by over 150 km. from the 2nd Belorussian Army Group's flank. This cannot be permitted now. You must wait until the 2nd Belorussian Army Group finishes operations in East Prussia and regroups its forces on the other side of the Vistula."

When I asked when the 2nd Belorussian Army Group would finish its operation and regrouping on the other side of the Vistula, Stalin answered: "In about 10–15 days." "Bear in mind," he added, "the 1st Ukrainian Army Group is now unable to move any farther and to protect your left flank since it will be busy for some time liquidating the enemy in the area around Oppeln and Katowice."

I asked the Supreme Commander in Chief not to stop the advance of the Army Group since later it would be more difficult for us to overcome the Meseritz fortified area.[34] I also asked him to strengthen our sector with an additional army for the purpose of protecting our right flank. He promised to think about it, but we didn't receive any answer that day.

On January 26 reconnaissance units of the 1st Guards Tank Army reached the Meseritz fortified area and captured a large group of prisoners. From interrogations we learned that German troops had not yet occupied many sectors of the fortified area. German units were still in the process of moving to this area.

On the basis of this information the Army Group command arrived at a decision to accelerate movement to the Oder by the main forces of the Army Group and to try to seize from the march the build-up areas on the west bank. In order to provide reliable protection in the event of possible enemy blows from East Pomerania against the main forces of the Army Group (1st and 2nd Guards Tank Armies, 5th Assault Army, and the main forces of the 8th Guards and the 69th and 33rd Armies) which were moving toward the Oder, it was decided to direct to the north and northwest in turn the 3rd Assault Army, the 1st Polish Army, the 47th and 61st Armies, and the 2nd Cavalry Corps. Part of the forces of the 8th Guards and the 1st Guards Tank Armies were left to destroy the garrison in Poznan'. At this time it was thought that not more than 20,000 troops were surrounded there, but later there proved to be actually 60,000, and the battle in the fortified city continued until February 23.[35]

According to our calculations the enemy could not organize a counterblow from Pomerania prior to the time the troops of our Army Group reached the Oder, and in case of serious danger we could still succeed in regrouping part of our troops from the Oder for the purpose of striking the enemy grouping in Pomerania. This is what eventually happened.

After many conversations Stalin agreed with the proposal of the Army Group command while ordering us to give thorough consideration to our right flank, but he refused to assign additional forces. The concern of the Supreme Commander in Chief about reliable protection for our right flank was completely justified. As the course of subsequent events proved, the threat of blows from East Pomerania constantly grew.

The offensive developed rapidly. The main forces of the Army Group, after destroying isolated enemy units and breaking his resistance in the Meseritz fortified region, brilliantly completed its march to the Oder on February 3 and seized a small bridgehead on the west bank in the area of Kuestrin. . . .

It seems to me appropriate to explain in more detail one question which is being raised at the present time by many who are writing their memoirs, particularly Marshal V. I. Chuikov: Why did the command element of the 1st Belorussian Army Group, after reaching the Oder in the first days of February, not secure permission from Supreme Headquarters to continue the offensive toward Berlin without stopping?

In his recollections, published in the magazines *Oktiabr'* and *Novaia i noveishaia istoriia*,[36] he asserts that: "Berlin could have been taken as early as February. This, naturally would have brought an earlier end to the war."

In our press many comrades have expressed their objections to Comrade Chuikov's point of view. . . . I feel constrained to say that with regard to the offensive toward Berlin everything was not as simple as V. I. Chuikov thinks. On January 26 when it became clear that the enemy could not contain our offensive on the fortified approaches to the Oder, we made a preliminary proposal to Supreme Headquarters, the essence of which amounted to the following: By January 30 the troops of the Army Group should reach Berlinkhen-Landsberg-Gretts line, bring up the rear, replenish supplies, and on the morning of February 1–2 continue the offensive in order to force the Oder from the march and subsequently to develop a fast-moving offensive toward Berlin, aiming mainly to envelop the city simultaneously from the northeast, north, and northwest. On January 27 Supreme Headquarters approved this proposal. On January 28 a suggestion was presented to Supreme Headquarters by the commander of the 1st Ukrainian Army Group, Marshal I. S. Konev. He proposed to destroy the enemy's Breslau grouping and by February 25–28 to reach the Elbe, while the right flank of his Army Group, in coordination with the 1st Belorussian Army Group, would take Berlin. On January 29 Supreme Headquarters also approved this proposal.

In fact, as V. I. Chuikov asserts, at that time the enemy had limited forces on the approaches to Berlin, and the defense was rather weak. As has already been stated above, however, in the first days of February there began to materialize the serious danger of a counterblow from East Pomerania against the flank and rear of the main force of the Army Group which was moving toward the Oder. This is what German Field Marshal Keitel said about this after the war:

> In February and March 1945 a counteroffensive against the troops advancing on Berlin was contemplated, using the base of operations in Pomerania for this purpose. It was planned that troops of Army Group Vistula, after remaining in covered positions in the area around Graundenz, would break the Russian front from the rear and advance along the valley of the Varta and Netze to Kuestrin.

This design is confirmed also by the former Chief of the General Staff of German ground forces, Colonel General Guderian. In his book he writes:

> The German command intended to strike a powerful counterblow with lightning speed, using the forces of Army Group Vistula, before strong Russian forces reached the front and before the Russians guessed our intentions.[37]

The cited evidence given by military leaders of fascist Germany leaves no doubt that the danger from the direction of East Pomerania was real. The Soviet command discovered the intentions of the enemy in time, however, and took the necessary measures to counteract them.

In the beginning of February, the 2nd and 11th German Armies were operating in the area between the Oder and Vistula rivers; they consisted of 16 infantry, 4 tank, and 3 motorized divisions, 4 brigades, and 8 combat groups. According to information supplied by our reconnaissance, they continued to be reinforced. Moreover, the 3rd Tank Army was deployed in the area around Stettin. The fascist German command could use this army on the approaches to Berlin as well as to reinforce the East Pomerania grouping (which actually happened). Could the Soviet command take the risk of continuing the offensive with the main forces of the Army Group in the direction of Berlin when a serious danger threatened from the north? V. I. Chuikov writes:

. . . as far as risk is concerned, in war it is often necessary to take risks. But in this case the risk was completely justified. In the Vistula-Oder operation our troops had already advanced more than 500 km., and from the Oder to Berlin there remained only 60–80 km.

Of course, it would have been possible to ignore this danger and to send both tank Armies and three or four combined-arms Armies straight for Berlin and to reach the city. But the enemy could easily have broken through our cover from the north, reached the crossings over the Oder, and placed the Army Group in the Berlin area in a very difficult position. History teaches that one must take risks but never go overboard. . . .

"If one evaluates objectively the strength of the grouping of Hitler's troops in Pomerania," says Comrade Chuikov, "then one must conclude that any threat to our strike grouping which was moving toward Berlin could easily have been contained by the troops of the 2nd Belorussian Army Group." Facts refute this assertion. At first it was intended to carry out the mission of destroying the enemy in East Pomerania using just these forces of the 2nd Belorussian Army Group, but they proved to be far from adequate. The offensive of the 2nd Belorussian Army Group, which started on February 10, went very slowly. For ten days the troops of this Army Group were able to move forward only 50–70 km. At this time the enemy launched a counterblow in the area to the south of Stargard and even succeeded in pushing our troops back and advancing 8–12 km. in a southerly direction. After evaluating the deteriorating situation, Supreme Headquarters decided to turn the four combined-arms and two tank Armies of the 1st Belorussian Army Group against Hitler's troops in East Pomerania. By this time these troops totaled forty divisions. As is known, the combat actions of the two Army Groups succeeded in destroying the East Pomerania grouping only toward the end of March. This is the kind of tough nut it was to crack.[38]

V. I. Chuikov thinks that for the offensive against Berlin in February 1945 the 1st Belorussian and 1st Ukrainian Army Groups could have allocated 8–10 Armies, including 3–4 tank Armies. With this, too, one cannot agree. In the beginning of February, of the eight combined-arms and two tank Armies of the 1st Belorussian Army Group, there were only four understrength Armies (5th Assault, 8th Guards, 69th and 33rd) on the axis of advance toward Berlin; the remaining forces of the Army Group we were obliged to turn in the direction of East Pomerania. As far as the 1st Ukrainian Army Group is concerned, in the period February 8–24 it was conducting an offensive operation to the northwest of Breslau. In this offensive the main forces of the Army Group (four combined-arms and two tank Armies, and the 2nd Air Army) were taking part. The enemy, after drawing up considerable forces, offered very stubborn resistance. In 17 days of offensive action, units of the Army Group moved ahead 100 km., reaching the Neisse river. Attempts to force the river and to develop the offensive did not meet with success, and troops of the Army Group reverted to the defensive.[39]

It is also necessary to bear in mind the fact that during the Vistula-Oder operation our units suffered serious losses, and by February 1 the strength in our rifle divisions averaged about 5,500 men and in the 8th Guards Army from 3,800 to 4,800 men. In the two tank Armies there were 740 tanks (in the tank brigades there was an average of 40 tanks, and in many of them there were only 15–20 tanks). The situation was similar in the 1st Ukrainian Army Group.[40]

Thus, in February 1945 neither the 1st Ukrainian nor the 1st Belorussian Army Groups was able to carry out the Berlin operation. It is just as dangerous to overestimate the strength of one's own troops as it is to underestimate the strength and capabilities of the enemy. The many-sided experience gained in war teaches us this lesson, and we must not ignore it.

And, finally, the difficulty of providing supplies to troops who advance more than 500 km. in 20 days of offensive action should not be forgotten. It is natural that with such fast forward movement the rear services will fall behind and troops will experience a shortage of supplies and especially of fuel. Also, the air force was not successful in shifting to forward bases. Comrade Chuikov had not analyzed all the complicated aspects of the situation in the rear when he wrote:

. . . If Supreme Headquarters and the headquarters of the Army Groups had organized supply as they should have and had succeeded in bringing the necessary quantities of ammunition, fuel, and food up to the Oder; and if our aviation had succeeded in moving up to airfields near the Oder; and if the pontoon-bridge building units had provided crossings for the troops at the Oder, then our four Armies—the 5th Assault, 8th Guards, and 1st and 2nd Tank—could have developed the offensive against Berlin further in the beginning of February. They could have covered another 80–100 km. and completed this gigantic operation by taking the German capital from the march.

Such reasoning with allusions to "if's" should not be entertained seriously, even by one who is merely writing his memoirs. But the very admission by V. I. Chuikov that re-supply was disrupted and aviation and pontoon-bridge units fell behind is evidence of the fact that under such circumstances it would have been the purest adventurism to undertake a decisive assault on Berlin.

V. I. Chuikov writes:

On February 4 the commander of the 1st Belorussian Army Group assembled Army Commanders Berzarin, Kolpakchi, Katukov, Bogdanov, and myself at a meeting at the 69th Army headquarters where he himself was present. We were already sitting at the table discussing the plan for an offensive against Berlin when the telephone rang. I was sitting almost alongside and heard the telephone conversation very well. Stalin was calling. He asked Zhukov where he was and what he was doing. The Marshal answered that he had assembled commanders of the Armies at the headquarters of Kolpakchi's Army and was working out with them the plan for the offensive against Berlin. After listening to the report, Stalin suddenly and, as I gathered, quite unexpectedly for the commander of the Army Group, demanded that he drop this and work out plans for destroying the German Army Group Vistula in Pomerania.

But no such meeting ever occurred on February 4 at the headquarters of the 69th Army.

On February 4–5, I was at the headquarters of the 61st Army which had deployed on our right flank for action against the enemy's grouping of forces in Pomerania. Therefore, the conversation on the telephone with Stalin of which V. I. Chuikov writes did not take place either.

Further, V. I. Chuikov asserts that the question of possibly taking Berlin in February 1945 was raised by him first during a military conference in Berlin in 1945 but was not discussed extensively at that time because it was in essence critical of Stalin. In fact, this question was brought up at the conference not by Comrade Chuikov, but by a representative of the General Staff, Major General S. M. Eniukov. Chuikov, as I remember and as is apparent from the stenographic record of his speech, made no reference to this question.

Now a few words about the Berlin operation itself. The details of the concept and plan for the operation were being worked out at Supreme Headquarters during the entire Vistula-Oder operation. At first Supreme Headquarters intended to begin the Berlin operation simultaneously with three Army Groups, but the 2nd Belorussian Army Group, which had to redeploy its forces from the area around Danzig and Gdynia to the lower reaches of the Oder following the completion of the action in East Pomerania, could not revert to the offensive with a forcing of the Oder before April 20.

Bearing in mind the developing military-political situation, Supreme Headquarters decided to begin the Berlin operation with two Army Groups not later than April 16. The commander of the 1st Ukrainian Army Group, Marshal I. S. Konev, and I were present at Supreme Headquarters for the last time at the beginning of April. At that meeting final approval was given to the plans of the Army Groups. The offensive on the main axis of advance and the capture of Berlin were assigned to the troops of the 1st Belorussian Army Group. The 1st Ukrainian Army Group was to develop the offensive from the Neisse River with the mission of destroying the enemy south of Berlin and isolating main forces of Army Group Center from the Berlin grouping of forces, in this way supporting the assault by the 1st Belorussian Army Group from the south.

Moreover, during this meeting at Supreme Headquarters Stalin gave instructions to Marshal I. S. Konev: In case of stubborn resistance on the part of the enemy on the eastern approaches to Berlin and possible delay in the offensive of the 1st Belorussian Army Group, the 1st Ukrainian Army Group was to be ready to strike a blow against Berlin from the south.

In connection with the fact that the 2nd Belorussian Army Group could begin the offensive on the western bank of the Oder no earlier than April 20, the 1st Belorussian Army Group during the initial, more difficult days of the operation was to attack with an open right flank. The enemy tried to take advantage of this.

"To the General Staff," stated General Jodl during his interrogation, "it was clear that the battle for Berlin would be decided on the Oder, and therefore the main mass of troops of the 9th Army which was defending Berlin was sent to the forward edge of the battle area. It was intended that reserves, which were being rapidly formed, would concentrate in the area north of Berlin in order to deliver subsequently a counterblow at the flank of Marshal Zhukov's troops."

The extraordinary and exceedingly complicated operation against Berlin demanded exceptionally careful preparation at all Army Group and Army levels. The troops of the Army Group were faced with the task of breaking through a continuous, deeply echeloned zone of strong defensive lines beginning at the Oder itself and ending in the strongly fortified city of Berlin.

During the course of the entire war we had never had to take such a strongly fortified city as Berlin. Its total area was equal to almost 900 sq. km. The subways and the extensive underground network afforded enemy troops flexibility of movement. The city itself and its environs had been carefully prepared for stubborn defense. Each street, square, crossroad, house, canal, and bridge was a component part of the overall defenses of the city.[41]

On six occasions our reconnaissance aircraft took photographs of Berlin, all approaches to it, and the defensive zones. Based on the results of the photographs, captured documents, and prisoner interrogations, detailed sketches, plans, and maps were drawn up and furnished to all command and staff levels down to and including company. Engineer units prepared an exact scale replica of the city and its suburbs for use in studying problems connected with the final storming of Berlin.

From April 5 to 7, we held a conference and war-gamed the operation on maps and mock-ups. Participating were the Army commanders and chiefs of staff, members of the military councils of the Armies, the chief of political administration of the Army Group, the artillery commanders of the Armies and of the Army Group, the commanders of all corps, and the chiefs of all service branches of the Army Group. The chief of the rear services of our Army Group, who had carefully studied all problems involved in providing supplies for the operation, was also present. From April 8 to 14, war-gaming at the Army Group level was supplemented by more detailed war-gaming and exercises at the level of Army, corps, division, and smaller units of all arms of the service as well as the air force.

In view of the Army Group's extremely extended lines of communication as well as the expenditure of large amounts of supplies in the unforeseen East Pomerania operation, at the beginning of the Berlin operation the Army Group did not have the needed quantities of supplies. Heroic efforts were required of our men in the rear services. As before, they measured up to what was expected of them.

In the process of preparing for the operation a question arose as to what additional measures could be taken to stun and demoralize the enemy. Bearing in mind the fact that troops are more impressionable at night, it was decided to launch the blow against the enemy's front two hours before dawn. In order to avoid possible accidents it was planned to illuminate the enemy's position and the targets under attack with 140 anti-aircraft searchlights. During the war-gaming at the Army Group level, the effectiveness of searchlights was demonstrated. All participants unanimously agreed to their use.

[*Editor's note:* The following is an excerpt from Marshal V. I. Chuikov's memoirs in which he describes the "effectiveness" of this new device under actual combat conditions:

The attack was being carried out in strict accordance with the plan, but life made its own corrections. The searchlight beams ran into a solid curtain of gunpowder, smoke, and earth. The most they could penetrate this curtain was 150–200 meters, no more. As has already been noted, the attack was begun before sunrise while it was still dark, and the searchlights were to provide the light. However, from my command-observation post, which was situated at elevation 81.5, several hundred meters from the row of searchlights, we could not observe the battlefield. We could only guess what was happening there from the shell bursts. Later, the gunpowder smoke enshrouded our elevation as well. Nor did the searchlights help the advancing troops. The searchlights were periodically turned on and off, and it seemed to the attackers that they were confronted by obstacles;

they lost their orientation. After all, human vision is not adapted to sudden changes from darkness to light. Even when an electric light is turned on in a dark room, a person remains blinded for an instant. When the light is turned off or when he goes out into the darkness from a lighted space, he also sees virtually nothing until his eyes get accustomed to the darkness. This is why the searchlights did not play the part in the attack that Marshal G. K. Zhukov, the author of this suggestion, hoped they would. They even brought harm rather than good. In many sectors, the sub-units stopped before brooks and canals which intersected the Oder Valley, deciding to wait for the dawn in order to examine the obstacle they would have to cross.

Subsequently, some historians, including military ones, have tried to represent this expedient of searchlights as virtually one of the principal reasons for the success of the offensive launched from the Oder base of operations. Among the actual participants in this fighting, however, it is unlikely that you will find anyone who would attest to the advantages of this "new weapon." [42]]

The employment of the tank Armies was the subject of serious discussion. Bearing in mind the existence of a strong tactical defensive position on the Seelow Heights, it was decided to commit both tank Armies to the battle after these heights had been seized. Naturally, we did not base our plans on the possibility that our tank Armies would rush into wide operational expanses following the rupture of the tactical defenses, as was the case, for example, in the preceding Vistula-Oder and East Pomerania operations. In the course of the battle, when the force of the blow by Army Group's first echelon proved to be inadequate for rapid reduction of the enemy's defenses, the danger arose that the offensive might be slowed. In the second half of the day on April 16, after taking counsel with the Army commanders, we decided to reinforce the attack of the combined-arms Armies with a powerful blow by all air and tank Armies. The enemy threw all that he could into the battle, but by sunset on April 17 and the morning of April 18, we nevertheless succeeded in shattering the defensive forces on the Seelow Heights and began to move forward. Hitler's generals took large forces from the Berlin defenses, including anti-aircraft artillery, and threw them against our troops. This somewhat slowed the tempo of the offensive. And this is altogether understandable. It was necessary to break the resistance of the fascist German units coming from inside Berlin.[43]

During these days Stalin feared a slowdown in the offensive by our troops. He therefore ordered the commander of the 1st Ukrainian Army Group to deliver a blow against Berlin from the south with part of his forces, as he had foreseen when he approved the plans of the operation at Supreme Headquarters on April 3.[44] After fierce battles on April 20, the enemy's defenses on the approaches to Berlin were shattered. "April 20," stated the commander of the German 56th Tank Corps, General

Weidling, during interrogation, "was the most difficult day for my corps and, probably, for all German units. They suffered huge losses during the preceding battles, were extremely battered and exhausted, and were no longer able to withstand the overwhelming onrush of superior Russian forces."

At 1:50 p.m. on April 20, the long-range artillery of the 79th Rifle Corps of the 3rd Assault Army commanded by Colonel General V. I. Kuznetsov was the first to open fire on Berlin, thereby starting the historic storming of the German capital. On April 21 units of the 3rd Assault, 2nd Guards Tank, and 47th Armies entered the outskirts of Berlin and began the struggle in the city.

In order to demoralize the enemy decisively, to destroy his will to fight, to give maximum help to our weakened combined-arms units, and also to accelerate the reduction of defenses in Berlin itself by all possible means, it was decided to commit the 1st and 2nd Guards Tank Armies together with the 3rd Guards, 5th Assault, and 8th Guards Armies against the city so as to defeat the enemy rapidly with the fire and avalanche effect of tanks. It should be added that at the time there was no space for maneuver, and no specific missions appropriate to the maneuvering capabilities of tank units could be set.

The struggle in Berlin approached its climax. We all wanted to finish off the enemy's grouping of forces in Berlin by May 1 in order to make the holiday for the Soviet people even more joyous. But the enemy, although he was in the last agony, continued to cling to every house, to every cellar, and to every floor and roof. Nevertheless, Soviet troops took block after block, house after house. The troops of Generals V. I. Kuznetsov, N. E. Berzarin, and S. I. Bogdanov drew closer and closer to the center of Berlin. Then came the long-awaited signal from Army Commander V. I. Kuznetsov: The Reichstag was taken and our red banner raised over it.[46]

How many thoughts went through our minds at this happy moment! The fierce battle at Moscow where our troops stood to the death, Stalingrad in ruins but unconquerable, the proud city of Leningrad which withstood long starvation while blockaded, thousands of destroyed villages and cities, many millions of dead Soviet people who had heroically withstood harsh years, the proud victory of the Kursk Salient, and, finally, the most important event for which the Soviet people had borne intense suffering—the complete defeat of fascist Germany, the defeat of fascism, and the glory of our righteous cause.

Marshal I. S. Konev
Strike from the South

ON APRIL 1, 1945 the commander of the 1st Belorussian Army Group, Marshal G. K. Zhukov, and I were summoned to Moscow to Supreme Headquarters. Stalin received us, as usual, in the Kremlin in his big study with the long table and the portraits of Suvorov and Kutuzov on the wall. In addition to Stalin, there were members of the State Defense Committee, the Chief of the General Staff, A. I. Antonov, and the Chief of Operations, S. M. Shtemenko.

We had just greeted each other, when Stalin asked:

"Are you aware of the way the situation is shaping up?"

Zhukov and I answered that we were aware of the situation from the data we had in our Army Groups. Stalin turned to Shtemenko and said:

"Read them the telegram."

Shtemenko read the telegram, the essence of which was the following: the Anglo-American command was preparing an operation to capture Berlin and was aiming to capture it before the Soviet Army. The chief grouping was being formed under the command of Field Marshal Montgomery. The direction of the main strike was planned north of the Ruhr along the shortest route separating the main grouping of the British forces and Berlin. The telegram listed a whole series of preliminary measures being taken by the Allied command—establishment of the grouping, deployment of forces. It ended by saying that, according to all data, the plan to take Berlin before the Soviet army was regarded at Allied Headquarters as entirely feasible, and preparations for its execution were in full swing.[47]

When Shtemenko had finished reading the telegram, Stalin turned to Zhukov and to me.

"Well, who is going to take Berlin, we or the Allies?"

It so happened that I was the first to reply to the question, and I

I. S. Konev, *Sorok piatyi* (Moscow, 1966), pp. 87–204.

said that we were going to take Berlin and that we would take it before the Allies did.

"So that's what you're like," Stalin said with a slight grin and then put this question point blank: "And how will you be able to build up a grouping for it? Your main force is on your southern flank, and apparently you will have to carry out a large-scale regrouping."

I replied:

"Comrade Stalin, you may rest assured that the Army Group will carry out all the necessary measures, and the redeployment for an offensive in the Berlin direction will be accomplished by us on time."

Zhukov spoke next. He reported that the troops were ready to capture Berlin. The 1st Belorussian Army Group, replete with troops and weapons, was by then aimed straight at Berlin and, moreover, was closest to it.

Having heard us both, Stalin said:

"Good. It is necessary for you both to prepare your plans right here in the General Staff in Moscow and to report to Supreme Headquarters when you are ready—say, in a day or two—so as to return to your Army Groups with approved plans in your hands."

We worked a little over twenty-four hours. Zhukov, as commander of the 1st Belorussian Army Group, had come prepared to discuss the main aspects of the forthcoming operation. By the time I had been summoned to Supreme Headquarters, I, too, had formed some ideas about how to redeploy the troops of the 1st Ukrainian Army Group from the southern to the Berlin direction.

Zhukov and I worked separately on our plans in the General Staff, but we discussed some questions that required coordination with the leading officers of the General Staff. We did not, of course, discuss details but strictly fundamental questions, such as the main directions, the planning of the timetable for the operation, and the date of its start. We were especially uneasy over the date for the start of the operation.

In view of Stalin's question as to who was going to take Berlin and the fact that, according to the telegram we had heard, the Allies were already preparing for the Berlin operation, we both realized that the dates of our readiness should be set as early as possible. On this question I had several exchanges of opinions with Zhukov. His chief grouping was basically ready and aimed against the enemy, but with me things were more complicated. After the recent Upper Silesia operation, a considerable part of my forces was still concentrated on the left flank of the Army Group, and this called for urgent and strenuous redeployment.

When on the morning of April 3 we came to Supreme Headquarters prepared to report our plans, the first plan to be examined was that of the 1st Belorussian Army Group, presented by Marshal Zhukov. Stalin made no substantive remarks on that plan. Then I reported on the plan of operations for the 1st Ukrainian Army Group. There were no substantive remarks on my plan either.

We discussed very carefully the starting date of the operation. For my part, I proposed for the 1st Ukrainian Army Group a date that was very close, considering the fact that we had to accomplish major regroupings.

Stalin accepted the date. In putting forward my proposals, I asked Supreme Headquarters to assign the 1st Ukrainian Army Group additional reserves to develop the operation in depth. Stalin agreed to this and said:

"Since the Army Groups in the Baltic area and East Prussia are beginning to get smaller, I can let you have two Armies from the Baltic Army Groups, the 28th and the 31st."

It was immediately estimated whether or not the Armies could arrive and be at the disposal of the 1st Ukrainian Army Group by the date set for the start of the operation. It turned out that the Armies would be unable to arrive by that time: the railways would be unable to transport them. I then suggested that the operation should be started with the available forces before the arrival of these two Armies. The proposal was accepted, and the final date agreed on between the commanders and approved by Supreme Headquarters was April 16.

After approval of the plans the draft directives of Supreme Headquarters to the two Army Groups were read. The drafts had been drawn up with our participation.

I shall mention in passing the practice of drawing up plans and directives that had been established at Supreme Headquarters. As a rule, an Army Group commander not only reported his plan and charted his views on the map, but he also drafted the Supreme Headquarters' directives with the participation of his staff. Starting with the general strategic design of Supreme Headquarters, the Army Group command planned the entire operation in all aspects connected with its execution and singled out the questions that went beyond its competence and entailed assistance from Supreme Headquarters to the Army Group.

Simultaneously, the draft directives were prepared, and their initial form reflected the views of the Army Group itself concerning the execution of the forthcoming operation and assumed that the Army Group would be given appropriate assistance from Supreme Headquarters. The number and nature of corrections in and additions to the draft directives depended on the discussion of the Army Groups' proposals at Supreme Headquarters and how close they were to the final decision. Even today

I find this method of planning worked out during the war rational and fruitful.

The directives to the Army Groups stated that Berlin was to be taken by the 1st Belorussian Army Group. The 1st Ukrainian Army Group was to rout the enemy in the Kottbus area and south of Berlin. In our subsequent offensive in the western and northwestern directions, we were to take the Beelitz-Wittenberg line, that is, a number of points south and southwest of Berlin, and to reach the Elbe no later than the tenth to twelfth day of the operation.

The Army Group was to deal its main blow with five combined-arms and two tank Armies. On the right flank of the Army Group it was proposed to create a density of at least 250 guns per kilometer in the breakthrough sector. For this purpose the Army Group was being reinforced with seven artillery breakthrough divisions. In the center the Army Group was to use two Armies to strike at Dresden and also to advance toward the Elbe. On the left flank the Army Group was to remain on the defensive. From the left flank, the 60th Army of Kurochkin was transferred to the 4th Ukrainian Army Group, which was operating in what may be called the Czechoslovak direction.

Except for these fundamental decisions—the direction of the attack, the composition of the groupings, and the artillery concentration—nothing more was discussed at Supreme Headquarters. Everything connected with the supply of matériel for the operation was handled in the usual manner without any special discussion. Moreover, the Army Group had a sufficient quantity of everything it needed.

Altogether the task of the 1st Ukrainian Army Group was to advance south of Berlin and contribute to its capture, to split the German front in two, and to link up with the Americans. In the course of the Berlin operation it developed that the Armies of the 1st Ukrainian Army Group not only assisted in taking Berlin but together with the troops of the 1st Belorussian Army Group took a direct part in storming it. The question arises: Did Supreme Headquarters envisage such a possibility when the plan for the Berlin operation was approved? If so, who actually envisaged it and to what extent?

My own thoughts at the time were as follows. Under the original plan Berlin was to have been taken by the 1st Belorussian Army Group. But the 1st Ukrainian Army Group's right flank, where our main strike grouping was concentrated, lay in the immediate vicinity of Berlin, just south of it. Who could say then how the operation would unfold, what unexpected developments we should be faced with in the various directions, and what new decisions or changes in the earlier decisions would have to be taken as we went on?

At any rate, I had already allowed for the contingency that a successful advance of our right-flank troops might put us in an advantageous position for a maneuver and an attack on Berlin from the south. I considered it premature to voice these ideas, although I did get the impression that Stalin, too, without saying anything about it, had allowed for such a variant in the long-range plan. I got this impression when, in approving the composition of the groupings and the directions of the attacks, Stalin began to pencil on the map the demarcation line between the 1st Belorussian and the 1st Ukrainian Army Groups. In the draft directives the line ran through Luebben, which was roughly 80 km. southeast of Berlin. He stopped there and went no farther. He did not say anything as he did this, but I think even Marshal Zhukov saw a definite meaning in it. The demarcation line stopped approximately where we were to be by the third day of the operation. From there on (apparently depending on the situation), it was tacitly assumed that the Army Group commanders could show their own initiative.

For me, at any rate, the stop of the demarcation line at Luebben meant that a swift breakthrough and rapid and mobile action on the right flank of our Army Group could subsequently create a situation in which our attack on Berlin from the south could have its advantages.

Was this failure to trace the demarcation line beyond Luebben to be taken as an implied call for competition between the Army Groups? I allow for such a possibility. At any rate, I do not rule it out. You will see why, if you think back twenty years and imagine what Berlin meant to us then and what a passionate desire was felt by all, from general down to private, to see that city with their own eyes and to capture it by force of arms. Of course it was my ardent desire, too. It would, indeed, be strange to say that in the final months of the war we were men bereft of passion. On the contrary, we all were fired with it. . . .

Both Marshal Zhukov and I were in a hurry to get back to the Army Groups, and our planes took off from the Central Airfield in Moscow within a two-minute interval. Each of us in his own Army Group was now to carry out his part of the Berlin operation assigned in the directives of Supreme Headquarters. . . .

In preparing for this extremely important strategic operation, we had to reckon with a number of specific factors, primarily with the probable strength of enemy resistance. Hitler's High Command had concentrated large forces to defend the capital and the approaches to it and had organized defenses in depth with a system of fortifications and all sorts of obstacles on the Oder and the Spree lines and on all the approaches to Berlin—from the east, southeast, south, and north. The very nature of the terrain around Berlin—forests, swamps, numerous rivers, lakes, and canals—presented many additional obstacles. This, like everything else that could complicate our operations, had also to be reckoned with.

Nor could we ignore the fact that Hitler's High Command and the German government persisted in their efforts to split the anti-Hitler coalition and had recently sought separate agreements with our Allies, hoping, should such agreements be reached, to shift troops from the Western to the Eastern Front against us.

As history has shown, the attempts made by Hitler and his associates to conclude separate agreements with our Allies were unsuccessful. At that time, during the war, we did not want to believe our Allies capable of entering into any separate agreements with the German command. But the atmosphere in those days was full not only of facts, but also of rumors, and we had absolutely no right to preclude that contingency.

This circumstance, I would say, lent particular urgency to the Berlin operation. At any rate, we had to take into account the possibility that, faced with a debacle, the Nazi leaders would prefer to surrender Berlin to the Americans and the British, to whom they would open the way, but would continue to fight us savagely to the last man. In planning the forthcoming operation we soberly took this possibility into account.[48] It later became reality, incidentally. Evidence of it, for instance, was the action of General Wenck's 12th Army, which was simply removed from the Western Front, where it was fighting the Allies, and was sent against us to lift the blockade of Berlin. . . .[49]

Then, early in April 1945, the German command had not yet shown its cards, but it was obvious that the Germans would do everything to keep us bogged down outside Berlin as long as possible.

The political calculations of the Germans were based to some extent on purely military considerations and hopes. The German command had indeed done a tremendous job of fortifying the approaches to Berlin and believed it would take our army a long time to overcome all these powerful engineering barriers, which were combined with natural obstacles and a well-organized defense.

The approaches to Berlin were difficult to negotiate. Take, for instance, the Seelow Heights. They would have been an extremely difficult obstacle even without the German army engineering installations there. Berlin itself was a huge, well-built city where practically every house was a ready-made strong point with brick walls from a meter to a meter and a half thick. In short, the German troops defending Berlin still believed they could stop us at Berlin, as we had stopped them at Moscow. This belief was kept alive by Goebbels' propaganda. . . .

The Germans based their plans on protracted action, while we wanted the utmost speed. The entire operation was to be completed within twelve to fifteen days so as to give the enemy no breathing space and to prevent him from prolonging the operation or escaping our blows.

That was how I saw the situation we had to prepare for. We had only twelve days to accomplish a major and complex regrouping of our forces. . . .

While assessing the prospects of the forthcoming operation, I came to the conclusion that after a successful and rapid breakthrough, the 1st Ukrainian Army Group would have better opportunities for large-scale maneuvering than the 1st Belorussian Army Group, which was advancing directly on Berlin.

When, after my return to the Army Group, we set out to plan the forthcoming operation, I deemed it necessary to provide for the possibility of such maneuvering from the outset. I inserted the first paragraph of the Supreme Headquarters' directives in our plan: "No later than ten to twelve days after the start of the operation the Beelitz-Wittenberg line is to be reached and an advance made farther down the Elbe river to Dresden"—and added: "Provision to be made with part of the forces on the Army Group's right flank for aiding the troops of the 1st Belorussian Army Group in the capture of Berlin." . . .

In the Army Group's plan the task of assisting the 1st Belorussian Army Group to capture Berlin was given in general outline. In the order issued to the 3rd Guards Tank Army it was stated specifically: "On the fifth day of the operation, the Trabbin-Zauchwitz area, Treuenbrietzen, Luckenwalde to be captured. Berlin to be attacked from the south by a tank corps reinforced with a rifle division of the 3rd Guards Army."

So even before the start of the operation one tank corps and a rifle division were earmarked for an attack on Berlin from the south.

The break-off of the demarcation line at Luebben had seemed to imply, or suggest, freedom of action close to Berlin. Indeed, how could it have been otherwise? I thought it strange and incomprehensible to advance on my right flank along the very southern outskirts of Berlin and deliberately to leave it untouched—especially in a situation where one could not predict how everything would work out. The decision to be ready to make such an attack seemed clear, comprehensible, and self-evident. . . .

I have seen in Western newspapers erroneous statements that on the first day of the Berlin operation the attack by the two Army Groups— the 1st Belorussian and the 1st Ukrainian—was carried out under a single plan. It is not so. Their operations were coordinated by Supreme Headquarters, while the Army Groups themselves only exchanged information and operational and reconnaissance reports. On the first day of the operation, each of the Army Groups naturally chose its own methods of attack, based on its assessment of the situation.

In the 1st Belorussian Army Group it was decided to carry out a powerful artillery preparation at night and to attack using searchlights. The 1st Ukrainian Army Group chose an entirely different method. We had planned a longer artillery preparation than our neighbors. It was designed to cover two stages—the forcing of the Neisse and the breakthrough of the enemy's main line of defense on the western bank of the river. The idea was to conceal the crossing operation as much as possible, so it was not in our interest to light up the breakthrough zone but to make full use of the darkness. The artillery preparation was to last two hours and thirty-five minutes, of which an hour and forty minutes were for covering the river crossing and forty-five minutes for preparing an attack on the western bank of the Neisse.

During that time we planned to suppress the entire German control and observation system and their artillery and mortar positions. The air force, operating at a still greater depth, was to complete the enemy's rout by concentrating blows against his reserves.[50]

On the eve of the offensive, I went from Breslau to General Pukhov's 13th Army observation post. It was an excellent post with a good field of vision and was located on the outskirts of an old pine forest. Below, immediately before us, was a steep slope to the river. One could see the Neisse and its western bank, although it was a fair distance away. . . .

The smokescreen was laid toward the end of the first phase of the artillery preparation. As far as I could see, it was very successful—powerful, of good density, and just the right altitude. It was laid skillfully by our assault planes. Flying at low altitude and high speed, they laid the smokescreen exactly on the bank of the Neisse. It must be mentioned that they had to lay the smokescreen along a front 390 km. long, no less and no more. This length of the smokescreen to a certain extent misled the enemy about the points where we crossed the Neisse. The smokescreen and the powerful artillery preparation made it very difficult for the enemy to control troops, and it upset their fire system and weakened the stability of their defenses. . . . During the crossing, our planes laid new smokescreens. It was very calm; wind velocity was only half a meter a second, and the smoke floated slowly over the enemy defenses, enveloping the entire Neisse valley, which was what we needed. . . .

Our forward battalions began to cross the Neisse under the cover of the smokescreen at 6:55 a.m., at the end of a forty-minute artillery barrage. The first echelon of our main forces got across very rapidly, within an hour. Immediately after the capture of bridgeheads on the western bank of the Neisse, we began laying bridges. . . . It took fifty minutes to lay light pontoon bridges, two hours to lay bridges for loads of thirty tons, and four or five hours for bridges capable of withstanding sixty tons. Part of the field artillery was drawn across by cable while the forward battalions were crossing.

The first 85mm. guns reached the western bank and were trained to fire point-blank against German tanks some ten or fifteen minutes after the first soldiers had crossed the river. This immediately created a feeling of stability at the initial small bridgeheads. Besides the bridges, we made use of ferries, sending across the first groups of tanks to be used for direct support of the infantry. . . .

Since the tank Armies entering the breakthrough would have to cross several rivers in their advance before the attack, I had categorically forbidden them to use any facilities of their own for crossing the Neisse. According to our plan, the tank Armies were to cross on specially prepared fording facilities and to use their own full and even extra equipment for forcing the next river—the Spree. The Neisse crossing was wholly the responsibility of the Army Group's engineer troops.

From the very outset, the plan provided for the tank Armies' rapid advance deep into the enemy lines. Their long-range blow was to be given every support.

The breakthrough both in the main direction and toward Dresden was successful. After fierce fighting, part of the 3rd and 5th Guards Armies and the 13th Army forced the Neisse, broke through the enemy defense lines along a 29 km. front, and advanced to a depth ot 13 km. . . .

Speaking of the unique features of this operation, I should like to say that the Neisse crossing, the capture of bridgeheads on its western bank, the breakthrough of the first enemy defense line, the attack on and breakthrough of the second line, the advance toward the Spree, the crossing of this river, and the break through the third German defense line all formed a single, continuous process. This was the first time in the Great Patriotic War that I had to cross a river and, without a pause, immediately to break through an enemy defense line with a well-developed system of fire, engineering installations, fortifications, and minefields, and then to breach a second defense line and a third and again to force a river. . . .

Later, analyzing the progress of our offensive in the first few days, I often wondered why the Germans had so hastily brought in their operational reserves and even some units from the High Command reserves on the second Neisse defense line. I think the fact that Berlin was quite close had a psychological effect on them. The space in which they could still try to hold us back was shrinking more and more. Moreover, the generals had guessed what our successful breakthrough southeast of Berlin could lead to. They were right to fear the advance of such a large group of forces, including tank Armies, into an operational area which offered the possibility of maneuvering in the direction of Berlin. However much of a smokescreen we may have laid—and there was enough smoke at the beginning of the operation—the German reconnaissance planes could not fail to detect our tank concentrations. It was this fear and Hitler's orders to hold the Neisse line at any cost that prompted the Germans to use the main operational reserves on the second defense line. Essentially, they made our future task all the easier.[51]

The German generals by this time were in a state of psychological breakdown, although I think they were not fully aware of the crisis and the virtual hopelessness of their position. Their already difficult position was made all the worse by the fact that Hitler kept attributing the defeats at the front to treason and made no exception for generals who were routed by the troops of the 1st Ukrainian Army Group on the Neisse. The report that Soviet troops had broken through in the Kottbus area shocked him, and he declared outright that it was a result of treason. I should like to say in retrospect that his generals on the Neisse line served him faithfully to the end, and, though realizing that disaster was imminent, they did everything to avert it or at least to delay it.

On the morning of April 17 I ordered that an advanced observation post should be prepared for me somewhere near the Spree, as soon as the situation permitted it, in the sector where Rybalko's 3rd Tank Army was to cross the river. After that I left in the same direction. . . .

In recalling the war and comparing its phases, in my opinion, we are often prone to underestimate what we achieved in mastering the art of war in those four years. In the fourth year of the war we regarded in a matter-of-fact way the execution of military tasks which in the early period of war would have been regarded as incredibly difficult and almost impossible. But in assessing the balance of forces at the beginning of the war, we underestimate to a certain extent one factor which added to the Germans' strength—the fact that they had combat experience and their offensive spirit had been built up by two years of steady victories on the battlefields of Europe. Then, in April 1945, we had driven back this army, one of the strongest in the world, almost all the way to Berlin. Nothing that remained to be done was insurmountable for our army, which was now mature, full of the offensive spirit, and determined to put an end to fascism once and for all. . . .

On my arrival at the Spree I learned from reconnaissance reports

and in fact saw myself that things were working out fairly well for us.
. . . Although the advance post was ready, I did not go there at once.
What kept me on the bank was not only the pleasant sight of the rapid
and successful crossing, not only the sight of a ferry already going from
one bank to the other and the bridge nearing completion, but also the
need to talk to the commanders of the tank Armies, which were to undertake a large-scale maneuver deep into the enemy rear. . . .

My talk with Rybalko and Leliushenko before their departure was
a kind of concise summary of everything we had discussed earlier. They
were to advance boldly into the operational depth without looking back;
they were not to fight the Germans for their support points but would
by-pass them, maneuver, and avoid frontal attacks; they were to spare
their tanks and not forget for a moment that they must have their reserves intact when the time came to accomplish their ultimate task. I
did not say this in so many words, but they knew very well that they
would obviously have to fight for Berlin. I left them both in good spirits.
My own mood was not bad either.

On reaching my command post in the castle, I rang up all the people I needed. . . . I spoke to Army Group headquarters, was informed
of the situation by several Army commanders, had another talk with the
tank Army commanders (who reported that their units had begun to advance successfully west of the Spree), and, after summing up the situation, called Supreme Headquarters by high-frequency telephone. I reported on the Army Group's offensive, the successful crossing of the
Spree, and said our tank Armies were outstripping the combined-arms
Armies and advancing deep in a northwestern direction.

A German battery continued to fire on the castle from somewhere
far off. . . . and there I was sitting and talking with Moscow. The audi-
bility was excellent. I must say that the high-frequency telephone system
was a godsend. It helped us out so much and was so reliable in the most
difficult conditions that I have nothing but praise for our equipment and
for our signalmen who took care of this communication line and in any
situation followed on the heels of those using it.[52]

I was nearing the end of my report when Stalin suddenly interrupted
me.

"Things are pretty hard with Zhukov," he said. "He is still hammering at the defenses."

After this Stalin was silent. I also kept quiet and waited to see what
he would say next. Suddenly Stalin asked:

"Is it possible to transfer Zhukov's mobile forces and send them on
to Berlin through the gap on your front?"[53]

When he had finished, I gave him my opinion.

"Comrade Stalin, this will take a lot of time and will greatly complicate the situation. There is no need to transfer tank forces from the 1st Belorussian Army Group into the breach we have made. Things are going well with us. We have sufficient forces and are in a position to turn both our tank Armies toward Berlin."

I then gave the direction in which the tank Armies would turn and named Zossen as a reference point—it was a little town 25 km. south of Berlin where we knew the Headquarters of the German General Staff was located.[54]

"By what map are you reporting?" Stalin asked.

I replied that the scale was 1 : 200,000. After a brief pause, during which he probably looked for Zossen on his own map in Moscow, Stalin said:

"Very good. Do you know that Zossen is the location of the German General Staff Headquarters?"

"Yes, I do," I replied.

"Very good," Stalin repeated. "I agree. Turn your tank Armies toward Berlin."

That was the end of our talk.

This decision was the only correct one in the situation that had arisen. While the 1st Belorussian Army Group, advancing on Berlin from the west, was finding it so difficult to break through the deep and well-prepared German defenses, it would have been strange to abandon such a promising maneuver as a tank assault on Berlin from the south through the breach we had made. . . .

As soon as Stalin had hung up, I called the commanders of the two tank Armies on the high-frequency line and instructed them to turn their Armies toward Berlin. These orders were later amplified in an Army Group directive, which three hours later was sent to Supreme Headquarters and to the troops. The tankmen could not afford to lose time while the directive was drawn up, sent, and received. They had to work through the night without losing a minute waiting for the official confirmation of my order. . . .

The nearer to Berlin, the more dense the German defenses and the greater the possibilities of support for their infantry. These included artillery, tanks, and great quantities of Faustpatronen.[55] By April 22 on the Teltow Canal, we had already come up against a system of solidly organized rifle, machine-gun, mortar, and artillery fire of an extremely high density, and we were unable to force a crossing of the canal from the march. . . .

The Germans had prepared a fairly strong defense line on the northern bank of the Teltow Canal. It consisted of trenches, reinforced concrete pillboxes, barriers, and dug-in tanks and self-propelled guns. On that side of the canal there was an almost solid wall of houses. They were all very solid buildings with walls a meter or so thick. A considerable section of the northern bank was occupied by large reinforced concrete factory buildings whose rear blank side faced the canal and formed a kind of medieval rampart running down to the water's edge. All of this was well adapted to a long, stubborn defense. Some of the bridges across the canal had been blown up; others had been mined. The canal itself was a serious obstacle, being forty to fifty meters wide and two or three meters deep.

Imagine this deep, wide moat filled with water and lined with steep concrete walls. On the 12-km.-long canal sector reached by Rybalko's tanks, the Germans had herded together everyone they could lay their hands on—some 15,000 men. A density of 1,200 men per kilometer is a very high figure, I must say, for fighting within a city. Besides that, they had more than 250 guns and mortars, 130 tanks and armored carriers, and more than 500 machine guns. They also had an unlimited quantity of Faustpatronen.

It should also be borne in mind that the German officers and men defending the Teltow Canal were aware that it was the last line on which they could hold us. Behind them was Berlin. In addition to Berlin and the desperate determination to fight to the end, to die but to keep us out of Berlin—and judging by the bitterness of the fighting, most of the men making their last stand in the German capital had that kind of determination—there were also the SS "blitz" tribunals to which all caught for desertion were sent.[56]

In that period Hitler, as we know, was behaving like one possessed, saying that the German people had proved unworthy of his leadership. He had come to hate his own people and was prepared to take revenge on them for the ignominious collapse of his bloody gamble. The atmosphere in Berlin was one of hysterically swift reprisals and the utmost cruelty. There is no doubt that it struck terror in the hearts of men and prolonged the agony of the German capital.

What a motley crowd it was that gathered along the Teltow Canal, especially in the Volkssturm battalions, where seasoned soldiers served alongside old men and weeping teenagers, who fought on nevertheless and set fire to our tanks with Faustpatronen. . . .

In their postwar writings, German generals who took part in this operation, including General Tippelskirch, heap responsibility for all the foolish orders issued in that period mainly on Hitler, but partially on Jodl and Keitel. There is considerable truth in this. In effect, Keitel, who initially took part in organizing Wenck's offensive, managed to misinform both sides, one might say. He did not give Wenck any idea of the tragic position of the encircled 9th Army and the 3rd Army half encircled north of Berlin, thereby giving him some false hopes. On the other hand, in his report to Hitler he exaggerated the actual possibilities of Wenck's army.

As a result, Hitler continued to believe that his plans were realistic. He thought he himself could be saved with Berlin by the joint efforts of the 9th, 12th, and 3rd Armies. It is possible that those were precisely the hopes on which he based his decision to stay in Berlin. Let me add that however fantastic the premises for such a decision, there was some logic in it. Add to this his hopes of pitting us against our Allies at the very last moment.

The fresh attempts made by Wenck's army on April 25 in the Beelitz-Treuenbrietzen area proved to be just as futile as the preceding ones. The attacks were fierce, but we beat them back successfully and our losses were minimal.

General Riazanov, supporting Ermakov's 5th Guards Mechanized Corps that day, was making particularly effective use of his assault planes. They came in, wave after wave, at hedge-hopping altitudes, showering the attacking German tanks with small antitank bombs. The German tank units were now having a taste of the medicine they gave our tankmen in 1941 and 1942, when German aircraft did not let them alone for a moment.[57]

It looked as if that day marked a psychological turning point for Wenck. He continued to carry out his orders, but you could feel that there was no real purpose behind his action and that he was merely going through the motions.

Events were developing in such a way that by April 25 all enemy efforts to break the ring around Berlin, to cut the 1st Ukrainian Army Group in half, and to sever its strike group from the rest of the force had quite obviously failed. Neither Hitler nor the remnants of his troops left in the ruins of Berlin could escape the trap in which they found themselves.

In the wake of the retreating German army, trees and poles bore the bodies of soldiers executed allegedly for cowardice and abandonment of positions without orders. I say "allegedly" because it was my impression that the German soldiers had fought hard in this situation. It was not Hitler, or Keitel, or Jodl but the soldiers in those days who were the only real force that postponed the inevitable end by hours or days. . . .

What is there to say about all this? If anything, it is that the whole affair was vile and reckless.

About 200,000 German troops were surrounded in Berlin proper. This grouping consisted of the remnants of six divisions of the 9th Army, one SS Guards Brigade, numerous police units, ten artillery batteries, a brigade of assault guns, three tank fighter brigades, six antitank batteries, one anti-aircraft division, the remnants of two other anti-aircraft divisions, and a few dozen Volkssturm battalions. In estimating the numerical strength of this grouping, it should be borne in mind that every day of the fighting it was receiving various reinforcements from the population.

All the inhabitants of Berlin who could be made to fight against our advancing troops were thrown into the battle. There were enough weapons to go around; in addition, civilians were used in the construction of defense installations and also as carriers of ammunition, medical orderlies, and even as scouts. When I say that some who fought against us in the streets of Berlin were in civilian dress, I must add that in the very last days and during the surrender, some officers and men of the German army donned civilian clothes and mixed with the population to avoid being taken prisoner.

On the whole, I think the figure of 200,000 taking part in the defense of Berlin is not quite accurate. I base my assertion on the intelligence reports of the 1st Belorussian Army Group. In all probability the figure was higher. . . .

I have come across the view that the battles in Berlin could have been fought with less ferocity, cruelty, and haste, and thereby with fewer losses. This is reasonable on the surface but ignores the main thing, namely, the actual intensity of the fighting and the state of men's minds. They were longing passionately to end the war as soon as possible. This must be borne in mind by those who wish to judge whether the losses were justified or not, and whether the city could have been taken a day or two later. Otherwise, the atmosphere of the Berlin fighting cannot be explained. . . .[58]

During the Berlin operation the Germans managed to destroy and damage more than 800 of our tanks and self-propelled guns, most of the losses occurring in the fighting in Berlin proper. In our efforts to reduce losses from Faustpatronen we worked out a very simple but effective device. The tanks were screened with tin plate or sheet iron. The Faustpatronen would go through the sheeting, the empty space beyond, and hit the tank's armor with their jet force quite spent. They would then ricochet quite harmlessly. Why did we think of these screens at such a late date? Apparently, because we only came up against the use of the Faustpatronen on a wide scale in street fighting; we did not pay much attention to them in field conditions.

It was the Volkssturm detachments, made up mostly of elderly people and teenagers, that had the greatest number of Faustpatronen. This was a weapon that could produce in untrained and physically unprepared men the conviction that they were really doing something tangible in the war. I must say that these Faustpatronen men usually fought to the end and at that final stage displayed greater steadfastness than soldiers who had been through thick and thin and were worn out by the many years of fighting and defeats.

The soldiers surrendered only when they had their backs to the wall. The same was true of the officers. But they lacked enthusiasm. They were grimly determined to fight on desperately until the surrender order came. There is only one way in which I can describe the mood of the Volkssturm in the decisive fighting for Berlin—hysterical self-sacrifice. These last defenders of the Third Reich, including some very young boys, regarded themselves as the final hope for a miracle that would take place at the very last moment against all odds. . . .

By April 27, as a result of the operations by the Armies of the 1st Belorussian Army Group, which had moved deep into the heart of Berlin, and of the operations of our Army Group, the German Berlin grouping was confined in the city to a narrow strip 2–5 km. wide running from east to west over a length of 16 km. All the territory it occupied was being shelled steadily by our guns. At the same time, the battle to liquidate the German Frankfurt-Guben grouping was progressing. The Germans were being hit from all sides by five Armies. . . . In turn, the German troops brought pressure to bear on the Armies of our Army Group which blocked their way to the southwest.

The harder they were hit from behind, the more energy they showed in trying to break through to our rear. We felt every blow they received over there through their blows at us here. They were consolidating their battle formations and striking at us with increasing force. What else could they do? Apart from surrender, they could do nothing but try to get through our formations and join up with Wenck.

That was what made the situation peculiar. The operations against other encircled groupings, say, in Stalingrad or Korsun'-Shevchenkovskii, had been concentric. In this case, the situation was quite different. The group itself was active and mobile and was trying to break out at any cost, putting all its resources into the effort. Since it was trying to break out in our direction, we were facing an increasingly difficult situation.

During the fighting, the German troops succeeded twice in breaking out of the encirclement. But they were stopped both times. As a result of their successive strikes they managed to move rather far, into

the Beelitz area, where on May 1 they had only some 5 km. to go to
link up with Wenck's army, which continued its attack from the west.

Of course, during this double breakthrough the Germans could not
reach our rear. They would break through and be stopped and break
through again and be stopped again. They moved inside a ring of our
troops, and whatever the outcome, they offered fresh proof that even in
the hardest conditions 200,000 men are always to be reckoned with,
especially when led by a strong hand and with a well-defined purpose.

Of these 200,000 men, roughly 30,000 got through to the Beelitz
area. Still they did get there, and to prevent them from escaping we
had to continue fighting back to front, facing Wenck in the west and
Gordov's 3rd Guards Army facing east and northeast. . . .

Almost 20 years later, when I visited Berlin in 1962, I went to the
Bayreuth area and saw there traces of this battle in the surrounding
villages. I saw rusty steel helmets and the remains of weapons; it was
still impossible to use the water from one of the lakes that had been
packed with corpses. Everything there was a reminder of the last days
of the breakthrough by the remnants of the German 9th Army, in which
the futility of the losses was combined with the courage of desperation
and the grim resolve of those doomed to destruction.

Western historians tend to exaggerate the number of men of the
9th Army who managed to break out of the encirclement toward the
west by May 2. Some say it was from 20,000 to 30,000. That is a very
great exaggeration. As commander of the 1st Ukrainian Army Group,
I can testify that no more than 3,000 to 4,000 men managed not so much
to break through as to creep through the forests in various sectors of
the front. . . .[59]

In a comparison of the operations conducted by Wenck's 12th Army
and the German 9th Army, which was trying to break through to meet
the former, I must say that the 9th Army did better. Wenck had taken
some strong blows in the very first battles and continued to fight, but
more, I should say, by way of going through the motions. But the 9th
Army, breaking out of the ring, fought boldly, to the death. And it was
precisely the determined nature of its actions that gave us such a lot of
trouble in those last days of the war.

Marshal V. I. Chuikov
Surrender

THERE IS a firm basis for saying that the leaders of the Third Reich were ready to surrender separately and unconditionally to the Western Allies in order to persuade Churchill and Truman to join them in an attack on the Soviet Union. We know that sometime between April 20 and 30, 1945, Goering and Himmler entered into negotiations with the Anglo-Americans and expressed their readiness to make a separate peace or truce even at the price of the physical removal of Hitler. Whether they came forward on their own initiative "to save Germany from communism" or were sent by Hitler himself, it is hard to say. This has remained a mystery.[60]

I am not one of those trusting souls who believes that the true picture of the end of the Third Reich came out at the Nuremberg trials, particularly when the chief leaders—Hitler, Goebbels, and Himmler—were already dead. Hermann Goering gave evasive testimony and then took his own life. It is entirely possible that the narrow circle of leaders of the Third Reich took the secret of their last days to the grave with them.

The objection could be raised that Hitler left a testament in which, before dying, he excluded Goering and Himmler from the Party. That, of course, is true. The author of these memoirs first heard the substance of this orally from the last Chief of the German Army General Staff, General Krebs,[61] and later held in his hands a letter signed by Goebbels and Bormann with Hitler's testament attached. However, knowing Hitler's artfulness and perfidy full well, I was always inclined to believe he would try to use even the report of his death for blackmail and deceit.

I first heard of the Fuehrer's suicide from General Krebs when he came to the command post of the 8th Guards Army for talks on the night of May 1. This is the way it happened. The preceding evening, when I returned from my observation post to the Army's headquarters in the region of Johannisthal, I had a telephone call from the commander of the Army Group, Marshal Zhukov.

"Is there any hope of mopping up Berlin entirely for the First of May holiday?" he asked.

V. I. Chuikov, "Kapitulatsiia gitlerovskoi germanii," *Novaia i noveishaia istoriia*, 1965, No. 2, pp. 11–13; V. I. Chuikov, "Konets tret'ego reikha," *Oktiabr'*, 1964, No. 5, pp. 138–61.

I replied that judging from the enemy's resistance, which, although weakening, still continued, there was no hope yet for a quick capitulation.

That same evening, the members of the political section of the Army invited me to supper. Just as we were sitting down to eat, the duty officer of the political section came to tell me I was urgently wanted on the telephone. The commander of the 4th Corps, Lieutenant General V. A. Glazunov, was on the line. In an agitated voice he reported that a lieutenant colonel of the German Army had come to the forward line of the 102nd Guards Infantry Regiment of the 35th Division with a white flag and an official letter addressed to the commander of the Russian troops. . . . I ordered that the lieutenant colonel be told we were ready to receive truce envoys and that they should proceed to the advance observation post, to which I would drive at once.

After reporting all this by telephone to Marshal Zhukov, I drove to the observation post with General Pozharskii. . . .[62] Then came the long moments of waiting. There was only the adjutant and myself in the room. One and a half hours passed. It was 2:00 a.m. by then, but we had no desire to sleep. We smoked one cigarette after another.

Memories of days, nights, weeks, and months of combat flashed through my mind—the war had already lasted four years. Before my eyes drifted—no, swept—a whirlwind of episodes of military life. There was the Volga, now so far away, and yet so near. Burning oil floated on it, the devouring flames consuming everything—barges and boats. There was Zaporozh'e, the night of the assault, then Nikopol', Odessa, Lublin, Lodz, and finally Berlin. The men of the 62nd Army, who had defended the sacred banks of the Volga, now stood on the Spree before a humbled Berlin, waiting, putting their arms aside for the moment. They were awaiting the truce envoys sent by the leaders of the Wehrmacht, envoys from the leaders of the Third Reich who not long ago had been certain of the imminent end of the Soviet state. They would come crying for mercy as though we had a short memory and had already forgotten about the millions killed, about the tens of millions of widows and orphans, about the gallows and gas chambers, and Maidanek and other death camps.

The adjutant was awake, too, and was looking at me with a rather proud expression. He was silent and I said nothing, but we understood each other without words. There was something to be proud of, too. We had reached Berlin. From the Volga to Berlin is a longer road than from La Manche to the Spree. And still we had reached Berlin. Ivan had outstripped Jack and Tommy and was stretching a hand to him across the Elbe to Torgau and Dessau as a comrade-in-arms. . . .

The door flew open with a bang. On the threshold was Vsevolod

Vishnevskii. . . . Behind him was the poet Evgenii Dolmatovskii, who had known the fighting men of the 62nd Army from the banks of the Volga and had been an eyewitness of the great battle of the Volga and the surrender of Paulus' army. Matvei Blanter, the composer, was also with them.[63]

General conversation flagged this time. Each was thinking about the impending events and appraising them in his own fashion. Everyone was smoking furiously, walking out into the large hall with black columns, counting off with even steps the seconds of the immeasurably long minutes. It was already 3:00 a.m. Dawn broke at 3:30 a.m. It was the morning of May 1. . . . At last, at 3:50, the door opened and in walked a German general with an Iron Cross around his neck and the fascist swastika on his sleeve.

I took his measure: average height, thick-set, with a shaven head and scarred face. With his right hand he made a gesture of greeting in his fashion, fascist-style. With his left, he handed me his documents—his service book. This was Germany's Chief of the Army General Staff, General Krebs. He was accompanied by the chief of staff of the 56th Tank Corps, Colonel of the General Staff von Dufwing, and an interpreter.

Krebs did not wait for questions. He announced:

"I shall speak of strictly secret matters. You are the first foreigner to be told that on April 30 Hitler chose to leave us and committed suicide."

After he spoke, Krebs paused as if checking the effect this announcement had on us. He obviously expected us to pounce on him with questions and generally to show a burning interest in such sensational news. However, I said calmly:

"We know that."

Then, after a pause to make him understand that this was no news to me, I asked Krebs to tell us exactly when it had happened.

Krebs, disconcerted by having his sensational announcement fall flat, replied:

"It happened at 3:00 p.m. today—" then, noticing that I was looking at my watch, he corrected himself, "yesterday, April 30, at about 3:00 p.m.—"

Krebs then read a message from Goebbels and Bormann to the Soviet High Command, which said:

In accordance with the testament of the departed Fuehrer, we entrust General Krebs with the following:

We inform the leader of the Soviet people that today at 3:30 p.m., the Fuehrer left this life voluntarily. On the basis of his lawful right as Fuehrer,

he transferred all authority to Doenitz, myself, and Bormann. I am empowered
by Bormann to establish contact with the leader of the Soviet people. This contact is necessary for peace talks between the powers which have borne the
greatest losses.

GOEBBELS

After reading Goebbel's statement, Krebs handed me two other
documents. One was authorization for the Chief of the General Staff,
General of Infantry Krebs, to conduct negotiations with the Russian
High Command (this was a form from the Chief of the Imperial Chancellery with a seal and Bormann's signature, dated April 30, 1945). The
second was Hitler's testament with a list of the members of the new
government and of the High Command of the German armed forces
(this document was signed by Hitler and witnesses and dated 4:00 a.m.,
April 29, 1945).[64]

Krebs seemed anxious to use these documents as a shield against
the questions he obviously expected. He was fully aware of his awkward position as a diplomat coming not just to represent one side to
the other, but to ask "pardon." On the one hand he had a natural desire
to try to find out whether there was not something to be gained by
playing on our well-founded feelings of distrust toward our allies, who
had dallied so long in opening the second front. On the other hand, it
was not so easy for him, an inveterate Nazi, to admit himself defeated.

Why did I tell Krebs that Hitler's suicide was not news to me? I
must admit that Hitler's death was news to me and that I hardly expected
to hear anything like that from Krebs. In preparing for the meeting
with Krebs, however, I had made up my mind in advance to remain
calm whatever the circumstances, to display no surprise whatever, and
to jump to no hasty conclusions. I knew that no experienced diplomat—
and that was precisely what Krebs was[65]—ever starts a conversation with
the issue which he regards as the main one. He always explores the
mood of his interlocutor to start with and then tries to bring the conversation around in such a way that the main issue is broached first
by the very person with whom the decision rests.

To me, and to all participants in the negotiations, Hitler's death
was indeed news of prime importance; to Krebs, it was the diplomatic
screen he used to conceal the main issue. Therefore, I immediately
brushed aside the fact of Hitler's death, thus forcing Krebs to come to
the point.

"Do those documents apply to Berlin alone or to all of Germany?"
I asked him.

"Goebbels has authorized me to speak on behalf of the entire German army," he answered.

I undertook to prove to him that in his answer and in the documents he had brought two notions were confused.

"You present yourself in two different capacities: that of military negotiator for a defeated army and of negotiator for a government which requests talks with my government. I am a military man, and I see no other way out for your army than to lay down arms immediately and to capitulate in order to avoid useless bloodshed. Under the given circumstances Goebbels and Bormann are not strengthening your armed forces or their combat capability. Wouldn't it be better if Goebbels and you were to order your troops to abandon all resistance?"

"There are other ways to end the war," Krebs answered. "We must be given the opportunity to assemble the new government, headed by Doenitz, which would settle this question through negotiations with the Soviet government."

"What kind of government could it be when your Fuehrer has committed suicide and by this very fact has admitted the failure of his regime? After him there could remain some one of his deputies who had the authority to decide whether or not there would be further bloodshed. Who now, and right now, is replacing Hitler?"

"Goebbels. He has been appointed chancellor. Before his death, however, Hitler formed a new cabinet headed by a president, Grand Admiral Doenitz."

I called Marshal Zhukov on the telephone and reported the situation. . . .

Marshal Zhukov said that he would immediately report to Moscow. I was to stand by the telephone; some questions might require further clarification.

A minute later he asked:

"When did Hitler commit suicide?" . . .

As I asked Krebs, I glanced at my watch. It was 4:27 a.m., May 1. Krebs hastened to specify:

"Yesterday, April 30, at 3:30 p.m."

I informed Zhukov who passed the information on to Moscow. After a while I heard the voice of the Marshal again:

"Ask Krebs whether they wish to lay down their arms and surrender or do they intend to occupy themselves with [protracted] peace negotiations?"

I asked Krebs bluntly:

"Are we discussing the surrender, and is this the purpose of your mission?"

"No, other possibilities exist."

"What are they?"

"Allow and help us to form the new government in accordance with Hitler's will; and this government will resolve the problem to your advantage."

Well, I thought, what a clever fellow. He is repeating the same thing—a favorite trick of diplomats for achieving an objective through insistent reiteration of the same idea phrased differently.[66] This time, however, he was far off the mark. On page 5 in Hitler's will I read: "So that Germany will have a government composed ot honorable men who will pursue the war with all available means, I as leader of the nation appoint the following as members of the new cabinet. . . ."

"What else can Krebs tell us?" Zhukov asked.

I put the same question to Krebs. He shrugged his shoulders. I then explained that we could negotiate nothing but total surrender to the Allies—the USSR, the USA, and Britain. On this subject we were united.

"To enable us to discuss your demands," Krebs said, "I request a temporary cessation of hostilities and your help for the new government to assemble here in Berlin." He stressed: "Precisely here, in Berlin, and nowhere else."

"We understand what your new government desires," I pointed out. "The more so, since we are aware of the attempt made by your friends, Himmler and Goering, to sound out our allies. Are you really unaware of this?"

Krebs tensed. Obviously he did not expect my question. Aimlessly, he fumbled in the side pocket of his uniform and produced a pencil for which he had absolutely no need.

"I have been accredited by the legal government formed according to Hitler's will," he finally answered. "A new government may be set up in the south, but it would be illegal. As yet, there is only a government in Berlin; it is the legal one, and we request an armistice to assemble all the cabinet members, to discuss the situation, and to conclude a peace which will be advantageous to both parties." . . .

Having declared that we put forth a single condition—general surrender—I went into the next room and rang up the Army Group commander. I put my views before Marshal Zhukov:

"Krebs is here not to discuss a surrender but, apparently, to find out what the circumstances are and what our mood is—whether or not we will engage in separate negotiations with the new government. They have no more forces with which to continue the fight. Goebbels and Bormann, faced with total defeat, have decided on a last move—to engage in negotiations with our government. They are looking for all possible rifts and breaches between us and the Allies to sow mistrust. Krebs is obviously dragging out his answers; he is playing for time even though this is not to their advantage, since our troops last night and today have not halted the offensive. The only quiet sector is the one where Krebs crossed the lines."

The Marshal asked a few more questions, said that he was reporting everything to Moscow immediately, and ordered me to go on talking to Krebs to find out the real purpose of his coming and to make him accept a general surrender.

I returned to the other room. It was 4:40 a.m. I was dizzy with fatigue and lack of sleep. I sat at the table facing Krebs. I had the feeling that during my absence he had thought about the developing situation and had thought up some new arguments with which to support his, or rather Goebbels', proposals. He resumed the conversation, again insisting on a temporary armistice.

"I cannot engage in any other negotiations," he said. "I am nothing but a representative and cannot answer for my government. It would be in your interest to engage in negotiations with the new German government. We know that the German Government is "finished" (here he laughed). You hold the strong hand. We both know that."

This was a queen's gambit. Krebs was moving in with his strongest piece. I could give him no quarter since obviously he wanted to involve me in discussing an armistice.

"You must realize, General," I said, "that we know what you want from us. You intend to warn us that you would continue the fight or, rather, the senseless resistance which would only raise the number of unnecessary casualties. Let me ask you a direct question: What is the sense of your fighting on?"

For a few seconds Krebs stared at me silently, not knowing what to say.

"We shall fight to the last man," he blurted out.

I was unable to conceal an ironical smile.

"General, what have you got left? What forces would you use to fight with?" After a short silence, I added: "I expect total surrender."

"No!" Krebs exclaimed with feeling. Sighing, he added: "In the case of total surrender we would no longer exist juridically as a government."

The negotiations were becoming more and more tiresome. Clearly Krebs' task was to convince us of the expediency of recognizing the "new" government. He had no right to amend his proposals without Goebbels' and Bormann's agreement and would go on repeating the same idea. One could sense hopelessness in his words, in his entire behavior. Yet, he did not leave; he expected something of me, possibly my statement that I was talking to him as to a prisoner of war.

Reports on the progress of combat operations led to the conclusion that there was no longer any firm enemy resistance along the line of encirclement. Only individual garrisons or SS units, which were still quite strong, offered resistance.

It was 5:00 a.m. Unable to restrain myself any longer I told Krebs:

"You are insisting on an armistice and suggesting peace negotiations while your own troops are surrendering of their own volition."

Krebs flinched.

"Where?" he asked rapidly.

"Everywhere."

"Without orders?" Krebs asked in amazement.

"Our troops are advancing, and yours are surrendering."

"These are, perhaps, individual occurrences," said the German general, clutching at a straw.

Just then we heard the thunder of a "Katiusha" volley. Krebs seemed to shrivel. . . .

The room next to ours had been converted into a dining room. We went there. Tea and sandwiches were brought in. Everyone was hungry. Krebs did not decline the invitation. He took a cup of tea and a sandwich; I noticed that his hands were trembling. I offered him brandy which he accepted.

We sat down wearily, feeling the closeness of the end of the war. Its final hours were exhausting, though. We were awaiting instructions from Moscow.

Front life, however, followed its own course. Army headquarters warned the troops, above all the artillery, to be ready to continue the attack. Scouts kept watch over the enemy, his reserves and supplies. The engineers built and improved the crossings over the Landwehr Canal. From time to time I left Krebs and went to other rooms to issue instructions and confirm staff orders. . . .

The guns were thundering outside the window. It was already light on the streets. The First of May holiday had also started in Berlin. We had conducted negotiations through the whole night, and the results were nil. Moscow's order was to wait for an answer, and every now and then we would be asked for some detail. . . .

There was a telephone call from Army Group headquarters. The Army Group commander informed me that he was sending his deputy to me, General of the Army Sokolovskii, and he requested more exact information on Himmler, on Ribbentrop's whereabouts, on who was now the Chief of the Nazi General Staff, and on where Hitler's body was. There were questions, questions, and more questions—

Returning to the room where the negotiations were taking place, I asked Krebs:

"Where is Hitler's body?"

"In Berlin. It was burned in accordance with his will. It happened today," Krebs answered.

"Who is the Chief of Staff of your High Command?"

"Jodl. Doenitz is the new Supreme Commander in Chief. They are both in Mecklenburg. Only Goebbels and Bormann are in Berlin."

"Why did you fail to inform us previously that Doenitz is in Mecklenburg?"

Krebs did not answer. I picked up the telephone, called Marshal Zhukov, and reported:

"The 'Supreme Commander in Chief,' Grand Admiral Doenitz, is in Mecklenburg with Himmler, whom Goebbels considers a traitor. Herman Goering, allegedly ill, is somewhere in the south. Only Goebbels, Bormann, Krebs, and Hitler's body are in Berlin. This fact alone would allow us to draw conclusions on the nature of Goebbels' and Bormann's proposals and documents."

Marshal Zhukov answered that the confusion of sending negotiators to us in Berlin and to the Allies in the west and south was delaying the decision of our government. The answer would be forthcoming soon and, in all likelihood, would be a demand for total surrender. . . .[67]

Krebs left. The truce envoy of the Third Reich did not yield. He did not agree to a surrender; he was unwilling to put an end to the destruction of Berlin and to the unnecessary casualties on both sides, including the civilian population.

What did he want of us, of the Soviet command, of the Soviet government?

Before leaving, Krebs stalled for a long time. He twice went to the staircase and twice retraced his steps—the first time he had forgotten his gloves which he had laid on the windowsill together with his cap; yet, he had put on his cap, forgetting his gloves. The second time Krebs came back claiming that he had forgotten his field case. He had not brought one in the first place. He insisted, nevertheless, that he had brought in it the documents from Goebbels and Bormann, even though— this I remember well—he had pulled the papers out of his side pocket.

Both his eyes and overall behavior indicated that the General was uncertain as to whether to go back into the hell or to throw himself on the mercy of the victor. Apparently, he expected us to declare him a prisoner of war, which he would have willingly accepted.

But why did we need such a prisoner of war? It was more expedient for us to have him go back because he might have had an influence in ending the bloodshed.

Still, what was Krebs' purpose in coming to us? Undoubtedly, he was the executor of Goebbels' and Bormann's will, which was also his own will. It seems that the three of them hoped to mitigate enmity between the Soviet Union and fascist Germany by informing us of Hitler's death. It was as though Germany had paid for the millions of victims with the fact that the principal culprit of the war had been cremated. Yet that was not all and not the main reason [for Krebs' mission].

The main reason was that they, and possibly all the other associates and adherents of Hitler, were hoping, as had Hitler until the final hours of his life, that the contradictions between the Soviet Union and her allies would intensify. The fact that certain differences existed between us was no secret.

We, the military, also knew this. However, I can state most emphatically that no conflicts whatsoever existed among the military allies, among the soldiers of the anti-Hitlerite coalition. We had one common objective, one common enemy, and we tried to finish him off as soon as possible. The closer the contacts between the Soviet and Allied troops became, the more the alliance strengthened, the greater became the respect they felt for one another.

The leaders of the Third Reich and some people in the West neither understood nor took this into consideration. . . .

General Krebs, no doubt an important intelligence agent and an experienced diplomat, left with nothing for his pains. It would seem that this was the last attempt at splitting the Allies. Having failed, Goebbels and company were forced to make some kind of decision.[68]

.   .   .   .

The command was given: Fire with all guns and finish off the enemy as quickly as possible!

"Katiusha" volleys thundered from all sides; thousands of artillery shells were fired at the government blocks, the Imperial Chancellery, and the Reichstag.

The results of the powerful and well-prepared strike were soon visible. Reports on the successful operations of our troops began coming in. . . .

General of the Army V. D. Sokolovskii, unable to hold out any longer, retired into the next house to get some rest. I also could hardly stand on my feet.

The telephone rang again. The 47th Guards Division reported that officers sent to the Potsdam Bridge had met there with German negotiators—a colonel and two majors. Colonel von Dufwing, chief of staff of the 56th Tank Corps, had declared that he had been authorized by the Corps commander, General of the Artillery Weidling, to inform the Soviet Command of General Weidling's decision to order the units of the 56th Tank Corps to cease any further resistance and to surrender.

The acting commander of the 47th Guards Division, Colonel Semchenko asked von Dufwing: "How much time does the corps command need to lay down its arms and surrender its personnel and the weapons of the corps units in an organized way to the Soviet command?"

Von Dufwing answered that three to four hours would be required. They intended to do this at night since Goebbels had issued the order that anyone who tried to surrender to the Russians would be shot in the back.

I gave the following order:

"Colonel von Dufwing to be sent back to General Weidling with the information that the surrender was accepted; the two German majors to remain with us."

I dozed off, awaiting results.

At 5:50 a.m. I was awakened with the news that a delegation from Goebbels had arrived. I leaped from the sofa and hastily washed in cold water.

There were three delegates wearing civilian clothes, accompanied by a soldier wearing a helmet and carrying a white flag. I ordered the soldier to leave. One of the delegates was the Councillor of the Ministry of Propaganda, Heinersdorf. I asked:

"What do you want, and what can I do for you?"

Heinersdorf presented me with a letter in a pink folder. As I was reading it, Vishnevskii, Pozharskii, Vainrub, and Tkachenko were straining to read over my shoulders.

The letter was signed by Dr. Fritsche. It read:

"As you have been notified by General Krebs, Goering cannot be reached. Dr. Goebbels is no longer among the living. I, as one of the survivors, ask you to take Berlin under your protection. My name is known. Director of the Ministry of Propaganda, Dr. Fritsche."[69]

So, that is what was happening in the final days and even hours! After Hitler, Goebbels departed from this world, and after Goebbels, who? Whoever it might be, this was the end of the war.

"When did Dr. Goebbels commit suicide?"

"Last evening, at the Propaganda Ministry."

"Where is the body?"

"Burned. It was burned by his personal aide and his chauffeur."

Hitler had also been burned. Apparently, the leaders of the Third Reich had chosen fire as a means for the expiation of their earthly sins.

"Where is Chief of the General Staff Krebs who was negotiating with us yesterday on Goebbels' instructions?"

"We do not know. General Einsdorf is the new Chief of Staff."

Later we learned that Krebs had shot himself. What else could he do after such a failure?

"Do you know our terms? We can discuss nothing but unconditional surrender."

"Yes, we know. That is why we are here to offer our help."

"How can you help your people?"

"Dr. Fritsche asks to be given the opportunity to address the German people and army over the radio and urge them to stop the unnecessary bloodshed and accept unconditional surrender."

"Will the troops obey Fritsche's orders?"

"His name is known throughout Germany, particularly in Berlin."

The telephone rang. It was General Glazunov reporting from the command point of the 47th Guards Division. It was reported from the forward line that German troops could be seen lining up in column formations.

At 6:00 a.m. on May 2 the commander of the 56th German Tank Corps, General of the Artillery Weidling, with two other generals from his staff, crossed the lines and surrendered. Weidling informed us that he was also in command of the Berlin defenses. He had been appointed to this position six days previously.

Asked by Colonel Semchenko whether the corps was surrendering with Goebbels' knowledge, Weidling answered that he had decided to surrender without informing Goebbels.

I ordered the cease-fire along the entire sector of the corps and asked that General Weidling, Lieutenant Colonel Matusov, and the interpreter be brought to me. I turned to Fritsche's emissaries:

"Do you and Fritsche know that the Berlin garrison has begun to surrender?"

They answered that at the time of their departure they had known nothing.

"At present the German troops are surrendering along all the sectors of the front. Where is Bormann?"

"Apparently he was in Hitler's Chancellery. There was a gas explosion. Bormann and Goebbels' family died there."

The news is fresh, yet hard to believe! I called Marshal Zhukov on the phone and reported the reason for the arrival of Fritsche's emissaries.

"Could we depend on Dr. Fritsche to say the things that should be said in his broadcast to the German people?" Zhukov asked.

I answered that we could, but under our supervision. We would be able to arrange it.

That marked the end of our conversation. I summoned Colonel Vaigachev, Deputy Army Chief of Intelligence for Political Affairs. Dawn was breaking. It was May 2, 6:45 a.m.

Marshal Zhukov rang up. I spoke to him and afterward announced to all those present, the emissaries from Fritsche above all:

"First. The Soviet command accepts the surrender of Berlin and is issuing the order for the cessation of military operations.

"Second. The remaining German civilian and military authorities must announce to all soldiers, officers, and civilians that all military property, buildings, and communal facilities and valuables must be preserved in good order. Nothing must be blown up or destroyed, particularly military property.

"Third. You, Herr Heinersdorf, will go with our officers to Dr. Fritsche, take him with you to the radio station for his broadcast, after which you will return here.

"Fourth. Once again I confirm that we guarantee the lives of soldiers, officers, generals, and civilians; and, whenever possible, we will render medical assistance to the wounded.

"Fifth. We demand that there be no provocations whatsoever on the part of the Germans—shooting or any other diversionary actions. Otherwise our troops will be forced to adopt countermeasures."

Heinersdorf asked that the personnel of the Ministry of Propaganda be protected.

"Those," I said, "who will voluntarily lay down their arms and will engage in no hostile activities against the Soviet people may rest assured that not a single hair on their heads will be touched."

Colonel Vaigachev came with an interpreter, Guards Master Sergeant Zhuravlev. I gave Vaigachev the following assignment:

"You will accompany Heinersdorf to Dr. Hans Fritsche. In the name of the German government, let this Hans Fritsche order the German troops to surrender, in full order, with weapons and equipment. Fritsche must broadcast the fact that the Soviet Command has accepted the request for surrender and is taking Berlin and its entire garrison under its protection. You will see to it that Fritsche gets to our radio station and that he broadcasts what I just said. After his broadcast he and his closest assistants are to come here. Here we shall discuss what will happen next. Is that clear?"

Colonel Vaigachev, Master Sergeant Zhuravlev, and the German delegation went to the door. There they unexpectedly bumped into Weidling. The latter looked at his compatriots malevolently and grumbled:

"This should have been done sooner."

General Weidling was a man of average height, lean, collected, wearing glasses, with hair smoothly combed back.

"Are you the commander of the Berlin garrison?" I asked.

"Yes, I am the commander of the 56th Tank Corps."

"Where is Krebs? What did he tell you?"

"I saw him yesterday at the Imperial Chancellery. I believe that he committed suicide. First he blamed me for the fact that, unofficially, the surrender had begun yesterday. Today the order to surrender was issued to the corps. Yesterday Krebs, Goebbels, and Bormann rejected the surrender. Soon afterward, however, Krebs convinced himself that the encirclement was very tight and decided, in defiance of Goebbels' wishes, to put an end to the senseless bloodshed. I repeat, I have ordered the surrender of my corps."

"What about the entire garrison? Does your authority extend over it?"

"Last night I issued a general order to continue fighting but then— issued another."

I could sense the disorder reigning in the German camp. Weidling showed me on a German map the location of his headquarters and of the corps units, the Volkssturm, and others. The surrender was to begin at 6:00 a.m.

General Sokolovskii came in. Now Weidling was under crossfire. "Where did Hitler and Goebbels go?"

"To the best of my knowledge, Goebbels and his family were to have committed suicide. The Fuehrer did this on April 30. His wife took poison."

"Were you told of this or did you see it?"

"On April 30 in the evening I was at the Imperial Chancellery. I was told this by Krebs, Bormann, and Goebbels."

"So, is this the end of the war?"

"In my view every unnecessary casualty is a crime, madness."

"You're right. How long have you been in the army?"

"Since 1911. I started in the ranks."

Suddenly Weidling had a nervous fit. Sokolovskii and I pretended not to notice anything and began to exchange a few words between ourselves. When the German calmed down, Sokolovskii told him:

"You must issue the order for total surrender."

"I could not issue a general order for surrender owing to lack of communications." Weidling explained. "Therefore, there can be many pockets of resistance still left. Many are unaware of the Fuehrer's death, since Dr. Goebbels forbade its proclamation."

"We have ceased military operations completely and even grounded our air force. Don't you know what's happening? Your troops began to surrender; then a civilian delegation was sent by Fritsche with a declaration of surrender; to facilitate its task we ceased military operations."

"I will willingly help stop military actions on the part of our troops."

He indicated on the map the location of the still remaining SS units. Most of them were around the Imperial Chancellery.

"Their intention is to make a breakthrough to the north," Weidling reported. "My authority does not extend to them."

"Give the order for total surrender—there should be no resistance even in isolated sectors."

"We have no ammunition. Therefore, resistance cannot last long."

"We know this. Write down your total surrender order and your conscience will be clear."

Weidling drafted the order. I glanced at my watch. 7:50 a.m.

"Do you need your assistant?" I asked Weidling.

"Oh yes, yes! That would be very good!" said the General eagerly.

I summoned the chief of staff of the 56th German Tank Corps. A man entered—tall, dark-haired, wearing a monocle, hair neatly parted, gray gloves on his hands. The Germans engaged in a discussion. Weidling clutched at his head but kept on writing. Then, he began to read aloud:

"On April 30 the Fuehrer committed suicide—"

General Sokolovskii interrupted:

"We have been told that Doenitz has announced this to the entire world."

"No," Weidling objected. "Yesterday Dr. Goebbels told me that Stalin alone had been informed of the fact."

"Yesterday an unidentified station of the German radio network reported that Hitler had died a heroic death."[70]

Puzzled, Weidling shrugged his shoulders and, silently, handed the draft order to me. Some of its formulations, perhaps, were not good. It read:

On April 30 the Fuehrer committed suicide and thereby left us, who had pledged our allegiance to him, on our own. The Fuehrer had ordered you, the German troops, to go on fighting for Berlin despite the fact that your ammunition was exhausted and regardless of the overall circumstances which made our further resistance senseless. I hereby order the immediate cessation of all resistance. Weidling, General of the Artillery, former Commandant of the Berlin Defense District.

"Not 'former'; you are still commandant," Sokolovskii corrected him.

General Pozharskii turned to me:

"Does the oath of allegiance have to be mentioned?"

"This should not be changed," I answered. "This is his own order."

Weidling was in a quandary whether to call this an appeal or an order.

"An order," I said.

"In how many copies?" the translator asked.

"Twelve. No, as many as possible—"

"I have a big staff," Weidling said. "I have two chiefs of staff and two more generals who came out of retirement and put themselves at my disposal. They will help organize the surrender."

A typewriter began to click.

Tea was brought in. The Germans were taken to another room and fed. We—Sokolovskii, Tkachenko, Pronin, Vainrub, Pozharskii, and I—reviewed over and over again the events of the last few days and hours. Some found strange the version of the burning of Hitler's and Goebbels' bodies and General Krebs' disappearance.

"Did you notice Weidling's nervous fit?" I asked.

"It's very difficult for him," Sokolovskii said.

"Naturally," Pronin pointed out. "But it is a clever order. He skillfully emphasized the oath of allegiance and the circumstances."

We were informed that the order was ready. I gave Army Chief of Staff General Beliavskii the following instruction:

"A Soviet and a German officer will get into a car; each will be given a copy of this order. They will ride through the streets and announce it to the troops and to the population."

It was a gray, cool morning. We reminisced about Stalingrad, joked and smoked. It was 11:30 a.m.

The adjutant reported that Fritsche was brought in on a self-propelled gun.

We were standing in a group when Fritsche entered. He was short, with glasses, wearing a gray coat. He was reading papers as he walked. He sat down silently with the interpreter by his side.

Fritsche also accepted the stipulations of unconditional surrender. Whether he liked it or not, this was the inevitable result of our negotiations.

SOKOLOVSKII (to Fritsche): We are interested in keeping Berlin calm. We can protect those who fear for their lives.

FRITSCHE: The German police force has scattered but could be reassembled.

SOKOLOVSKII: We are not interested in the police. The police will be considered as prisoners of war. We are interested in the administrative officials. We shall give them protection, and no harm will come to them.

FRITSCHE: I do not understand. Who could cause them any harm and where? Who would dare indulge in any excesses?

SOKOLOVSKII: Some of our soldiers or the German population might be cruel toward you for the conduct of the Gestapo and other such activities.

FRITSCHE: Yes, that is possible.

SOKOLOVSKII: We have planned for everything and made suitable announcements. We have appointed a commandant for Berlin—Soviet General Berzarin. District commandants' offices have been set up. They will take all necessary measures. Do you have any other wishes?

FRITSCHE: I wrote you a letter as the last man in charge of the government. I wrote it to prevent bloodshed.

SOKOLOVSKII: We understand the gesture forced on you by circumstances.

FRITSCHE: I should like to expand this document, for which reason I would have to get in touch with Doenitz.

"At 10:00 a.m. this morning," I said, "Doenitz turned to the army and the people with the statement that he had assumed the leadership and would continue the struggle against Bolshevism to the end and that he would also fight the Americans and the British should they stand in his way. He does not frighten us, however!"

FRITSCHE: I was unaware of this. Where am I to remain?

SOKOLOVSKII: Here. Wait for our further instructions.

Fritsche was taken out. Was he not perhaps a "plant"?[71] I went on, thinking aloud:

"Doenitz has proclaimed Himmler a traitor. Thus, Berlin has surrendered separately. Could it be that Hitler has gone underground? All in all, we have finished them off. You can imagine the disintegration and political disorder in their ranks for Goebbels to turn to us!"

My irony was understood, and everyone laughed.

Happy news from Army headquarters. Our units had come in contact with troops of General Kuznetsov's Assault Army. The fighting in the area of the Reichstag and the Imperial Chancellery as well as along the entire Tiergarten had come to an end. Everything was quiet in Berlin.[72] . . .

PART III   THE VICTORS

Introduction

THE CONCLUDING EXCERPTS recreate mood and atmosphere during the first days and weeks following the war's end in Europe. They begin with an account of the meeting in the heart of Germany between the Allied commanders, Marshal Konev and General Bradley, and then move to the jubilant victory celebrations and receptions in Moscow which were crowned by the imposing military parade of June 24, 1945 in Red Square. The memoirs of Soviet military leaders convey the indescribable relief which peace brought, the elation, joy, and pride that for a moment obscured the memory of war's hardship and sorrow.

The optimistic mood of those happy days colored popular expectations of the future. Widespread hope existed among all groups in Soviet society that sacrifice and effort had earned them a better· life, one far different from the terror of the 1937–41 period. At the same time, some feared that the return to peace might also bring a return to those methods of internal rule, recol-

550

lection of which even war could not efface. These two aspects of popular feeling in those first days of victory are vividly expressed in the memoirs of the Soviet writer, Il'ia Ehrenburg:

And how would things be in our country after the war? This preoccupied me even more. . . . Above all, what would Stalin do now? . . . On that day [of victory] everyone must have felt that this was one more milestone, perhaps the most important one: something had ended, something was beginning. I realized that the new, postwar life would be hard: the country was devastated and impoverished; the war had killed off the young, the strong, probably the best; but I also knew how much our people had gained in stature. I remembered the wise and hopeful words about the future which I had more than once heard in trenches and dugouts. And if anyone had told me that evening that ahead of us lay the Leningrad case, the indictment of the doctors . . . I should have taken him for a madman. No, I was no prophet.*

*Il'ia Ehrenburg, *The War, 1941–45* (London: MacGibbon and Kee, 1964), pp. 190–91.

Marshal I. S. Konev
Meeting with Bradley

[IN THE BEGINNING of May] I met the commander of US forces in Europe, General Omar Bradley. I should like to describe our meeting, especially in view of the fact that General Bradley has already done so in his book, *A Soldier's Story*. I see no need to enter into a debate with him over the way certain facts are presented in his book, but I think it useful to give the reader an idea of these meetings from my viewpoint.[73]

I first met him a week after our troops joined up with the Americans on the Elbe. This took place at my command post, some 40 km. northeast of Torgau. Bradley arrived with a retinue of generals and officers and a great—I might say excessive—number of correspondents and photographers. On our side, in addition to myself, there were members of the Army Group's military council, the Army Group chief of staff, Commander of the 5th Guards Army Zhadov, and Commander of the 34th Guards Corps Baklanov, whose troops were the first to meet the Americans on the Elbe. There were also a number of correspondents from our newspapers, cameramen and photographers, but in far more modest numbers than the Americans.

There have been various times in the past and also the present when, through no fault of ours, Soviet-American relations have left much to be desired. In the interests of historical accuracy, I must say that on that day, May 5, 1945, the meeting of the two commanders—American and Soviet—was friendly and took place in an atmosphere of frankness and straightforwardness. After all, Bradley and I were soldiers, not diplomats, and this left its mark on both our meetings: they were official and friendly at the same time.

Bradley and I examined his map, on which the position of American troops on that day—May 5, 1945—had been marked. Bradley explained briefly which of his forces had advanced to which points along the line agreed upon, and then asked me how we intended to take Prague and whether American forces should not assist us in its capture.

I. S. Konev, *Sorok piatyi* (Moscow, 1966), pp. 220–28.

The question did not surprise me. Although the advance of the 2nd, 4th, and 1st Ukrainian Army Groups against Schoerner's group had not yet begun, the Americans could no longer have any doubt that the advance was to start in the very near future. I told Bradley that there was no need to give us any assistance in taking Prague, and that any advance of the American troops east of the agreed line of contact with us could lead to confusion and a mixing of troops. This was undesirable, and I asked him not to do it.[74] Bradley agreed with me and said the forces under his command would continue strictly to observe the established line.

I answered Bradley's question about how we intended to take Prague in a general way, saying that Soviet troops directed against Czechoslovakia were in a position to cope with the task and certainly would cope with it. I did not go into details about forthcoming action by our Army Group. I did not consider it possible to give information on my own operational plans. Although I believed in my heart that the troops of the 1st Ukrainian Army Group would play a decisive role in the liberation of Prague, even had I felt I had the right to speak of it, I would have tried to avoid any predictions on that score.[75]

At dinner I spoke in my first official toast of the trials and tribulations the Soviet army had gone through on its way to victory. I also spoke of the importance of President Roosevelt's role in the formation of the anti-Hitler coalition and in all of its subsequent action. Roosevelt's death was still a fresh memory, and I was one of those who felt his loss deeply and sincerely. Therefore, in giving my official condolences on the untimely end of the American President, I introduced my own personal feelings too and expressed the hope that the new president would continue to work for the cause for which Roosevelt had fought. (Unfortunately, this hope was not realized. Roosevelt's successor was very soon to make his first contribution to the aggravation of relations between our countries.) In speaking of our mutual struggle against the fascist aggressors, I singled out and praised the incontestable services of the officers and men of the 12th American Army Group in this struggle.

In his answering toast, General Bradley spoke of the courage of Soviet soldiers and the bravery of the troops of the 1st Ukrainian Army Group who, in his words, set an example for American soldiers, officers, and generals. After dwelling on Roosevelt's services, he expressed regret that the President had not lived to see the happy days of victory, and then proposed a toast to our meeting.

After the preliminary official toasts, a friendly conversation began at the table, interrupted, so to speak, by local toasts in honor of our staff officers, American staff officers, army commanders, and officers of various branches of the service. These toasts were warm and friendly. They bore witness to the genuine respect we had for one another and to the value we placed on our wartime friendship born and strengthened in the fight against a common enemy.[76] I shall not relate all the conversations that followed at dinner—they were fairly long and generally on the same themes touched upon in our mutual toasts.

After dinner I invited Bradley and his companions to attend a performance by a song and dance ensemble of the 1st Ukrainian Army Group. This ensemble, formed in Kiev in 1943 under the leadership of Lidiia Chernysheva, was very popular with us. It had some truly outstanding musicians, singers, and dancers. When the ensemble sang the US national anthem, the Americans joined in and applauded our musicians warmly afterward. They also applauded when the ensemble sang the Soviet national anthem.[77]

The artists of the ensemble were in particularly good form that day. In addition to our songs, they sang the humorous American song, "There Is a Tavern in the Town," and the English song, "It's a Long Way to Tipperary," both enthusiastically received by our guests. Then there was a performance of a Ukrainian *gopak* and a Russian folk dance—our dancers' star numbers—which make a vivid impression under ordinary circumstances and made an even more vivid one that day, thanks to the happy holiday mood we and our guests shared.

General Bradley, who sat next to me, was interested in knowing what the ensemble was and how the artists had gotten to the front. I told him that the ensemble was made up of our own soldiers, who had covered the big battle circuit along with the troops of the Army Group. I thought, however, that he did not quite believe me, and a pity it was, too, because most of the members of the ensemble had actually begun the war as soldiers, and later, after the ensemble had been created, had performed many times in the battle zones, sometimes under far from safe conditions.

When it had ended, Bradley thanked me for the concert and announced the US Government's decision to award me, as commander of the 1st Ukrainian Army Group, an important American medal. He thereupon presented me with the medal, and, as is customary in such circumstances, congratulated and embraced me. My comrades of the Army Group who took part in this meeting sincerely approved of the award. They correctly interpreted it as an American testimonial to the military feats performed by the troops I had the honor to command.

After the brief presentation ceremony, Bradley and I left the building in which the dinner and concert had taken place. There in the open air—in the presence of a large audience, which had gathered in connection with the arrival of our American guests—I presented General Bradley, in the name of the fighting men of the 1st Ukrainian Army Group, a Red flag as a symbol of our friendship and our meeting. I was already aware that Bradley intended to give me the Willys jeep he had brought with him from his headquarters in his plane. I, too, had a personal gift ready for him—my war horse—which I presented first. This horse had gone everywhere with me since I assumed command of the Steppe Army Group in the summer of 1943. It was a handsome, well-trained Don stallion. With it, I gave Bradley my saddle, bridle, and all the trappings.

It seemed to me that he was truly pleased with the gift. After accepting the horse, he in turn presented me with the light-weight Willys, which bore the inscription "to the Commander of the 1st Ukrainian Army Group from the soldiers of the 12th US Army Group." With it he gave me an American flag and an American submachine gun.[78]

A few days later, I paid a return visit to Bradley's headquarters. We drove in our own cars to Torgau, where we were met by a senior officer of Bradley's staff and an interpreter, who accompanied us as far as Leipzig. In Leipzig, Bradley himself met me and suggested I fly in his personal plane the rest of the way to his headquarters, which was a good distance.

We boarded his C-47, which was escorted the entire way by two fighter squadrons. They kept making every possible kind of maneuver in the air, reforming and demonstrating a superior class of group flying. When our plane landed not far from Kassel, the fighters went off spectacularly at various graded heights, down to the very lowest, to zero altitude. I must admit, I thought at the time that the fighter escort was there not just to do us honor, but to demonstrate its master piloting.

We had an escort from the airport to the region of Kassel, too. First came some armored vehicles, behind them a car with a powerful siren, followed by the car in which Bradley, the translator, and I rode. Behind us there were armored carriers again and, at the end, three tanks. Troops were lined up at intervals on the way from the airport to Bradley's residence—representatives of every service with, I believe, the sole exception of the navy. We were met by numerous officers of Bradley's staff and even more numerous correspondents when we drove up to the buildings.

In the main reception room, Bradley offered us a cocktail made, he told us, from his own recipe. The cocktail was ladled from a huge, brass pot into soldiers' mugs. I was told this was traditional. Well, traditions are what they are.

Immediately after cocktails, Bradley took me to his staff quarters at the other end of town. An honor guard composed of all types of troops was drawn up in front of the building. Bradley and I reviewed the unit.

I requested then that the General order the troops to stand at attention. When this had been done, on instructions of the Soviet government I presented General Bradley in front of the honor guard with the Order of Suvorov, First Class. Bradley is a reserved man, but I thought he was moved at that moment. We embraced, and I congratulated him.

Then Bradley and I entered the hall in which the table had been set for dinner. And the affair again started, as is customary, with toasts. The first toast was proposed by the host, the second one by me—to our meeting, to Bradley, and to his brothers-in-arms and friends gathered at the table.

During dinner the conversation hardly touched on military subjects. The only military topic we did discuss at this time was Suvorov. Having been given the Order of Suvorov, Bradley was interested in this historical personage. It became clear that he had known nothing about Suvorov before, and right there at the table I had to recount Suvorov's major campaigns, including the Italian campaign and the Swiss expedition.[79] In conclusion, I told Bradley that Suvorov was the greatest military genius in the history of the Russian army and that the order I had presented to him that day was primarily an award for military leadership, a tribute to a man's contribution as a military commander. I told him it was the highest award we had for commanders of large formations, and that Marshal Stalin had personally instructed me to present this order to him, General Bradley.[80]

After dinner, two violinists in American uniform, one much older than the other, played several magnificent duets. I should say at once that the superlative violin playing that I had the opportunity of hearing in Bradley's headquarters that day was not surprising: these two soldiers were the famous violinist Jascha Heifetz and his son.

In the pauses between numbers, Bradley looked at me somewhat ironically. Obviously my supposition had been correct. He had not believed me when I told him at our first meeting that our song and dance ensemble was made up of soldiers from our Army Group. He apparently believed I had played a little trick on him and decided to retaliate in a friendly way by masquerading Jascha Heifetz and his son as American soldiers.[81]

There was a warm atmosphere at dinner. The Americans present included generals, commanders of armies, corps, and divisions. During the dinner conversation, I remember Bradley's expressing his regret several times that General Patton was not there. He referred to Patton's army as the best American army and to Patton as the most outstanding American general, a man capable of bold tactics and decisive use of tank troops.

Once or twice Bradley introduced General Eisenhower's name into the conversation. Bradley spoke of him with respect but had more esteem for him as a diplomat than as a military commander. From what Bradley said, it was obvious that a very great deal of Eisenhower's time and energy was taken up with the coordination of action between the Allied commands and governments, so that almost the entire burden of the practical leadership of American troops in Europe fell to Bradley, who did not see eye to eye with Eisenhower on a number of points.

We spoke through interpreters, and for that reason, I may not have caught some shades of meaning quite accurately, but this was the general impression I had of the conversation.

Bradley himself made a favorable impression on me as a man and as a soldier at both our meetings. He was no longer young in May of '45—he was already about sixty. A professional soldier, he was strong, calm, and reserved. Judging from our exchange on military subjects, his analysis of events was accurate and interesting, and he realized the importance that powerful artillery, tanks, and aviation had acquired during the war. He understood the nature of modern warfare well and accurately differentiated the primary from the secondary. I felt he also had a profound understanding of artillery matters and appraised our tanks, their armament, armor, engines, etc. with a knowledgeable eye. In sum, I both felt and could see that the man beside me was well oriented in the use of all arms of the service, and this, in my opinion, is the primary mark of a highly qualified commander. I had the impression that here was a military man in the full sense of the word, an army leader worthy of representing American troops in Europe.

In our talks, he appeared well disposed toward our people and our army and, it seemed to me, he was sincere in praising our latest combat operations. He also showed that he understood the full extent of the difficulty of the fight the Soviet army had been waging with the Germans. In one of our conversations he told me outright that our army had borne the brunt of the war in the fight with the Germans. In other words, he said precisely what many other generals in the West, who had once been our allies, subsequently so stubbornly ignored or even tried to refute. Bradley, judging by our conversation, understood very well that the big, difficult, prolonged, and stubborn fight had fallen to the lot of the Soviet army.

Our conversation showed that we also agreed on our evaluation of the enemy. He considered the German army strong, battle-hardened, and capable of waging a stubborn fight with great skill and fortitude.

Our meeting began and ended in a relaxed atmosphere that testified to the genuinely good, friendly relations we then had. When I left Bradley, I was in the best of spirits, and it was only on the way back that my mood was a little clouded by one small detail.

It was this. When we sat down to dinner, I noticed a microphone in front of me. I saw no need to broadcast the toasts made at the table and asked that the microphone be taken away. Bradley immediately gave orders to this effect. But as I was returning to my own command post, I turned on the radio and heard my own voice on the air. The toast I had made at Bradley's dinner had been recorded, nevertheless, and was now being broadcast. True, I did not attach any basic importance to this, but I shall not hide that, inasmuch as we had agreed earlier to eliminate it, the breaking of a promise in even so insignificant a matter left me with a rather unpleasant aftertaste. However, I assume it was done without Bradley's knowledge and that he himself was tricked by the correspondents in this instance. It goes without saying that for me both meetings with Bradley were, at the time, events of considerable importance and interest.[82]

Chief Marshal of Artillery N. N. Voronov
First Weeks of Peace

AFTER MIDNIGHT on May 7, 1945 a large Hitlerite group of forces ceased resistance on the second front in the region of Reims and began to surrender. Our Allies officially formalized this event through the surrender protocol of the fascist German troops in the above-mentioned region, a protocol which was signed by Major General of the Artillery I. Susloparov, as a representative of the USSR. Having learned this, Chief of the General Staff, General of the Army A. I. Antonov sent early in the morning to the heads of the English and US military missions in Moscow, Admiral Archer and General John Dean, a document which demanded the signing of the general act of unconditional surrender in Berlin on May 8, 1945, to supersede the temporary protocol signed in Reims. This demand was legitimate and had full legal justification. On the same day a message was received from General Eisenhower who agreed to the arrival of Allied representatives in Berlin on May 8, 1945, for the purpose of signing the final act of unconditional surrender by the German armed forces.

During the day on May 7 Stalin telephoned me and began to ask questions in an irritated tone: Who the hell is the "famous" General of

N. N. Voronov, "Podvig sovetskogo naroda," *Istoriia SSSR*, 1965, No. 3, pp. 24–26.

the Artillery Ivan Susloparov, and did I know that he had dared without telling the Soviet government and without its permission to sign a document of such tremendous international importance—the capitulation to the Allies of the Hitlerite forces in the Reims region. At the same time many harsh words were thrown at me for failing to educate artillery officers properly. In conclusion Stalin added that Susloparov had been called to Moscow immediately and that he would be punished harshly. The conversation ended on this. The blunder committed by Major General of the Artillery I. Susloparov did not give me any peace. I did not know how and why he was in the Reims area. During the historically memorable and joyful days of May 7–9, 1945 all kinds of ideas about how to defend the good general were constantly in my head. A number of measures were taken, and, of course, the long awaited victory and the general rejoicing in our country and throughout the world helped.[83]

After the act of unconditional surrender of Hitler's Germany had been signed, in my joy I proposed that Supreme Headquarters mark the victory with a more powerful salute than usual—a 30-salvo artillery salute from a thousand guns. The proposal was adopted, and we had to prepare such a mighty Moscow salute immediately. New firing positions were chosen to ensure safety and to preserve the window panes of the capital, and reliable communications and control were organized. . . .

Before the historic salute in honor of Victory Day began, I could not resist joining the jubilant people on the street. This was an unforgettable sight. People were embracing each other, singing, looking at beautiful, multicolor fireworks that lit up the sky, and applauding the powerful gun salvos.

Preparations were begun for the forthcoming victory parade on June 24. At the same time the most energetic preparations and transfer of artillery units and formations to the Far East proceeded in accordance with the decision of Supreme Headquarters, and the shipment of artillery supplies there continued. How grateful I was for the timely information concerning the decisions of the Teheran conference which dealt with the problem of war with imperialist Japan! We made full use of the time given to us. For us, artillerymen, the Far East had become the most important area.[84]

A conference chaired by Stalin was held on May 21 to discuss problems of the forthcoming demobilization and of transportation not only of the demobilized soldiers but also of liberated Soviet citizens.[85]

With regard to the reduction of our armed forces Stalin said that, first of all, we had to cut back anti-aircraft defense units and cavalry by 50 percent and the infantry by 35–50 percent, as well as aviation and artillery to some extent. I was greatly surprised by Stalin's statement and general attitude toward anti-aircraft defense. Stalin's position gave grounds for the officials in the central apparatus to start an immediate and irrevocable reduction of our military forces precisely with anti-aircraft defense. Yet in three or four months we were supposed to enter into a war against Japan—the anti-aircraft defense forces were sorely needed in the Far East. It became necessary for me, my deputies, and the Main Headquarters of Anti-aircraft Defense to oppose these measures, arguing the necessity of delaying the reduction in our anti-aircraft defense forces for a longer period of time. The argument was decided in our favor.

I was anxious to hold a conference with the artillery commanders of Army Groups as soon as possible in order to exchange views about our war experience, about the reduction of forces and the imminent demobilization of older conscripts, and other important questions. However, N. A. Bulganin,[86] from whom I requested permission to hold such a conference, refused categorically. His reasons were unconvincing and hard for me to understand. In the end, after persistent requests, I was allowed to summon the Army Group artillery commanders a few at a time, quietly and unobtrusively! Why did he make me play hide and seek? Apparently it was simply the old maxim—"inaction never harmed anybody. . . ."

The day of June 24, 1945 is forever engraved on my memory. On that day, the victory parade took place in Moscow. . . . The next day a reception was held in the Kremlin for those who took part in the victory parade. Toasts rang out for the military councils of the Army Groups and for individual generals, including artillery commanders. After the second or third toast, Stalin said: "That's not right. The artillery deserves a separate toast." He called me up and asked for a list of marshals and generals of artillery.

I had to leave the Georgievskii Hall, find two sheets of paper, sit down at a small table outside the entrance to the hall, and carry out my commission. When I reentered the hall, Stalin immediately asked for my list, and then a toast was drunk to Soviet artillery, its marshals and generals, and all its soldiers. All those marshals and generals of artillery who were cited in the toast and were present in the hall, went up to the table where the governmental leaders were seated to be congratulated. The next day all newspapers described our celebration at the Kremlin and mentioned all the names of the artillerymen announced in Georgievskii Hall.[87]

The victory parade and the reception in the great Kremlin Palace were, in essence, a national celebration in honor of the victors. . . . The celebration and unforgettable victorious jubilation continued long past midnight.

Lieutenant General A. S. Iakovlev
The Capital Victorious

In HONOR of the victory, the Soviet government gave a reception at the Kremlin on May 24, 1945. While I had visited the Kremlin often before, on this occasion it was as if I were going there for the first time. I was filled with excitement and anticipation of what lay ahead.

A bumper-to-bumper line of automobiles carrying personages to the government reception passed under the arc of the Borovitskie Gates.

The Great Kremlin Palace was brightly illuminated, festive and ceremonious. The broad marble staircase, the red carpet, the light from innumerable candelabra reflected in the gilded decorations, and the huge paintings in their massive frames—all the familiar things seemed to have a special effect now.

The last reception here had been on May 2, 1941, just before the war. And here we were again in the same palace after a four-year interval—decked out in our dress uniforms, happy and proud of our victory.

The guest list included renowned marshals, generals, and admirals, distinguished government leaders, designers, actors, scientists, and workers. Many of these people had not seen one another for a long time. Everyone was excited. Friends were calling out greetings to each other, shaking hands and embracing one another. In the Georgievskii Hall, just as before the war, the tables were arranged festively and decorated with flowers.

For some reason, I remembered 1931, when, as a very young military engineer just graduated from the Air Force Academy, I attended a reception at the Kremlin. I recalled the excitement of my comrades and myself; how we stood at attention and held our breath listening to the decree which made us officers for the first time. How many years had passed since then, how many things had happened! But it seemed as if this had happened only yesterday.

Everyone looked for the seat indicated in his invitation and sat down

A. S. Iakovlev, *Tsel' zhizni* (Moscow, 1966), pp. 373–77.

at the tables. At 8:00 p.m. on the dot, Party and government leaders appeared. Ovations and shouts of "Hurrah" shook the vaulted halls of the ancient Kremlin palace with a deafening roar. They seemed endless.

As the tumult gradually subsided, Marshals of the Soviet Union were invited to the table of the Presidium. They rose from their seats in various parts of the hall and one after another—to the applause of those present—approached the table at which the Party and government leaders were seated.

The chairman, V. M. Molotov, rang a bell and, in the silence that for a moment followed, proposed a toast to the soldiers, sailors, officers, generals, and admirals of the Soviet armed forces. The first toast was met with a tumultuous ovation. Following this, there was a toast to the great Communist Party.

A delegation of Polish miners who had brought a trainload of coal to Moscow as a gift was present at the reception. The Polish guests went up to the table of the Presidium and presented their greeting.

In the intervals between the toasts Moscow's best actors and actresses performed on the stage of the Georgievskii Hall; Galina Ulanova and Ol'ga Lepeshinskaia were at the height of their glory and everyone was enchanted by the singers—Maksim Mikhailov, Mark Reizen, Valeriia Barsova, and Vera Davydova. A. V. Aleksandrov, founder and director of the Red Army Ensemble, was still alive at that time. That evening, the stars of our ballet and music truly shone. . . .[88]

The evening passed in an atmosphere of unusual enthusiasm and gaiety. The war with Hitler's Germany actually ended on May 8 with the signing of the unconditional surrender, but for all of us present at that reception, the concluding chord of the four years of war was the unforgettable evening in the Georgievskii Hall of the Kremlin Palace on May 24, 1945.

And exactly one month later, it was my good fortune to view the great apotheosis of our victory—the famous parade of our troops in Red Square on June 24, 1945. This was not the traditional parade that was held on May Day or the October holidays. . . . Between 1925 and 1945 I had seen at least 20 military parades in Red Square, but none could compare with this one. Guns with stars on their barrels still seemed to smell of gunpowder.[89] There were "Katiushas" which a short time ago had raked the enemy with withering fire. A solemn procession of tanks and military vehicles that had traversed the land of the defeated fascist Reich moved across the cobblestones of Red Square.[90]

A stunning moment of the victory parade, one that would be remembered all one's life, was the point at which the captured enemy banners were consigned to infamy. The huge orchestra suddenly stopped playing.

Red Square was immersed in silence. Then a menacing staccato beat of hundreds of drums could be heard. Marching in precise formation and beating out an iron cadence, a column of Soviet soldiers drew nigh: 200 soldiers carrying 200 enemy banners. Upon reaching the Mausoleum, the soldiers did a right turn and flung the captured enemy banners and standards with the black swastikas at the base of the Mausoleum.

There was a downpour of rain. It was impossible to tear one's eyes from the dirty banners that had been cast down onto the wet granite. The enemy had been conquered. This memory brought back the incredible difficulties, the sufferings that the nation had gone through during the war years; and now, how deep was our satisfaction at the just vengeance!

On the evening of June 24, Moscow rejoiced. It seemed as if all Muscovites were in the streets on that night. The people were celebrating their victory.

Admiral N. G. Kuznetsov
The Leader Victorious

THE WAR in Europe was over, although Japan was still resisting stubbornly. The month of May began in an atmosphere of tremendous enthusiasm over the recent victory. Everywhere preparations were being made for a parade in honor of this momentous occasion. The decision to have a parade was made in early June during one of the Kremlin conferences at which I happened to be present. Someone suggested it would not be a bad idea to follow the old way of celebrating victories and arrange a victory parade in Moscow. The idea, I recall, was immediately accepted and preparations were under way in a few days.

For the parade on June 24th, we of the navy drilled a composite unit which passed in front of Lenin's Mausoleum in Red Square under the command of Vice Admiral V. G. Fadeev, the hero of the battle for Sevastopol'. It happened to be rainy, but everyone was in an excellent mood. The parade was led by Marshal K. K. Rokossovskii. The supreme

N. G. Kuznetsov, "Na potsdamskoi konferentsii," *Voprosy istorii*, 1965, No. 8, pp. 86–88.

and unforgettable moment was when the Soviet soldiers flung the defeated enemy's flags at the foot of the Mausoleum. It seemed as if that was the end of fascism forever, then and there. The mood reigning throughout Moscow and the entire country that day certainly needs no description.

When the parade was over, the high officials stayed on in a rather small room right at the Kremlin wall. On ordinary occasions, it was pleasant to drop in there to warm up when the weather was bad during the parades and demonstrations for the First of May or the Seventh of November. This time the tradition was broken. Everyone, without exception, stood on the platform of the Mausoleum to the very end and then poured into this building. There was an impromptu banquet. The building, never designed for such large numbers of people, was crowded. All those who could, found places near the table. There was a relaxed atmosphere, unusual for those days.

Stalin, of course, was the center of attention. All successes and victories were attributed to him alone. In reviewing his contributions (which was the order of the day), the speakers manifestly exaggerated them. It was here that the proposals were made to give him the title of Generalissimo, award him the Order of Victory, and confer the title of Hero of the Soviet Union. This was rather a lot for one day, but at the time, in the flush of victory, it did not seem unusual.

There was something else I remember with particular clarity. When the numerous toasts had done their work and spirits were lifted still higher, Stalin took the floor. He thanked those present for the honor they had shown him and for their wishes for many long years to come, and, after remarking that he was already in his 67th year, he unexpectedly began talking about how many years he would be able to remain at his post. "I'll work another two or three years and then I'll have to retire"—that was the gist of what he said.

I would not venture to say whether he meant what he said or simply wanted to see the effect of such an unusual declaration on those present. As was to be expected, the cry rang out that he would live to rule the country a long time yet. Stalin did not insist. Once later, in 1952, I heard an official request for his partial retirement—at the plenary session of the Central Committee of the Communist Party of the USSR, following the 19th Party Congress. He was then relieved of the post of Minister of Defense, but kept his major offices in the Party Central Committee and the Council of Ministers. His retirement, however, was already quite inevitable by then.[91]

NOTES

CHAPTER ONE

1 An officer rank in the engineering troops equivalent to that of major.

2 Top Red Army commanders arrested in May 1937, allegedly tried by a military tribunal, sentenced to death as agents of foreign powers, and shot. Marshal Tukhachevskii served in the late 1920's as Chief of the Red Army General Staff and was at the time of his arrest a Deputy People's Commissar of Defense. He was generally recognized both within the Soviet Union and abroad as the foremost military theoretician of the Red Army. Army Commander First Rank Uborevich before his arrest commanded the Belorussian Military District. Army Commander First Rank Iakir before his arrest commanded the Red Army in the Ukraine. Army Commander Second Rank Kork served until 1935 as commander of the Moscow Military District and at the time of his arrest headed the Frunze Military Academy. Army Commander Second Rank Primakov was before his arrest Deputy Commander of the Leningrad Military District.

3 Voroshilov, a close associate of Stalin from the time of the Civil War and a veteran of the pre-revolutionary underground Party, occupied from 1934 until May 1940 the position of People's Commissar of Defense, that is, official head of the Soviet military establishment.

4 According to the Table of Ranks of the Red Army of that period, Division Commander was equivalent to Lieutenant General. The Soviet state security forces had at that time their own table of officer ranks which, as Starinov notes, were not equivalent to regular Army ranks and carried much greater weight. During the war the state security forces adopted the Red Army Table of Ranks. The head of the Soviet state security establishment, Beria, received toward the end of the war the highest military rank, that of Marshal of the Soviet Union.

5 Kotovskii, a famous Red cavalry commander in the Civil War who fought in Bessarabia and the Ukraine.

6 Starinov refers here to guerrilla schools and bases organized by the Red Army command in the Ukraine during the late 1920's and early 1930's to prepare cadres for the eventuality of foreign invasion and struggle on enemy-occupied territory. During the Great Purge all schools and bases were dissolved and their leaders arrested and accused of preparing guerrilla warfare against Soviet power. When the war broke out and the Germans occupied a large part of European Russia, the Soviet command had to organize guerrilla warfare from scratch.

7 The Order of the Red Banner was the first Soviet military decoration to be established in 1918 during the Civil War. Awarded for military valor in combat, it remains even today one of the highest combat decorations of the Soviet Union. During the Second World War 238,000 individuals received this decoration. In the early 1930's a civilian equivalent was established—the Order of the Red Banner of Labor. The Weapon of Honor, a form of military reward used in the early years of Soviet power, was usually a saber or a revolver engraved with the name of the recipient, a brief description of his accomplishment, and the name of the rewarding commander or institution.

8 Well-known commanders of the Red Army shot during the Purge. Zhelezniakov was a popular Civil War hero. The Latvian Avgust Ivanovich Baar served under Iakir, commander of the Red Army in the Ukraine, as his deputy in charge of special forces.

9 From the Great Purge in the mid-1930's the term "enemy of the people" was used in Stalin's Russia to characterize all individuals accused of conscious anti-state activity, regardless of its particular type, form, etc. In other words, it served to identify individuals who were considered political criminals.

10 Head of the Soviet secret police from 1935 through the Great Purge and, previously, a Secretary of the Party's Central Committee. The entire period of the Great Purge in Russia takes its name from

565

him—"Ezhovshchina." The behavior of Voroshilov and his conversation with Ezhov, as reported by Starinov, are better understood if one remembers that at this time Ezhov was undoubtedly the most powerful man in Russia after Stalin. Following his fall at the end of the Great Purge, no associate of Stalin has ever achieved comparable power.

11 Units of the Red Army were and are identified not only by numbers but very often also by geographic names associated with the place of their formation or the place where they fought battles, achieved victories, etc. (In this case "Korosten'" is a town in the Ukraine.) Moreover, units of the Soviet army are awarded military decorations for special accomplishments in combat or training. These decorations are also listed in the identification of the unit. In this case the 4th Korosten' Regiment was decorated with the Order of the Red Banner

12 Detachments of armed workers organized by the Bolshevik Party during the October Revolution in 1917 were called Red Guards. In February 1918 the Soviet government began to organize its regular military force, the Red Army, on the basis of Red Guards and units of the disbanded tsarist army. After the victorious war with Germany in 1945 the name Red Army was changed to Soviet Army.

13 At the Twentieth Party Congress in 1956 Khrushchev quoted a document which confirmed not only the use of torture by the Soviet secret police as a method of investigation, but the legalization of this practice on the authority of the Central Committee of the Party. This document, a telegram dispatched to local Party authorities by Stalin on January 20, 1939, reads as follows:

"The Central Committee of the All-Union Communist Party (Bolsheviks) explains that the application of methods of physical pressure in NKVD practice is permissible from 1937 on in accordance with permission of the Central Committee of the All-Union Communist Party (Bolsheviks). . . . It is known that all bourgeois intelligence services use methods of physical influence against the representatives of the socialist proletariat and that they use them in their most scandalous forms.

"The question arises as to why the socialist intelligence service should be more humanitarian against the mad agents of the bourgeoisie, against the deadly enemies of the working class and of the kolkhoz workers. The Cen-

tral Committee of the All-Union Communist Party (Bolsheviks) considers that physical pressure should still be used obligatorily, as an exception applicable to known and obstinate enemies of the people, as a method both justifiable and appropriate."

(N. S. Khrushchev, "Special Report to the Twentieth Congress of the Communist Party of the Soviet Union," *The New Leader*, 1956, Supplement, pp. S34–S35.)

14 Special Sections constituted a separate organization within the armed forces responsible to the leadership of the secret police and virtually independent of the military chain of command. Established almost at the beginning of the Red Army, they were attached to all units from battalion or regimental level, depending on the period. They engaged in counterintelligence within the military and, together with the Red Army's political apparatus, supervised the loyalty and behavior of military personnel.

15 The famous Soviet airplane designer whose two-engine dive bomber Pe-2 was the Soviet response to the German Stuka (Ju-87) dive bomber during the Second World War. The test model of the Pe-2 was flown for the first time in the Soviet Union at approximately the time described by Starinov. In other words this major Soviet weapon, which accounted for about two-thirds of all Soviet bomber aircraft produced during the Second World War (11,000 Pe-2 bombers), was designed and tested by Petliakov while in prison. Incidentally, Petliakov was not the only successful aircraft designer imprisoned during the Great Purge. So also was Tupolev, the Soviet bomber designer, best known for his jet aircraft, which is used by every Russian statesman who travels abroad.

16 Ezhov was dismissed from his post in December 1938 and disappeared. Soviet authorities have never made an official announcement concerning his fate, but he was undoubtedly executed as a victim of the same purge to which he gave his name. Beria, who succeeded Ezhov as head of the secret police, remained in office until a few months after Stalin's death when he was accused of treason and executed by his colleagues in the Party leadership during the struggle for Stalin's succession.

17 The intra-Party discussion refers here to a debate within the Soviet Communist Party during the middle and late 1920's between supporters of Stalin and those of his opponents, Trotsky, Zinoviev, and

Kamenev. During the Great Purge, at a time when arrest and execution befell even those Party members who had unflaggingly supported Stalin, those who opposed Stalin during the intra-Party discussion or merely wavered were obvious targets for arrest.

18 At the Twentieth Party Congress in February 1956 the campaign to discredit Stalin's methods of rule started.

19 Iagoda was Ezhov's predecessor as head of the Soviet secret police. He was arrested in 1935 and was later tried and executed as an agent of a foreign power.

20 A military academy named in honor of one of the creators of the Red Army and its leader in the 1920's, Mikhail Frunze. The Frunze Academy, the second highest military school in the Soviet Union, is the command and staff academy and at the same time serves as a higher infantry school. Its status is higher, therefore, than that of the military branch academies, e.g., armor, artillery, air force, etc. The overwhelming majority of Soviet officers of general rank were graduated from this academy.

21 A colonel of the tsarist army who enlisted in the Red Army in 1918 and was appointed its first commander in chief, which post he occupied until July 1919. His rank, Army Commander Second Rank, was equivalent to Colonel General. He was executed in the summer of 1938 as an "enemy of the people."

22 Soviet officers who fought in the Civil War in Spain in 1936–38 under orders of the Soviet government were automatically suspected of disloyalty upon their return. Their travel abroad, their association with foreigners, their contact with non-Communist participants in the Spanish Civil War were believed to have afforded then possibilities for recruitment by foreign intelligence and for infection by disloyal thoughts. The decoration and title Hero of the Soviet Union received by Major Arman was and remains the highest Soviet military decoration for valor (equivalent to the American Medal of Honor). It consists of a small gold star worn on the left breast above all other decorations. With the gold star of the Hero, the recipient automatically receives the Order of Lenin. Established in 1934, the decoration has been awarded to about 12,000 individuals, of whom only 600 received it prior to the outbreak of the Nazi-Soviet war.

23 The Main Political Administration of the Red Army is the headquarters of Party machinery responsible for political indoctrination and control within the Red Army. It directs a vast army of political officers on all command and staff levels. Gamarnik, a veteran Party leader, headed it from 1929. He either committed suicide or was killed while resisting arrest on May 31, 1937.

24 In the 1945–56 period a large number of Soviet officers occupied command and staff positions in the Polish army, then a satellite of the Soviet Union. In many cases they were selected because of their Polish origin and Polish sounding names. The most famous of these officers, Marshal Rokossovskii, whose father was Polish and whose mother was Russian, was appointed Polish Minister of Defense in 1949. General of the Army Poplavskii was his deputy in charge of ground forces. In 1956 after the bloodless Polish revolution the Polish government requested that an overwhelming majority of these Soviet officers, including Rokossovskii and Poplavskii, leave Poland. They resumed service in the Soviet army.

25 Lieutenant General Lev Dovator, one of the heroes of the battle of Moscow where he commanded a cavalry corps. He died in combat during the Soviet counteroffensive in December 1941 and was posthumously awarded the title Hero of the Soviet Union.

26 Stuchenko refers here to the meeting of the Party's Central Committee in January 1938 at which some expulsions from the Party and arrests were criticized as unjustified. This meeting, however, at the same time praised the Purge in general and the secret police and Ezhov, its head, in particular. Only by the end of 1938 or the beginning of 1939 did the intensity of mass terror appreciably decline.

27 L. M. Kaganovich, a close associate of Stalin and member of the Party's ruling Politburo. Throughout most of his career he was in charge of the Soviet railroad system.

28 From another place in Stuchenko's account, it seems that Nichiporovich was released from prison and reinstated in the army shortly before the outbreak of the Nazi-Soviet war. As commander of a motorized infantry division he fought the Germans in Belorussia in the summer of 1941. After his division was encircled, he formed a guerrilla detachment from the remnants of his troops and died later in combat.

29 At the time, summer 1944, Marshal Biriuzov served as chief of staff of the 3rd Ukrainian Army Group fighting on the Soviet-Rumanian border; Lieutenant

General Berzarin, whom he mentions, was commander of the 5th Assault Army in Biriuzov's Group. The chief of staff of the 5th Army to whom he refers on the following pages of his account was Major General A. M. Kushchev whose subsequent fate is not known.

30   Until the late 1930's, Iakovlev designed only sports aircraft. His UT-1 and UT-2 monoplanes were the basic training aircraft used by the Soviet air force and civilian aviation in the prewar period.

31   During that period of Soviet history the burden of proof rested with the accused. A presumption of guilt by the court was sufficient legal proof of guilt. Moreover, most of the defendants were tried not by a regular civilian or even military court but by the so-called "troikas"—groups of three secret police officers constituted as a tribunal. The police therefore accused a man of a crime, arrested him, collected the "evidence," tried and sentenced him, then executed the sentence.

32   One of the men most hated by the Soviet military, Mekhlis worked during the early 1930's in Stalin's personal secretariat and later headed the main Party daily newspaper *Pravda* (*Truth*). During the Great Purge he played a major role in organizing the purge of the armed forces. Toward the end of the Purge he was appointed Chief Political Commissar of the Red Army.

33   Chkalov, the most famous Soviet pilot of the late 1930's. In 1937 with a crew of two he made a 63-hour, non-stop 7,000-mile flight from Moscow to Vancouver over the North Pole. He died accidentally in December 1938 while testing a new fighter plane.

34   The main daily newspaper of the Young Communist League (*Komsomol*).

35   Noril'sk, a town in Siberia above the Arctic Circle and a center of Soviet nonferrous metallurgy. The basic labor force of the mines and factories in the area consisted of prisoners from numerous local concentration camps.

36   Zaveniagin, a prominent industrial manager, director of the largest Soviet steel enterprise of the 1930's, Magnitogorsk, was appointed Deputy Chief of the NKVD (secret police) for Economic Affairs in 1939. He was in charge of the NKVD's vast economic empire which employed, according to some estimates, close to 15 million slave laborers.

37   A direct telephone line, limited to "subscribers" in Moscow alone, which connected the offices of key personnel in the central Party, government, military,

and police establishments through a special switchboard in the Kremlin. Concerning the telephone network which connected the entire country, see below, Chapter Two, n. 27.

38   The Supreme Naval Council was set up in 1938 to supervise the work of the naval command. It was headed by Stalin's trusted lieutenant, Zhdanov, and consisted of a group of top naval commanders, economic managers in charge of ship-building, and Party leaders. At the time when Kuznetsov's account starts, he was commander in chief of the Soviet Pacific Fleet

39   Kuznetsov clearly minimizes Frinovskii's importance. A senior assistant to Ezhov, with a rank equivalent to Colonel General, Frinovskii was in charge of the militarized units of the NKVD for many years. (In the mid-1930's almost 200.000 NKVD men were organized in divisions, brigades, and support units.) Before Frinovskii's appointment as People's Commissar of the Navy in the fall of 1938, he headed the entire secret police organization within the Red Army, the so-called Special Sections. His appointment to the navy was an example of the extension of the powers of the secret police in the last months of Ezhov's rule.

40   In 1938 the Soviet leadership publicly proclaimed a program of building a powerful navy in place of a relatively small and defensively oriented naval force. Soviet economic development, starting from the late 1920's, was usually planned ahead in periods of five years. The naval program initiated in 1938, as Admiral Kuznetsov reports in another place, was to encompass at least three five-year periods.

41   A major seaport on the Pacific Ocean and the main base of the Soviet Pacific fleet. It is the administrative center of the Soviet Pacific Maritime Province and is located almost 4,000 miles from Moscow.

42   In accordance with Party statutes, periodic congresses of the Party were to inform political, economic, military, and cultural leaders from the capital and the provinces about the current internal and international situations and instruct them about those tasks the top leaders had set for the near future. At such meetings there are "elections" of members of leading Party organs which reflect changes that have taken place in the power configuration within the Soviet elite during the intervals between congresses. The Eighteenth Party Congress in March 1939 was the first to meet after the start of the Great Purge. Its composition regis-

tered the wholesale renewal of the upper echelons of the Soviet elite—about 80 percent of the Party's Central Committee elected at this Congress consisted of newcomers. It was also the last congress to assemble prior to the start of World War II. Stalin in his speech to the congress gave the first public hint that the Soviet Union was not irrevocably committed to an anti-Nazi stand.

43 Army Commander Second Rank (Colonel General) Shtern, who like Kuznetsov had been a Soviet "volunteer" in Spain, served at this time as commander of the 1st Far Eastern Army, which faced the Japanese Kwantung Army across the border in northern China.

44 Marshal of the Soviet Union and Civil War hero Bliukher was the top Soviet military expert on the Far East. He commanded Soviet troops in the Far East from the early 1920's. Untouched by the first wave of military purges, he signed the verdict of the Military Tribunal which condemned the top Soviet military leaders to death in 1937. He was himself arrested and executed in the fall of 1938. The previously mentioned General Shtern was his successor.

45 Admiral Kuznetsov must have had some idea "of the true scale of the violations of legality" because the theater in which he was serving was especially hard hit by the purges—about 80 percent of the command staff of the Soviet Far Eastern forces was removed. Incidentally, the commander with whom he traveled to Moscow, Shtern, was soon arrested and executed, a scant few weeks before the start of the Nazi-Soviet war.

46 At the beginning of each Party congress a presidium of the congress is elected. Composed of a few dozen individuals, including top Party and government leaders and representatives from all principal areas of the Soviet Union, it sits throughout the congress on the proscenium facing the delegates. While the presidium is a purely decorative body, selection for it is a great honor which signifies recognition by Party leaders of an individual's accomplishments or importance. The fact that Kuznetsov was selected to the presidium and his superior, the People's Commissar of the Navy, was not, provided a clue of forthcoming changes in the naval command.

47 The author refers here to the clash between Japanese troops occupying Korea and Soviet troops at Lake Khasan (Changkufeng) on the Soviet-Korean border in August 1938 in which the Soviet

side gained the upper hand. This victory was loudly praised in the Soviet press at the time and was presented as proof of the Red Army's invincibility and of the alleged fact that the military purge, far from impairing the Red Army's effectiveness, had strengthened it.

48 Stalin's closest associate, in fact his second in command. At the time he was Chairman of the Council of People's Commissars, i.e., Prime Minister of the Soviet government, a position he held from 1930.

49 Frinovskii's "request" to be relieved of his post was in fact part of a new purge which started in December 1938 and was directed against secret police officials associated with the ousted police chief Ezhov. Thousands of police officials who conducted the purge in 1937–38 disappeared without trace and were replaced by men loyal to the new police chief Beria.

50 Admiral Kuznetsov's speech dealt with more themes than he reports here. As a matter of fact one of his principal subjects was the vilification of executed army and navy commanders.

51 The Central Committee of the Party, formally the highest Party authority in the interval between congresses, had in reality no policy-making role whatever during Stalin's lifetime. While the Central Committee had no real power as a collective body and seldom met in plenary session—during the four years of the Nazi-Soviet war it met only once, in the winter of 1944—the individuals elected to the Central Committee included all top executives of the Party, government, industry, and the diplomatic and military establishments. Selection to the Central Committee constituted symbolic recognition by the top leadership of an individual's prominence in any of these areas. The Central Committee elected at the Eighteenth Party Congress had 68 full members. Kuznetsov and Shtern were among the group of 71 executives selected for the somewhat lower echelon, alternate membership in the Central Committee.

52 Zhdanov, Secretary of the Central Committee and Party boss of Leningrad, was at the time the rising star in Stalin's entourage. In 1938 he was appointed Stalin's watchdog over naval affairs. In the 1939–41 period he was also used frequently by Stalin to supervise general military affairs.

53 Soviet sources make no reference to the identity of Smirnov-Svetlovskii. It seems

almost certain that this is the same Smirnov, previously mentioned by Kuznetsov, who was appointed People's Commissar of the Navy when the commissariat was created in 1937. He was replaced later by Frinovskii and served as Frinovskii's deputy until Kuznetsov was appointed People's Commissar.

54 Supreme Naval Staff was the naval equivalent of the Soviet General Staff, subordinate to the People's Commissar of the Navy. Vice Admiral Galler, its chief in the 1938–40 period, was a former tsarist naval officer who joined the Soviet navy in 1918 and who before his appointment to Moscow commanded the Baltic Fleet. During the war he served as Deputy People's Commissar of the Navy in charge of shipbuilding and armament. From 1947 he served as commandant of the Naval Academy in Leningrad. In 1949 during the purge of the Leningrad leadership he was arrested and a year later died in prison.

55 One of the rising Soviet industrial managers, Tevosian was at the time People's Commissar for Shipbuilding. During the war and in the postwar period he became one of the most prominent executives in Soviet defense industries.

56 Pre-Purge leaders of the Soviet navy. Orlov, a career naval officer, was commander in chief of the Soviet navy from 1931 until his arrest in 1937. Muklevich, a Party leader assigned to the navy, served as its commander in chief in the late 1920's and later as Director of Naval Construction. He was arrested and executed in the spring of 1937. Pantserzhanskii was commander in chief of the navy in the mid-1920's and later Deputy Commander of the Navy in charge of Combat Training. He was arrested in 1937. Kozhanov, commander of the Black Sea Fleet, was arrested in 1937. Viktorov was a career naval officer who before his arrest in the fall of 1938 served as commander of the Pacific Fleet, Kuznetsov's predecessor in the Far East.

57 The Supreme Soviet of the USSR—the bicameral legislature of the Soviet Union—was an institution of purely ritualistic importance during Stalin's lifetime. Its executive body, the Presidium, issued decrees concerning top governmental appointments which were later ratified by the plenary session of the Supreme Soviet.

58 At the time described in his memoirs Iakovlev headed a fighter aircraft design bureau. In 1939 he designed the famous fighter aircraft "Iak" which accounted for over half of all Soviet fighters produced during the war (37,000 Iak-1 and modified Iak-3 fighters).

59 Poskrebyshev headed Stalin's personal secretariat. He played a key role in Kremlin politics and disappeared immediately after Stalin's death.

60 M. M. Kaganovich, one of three brothers who played an important part in Soviet politics during the 1930's. The most famous of the three, L. M. Kaganovich, was a Politburo member and chief of Soviet railroads. The brother described here was one of the managers of Soviet heavy industry during the 1930's. After his dismissal in 1940 he disappeared from public view, and his fate is unknown. The third brother, a Party secretary of the large industrial center of Gor'kii, also disappeared about the same time. The fall into disfavor of the two brothers may have been related at least in part to the dismissal of a large number of Soviet leaders of Jewish origin while the Nazi-Soviet Pact was in force. L. M. Kaganovich, however, remained in Stalin's good graces through the period, although his public visibility clearly declined.

61 This curious argument—don't worry about being able to handle your job because your superior also lacks experience—was standard in the post-Purge period. The newly appointed Commissar for the Aviation Industry Shakhurin occupied the position throughout the war. In 1946 he was dismissed for alleged misdirection of aviation development and excessive expenditure of state funds. Only in 1956 was he rehabilitated and appointed First Deputy Minister of the Aviation Industry.

62 *Izvestiia (News),* the principal daily newspaper of the Soviet government.

63 In all probability the newspaper mentioned here was being published by Russian emigrés in eastern Poland prior to its occupation by Soviet troops in September 1939. The northern part of this territory was incorporated into Belorussia, thus the name Western Belorussia.

64 One of the key designers of Russian small arms. His sub-machine gun was a basic weapon of Soviet infantry in the Second World War.

65 Soviet industry at that time was administered by several People's Commissariats (Ministries), each responsible for one or more branches of production. A Commissariat was subdivided into a number of Main Administrations (*Glavki*), each in charge of the manufacture of a particular

type of product. With the exception of the 1957–65 period this organizational form of industrial state management has prevailed in the Soviet Union.

66 General of the Army Pavlov commanded a tactical tank unit until 1936. In 1936–37 he was in charge of Soviet tank forces in the Republican Army during the Spanish Civil War. Shortly after his return he was catapulted into the position of directing all Soviet armor and motorized forces.

67 Before Emelianov became an industrial executive, he was engaged in research and teaching at Moscow technical institutes and continued to do so while occupying various governmental posts. A Doctor of Science, he wrote four books on metallurgy and in 1953 was elected to the Soviet Academy of Sciences, one of the highest marks of recognition for scholarly achievement.

68 In order to provide convincing proof of the groundlessness of the military's defense of screen armor, a defense based on experience during the Spanish Civil War, Emelianov contrived to borrow from General Pavlov a sample of the armor used by Soviet tankmen in Spain and to demonstrate in an actual test its vulnerability to machine-gun fire.

69 The following episode took place half a year after that concerning the screen armor. Frustrated by the difficulties of expanding the output of tank turrets produced by a stamping process, the only one in use at the time, Emelianov suggested as an alternative the application of the casting method for which Soviet industry was better prepared. His suggestion was approved by the governmental Defense Committee chaired by the People's Commissar of Defense, Marshal Voroshilov. On this basis Emelianov issued orders to defense plants to switch to the new process. His narrative begins three days after this order was issued.

70 Colonel General (later Chief Marshal of Armored Troops) Fedorenko assumed command of Red Army armored units from General Pavlov in June 1940. He occupied this post throughout the war and until his death in 1951.

71 The use of the surname is the most formal form of address in Russian. The use of the name and patronymic in Russian does not compare in familiarity with the use of the first name in English. The use of name and patronymic is usually accompanied by the second person plural. It establishes a certain distance between

the speakers and may connote deep respect and even a warmth of feeling.

72 Nosenko, the People's Commissar of Machine Building and Emelianov's superior.

73 The trade agreement was signed in February 1940. It was a barter agreement according to which the Soviet government was to deliver over 1,000,000 metric tons of feed grains, about 900,000 tons of oil, 100,000 tons of cotton, 100,000 tons of chromium, half a million tons of iron ore, 2.5 metric tons of platinum, and a number of other items with a total valuation of 600 million German marks in return for German industrial products, machinery, and armaments.

74 Aside from Iakovlev, the two best known members of the delegations were Dement'ev, at the time director of a large aircraft plant who during the war was in charge of receiving aircraft plant equipment from the United States under the Lend-Lease program and is today the Minister of the Aviation Industry, and Polikarpov, a well-known aircraft designer whose fighter planes constituted the mainstay of the Soviet air force during the 1930's.

75 Ernst Udet, one of the greatest German fighter pilots during the First World War, second only to Richthofen in the number of aircraft he shot down. In the 1930's he headed the technical department of the German air ministry and in the first years of the Second World War was in charge of air force supplies. In November 1941 the Germans announced that General Udet had died while testing a new weapon. It was later learned that he shot himself because of intolerable relations with his superior, Marshal Goering. He was one of the few German air force generals who was well liked in the West and, as Iakovlev's account shows, also in the Soviet Union.

76 For an account of the Nazi-Soviet negotiations in November 1940, see the following excerpt from the memoirs of V. M. Berezhkov.

77 German accounts confirm Iakovlev's supposition. The following excerpt from the memoirs of the famous German armor commander, General Guderian, is interesting because it shows the German reaction to the disbelief of the Soviet visitors. Guderian writes:

"In the spring of 1940 Hitler had specifically ordered that a Russian military mission be shown over our tank schools and factories; in this order he had insisted that nothing be concealed

from them. The Russian officers firmly refused to believe that the Panzer IV was in fact our heaviest tank. They said repeatedly that we must be hiding our newest models from them and complained that we were not carrying out Hitler's orders to show them everything. They were so insistent on this point that eventually our manufacturers and the Ordnance Office officials concluded: It seems that the Russians must already possess better and heavier tanks than we do.' It was at the end of July 1941 that the T-34 tank appeared at the front and the riddle of the new Russian model was solved."
(Heinz Guderian, *Panzer Leader* [New York: E. P. Dutton and Co., 1952], p. 143.)
These conclusions were more justified in the case of tanks than in the case of airplanes. But one must assume that even had the Russians not possessed the T-34 tank, Soviet officers would still have refused to believe that the Germans were showing them the real state of their armor. Aside from the fact that such openness was very unusual in itself, it ran counter to everything that the Soviet military was taught and led to believe.

78 The Soviet delegation led by V. M. Molotov, the Prime Minister and Minister of Foreign Affairs, included Dekanozov, who was shortly afterward posted to Berlin as Soviet ambassador, and about 60 other Soviet functionaries. The author of the memoirs was an official in the People's Commissariat of Foreign Trade who served for half a year in 1940 in the Soviet Embassy in Berlin and was attached to the delegation as a consultant and translator. He and V. N. Pavlov, then First Secretary of the Soviet Embassy in Berlin and later Stalin's personal translator, were present at all meetings between the head of the Soviet delegation and the top Nazi leaders. Molotov came to Berlin on November 12, 1940 and stayed 48 hours. At the time of the meeting with Hitler which is described in the memoirs, Molotov had already conversed at length with German Foreign Minister von Ribbentrop. (At present Berezhkov is deputy editor in chief of the Soviet weekly foreign affairs magazine *New Times*.).

79 After the war the latter published an excellent account of German-Soviet relations in the 1923–41 period which included his impressions of the November 1940 meeting. See G. Hilger and Alfred G. Meyer, *The Incompatible Allies* (New York: The Macmillan Company, 1953).

80 According to the German Foreign Office's transcript of the meeting, which was later published in the United States in a collection of captured German documents, Molotov interrupted Hitler's speech several times to express his agreement with Hitler's arguments. See *Nazi-Soviet Relations 1939–41* (Washington, D.C.: U.S. Department of State, 1948), pp. 226–32.

81 According to the German transcript, Molotov's behavior was much less belligerent than Berezhkov's memoirs indicate. At the same time it seems certain that the question of Finland was the central point raised by Molotov. The Soviet government regarded with anxiety the development of closer relations between Finland and Germany.

82 The German transcript tells a somewhat different story: "Molotov expressed his agreement with the statements of the Fuehrer regarding the role of America and England. The participation of Russia in the tripartite pact appeared to him entirely acceptable in principle, provided that Russia was to cooperate as a partner and not be merely an object. In that case he saw no difficulty in the matter of participation of the Soviet Union in the common effort." (*Nazi-Soviet Relations 1939–1941, op. cit.,* pp. 233–34.)

83 This would tend to confirm the impression of many commentators that Hitler's friendly behavior in the first days of conversation led the Soviet government to increase its pressure in the negotiations on the second day, when Molotov was much more belligerent and demanding than previously. George F. Kennan makes the following comment: "Stalin, it seems to me, must have been under a serious misapprehension as to the strength of his position. He was probably misled by the interest Ribbentrop had shown in trying to bind Russia to the Axis side in the war. He evidently thought this reflected a sense of weakness on the part of the Germans, and that this in turn increased Russia's bargaining power. . . . In this, he grievously miscalculated. Hitler, whose head had now been turned with a series of brilliant military successes, was in no mood to trifle with Russia." (George F. Kennan, *Russia and the West under Lenin and Stalin* [Boston: Little, Brown and Co., 1960], pp. 343–44.)

84 According to the German transcript this remark by Molotov was not made in his conversation with Hitler but later

while talking with Foreign Minister von Ribbentrop. (See *Nazi-Soviet Relations, 1939–1941, op. cit.*, p. 254.) It seems that the evaluation of the strength of British resistance and of the Nazi entanglement in the West is crucial for understanding Soviet behavior in 1940–41. Stalin, it seems, did not believe there was great danger of Hitler turning against the Soviet Union so long as England was not defeated. This view was based on Hitler's own statement that he would not repeat the German error of World War I—a struggle on two fronts. While not devoid of logic, Stalin's view failed to take into consideration Hitler's overestimation of German military power and his belief on the one hand that England could cause little injury to Germany during any attack on the Soviet Union and on the other hand that the campaign against Russia could be won in a matter of a few months.

85 Summing up his impression of the talks between Molotov and Hitler, Hilger writes: "Two things became clear in the discussions: Hitler's intention to push the Soviet Union in the direction of the Persian Gulf, and his unwillingness to acknowledge any Soviet interest in Europe." (Hilger and Meyer, *op. cit.*, p. 324.)

86 This episode is also reported by Churchill, who heard it from Stalin. It should also be mentioned that the air raids on Berlin were deliberately staged by the British to coincide with Molotov's arrival for a conference to which they had not been invited. (Winston S. Churchill, *Their Finest Hour* [Boston: Houghton Mifflin Co., 1949], p. 586.)

87 Eight days after Molotov's return to Moscow, on November 26, 1940, the Soviet government sent a reply to Hitler's invitation to join the Four-Power Pact: "The Soviet Government is prepared to accept the draft of the Four-Power Pact . . . provided that the German troops are immediately withdrawn from Finland, which, under the compact of 1939, belongs to the Soviet Union's sphere of influence . . . ; provided that within the next few months the security of the Soviet Union in the Straits [Bosporus and Dardanelles] is assured by the conclusion of a mutual assistance pact between the Soviet Union and Bulgaria, which geographically is situated inside the security zone of the Black Sea boundaries of the Soviet Union . . . ; provided that the area south of Batum and Baku in the general direction of the Persian Gulf is recognized as the center of the aspirations of the Soviet Union; provided that Japan renounces her rights to concessions for coal and oil in Northern Sakhalin." (*Nazi-Soviet Relations, 1939–1941, op. cit.*, pp. 258–59.) Needless to say, Hitler was not willing to accept these conditions, which served only to strengthen his fears about his Soviet ally and his resolve to strike before Soviet strength matched its great power appetite.

88 The view that the Soviet Union in 1939 had no other choice than to conclude a pact with Hitler runs through all Soviet writings and, one suspects, is honestly believed by most Soviet writers even, as in this case, by a writer who criticizes Soviet behavior during the period of Nazi-Soviet friendship. This belief is based on the assumption that without the pact Hitler would have attacked Russia in 1939. There are no valid reasons, however, to believe that this would have been the case or that England or France would not have declared war on Hitler when he attacked Poland had the Nazi-Soviet Pact not existed. At the same time it does not seem valid to assume, as do some commentators, that without the pact with Russia Hitler would not have attacked Poland, thus at least postponing the war in Europe.

89 General Meretskov was the commander of the Leningrad Military District which bordered on Finland. (Leningrad itself was located only 20 miles from the Russo-Finnish frontier.) During the Winter War with Finland he commanded the 7th Army (composed of 12 rifle divisions and a tank corps) which was deployed along the axis of the main Soviet assault against Finnish fortifications on the road to Helsinki. The conversation reported by Voronov took place at the command post of the 7th Army. Marshal Kulik was Deputy People's Commissar of Defense in charge of Soviet artillery and as such was Voronov's immediate superior. General Mekhlis was at the time Chief Political Commissar of the Red Army, a position which he occupied from 1938.

90 All Soviet writers on the subject still persist in asserting that the Finns started the Winter War. Some who are not ready to state explicitly that the Finns attacked the Soviet Union make a fine distinction and say that the Finns provoked the war. The "provocation" consisted in refusing Soviet demands for large pieces of Finnish territory.

91 The right flank in the Finnish defense fortifications against which the main Soviet strike in the February 1940 offen-

sive was directed. The breach of the defenses in the Summa sector opened the way to Soviet advance up the western coast of Finland toward the port of Viipuri (Vyborg) and precipitated Finnish acceptance of peace terms dictated by the Russians.

92 See n. 47 above. The battle of Khalkhin-Gol on the Mongolian-Chinese border in August 1939 was a repetition on a larger and bloodier scale of earlier fighting between units of the Japanese Kwantung Army and Soviet troops. In this battle the future Marshal Zhukov commanded the main Soviet grouping (35 rifle battalions, 20 cavalry squadrons, 500 tanks, and 500 aircraft). He passed his first major test of high level combat command with flying colors. The performance of Soviet troops, especially of mechanized units and the air force, tended to reassure the Soviet leadership about the Red Army's capacity for mobile warfare. The shortcomings of the Red Army during the war with Finland, its inability to break through fortified defense lines in difficult terrain came then as an even greater shock to Soviet leaders.

93 Until 1937 the Soviet navy was controlled by the People's Commissariat of Defense. In December 1937 a separate Commissariat of the Navy was established which existed throughout the Second World War. At present the navy is again integrated into the organization of the Soviet Ministry of Defense.

94 A Finnish port at the southern end of the Gulf of Bothnia.

95 The major Soviet weaknesses are pointed out by the Finnish Marshal Mannerheim in his memoirs. The following are especially important: "The Russian officers were generally brave men who were little concerned about casualties, but in the higher ranks there were signs of a kind of inertia. This displayed itself in the formalism and simplicity of the operative plan, which excluded maneuvering and was obstinately pursued to victory or defeat. The Russians based their art of war on the weight of material, and were clumsy, ruthless and extravagant." (*The Memoirs of Marshal Mannerheim* [New York: E. P. Dutton and Co., 1954], p. 261.) Marshal Mannerheim further criticizes Soviet armor and the air force but considers the performance of Soviet artillery decisive for the Soviet victory and judges artillery equipment up to modern standards.

96 Admiral Kuznetsov enumerates in another place the navy's shortcomings during the Finnish campaign: lack of established procedures for coordination with ground forces, insufficient tactical use of airplanes and submarines, poor marksmanship and utilization of ship artillery against shore targets. It was clear, he concludes, that the Soviet navy had been prepared to fight in conditions less arduous than those faced against the Finns.

97 This would appear to be the only occasion when anything favorable was said about Mekhlis by a Soviet memoirist. Incidentally, while Mekhlis had been abused at the conference for criticizing the leadership of the Commissariat of Defense, Stalin himself did not wait long to draw the appropriate conclusions. In a speech at the conference on April 17 he stated that "the attachment to tradition and the experience of the Civil War hindered . . . the reconstruction [of the Red Army] according to new patterns and in conformity with the requirements of modern warfare." (See *Istoriia Velikoi Otechestvennoi voiny Sovetskogo Soiuza, 1941–1945* [Moscow, 1963], I, 277.) A month later in May 1940 Marshal Voroshilov, the Civil War hero, was dismissed from his post, and in his place Marshal Timoshenko assumed leadership of the Soviet armed forces. Timoshenko was sent to the Finnish front after the initial disaster and was responsible for the victorious offensive of February–March 1940. With the new appointment a whole series of reforms was initiated in the Red Army. Its major direction was to increase discipline and the authority of the professional officer and to train troops for operations in difficult conditions. Work on new field regulations was begun, and the proper coordination of infantry units with other arms was stressed.

98 Belt of defenses running along the Soviet-Finnish frontier. A large part of the belt relied mainly on the naturally difficult terrain, the river Vuokso, the numerous lakes, and marshy ground. The more exposed places were reinforced by pill-boxes, antitank traps and barriers, and trenches. Concrete fortifications had been constructed mainly in the exposed southern sector, especially around Summa.

99 The author's contention is not without justification. The German Field Marshal von Kesselring, for example, notes: "In the 1920's we had developed tanks and aircraft side by side with the Russians, but since then we had a record of years of progress, improved experiment, whereas the Finnish war had exposed Russian weaknesses." (Albert von Kesselring, A

Soldier's Record [New York: William Morrow and Co., 1954], p. 94.) The numerous writings by Soviet military leaders of the early 1930's which survived their authors who died during the Great Purge were, according to Western specialists, much more mature and modern in their outlook than the concepts which dominated Soviet military thinking in the immediate post-Purge period.

100 Before the war the Soviet Union was divided into ten military districts. The command of the military district was in charge of all troops stationed in its area. The leadership of the military district was provided by so-called military councils, each consisting of the commander, the chief of staff, and the political commissar of the district. A number of large units of the Red Army were directly responsible to Moscow. They were so-called "special" or "detached" armies deployed in the Far Eastern territories of the Soviet Union facing the Japanese.

101 Meretskov's appointment to this post in August 1940 was part of the reorganization of the Soviet army after the Finnish war and a recognition of Meretskov's performance during this war as commander of the key Soviet assault Army. In addition, Meretskov was named a Hero of the Soviet Union and promoted to the rank of General of the Army.

102 The two principal reports were made by General Zhukov on "The Nature of Contemporary Offensive Operations" and by General Tiulenev on "The Nature of Contemporary Defensive Operations." Other reports included that by General Pavlov on the employment of a mechanized corps in an offensive and that of General Rychagov on the air arm in an offensive operation and on gaining air supremacy.

103 An area of operation over 200 miles long. Given full-strength divisions, the Army Groups participating in the game were composed of about 600,000 to 900,000 troops without supporting units. During the Nazi-Soviet war, especially in its earlier period, an average Army Group was composed not of 50 to 80 but 15 to 20 divisions.

104 The Main Military Council of the Red Army, established in 1938, had 11 members with Voroshilov, the People's Commissar of Defense, as its chairman. The Council was concerned primarily with policy-making in matters concerning the organization and armament of the Red Army.

105 While generally correct, in the par-

ticular case of the Nazi-Soviet balance of military power, Stalin's view may have led to a false sense of security. In a war with Russia Germany could count on achieving only local superiority of manpower. When the Germans invaded Russia, they did exactly what Stalin regarded as ineffectual—they attained overwhelming local superiority along the main axis of their advance. The point is that Stalin's view was based on a condition which in the case of the Nazi-Soviet struggle did not obtain—an equal mobility of opposing forces. Indeed, Stalin's objection was in flagrant disregard of the tactics on which the entire German blitz warfare was based.

106 In early 1934 the Soviet icebreaker *Cheliuskin* was trapped in Arctic ice. The Soviet government organized a successful air rescue operation, under very difficult conditions, of the 100-man crew stranded on polar ice. Seven pilots who led the rescue were the first to be decorated with the newly established, highest Soviet military decoration, the Golden Star of the Hero of the Soviet Union.

107 Marshal Kulik seems to receive more criticism in the military memoirs than any other top military official. A Civil War artillery commander, he rose rapidly during the Purge and in 1941 was one of four Soviet Marshals. His decline during the war was almost as rapid as his promotion before it. According to one author, he was demoted to Major General in the fall of 1941 when he emerged from German encirclement without identification papers and without his soldiers. In 1942 he commanded artillery in a corps unit but by the summer of 1943 was promoted to Lieutenant General and given an assault army. After his army was decimated in the disastrous Khar'kov operation in the summer of 1943, he was again demoted and completely disappeared from the scene. (See N. K. Popel', *Tanki povernuli na zapad* [Moscow, 1960], pp. 184–85.)

108 From Kazakov's account it would appear that at the conference itself Marshal Kulik was the only member of the Soviet High Command to be criticized by name. By inference, however, Stalin tried to place blame for the state of Soviet armaments on Marshal Voroshilov who shortly before had been the head of the Soviet armed forces.

109 In November 1939 the Soviet leadership decisively downgraded the independent role of armor and dispersed its existing tank force (organized in corps of

500 tanks each) among large infantry
units. The decision was based on Soviet
experience during the Spanish Civil War
where mountainous terrain limited the
use of tanks to small units in direct support of infantry. It is notable that this
decision was adopted after the German
campaign in Poland had disclosed the
significant role of deep penetrations by
large armor formations. In a way the
development of German and Soviet military thought with regard to tank forces
went in opposite directions. In the early
and mid-thirties the Soviet Union pio-
neered the establishment of large tank
formations while in Germany the tank
forces were still considered as a support
arm only. In the late thirties when the
Germans adopted a new organization with
tank forces massed in powerful assault
groups, the Soviets reversed their previous
stand. Only after the fall of France was
the decision adopted to reestablish tank
corps. The organization of the first tank
corps had begun by July 1940, but most
corps began to form only in March–June
1941. Moreover, the Soviet leadership
committed a grave error in scattering
the insufficient quantities of new tank
equipment among all newly formed units.
As a result, at the outbreak of the war
no tank corps was completely formed,
and the existing modern tanks were dispersed among a large number of units
and could not be used effectively. (There
were 14 tank corps being formed in
frontier districts with an authorized establishment of 1,031 tanks in each.)
110 Vatutin was at this time Chief of
Operations of the Soviet General Staff.
Vasilevskii and Anisov were his deputies.
111 Shaposhnikov, a highly professional
soldier, former colonel in the tsarist army,
was Chief of the Soviet General Staff
from 1937 until 1940 when he left the
office owing to ill health. Until the beginning of the war, when he again assumed leadership of the General Staff,
he retained his membership in the Main
Military Council and could be considered a senior military consultant to Stalin.
112 Meretskov escaped further punishment.
He never regained a leading position in
the Soviet military establishment, however. During the war he was in command
of an Army and later an Army Group but
in most cases on front sectors of secondary importance.
113 Eremenko was perhaps the one Soviet Marshal most closely identified with
Khrushchev, his wartime commissar during the Stalingrad battle. His general
criticism of the Soviet High Command

under Stalin is more outspoken than that
of other memoirists.
114 Lieutenant General Rychagov, Commander in Chief of the Soviet Air Force.
According to some accounts, he committed suicide in the first week of the
war when faced with the wholesale destruction of the Soviet air force. According to other accounts, he was held responsible for this destruction and executed
for treason on Stalin's order.
115 The author does not provide proof
for his assertion, and his accusation is
not repeated by any other memoirists,
nor is it recorded in the official Soviet
history of the war published during the
Khrushchev period and generally very
critical of Stalin.
116 In the previous account by General
Kazakov there is no mention of any serious difference of opinion between Stalin
and the military men participating in the
meeting. In the highly critical—one may
say devastating—review of Eremenko's
book, which was published in the Soviet
Union in 1965, the critics accuse him of
trying to create the impression that only
he and a few other generals expressed
opinions at the meetings which are now
ex post facto obviously correct. As a matter of fact, the reviewers say, what Eremenko presents as his own views were
expressed by most of the participants at
the conference. (See V. Ivanov and K.
Cheremukhin, "O knige 'V nachale
voiny,'" Voenno-istoricheskii zhurnal,
1965, No. 6, pp. 72–80.)
117 Eremenko is obviously in error. At
that time Stalin was not yet Chairman
of the Council of People's Commissars.
He assumed the position only in May
1941.
118 According to Marshal Bagramian the
operational war plans for frontier districts were discussed in the General Staff
with the district commands and approved
in April 1941. In the approved form they
were based on the assumption that in
case of war the country would have weeks
not days to bring its armed forces to a
state where they could repulse the invasion. Beginning in May 1941 the plans
were somewhat altered, and troops from
the interior, especially from the Caucasus
and the Far East, began to arrive in frontier districts. The new plan envisaged a
much greater concentration of first echelon
troops, that is, those deployed in the
immediate vicinity of the frontier. (I. Kh.
Bagramian, "Zapiski nachal'nika operativnogo otdela," Voenno-istoricheskii zhurnal, 1967, No. 1, pp. 58–62.)
119 It would appear that Marshal Ere-

menko is confusing two separate questions—the deployment plan and its implementation. The plan itself was based on an idea very similar to that expressed by Marshal Eremenko. Its implementation, however, was not accomplished prior to the outbreak of the war. For a broader discussion of the deployment plan and its implementation, see Chapter Two, n. 67.

120 While Vannikov's claim seems exaggerated, artillery was the arm in which the Russians had a tradition of excellence and the strongest weapon in Soviet armament. Both before and throughout the war insistence on fire power lay at the heart of Soviet operational doctrine. The exalted place of artillery was well expressed in Stalin's phrase—"artillery is the god of war."

121 Designed and tested in the late 1930's, the T-34 was not produced until 1940. In all, 115 tanks were built in 1940; 1,100 were built in the first six months of 1941. A Western expert evaluated the T-34 medium tank as follows: "By comparison with contemporary medium tank designs it represented an advance both in armament and armor and was superior in this respect not only to the German light medium Panzer-3 but also to the most powerful German tank at the time, the medium Panzer-4. . . . The most notable feature about the T-34 was its main armament in the shape of the 76.2mm gun, model 1939, 30.6 calibers long, which placed it well ahead in the armament race." (R. N. Ogorkiewicz, "Soviet Tanks," in B. H. Liddell Hart, ed., *The Red Army* [New York: Harcourt, Brace and Company, 1956], p. 300.)

122 Voznesenskii, then and throughout the war the chief Soviet economic planner with the rank of Deputy Prime Minister. The Economic Council of the defense industries was a policy-making body which coordinated the activities of all commissariats engaged in armament production.

123 Stalin obviously regarded Zhdanov as the main artillery expert among the political leaders. (NB: Stalin also entrusted Zhdanov with supervision of the Soviet navy.) In fact, Zhdanov had no military experience whatever aside from participation in the Civil War as a political commissar. Nor did he have a technical education which would prepare him for the responsibilities he assumed. (It should be noted that after the war he was regarded by Stalin as his main propaganda expert.)

124 A fatal shortcoming of German armor

until 1943 was its total lack of medium heavy and heavy tanks. The light Panzer-1 and Panzer-2 tanks (T-1 and T-2) had such thin armor that they were called by officers in the field "tin coffins" (and by 1942 were withdrawn from the Russian theater). The armor of the medium Panzer-3 and Panzer-4 was penetrated by shells of the T-34 tank gun from a distance of 1,500 to 2,000 yards, whereas its own fire was effective against the T-34 at a distance of not more than 500 yards.

125 Vannikov returned to his old post directly from prison. He remained one of the key executives in Soviet defense industries until his death in 1962. After the war he was one of those responsible for producing the Soviet atomic and hydrogen bombs.

126 Until the beginning of 1941 the leadership of Soviet artillery was divided between two institutions—the Main Artillery Directorate and the Office of the Chief of Artillery of the Red Army. The first was a supervisory administrative body, and the latter was concerned with questions of actual combat training. In early 1941 the two institutions were merged, and Voronov, previously Chief of Artillery of the Red Army, was appointed First Deputy to Marshal Kulik, who retained the post of Chief of the Main Artillery Directorate.

127 Lieutenant General Savchenko and Colonel General Grendal' were Deputy Chiefs of the Main Artillery Directorate.

128 In early 1940 the Red Army received a draft of new Field Service Regulations which took into account the experience of battles with the Japanese at Lake Khasan and Khalkhin-Gol. But the war with Finland demonstrated the need for even more drastic revisions. In the summer of 1940 a special commission assumed the task of re-editing the draft. The new version was not considered satisfactory, however, and was not adopted before the outbreak of the Nazi-Soviet war. Only in 1942 and 1943 did the Red Army receive field regulations, which, incidentally, bore scant resemblance to the prewar draft.

129 At the beginning of the war Voronov replaced Marshal Kulik as Chief of the Main Artillery Directorate, retaining simultaneously general control over antiaircraft defense.

130 Khrenov was Chief of Engineers of the 7th Army under the command of General Meretskov during the Finnish war. His promotion and appointment to Moscow were part of the general army reorganization at the end of that war. (He was probably brought to Moscow by his former

C.O., who had become Chief of the General Staff.)

131 Starinov refers here to the occasion when Marshal Kulik was stranded on a front road in Finland because no engineers could be found to clear the road of mines. Only after Starinov arrived and took care of the mines was Kulik able to proceed.

132 Famous Soviet flyers and test pilots of the late 1930's. Gromov repeated the record long-distance flight of Chkalov from Moscow to the USA. Vodop'ianov was the hero of the previously mentioned rescue of the icebreaker *Cheliuskin*'s crew. Kokkinaki established a number of world high altitude records.

133 According to available estimates, Soviet "volunteers" in Spain numbered close to 1,500 of whom about 140 were military pilots. Among the Soviet officers sent to Spain were the future Marshals Kulik, Malinovskii, Meretskov, and Voronov and future Generals Shtern, Batov, Pavlov, and Rodimtsev.

134 Iakovlev obviously errs. The two commanders mentioned were rapidly promoted after their return from Spain and attained the highest position in the air force, that of Commander in Chief. The first commander was dismissed in 1940 and arrested and executed shortly before the outbreak of the Nazi-Soviet war; the latter died at the beginning of the war (see n. 114).

135 This would appear to be the first time a Soviet publication quotes Stalin's view of Ezhov and mentions the fact of his execution.

136 The new Soviet fighter aircraft can be compared to German Messerschmitt fighters as follows: Iak-1—a light, maneuverable fighter with a maximum speed of 340 mph; Lag-3—of wooden construction with a maximum speed of 365 mph; Mig-3—the fastest fighter with a maximum speed of slightly over 400 mph (produced in very small numbers throughout the war). All new Soviet fighters were equipped with 20mm cannon and machine guns. The star German performer, the Messerschmitt-109 fighter, had a maximum speed of 354 mph. The Focke-Wulf-190 fighter introduced later was faster by about 20 mph and heavily armed with four cannon.

137 In 1939 heavy long-range bombers constituted 20.6 percent of the total Soviet air power (as compared with 10.6 percent in 1934). Light bombers, assault planes, and reconnaissance aircraft accounted in 1939 for 26 percent of Soviet air power (as compared to 50.2 percent

in 1934). Fighter aviation accounted for 30 percent in 1939 as compared to 12.3 percent in 1934. During the war the proportions were completely reversed. It is sufficient to say that throughout the entire war no more than 79 heavy bombers (Pe-8) were produced. The main stress was on fighter planes and assault planes to support troops in the field.

138 The two main types of Soviet heavy bombers were the SB bomber with a maximum speed of about 280 mph and range of about 630 miles and the TB-3 bomber with the same speed but with a 2,500-mile range. Both bombers carried a three-man crew.

139 Kuznetsov refers here to Colonel Mitchell's experiment to demonstrate the combat potential of air power against surface warships in a practical test.

140 One should note that to this day the Soviet navy has never possessed a single aircraft carrier.

141 In another place in his memoirs Kuznetsov reports the following characteristic item: "In the postwar discussion of naval construction—before rockets came on the scene—we navy men insisted that cruisers should have nothing heavier than 9-inch guns. Such cruisers successfully beat off all ships of their class and were relatively small and cheap. Stalin waited a long time before accepting this proposal. He did accept it finally, but in 1949 when I served in another post, I learned that at his insistence one heavy cruiser with 12-inch guns was to be built after all."

142 The capital of Estonia and a Baltic seaport. In the summer of 1940 after Estonia's incorporation into the Soviet Union it became the chief base of the Soviet Baltic Fleet.

143 As a matter of fact the Soviet Union wanted to buy from Germany not one but two cruisers, and only German refusal prevented the duplication of the *Luetzow* error.

144 In the years 1939–41, the Soviet navy commissioned new surface ships with a total tonnage of 108,000 tons and submarines with a total tonnage of 50,000 tons. But by the end of 1940 there were still 269 ships of all types on the stocks, an overwhelming majority of which were not finished before the start of the war. Owing to the fact that naval ship-building yards were located primarily in western territories of the Soviet Union, which were quickly occupied by the Germans, most of these ships were lost. At the start of the war the Soviet navy consisted of three battleships, seven cruisers, 59 destroyers, 269 torpedo boats, and 218 submarines.

CHAPTER TWO

1 The headquarters of the Central Asian Military District where General Kazakov served as chief of staff was located in Tashkent, the capital of the Soviet Uzbek Republic.

2 Hanko (Hangö), a peninsula jutting into the Baltic Sea at the entrance to the Gulf of Finland, leased to the Soviet Union as a result of war with Finland in 1940. Poliarnyi, the main naval base of the Soviet Northern Fleet in the Arctic Circle.

3 Despite such warnings, Soviet ships continued to pass through German territorial waters until the very hour of invasion. The Soviet Ambassador in London at the time, I. N. Maiskii, writes about his request to Moscow on June 20, 1941 for permission to reroute a Soviet ship about to depart from Britain to the Soviet Union away from the Baltic Sea. The answer, sent from Moscow on June 21, arrived in London on the evening of June 22 after the war had already started. It stated—Request denied. (I. N. Maiskii, *Vospominaniia sovetskogo posla—voina* [Moscow, 1965], pp. 138–39.)

4 As was mentioned previously by Kuznetsov, German ships began to leave Soviet ports a few days before the start of the war. On June 21 all German ships without exception left Soviet ports. When the Nazi-Soviet war broke out, according to Admiral Panteleev, there were more than 40 Soviet ships in German ports with a combined tonnage of over 123,000 GRT which were confiscated as war booty by the German authorities. (Iu. A. Panteleev, *Morskoi front* [Moscow, 1965], p. 36.)

5 Dictatorial governments are especially susceptible to certain hazards in the compilation and interpretation of intelligence. While the dictator wishes to know everything that his subordinates and associates know, the latter often hesitate to report information contrary to opinions known to be held by the dictator; they withhold or tamper with it so as to make it more palatable to the leader. One suspects, therefore, not only that Stalin brushed aside unpleasant facts about German intentions and preparations but that his informants presented these facts to him in a biased manner. As a matter of fact, a recent, apparently authentic Soviet document published in the West makes exactly this point with regard to the author of these memoirs, Admiral Kuznetsov. The document is a verbatim report of a discussion held in Moscow by historians and military leaders concerning a recent Soviet book on World War II. One of the discussants said about Kuznetsov: "When he received from Vorontsov, the Soviet Naval Attaché in Berlin, a report giving plans and date of the German attack, he immediately gave the information to Stalin. True enough, but in what light did he present it? If you could read it, you could see that he claims Vorontsov's communication to be a trick of German counterespionage." (*Der Spiegel*, March 20, 1967, p. 135.)

6 Kuznetsov's caution is not surprising when one considers that Ivan Rogov, Chief Political Commissar of the Navy and a member of the Party's Central Committee, was dubbed by navy men "Ivan the Terrible."

7 High-ranking executives in the Soviet defense industry, the first in charge of heavy machine building, the second in charge of ship building.

8 Kuznetsov refers here to the line adopted by Stalin in the face of numerous warnings about an impending German invasion given to the Soviet Union by Western statesmen. According to this line, Western governments were engaged in a conspiracy to provoke a war between the Soviet Union and Nazi Germany.

9 A port on the Manchurian coast of the Yellow Sea, scene of major fighting in the Russo-Japanese War of 1904 in which the Russian land and sea forces were decisively beaten. Until 1886 Port Arthur was a Chinese possession. It was returned by Russia to Communist China in 1954.

10 Clear allusion is made to Soviet Foreign Minister Molotov's speech on the first day of the war in which he complained bitterly about the perfidy of Nazi Germany which violated the pact with Russia.

11 Admiral Kuznetsov was in 1936–37 the main Soviet naval adviser to the Republican forces during the Spanish Civil War. Cartagena, a Spanish seaport on the Iberian coast, the main reception point for Soviet arms shipments.

12 The Soviet navy prior to the war followed a procedure for alert which consisted of three stages. When No. 3 was

in force, the fleets continued their normal training and exercises, and shore leaves were granted, but ships were kept fully fueled and no major repairs were undertaken. When No. 2 was in force, ships received all necessary munitions and stores; shore leaves were restricted; preparations were made so that ships could put out to sea on short notice; battle shifts were established for some guns. No. 1 was the full combat alert, with ships under their own power and all crews manning battle stations.

13 No better indication of the atmosphere in the Red Army on the eve of Nazi invasion can be found than this strange question repeated in the memoirs by commanders of many attacked units. Low- and high-ranking officers feared to assume responsibility for any action without direct and explicit instructions from their superiors. Their anxiety, characteristic in the post-Purge period, was magnified enormously by command warnings and admonitions to avoid provoking an armed incident with the Germans. On a later page of the memoirs Admiral Kuznetsov expressed his disgust when one of his fleet commanders asked this question, which he himself had put just a few hours earlier.

14 Vice Admiral Tributs, Commander in Chief of the Soviet Baltic Fleet throughout the war.

15 Vice Admiral Golovko, from 1940 until 1946 Commander in Chief of the Soviet Northern Fleet.

16 Seaport on the Crimean peninsula, the main naval base of the Soviet Black Sea Fleet.

17 Vice Admiral Oktiabr'skii, Commander in Chief of the Soviet Black Sea Fleet from 1939 until 1948.

18 G. M. Malenkov, Secretary of the Party's Central Committee, Stalin's right hand man in Party affairs. He was apparently groomed by Stalin for the succession. He was Soviet Prime Minister from Stalin's death until February 1955 and in 1957 was expelled from the leadership by Khrushchev after which he disappeared from public life.

19 Kuznetsov does not mention that his message still contained the self-insuring phrase "Don't succumb to provocations."

20 The major danger to the Soviet navy did not come from the sea, for which their entire peacetime training and planning had prepared them, but from land and air. Within two months all Baltic bases except Kronshtadt (near Leningrad) had been captured. In another place Admiral Kuznetsov writes:

"Events were unfolding with a rapidity that would have been difficult to foresee. In a very short time, our bases in the Baltic were under threat of an attack from the rear. Our excessive self-confidence turned against us. In those days, I recalled a talk I had had shortly before the war with F. I. Kuznetsov, Commander of the Baltic Military District. I asked him how the perimeter defense of Libava and Riga, where many of our ships were based, was planned.

" 'Do you really believe that we will let the enemy get as far as Riga?' he asked in an offended tone.

"'The Lord helps those who help themselves,' I replied with the old saying.

"And now that had happened! The energetic German advance threatened not only Riga but also the main base of the fleet—Tallin. The position of Libava from the land side had become hopeless a mere two days after the start of the war. And still worse things lay ahead of us. In the space of two months, the Baltic Fleet had to make the painful journey from Libava to Kronshtadt, abandoning its bases."

21 Code name for the German plan to invade Great Britain in 1940. After numerous delays the plan was indefinitely postponed in favor of the invasion of Russia. One suspects that Kuznetsov was wrong in supposing that more active Soviet preparations against the invasion would have induced Hitler to postpone or abandon Plan Barbarossa. After victories in western Europe, in Africa, and in the Balkans Germany's actions were determined by Hitler's limitless faith in the invincibility of the German war machine and very little influenced either by the appeasement or the resistance of his opponents. The comparison with the late 1930's when Hitler's confidence in his military strength was rather moderate and when the appeasement policy of the Western powers encouraged his expansion does not seem to be valid.

22 On June 10, 1941 the British permanent Undersecretary of State for Foreign Affairs, Sir Alexander Cadogan, informed the Soviet government through diplomatic channels about the impending German attack. He provided the Soviet ambassador to London with a detailed list of German troop movements and

preparations for the invasion and on behalf of the British Prime Minister Churchill requested that this information be communicated to the Kremlin. The Soviet reaction to the British warning is described in Churchill's memoirs as follows: "At this time the Soviet government, at once haughty and purblind, regarded every warning we gave as a mere attempt of beaten men to drag others into ruin." (Winston Churchill, *The Grand Alliance* [Boston: Houghton Mifflin Co., 1950], p. 205.)

23 Stalin's behavior during the months preceding the German invasion was more complex and contradictatory than Kuznetsov suggests in his explanation. While there is ample evidence to support his contention that Stalin went out of his way to pacify Hitler, there were also attempts by Stalin to expand Soviet influence in the Balkans in direct competition with the Germans. About one such attempt George Kennan says: "He infuriated Hitler beyond words by interfering in Yugoslavia on the very eve of the German attack on that country. He just couldn't leave the Balkans alone." (George F. Kennan, *Russia and the West* [Boston: Little, Brown and Co., 1961], p. 345.)

24 The text of the TASS (official Soviet news agency) communiqué is quoted in the introduction to this chapter. During the Khrushchev period its denial of German intentions to attack Russia was presented as major proof of Stalin's faith in the Nazi-Soviet pact. Today many Soviet authors, while still criticizing its harmful tranquilizing effect on the Red Army, regard it primarily as an attempt to test German intentions, that is, a reflection of Stalin's anxiety about rather than faith in his German "friends." (See, e.g., Berezhkov's memoirs, p. 214.)

It is interesting to note that Hitler shrewdly guessed what lay behind the TASS announcement. There is the following entry in Goebbels' diary on the day after the communiqué was issued: "In the Fuehrer's opinion the TASS denial is merely the result of fear. Stalin is trembling in the face of oncoming events."

25 The date most commonly accepted as the starting point of German planning for war with Russia is July 29, 1940. On this day the Chief of Staff of the Wehrmacht, General Jodl, instructed military planners concerning Hitler's wish to prepare an assault against Russia. The final

detailed plan for invasion of December 18, 1940, incidentally, was Directive No. 21 and not No. 1 as Tiulenev asserts. The present Soviet Defense Minister, Marshal Grechko, had this to say about this plan in a recently published article: "It is not without interest to note: Eleven days after Hitler had accepted the final plan for war against the Soviet Union (December 18, 1940), this fact and the basic data for the decision by the German command became known to our intelligence." (*Voenno-istoricheskii zhurnal,* 1966, No. 6, p. 9.)

26 Tiulenev quotes the words of a song very popular in the Soviet Union on the eve of the war, the major theme of which was the constant vigilance and invincibility of the Red Army. The title of the song was "If War Comes Tomorrow."

27 In Russian: *V. Ch. (Vysoko chastotnyi).* The *V. Ch.* was a separate telephone network used for military and governmental communications throughout Russia. Serviced by special units of the Soviet secret police, it provided for speed and security against "bugging."

28 A number of writers repeat the story—too incredible to have been invented—that Stalin seriously entertained the possibility that the Nazi invasion was the "private war" of German generals who were trying to force Hitler to wage war against Russia. A Soviet response in force to this "provocation" would only serve to escalate it into a major conflict. This view, however shortlived, betrays an extraordinary failure to comprehend Nazism.

29 Minsk was located about 200 miles from the Soviet frontier. L'vov, the largest city in the western Ukraine, was located about 25 miles from the frontier.

30 According to an article written by a Soviet Air Force Major General: "During the day of June 22 the enemy air force attacked about 65 percent of the air fields in the frontier military districts to a depth of up to 400 km. from the frontier. As a result almost 21 percent of the combat aircraft of the four frontier districts (Baltic, Western, Kiev, Odessa) was destroyed." (G. Psheanianik "Borba s aviatsiei protivnika v letne-osennei kampanii 1941 goda," *Voenno-istoricheskii zhurnal,* 1961, No. 3, p. 37.) The admitted losses of the Soviet air force increased on the second day of war to 2,000 aircraft and by the end of the year reached about 8,000. Before the war the Soviet air force was numerically

the strongest in the world. A commonly accepted estimate puts its strength in June 1941 at over 10,000 combat aircraft. (Raymond L. Garthoff, *How Russia Makes War* |Glencoe, Ill.: The Free Press, 1953], p. 429.) The Luftwaffe started the campaign in Russia with about 2,000 aircraft, and its initial losses were negligible. The decisive factor was not of course numbers but the qualitative differences of the machines, the experience of pilots, and combat tactics, in which areas the inferiority of the Red air force was as pronounced as its quantitative superiority.

31 General Douhet, Italian exponent in the interwar period of an extremist view on air power. The experience of World War II has shown that his doctrine exaggerated the capacity of mass bombing to destroy the morale of the population and to cripple modern industry and underestimated the prospects for air defense.

32 Older types of fighter aircraft, mainly the I-15, I-153, and I-16 with maximum speeds ranging from 240 to 300 mph, not only constituted the mainstay of the Soviet air force at the time of invasion and in subsequent months; they were still being produced in large numbers until October 1941. The relative weight of modern fighter aircraft (Iak, Lag, Mig) in Soviet fighter aviation was at the end of 1940—1.3 percent; in June 1941—11 percent; at the end of 1941—41.2 percent; and in June 1942—77 percent. (Colonel F. Shesterin, "Borba za gospodstvo v vozdukhe," *Voenno-istoricheskii zhurnal*, 1965, No. 11, p. 21.)

33 The striking success of the transfer of the Soviet aircraft industry thousands of miles to the east and of its expansion can be seen from statistics on annual aircraft production in the 1939-44 period (German production figures for comparison).

Number of Aircraft Built	1939	1940	1941
USSR	8,870	10,560	15,200
Germany	2,500	10,250	12,400

Number of Aircraft Built	1942	1943	1944
USSR	25,430	35,000	40,300
Germany	14,700	25,220	37,950

(Source: **ibid.**, p. 20.)

34 For a description of the Soviet command structure during the war, see the introduction to Chapter Four.

35 According to a story told by Voronov in another part of his memoirs the spade-mortar, an "invention" which aroused the fancy of Stalin and his colleagues, was "designed" as a combination of tool for trench digging and individual weapon. The spade had a hollow handle that doubled as a mortar tube and a removable blade that was to serve as the mortar base. Only after many tests and accidents did the Defense Committee agree to abandon the "project."

36 "Rote Kapelle" (Red Choir), the best-known Soviet intelligence network in Nazi Germany. It included a number of German officers, most notably Harro Schulze-Boysen, an intelligence officer in the German Air Ministry. The network supplied invaluable information on the plans of the German High Command until the fall of 1943 when it was uncovered and destroyed. (David J. Dallin, *Soviet Espionage* [New Haven: Yale University Press, 1955], pp. 246–47.)

37 Admiral Kuznetsov recalled in his memoirs: "I received a telegram from M. A. Vorontsov, Naval Attaché in Berlin. He not only spoke about the Germans' preparations but gave almost the precise date for the beginning of the war. Among a multitude of similar materials such a report no longer seemed extraordinary; it was a document sent by an official and responsible person. At that time such reports were automatically sent to certain addresses. I ordered a check on whether Stalin had received the telegram. I was told: Yes, he had." (*Oktiabr*, 1965, No. 11, p. 161.) The same information on the impending German attack was also received from the famous Soviet spy Richard Sorge in Tokyo. A Soviet author writes that Sorge in his dispatch of May 15, 1941 specified the day of invasion as June 22 and, in addition, provided a general scheme of the military operations that the Nazis were planning, including the number of troops involved. (*Pravda*, September 4, 1964.)

38 The initial invasion date was set for May 15 but later postponed, partly because of the late spring thaw in 1941 but primarily because of the German invasion of Yugoslavia and Greece.

39 Berezhkov refers here to the view apparently held by Stalin that Germany was preparing the ground by its threatening moves for extensive economic and political demands on the Soviet Union. This belief that Germany intended to blackmail Russia but not to make war

and Soviet willingness to pay the blackmail price if only the Germans would name it were expressed in a number of Soviet communications to Berlin up to the very day of invasion. (cf., the conversation between Molotov and the German Ambassador to Moscow on the evening of June 21, 1941 reported in *Nazi-Soviet Relations, 1939–1941* [Washington, D.C.: U.S. Department of State, 1948], p. 355.)

40 At the time war broke out there were about 1,500 Soviet citizens in Germany, including 900 sailors, and 120 German citizens in Russia.

41 According to German Foreign Office documents, Berezhkov errs in asserting that the Soviet note was not delivered to the German authorities. State Secretary Weizsacker in the German Foreign Office addressed a memorandum dated June 21 to Foreign Minister von Ribbentrop which reads as follows: "The Russian Ambassador who wanted to call on the Reich Foreign Minister today and had been referred to me instead called on me this evening at 9:30 p.m. and handed me a note [with complaints about the flight of German aircraft over Soviet territory]. . . . In conclusion the note expresses confidence that the German government would take steps to put an end to these border violations. . . . I told him that since I had an entirely different opinion than he and had to obey the opinion of my government, it would be better not to go more deeply into the matter just now. The reply would be forthcoming later. The ambassador agreed to the procedure and left me." (*Nazi-Soviet Relations, 1939–1941, op. cit.*, pp. 353–54.)

42 Berezkhov apparently tries to imply that the German description of the meeting (which describes von Ribbentrop's behavior as more dignified than the Russian version) is untrustworthy because its author, Dr. Paul Schmidt, who usually acted as Ribbentrop's interpreter, could not hear the conversation.

43 It is characteristic that Berezhkov throughout his narrative does not mention the name of the Soviet ambassador in Germany at that time, Dekanozov. The reason for this omission is simple. Dekanozov, formerly a Deputy Foreign Minister, was a close associate of Beria, the head of the Soviet secret police, and was executed in 1953 together with his patron.

44 While there is no basis to question Berezhkov's account, there is no evidence that von Ribbentrop, one of Hitler's most

subservient ministers to the end, at any time opposed the attack. He may personally have regretted the termination of Nazi-Soviet cooperation, however, which was his crowning if not sole achievement as German Foreign Minister.

45 The official declaration of war took place two and a half hours after the invasion started when the German ambassador in Moscow, accompanied by his Counselor Hilger, went to see Soviet Foreign Minister Molotov. This is how Hilger describes the scene: "Shortly after four in the morning [Moscow time] we were once more entering the Kremlin, where Molotov received us at once. He wore a tired and worn-out expression. After the ambassador delivered his message [that the German government had decided to take appropriate counter measures against Soviet troop concentrations near the German border], there were several seconds of deep silence. Molotov was visibly struggling with deep inner excitement. Then he asked: 'Is this supposed to be a declaration of war?' The ambassador shrugged in silence. . . . Then Molotov said, with slightly raised voice, that the message he had just been given could not, of course, mean anything but a declaration of war, since German troops had already crossed the Soviet border, and Soviet cities . . . had been bombarded by German airplanes. . . . And then Molotov gave free reign to his indignation. He called the German action a breach of confidence unprecedented in history. . . . 'Surely we have not deserved that.' With these words Molotov closed his declaration." (G. Hilger and A. G. Meyer, *The Incompatible Allies* [New York: Macmillan Company, 1953], p. 336.)

46 A city on the Bug River, which in 1941 constituted the German-Soviet frontier. Brest was the main railroad junction on Soviet western borders.

47 Soviet mineral water.

48 In Russian the term used with regard to Stalin is *Khoziain*, which means literally master, proprietor, landlord.

49 Starinov's account of Stalin's May 5 speech differs radically from the account by Alexander Werth. According to Werth, who reconstructed Stalin's speech from information gathered from a number of Russians, its line was exactly the opposite of that reported by Starinov: The Red Army is not sufficiently strong to smash the Germans, its equipment is still far from satisfactory. (Alexander Werth, *Russia at War, 1941–45* [New York: Avon Books, 1965], pp. 135–36.)

584

One could hardly expect of course that the substance of the Werth account, if correct, would be recorded in Soviet memoirs at the time when Khrushchev's anti-Stalin campaign was in progress. It is curious, however, that in the last three years no memoirs mention the conference in terms similar to those of Werth.

50 A town in the Pripet marshes about 100 miles from the Soviet frontier.

51 Major General K. D. Golubev, Commander of the 10th Army. Colonel (presently Colonel General) L. M. Sandalov, chief of staff of the 4th Army. The 4th and the 10th Armies were covering the main direction of the German assault (Brest, Bialystok).

52 The intelligence report which accurately estimated the strength of the attacking German infantry underestimated by more than one half the strength of armored and motorized troops.

53 A city in the Soviet frontier zone about 200 miles west of Minsk where the headquarters of the Western Military District was located.

54 All cities located within a maximum of 50 miles from the Soviet-German frontier.

55 Pavlov's orders followed from Directive No. 3 of the People's Commissar of Defense which was issued in Moscow at 9:15 p.m. of the first day of war. The Directive demanded that the Western Army Group mount a counterattack with the aim of encircling the German assault grouping, of advancing 60-100 miles, and of capturing within three days the town of Suvalki located in territory held by Germany prior to the invasion.

56 Not only was Boldin unable to mount a counterattack, but even his attempt to assemble the strike group did not succeed. The troops of the Western Army Group became victims of the first two gigantic German encirclement operations. In the so-called Bialystok-Slonim pocket 150,000 prisoners were taken by the Germans and 1,200 tanks and 600 guns captured or destroyed and in the Minsk pocket 300,000 prisoners, 2,500 tanks, and 1,400 guns. Boldin himself spent 45 days behind enemy lines and only on August 11 fought his way out of encirclement with 1,600 men and officers at a point over 400 miles east from his starting point.

57 On June 10, 1941 Marshal Eremenko received an order to turn over the command of the 1st Special Far Eastern Army to his chief of staff and to depart for Moscow where a new assignment awaited him.

58 Mogilev, located about 350 miles from the Soviet frontier. At the time of Eremenko's departure German troops were still about 60 miles from the location of Western Army Group headquarters.

59 Eremenko was in command of the Western Army Group for less than a week. On July 4 Marshal Timoshenko, People's Commissar of Defense, personally assumed command of this crucial front. Eremenko was appointed his deputy.

60 Soviet memoirists and war historians inconsistently employ two arguments which are in part mutually exclusive—that the Red Army did not have sufficient new weapons, that its cadres were inexperienced and insufficiently trained, that it lacked training and operational planning for protracted defensive action, etc., and at the same time that the situation in June 1941 would have been strikingly different had the command been warned in time, the troops alerted, and the units deployed in advance.

In most cases one can discern a tendency among Soviet historians and military writers to assert that the lack of warning to the troops on the eve of invasion was not only a reinforcing factor, but the main reason for the events which followed. After listing a number of shortcomings in the training, structure, and weaponry of the Red Army on the eve of the German attack, the authors of the official Soviet war history declare:

"However, the *main* reason for the extremely unfavorable situation in which the Red Army found itself at the beginning of the Great Patriotic War consisted in the fact that Soviet troops were not brought in good time to full combat readiness. . . . [The troops] did have sufficient strength and matériel to repulse the first strikes of the enemy and to withstand his onslaught."

(*Istoriia Velikoi Otechestvennoi voiny Sovetskogo Soiuza 1941–1945* [Moscow, 1965], VI, 191. Italics mine—*Ed.*)

While one should not minimize the effects that the shock of surprise had on the Red Army's overall performance, it seems that the shock of German arms was sufficiently strong to produce a calamity. Even had the element of tactical surprise been lacking, the Soviet leadership and the Red Army would still have been exposed to the surprise of modern warfare for which neither their maneuvers and exercises nor the Winter War with Finland nor the Civil War in Spain had prepared them well. In the later stages of the war, in 1942 or even after Stalingrad in 1943, where both the element of surprise and many of the factors which contributed to the initial Soviet defeats had disappeared or were substantially reduced and the elements of weakness in the German capacity for waging a total war were much more pronounced than in the summer of 1941, German strength was still sufficient to inflict on the Soviets enormous losses of manpower and territory.

61 All cities mentioned by Fediuninskii were located in the former Polish territories incorporated in 1939 into the Soviet Union. Their population, both Polish and Ukrainian, was far from friendly toward the Soviets. While the Poles saw very little to choose from between the Russians and the Germans, many Ukrainians hoped that a German victory would enable them to attain national independence, a hope, incidentally, which German occupation policy quickly dispelled.

62 Lieutenant General Kirponos, Commander of the Kiev Military District, occupied the post from February 1941 when he replaced Marshal Zhukov, who was promoted to Chief of the Soviet General Staff. A divisional tank commander in 1939, he distinguished himself in the war with Finland and was awarded the title Hero of the Soviet Union. Promoted with dizzying speed, at the outbreak of the Nazi-Soviet war he was in charge of one of the largest and strategically crucial Soviet military districts. Bagramian evaluates Kirponos as follows:

"By the end of January [1941 the Chief of Staff] General Purkaev invited me to accompany him to the railroad station to meet the new [district] commander. Until then I had met Kirponos only once in 1937 . . . when he occupied the modest post of infantry school director in Kazan'. . . . But, I was thinking, his military talents must be quite considerable to advance in one year from division chief to commander of one of the most important military districts. For a long time General Purkaev who . . . had met Kirponos frequently did not answer my question about what he thought of Kirponos. Then, with a shrug of his shoulders, he said: 'We became very poor in higher commanding personnel—There

is nobody to choose from. It is quite possible that Kirponos ranks at present among our most prominent generals. I don't know. I didn't serve with him, and at meetings and conferences he kept silent for the most part. . . . He is an old and worthy soldier, but his military talents are, apparently, not striking. He doesn't stand out very much. And as far as what people say about his enjoying the respect of Iosif Vissarionovich [Stalin], this depends to a large extent on Comrade Timoshenko, under whose command Kirponos fought. Timoshenko became People's Commissar, and Stalin appointed Kirponos to our district not without his recommendation.' "

(*Voenno-istoricheskii zhurnal*, 1967, No. 1, pp. 57–58.)

63 The chief of staff of the Kiev Military District. A career Red Army officer and graduate of the General Staff Academy, Lieutenant General Purkaev occupied prior to this the post of Soviet Military Attaché in Berlin. In the 1930's he was regarded in the Red Army, according to Bagramian, as one of its most professional and well educated generals.

64 Corps Commissar (Lieutenant General) N. N. Vashugin was a regimental commander until 1938 when he was advanced thanks to his zeal during the Great Purge to one of the top political posts in the Red Army—Chief Political Commissar (and military council member) of the Leningrad Military District. He was transferred to Kiev in February 1941.

65 The peacetime command and headquarters of the Soviet frontier military districts were to be immediately transformed on the outbreak of war into headquarters of field Army Groups. These Army Groups would encompass all units located in the territory of the military districts. The troops of the Kiev Military District were to form the Southwestern Army Group. While the headquarters of the military districts were located in the capital of the Ukraine, Kiev, the field command post of the Southwestern Army Group was prepared in advance in Tarnopol', a city over 200 miles west of Kiev and no more than 130 miles removed from the Soviet-German frontier. The city was captured in the second week of war.

66 The story of the German deserter has already become an element of folklore in Soviet history concerning the eve of the invasion. It was mentioned in Khrushchev's Secret Speech; it is recorded in

the official war history; it is recounted in
a number of memoirs. Almost every time
it appears in a slightly different form—
in some accounts it happened a few days
before the invasion, in others during the
night of the invasion, in some accounts
the soldier was a "communist sympa-
thizer," in others he struck his officer
and fled from punishment. Of course,
there may have been more than one
German deserter, but after comparing
descriptions of circumstances, place, Soviet unit numbers, etc., one suspects
that all accounts deal with one and the
same deserter.

67 The question of the delayed deployment of Soviet troops seems to create
for the memoirists difficulties similar to
those discussed in n. 60. On the one hand
they admit that the deployment plan
was faulty; on the other hand they argue
that were it not for its delayed implementation, the outcome of the first weeks
of war would have been radically different.
If one discards exaggerated claims of
what timely deployment and combat
alert might have accomplished, however,
both parts of the argument can be reconciled. The deployment plan of Soviet
troops of cover in the frontier defense
zone would have invited disaster in a
war against a highly mobile and operationally mature opponent, well trained
in the art of blitzkrieg, even had it been
implemented in advance. According to
this plan the bulk of Soviet forces was
to be massed in the first echelon zone
and the bulk of first echelon troops was to
take up defensive positions in the immediate border area. Development of
secondary defense lines and concentration of mobile reserves in depth were
clearly neglected. As a result of the Soviet High Command's delay in implementing the deployment directive until
literally the last moment, the worst features of the original plan were more
strongly pronounced and the basic weaknesses of the Red Army (e.g., its low level
of mobility) were more blatantly exposed.
The 56 divisions massed in the immediate
frontier zone (i.e., 32 percent of the total
strength in frontier districts) were not
alerted; field communication and control had to be organized under devastating fire; the divisional and corps units
were caught in a situation much worse
than that envisaged by the war deployment plan, namely, they were attacked
from air and land while on the march
toward the frontier or thrown into battle directly from their forced march. In

other words, the Soviet High Command
committed a triple error—when it designed its deployment plan, when it delayed its implementation, and when it
tried to implement it under fire instead
of concentrating on the creation of strong
secondary defense lines.

68 During the first and second days of
war the Soviet Command committed the
bulk of its bomber force to massive ineffectual strikes during which it was virtually destroyed. Field Marshal von Kesselring, Commander of the German 2nd
Air Army, describes the Luftwaffe's encounter with these bombers which were
flying in tactically impossible formations
without fighter escort as "infanticide."
(Albert von Kesselring, *A Soldier's Record* [New York: William Morrow and
Co., 1954], p. 90.)

69 The order envisaged that almost the
entire armored strength of the Army
Groups would take part in the counterattack and penetrate to a depth of 100
miles in two days. Lublin, a city in
German-occupied Poland 60 miles from
the Soviet border.

70 Lieutenant General Popel', political
commissar of the 8th Motorized Corps,
provides a vivid account of Commissar
Vashugin's activity during the counterattack. The following episode took place
on June 27 at the corps command post
in a forest clearing. The corps, after a
250-mile forced march and two days of
heavy fighting, could not assemble its
divisions for an attack ordered by the
Army Group. The corps commander,
Lieutenant General Riabyshev, was informed that a group of cars was approaching the clearing.

"Riabyshev . . . moved to meet the
lead car out of which stepped a short
military man with a black mustache.
Riabyshev stood at attention:

" 'Comrade member of the Army
Group Military Council—'

The doors of other cars opened.
Numerous new people began to appear—colonels, lieutenant colonels.
Some I recognized—the prosecutor,
the chairman of the military tribunal.

The general to whom Riabyshev reported did not listen to him and did
not return his greeting. He moved
straight toward Riabyshev, and when
he came close he looked up at the
wrinkled face of the corps commander and asked in a voice tight with
fury:

" 'How much did you get to sell
out, Judas?'

Riabyshev started to speak:
" 'Would you listen to me, Comrade Corps Commissar—'
" 'The field tribunal will listen to you, traitor. Here under the pine we will listen to you, and under the pine we will shoot you. . . .'
"The commissar is accusing him of treason. How can it be otherwise? We are suffering failure after failure. The corps was ordered to attack at 9:00 a.m., and now at 10:00 a.m. its divisions have not yet taken up jump-off positions. . . . I could not restrain myself and stepped forward:
" 'You can accuse us of whatever you wish, but take the trouble to hear us out beforehand.'
" 'Oh, it's you, the court-appointed defender of the traitor—'
" 'Now a stream of abuse descended upon me. . . .
"[After listening at last to explanations, Vashugin quieted down.] He looked at his watch and ordered Riabyshev:
" 'In twenty minutes time you will report to me your decision [about how to continue the attack].'
"He left quickly for his car. . . . The corps commissar did not give time for reconnaissance or for regrouping the divisions. What can we attack with? Riabyshev went to the commissar who was pacing near the car.
" 'The corps can complete its redeployment only by tomorrow morning.'
"The commissar almost whispered in his anger:
" 'In twenty minutes the decision—and forward.'

" 'What can we go "forward" with?'
" 'I order you to start the attack immediately. If you don't start, I will relieve you of your command and turn you over to the tribunal. . . .'
"The corps commissar turned to me:
" 'If by evening you occupy Dubno you will receive a decoration. If you don't—we will expel you from the Party and shoot you.' "
(N. I. Popel', *V tiazhkuiu poru* [Moscow, 1959], pp. 137–41.)
The attack on Dubno took place as ordered by Vashugin with predictable results. Three days later Vashugin, ordered by the Army Group commander to mount a counterattack with a tank division, led the tanks into a swamp where they had to be abandoned. Then and there Vashugin committed suicide. (*Ibid.*, p. 269.)

71 German Generals agree that the actions of the Southwestern Army Group caused considerable initial difficulties for the invading armies. Colonel General Hoth, Commander of the 3rd Panzer Group, writes:
"The greatest difficulties were encountered by Army Group South. . . . A considerable obstacle to the assault of German units came from the enemy's strong counterattacks . . . which forced a large part of the 1st Tank Group to change the direction of its offensive and instead of moving toward Kiev to move northward and engage in battles of local importance."
(Herman Hoth, *Panzer Operationen* [Heidelberg: Scharnhorst Buchkameradschaft, 1956], p. 68.)

CHAPTER THREE

1 Until then Konev had commanded the 19th Army in the Smolensk sector. The command of the Western Army Group included, besides Konev (then a Colonel General), Lieutenant Generals Sokolovskii as chief of staff and Lestev as political commissar. When the German assault against Moscow began, N. A. Bulganin, the future Prime Minister of the USSR, was appointed the political commissar of the Western Army Group. (General Lestev was killed in an air raid on October 18.)

2 Aside from errors of detail (e.g., that Keitel and Goering would direct the Moscow offensive from Smolensk), Konev's report is fairly accurate in predicting

the date and directions of the assault. It even exaggerates German strength but curiously does not contain any expression of alarm. Only this failure to recognize the approaching danger, despite knowledge of pertinent facts, can explain the degree of astonishment evinced by the Soviet High Command when the German assault produced enormous initial successes.

3 The Volkhov sector near Leningrad, in September 1941 the scene of fierce fighting during the German offensive against Leningrad. The transfer of troops from the Moscow to the Volkhov sector reflects not only the desperate situation near Leningrad (where Zhukov was then dis-

patched) but also Stalin's disbelief that an offensive against Moscow would still be launched by the Germans during the 1941 campaign and at the same time his faith in the level of preparedness of the Smolensk-Briansk defense line.

4   The Reserve Army Group and the Mozhaisk defense line—at the beginning of the German assault the last Soviet troop concentration and the closest fortified defense line in front of Moscow. Marshal Zhukov's memoirs which follow explain the general disposition of opposing forces in the battle of Moscow.

5   Tula, a city about 100 miles south of Moscow, the traditional center of Russian arms production. Orel, a city about 200 miles south of Moscow and a key railroad junction, was at the start of the German offensive still 140 miles behind the front line. Its capture on the third day of the battle was totally unexpected by the Soviet command. It is described by General Guderian whose tanks achieved the breakthrough:

"On October 3rd the 4th Panzer Division arrived at Orel. We had thus reached a good road and captured an important rail and road center which would serve as a base for our future operations. Our seizure of the town took the enemy so completely by surprise that the electric trams were still running as our tanks drove in. The evacuation of industrial installations, carefully prepared by the Russians, could not be carried out. Along the streets leading from the factories to the station lay dismantled machines and crates filled with tools and raw materials."

(Heinz Guderian, *Panzer Leader* [New York: E. P. Dutton and Co., 1952], pp. 230–32.)

6   Hitler made the radio speech to which Telegin refers on October 3. It was based on his Order of the Day which had been read to the men on the Eastern Front one day earlier, at the start of the battle. Its actual wording was as follows:

"The last great decisive battle of this year will mean the annihilation of the enemy. . . . I say this today because for the first time I am entitled to say it: the enemy is already beaten and will never be in a position to rise again."

7   Soviet defense line 80 miles southwest of Moscow which the Soviets believed at this moment to be over 100 miles away from the front line.

8   A town 130 miles southwest of Moscow,

deep inside the region where, according to Soviet expectations, the Reserve Army Group should have been deployed.

9   While Soviet sources do not conceal that the easy destruction of the Red Army's defense near Viaz'ma and Briansk was totally unexpected by the Soviet leadership, Telegin's account indicates that the vacuum of leadership on the Soviet side at the start of Operation Typhoon was much greater than one would expect. In the light of Telegin's story the conversation between Stalin and Zhukov after the latter's recall from Leningrad (see p. 278) may be better understood and Zhukov's achievement in assuming control in the field better appreciated.

10   Lieutenant General P. A. Artem'ev. Commander of the Moscow Military District and Telegin's direct superior, who before the war commanded the internal security troops of the NKVD. On October 5 he was organizing defenses in Tula.

11   A close associate of Beria, Abakumov was after the war the Minister of State Security. After Stalin's death and Beria's downfall, he was tried and executed by the Malenkov-Khrushchev government in December 1954. During the war counterintelligence in the armed forces (Special Sections and then *Smersh*, so well popularized by Ian Fleming's James Bond) was independent of military authority and directly controlled by Beria through Abakumov.

12   Air Force Lieutenant General N. A. Sbytov, former commander of the air force of the Moscow Military District and the Moscow Defense Zone, provides the following account of the incident which supplements and in some respects differs from that of Telegin:

"The fascists were already approaching Iukhnov. On October 5, at 2:00 p.m., I was summoned to the Chief of Military Counterintelligence Abakumov.

"'Where did you get it from—that the Germans are moving on Iukhnov?'

"'Air reconnaissance has not only discovered but several times confirmed the fact that fascist tanks and motorized infantry are on the move in this direction.'

"I was not believed. Then I requested that one of the commanders of the air formations be summoned to corroborate my statement. The air force officer who was summoned, however, displayed a lack of courage and said that he didn't know anything. I asked that the chief of staff [of Moscow's

Notes

589

Defense Zone Air Force], Colonel I. I. Komarov, be summoned. He brought with him the combat report log. But even that did not prove to be sufficient. They asked me to present the photos made by air reconnaissance. I answered:

" 'The reconnaissance was conducted by fighter aircraft and they have no cameras. But they didn't need any cameras. They were flying at the height of 200–300 meters and saw everything perfectly. We cannot disbelieve our pilots.'

"They tried to confuse me, they tried to force me to deny that the information brought by the reconnaissance was correct and to admit that there were no enemy troops near Iukhnov. Finally the interrogation ended and I was permitted to leave.

"Returning to headquarters, I tried in vain to get in touch with the Supreme Command. About 4:00 p.m., I approached the commander of the military district, General P. A. Artem'ev. Together we got in touch with the Deputy Chief of the General Staff, Lieutenant General A. M. Vasilevskii, who confirmed that the pilots could not have mistaken our tanks for fascist tanks because we simply did not have such a large number of tanks in the Iukhnov region. . . .

"About 7:00 p.m., on this same day, a representative of counterintelligence arrived at my command point with the transcript of my interrogation and asked me to sign it. I wrote on the transcript: 'The latest reconnaissance has established that fascist tanks are already in the Iukhnov region and that by the end of October 5 they will capture the city.' I signed it.

"Local Communists and anti-aircraft defense posts which reported to Moscow that on the night of October 5 the Hitlerites had captured Iukhnov quickly cleared up the whole story. On October 6 before dawn we were told:

" 'Your reconnaissance was correct. Those tanks were fascist. Do whatever you want but see to it that there are no enemy troops east of the Ugra River.'

"We declared a combat alert not only in all air force units but also in all air force schools."
(N. A. Sbytov, "Aviatsionnyi shchit stolitsy," in *Bitva za Moskvu* [Moscow, 1966], pp. 402–404.)

13 Guards mortars, mobile (truck-mounted)

multiple rocket launchers nicknamed "Katiusha" (Little Cathy).

14 Operational group, a multidivisional field formation created for a specific task and ,dissolved after its fulfillment. The group in question, commanded by Lieutenant General Ermakov, was composed of 5 infantry divisions and 2 motorized brigades.

15 The Reserve Army Group (dissolved on October 10, 1941) was commanded by Marshal Budennyi, whose political commissar, Kruglov, was the future head of the Soviet secret police; his chief of staff was Lieutenant General Anisov. Colonel General Eremenko commanded the Briansk Army Group (dissolved November 9, 1941); his political "assistant" was Divisional Commissar Mazepov, and his chief of staff was Major General Zakharov. As was mentioned previously, Colonel General Konev commanded the Western Army Group.

Recently published statistics on the composition of Soviet forces at the start of the Moscow battle somewhat modify the data given by Marshal Zhukov. The pertinent figures are as follows:

	Combined total: 3 Army Groups	Total: Western Army Group
Personnel: total	1,252,000	540,000
in combat units	868,000	321,000
Aircraft: total	936	272
fighters: total	285	146
Tanks: total	849	464
Heavy	47	19
Medium	94	32
Light	708	413
Artillery pieces	5,637	2,351
Mortars	4,961	1,685
Trucks	62,600	30,400
Horses	226,600	96,800

("Moskovskaia bitva v tsifrakh [Period oborony]," *Voenno-istoricheskii zhurnal,* 1967, No. 3, pp. 70, 72.)

It is interesting to compare with recently published Soviet data the official German estimates of Soviet forces defending Moscow which were made at the start of the battle.

	German estimate	Soviet figures
Field Armies (including reserves)	14	15
Infantry Divisions	65	83
Tank Divisions	9	1
Cavalry Divisions	6	9

(For German estimates, see Field Marshal von Bock's War Diary of December 1, 1941, quoted in H. A. Jacobsen and J. Rohwer, eds., *Decisive Battles of World War II: The German View* [New York: G. P. Putnam's Sons, 1965], pp. 144–45.)

16 The German forces under Field Marshal von Bock consisted, according to Soviet sources, of 14 tank and 8 motorized divisions, 2 motorized brigades, and 50 infantry divisions, i.e., about one-third of the total number of active infantry divisions and two-thirds of active tank and motorized divisions from Germany and its satellites on the Eastern Front. The German Army Group Center had invaded Russia on June 22 with only three tank divisions fewer than the number which took part in Operation Typhoon. Moreover, its perimeter of action in early October was but a fifth of its line on June 22. The Soviet claim that the Germans enjoyed numerical superiority from the very start of the battle, however, seems to be based on their calculation of full-strength divisions, which would result in Zhukov's figure of over one million men (50 infantry divisions with 15,200 men each, 14 tank divisions with 14,400 men each, 8 motorized divisions with 12,600 men each). Yet the German divisions were no more the fresh units of the summer campaign, and some reportedly had lost up to a third of their original strength.

17 The three Army Groups on the defense perimeter in front of Moscow formed the Western Strategic Sector, the commander of which was responsible directly to Supreme Headquarters. Until September 12, 1941 the sector was under the command of Marshal Timoshenko, who then left for the Ukraine to preside over the destruction of the Soviet troops in the Southwestern Strategic Sector. During the battle of Moscow, Supreme Headquarters dealt directly with the command of the Army Groups. No commander was appointed to replace Timoshenko, although in actuality Zhukov was in control of almost all troops on the approaches to Moscow. The Western Strategic Sector was formally dissolved in late spring of 1942.

18 The Mozhaisk line of defense was located on its closest approaches about 70 miles west of Moscow. The distance between the forward front line at the start of Operation Typhoon and the Mozhaisk perimeter was over 130 miles.

19 District soviet, the seat of the district (county) state authority. The chairman of the executive committee of the soviet is the official head of local administration.

20 Of all top Soviet commanders of the first half of the war Marshal Budennyi perhaps best personified the type of brave, dashing, but uneducated cavalry officer who tended to view combat as an extension of the Civil War. His luck in the fall of 1941 seemed especially poor. Until September 12 he was in charge of the entire Southwestern Strategic Sector (Ukraine) where his troops were encircled. Shortly after his appointment to the much lower Reserve Army Group command, he witnessed the total disintegration of his units. On the same day that his conversation with Zhukov took place, he was relieved of his command. He reappeared in 1942 as commander of the Caucasus Sector. After the war he was given charge of horse racing and stud farms in the Soviet Union, a position which he continues to hold at the present time.

21 In the first ten days of Operation Typhoon, German forces more than halved the distance separating them from Moscow. At their farthest points of advance, there remained 100 miles to the Soviet capital.

22 Konev's analysis of the initial stage of the Moscow battle is taken from his memoirs, "Nachalo Moskovskoi bitvy," *Voenno-istoricheskii zhurnal*, 1966, No. 10, pp. 65–67. His account of the "objective factors" in the battle is intended to counteract Zhukov's criticism and, incidentally, to imply that he was not dismissed from his command but himself suggested the appointment of Zhukov in his stead.

23 The wartime rivalry and postwar enmity between Zhukov and Konev are well established. In 1957, when Zhukov was forced by Khrushchev to retire, owing to alleged resistance to Party control, it was Marshal Konev who wrote a vicious article indicting Zhukov for past and present deeds. Zhukov is clearly trying to stress his fairness with regard to Marshal Konev at a time when he had an opportunity to harm him.

24 For the story behind the formation of the antitank artillery "regiments," see the memoirs of Chief Marshal of Artillery N. N. Voronov (p. 303).

25 According to German sources, 673,000 prisoners were taken along with 1,200 tanks and 3,500 guns in the Viaz'ma pocket together with the Briansk trap (where the 3rd, 13th, and units of the 50th Soviet Armies were encircled). (See von Bock's War Diary of October 19, 1941,

quoted in *Decisive Battles of World War II: The German View, op. cit.*, p. 150.) On the other hand, the figures given by Zhukov of total Soviet strength in the Moscow sector at the beginning of the German offensive (800,000 first-line soldiers, 770 tanks, and 9,150 guns) render the German claim rather unrealistic. The important thing, however, is not the exact estimation of Soviet losses in the first phase of Operation Typhoon, but the fact (with which Zhukov concurs) of the disappearance following the first German strikes of the continuous, solid line of Soviet defenses built up during the July–September stabilization of the Central sector. According to official Soviet war history, the forces encircled near Viaz'ma, owing to their active resistance, delayed for a week the drive of the German 4th Army and 4th Tank Group toward Moscow.

26 These points were located along a radius 60–70 miles from Moscow. They stretched in a half circle from the north to the west of the capital.

27 Kuibyshev, a large industrial center on the Volga about 500 miles east of Moscow with a population of about 500,000. The evacuation involved not only civilian authorities but even central military institutions as, e.g., the Artillery, Armor, and other Directorates of the People's Commissariat of Defense.

28 This defense line formed a half circle stretching from north through west to south around Moscow. Its northern point was 45 miles from the capital, its southern point 60 miles, and its western point 30 miles.

29 A historical study of the U.S. Department of the Army presents the following conclusion:

"Large-scale operations are impossible during the muddy season. In the autumn of 1941, an entire German army was completely stopped by mud. The muddy season of that year began in mid-October and was more severe than any other muddy season experienced in World War I or World War II. During the first stages cart and dirt roads were impassable, and then the road from Roslavl' to Orel became mud-choked. Supply trucks broke through gravel-top roads and churned up traffic lanes until even courier service had to be carried out with tracked vehicles. Finally only horse-drawn vehicles could move; all other transport and the bulk of the tanks and artillery were stopped dead. The muddy season lasted a month."

(*Effects of Climate on Combat in European Russia* [Department of the Army Pamphlet No. 20–291, February 1952], p. 31.)

30 During the Moscow battle about half a million Muscovites (three-fourths of them women) participated in constructing defense lines on the approaches to the capital. They built over 400 miles of antitank ditches, 250 miles of antitank obstacles, 800 miles of barbed wire barriers and 30 thousand various fire points. Moscow itself was divided into two defense sectors, each with three rings of defensive fortifications. (See P. Andreev and K. Bukov, *Podvig goroda-geroia* [Moscow, 1965], p. 78.)

31 That is, Zhukov anticipated a German pincer movement originating from the north and south of Moscow.

32 The Germans chose the date for their final assault primarily on the basis of climatic conditions. General Guenther Blumentritt, chief of staff of the German 4th Army, describes the conference of front-line commanders with the Chief of the General Staff concerning the plan of battle as follows:

"The final decision was that one last attempt would be made, one final attack launched, with Moscow as objective. The Supreme Command was well aware that this could not begin before the end of the mud period, when the soil would be frozen solid once again. . . . By mid-November the mud period was over and frost heralded the approach of winter. Both the roads and the open country were now passable for vehicles of all kinds. Tractors extricated the heavy artillery from the mud far behind the front and one gun after another was towed forward."

(Guenther Blumentritt, "Moscow," in Seymour Freiden and William Richardson, eds., *The Fatal Decisions* [New York: Berkley Publishing Co., 1963], pp. 73–74.)

33 The huge artificial lake from which the 70-mile-long Moscow-Volga Canal leads directly to the capital. It is also known as the Volga Reservoir.

34 This emergency transfer of a division from Serpukhov to Solnechnogorsk, i.e., from the southern flank of the Western Army Group to its critical right flank over a distance of hundreds of kilometers, points out the extremely important advantage of Zhukov's troops over the attacking German formation. The highly developed and extensive Moscow railroad nexus just behind the Soviet lines pro-

vided for exceptional maneuverability and thus compensated for the scarcity of reserves. This should also be taken into account when one considers Zhukov's argument about the "equality" of winter road conditions for both German and Soviet forces.

35 What Zhukov probably has in mind is that German forces had not attained any of the goals of either the initial or the revised Plan Barbarossa—Moscow, Leningrad, the Caucasus oil fields, and the occupation of the entire Crimea. One might add, however, that the capture of the industrial and coal-mining area of the Donets Basin, a primary target of Hitler's famous Directive No. 34 which revised the initial plan of the Russian campaign, had by then largely been achieved, and Leningrad had been isolated and neutralized.

36 At the time when Soviet forces according to Zhukov's estimate were ready for a counteroffensive, the German General Staff evaluated the Red Army on December 1, 1941 as follows:
    "The numerical strength of the majority of Soviet combat units is low, their equipment with heavy weapons and guns is unsatisfactory. New units were appearing with less frequency in recent days; individual units are being transferred from quiet to endangered front sectors. On this basis it should be assumed that no significant reserve units exist at present. . . . The combat strength of the enemy has been weakened decisively as a result of losses in personnel and matériel which have surpassed all expectations."

37 The Great Purge contributed to Rokossovskii's slow advance as compared to that of Zhukov. While opening many vacancies for Zhukov, it claimed Rokossovskii, then a cavalry corps commander, as its victim in August 1937. He was released from prison and reinstated in his former rank and position only in March 1940.

38 The events described by Rokossovskii took place during the November Nazi offensive near Moscow. His narrative starts with the critical days of November 19, 1941. For a survey of the fighting near Moscow in this critical period, see Marshal Zhukov's memoirs, pp. 291–93 above.

39 Rokossovskii's action in appealing his superior's decision directly to Supreme Headquarters and without informing Zhukov was unprecedented to say the least. The only other comparable occasion mentioned in the memoirs concerns

a field commander, General Volskii, who wrote to Stalin that the plan for the Stalingrad counteroffensive which was about to start was unrealistic.

40 Rokossovskii refers here to what was commonly known among high Soviet military commanders—that Marshal Shaposhnikov never made a decision of even slight importance without asking Stalin's approval or reporting it personally to Stalin. Shaposhnikov's cautiousness may have been related to the fact that as a former colonel of the General Staff in the old tsarist army who switched to the Bolsheviks during the Civil War, he was even more vulnerable than an "ordinary" Red Army commander in the atmosphere of suspiciousness which reigned in the Kremlin.

41 Rokossovskii's troops were unable to hold their defense line. On the same day German forces hurled them back to the east, forced the Istra River from the march, and seized bases of operations on its east bank. Simultaneously, German units began to advance in the Solnechnogorsk area, by-passing the Istra Reservoir from the north.

42 Lieutenant General Zhigarev was Commander in Chief of the Air Force from July 1941 until winter 1942, when General A. A. Novikov assumed command for the remainder of the war.

43 The former commander of anti-aircraft units defending Moscow, Colonel General D. A. Zhuravlev recounts in his memoirs that the exercise took place on the evening of July 21, 1941. It ended after 8 p.m., and scarcely two hours later the Germans sent 250 bombers over Moscow in the first air raid on the capital. During the next three weeks the Luftwaffe carried out 17 night raids lasting from four to five hours each with an average number of 150 bombers per raid. From mid-September, instead of a single successive daily raid, each day the Germans attacked Moscow in small groups, even with single planes, and with great frequency. In November, the last month of frequent air attacks against Moscow, 41 raids took place, 24 of them at night. Zhuravlev asserts that German losses averaged 10 percent of aircraft participating in each raid and that only two to three percent of the bombers were able to reach the city and unload their bombs on target. (D. A. Zhuravlev, "Protivovozdushnaia oborona stolitsy," Bitva za Moskvu [Moscow, 1966], pp. 384–90.)

44 It would seem from the Soviet memoirs that this "method" of securing an indi-

vidual's release from labor camp or prison explains the rehabilitation and return to active duty of certain purged generals. More effective than normal "legal" efforts, it required "only" Stalin's good humor and a friend with access to Stalin and the courage to make the request. Iakovlev himself quotes another such example in his memoirs (see p. 88).

45 Stalin refers here to a prior incident when Voronov reported that he had saved for emergency use over one million artillery shells by cutting deliveries to the front. At that time Stalin was so glad to have an unexpected ammunition reserve that Voronov's action went unpunished.

46 A prominent Russian scientist, specialist in mechanics and rocketry. Presently Vice President of the Space Research Commission of the International Council of Scientific Societies.

47 Moscow was the largest Soviet industrial center, accounting for 22 percent of total Soviet industrial production. The evacuation of Moscow industry commenced as early as summer 1941 and proceeded on a crash basis from October. From the start of the evacuation to the Soviet counteroffensive on December 5, about 500 industrial enterprises together with about 200,000 workers and technical personnel were evacuated to the east from Moscow.

48 While somewhat more realistic than Zhukov's description, that of Telegin still does not convey the extent of what happened in those few days. It may be argued that the spontaneous flight of the population and officials, the disappearance of police from the streets of Moscow, the looting of stores, etc., warrant more than a few lines in the memoirs of the chief political commissar of Moscow at that time. On the basis of eyewitness accounts, however, one is inclined to agree with the conclusion of one western investigation that "at the height of the crisis the majority of the population of Moscow did not rebel against their rulers. And, on the basis of available evidence, they had no intention of doing so." (Leon Goure and Herbert S. Dinerstein, *Moscow in Crisis* [Glencoe, Illinois: The Free Press, 1955], p. 225.)

49 A Secretary of the Central Committee of the Communist Party and head of the Moscow Party organization. Later during the war, the Chief of the Main Political Administration of the Red Army. Died in 1945.

50 V. P. Pronin, the wartime Mayor of Moscow (Chairman of the Moscow Soviet), provides in his memoirs the following account of the meeting:

"On October 19, a damp, dank evening, A. S. Shcherbakov and I were in the Kremlin. . . . The meeting started. Stalin stepped up to the table and said: 'The situation is known to all of you. Should we defend Moscow?' He was silent for a moment and then addressed this question to all members of the State Defense Committee. After receiving affirmative answers, Stalin dictated the decree on a state of siege in Moscow. . . . Immediately afterward, the Supreme Commander in Chief began to telephone the military district commanders of the eastern regions and issued orders to dispatch additional divisions to Moscow. He named [the numbers] of many of these divisions from memory, glancing only occasionally at his notebook."

(V. P. Pronin, "Gorod-voin," *Bitva za Moskvu* [Moscow, 1966], p. 465.)

51 The decree stated among other things that "for the purpose of putting a stop to the subversive activities of spies, saboteurs, and other agents of German fascism," the movement of unauthorized persons and vehicles on the streets of Moscow is prohibited from twelve midnight to 5:00 a.m. and that troops of the NKVD are put at the disposal of the Commandant of the city of Moscow for the maintenance of order. A key paragraph declared: "All persons fomenting disorder are to be immediately turned over to the Military Tribunal and the *agents provocateurs*, spies, and other agents of the enemy, apprehended for inciting disturbances, are to be shot on the spot." According to General Artem'ev, Commander of the Moscow Military District, there were in all two occasions when the right to on-the-spot execution was used. (*Ogonek*, 1966, No. 45, p. 6.)

52 The parade was conducted annually from the 1920's. In 1941, however, only military units took part, while in peacetime the march of civilian columns took up at least half the time assigned to the parade. Each parade marched in front of Lenin's mausoleum above which the reviewing stand was placed for key Party, government, and military leaders. (The October Revolution is celebrated on November 7 due to the calendar change by the Soviet government in 1918. According to the old calendar the Revolution took place on October 25.)

53 The parade was deliberately planned to start earlier than usual as additional insurance against air raids.

54 In 1941, 12 Home Guards (narodnoe opolchenie) divisions were formed from the Moscow civilian population. Their 120,000 members, very poorly armed and possessing only rudimentary training, were used to bridge the gaps in Soviet defenses during the October and November fighting until the arrival of regular units.

55 On that day over 500 fighter aircraft, practically the entire fighter force of the whole Western Strategic Sector, was kept ready for instant takeoff. According to Soviet sources, despite the weather about 250 German bombers headed for Moscow in several waves but all were turned back by anti-aircraft defense without having been able to drop their bombs on the capital.

56 Moscow's principal department store on Red Square, directly across from the Lenin Mausoleum.

57 Directly before the war Golikov was Chief of Intelligence of the Soviet General Staff (GRU). He spent several months at the beginning of the war in the US where he headed a Soviet military mission which negotiated the terms of lend-lease aid to Russia.

58 A region over 500 miles southeast of Moscow.

59 In other words 85 percent of the political officers in the Army were civilian Party workers, government and trade union officials, etc., without military preparation.

60 A nationality group over one million strong which is related to the Tartars. Their greatest concentration is in the Mordva Autonomous Republic in the region of the Volga River.

61 After entering the Party, the new member retains candidate status for the first year. In other words, Golikov states that one-third of the Party members in his Army had been members for less than one year.

62 With those reinforcements the Communists in Golikov's Army still composed less than 6 percent of the total personnel. If one takes into consideration the fact that among officers the percentage of Communists was much higher and that the entire political apparatus of the Army belonged to the Party, one can conclude that the number of Communists among enlisted men and non-commissioned officers was much lower, probably not in excess of 2-3 percent.

63 Pravda (Truth), the main Party daily; Izvestiia (News), the main government daily; Komsomol'skaia Pravda (Komsomol Truth), the daily of the Young Communist League; Krasnaia Zvezda (Red Star), the main newspaper of the People's Commissariat of Defense.

64 In the Red Army enlisted personnel and even officers wrapped square pieces of cloth around their feet instead of wearing socks. It is believed to be a better protection against frost and blisters.

65 A map with a scale of one inch to one and a half miles, ideal for a motorist's excursion and useless for military purposes.

66 Golikov's staff was also taking part in planning the defenses and the construction of fortifications in the area of their formation (along the Sura and Volga rivers) where Stalin, uncertain about the results of the Moscow battle, ordered the preparation of a last ditch stand.

67 Nine new Armies were being formed in October and November (10th, 26th, 57th, 28th, 39th, 58th, 59th, 60th, and 61st). Their formation sectors were distributed from Lake Onega in the north through Iaroslavl', Gor'kii, Saratov, Stalingrad, to Astrakhan in the south. They began to arrive at the Moscow front at the end of November.

68 Sector in the southernmost tip of the left wing of the Western Army Group.

69 The major source of manpower and weapons for the partisan movement at that stage was units of the Red Army trapped deep in the German rear. The actual role of the partisans in the battle of Moscow would seem very small; the stress on their accomplishments in Soviet accounts derives rather from the movement's contribution to the image of war against the Nazis as the "holy war of the people."

70 The deployment of the troops of the Western Army Group on the eve of the counteroffensive reflected the proposed order of the battle. The Armies of the center (33rd, 43rd, 49th Armies and part of the 5th Army) with their limited tasks included 16.5 divisions. The right (north) wing of the Army Group (30th, 1st Assault, 20th, 16th Armies and part of the 5th Army) where the center of gravity of the whole counteroffensive rested was composed of 45.5 divisions. The left wing (south) which was intended to provide the other part of the Soviet pincers (50th, 10th Armies, part of the 49th Army, and Belov's Group) was composed of twenty-four divisions. Five divisions were held as Army Group reserve.

The key role of the north flank as compared to the secondary task of the center is most strikingly expressed in the following figures: the tactical density of troop deployment constituted in the center 1,198 and in the north flank 2,026 fighting men per one km. (the relevant figures for guns and mortars: north—7.5, center—5.2 per one km.). The 16th Army, which was supposed to spearhead the major breakthrough on the north flank, had at its disposal one division for each 1.7 km. of its assigned perimeter as compared to 7-11 km. for a typical division of the center Armies. The quoted figures indicate also that the major Soviet breakthrough force consisted of mass manpower which could expect a very low level of artillery support. (For the source of this data see "Moskovskaia bitva v tsifrakh [Period Kontrnastupleniia]," in *Voennoistoricheskii zhurnal*, 1967, No. 1, pp. 70–79.)

71 As usual, both sides claim that the other was significantly superior in numbers on the ground at the start of the operation. According to Soviet sources, even the crucial right wing of the Western Army Group had on the axis of its main thrust only a 1.6 superiority over the Germans in manpower and remained inferior in artillery and tanks. The latest Soviet figures of the strength of Zhukov's Western Army Group on December 1, 1941 are as follow: 787,000 men (of which 578,000 were in combat units), 1,794 field guns, 2,973 mortars, and 618 tanks (of which 205 were the superior T-34 and KV type). On paper the German armor and artillery strength seems superior to the Soviet. One suspects, however, that in terms of units and equipment fit for combat, the German advantage was to a large extent illusory, due to their unpreparedness for waging war in winter conditions on the one hand and the Soviet edge in logistics and air support on the other hand.

72 General Vasilevskii apparently had in mind the high probability that the German forces would halt their push toward Moscow and shift to defensive positions, which, when left to stabilize, would be extremely difficult to breach with the available Soviet forces. As a matter of fact, it appears that the Germans (at least at the Army Group command level) recognized at the beginning of December, almost simultaneously with the Soviet decision to mount a counteroffensive, that Moscow could not be taken without reinforcements which were denied to them. The German tank leader Guderian,

for example, admitted on the eve of the Soviet counteroffensive the failure of the attack against Moscow and ordered his units to assume defensive positions. General Vasilevskii's assessment was validated also in the Soviet strategic offensive of winter 1942, the limited results of which can be explained in part by the stabilization of the German defensive line before the Soviet attack had started.

73 The Kalinin Army Group and the right wing of the Southwestern Army Group together had 273,000 men (of whom 182,000 were in combat units), 763 field guns, 702 mortars, and only 60 (!) tanks. (Incidentally, while all three Army Groups in front of Moscow had available only 678 tanks, they had at their disposal 166,000 horses in their combat units.) The Kalinin and the right wing of the Southwestern Army Groups had, at the start of the counteroffensive, 34.5 divisions deployed on a front of almost 500 km. The Western Army Group had 91 divisions on a 650 km. front line.

74 At the beginning of the counteroffensive, the total number of Soviet aircraft in the Western Strategic Sector was 1,376 (of which 859 were in working order). The German strength was 580 airplanes.

75 Stalin's alarm is understandable if one considers that the town is located about ten miles from the city limits of Moscow, and that the front line at that time was about twenty miles more to the northwest.

76 Zhukov remained a member of Supreme Headquarters even after he left the post of Chief of the General Staff in July 1941 and assumed command of field Army Groups.

77 According to this order, the major objective of the offensive was the encirclement of the Mozhaisk-Gzhatsk-Viaz'ma German grouping. The plan of the operation anticipated the accomplishment of its first phase not later than January 12, i.e., five days after the initial order was issued and two days after the operation actually started. It should be noted that the German positions in the direction of the main thrust on the Lama River were relatively well fortified.

78 Attempting, on Zhukov's order, to capture the city of Viaz'ma before the arrival of German reinforcements, the 33rd Army under the command of Lieutenant General Efremov dangerously exposed its flanks. On February 4, 1942, when General Efremov was already on the approaches to the city, the Germans counterattacked from the flanks and encircled a large part of his Army. Also, the 1st Guard Cavalry

Corps of General Belov found itself in the new Viaz'ma pocket (the first encirclement was achieved here by the Germans in early October 1941 at the start of Operation Typhoon). The drop of the 8th Airborne Brigade into the pocket to help the encircled troops was to no avail.

The encircled Soviet units, with the help of the partisans, continued to fight in the German rear, but in April the situation became critical. In coordination with Zhukov's Headquarters, Belov and Efremov attempted a breakthrough to the east to rejoin Soviet units. Belov succeeded in reaching Soviet lines with a substantial part of his cavalry and of the airborne brigade. Efremov, fearing that his troops were too exhausted to reach the agreed-upon front-line sector, went over Zhukov's head and asked Stalin by radio for permission to attempt a breakthrough at a closer point. Permission, according to Zhukov, was granted, but the whole group was destroyed or captured on the approaches to the front line. General Efremov died allegedly from wounds received in the battle and is celebrated in the Soviet Union as one of the heroes of the winter campaign. Recently (February

1967), however, an official Soviet source disclosed that General Efremov committed suicide when it became evident to him that the breakthrough would not succeed.

79 The 29th Army had consisted initially of five full-strength divisions, a total which exceeded by at least six or seven times the 6,000 men that fought their way out of encirclement.

80 According to German sources, these figures are inflated. Colonel General Halder, Chief of the German General Staff, estimates the total German losses on the eastern front as of February 28, 1942, to be 1,005,000 killed, wounded, and missing. The losses as of November 26, 1941, were 743,000. Therefore, the German figure for losses in the period of the Soviet counteroffensive near Moscow, in all sectors of the Soviet-Nazi front, are estimated at 262,000, which is half as much as Zhukov's estimate for the Western Strategic Sector alone. Even Halder's figures, however, tell the tale. As of November 1941, the German losses constituted 23 percent of their Eastern Front force and, as of February 1942, 31 percent.

CHAPTER FOUR

1 Stalin did not assume formal leadership of the Soviet government in 1940 but in May 1941.

2 Stalin finally spoke to the Soviet people on July 3, 1941, the twelfth day of war. His speech is remembered mainly for the form he used to address them— "Brothers and sisters, my dear country-men." The form was used on that occasion for the first and the last time.

3 Soviet sources have never explained why Zhukov was replaced by Shaposhnikov within a month after the invasion. The change cannot be considered a demotion for Zhukov because he remained in Stalin's favor and shortly thereafter became Stalin's key troubleshooter. Kuznetsov's implication that the change was necessary refers, it would appear, to the fact that Zhukov's temperament and experience made him best suited for line not staff positions, while Shaposhnikov was the natural choice for General Staff leadership.

4 This theme appears repeatedly in Soviet memoirs. For the most striking example see pp. 460-61. At the same time it seems characteristic of Stalin's style of work that he dealt with his subordinates in the presence of others.

Private interviews with Stalin are rarely recorded in the memoirs.

5 This view was expressed not only by "certain Army Group commanders," as Shtemenko asserts, but it was adopted during Khrushchev's tenure in office as the dominant line and found its way into the official Soviet war history and important military publications. One reads, e.g., in the authoritative book on military strategy collectively produced by fifteen leading Soviet military theoreticians:

"The representatives of the Supreme High Command helped the command of the Army Groups to carry out the plans of the Supreme High Command, to make decisions depending on the role and place of the Army Group in a given operation, and also to solve on-the-spot problems concerning operational and strategic cooperation. However, there were substantial shortcomings in the work of these representatives, mainly when they substituted for the Army Group troop commanders and restrained the latter's initiative, and also when preferential reinforcement of troops and supply of materials was given to one Army Group at the ex-

pense of others on the insistence of a representative."
(Marshal V. D. Sokolovskii, ed., *Military Strategy* [New York: Frederick A. Praeger, 1963], p. 365.)

6 General of the Army Antonov, former junior officer of the tsarist army, enlisted in the Red Army in 1919, was graduated from the Frunze and General Staff Academies in the 1930's, and served during the first period of the war as an Army Group chief of staff. In December 1942 he was transferred to Moscow and appointed Chief of Operations of the General Staff.

7 The difference between the General Staff's work schedules described by Shtemenko and by Marshal Vasilevskii in the preceding account probably reflects the difference in the resp xtive periods of war—1944 in the first case, 1942 in the second.

8 From Shtemenko's account and others it would appear that Stalin conducted his business during the war from three places—his office in the Kremlin, the Supreme Headquarters shelter in the Kremlin, and his country house. The country house was situated in Kuntsevo just outside Moscow and was called in Shtemenko's account "nearby" *(blizhnaia)* to distinguish it from Stalin's other, more distant country houses.

9 Clearly an allusion to Khrushchev's allegation that Stalin directed military operations from a globe in his office.

10 Of all the generals who "did not fill the bill" only one, Colonel General Bogoliubov, later held important field positions. He was chief of staff of several Army Groups until the end of the war.

11 A political commissar was attached to chiefs of staff as well as to commanders of every Red Army unit or institution. The commissar automatically assumed the duties of the officer to whom he was attached during the latter's absence. Shtemenko's disclosure that this could happen even in the General Staff is quite revealing. Probably, General Bokov's performance of the duties of Chief of the General Staff were limited to internal, mainly administrative questions. It would seem hardly credible that at the time Stalin would want or tolerate operational reports from a general who was merely "a wonderful person and a good Party leader" but who knew very little about the business of war.

12 Senior staff officers in the Office of Operations who were assigned responsibility for the major strategic sectors of the front. It would appear that such divi-

sion of responsibility continued even after 1942 when formal division of the entire Nazi-Soviet theater of operations into several strategic sector commands was abolished.

13 Shtemenko reports that Stalin put Antonov to yet another test:
"Less than a month after his arrival at the General Staff, Antonov received an extremely important and difficult mission. As a representative of Supreme Headquarters he was to analyze the situation of the Voronezh, Briansk, and somewhat later of the Central Army Groups, and to make suggestions as to future operations. As we all realized, in carrying out this mission Antonov had to reassure the Soviet Supreme High Command that it had acted correctly in appointing him to one of the highest military posts."

14 In all likelihood the reference here is to General F. K. Korzhenevich, Chief of Staff of the 1st Ukrainian Army Group during the battle for Kiev in 1943. (The commander was General Vatutin, and the chief commissar N. S. Khrushchev.)

15 Shtemenko recalls in another place that Antonov deserves credit especially for the original design of the summer 1944 offensive in Belorussia, which led to the annihilation of the German Army Group Center.

16 The Order of Victory, established on November 8, 1943, was awarded to senior military commanders for successful execution of large-scale military operations. Oriental in its splendor, it was probably the most expensive decoration to come out of World War II. The order consists of a five-pointed platinum star, two inches in diameter, covered by red and blue enamel on which 135 diamonds are studded.- In addition to Antonov the following military leaders were awarded this decoration: Marshals Govorov, Konev, Malinovskii, Meretskov, Rokossovskii, Timoshenko, Tolbukhin. Stalin and Marshals Vasilevskii and Zhukov received this decoration twice. Five foreigners have also been awarded the decoration: General Eisenhower, Field Marshal Montgomery, Marshal Tito, the Polish Marshal Rola-Zymierski, and King Michael of Rumania. (See "Orden Pobedy," *Voenno-istoricheskii zhurnal,* 1965, No. 5, pp. 124–25.)

17 General Antonov was the senior military member of the Soviet delegation to Yalta and Potsdam. The other military representatives were Air Marshal S. A. Khudiakov and Admiral N. G. Kuznetsov.

Incidentally, the latter published in 1965 in the Soviet historical journal *Voprosy istorii* the only Soviet memoir account of the Yalta and Potsdam meetings.

18 From 1948 until 1954 Antonov was demoted for unknown reasons to deputy commander and then commander of the Transcaucasian Military District. From 1955 until his death in 1962 he held the position of Chief of Staff of the Armed Forces of the Warsaw Pact countries, the Soviet bloc equivalent of NATO.

19 The summer 1943 battle of Kursk-Orel in central Russia was the last, unsuccessful German attempt to retain the strategic initiative on the Eastern Front. The greatest tank battle in history (about 6,000 tanks of the two protagonists were concentrated in a very small area), it resulted in losses of matériel to Germany which could not be replaced. Zhukov as representative of Supreme Headquarters exercised overall leadership of the five Soviet Army Groups participating in the battle. His account of the battle was recently published in *Voenno-istoricheskii zhurnal*, 1967, Nos. 7, 8.

20 See n. 11, Chapter One.

21 The odd number of 124 guns used for the salute is explained as follows: The salvos of the salute were fired by the Kremlin artillery. When the first salute was being planned, Stalin summoned the military commandant of the Kremlin and asked him how many guns there were in the Kremlin. The commandant was unsure but felt he should know and replied 120. Stalin ordered him to organize the salute from "all available guns." Upon leaving Stalin, the commandant checked and discovered there were 124 guns of all makes and types in working order. To be on the safe side he took Stalin's order literally and fired the salvos "from all available guns."

22 Khar'kov, the large industrial center in the Don Basin with a Russian majority among its population, was the capital of the Ukrainian Republic until 1934, after which time Kiev, the traditional Ukrainian center, became the capital.

23 Soviet cities ranging in population from 5,000 to 800,000.

24 During the war Colonel General M. V. Zakharov served as chief of staff of several Army Groups (Kalinin, Leningrad, Steppe, 2nd Ukrainian). Presently he is Chief of the Soviet General Staff and First Deputy Minister of Defense.

25 It is very interesting to note that the orders of the day were not addressed,

inter alia, to the member of the military council of the Army Group, i.e., the Party's representative in the field command. This reflected the diminished role of political cadres in the Red Army starting with the Stalingrad battle and their increasing exclusion from interference in operational leadership. It reflected as well the growing status of top field commanders after they began to achieve victories.

26 During the period of Soviet rule the names of a large number of cities have been changed to commemorate revolutionary events, to honor Soviet leaders, etc. In some cases the names were changed more than once as, e.g., in the case of Stalingrad (Stalin's city), the former Tsaritsyn (Tsar's city), which became in 1961 Volgograd (city on the Volga).

27 "Guards" status was conferred on army, navy, and air force units which distinguished themselves in combat. Soldiers of Guards units had the right to wear on their uniforms a special metal badge and to precede their military ranks with the word "Guards" (e.g., Guards sergeant, Guards major, etc.). The title, in addition to prestige, carried several privileges—quicker promotions for officers and noncommissioned personnel, one and a half pay for officers and double pay for enlisted men, first priority in supply and equipment allocation, a larger number of heavy and automatic weapons, and higher ammunition norms. An order of Supreme Headquarters dated April 16, 1943 declared that Guards units were to be used in offensive operations on the axis of the main assaults and in defensive operations for counterattacks. The first Soviet Guards units were established on September 18, 1941 when the 100th, 127th, 153rd, and 161st Rifle Divisions were renamed the 1st, 2nd, 3rd, and 4th Guards Rifle Divisions. By the end of the war 148 rifle, 20 cavalry, 67 aviation divisions, and 6 tank armies had been designated Guards units. (See "Sovetskaia gvardiia," *Voenno-istoricheskii zhurnal*, 1966, No. 8, pp. 117–19.) It should be noted that the Soviets followed the traditional practice of the tsarist army in this regard.

28 B. S. Pusin, during the war the director of the Soviet state radio network.

29 Yurii Levitan, announcer on Moscow Radio, who throughout the war read all important government communiqués.

30 The statistics concerning the salutes for the 1943–45 period are as follows: Salutes of the I category (24 salvos from

324 guns) were given 22 times, II category (20 salvos from 224 guns) 210 times, III category (12 salvos from 124 guns) 122 times. Altogether there were 354 salutes for the 540 days of war which followed the first salute. On many days more than one salute was fired in Moscow. In 1943 two salutes daily were made five times and three salutes twice; in 1944 two salutes daily were made 26 times, three salutes four times, and five salutes once; in 1945 two salutes were made 25 times, three salutes 15 times, four salutes three times, and five salutes twice. The greatest number of salutes (68) was fired to honor the troops of the 1st Ukrainian Army Group commanded in the 1943–45 period successively by General of the Army Vatutin, Marshal Zhukov, and Marshal Konev.

31 The evacuation of population and property from endangered territories to the eastern provinces was carried out twice—once from June to December 1941 (it was halted during the Soviet counteroffensive near Moscow) and again from May to October 1942 (from the start of the German summer offensive to the stalemate stage of the battle for Stalingrad). The evacuation was organized by a State Council established on June 24, 1941 which was first headed by L. M. Kaganovich, People's Commissar of Transport, and later (from July 16) by N. M. Shvernik, head of Trade Unions. The present Soviet Prime Minister, A. N. Kosygin, served as Deputy Chairman. The evacuation of population involved resettlement of about 25 million people of whom 17 million were moved in 1941. According to the latest Soviet figures 1,523 industrial plants were evacuated to the east from June to December 1941 of which over 40 percent went to the Urals and about 20 percent each to Siberia and Central Asia. (Source: *Eshelony idut na vostok* [Moscow, 1966], pp. 6–13.)

32 Owing to the loss or deliberate destruction of military equipment stored in western territories of the Soviet Union, even simple infantry rifles, not to mention guns, tanks, and other heavy equipment, were in critically short supply. Iakovlev recalls a conversation with Stalin in the second half of August 1941 during which Stalin replied as follows to the remark of the aircraft designer Iliushin that population on territories from which the Red Army was retreating should be armed:

"We would arm them, but we do not even have sufficient rifles and weap-

ons with which to arm the regular army. We organize reinforcements, but we have nothing to arm them with. We had thought at first to order rifles from England, but the cartridges there are different. This would have resulted in confusion. Therefore, it was decided to expand the domestic production of rifles and cartridges in every way." (A. S. Iakovlev, *Tsel' zhizni* [Moscow, 1966], p. 271.)

Chief Marshal of Artillery Voronov recalls in his memoirs that as of December 31, 1941 the entire available reserve of sub-machine guns in Moscow consisted of 250 weapons. (N. N. Voronov, *Na sluzhbe voennoi* [Moscow, 1963], p. 232.)

33 The Chairmanship of the State Planning Commission and, presumably, the coordination of war industry were taken over by M. Z. Saburov, who was until then Voznesenskii's first deputy. Voznesenskii himself was appointed First Deputy Chairman of the Council of People's Commissars for Economic Affairs and in 1942 became a full member of the State Defense Committee.

34 Throughout the war the total industrial production of the Soviet Union reached its prewar (1940) level in only one year, 1944. Calculating on a monthly basis, the low point of overall industrial production came in November 1941, when it was barely 51.7 percent of the prewar level. Only a drastic reduction in the output of non-defense industries made possible the significant increase in Soviet manufacture of munitions and war equipment. Thus the machine-building industry which was engaged almost entirely in direct defense production expanded its output in 1941 ($1940 = 100$) to 112 and in 1942 to 119, while the index of the consumer goods industry (*including* supplies for the armed forces) declined to 77 in 1941 and to 41 in 1942. (Source: Ia. E. Chaadaev, *Ekonomika SSSR 1941–1945* [Moscow, 1965], pp. 65–67.)

35 In an earlier part of Khrulev's memoirs, omitted here, he recounted how impressed he was with ideas on the organization of quartermaster services which were contained in the 1914 Regulations of the tsarist army. His proposals for the reorganization of the Red Army supply system which were later approved by Stalin incorporated major principles from these Regulations.

36 Khrulev apparently has in mind the heavy losses encountered by the 39th Army during the December 1941 counteroffensive of the Kalinin Army Group

northwest of Moscow, which were due to a large extent to the breakdown of supply.

37 Horse-drawn trains remained a crucial form of Red Army transportation until the very end of the war. While supplies at the Army Group level were delivered by railroad and distributed mainly by truck convoys, lesser units had to rely largely on horse transport. For example, in the final operations of the war in 1945 the 8th Guards Army (about 100,000 men strong) which was deployed on the main axis of Soviet advance against Berlin disposed of only 323 trucks. (*Voenno-istoricheskii zhurnal*, 1965, No. 3, p. 74.) It should be mentioned that of all armies fighting in Europe only the Anglo-American expeditionary forces were fully motorized. The German army from the beginning of the war relied heavily on horse transport.

38 The daily norms for combat infantry, e.g., included 1.5 lb. bread, 3.5 oz. meat, about 1 oz. sugar, 1 oz. fat, and 0.5 oz. tobacco. A daily ration of spirits (approximately a quarter of a pint) was also issued to frontline soldiers.

39 The "substitutions," far from being made "without any reason," were probably made with the good reason that the substituted products, while of equal caloric value, were in greater demand and could secure for the supply officers a higher price on the thriving black market.

40 Throughout the war the Red Army had penal units of company or, at most, battalion size to which officers (and enlisted personnel) who were accused of dereliction of duty, cowardice, etc., were assigned to fight as privates. The penal units, with police detachments behind them, were used in the most dangerous front sectors and in the bloodiest actions. If an officer survived a few such actions and displayed personal courage, he might be reinstated in his rank and in his command.

41 The supervision of rear services became one of the main duties of Party officials assigned to the military councils of Armies and Army Groups after the abolition of the institution of commissars. In this connection it is perhaps worth mentioning that both Khrushchev and his successor Brezhnev, who served in this capacity during the war, received long after the war a decoration which is usually associated with heroic feats—the Gold Star and the title Hero of the Soviet Union.

42 The Il-4 remained throughout the war the principal Soviet bomber aircraft for both day and night bombing. The Soviet stress on fighters and troop-support assault planes to the neglect of bombers is best illustrated by the fact that of the 142,800 military aircraft produced in the USSR in the 1941–45 period, fighters accounted for 41 percent, assault planes for 26 percent, and bombers for only 12 percent of the total. The extent to which the air force was used for direct battle support can be seen in the fact that 93 percent of all Soviet bomber sorties during the war was limited to an area within 33 miles of the forward battle lines. (See *Voenno-istoricheskii zhurnal*, 1966, No. 4, p. 45; 1967, No. 9, p. 35; *Istoriia Velikoi Otechestvennoi voiny Sovetskogo Soiuza 1941–1945*, [1965] VI, 51.)

43 The La-5 Soviet fighter plane had a maximum range of 320 miles. A fighter of Iakovlev's own design, the Iak-9, the serial production of which began in 1944, had the longest range of all Soviet fighter aircraft (580 miles). (One of its models, the Iak-9D, was able to attain the maximum range of 800–900 miles.) Soviet aircraft were clearly inferior in range to both German and Allied fighters. The range of German fighters varied from a low of 480 miles (ME-109) to the maximum of 600 (ME-109F) and 900 (ME-110) miles. The fighter planes of the Western Allies which were used as escorts for the strategic bombing of Germany had a range of up to 1,200 miles.

44 Like all Soviet fighter planes manufactured during the war (with the exception of the Mig-3), the Iak-9 was built of plywood covered with fabric.

45 According to Iakovlev's account, Dement'ev organized a few dozen working teams of carpenters and painters from all Soviet aircraft plants and sent them by plane to the Kursk sector. These teams were able in two or three weeks to reinforce the wing coverings of several hundred Iak planes and make them serviceable for the start of the Kursk battle.

Incidentally, the Soviet reviewer of Iakovlev's book, an air force Lieutenant General, corrects certain details in this account. He writes that some Iak fighters had crashed during control flights at the plant before being sent to the front, but that officials in the People's Commissariat of the Aviation Industry to all intents and purposes ignored the accidents. Moreover, he alleges, even after complaints from the front reached the Commissariat, the crashes were blamed on pilot error. Only when the pilots addressed a letter to Stalin personally, attaching thereto a piece of the torn wing covering, did the reckoning described by Iakovlev take place. According to the author, it was later learned that the quality of paint or glue was not responsible for the trouble, but that the fabric covering had been glued to the plywood wing without a priming in order to speed production. (*Voenno-istoricheskii zhurnal*, 1967, No. 10, pp. 102–106.)

46 During the first two months of the Nazi-Soviet war the Germans advanced along two key axes—in the center toward Moscow and in the north toward Leningrad. In the south while the German armored divisions advanced by the end of the third week of war to points only ten miles west of Kiev, 'heir further successes were limited until the second half of August. They neither succeeded in capturing Kiev nor were they able to destroy Armies covering the flanks of the Kiev zone from north and south. On August 21 Hitler issued an order which switched the major direction of German attack away from Moscow toward the south. The order stated: "Of primary importance before the outbreak of winter is not the capture of Moscow but rather the occupation of the Crimea, of the industrial and coal-mining area of the Donets basin, the cutting of the Russian supply routes from the Caucasian oilfields, and, in the north, the investment of Leningrad and the establishment of contact with the Finns." Defending the Ukraine was the Southwestern Army Group composed of five Armies (about three-quarters of a million strong). At the onset of the final German assault it was holding lines along the Dnepr River southeast of Kiev and the Dnepr and Desna Rivers northeast of Kiev. The Southwestern Army Group was commanded from the start of the war by Colonel General Kirponos (see n. 62, Chapter Two). The political commissars attached to the Army Group were M. A. Burmistenko, Second Secretary of the Communist Party of the Ukraine, and E. P. Rykov, a career political officer. From the end of July the Army Group chief of staff was Major General V. I. Tupikov, previously the Soviet military attaché in Berlin and chief of staff of the Khar'kov Military District. Only 40 years old at the time, Tupikov was a graduate of the Frunze Military Academy and a highly professional soldier. The future Marshal Bagramian, then a Major General, served as Army Group chief of operations and in that capacity was Tupikov's deputy. The fragment of Bagramian's memoirs included here relates to the final sixteen days of the Battle of Kiev (September 10–26, 1941).

47 The German plan of the operation consisted of an attempt to trap the troops of the Southwestern Army Group by a deep enveloping maneuver from the south and north simultaneously. From the south the tanks of Field Marshal Kleist and from the north the Tank Army of Colonel General Guderian, redirected from its Moscow axis of advance, broke through the Soviet flanks and pressed toward a meeting point in the city of Romny, about 140 miles east of Kiev. On September 10 Guderian took Romny, and Kleist completed his concentration on the Kremenchug bridgehead for the push which was to close the gigantic pocket.

48 The Briansk Army Group commanded by Lieutenant General Eremenko was the Southwestern Army Group's neighbor to the north. Formed on August 14, it aimed initially to check Guderian's advance toward Briansk and Moscow. When Guderian turned his tanks southward instead, Eremenko's main task was to prevent him from breaking through on the flank of the Southwestern Army Group. Eremenko in his memoirs describes his task as follows: "Acting on the Supreme Command order of August 30, we worked out a plan of operations for August 31 to September 15. The plan was aimed at annihilating the Guderian panzer force opposing the Briansk Army Group." (Marshal A. I. Eremenko, *V nachale voiny* [Moscow, 1964], p. 223.) Eremenko tries to present his singular failure to achieve this goal as a patent success. He writes: "Although we failed to reach the line designated in the order of the Supreme Command, the counteroffensive was a distinct success. Our Army Group moved forward an average of 10–12 km. and considerably more at some points. . . . The territorial gain made in the offensive was not very great, but the operational impact was." (*Ibid.*, p. 224.) This part of Marshal Eremenko's memoirs was criticized by his Soviet military reviewers with justifiable harshness.

49 In July 1941 the entire Russo-German front was divided into three sectors (*napravlenie*), each with a commander in chief (*glavkom*) and each encompassing several Army Groups. The Southwestern sector with Marshal S. M. Budennyi as its commander in chief included the Southwestern and Southern Army Groups and the Black Sea Fleet.

50   At another place in his memoirs Bagramian quotes an interesting conversation on August 25 between Stalin and Eremenko which shows that they both strongly believed that Guderian's forces could be destroyed by the Briansk Army Group. To Stalin's question: Can you promise to defeat Guderian in which case we will send you reinforcements, Eremenko replied: "I want to destroy Guderian and will smash this scoundrel without any doubt." (I. Kh. Bagramian, *Gorod-voin na Dnepre* [Moscow, 1965], p. 104.) Bagramian commented: "This was a rather bold statement."

51   A member of Budennyi's military council at that time was none other than Khrushchev, whose experience during the Kiev debacle became one of his major indictments against Stalin's war leadership.

52   While the Russian armies in the developing encirclement were very large in numbers, they had almost no armor and were critically short of fuel and shells. Their lack of mobility would have rendered extremely difficult a countermaneuver against the German tank pincers even had Moscow's orders not reduced them to stationary defenses around Kiev.

53   The following conversation between Guderian and his chief of operations, Lieutenant Colonel Bayerlein, on August 29, 1941, provides vivid confirmation of Bagramian's point:

"Next to Guderian sat Lieutenant Colonel Bayerlein, the situation map spread out on his knees. Thick red arrows and arcs on the map indicated the strong Russian forces in front of the German spearheads and along their flanks 'Eremenko is going all out to reduce our bridgehead,' Guderian was thinking aloud. 'If he succeeds in delaying us much longer, and if the Soviet High Command discovers what we are trying to do to Budennyi's Army Group, the whole splendid plan of our High Command could misfire.'

"Bayerlein confirmed the anxieties of his Commander. 'I was on the phone to Second Army yesterday. Freiherr von Weichs seems to be worried about it too. Lieutenant Colonel Feyerabend, their chief of operations, has had reports from long-range reconnaissance about the Russians beginning to withdraw from the Dnieper front below Kiev. At the same time, work has been observed in progress on positions in the Donets area.'

" 'Well, there you are.' Guderian was getting heated. 'Budennyi has learnt his lesson at Uman. He's slipping through the noose. Everything now depends on which of us is quicker.' " (Cited in Paul Carell, *Hitler Moves East 1941–1943* [New York: Bantam Books, 1966], p. 122.)

54   According to German records, the battle of Kiev yielded the Germans 665,000 prisoners, 3,718 guns, and 884 armored vehicles. Thus it was the largest encircling operation of World War II in size of territory within the pocket and in number of prisoners taken. The official Soviet war history disputes these figures but provides only fragmentary data. According to this data the Southwestern Army Group consisted of 677,085 men at the outset of the Kiev battle. Of these, 150,541 belonged to units which escaped encirclement and withdrew to new defensive positions. Taking into consideration the heavy casualties suffered by the encircled forces and the fact that a large number succeeded in breaking out of the pocket, the Soviet source states that at most "only" 175,000 were captured by the Germans (*Istoriia Velikoi Otechestvennoi voiny Sovetskogo Soiuza*, II [1961], 110–11.) While German figures may well have been inflated, particularly by the addition of captured Home Guard detachments and the civilian male population to the totals, the Soviet figure seems low. It excludes from its estimate, *inter alia*, the numerous units which reinforced the Southwestern Army Group after the battle of Kiev had started.

55   Until only ten years ago Soviet war histories never mentioned the fate of Kirponos, Burmistenko, and their comrades. Rumors circulating during and after the war alleged even that Burmistenko surrendered to the Germans and served their cause. After an account similar to that of Bagramian concerning the fallen leaders of the Southwestern Army Group had been published in the official Soviet war history in 1961, many conflicting reports on this event continued to appear in print. It was alleged by writers of memoirs who did not take part in Kirponos' attempt to lead a group of commanders out of encirclement that Kirponos committed suicide. Only in 1964 did a well documented report appear in the *Soviet Journal of Military History* on the deaths of Kirponos, Burmistenko, and Tupikov, a report based on eyewitness testimony and on an investigation conducted by a military commis-

sion. This report was the basis for Bagramian's account. ("Pravda o gibeli generala M. P. Kirponosa," *Voenno-istoricheskii zhurnal*, 1964, No. 9, pp. 61–69.)

56 Guderian's memoirs contain the following entry about the captured Major General Potapov:

"The Commander of the Fifth Army was among the prisoners captured. I had an interesting conversation with this officer, to whom I put a number of questions:

"1. When did you learn that my tanks had penetrated behind you? *Answer:* 'About the 8th of September.'

"2. Why did you not evacuate Kiev at once? *Answer:* 'We had received orders from the Army Group to evacuate the area and withdraw eastward and had already begun to do so, when we received contrary orders to turn about and to defend Kiev in all circumstances.'

"The carrying out of this second order resulted in the destruction of the Kiev Army Group. The enemy was never to make the same mistake again. Unfortunately, though, we were to suffer the direst calamities as a result of just such interference from higher levels." (H. Guderian, *op. cit.*, p. 225.)

57 For an analysis of the Soviet winter offensive 1941–42, see Marshal Zhukov's memoirs, pp. 331–35.

58 Not one of the variants of the German summer offensive prepared during the winter and spring of 1941–42 envisaged a direct attack on Moscow. The discussion centered mainly on the magnitude of the strike in the south and its direction along one (Stalingrad) or two (Stalingrad, Caucasus) axes. It is true that one of the aims of the strike in the Stalingrad direction as described in Hitler's Directive No. 41 (April 1942) was to cut the communications of Russian armies defending Moscow and eventually to turn north against the Soviet capital. This long-range aim was used during Stalin's lifetime to cover up the Soviet leader's erroneous evaluation of German intentions and to prove that the real aim of the German summer offensive was Moscow.

59 The sectors selected for the offensive operations were located along the entire length of the Eastern Front, from Leningrad—virtually the northernmost sector of the front—through Demiansk 170 miles to the south, Smolensk in front of Moscow in the center, Lgovsk-Kursk 270 miles and Khar'kov 400 miles south of Moscow, to the Crimea—the southernmost tip of the front. The dispersal of the Red

Army's strength in numerous offensive actions while faced with a new German assault demonstrated, aside from the error in predicting the main axis of the German summer offensive, a gross miscalculation of the true balance of forces. Moreover, adherence to the principle of carrying out offensive operations while at the same time trying to strengthen defensive positions led to the anomalous situation where the Army Groups involved could commit only a part of their forces to attack because they had to prepare for defense and only a part of their forces to defense because they had to attack.

60 About 90 miles apart, the Kursk and Orel sectors were located on the flanks of the Briansk Army Group—Kursk on the southern flank adjacent to the Southwestern Army Group, Orel on the northern flank adjacent to the Western Army Group that covered Moscow. The decision to concentrate the Army Group's forces in the Orel sector reflected therefore Stalin's belief that the main German thrust would be directed against Moscow.

61 The battle of Khar'kov in May 1942 was one of the worst disasters suffered by the Red Army. The Soviet High Command planned to recapture this largest industrial center of the Ukraine by simultaneous blows from the north and south of the city. The Germans for their part planned their own offensive from the Khar'kov sector to start on May 18. The Russians started their offensive first on May 12 but after an initial advance met with a powerful counteroffensive on their own southern flank. On orders from Moscow they continued their assault without sufficient reserves, and in the ensuing trap many units were wiped out and several Soviet generals killed. Moreover, a crucial Soviet front sector, the jumping-off point for the main German thrust south toward Stalingrad, was disastrously weakened.

62 The battle of Kursk in July 1943 constituted one of the Red Army's greatest victories of the war. The bulk of the German armored forces was decisively crushed. This battle represented the last German attempt to mount a major offensive on the Eastern Front and the first major Soviet victory which was not "snatched from the jaws of defeat" as were the battles of Moscow and Stalingrad.

63 The events described by General Shtemenko were taking place in the summer of 1944 when the Red Army was preparing an offensive to clear Germans from Soviet territory. The main thrust of the Soviet

summer 1944 offensive which started on June 23 was directed against the German Army Group Center in Belorussia. Carried out by 14 combined arms Armies, one tank, and four air Armies (over 2,500,000 men and more than 6,000 tanks and 7,000 aircraft), the offensive led to the collapse of the defensive lines held by Army Group Center (Field Marshal Busch) and destruction of 28 German divisions (out of 45 in the Army Group at the start of the operation) and the loss of 350,000 men. As a result of the offensive the Red Army rolled back the German front as far as the Vistula River and the East Prussian frontier and cut off German forces in the Baltic area. (For figures on Russian forces, see "Belorusskaia operatsiia v tsifrakh," *Voenno-istoricheskii zhurnal*, 1964, No. 6, pp. 74–86. For data on German forces, see H. A. Jacobsen and J. Rohwer, eds., *Decisive Battles of World War II: The German View* [New York: G. P. Putnam's Sons, 1965], pp. 355–82.)

64 The Soviet forces participating in the operation were organized into four Army Groups: (from south to north) the 1st Belorussian, commanded by Marshal K. K. Rokossovskii; the 2nd Belorussiar under General of the Army G. F. Zakharov (to which General Shtemenko was attached as Moscow's representative); the 3rd Belorussian under Colonel General Cherniakhovskii; and the 1st Baltic under General of the Army I. Kh. Bagramian. Of these the strongest in men and weapons was Rokossovskii's and the weakest, Zakharov's.

65 Cherniakhovskii, who was promoted during the Belorussian operation to the rank of General of the Army, was then at the age of 38 the youngest of all Soviet Army Group commanders. He entered the Red Army in 1924, was promoted to officer rank in 1928, and started the war as a commander of a tank division with the rank of colonel. Prior to the Belorussian operation he had commanded the 60th Army for about a year and a half and was appointed in April 1944 to the Army Group Command on the suggestion of Marshal Vasilevskii. One of the most promising senior Soviet officers who came to the fore in the second half of the war, he was killed in action in February 1945 during the assault on East Prussia.

66 The career of General of the Army I. E. Petrov was, as his biographer, the Soviet writer Konstantin Simonov, remarks, "far from smooth and at times even strangely thorny for reasons which are still not entirely clear." (K. Simonov, "Shtrikhi portreta," *Voenno-istoricheskii zhurnal*, 1966, No. 6, pp. 47–48.) A divisional commander with the rank of Major General at the beginning of the war, he assumed command of the Army defending the Black Sea port of Odessa in October 1941. After Odessa's fall, he was in charge of all ground forces which for nine months defended the principal base of the Black Sea Fleet, Sevastopol'. After its fall, throughout 1943 he commanded an Army and later an Army Group engaged in a defense and later counteroffensive on the approaches to the Caucasus. At the beginning of 1944 he was removed from his command following an unsuccessful landing operation in the Crimea and demoted from General of the Army to Colonel General. But two months later he was appointed to an even higher position than that held previously—Commander of the 2nd Belorussian Army Group. As Shtemenko reports, after only a month and a half, on the eve of the summer offensive, he was again removed from his position but two months later was appointed Commander of the 4th Ukrainian Army Group and in October of that year was reinstated in the rank of General of the Army. The promotion-demotion seesaw did not end there. In March 1945 he was suddenly and for no apparent reason relieved of his command again but a few days later was appointed chief of staff of Marshal Konev's 1st Ukrainian Army Group which in number of troops and weapons was at least four to five times larger than Petrov's former command. Simonov comments: "Recalling this seesaw of Petrov's appointments and dismissals, one comes to think that the iron will [of Stalin] so well known to all of us was not always accompanied by iron logic." (*Ibid.*, p. 49.) The clue to Petrov's dismissal in 1945 probably lies in the fact that at approximately the same time (spring 1945) the man who, according to Shtemenko, was responsible for Petrov's misfortune in 1944, L. Z. Mekhlis, was again appointed chief political commissar to Petrov's Army Group. After the war from 1945 to 1952 Petrov commanded the Turkestan Military District (in Soviet Central Asia) and from 1952 until his death in 1958 worked in the Ministry of Defense in Moscow.

67 General Zakharov started the war as chief of staff of the Ural Military District and was soon sent to the front as chief of staff of the 22nd Army, which

was engaged in heavy fighting near Smolensk in central Russia. He was promoted to chief of staff of the Briansk Army Group (commanded by Marshal Eremenko) and then until summer 1943 occupied the posts of chief of staff or deputy commander in a number of Army Groups (among others, at the battle of Stalingrad). From summer 1943 until his arrival in Belorussia to replace Petrov he commanded the 51st and then the 2nd Guards Armies. His promotion to Army Group command in summer 1944 was probably the result of his success in leading the 2nd Guards Army's assault on the strong German defense line in the Crimean peninsula in April–May 1944.

General Zakharov was one of the few military commanders of World War II about whom almost every Soviet memoirist and military writer has something derogatory to say without any known political reason. Only strong dislike by colleagues who now lead the Soviet armed forces can explain the following passage in a biographical essay published in an official journal of the Soviet Ministry of Defense to commemorate his 70th birthday: "Together with favorable evaluations, the service characteristics of Zakharov [for the prewar period] also stressed quite serious shortcomings—excessive self-confidence, short temper, harshness, and sometimes even rudeness toward subordinates. Unfortunately, those traits proved to be firmly established in his subsequent service as well." (*Voenno-istoricheskii zhurnal*, 1967, No. 4, p. 126.)

68 The offensive operation of Zakharov's Army Group was very successful, and by the end of July he was promoted to the rank of General of the Army. In November 1944 he was removed from the Army Group, however, and assigned to a much lower position—commander of the 4th Guards Army fighting in Hungary. During the battle for Budapest Zakharov committed serious errors in the organization and leadership of his troops which permitted the Germans to break out of Soviet encirclement. Removed from his command, Zakharov served during the closing months of the war as one of the deputies of the 4th Ukrainian Army Group commander. After the war he commanded small military districts (South Ural, East Siberia) and then served as Deputy Chief of the Main Directorate of Combat Training in the Soviet Ministry of Defense. He died in 1957 at the age of 60.

69 Marshal Voronov was attached at the time to the Western Army Group in the capacity of Supreme Headquarters representative. The Army Group was developing the Soviet success in the Kursk battle by conducting an offensive operation in the direction of Smolensk. The Kalinin Army Group, its neighbor to the north, was preparing a supporting thrust against the flank of German troops defending Smolensk.

70 In another place Marshal Voronov recounts a number of similar episodes when Stalin reacted sharply to his representatives' requests for changes in the established operational timetable (and so also does Marshal Vasilevskii in his reminiscences of the Stalingrad battle).

71 Batov (then a Lieutenant General) was commanding the 65th Army in Marshal Rokossovskii's 1st Belorussian Army Group. The events described took place during the preparation for the Red Army's Belorussian offensive in June 1944 (see n. 63 and n. 64 above).

72 Advised about the forthcoming offensive by Rokossovskii, Batov, whose Army's sector of deployment included the Pripet Marshes, proposed that his main strike be staged from the marshy areas where the Germans would least expect it. After Zhukov's inspection his proposal was accepted and subsequently carried out successfully.

73 The circumstances of the encirclement of the German 4th Army virtually paralleled those in which the Red Armies suffered a similar fate in the first year of war (e.g., Kiev). Forbidden to make a timely retreat, too weak to hold extended defense lines, without reserves to counteract deep flanking thrusts by Soviet armor, it suffered prohibitive losses in manpower and matériel.

74 Voronezh, a city at the strategic midpoint between Moscow and Stalingrad, was a key initial objective of the German summer 1942 offensive. Although the Germans succeeded at first in breaking the Soviet defense lines in the Voronezh sector and crossing the river Don both south and north of the city, they were prevented by stiffened Red Army resistance and by the concentration of their own forces on the Stalingrad axis of advance from taking the entire city and securing the northern flank of von Paulus' Army.

75 See n. 61 above.

76 According to German claims, 239,000 prisoners were taken and 1,250 tanks and 2,026 guns destroyed or captured in the Khar'kov battle.

77 Kazakov had served previously under

Marshal Eremenko and expresses an unflattering opinion of Eremenko's style of work, relations with his subordinates, and professional abilities. At the same time he praises Eremenko's personal courage in the field. One gains the impression from numerous memoirs that Rokossovskii was one of the most respected and liked senior officers in the Red Army. The way in which dozens of memoirists recall with sympathy their service or their encounters with Rokossovskii has a warmth that seldom appears in descriptions of other military leaders. What apparently impressed them was first and foremost Rokossovskii's "kul'turnost' "—culture, good manners, civility—a relatively rare commodity among senior officers during the war.

78 At the time of the events described, L. M. Sandalov (then a Lieutenant General) served as chief of staff of the Briansk Army Group (composed of the 50th, 11th, 63rd, and 11th Guards Armies, and the 15th Air Army) which was advancing on a 90-mile front south of Smolensk. The commander of the Briansk Army Group was General of the Army M. M. Popov (formerly commander of the 5th Assault Army in the battle of Stalingrad). Its chief political commissar was Lieutenant General L. Z. Mekhlis.

79 The Briansk Army Group was disbanded on October 10, 1943 and the command of most of its troops was transferred to its southern neighbor, the Central Army Group, which ten days later was itself dissected into the newly formed Belorussian and 1st Ukrainian Army Groups. The region of Velikie Luki, to which the former Briansk Army Group headquarters with the remaining troops was transferred, is situated about 350 miles to the north on the approaches to the Baltic republics of Latvia and Estonia.

80 Operations against the German Army Group North and Operational Group Narva in the Baltic provinces were conducted by five Army Groups: (from north to south) Leningrad, Volkhov, 3rd, 2nd, and 1st Baltic. In the winter offensive of 1943–44 the Red Army succeeded in reaching only the frontiers of the Baltic regions (and breaking the blockade of Leningrad). Only in the summer–fall offensive of 1944 did the Red Army recapture Lithuania and Estonia and most of Latvia.

81 It would appear that the transfer of the Army Group Commander, M. M. Popov, reflected dissatisfaction with his performance. Popov was appointed chief

of staff of the Leningrad Army Group and reduced in rank from General of the Army to Colonel General. (For Popov it was already a second demotion—in 1941 he had occupied the post of Commander of the Leningrad Army Group and was subsequently demoted to Army commander). On the other hand, the member of the military council, Lieutenant General N. A. Bulganin (the future Soviet Prime Minister), was transferred to the same position in Rokossovskii's 1st Belorussian Army Group, which was assigned a key role in the forthcoming Soviet summer offensive.

82 On August 28, 1941 a group of representatives of Supreme Headquarters, including Molotov, Malenkov, and—from the military—the Chief of Soviet Artillery Voronov, arrived at Leningrad to evaluate for Stalin the rapidly deteriorating situation in this front sector. By September 8 the German advance had effectively isolated Leningrad from the rest of the country, the start of a 900-day siege. The general German assault on the city was launched on September 9. By September 12, the day of Kuznetsov's departure for Moscow, German troops to the southeast and south of Leningrad had reached points 8–12 miles from the city limits.

83 The name of the city before the 1917 revolution was St. Petersburg, after Peter the Great who founded it in 1703. During World War I it was renamed Petrograd and after the death of Lenin in 1924 was changed to Leningrad. Both before and after the revolution it was familiarly called "Peter."

84 At the start of the Leningrad blockade the Baltic Fleet was composed of more than 150 surface warships, including two battleships (*October Revolution* and *Marat*) and three cruisers (*Kirov, Maksim Gor'kii,* and *Petropavlovsk*). Its main role during the 900-day blockade was to provide artillery support for defending ground forces.

85 Throughout the blockade the leaders of the Leningrad Party organization (Zhdanov, First Secretary of the Leningrad municipal and provincial Party committees; Kuznetsov, Secretary of the municipal Party committee; Popkov, head of the Leningrad soviet) served as members of the military council of the defending Army Group. Army Group headquarters was located in the famous Smolnyi Institute from which Bolshevik leaders in 1917 directed the revolutionary coup that brought them to power. (Smolnyi

had been established as a school for well-born young ladies in the eighteenth century.)

86 Leningrad is situated on a narrow (30-mile-wide) strip of land between the Gulf of Finland in the west and Lake Ladoga in the east. Its land communications with the rest of the country were entirely cut off when the Germans reached a line stretching in a 40–50 mile half circle from the southwest to the east of the city with its terminal points in Strel'na on the Finnish Gulf and Shlissel'burg on Lake Ladoga. The city was blockaded on the north by Finnish troops. (About 40 miles separated the Finnish half circle of the blockade from the German.) From then on Leningrad's only link with the rest of the country remained through Lake Ladoga by ship or in winter by trucks across the ice. (The shortest ice route over the lake was about 35 miles long.) The blockade of Leningrad, partly broken in the winter of 1943, was finally lifted only in the winter of 1944.

87 It is sometimes argued that the survival of the city in the September assault was due primarily to the fact that Hitler did not actually intend to take the city but rather to starve it into submission. It is certainly true that at the beginning of September, Hitler intended, as his Directive No. 35 of September 6 indicates, to reduce the Leningrad sector to a subsidiary status, entrust the siege to limited forces of 6–7 divisions, and transfer the main armor and air power of Von Leeb's Army Group North to the German concentration in front of Moscow and in the south. As Alan Clark convincingly shows in his study of the Nazi-Soviet war, von Leeb hoped nevertheless to capture the city in the beginning of September. The attacks launched by his troops in the September 12–17 period certainly represented an attempt to take the city by storm, while the subsequent tightening of the blockade was from von Leeb's point of view a solution forced only by the staunch defense and by his inability to delay further the transfer of his armor to Army Group Center. (See Alan Clark, *Barbarossa, the Russian-German Conflict 1941–45* [New York: William Morrow and Co., 1965], pp. 119–28.)

88 Kirov plant—one of the largest and oldest Soviet defense plants, a producer mainly of tanks, located in the southern part of the city. Prior to the Revolution it was known as the Putilov Plant and was one of the key strongpoints of the Bolshevik underground organization.

89 General Fediuninskii remained in command of the 42nd Army until October 10 when he assumed temporary command of the entire Leningrad Army Group in place of Zhukov, who was recalled by Stalin in order to organize the defense of Moscow. At the end of October Fediuninskii was transferred to the adjacent Volkhov Army Group where he assumed command of the 54th Army.

90 Until August 23, 1941 Soviet troops in the northern theater which stretched from Murmansk to about 220 miles south of Leningrad were organized into two Army Groups (Northern and Northwestern) and together with the Baltic and Northern Fleets were subordinated to the Northwestern Strategic Sector command headed by Marshal Voroshilov. On that day the Northwestern Sector command was dissolved and the Army Groups reorganized (the Northern Army Group into the Karelian and Leningrad Army Groups with the latter assuming operational command of the Baltic Fleet; the Northwestern Army Group later divided into Northwestern and Volkhov Army Groups). Supreme Headquarters in Moscow assumed direct leadership of the Army Groups in the north. On August 28 Marshal Voroshilov took over command of the Leningrad Army Group until his replacement by Zhukov two weeks later.

91 The author, it seems, unfairly minimizes Zhukov's role in stabilizing Leningrad's resistance in the crucial September days. While he is correct in his assertion that the basic operational decisions made during Zhukov's first days of command did not differ much from those of his predecessors, his own account clearly shows that Zhukov supplied the defense with sorely needed qualities of decisiveness, will power, cool-headedness, and professionalism, even though they were accompanied by pronounced harshness in the treatment of subordinates. In the pages of his memoirs which were omitted here, Bychevskii describes Voroshilov's style of command and displays considerable sympathy for the Marshal as a person and respect for his courage while at the same time implying that Voroshilov was unfit for a field command position of such key importance. For example, Bychevskii's account of Voroshilov personally leading a Soviet marine brigade in counterattack on September 9 demonstrates either the limitations of his command or perhaps confirms the story reported by Alexander Werth: "The dramatic story I heard from several peo-

ple in Leningrad . . . was that about September 10, when there was practically complete chaos at the front, Voroshilov, believing that everything was lost, went into the front line, in the hope of getting killed by the Germans." (Alexander Werth, *Russia at War, 1941-1945* [New York: Avon Books, 1964], pp. 296-97.)

92 Belt *(Okruzhnaia)* Railway—a railway running on the southern and western outskirts of Leningrad. In the beginning of September it was transformed into a secondary antitank fortified defense line.

93 On June 27, 1941 the Leningrad Party and military authorities adopted a resolution to create from the civilian population auxiliary military units of home guards. Each of the 15 city precincts was expected to form one division. During the siege the Leningrad Home Guards Army consisted of 159,000 people of whom about 20,000 were Party members and 18,000 were members of the Young Communist League. Poorly armed, untrained, and lacking professional leadership, they were mainly used in emergency situations to fill gaps in the defense line. (*900 geroicheskikh dnei* [Moscow, 1966], pp. 122, 406.)

94 Marshal Voronov was at that time the Supreme Headquarters representative with the Western Army Group which was deployed in the central sector of the front about 160-200 miles west and southwest of Moscow. The town Iukhnov to which he, the Western Army Group commander, Colonel General V. D. Sokolovskii, and an officer on Voronov's staff, General Kamera, were summoned was located about 120 miles southwest of Moscow and over 70 miles from the front line.

95 Khrushchev in his Secret Speech to the Twentieth Party Congress in 1956 had the following to say about Stalin's visit to the "front":

"Stalin was very far from an understanding of the real situation which was developing at the front. This was natural because, during the whole Patriotic War, he never visited any section of the front or any liberated city except for one short ride on the Mozhaisk highway during a stabilized situation at the front. To this incident were dedicated many literary works full of fantasies of all sorts and so many paintings." (N. S. Khrushchev, "Special Report to the 20th Congress of the Communist Party of the Soviet Union," *New Leader Supplement*, 1962, p. S40.)

The most famous painting of Stalin

at the front, which was reproduced innumerable times on posters, postcards, in books, etc., had the title "Stalin at the front near Moscow—1941" and showed him standing at the edge of a forest in a heavy fur coat with binoculars trained on Soviet troops who were attacking German positions.

96 The events described took place at the height of the German summer 1942 offensive in the south of Russia. The offensive developed in two directions—against Stalingrad and against the Caucasus—with the aim of capturing Soviet oil fields. The far approaches to the Caucasus where the author served were covered by two Soviet Army Groups, the Southern (G.O.C. Marshal Malinovskii) and North Caucasian (G.O.C. Marshal Budennyi). (The immediate approaches to the Caucasus were covered by the Transcaucasian Army Group which constituted the secondary defense line.) By the end of July, after telling defeats, the two Army Groups were reorganized into one command (the North Caucasian Army Group) with Marshal Budennyi as G.O.C. and the future Chief of the General Staff, Lieutenant General A. I. Antonov, as chief of staff. The author, until then Chief of the Transportation and Highway Service of the Southern Army Groups, was appointed to the same position in the new North Caucasian Army Group. Its headquarters was located in Georgievskoe, close to the Black Sea about 100 miles behind the front lines.

97 The military council of the North Caucasus Army Group had two political members—the senior one, L. M. Kaganovich, a member of the Party's Politburo, and the junior, L. P. Korniets. The latter occupied various Party and governmental positions in the Ukraine both before and after the war of which the highest was First Deputy Prime Minister of the Ukraine.

98 In another place Strakhov described the state of his equipment as follows: "There were hardly any local repair installations in the Caucasus. We had only military repair facilities—low grade mobile repair detachments and battalion repair shops with primitive equipment. But it was the lack of tire rubber that gave us the greatest trouble. No supplies had come in since the beginning of the war. The use of chains on bad roads, mountain road driving, the heat and long trips took a heavy toll of tire coverings and inner tubes. On every trip, motorized companies had to carry a vulcanizing ap-

paratus therefore in order to make the needed repairs on the way; sometimes instead of inner tubes they had to stuff a tire cover with old rags. It was difficult with such 'rubber' to complete assignments on schedule."

99 On September 1, 1942, when the German advance brought them to the close approaches of the Caucasus range and of the borders of the Soviet republics of Georgia and Azerbaidzhan, the North Caucasian Army Group was dissolved (and Marshal Budennyi recalled to Moscow). Its troops were organized into a Black Sea Operational Group subordinated to the Transcaucasian Army Group command, which assumed responsibility for defense of the entire Caucasus theater of operations. The Black Sea Operational Group composed of three Armies was responsible for the left (west) flank of the Transcaucasian Army Group defenses along a 130-mile strip of the Black Sea.

Colonel General Cherevichenko, who was appointed to command the Black Sea Group, served directly before the war as commander of the Odessa Military District and during the war commanded the Southern (fall 1941) and Briansk (winter 1941–42) Army Groups. From July to September 1942 he was Budennyi's deputy in the North Caucasian Army Group.

100 Kaganovich's first name was Lazar, a typical Jewish name in Russia.

101 In mid-October 1942 the German assault against the center of the line held by the Black Sea Operational Group succeeded in breaking Soviet defenses in front of the important Black Sea port of Tuapse and placing the main forces of the Group in danger of encirclement. By October 20 Kaganovich was recalled to Moscow, and General Cherevichenko was removed from command, never again to lead large field units. Cherevichenko's successor, General Petrov (see n. 66 above), reinforced with reserve units, succeeded in preventing the capture of Tuapse and by a series of counterassaults stabilized Soviet positions in this sector.

102 On July 13, 1944, three weeks after the start of the Soviet offensive against the German Army Group Center in Belorussia, Soviet troops in the Ukraine launched an offensive against the German Army Group Northern Ukraine. The offensive, conducted by the 1st Ukrainian Army Group led by Marshal Konev, managed in the first two weeks to capture the major center of the western Ukraine, L'vov, and to advance westward beyond

the frontiers of Poland. The main German forces were retreating to the south, however, toward the Carpathian Mountains which separate the Soviet Union from Czechoslovakia and were able to slow down the Soviet advance in this direction significantly.

103 In the beginning of August 1944 Supreme Headquarters decided to direct the offensive effort of Marshal Konev's 1st Ukrainian Army Group solely in the western direction against German troops in Poland and to create a separate command to pursue the advance against German troops retreating south into the Carpathians and eventually into Czechoslovakia and Hungary. For this purpose the 4th Ukrainian Army Group, composed of the troops of the left wing of the 1st Ukrainian Army Group and large units from the Supreme Headquarters reserve, was created on August 5, 1944. It was commanded by Colonel General I. E. Petrov with Colonel General L. Z. Mekhlis as political commissar (see n. 66 above). One of the units transferred from the 1st Ukrainian to the new Army Group was the 1st Guards Army which included the 11th Rifle Corps commanded by the author of these memoirs. The commander of the 1st Guards Army, Colonel General A. A. Grechko, is presently the Soviet Minister of Defense.

104 General Zamertsev refers here to the December 1941–May 1942 Soviet campaign to recapture the Crimea. Soviet troops managed in the winter of 1941 to recapture in a landing operation the Kerch Peninsula at the eastern extremity of the Crimea and thus to endanger the entire German Crimean group (Field Marshal von Manstein's 11th Army) and to reduce its pressure on the besieged naval base of Sevastopol'. Their initial success was not followed up, however, and in May 1942 von Manstein's offensive led to a disastrous defeat in which few Soviet troops were able to evacuate to the Caucasus (five miles across the Kerch Straits), and large quantities of military equipment were captured by the Germans.

Blame for the operation's failure was assigned by the Soviet Supreme Command to the leadership of the Crimean Army Group which conducted the Kerch operation. Its commander, his deputies, his commissar, and several unit commanders were dismissed and demoted in rank. Mekhlis, at that time Deputy People's Commissar of Defense and Chief Political Commissar of the Red Army, was attached during the operation to the

Crimean Army Group as Supreme Headquarters representative. He too was
removed from his high posts and demoted
to the rank of corps commissar.

105 General Zamertsev was not returned
to his corps command after all. In February 1945, after Soviet troops captured
Budapest, he was appointed its military
commandant and remained in this position until 1947.

106 The original geographic base of Beria's
power was the Soviet Caucasian republics, primarily Georgia. Prior to his appointment in January 1939 to the all-
powerful position of secret police chief
in the central government, Beria occupied
the post of First Secretary of the Transcaucasian branch of the Communist Party
and controlled through his protégés all
key positions in the local government.
When he went to Moscow, he took some
of his Georgian assistants with him and
kept tight rein on the Caucasus through
associates whom he left behind. Of those
mentioned by General Tiulenev, Kabulov
and Mamulov were at that time his deputies in the central police establishment
in Moscow; the remaining two directed
police operations in the Caucasus. All
were sentenced to death together with
Beria after Stalin's death.

107 Beria's protégés from the NKVD were
sometimes to be found also in command
positions in the regular army. For example, during the defense of the Caucasus the Northern Operational Group
(three Armies) of the Transcaucasian Army
Group was under the command of Lieutenant General I. I. Maslennikov, who
both before and after the war served as
Beria's deputy in charge of frontier troops.

108 Needless to say, until 1953 Beria's
contribution to the successful defense of the
Caucasus received the highest praise in
Soviet sources. Aside from the "political
general" Bulganin, who for a number of
years after the war occupied the position
of Soviet Minister of Defense, Beria was
the only non-military man to achieve at
the end of the war the highest military
rank, Marshal of the Soviet Union.

109 With the outbreak of the war the
author of the memoirs, who headed the
Siberian Military District, was ordered
to form the 24th Reserve Army from
troops stationed in his district and to
occupy a secondary fortified defense line
about 200 miles in front of Moscow. At
the time of the described episode the
rapidly advancing German troops were
still 40–80 miles from the 24th Army's
perimeter of defense.

110 The incident described took place at
the height of the Stalingrad battle on
September 14, 1942. On that day the
Germans broke through Soviet defenses
in one sector of the city, captured the
railroad station, and reached the banks
of the Volga. Soviet troops fighting in the
city on the right (west) bank of the Volga
were thereby cut off from remaining
Soviet forces to the north and the south.
Their only remaining communication
line was across the river itself. Constant
air attacks disrupted the Volga crossings.
Supply and reserve divisions on the left
bank were unable to reach the armies
defending Stalingrad.

The author of the memoirs, twice Hero
of the Soviet Union with 43 destroyed
enemy planes to his credit, commanded
a fighter regiment in the 8th Air Army
attached to the Stalingrad Army Group
during the Stalingrad battle (with the
rank of captain). On September 14 he
and other air unit commanders of the
Stalingrad sector received an order to
report to Army Group headquarters.
The pilots were expecting to be decorated
by the Army Group leadership.

111 In addition to Stalin's son, sons of
two Politburo members participated in
the Stalingrad battle as fighter pilots—
Vladimir Mikoyan and Leonid Khrushchev. According to Luganskii, who
knew them personally, both died in air
combat during the battle. With regard
to Vasilii Stalin, it should be noted that
Svetlana Stalin reports in her memoirs
that her brother often visited Moscow
during the Stalingrad battle and shortly
after the event described in this excerpt
became involved in making a movie about
the air force. (*Life*, September 22, 1967,
p. 96.)

112 At the start of the war Colonel Starinov was a mine specialist in the Main
Military-Engineering Directorate of the
Red Army in Moscow. At the end of
September 1941 he was sent to help
organize the defense of Khar'kov, the
largest industrial center of the Ukraine.
When it became clear that the city would
be captured, Starinov was ordered to
destroy all objectives of economic and
military importance and to place delayed-
action and remote-control mines in a few
selected buildings which were likely to
be occupied by various German headquarters. (Khar'kov fell on October 24,
1941 and on November 14 Starinov
detonated several mines in the city by
remote radio signal. One of the mines
exploded in the quarters of the German

military commandant of Khar'kov, Lieutenant General von Braun, killing him and some other senior officers.)

During his Khar'kov assignment Starinov was in close contact with Nikita Sergeevich Khrushchev, who was then the chief political commissar with the Southwestern Army Group defending the city. After Starinov complained that the government was not paying due attention to the production of mines, Khrushchev gave him a personal letter to officials in the Party's Central Committee asking them to help the colonel. Starinov returned to Moscow in the second half of November.

113 It appears to have been normal procedure throughout the war for high-ranking field commanders to surrender their weapons before seeing Stalin. The Chief Marshal of Armored Troops, M. E. Katukov, records in his memoirs an experience similar to that of Starinov:

"In the first half of September 1942 I received an order to appear before Stalin in the Kremlin.

"The first question I heard at the entrance control point of the Kremlin was: 'Are you carrying firearms?'

" 'Well,' I thought, 'this is nice: it's wartime, and I don't have a pistol. It must be a violation.'

"But everything was in order: it was forbidden to go to Stalin carrying firearms."

(M. E. Katukov, "Podniavshii mech ot mecha i pogibnet," *Oktiabr'*, 1965, No. 5, p. 199.)

114 Starinov's superior at that time, Major General L. Z. Kotliar, was Chief of the Red Army's Main Military-Engineering Directorate.

115 The Soviet artillery, unlike that of the Western Allies, included during the Second World War major single-arm formations. Organized in divisions (20 to 24 battalions) and corps (72 to 96 battalions), it was the most significant supporting arm of the Red Army both in defense and offense. The bulk of heavy artillery was assembled in units directly subordinate to Supreme Headquarters. At the time described by Voronov (summer 1944) new large artillery reserve units were being rapidly formed on an unprecedented scale. They were equipped with the new 100 mm. antitank guns, 152 mm. howitzers, and 160 mm. mortars. These units were intended for use as the principal breakthrough force in the Red Army's offensive against the deep field fortifications on which the German defense was based.

116 The episode described in this part of Voronov's memoirs took place in August 1941. At that time almost every piece of equipment and every round of ammunition at Moscow's disposal could be issued to field units only on Stalin's signature. It seems that this procedure persisted even after the crucial shortages of 1941 and 1942 were overcome (although with less attention to minute details).

117 At the May 22-23, 1944 meeting at Supreme Headquarters in Moscow the final plan of the major Soviet offensive operation of 1944—the combined assault of four Army Groups against the German Army Group Center in Belorussia—was adopted. For the overall aim and result of the operation see n. 63 and n. 64 above.

118 This incident has been described in several Soviet sources, each conforming in the main to the fragment presented here. Marshal Rokossovskii himself wrote twice about it—once in his reminiscences about the Belorussian operation which were included in the same anthology from which the account of Nepomniashchii was taken (K. K. Rokossovskii, "Ot Gomelia do Bresta," *Polki idut na zapad* [Moscow, 1964], pp. 21–47) and once in an extensive interview granted to the editors of the Soviet *Journal of Military History* on the twentieth anniversary of the operation (K. K. Rokossovskii, "Dva glavnykh udara," *Voenno-istoricheskii zhurnal*, 1964, No. 6, pp. 13–18). The following excerpt is from the second source with an insert in brackets from the first source:

"At the beginning of May 1944, we began to work out a plan of operations the aim of which was to free the southern part of Belorussia and, passing beyond her borders, to free the eastern districts of Poland. Our plan called for the Armies of the right wing to begin the attack on the Bobruisk front, and we intended to strike from the Kovel sector only when they had reached the line of Svisloch-Pruzhany.

"Painstaking study of the terrain and the state of the enemy's defense convinced us that on the Bobruisk line we must strike two main blows from different sectors (one against Bobruisk and Osipovichi from the Rogachev sector, the other in the general direction of Slutsk from the lower Berezina-Ozarichi sector). And both strikes should be approximately equal in strength. This contradicted our established theoretical view that an Army

Group should attack by delivering one major strike for which our main forces and equipment should be concentrated. In deciding to deliver two strikes, we allowed a certain dispersion of our forces, but no other solution promised success in view of the forest and swamp terrain and the enemy's troop distribution.

["Such a decision made possible the application, in the first attack, of maximum force in two different directions and prevented the enemy from moving troops from one sector to another. More than that: A successful attack even in one direction would immediately help the attack in the other, in case the enemy's defense had not been immediately broken over there.

["This decision violated the established rule that in the beginning of an offensive, the Army or Army Group should strike one major blow, in which the greater part of its forces and equipment would be concentrated, while auxiliary blows would be organized in other sectors, with the primary task of paralyzing the enemy. In this way, a dispersion of forces was avoided. But in this particular case, we resorted to a dispersion of forces because the forest and swamp terrain did not allow us to put the whole enormous force which was at the Army Group's disposal into a blow by one sector. A considerable number of troops would have been idle part of the time."]

"The plan of the Belorussian operation was approved at Supreme Headquarters on May 22–23. Our arguments for starting the attack first with the troops of the Army Group's right wing, followed somewhat later by the rest, were approved. We were also advised to keep in mind the necessity for close cooperation with the 1st Ukrainian Army Group. But when the operation in the Bobruisk sector came up for discussion, a heated argument developed.

"Our decision to deliver two equal blows from the Army Group's right wing was subjected to strong criticism. Stalin and certain members of Supreme Headquarters did not agree. They insisted upon striking a single main blow from the Dnepr bridgehead in the 3rd Army sector. My arguments that few troops could be used there, that the terrain was difficult, and that a strong enemy grouping was waiting to the north were ignored. Stalin's concep-

tion of 'the main blow' was evidently the cause of his stubborn insistence on dealing a single powerful strike. But in the given instance, the unique conditions demanded clearly a departure from the stereotype. It was precisely the infliction of two strikes, more than anything else, which led to the encirclement and defeat of the enemy's large Bobruisk grouping and speeded up our breakthrough in depth, while the single blow from the district north of Rogachev only helped to push the enemy out.

"Stalin twice invited me to go to the next room in order to think over Supreme Headquarters' proposal and reconcile my own thinking to accord with it. During my second period of reflection, Molotov and Malenkov came into the room. They disapproved of my arguing with the Supreme Commander in Chief himself and insisted that I accept the proposals of Supreme Headquarters. I replied that I was sure I was right and that *if Supreme Headquarters ordered a single blow, I would ask to be relieved of the Army Group command.* When I returned again to the meeting, I tried once more to present our arguments for two main blows as persuasively as possible. Only after my third report did Stalin at last approve our plan of attack." [Italics added, Ed.]

Both the Nepomniashchii fragment and Rokossovskii's articles were published before Khrushchev's ouster. In 1966, when Khrushchev's successors were clearly playing down the criticism of Stalin, the incident was retold in a biographical essay on the occasion of Rokossovskii's seventieth birthday by his comrade-in-arms, General of the Army P. I. Batov, and P. I. Troianovskii, a well-known war correspondent of the main military daily *Red Star.* It is noteworthy that their account is in the main similar to those of the Khrushchev period. It adds one interesting detail, however—that the first wait of Rokossovskii in the room adjoining Stalin's office lasted two hours—and presents Stalin's final reaction to the Marshal's obstinacy in somewhat more benevolent terms. After the Marshal argued the merits of his operation plan for the third time, Stalin's reaction was said by Rokossovskii's biographers to be as follows:

"There was a pause. Stalin smoked his pipe in silence. Then he approached Rokossovskii, put a hand on his shoulder, and said:

" 'You know, Rokossovskii is right. And generally I like a commander who sticks to his guns. I confirm your decision, Comrade Rokossovskii.' "

(P. I. Batov and P. I. Troianovskii, "Chelovek, bol'shevik, polkovodets," *Voenno-istoricheskii zhurnal*, 1966, No. 12, p. 41.)

CHAPTER FIVE

1 Shtemenko's presentation here has very little relation to the real state of affairs. While it is true that the Red Army's advance in summer 1944 led to an extension of Soviet lines of communication and to an inevitable weakening of combat units after the prolonged offensive operation, the German losses in Poland were enormous, their defensive position weak, and their reserves almost completely dissipated. Far from being true that the German High Command shifted part of its forces from the western to the eastern theater of operations, as Shtemenko asserts, the reverse was the case. After the successful Anglo-American landing in Normandy and later during German preparation for their last major gamble, the Ardennes offensive, the German High Command mobilized every available reserve for the western theater and even transferred to the west several major units from the Nazi-Soviet front. One may note, e.g., that only one-third of the total German production of new tanks and assault guns in November–December 1944 was assigned to the Eastern Front. The total number of German divisions in Poland was lower by one-fifth than that available at the start of the Soviet summer offensive. The Soviet decision to stabilize the central sector of the Nazi-Soviet front from August 1944 until January 1945 and to shift the center of gravity to the Balkans was a political one, as discussed in the introduction to this chapter.

2 General Guderian has the following to say about Germany's Hungarian allies at this stage of the war: "Apart from our own troubles we were also most anxious about the fighting ability and the loyalty of our Hungarian Allies. . . . The Head of the Hungarian State [Horthy] was hoping for a rapprochement with the Anglo-Saxon powers. . . . A number of senior Hungarian officers were deserting to the common enemy, among them . . . the Chief of the Hungarian General Staff Voros, who had recently visited me in East Prussia, had assured me of his loyalty to the alliance, and had accepted a motor-car as a present from me. In this car, my own Mercedes, he drove off a few days later to the Russians. No reli-

ance could be placed on the Hungarians any more. Hitler therefore overthrew Horthy's government and put Szalasi in his place; this latter was a Hungarian Fascist of little ability and less tact. . . . Conditions in Hungary were in no wise improved as a result." (General Heinz Guderian, *Panzer Leader* [New York: E. P. Dutton and Co., Inc., 1952], pp. 378–79.) Nevertheless, mainly because of the importance Hitler attached to the Hungarian theater (Hungarian oil remained after Rumania's loss the major source of fuel for German aircraft and tanks) and his subsequent transfer of large mobile reserves from other sectors of the Nazi-Soviet front to Hungary, Soviet advances in this theater were very costly and slow. Even though the newly formed Hungarian government on Soviet-occupied territories signed an armistice on January 20, 1945 with Russia and the Western Allies, 11 Hungarian divisions and brigades (over 200,000 strong) fought on the German side as late as March 1945.

3 The Soviet military assigns to Stalin much of the blame for Soviet failure to capture Budapest at an earlier date. In an anthology devoted to the final Soviet operations in the Balkans and southeast Europe and edited by the then Soviet Minister of Defense, Marshal Malinovskii, one finds the text of a telephone conversation between Stalin and the commander of the 2nd Ukrainian Army Group, Malinovskii, which sheds interesting light on the subject:

"This conversation took place by telephone on the eve of the 46th Army's assault on Budapest, which began October 29 [1944].

"*Stalin:* It is imperative that you capture the Hungarian capital [Budapest] as soon as possible, literally within the next few days. It must be done at any cost. Can you do this?

"*C.O. of the 2nd Ukrainian Army Group* [Malinovskii]: This mission can be carried out five days from now, after the 4th Mechanized Guards Corps links up with the 46th Army. We expect its arrival by November 1. Then the 46th Army, reinforced by two Mechanized Guards Corps (the 2nd and 4th), can inflict a powerful, entirely unexpected blow and take Budapest in two or three days.

"*Stalin:* We cannot give you five days. Try to understand that for political reasons we must take Budapest as soon as possible.

"*Malinovskii:* I understand perfectly that we must take Budapest precisely for political reasons. [At that time a democratic Hungarian government was being formed, and the liberation of the capital from German-Fascist occupation would have hastened the process of its formation and would have had a definite influence on certain wavering elements among the bourgeois parties and factions.—*The author.*] We should, however, wait for the arrival of the 4th Mechanized Guards Corps. Only then can we count on success.

"*Stalin:* We cannot postpone the attack for five days. We must attack Budapest immediately.

"*Malinovskii.* If you give me five days now, then in another few days, five at most, Budapest will be taken. But if we attack at once, the 46th Army will not be able to make rapid progress owing to insufficient forces. It will be dragged inevitably into long, drawn-out battles at the very approaches to the Hungarian capital. In short, we will not be able to take Budapest from the march.

"*Stalin:* You are being needlessly stubborn. You don't understand the political necessity of an immediate strike against Budapest.

"*Malinovskii.* I well understand the political importance of taking Budapest and that is why I'm asking for five days.

"*Stalin:* I order you categorically to attack Budapest.

"Stalin then hung up, which meant that the conversation was finished. A few minutes later, the phone rang again. General of the Army A. I. Antonov, the Chief of the General Staff, asked for the precise time when the 46th Army would attack, in order to report it to Stalin.

"Malinovskii spoke to Stalin and Antonov directly from the headquarters of the 46th Army. And right then and there, he ordered the Army commander to attack on the morning of October 29. Naturally, the attack developed slowly, and the German-Fascist command had time to transfer enough forces and matériel to organize a stubborn resistance. That was the only reason why protracted battles were fought for Budapest. They were eloquent testimony to misplaced haste or rather to error in deciding such an important strategical mission as the capture of the Hungarian capital. One could not help but remember the motto of a military leader: 'I don't hurry, because I intend to act quickly.' We might point out that afterward, Stalin avoided the subject of Budapest in his telephone conversations with Malinovskii for quite a while."

(*Budapesht—Vena—Praga* [Moscow, 1965], pp. 81–83).

4 As mentioned previously, Shtemenko's claims of German strength in Poland and of the existing balance of forces are unfounded. Moreover, the Soviet grouping in the central sector could have been very substantially reinforced by the transfer of forces from the south and north, had the Soviet High Command planned to pursue its offensive on the Berlin axis of advance.

5 In actuality, Soviet troops reached the Banska Bystritsa–Komarno–Nad'kanizhe line, which stretched 200 miles across Slovakia and Western Hungary to the Yugoslav border, only in late March 1945, and Vienna was captured in mid-April.

6 Shtemenko's admission here clearly contradicts his previous assertions about the strength of German positions in the central (Polish) front sector. It may well be, however, that both statements—that the main German strength was concentrated in the central sector and that Hitler, expecting the main Soviet thrust against Germany to be directed from the south, concentrated his major forces there—are true, the first as a reflection of a Soviet assumption that Hitler must surely concentrate his maximum strength on the direct line of Soviet advance against Berlin even if it meant a weakening of other front sectors, the second as a reflection of Hitler's actual behavior.

7 In the period September–December 1944 twelve rifle and seven tank divisions were transferred from Army Group A, which was holding the central sector of the Nazi-Soviet front, to the East Prussian and Balkan sectors and the Western Front.

8 According to the plan disclosed by Shtemenko, the capture of Berlin should have been accomplished after 45 days of major offensive operations. In actuality, of the 110 days from the start of the Soviet offensive on January 12 to the capture of Berlin on May 2 the Red Army was en-

gaged in major offensive actions for 36 days. What Shtemenko does not mention, however, is that according to his own testimony, the Supreme High Command did not anticipate in its initial plan any pause between the first and second stages of the operation, not to speak of one lasting 70 days. Moreover, the major change from the initial plan was its "over-fulfillment" in the first stage which brought Soviet troops to the very approaches of the Berlin defense zone without a halt on the Bydgoszcz (Bromberg)–Poznan' line.

9 See pp. 409–10.

10 From other accounts it is clear that the date for the meeting of Army Group commanders at Supreme Headquarters was deliberately chosen to coincide with anniversary celebrations and thus to provide a convenient reason for gathering the senior officers in Moscow without arousing the enemy's suspicions.

11 Marshal Rokossovskii recounts in his memoirs his deep disappointment at being denied the chance to participate personally in the assault on Berlin by Stalin's decision to place Zhukov in command of his Army Group. He writes:

"In the middle of November 1944 I received a call from Stalin. After hearing out my report on the situation [in the sector of the 1st Belorussian Army Group], he said that Supreme Headquarters had adopted a decision to appoint me commander of the 2nd Belorussian Army Group. Such a decision was highly unexpected for me. I had very recently been at Supreme Headquarters reporting my suggestions for the organization of the 1st Belorussian Army Group's offensive on the Berlin axis. All our suggestions were accepted without any remarks whatsoever and here suddenly a new assignment. Involuntarily, I asked the Supreme Commander in Chief—'Why such disfavor?' Stalin answered that his deputy, Marshal Zhukov, was being appointed commander of the 1st Belorussian Army Group and that I would learn all other details when I came to Supreme Headquarters."

(K. K. Rokossovskii, "Na berlinskom i vostochno-prusskom napravleniiakh," *Voenno-istoricheskii zhurnal*, 1965, No. 2, p. 25.)

12 See n. 65, Chapter Four.

13 Shtemenko, in another part of his memoirs, discloses an interesting change in the planned direction of the main strike of Zhukov's and Konev's Army

Groups. Initially, Zhukov's troops were supposed to attack directly westward toward Poznan', the shortest route to Berlin. Zhukov's neighbor to the south, Konev, was to strike northwest toward Kalish in support of Zhukov. His strike therefore was clearly of secondary, supporting importance. By the end of November, however, on the suggestion of Zhukov, who feared that an advance directly westward would be very difficult because of strong enemy defenses, the plan was amended, and Zhukov's troops directed their main strike southwest toward Lodz. The supporting strike of Konev toward Kalish lost its significance, therefore, and Konev's troops were ordered to direct their main strike directly westward toward Breslau.

14 The Silesian basin was, after the Ruhr, the second largest industrial and mining center of Germany, covering a total area of close to 6,000 sq. km. The entire area was incorporated by Poland after the war. Poland was thus reimbursed at German expense for territories annexed by the Soviet Union in 1939. A large part of Silesian industrial equipment was dismantled and moved to the Soviet Union as part payment of reparations owed by Germany to the USSR. (For example, the first new compact passenger car produced in the Soviet Union after the war—the Moskvich—was simply the German Opel produced on complete assembly lines from the Opel factory in Breslau which were transferred to the Moscow ZIS factory.)

15 Soviet forces participating in the Vistula-Oder operation were almost evenly divided between the Army Groups of Marshals Zhukov and Konev. Zhukov had a slight advantage in the number of men and in assault guns and motor transport, while Konev possessed a stronger tank concentration. In one respect, however, Zhukov had a clear advantage—his supply reserves were considerably larger than those of Konev, with the single exception of fuel for land vehicles. (*Voenno-istoricheskii zhurnal*, 1965, No. 1, pp. 71, 73.)

16 In the light of Soviet insistence that the original starting date of the offensive was to be January 20 and that only on the request of the Western Allies was it moved ahead to January 12, it is interesting to note that at the beginning of January the German High Command anticipated the start of the Soviet attack on January 12. (See H. Guderian, *op. cit.*, p. 386.)

17 As Konev explains in another place.

he was afraid that the normal procedure followed by the Red Army at the start of an offensive operation—a reconnaissance in force conducted a day before the offensive and an all-out attack after a single powerful artillery preparation on the day of the offensive, a method familiar to the Germans—would be countered, as had so often been done in the past, by a German pullback prior to the start of the Soviet attack which would prevent the artillery barrage from hitting the major enemy concentration. This time Konev decided to forego the reconnaissance on the day before the offensive and planned two artillery attacks on the day of its start.

18 The fatal German error in deploying reserves in the sector of Army Group A is explained in detail in the memoirs of General Guderian, at that time Chief of the General Staff of the German Ground Forces. He writes:

"The officers at the front wished to build the major defensive line some 12 miles behind the main [forward] line of defense, to camouflage it carefully, and to install a holding garrison inside it. They further wanted a standing authority to withdraw the bulk of their forces into this major defensive line as soon as the Russian artillery preparation that heralded a forthcoming attack should begin. . . . The Russians' barrage would thus be wasted. . . . I approved [their plan] and submitted it to Hitler. He lost his temper, saying that he refused to accept the sacrifice of 12 miles without a fight and ordered that the major defensive line be built from one–two miles behind the main line of defense. . . . This mistake of his was to cost us dear when the Russians broke through in January 1945 and our reserves—again on a direct order of Hitler's and against my judgment—were once again too close to the front."

(Guderian, *op. cit.*, pp. 377–78.)

19 The density of artillery concentration on the breakthrough sectors in the Vistula-Oder operation was the highest ever achieved by the Soviet army, or any other army, during the Second World War. (It was not exceeded even in the Berlin operation.) The enormous density of artillery fire at the start of the offensive reflected on the one hand the very large number of artillery units in Zhukov's and Konev's Army Groups and on the other hand their enormous concentration on the axes of the main assault. Zhukov's and Konev's Army Groups had at the

beginning of the operation 13,700 guns and mortars each (not counting antitank, rocket, anti-aircraft, and self-propelled artillery), of which over half (7,500–8,500) was concentrated in the sector of the main strike. For a comparison, one may add, the entire German Army Group A had 4,100 guns and mortars at its disposal. (Source: "Vislo-Oderskaia operatsiia v tsifrakh," *Voenno-istoricheskii zhurnal*, 1965, No. 1, p. 75.)

20 Konev's memoirs are a striking example of the departure of Soviet military writers and memoirists, especially in the last two years, from the previously prevailing, almost caricature-like portrayal of the German army in Soviet publications. While Soviet military writers characterized the German army in their general statements as powerful and effective, seldom would one find such descriptions of individual operations and even grudging praise of the fighting ability and courage of German soldiers and the military talent of German generals as appear in Konev's memoirs. The failure to pay due respect to the military qualities of the German army is now being criticized in Soviet articles, the authors of which logically point out that to minimize the skill of the opponent is also to minimize that of the victor. General of the Army Ivanov, for example, together with five other senior officers, recently commented on the publication of the latest one-volume Soviet history of the Nazi-Soviet war as follows:

"The authors of the book may be reproached for the fact that when describing Soviet operations [in 1944–45] they fail to pay sufficient attention to descriptions of the enemy and above all to those of his strong points which enabled him to resist Soviet troops bitterly until almost the last day of the war. The Soviet armed forces achieved a victory over an enemy which was experienced and skillful. Therefore, the book would only have gained from a thorough presentation of the strength of the German fascist army and the state of its military art. . . . Otherwise, the victories achieved by our nation are minimized to some extent."

(V. Ivanov et al., "Novaia kniga o velikoi pobede Sovetskogo Soiuza," *Voenno-istoricheskii zhurnal*, 1965, No. 12, p. 72.)

21 Marshal Konev in another part of his memoirs explains the term "combat group" as applied to German army units of the period:

"German 'combat groups came into

existence as emergency measures in the organization of troops. When a unit lost more than half its personnel in battle and could no longer be considered the old combat unit, it was registered with the new name 'combat group.' In 1945 composite combat groups emerged from remnants of several routed units. They were most frequently designated by the name of their commander. Their numerical strength varied, depending on whether the original unit had been a regiment, a brigade, or a division—ranging from 500 to 700 men and sometimes from 1,000 to 1,500. As a rule the combat groups fought very stubbornly. They were led by experienced commanders who had a good knovledge of their subordinates."

22 The Vistula-Oder operation was the largest single Soviet offensive of World War II in terms of the numerical strength of the Armies involved and the number of heavy weapons and equipment utilized as well as in terms of the rapidity of the Red Army's advance and the size of territory seized. During the January 1945 offensive, which lasted for 20 days, Soviet troops achieved an average daily rate of advance of between 15–20 miles. The two participating Army Groups were composed of 2,200,000 men of whom almost 1,600,000 were in combat units, with 4,529 tanks, 2,513 self-propelled artillery weapons, and over 5,000 aircraft. To gain perspective one may mention that the two Army Groups possessed more tanks and aircraft than the entire Red Army in May 1942. According to German sources the Red superiority in this operation was as follows: in infantry 11:1, in tanks 7:1, in guns 20:1, in air power 20:1. According to Soviet claims 31 enemy divisions were totally destroyed during the operation and 25 divisions had casualties of 60–70 percent. 147,000 enemy soldiers were taken prisoner.

23 Zhukov's demarcation line kept the northern, eastern, and southern parts of the Berlin defense zone entirely within the area of operation of his own Army Group. The closest that Konev's Army Group would have come to Berlin was in an encircling strike southwest of Berlin toward the city of Brandenburg about 20 miles west of Berlin.

24 Lieutenant General Telegin, Marshal Zhukov's deputy for political affairs, provides in his memoirs an interesting account of the supply difficulties and their causes:

"Why did some of our Armies suffer a shortage of ammunition? There were, after all, sufficient quantities in the Army and Army Group dumps. It happened because a large part of the auto transport of divisions and even Armies was released from carrying supplies and transferred to forward units for pursuit of the enemy. . . .

"Why did the Armies experience an even more acute shortage of fuel? Here it happened as the folk saying goes—'You extract your tail and your nose gets stuck.' Indeed, our railroad repair units were not quick enough to make the railway operative. . . . This forced us to organize the unloading of supplies at a considerable distance from the combat troops. Consequently, the importance and scale of auto supply lines expanded significantly. This in turn meant that a considerable part of the fuel which should have been supplied to the troops under normal conditions was now consumed by supply trucks in their 300–400 and sometimes even 500 km.-long trips. Another acute problem was created by the shortages of containers for fuel transport."

(K. F. Telegin, "Na zakliuchitel'nom etape voiny," *Voenno-istoricheskii zhurnal*, 1965, No. 4, p. 63.)

25 For an example of one such "comrade" see Marshal Chuikov's memoirs which follow.

26 The last and sole chance for the Germans to disorganize the Soviet concentration in front of Berlin and to delay its final assault on the capital was to strike from eastern Pomerania against Zhukov's northern flank. Any possibility that such a strike with all available forces could be mounted, especially prior to the time the Red Army would be able to bring up its own reserves, disappeared when Hitler, despite Guderian's objections, persisted in his own plan to withhold the few available reserves from this sector. The German attack launched on February 15 in the Arnswalde sector (about 90 miles northeast of Berlin) petered out after only a few days.

The Soviet High Command reinforced Marshal Rokossovskii's 2nd Belorussian Army Group in Pomerania and redirected Zhukov's right flank Armies for a strike north. In an offensive operation which lasted from February 24 to March 20 the German grouping in East Pomerania was defeated. Soviet troops north of Zhukov reached the Baltic Sea and occupied positions along the entire length of the Oder River, starting from the seaport of Stettin.

27 The battle of Lake Balaton in south-western Hungary (March 6–16), the last offensive launched by the German army during the Second World War, absorbed most of the reserves sorely needed to defend Berlin (e.g., the 6th Tank Army under SS Colonel General Sepp Dietrich which was withdrawn from the Western Front). According to Soviet sources, at the start of the battle the German grouping with 430,000 men and almost 900 tanks and assault guns was equal in numerical strength and superior in tank support to the opposing Russian armies of Marshal Tolbukhin. It was able to achieve only an initial success, breaking Soviet lines on a 30-mile-wide sector and pushing 15–20 miles deep. On March 16 Soviet troops started their offensive and within two weeks cleared western Hungary and moved into Austria. It should be noted, however, that their major aim—the encirclement and destruction of the German 6th Army—was not accomplished. (Data from Colonel General M. N. Sharokhin and Colonel V. S. Petrukhin, *Put' k Balatonu* [Moscow, 1966], pp. 96–132.)

28 At the Yalta conference in February 1945 the Soviet Union and the Western Allies agreed to divide defeated Germany into four zones of occupation. The advance of the troops of any party to the agreement into territory assigned to the occupation zone of another party would be followed after Germany's capitulation, according to the agreement, by withdrawal in favor of the party authorized to occupy it. At the time described by the author, the Western Allies had already advanced about 100 miles into their own zones of Germany, while the Soviet army had not yet reached what was to become the Soviet zone of occupation.

29 Shtemenko refers here to Churchill's telegram to President Roosevelt dated April 1, 1945 which reads in part:
"I say quite frankly that Berlin remains of high strategic importance. Nothing will exert a psychological effect of despair upon all German forces of resistance equal to that of the fall of Berlin. It will be the supreme signal of defeat to the German people. On the other hand, if left to itself to maintain a siege by the Russians among its ruins, and as long as the German flag flies there, it will animate the resistance of all Germans under arms.
"There is moreover another aspect which it is proper for you and me to consider. The Russian armies will no doubt overrun all Austria and enter Vienna. If they also take Berlin, will not their impression that they have been the overwhelming contributor to our common victory be unduly imprinted in their minds, and may this not lead them into a mood which will raise grave and formidable difficulties in the future?"
(Stephen E. Ambrose, *Eisenhower and Berlin 1945* [New York: W. W. Norton & Co., Inc., 1967], pp. 101–102.)

30 As Marshal Konev makes clear in the memoirs reprinted below, Stalin was not so explicit with regard to the meaning of his curious demarcation line when Zhukov and Konev were still present. Konev's memoirs show at the same time, however, that even without Stalin's verbal agreement he, Konev, felt that his hopes of participating in the Berlin assault were tacitly encouraged.

31 See n. 26 above.

32 General Guderian acknowledges what Chuikov asserts—that the possible German counterblows against Zhukov's Army Group from Pomerania did not present a serious danger to the Russians in view of the small size of the German forces involved. It should be noted, however, that this admission concerns the situation as it developed *after* Hitler persisted in throwing most of the available reserves into an offensive operation in Hungary and *after* the advance Soviet units were reinforced during February. Needless to say, the Soviet High Command had no way of knowing how the German High Command would utilize its reserves and, moreover, was absolutely correct in anticipating what Guderian's *plans* would be (i.e., that he would, if able, counterattack on the exposed northern flank of Zhukov's Armies). (See Guderian, *op. cit.*, p. 406.)

33 According to General Shtemenko in the preceding memoir fragment, this is exactly what the Soviet General Staff did when the January offensive of Zhukov's and Konev's Armies continued to advance beyond the line initially envisaged for the first stage of the operation.

34 Meseritz, a town 40 miles east of the Oder river. According to the initial plan of Supreme Headquarters for the January offensive, Zhukov's advance was to stop short of there.

35 On the orders of Hitler German garrisons in important strongpoints on the path of the Soviet advance were forbidden to withdraw even when faced with imminent encirclement. Their continuing resistance behind enemy lines, it was hoped, would complicate and slow the Red Army

advance. To what extent these hopes were justified or to what extent the troops which were immobilized in isolated fortresses could have been utilized more effectively after withdrawal to main defense lines is difficult to establish and in all probability differed from one case to another. Retention of troops in Poznan' (a large Polish city about 100 miles east of the Oder on the Berlin axis) would appear to have been justified in view of the city's importance as a communications center on the main line of Soviet advance and the fact that some of Zhukov's best assault units were tied down in an effort to capture it.

36 In an article for the journal *Novaia i noveishaia istoriia* (1965, No. 2), Marshal Chuikov repeated and expanded the arguments which had appeared in *Oktiabr'*, a part of which was reproduced above. In most cases the quotations from Marshal Zhukov which follow come from this article.

37 Marshals Zhukov and Chuikov are both quoting from General Guderian's memoirs to support their respective points of view. They both omit what does not support their arguments. It would appear that they can both look legitimately to Guderian for support, Zhukov for the description of the *intentions* of the German General Staff and the *potential* danger to his right flank from Pomerania and Chuikov for the assessment of the *actual* danger. (See also n. 32 above.)

38 See n. 26 above.

39 The advance of Konev's 1st Ukrainian Army Group in the February–March period was hampered by the stubborn defense of the largest city in southeast Germany, Breslau. While the Soviet army at that stage of war adopted the old German tactic of avoiding frontal attacks against fortified cities, leaving them to second-echelon units, the defense of the important communications center of Breslau made it difficult for Konev's Armies to concentrate and maneuver and reduced the reserves available for continuing the thrust into Germany. The surviving 41,000-strong garrison of Breslau laid down its arms only on May 6, 1945.

40 From Zhukov's figures it would appear that the casualties suffered by Soviet units during the 20 days of the January offensive were of the order of 35–45 percent in personnel and almost as high in loss of tank equipment.

41 The major difficulty for the Soviet advance in the Berlin operation was the character of the combat itself rather than the number or quality of the defending troops. The peculiar nature of street fighting nullified in part the Russian superiority in numbers and equipment. Lieutenant General Telegin, Zhukov's political deputy, writes in his introduction to an anthology of memoirs on the Berlin battle as follows:

"The Berlin operation which was conducted on the Kuestrin-Berlin axis to a depth of 100 km. lasted 16 days, of which 5 days were used to cover the 60 km. distance from the Oder to Berlin and 11 days for the assault on the city itself. On some days our advance in Berlin measured only a few hundred meters."

(*Poslednii shturm* [Moscow, 1965], pp. 12–13.)

42 V. I. Chuikov, "Konets tret'ego reikha," *Oktiabr'*, 1964, No. 5, pp. 144–45.

43 The forward line of German defense, three to six miles deep, was situated on the west bank of the Oder. The second line of defense ran through the Seelow Heights which commanded the approaches to the principal and shortest route to Berlin. Only three-quarters of a mile to three miles deep, it possessed a well-organized cross-fire system and extensive fortifications and caused Zhukov's troops to fall behind the planned schedule of advance after the first hours of the offensive, a fact which Zhukov neglects to mention. The commander of the 77th Rifle Corps in Zhukov's Army Group, Lieutenant General V. Pozniak, describes the situation as follows:

"The troops of the 1st Belorussian Army Group . . . succeeded with relative ease in breaking through the first and second positions of the enemy forward defense line. But the tempo of the further advance of our troops dropped sharply. . . . On the first day of the operation we expended about 2,500 railroad cars of ammunition (1,236,000 artillery and mortar shells) in the artillery assault on enemy positions. Our air force conducted 6,550 sorties. But despite such strong artillery and air support our infantry and tanks advanced only four to eight km. on April 16 and did not execute the task assigned for the first day of the operation. Only on April 17 with the support of the 1st and 2nd Guards Tank Armies which were introduced into combat were we able to break through the second enemy defense line and attain the goals planned for the first day of the operation.

"But even after breaking through the second defense line, the tank Armies of the 1st Belorussian Army Group did not achieve operational maneuvering space. . . . Only at the end of the fourth day of fighting did the Army Group effect the breach of the Oder defense zone, advancing 30 km. The speed of advance was considerably below what had been planned, and this fact endangered the design of the entire operation."

(V. Pozniak, "Zavershaiushchie udary po vragu," *Voenno-istoricheskii zhurnal*, 1965, No. 5, p. 30.)

44 Zhukov tries to present Konev's strike from the south against Berlin as part of a plan prearranged as early as April 3, 1945 at the Supreme Headquarters meeting rather than as a move to compensate for the slow progress of Zhukov's own troops in assaulting the German capital from the east. The reader will recall from Shtemenko's account of the meeting and will see below in Konev's reminiscences that no such plan was formulated at this meeting. When Marshal Konev opposed the initial demarcation line established by Stalin, which assigned the Berlin sector to Zhukov's zone of operation, he counted precisely on the contingency that developed, namely, Zhukov's slow advance.

45 Marshal Zhukov is answering here criticism concerning his handling of tank units in the Berlin battle which was directed against him by Marshal Chuikov, his subordinate in this operation. Chuikov's argument is as follows:

"The Army Group commander ordered the 1st Tank Army to operate in the same area as the 8th Guards Army and assigned it a separate zone. In my estimation, the decision to employ a tank Army for an offensive in such a city as Berlin was incorrect. Tanks are strong in the field. During fighting in a city, the streets and squares are empty. The enemy organizes his defense in buildings, in attics, and cellars, and the tankers do not see him. At the same time tanks are a good target for antitank riflemen armed with 'Faustpatronen.'

"Of course, this does not by any means signify that tanks are completely unsuited to street fighting. I am far from such a thought. They are needed not as an independent force but for joint operations with troops of other arms and in assault groups. . . .

"In this connection, I could not understand why, on April 19, 1945, the tankers of the 1st Army—having

gained considerable operational maneuvering space after seizing Muenchenberg and having successfully developed the offensive in the direction of Fuerstenwald and Erkner, i.e., to the southeastern suburbs of Berlin—received the order to turn toward Berlin to attack it from the east. Why did this Army not receive the mission to attack to the southwest, in particular along the Frankfurt-Berlin Autobahn, and subsequently along the Magdeburg-Leipzig [Autobahn], enveloping Berlin from the south?

"The first error, that of putting the tank Army into the fighting before the combined-arms formations had gained the Seelow Heights, engendered the second error of the commander of the Berlin operation: now he aimed the tank Armies at the very city of Berlin, rather than enveloping the city from the south and the north. These miscalculations of the command and the headquarters of the Army Groups were then placed on the shoulders of the lower-echelon commanders. . . ."

(*Oktiabr'*, 1964, No. 5, p. 152).

46 The storming of the Reichstag, the seat of the German Parliament, was chosen by the Soviet Command to symbolize Soviet victory. Elaborate plans were made by the attacking units prior to the event. Special squads were selected and entrusted with flags to raise on the Reichstag dome. There was fierce competition for reaching the top first. The three non-commissioned officers who succeeded happened by "lucky" coincidence to be Georgian, Ukrainian, and Russian and were made Heroes of the Soviet Union. One possible reason for the choice of the Reichstag may have been its central location and its height.

47 It is impossible to determine the source of the telegram. It seems almost certain, however, that it came from a Soviet source at Allied (probably British) headquarters or that it was not a telegram at all but an evaluation concocted in Moscow. Of greater interest than the telegram itself, however, are the known facts concerning Soviet-Allied communications in this period which shed light on Stalin's behavior. Three days earlier, Stalin received a cable from Eisenhower which contained a copy of his plan of Allied operations in Germany, which was communicated simultaneously to Washington and London. The cable disclosed that the thrust of the Western Allies into Germany would concentrate in the northern and southern sectors and that Berlin was no longer

considered "a strategically important objective." (See Dwight D. Eisenhower, *Crusade in Europe* [New York: Doubleday and Co., Inc., 1948], p. 398.)

Opposed with determination by Churchill (see n. 29) the plan was nevertheless endorsed by Washington. On the same day of the meeting described by Shtemenko, Stalin sent Eisenhower a reply in which he expressed full agreement with Eisenhower's plans and added that the principal blow of Soviet forces would be made in the Leipzig-Dresden direction and that the Red Army's final assault would take place approximately in the second half of May. "Berlin," wrote Stalin, "has lost its former strategic importance. . . . The Soviet High Command therefore proposes to allot secondary forces to the Berlin direction."

Stalin's endorsement of Eisenhower's phrase—Berlin has lost its strategic importance—should not be regarded solely as hypocrisy. In military terms this was indeed the case. At that stage of the war, however, very few military plans of Stalin were based primarily on military considerations, and the capture of Berlin was of primary interest politically with a view toward the shape of Europe after the war. Stalin evidently considered essential the quickest possible resumption of Zhukov's and Konev's offensive in the Berlin direction. His reasoning was based on the patent disagreement between the Anglo-American Allies about Berlin, the successful destruction by Anglo-American armies from March 23 to April 1 of the Rhine barriers, the fear that the Western Allies in time might reconsider their decision, and the fear that Germans would cease to resist in the West and invite an Allied march into Berlin.

48 While the Germans had no general plan of surrender in the West and continued resistance in the East, the comparative figures of casualties in both theaters shows a striking difference. The last available summary of the Army's General Staff (OKW) concerning casualties suffered by German ground forces in the ten-day period from April 11 to 20, 1945 provides the following figures for the Western and Eastern Fronts:

	West		East	
	All ranks	Officers only	All ranks	Officers only
Killed	577	18	7,587	286
Wounded	1,951	68	35,414	908
Missing	268,229	7,742	25,823	434
Total	270,757	7,828	68,824	1,628

(The document is reproduced in a study by a Polish colonel published in the Soviet *Journal of Military History:* Janusz Przymanowski, "Novye dokumenty o liudskikh poteriakh vermakhta vo vtoroi mirovoi voine," *Voenno-istoricheskii zhurnal*, 1965, No. 12, p. 68.) The figures reflect the difference in the will to fight displayed by the German soldier as well as differences in the degree of bitterness against the Germans felt by the Western and the Soviet soldier.

49 There is no shred of evidence to indicate that Hitler planned or even contemplated the deliberate surrender of Berlin to the Western Allies. While one may well accept Marshal Konev's statement that such rumors were rife in Red Army command circles in spring 1945 and readily believed, his reaffirmation of this belief today, over twenty years and thousands of published documents later, must be considered an example of the impressive vitality of rumors that people wanted to believe. The rumors would explain one element behind the urgency with which the Berlin operation was mounted but can hardly serve today as an argument that the urgency was justified. Marshal Konev does not even raise the important question on Berlin which is still disputed by Western military writers—would the Western Allied forces have been able to enter Berlin first had it not been for the crucial decision of March 28? Konev is obviously unwilling to admit that the Western Allies did not intend to attack in the Berlin direction and that the Soviet race to Berlin was directed mainly against the *possibility* of an Allied change of mind.

50 Konev's plan called also for the laying of a smoke screen by the air force along the entire length of the German defense lines in front of his Army Group. His intention was to blind the Germans' observation posts and to confuse their fire system rather than to mask the Soviet crossing.

51 The disposition of German troops in front of Konev, which he rightly criticized, was clearly different from that in front of Zhukov. The skillful, well-camouflaged, and well-timed withdrawal of German troops by the commander, General Heinrici, from the preparatory Soviet artillery barrage to secondary positions accounts in large part for the difficulties of Zhukov's Army Group on the Seelow Heights.

52 The high-frequency telephone line is explained in n. 27, Chapter Two. The

line which was serviced by special units of NKVD signal troops was expanded westward beyond Soviet borders as the Red Army advanced.

53 The battle of Berlin illuminates an interesting aspect of Stalin's attitude toward his first deputy, Marshal Zhukov. While Stalin was not above the exploitation of competition between Konev and Zhukov in order to speed the Soviet offensive, he still planned initially to give Zhukov the glory of capturing Berlin, and, as Konev discloses here, when Zhukov's troops bogged down on the Seelow Heights, Stalin still considered the possibility of using *Zhukov's* tanks to attack Berlin through the breach in German lines made by *Konev's* troops. The cordial relations between Zhukov and Stalin which, one assumes, provided the background for Stalin's magnanimity toward his most famous commander are mentioned by Eisenhower when he recounts his August 1945 visit to Moscow:

"At that time Marshal Zhukov was patently a great favorite with the Generalissimo. Zhukov was included in every conversation I had with Stalin and the two spoke to each other on terms of intimacy and cordiality. This was highly pleasing to me because of my belief in the friendliness and cooperative purpose of Marshal Zhukov." (Eisenhower, *op. cit.*, p. 462.)

Shortly thereafter, however, the magnanimous and cordial Stalin sent Zhukov into semi-exile as commander of a remote Soviet military district.

54 Zossen, the location of the headquarters of the German Army's (ground forces) General Staff (OKH). At the time the post of Chief of OKH was occupied by General Krebs. The General Staff of the German Armed Forces (OKW) headed by Field Marshal von Keitel with Field Marshal von Jodl as his deputy was at that time in Berlin itself.

55 A German bazooka-type antitank weapon, easy to produce and operate, of scant effectiveness in field operations but deadly in street fighting, the "faustpatronen" accounted for most Soviet tank losses in the Berlin operation.

56 The atmosphere in Berlin is well conveyed in the following description by a German civilian eyewitness:

"Panic had reached its peak in the city. Hordes of soldiers stationed in Berlin deserted and were shot on the spot or hanged on the nearest tree. A few clad only in underclothes were dangling on a tree quite near our house.

On their chests they had placards reading: 'We betrayed the Fuehrer.' The Werewolf pasted leaflets on the houses:

Dirty cowards and defeatists
We've got them all on our lists!

"The SS went into underground stations, picked out among the sheltering crowds a few men whose faces they did not like, and shot them then and there.

"The scourge of our district was a small one-legged *Hauptscharfuehrer* of the SS who stumped through the street on crutches, a machine-pistol at the ready, followed by his men. Anyone he didn't like the look of he instantly shot. The gang went down cellars at random and dragged all the men outside, giving them rifles and ordering them straight to the front. Anyone who hesitated was shot."
(Quoted in Desmond Flower and James Reeves, eds., *The Taste of Courage* [New York: Harper & Brothers Publishers, 1960], p. 1011.)

57 Soviet air power in the Berlin battle was the greatest ever assembled for any Soviet offensive operation (even the winter 1945 drive from the Vistula to the Oder). The participating Army Groups were supported by three air Armies with 7,500 war planes of which almost half consisted of fighter aircraft. In addition, Zhukov's assault was supported by 800 bombers of the Strategic Air Command which remained under Supreme Headquarters direction. During the 17 days of assault on Berlin (April 16–May 2) over 91,000 Soviet combat sorties were flown. (Source: "Berlinskaia operatsiia v tsifrakh," *Voenno-istoricheskii zhurnal,* 1965, No. 4, pp. 81, 87.)

58 It seems pertinent to note that in the 22 days from the commencement of the offensive on April 16 to May 8 Soviet troops participating in the Berlin battle suffered what can be considered exceptionally heavy casualties—304,877 dead, wounded, or missing. Losses of equipment were also very high—2,156 tanks and assault guns, 1,220 guns and mortars, 527 aircraft. (See *Istoriia Velikoi Otechestvennoi voiny Sovetskogo Soiuza* [1963] V, 290.)

59 According to the commander of the German Ninth Army, General Busse, about 40,000 of his men succeeded in breaking the Soviet ring to reach the positions of the German Twelfth Army. (Theodor Busse, "Die letzte Schlacht der 9 Armee," *Wehrwissenschaftliche Rundschau,* 1955, p. 168.)

60 It is almost incredible that one of the

most senior Soviet military leaders, who was at the time of writing his memoirs Deputy Minister of Defense and Chief of Soviet Ground Forces, could today continue to speculate that the desperate attempts of Himmler and Goering to establish communications with the Western Allies in the final days of the war were part of a conspiracy supervised by Hitler. One may assume that his uncertainty stems from a combination of the well-known overdeveloped Soviet suspiciousness and from lack of knowledge of rich documentary material published on this matter in the West.

61 On March 28, 1945 General Guderian was replaced as Army Chief of Staff by General Krebs. Guderian writes the following about his successor·
"He was a clever officer, with a good military education behind him, but he lacked experience as a commander since he had spent the whole war in various staff appointments. During his long career as a staff officer he had proved himself highly capable at staff work and had also shown a great talent for being adaptable and accommodating, qualities which hardly fitted him to stand up to a man like Hitler. Furthermore he had been a close friend of General Burgdorf, the head of the Army Personnel Office ... [who] soon drew Krebs into ... the circle that revolved about Bormann and Fegelein, and with them, too, Krebs soon struck up an intimate friendship. These personal relationships finally deprived him of his freedom of action and independence of thought."
(Guderian, *op. cit.*, pp. 415–16.)

62 General Pozharskii was Chuikov's chief of artillery.

63 In the last days of the Berlin operation Chuikov was host to a group of men prominent in the cultural world—Vishnevskii, one of Stalin's favorite playwrights; Dolmatovskii, a poet laureate; and Blanter, composer of popular songs for soldiers and civilians.

64 Hitler in his testament expelled from the Party and from all offices Reichsmarshal Goering and SS Chief Himmler and appointed Grand Admiral Doenitz, head of the navy, as Reichspresident and Supreme Commander of the Armed Forces. Goebbels was assigned the post of Reichs Chancellor and Bormann the Party leadership. (See H. R. Trevor-Roper, *The Last Days of Hitler* [3rd ed.; New York: Collier Books, 1962], pp. 238–39.)

65 Shortly before the Nazi-Soviet war Krebs occupied the post of assistant military attaché in the German Embassy in Moscow. He spoke Russian and knew many Soviet military leaders personally—partial explanation at least for his selection. There is one final irony in selecting Krebs to inform Stalin about Hitler's death. He was probably the only German general to be publicly embraced by Stalin. This event took place on April 13, 1941 at the Moscow railroad station and is reported by Gustav Hilger (G. Hilger and A. G. Meyer, *The Incompatible Allies* [New York: The Macmillan Co., 1953], p. 327.)

66 In Chuikov's account of negotiations with Krebs, he frequently takes pleasure in displaying a knowledge of what he calls "diplomatic tricks." His apparent belief in his ability to see through "the deviousness of diplomatic behavior" probably derives from personal experience with a diplomatic mission. In the years 1941–1942, Chuikov served as Soviet military attaché in China (Chungking) and chief Soviet military adviser to Chiang Kai-shek.

67 Shortly afterward, General Sokolovskii arrived at Chuikov's headquarters and the answer came from Moscow by telephone—anything less than a general unconditional surrender or the surrender of Berlin alone would not be accepted. Additional talks followed during which Sokolovskii tried to discover from Krebs details of the situation in the German leadership. Then at 1:00 p.m. on May 1, after nine hours, the "negotiations" ended. Five hours after Krebs' departure, at 6:00 p.m., a German truce envoy delivered to Chuikov a letter from Bormann and Krebs rejecting the unconditional surrender.

68 Their decision was first to inform Doenitz that he was now in full charge of Germany's government, a decision which they delayed in the hope that the Russians would permit Doenitz to come to Berlin. A day later Goebbels committed suicide, followed shortly thereafter by General Krebs.

69 Hans Fritsche, a former radio commentator who made a career in the Nazi Propaganda Ministry and became one of Goebbel's deputies. He was the only defendant at the Nuremberg trials to be acquitted, probably because of his insignificance in comparison to the other defendants.

70 The broadcast mentioned by Chuikov was made by Hamburg Radio on the evening of May 1, and the version of Hitler's "heroic death" was repeated shortly afterward by the new chief of state,

Doenitz. It appears that the first radiograms informing Doenitz of Hitler's death made no mention of suicide.

71 The meaning of Chuikov's remark is not quite clear. The Russian words *podstavnoe litso* suggest that Chuikov either had doubts whether this was indeed Fritsche or that Fritsche had been sent to the Russians in order to cover up some kind of intrigue by higher Nazi leaders.

72 Following the capitulation of the Berlin garrison, Chuikov and his troops remained in Berlin only for a brief period. He was stationed in Germany until Stalin's death, as commander of Soviet occupation troops in Thuringia until 1949 and then as commander in chief of all Soviet forces in Germany.

73 General Omar Bradley commanded the American 12th Army Group at the time, not US forces in Europe.

74 Czechoslovakia remained the only territory in east-central Europe which had not yet been overrun by the Red Army. Immediately after the end of the Berlin battle Konev's left-flank tank troops were ordered to make a forced march from southeast Germany to Prague (100 miles). They entered the Czech capital on May 9. The Soviets maintain officially that they saved Prague from destruction by Field Marshal Schoerner's army, which was allegedly poised to quell a Czech uprising that had erupted on May 2. In the light of the general situation at the time, however, one could hardly speak of any real danger to Prague, not to speak of destruction, from disintegrating German units. Moreover, in one of the final ironies of World War II, units of the anti-Soviet army of General Vlasov, formed by the Germans from Soviet prisoners of war, were at that time in control of Prague, having turned their guns against the Germans. The danger that "threatened" Prague, from the Soviet point of view, was its liberation by the American army, which had already crossed the western frontier of Czechoslovakia and was closer to Prague than Soviet troops. Since an agreement existed between the Soviet Union and the United States that American units would not move beyond the city of Pilzno, 50 miles southwest of Prague, Konev's rapid advance was apparently intended to preclude any American change of plan.

75 Konev here is obviously at pains to explain his secretiveness about the disposition of the Red Army which Bradley describes in his memoirs as follows:

"Konev took me first to his office for a moment of private conversation through our interpreters. I gave him a map I had prepared for the occasion, showing the disposition of every US division across his group front. The marshal started in surprise but did not volunteer to show me his own dispositions. Had he wanted to, he would probably have had to ask permission from the Kremlin. American lieutenants were delegated greater authority on the Elbe than were Russian division commanders."

(Omar N. Bradley, *A Soldier's Story* [New York: Henry Holt and Co., 1951], p. 551.)

76 Bradley describes the banquet as follows:

"The banquet table had been banked lavishly with fresh caviar, veal, beef, cucumbers, black bread, and butter. A row of wine bottles filled the center. Vodka decanters were spread liberally about for the toasts, which started as soon as we sat down. Konev rose and lifted his glass. 'To Stalin, Churchill, and Roosevelt—' he said, not yet having learned of Truman's succession.

"After seating himself, Konev shifted to a smaller glass which he filled not with vodka but with white wine.

"'The marshal has stomach trouble,' his interpreter explained. 'He can no longer drink vodka.' I smiled and reached for the wine myself, relieved to know there would be no need for the mineral oil I had already swallowed."

(Bradley, *ibid.*)

77 Konev registers his reaction to the Americans' applause of the national anthem because the playing of the national anthem is considered too solemn an occasion in Russia (and in Europe) for applause. Incidentally, the Russian chorus had memorized the American anthem without knowing a word of English.

78 One might juxtapose to Konev's description of the gift exchange the comment of Bradley:

" 'I'll probably get stuck by the comptroller and have to pay for this thing 20 years after the war,' I told Hansen when he ordered the jeep from Antwerp, 'but what the dickens, I don't suppose we can go up empty-handed.' "

(Bradley, *op. cit.*, p. 553.)

79 A. I. Suvorov (1729–1800), the famous Russian military leader of the end of the 18th century who led Russian armies against Napoleon Bonaparte. The commemoration of Suvorov reverses an ear

lier Soviet line which had attempted to erase the memory of military victories achieved by tsarist generals. The departure was part of a major attempt to associate Soviet power with historical military victories in order to encourage patriotic feelings.

80 The order of Suvorov came in three ranks. The first rank, given to Bradley, was awarded to 340 military leaders from the time of its establishment in 1943.

81 Bradley describes the incident as follows:

"[When the Russian dance troupe began to perform] Konev shrugged his shoulders. 'Just a few girls,' he explained, 'from the Red Army.'

"Two weeks later when Konev repaid our call with one to our CP, he was enthralled with the violin virtuosity of a thin khaki-clad man.

" 'Magnificent,' the marshal cried in delight.

" 'Oh, that,' I said. 'Nothing, nothing at all. Just one of our American soldiers.'

"We had pirated the violinist from Special Services in Paris for the day. His name was Jascha Heifetz."
(Bradley, *op. cit.*, pp. 551–53.)

82 In addition to the Konev-Bradley meetings in May 1945, other encounters took place in Germany between leading Soviet and Western military figures, e.g., the commander of the Soviet northern sector Marshal Rokossovskii with Field Marshal Montgomery and, of course, General Eisenhower with Marshal Zhukov. As Eisenhower describes the meeting, the banquet and entertainment routine was virtually identical with that described by Bradley with the exception of the decoration—Eisenhower received the highest Soviet military order "Victory," which has been awarded to only 16 people from the time it was established.

83 On May 5 General Eisenhower asked the Soviet High Command to assign a Red Army officer to his headquarters for the specific purpose of representing Russia in any surrender negotiations that the Doenitz government might propose. The Russians sent Major General Ivan Susloparov. (See Eisenhower, *op. cit.*, p. 425.)

From the Russian point of view the trouble with the act of unconditional surrender signed in Reims on May 7 (not for the Reims German grouping as Voronov asserts but for the entire German Armed Forces and signed by General Jodl as Admiral Doenitz' representative)

was that the ceremony took place in territory occupied by the Western powers and not Russia and that the act was signed by Eisenhower but not by a senior Soviet leader as well and therefore accentuated the Western contribution to the victory over Germany. Moreover, owing to a mistake by General Smith, Eisenhower's Chief of Staff, the surrender document was different from the one agreed upon by Russia, the US, and Great Britain at the end of March 1945, a fact which the Russians interpreted as a sinister double-cross. As Robert Murphy, General Eisenhower's political adviser, recounts in his memoirs:

"When Smith asked him [Susloparov] to certify the improvised documents, the obliging Russian did so. Susloparov told us later that his government never had informed him of any other terms, which doubtless was true, but he was abruptly recalled to Moscow when he admitted that he had certified the terms which Smith had hastily adapted."
(Robert Murphy, *Diplomat Among Warriors* [New York: Pyramid Books, 1965], p. 271.)

84 In another place Marshal Voronov provides an interesting account of the preparations which were being made in the Red Army for the war against Japan during the later stages of the war in Europe. He writes:

"Soon after the Teheran conference ended, I and the present Marshal of the Soviet Union V. D. Sokolovskii heard from Stalin the important news that at the conference he had accepted the proposal of Churchill and Roosevelt to take part in the war against imperialist Japan three or four months after the end of the war in Europe. He told us that we should make use of the favorable international situation to return everything that Japan had seized as a result of the Russo-Japanese War. He added: 'But we don't need anything that isn't ours.' This was a great military secret which wasn't supposed to be mentioned to anyone, but at the same time we had to be very active in a quiet way. No one would have forgiven me if there had not been a sufficient quantity of artillery, ammunition, and trained cadres for the beginning of our military actions in the Far East. Therefore, as soon as a small reserve of ammunition was collected, it was quietly sent off to somewhere on the Amur, evoking not a little surprise from people who in some way took part in this shipment. The ammunition in the railroad cars was completely camouflaged. From time to time protests burst from the Far East army commanders over the dispatch of ammunition for guns of large caliber and special power, which they did not even have. These protests demanded that those in the Main Artillery Administration guilty of confusion in their planning and sending ammunition east instead of west should be brought to account.

"Quietly, with great caution, we continued to select artillery personnel for the Far Eastern troops. Generals and officers with extensive combat experience were sent there. How many objections filled with smouldering indignation we had to hear from them in those days!

"'Why this punishment?!,' they would ask. 'This is unjust. I want so much to take part in the final battles, to finish the war in Berlin, and you are sending me into the remotest reserves, into virtual retirement.'

"One so wanted to calm them, to explain to them that they would have battles there—but military secrecy came first.

"On the other hand, how the generals and officers of the Far East rejoiced when we sent them to the western front!"

(N. N. Voronov, "Podvig sovetskogo naroda," *Istoriia SSSR*, 1965, No. 4, pp. 17–18.)

85 There were about two million Soviet citizens in Germany who had come as forced laborers, prisoners of war, or evacuees with the retreat of German armies. Most of them lived in the western occupation zones. Soviet authorities were determined to secure their return regardless of private wishes, and in the initial period at least they received full cooperation from the Western authorities who organized voluntary and compulsory repatriation. Those repatriated were treated by Soviet authorities as political suspects; and prisoners of war, who were virtually regarded as traitors, went almost directly from German camps to camps in Siberia.

86 N. A. Bulganin, then a General of the Army, was at the time the Deputy People's Commissar of Defense. He was promoted to the rank of marshal in 1947 and appointed USSR Minister of Armed Forces, a post he held until 1949 and again from 1953–55.

87 At the Kremlin celebration Stalin made his famous toast in which he singled out the Russian people as "the most remarkable of all the nations of the Soviet Union, the leading nation." His stress on the contribution of the people rather than the military professionals presaged the campaign which followed soon after, the aim of which was to denigrate the services of military leaders.

88 The program of entertainment as described by Iakovlev in his memoirs consisted of over 40 acts from the finest to the most tawdry examples of Soviet culture. It was remarkable for the absence of any performances related to the revolutionary experience of 1917.

89 Each star on the gun barrel represented the destruction of some enemy object.

90 The parade was opened by the ceremonial march of students from Soviet military academies and then followed by 12 columns of regimental size, composed of soldiers and led by the commander and staff of each Soviet Army Group. The order in which the Army Group columns marched was decided upon in the following manner described by Colonel General Stuchenko:

"Long before the day of the parade, a conflict developed among the Army Groups as to who would open the victorious procession. Naturally, everyone considered his own Army Group the most important one. Everyone wondered whose column would go first, second, or third. The other places, except for the last, did not bother anybody.

"At first it was proposed that the Leningrad Army Group would go fourth, following the 1st Belorussian, 1st Ukrainian, and 2nd Belorussian, which had all taken part in the Berlin operation. Debates flared up again in mid-June. At last, a wise decision was reached: the Army Groups would go in the order of their location at the end of the war, from north to south. This put an end to all arguments. We men of Leningrad would now go second, behind the Karelian Army Group."

(A. T. Stuchenko, *Zavidnaia nasha sud'ba* [Moscow, 1964)], p. 250.)

91 At the XIX Party Congress in October 1952 there was indeed an indication that Stalin had decided to delegate to some of his associates certain of his responsibilities. For example, this was the first congress from the time Stalin achieved power that the major programmatic report to the delegates was made by some-

one other than Stalin himself, in this case by Malenkov, who was generally considered the heir apparent. Kuznetsov's statement that Stalin made some kind of official request for partial retirement at the Plenum of the Central Committee which followed the Congress is completely new and difficult to evaluate without additional information. His assertion that Stalin was relieved at that meeting of the post of Minister of Defense must surely be inaccurate for the simple reason that Marshal Vasilevskii held this post from 1949 until Stalin's death.

BIOGRAPHICAL INDEX

Antonov, A. I. (1896-1962) General of the Army. Russian. Son of artillery officer. Junior officer in tsarist army during World War I. Entered Red Army 1919. Staff duties at division level during Civil War. Entered Party 1926. Studied in command section (1928-30), then in operational section (1931-33) of Frunze Military Academy. Divisional Chief of Staff, then Chief of Operations of Khar'kov Military District 1933-36. Studied in Academy of General Staff 1936-38. Chief of Staff of Moscow Military District, then lecturer in Frunze Academy 1938-40. Deputy Chief of Staff of Kiev Military District 1941. Chief of Staff Southern Army Group from August 1941. Chief of Staff of North Caucasian then Transcaucasian Army Groups from July 1942. Appointed Chief of Operations of General Staff December 1942. Simultaneously served as First Deputy Chief of General Staff from April 1943. Chief of General Staff February 1945-March 1946. First Deputy Chief of Staff March 1946-November 1948. First Deputy Commander, then Commander of Transcaucasian Military District 1949-54. Chief of Staff of Warsaw Pact Forces from 1955.

Artem'ev, P. A. (1897-   ) Colonel General. Russian. Peasant origin. Laborer. Entered Red Army 1918. Entered Party 1920. Political officer during Civil War. Political commissar battalion, regiment 1922-28. Served in border troops 1929-33. Attended Frunze Military Academy 1934-38. Commander Dzerzhinskii NKVD division, Deputy Commander, then Commander in Chief of NKVD troops (militarized security forces) 1938-41. Commander Moscow Military District July 1941-47, 1949-53. Attended Academy of General Staff 1947-49. Disappeared from public life after execution in June 1953 of former superior, Chief of Secret Police Beria. In 1961 identified as First Deputy Commander Ural Military District.

Bagramian, I. Kh. (1897-   ) Marshal of S.U. Hero of S.U. Armenian. Son of railroad worker. Worked as railroad technician. Junior officer in tsarist army during World War I. Officer in army of Armenian nationalist movement ("Dashnak") 1918-21. Entered Red Army 1921. Entered Party 1941. Commander cavalry squadron 1921-23. Commander cavalry regiment 1923-24, 1925-30. Attended Higher Cavalry School 1924-25. Graduate of Frunze Military Academy 1934. Chief of staff of cavalry division 1934-36. Graduate of Academy of General Staff 1938. Senior lecturer, Academy of General Staff 1938-40. Chief of Operations 12th Army 1940. Chief of Operations and Deputy Chief of Staff Kiev Military District 1941. Chief of Operations and Deputy Chief of Staff of Southwestern Army Group in the Ukraine June 1941-March 1942. Chief of Staff, Southwestern Army Group, March-June 1942. Commander of 16th (11th Guards)

628

Army July 1942–November 1943 in the Kursk and Briansk battles. Commander of 1st Baltic Army Group 1943–45. Commander, Baltic Military District 1945–54. Chief Inspector of Soviet Ministry of Defense 1954–55. Deputy Minister of Defense 1955–56. Commandant, Academy of General Staff 1956–58. From 1958 Deputy Minister of Defense, Chief of Rear Services of Armed Forces.

Batov, P. I. (1897–   ) General of the Army. Twice Hero of S.U. Russian. Peasant origin. Junior officer in tsarist army during World War I. Entered Red Army 1918. Administrative duties during Civil War. Entered Party 1929. Commandant of regimental school, commander of battalion, then regiment 1921–33. Graduate of Frunze Military Academy 1936. Soviet adviser in Spain during Civil War until fall 1937. Upon return to USSR appointed commander of rifle corps. Took part in Soviet occupation of Poland 1939 and in Finnish War 1939–40. First Deputy Commander Transcaucasian Military District 1940. Commander 9th Rifle Corps 1941. Commander of 51st Special Army fighting in Crimea and 3rd Army in Briansk sec.or 1941–42. Commander of 65th Army in battles for Stalingrad and Kursk, in Dnepr crossing and Belorussian offensive, in assault on East Pomerania and crossing of Oder estuary 1942–45. Commander of Army in Germany 1945–49. Commander of Kaliningrad, Carpathian, and Baltic Military Districts 1949–62. Chief of Staff of Warsaw Pact Forces 1962–66. From 1966 Inspector General in Soviet Ministry of Defense.

Belov, P. A. (1897–1962) Colonel General. Hero of S.U. Russian. Son of clerk. White collar worker. Non-commissioned officer during World War I. Entered Party 1918. Entered Red Army 1919. Squadron commander in Civil War. Cavalry regiment commander 1922–29. Graduate of Frunze Military Academy 1934. Deputy commander, commander cavalry division. Chief of staff cavalry corps 1935–40. Commander 2nd Cavalry Corps 1940–41. Commander of 1st Guards Cavalry Corps and of operational group (cavalry corps, tank and rifle divisions) in Moscow counteroffensive 1941–42. Commander 61st Army in Kursk battle, Dnepr crossing, advance into Poland, assault on Berlin 1942–45. Commander Southern Ural Military District 1945–55. Chairman Voluntary Association of Support of Army, Air Force, and Navy (DOSAAF) 1955 until retirement in 1960.

Biriuzov, S. S. (1904–1964) Marshal of S.U. Hero of S.U. Russian. Worker origin. Entered Red Army 1922. Entered Party 1926. Graduate of officers school 1926. Commander of platoon, then battalion and regiment 1926–34. Attended Frunze Military Academy 1934–37. Chief of Staff (from 1937) then commander of rifle division 1939–41. Commander 132nd Rifle Division in retreat to Moscow and during winter counteroffensive 1941–42. Commander 48th Army in Voronezh sector 1942. Chief of Staff, 2nd Guards Army in Stalingrad counteroffensive 1942–43. Chief of Staff of Southern, 4th and 3rd Ukrainian Army Groups in battles for Ukraine and Crimea and conquest of Rumania and Bulgaria 1943–44. Commander of 37th Army and Deputy Head of Allied Control Commission in Bulgaria October 1944–April 1946 and July 1946–April 1947. Deputy Commander in Chief of Soviet Ground Forces April–July 1946. Commander of Far Eastern Military District 1947–53. Commander in Chief of Soviet forces in Hungary 1953–54. First Deputy Commander (1954–55) and Commander in Chief (1955–62) of Anti-aircraft Defense Forces of USSR. Commander in Chief of Strategic Rocket Forces 1962–63. From March 1963 to his death in plane crash Chief of General Staff and First Deputy Minister of Defense.

Budennyi, S. M. (1883–   ) Marshal of S.U. Hero of S.U. Russian. Peasant origin. Drafted into army 1903. Served in cavalry until Revolution. Fought in Russo-Japanese War and in World War I as sergeant-major. Entered Red Army 1918. Entered Party 1919. One of creators of Red Cavalry. Commander 1st Cavalry Army during Civil War. Inspector of Red Army cavalry during 1920's. Graduate of Frunze Military Academy 1932. Again Inspector of Red Cavalry. Commander Moscow Military District 1937–39. Deputy, then First Deputy People's Commissar of Defense 1939–41. Commander in Chief Southwestern Strategic Sector, then Commander Reserve Army Group summer–autumn 1941. Commander Transcaucasian Army Group 1942. Commander in Chief of Cavalry 1943–53. After 1953 honorific appointments and Deputy Minister of Agriculture in charge of horse breeding.

Cherniakhovskii, I. D. (1906–1945) General of the Army. Twice Hero of S.U. Ukrainian. Son of railroad worker. Worked on railroad. Entered Red Army 1924. Entered Party 1928 and commissioned an officer. Junior commander and political worker in artillery regiment 1928–31. Studied in command-engineering section of Military Academy of Motorization and Mechanization 1931–36. Chief of staff of tank battalion, then regimental commander 1936–40. Deputy commander, then commander of tank division 1940–41. After month of heavy fighting and retreat his division lost almost all combat vehicles and reformed into rifle division. Fights with division south of Leningrad until summer 1942. Commander 18th Tank Corps, then 60th Army July 1942–April 1944. Took part in battle for Kursk 1943 and offensive operations in Ukraine. Appointed Commander of 3rd Belorussian Army Group on recommendation of Marshal Vasilevskii, Chief of the General Staff. Youngest Soviet general (38 years of age) to reach such high position. His Army Group advanced through Belorussia to borders of East Prussia in early fall 1944. Virtually until war's end engaged in heavy fighting in this sector. Killed by enemy shell while inspecting field unit February 1945 during final assault of East Prussia.

Chuikov, V. I. (1900–   ) Marshal of S.U. Twice Hero of S.U. Russian. Peasant origin. Entered Red Army 1918. Entered Party 1919. Regimental commander during Civil War. Graduate of Frunze Military Academy 1925. Graduate of Military Academy of Armored Troops early 1930's. Commander mechanized brigade 1937. Commander rifle corps, then 4th Army 1938–40. Took part in occupation of Poland and Finnish war. Military attaché in China, adviser to Chiang Kai-shek 1941–May 1942. Commander 62nd Army 1942–45. Participated in battle of Stalingrad and final assault on Berlin. Deputy Commander, then Commander in Chief Soviet occupation forces in Germany 1946–53. Commander Kiev Military District 1953–60. Deputy Minister of Defense and Commander in Chief of Soviet Ground Forces 1960–65. From 1965 Chief of Civil Defense.

Emelianov, V. S. (1901–   ) Hero of Socialist Labor. Twice recipient of Stalin Prize. Correspondent member of Soviet Academy of Sciences. Russian. Son of carpenter. Entered Party 1919. Graduate of Moscow Mining Academy 1928. Doctoral research and assistantship in Academy 1928–32. Engineering and executive positions in metallurgical industry 1933–38. Official in central administration of defense industries 1938–40. Deputy Chairman of State Standards Committee, Director Moscow Physico-technical Institute 1940–46. Senior executive in atomic program 1946–56. Chairman Main Board on Use of Atomic Energy of Council of Ministers 1957–60. Chairman (1960–62), then Deputy Chairman State Committee on Use of Atomic Energy. Key Soviet representative abroad on matters concerning atomic energy. Alternate member of Central Committee of Party from 1961.

Eremenko, A. I. (1892–   ) Marshal of S.U. Hero of S.U. Russian. Peasant origin. Drafted in tsarist army 1913. Non-commissioned officer World War I. Entered Party and Red Army 1918. Red Cavalry officer during Civil War. After training in Higher Cavalry School appointed regimental commander 1923. Attended Frunze Military Academy 1931–35. Commander cavalry division 1935–38. Commander 6th Cossack Corps, took part in occupation of Poland 1938–40. Commander 1st Special Red Banner Army in Far East 1940–41. Commander Western, then Briansk Army Groups in battle for Moscow July–October 1941. Commander 4th Assault Army winter 1941–42. Commander Stalingrad Army Group in battle for Stalingrad. Commander Southern, then Kalinin Army Groups 1943. Commander Special Maritime Army in Crimean offensive 1944. Commander 2nd Baltic Army Group April 1944–March 1945. Commander 4th Ukrainian Army Group during advance into Czechoslovakia. Commander Carpathian, West Siberian, North Caucasian Military Districts 1945–58. From 1958 Inspector General of Ministry of Defense.

Fediuninskii, I. I. (1900–   ) General of the Army. Hero of S.U. Russian. Entered Red Army 1919. Entered Party 1930. Commander 82nd Motorized Rifle Division in Far East 1939–40. Attended training courses for senior commanders in Academy of General Staff 1940–41. Commander 15th Rifle Corps April–August 1941. Commander 42nd, then 54th Army in defense of Leningrad and Volkhov October 1941–42. Commander 5th Army in Moscow, then Leningrad sectors June 1942–43. Commander 2nd Assault Army in offensive near Leningrad and assault on East Prussia December 1943–45. Army commander with Soviet forces in Poland, Deputy Commander in Chief of Soviet occupation forces in Germany 1945–52. Deputy Commander, then Commander Transcaucasian Military District 1952–57. Commander Turkestan Military District since 1957.

Golikov, F. I. (1900–   ) Marshal of S.U. Hero of S.U. Russian. Peasant origin. Joined Party and Red Army in 1918. Fought in Civil War. Political work in Red Army during 1920's. Rifle regiment commander 1930. Graduate of Frunze Military Academy 1933. Division, then corps commander 1934–38. Commander 6th Army, took part in occupation of Poland 1939. Deputy Chief of General Staff, Chief of Military Intelligence 1940–41. Headed military mission to London and Washington 1941. Commander 10th Army in battle of Moscow 1941–42. Commander 4th Assault Army, Briansk, then Voronezh Army Groups 1942. Deputy Commander Stalingrad Army Group 1942–43. Deputy Minister of Defense and Chief of Main Directorate of Personnel of Red Army 1943–50. Chief of Soviet Repatriation Commission 1944–46. Commander Special Mechanized Army 1950–56. Commandant of Military Academy of Armored Troops 1956. Chief of Main Political Administration of Soviet Armed Forces 1957–62. From 1962 official in Soviet Ministry of Defense.

Grechko, A. A. (1903–   ) Marshal of S.U. Hero of S.U. Ukrainian. Peasant origin. Entered Red Army 1919. Fought in Red Cavalry during Civil War. Graduate of cavalry officer school 1926. Squadron commander, chief of staff cavalry regiment 1927–31. Attended Frunze Military Academy 1932–36. Commander cavalry regiment, then Chief of Staff 36th Cavalry Division 1937–39. Graduate of Academy of General Staff 1941 and assigned to General Staff. Cavalry division, corps commander July 1941–April 1942. Commander 12th, 18th, 47th then 56th Armies in Caucasian sector 1942–43. Commander 1st Guards Army in offensive operations from the Ukraine to Czechoslovakia 1944–45. Commander Kiev Military District 1945–53. Commander in Chief of Soviet occupation forces in Germany 1953–57. First Deputy Minister of Defense and Commander in Chief of Ground Forces 1957–60. First Deputy Minister of Defense and Commander in Chief of Warsaw Pact Forces 1960–67. From 1967 Minister of Defense.

Iakovlev, A. S. (1905–   ) Colonel General of the Air Force. Six-time recipient of Stalin Prize. Twice Hero of Socialist Labor. Correspondent member Soviet Academy of Sciences. Russian. Son of clerk. Worker in airplane shop at Moscow Airport 1924–25. Technician in Red Air Force 1925. Designed first plane 1927. Studied in Engineering Department of Air Force Academy 1927–31. Designed training aircraft 1930's. Visited France, England, Germany, Italy. Entered Party 1938. Designed first fighter aircraft in "Iak" series 1939. Iak-1 accepted for serial production 1940. Deputy People's Commissar (Minister) of Aviation Industry for development and research 1940–48. Subsequently and presently Designer in Chief Experimental Design Bureau. Designed jet fighter Iak-15, jet all-weather interceptor Iak-23, heavy helicopter Iak-24, jet trainers Iak-30 and 32, short-range, three-engine jet transport Iak-40.

Kalinin, S. A. (1891–   ) Lieutenant General. Russian. Son of laborer. Textile worker. Drafted 1912. Sergeant in tsarist army World War I. Entered Party May 1917. Entered Red Army 1918. Brigade commander and officer with security troops during Civil War. Attended senior training courses and commanded rifle division in early 1920's. Deputy Chief of Staff of Ukrainian Military District 1926–28. Commander of rifle division 1928–35. Deputy Chief of Staff Moscow Military District, Commander 12th Rifle Corps, Deputy Commander Siberian, then Kiev Military Districts 1936–38. Commander Siberian Military Districts 1938–41. Commander 24th Army near Smolensk July 1941. Aide to Commander of Western Army Group August–September 1941. Supreme Headquarters representative in Siberia for formation of new units October–December 1941. Commander Volga Military District 1942–44. Commander Khar'kov Military District 1944 until retirement 1954.

Khrulev, A. V. (1892–1962) General of the Army. Russian. Son of blacksmith. Factory worker. Entered Red Guards in 1917. Entered Party and Red Army 1918. Political commissar in Red Cavalry during Civil War. Graduate of military-political school 1925. Political commissar of 4th Cavalry Division (1921–24), 10th Cavalry Division (1926–29). Executive positions in quartermaster branch of Red Army 1930–38. Chief of Supply then Quartermaster General of Red Army 1939–41. Deputy People's Commissar of Defense and Chief of Red Army Rear Services 1941–45. Simultaneously, People's Commissar of Transport 1942–43. Deputy Minister of Defense in charge of supply and construction 1945–51. Deputy Minister of Construction Materials Industry, then of Automobile Transport and Highways 1951–56. Deputy Minister of Construction 1957. Subsequently, Deputy Chairman of Soviet War Veterans Committee.

Kirponos, M. P. (1892–1941) Colonel General. Hero of S.U. Ukrainian. Peasant origin. Private, then medical aide in tsarist army in World War I. Entered

Party 1918. Formed guerrilla detachments in Ukraine. Entered Red Army 1918. Commanded regiment during Civil War. Graduate of Frunze Military Academy 1927. Chief of staff of rifle division until 1934. Commandant of infantry officer school in Kazan' 1934–39. Commander of rifle division during Finnish war 1939–40. Commander of Leningrad and, directly before war, Kiev Military Districts June 1940–July 1941. Commander of Southwestern Army Group defending Ukraine after German attack. His entire Army Group encircled near Kiev September 1941. Mortally wounded during attempt to break out of encirclement with group of headquarters officers.

Konev, I. S. (1897–   ) Marshal of S.U. Twice Hero of S.U. Russian. Peasant origin. Lumberjack. Non-commissioned officer in the tsarist army during World War I. Entered Red Army and Party 1918. Political commissar of armored train during Civil War. Political commissar of 17th Maritime Rifle Corps until 1927 when he was graduated from command training courses. Regimental then divisional commander 1927–32. Graduate of Frunze Military Academy 1934. Division (1934–37) Corps (1937–38) commander. Commander 2nd Red Banner Far Eastern Army 1938–40. Commander Trans-Baikal, then Transcaucasian Military Districts 1940–41. Commander 19th Army and Western Army Group in battle for Moscow 1941. Commander Kalinin Army Group 1941–43. Commander Steppe, 2nd Ukrainian, and 1st Ukrainian Army Groups in Soviet offensives in the Ukraine, Poland, and the battle for Berlin 1943–45. Commander in Chief Soviet occupation forces in Austria and Hungary 1945–46. Commander in Chief of Soviet Ground Forces and Deputy Minister of War 1946–50. Chief Inspector of the Soviet Army 1950–51. Commander Carpathian Military District 1951–55. First Deputy Minister of Defense and Commander in Chief of Warsaw Pact Forces 1955–60. Commander in Chief of Soviet occupation forces in Germany 1961–62. From 1962 Inspector General of the Ministry of Defense.

Kulik, G. I. (1890–   ) One-time Marshal of S.U. Hero of S.U. Russian. Peasant origin. Laborer. Drafted into tsarist army 1912. Non-commissioned officer in artillery during World War I. Entered Party 1917. Entered Red Army 1918. Chief of Artillery of 1st Horse Cavalry Army during Civil War. Attended courses for senior commanders in early 1920's. Chief Quartermaster of Red Army 1926–29. Attended Frunze Military Academy 1930–32. Commander rifle corps 1933–36. Senior military adviser in Spanish Civil War 1936–37. Inspector General of Artillery 1937–39. Deputy People's Commissar of Defense and Chief of Main Artillery Directorate of Red Army 1939–41. Field representative of Soviet High Command during Finnish War. Named Marshal of S.U. June 1940. Commander 54th Army in Volkhov sector fall 1941. Demoted from Marshal of S.U. to Major General. Representative of High Command concerned with formation of reserve units in interior. Commander of corps artillery 1942–43. Promoted to Lieutenant General and appointed Commander 8th Assault Army summer 1943. Demoted shortly thereafter for unsuccessful operation. Disappeared from public view.

Kuznetsov, N. G. (1902–   ) Admiral of the Fleet. Hero of S.U. Russian. Peasant origin. Entered Red Navy 1919. Served as sailor in North Dvina flotilla during Civil War. Entered Party 1925. Studied in Naval Officer School 1922–26. Gunnery officer on cruiser *Red Ukraine* in Black Sea 1926–29. Graduate of

Naval Academy 1932. First officer on cruiser *Red Caucasus* in Black Sea 1932–34. Commander of cruiser *Red Ukraine* 1934–36. Soviet Naval Attaché and Chief Naval Adviser during Civil War in Spain 1936–37. First Deputy Commander, then Commander of Pacific Fleet 1937–39. People's Commissar of the Navy, Commander in Chief of Naval Forces 1939–45 and 1951–53. First Deputy Minister of Defense, Commander in Chief of the Navy 1946 and 1953–56. Deputy Commander in Chief of the Navy 1947–50. After 1956 on Staff of Ministry of Defense.

Luganskii, S. D. (1919–   ) Major General. Twice Hero of S.U. Russian. Worker origin. Entered Red Army 1936. Took part in Finnish War as fighter pilot 1939–40. During World War II squadron, fighter regiment commander. Took part in battles for Stalingrad, Kursk, and in operations in Poland and Germany. Credited with 43 enemy planes destroyed. After war attended Air Force Academy and commanded fighter units.

Malinovskii, R. Ia. (1898–1967) Marshal of S.U. Twice Hero of S.U. Ukrainian. Son of worker. Non-commissioned officer in tsarist army during World War I. Entered Red Army 1919. Battalion, regiment commander in Civil War. Entered Party 1926. Attended Frunze Military Academy 1926–30. Military adviser in Spanish Civil War 1936–38. Instructor Frunze Military Academy 1939–40. Commander 48th Rifle Corps on Rumanian border 1940–41. Commander 6th Army in Ukraine 1941. Commander Southern Army Group, then Don Operational Group and 66th Army 1942. Commander 2nd Guards Army in Stalingrad counter-offensive 1942–43. Commander Southern, Southwestern, 3rd and 2nd Ukrainian Army Groups in offensive operations in Ukraine, Rumania, Hungary, Austria, Czechoslovakia 1943–45. Commander Transbaikal Army Group in war with Japan 1945. Commander Far Eastern Military District, Commander in Chief Soviet Forces in Far East 1945–56. First Deputy Minister of Defense and Commander in Chief of Soviet Ground Forces March 1956–57. From October 1957 Minister of Defense.

Mekhlis, L. Z. (1889–1953) Colonel General. Jewish. Son of clerk. Private tutor and clerk. Artilleryman in tsarist army during World War I. Entered Party 1918. Political commissar of brigade, division, and army during Civil War. Senior official in People's Commissariat of Workers and Peasants Inspection 1921–22. Official in apparatus of Central Committee of Party and in Stalin's personal secretariat 1922–27. Graduate of higher Party school 1930. Editor of *Pravda* 1930–37. Deputy People's Commissar of Defense and Chief of Main Political Administration of Red Army 1937–September 1940. People's Commissar of State Control 1940–June 1941. During Nazi-Soviet war member of military councils of several Armies and Army Groups. Minister of State Control 1945–49. Alternate Member from 1934, Full Member of Central Committee of Party from 1939. From 1949 inactive owing to illness.

Meretskov, K. A. (1897–   ) Marshal of S.U. Hero of S.U. Russian. Peasant origin. Factory worker in Moscow. Entered Party May 1917. Red Guard. From 1918 political commissar in Red Army. Attended training courses of General Staff during Civil War and served as assistant to divisional chief of staff. Divisional chief of staff 1921–24. Assistant to Chief of Staff of Moscow Military District and commissar of district headquarters 1924–30. Divisional commander

1930. Chief of Staff of Moscow then Belorussian Military Districts 1931–35. Chief of Staff of Special Red Banner Far Eastern Army 1935–36. Soviet adviser in Spain during Civil War summer 1936–37. Deputy Chief of General Staff June 1937–September 1938. Commander of Volga, then Leningrad Military Districts 1938–39. Commander of 7th Army during Finnish War. Chief of General Staff August 1940–January 1941. Deputy People's Commissar of Defense and Chief of Combat Training Directorate 1941. Supreme Headquarters representative in northern sector fall 1941. Commander Volkhov, then Karelian Army Groups 1941–45. Commander 1st Far Eastern Army Group in war with Japan. Commander of Maritime, Moscow, and Northern Military Districts consecutively 1945–54. From 1954 until retirement in 1961 assistant to Minister of Defense for higher military education.

Pavlov, D. G. (1893–1941) General of the Army. Hero of S.U. Russian. Son of lumberjack. Non-commissioned officer during World War I. German P.O.W. camp. Entered Red Army 1918. Squadron commander during Civil War. Attended training courses for senior cavalry officers in early 1920's. Commander cavalry regiment 1924–28. Attended courses for tank officers in early 1930's. Divisional tank commander until 1936. Commander Soviet tank units in Spanish Civil War 1936–37. Tank corps commander 1937–38. Deputy Chief, then Chief Main Directorate of Motorized and Mechanized Forces 1938–40. Commander of tank reserve group in Finnish War 1940. Commander Western Special Military District from January 1941. Commander Western Army Group from June 22. Accused of treason and shot July 1941.

Petrov, I. E. (1896–1958) General of the Army. Hero of S.U. Russian. Son of shoemaker. Attended normal school. Junior officer in tsarist army 1916–17. Entered Party and Red Army 1918. Began Civil War as platoon commander and ended as political commissar of cavalry regiment. From 1921 to Nazi-Soviet war served in Central Asia—in 1920's as regimental, then brigade cavalry commander, in 1930's as Commandant and Political Commissar of Central Asian Military School. Commander of mechanized corps 1940–41. Commander 2nd Cavalry, then 25th Rifle Division in defense of Odessa 1941. Commander in Chief of ground forces in defense of Sevastopol' October 1941–June 1942. Commander 44th Army, Black Sea group of forces, then North Caucasian Army Group in defense of Caucasus 1942–43. Commander, Special Maritime Army 1943. Removed in early 1944 and demoted to colonel general for unsuccessful landing operation in Crimea. Commander 2nd Belorussian, then 4th Ukrainian Army Groups 1944–45. Chief of Staff 1st Ukrainian Army Group March–June 1945. Commander Turkestan Military District 1945–52. From 1952 on Staff of Ministry of Defense.

Rokossovskii, K. K. (1896–1968) Marshal of S.U. Twice Hero of S.U. Son of Polish father, Russian mother. Father a locomotive driver. Orphaned at age 14; began work as construction worker. Drafted into tsarist army 1914. Ended World War I as cavalry sergeant. Red Guard 1917. Entered Red Army 1918. Commanded squadron, cavalry regiment in Civil War. Entered Party 1919. Regimental commander and student in training course for junior, then senior cavalry officers during 1920's. Commander of cavalry brigade 1929. Commander of division 1930. Commander of corps 1936. Arrested August 1937 and jailed for almost three years. Released from prison March 1940 and reinstated as 5th

Cavalry Corps Commander. Commander 9th Mechanized Corps in Ukraine June 1941. Commander operational group of forces near Smolensk July 1941. Commander 16th Army in battle for Moscow 1941–42. Commander Briansk Army Group July–September 1942. Commander Don Army Group in battle for Stalingrad 1942–43. Commander Central Army Group in Kursk battle 1943. Commander 1st, then 2nd Belorussian Army Groups 1943–45. Commander in Chief of Soviet forces in Poland 1945–49. Minister of Defense and Deputy Prime Minister of Polish People's Republic; Marshal of Poland 1949–56. Chief Inspector and Deputy Minister of Defense of USSR 1956–62. From 1962 Inspector General of Soviet Ministry of Defense.

Sandalov, L. M. (1900–   ) Colonel General. Russian. Entered Red Army 1919. Staff officer in operations section of Kiev Military District 1934–36. Attended Academy of General Staff 1936–37. Chief of Operations Belorussian Military District 1938–40. Chief of Staff 4th Army 1940–July 1941. Chief of Staff Briansk Army Group in defense of Moscow, Chief of Staff 20th Army in Moscow counteroffensive 1941–42. Chief of Staff Briansk Army Group 1942–43. Chief of Staff 2nd Baltic Army Group October 1943–45. Chief of Staff 4th Ukrainian Army Group in Czechoslovakia March–May 1945. After war Chief of Main Staff of Soviet Ground Forces. Retired in 1951 after plane crash which left him paralyzed.

Shaposhnikov, B. M. (1882-1945) Marshal of S.U. Russian. Son of junior administrative official. Career officer in tsarist army. Graduate of Academy of General Staff 1910. Staff position and regiment commander with rank of colonel during World War I. Entered Red Army 1918. One of key staff workers of Red Army during Civil War. Assistant to Chief of Staff of Red Army 1921–24. Assistant to People's Commissar of Military Affairs, then Commander Leningrad Military District 1925–27. Commander Moscow Military District 1927–28. Chief of Staff of Red Army 1928–31. Entered Party 1930. Commander Volga Military District 1931. Commandant Frunze Military Academy 1932–37. Chief of General Staff of Red Army 1937–40, 1941–42. Retired in July 1942 owing to ill health. Until death in 1945 Chief of Historical Administration of People's Commissariat of Defense.

Shcherbakov, A. S. (1901-1945) Colonel General. Russian. Worker origin. Entered Party 1918. Official in Young Communists League 1919–21. Studied at Sverdlov Communist University 1921–24. Party official in central Russia 1924–30. Studied in higher Party school 1930–32. Deputy Head Organizational Department of the Party's Central Committee 1932–34. Head Department of Propaganda of Central Committee 1935. Secretary Leningrad, East Siberian, Donets, and Stalino Party committees, consecutively, 1936–38. First Secretary Moscow provincial and city Party committees 1938–41. From 1941 Secretary of Central Committee of Party. From 1942 Chief of Main Political Administration of Red Army.

Shtemenko, S. M. (1901–   ) Colonel General. Entered Red Army 1919. Graduate from Military Academy of Armored Forces in 1930's. Officer of General Staff of Red Army from 1939. Section Chief in Office of Operations of General Staff 1940–42. Deputy Chief of Operations of General Staff 1943. Chief of Operations, Deputy Chief of General Staff 1943–48. Chief of General Staff, Deputy Minister of Defense 1949–52. Reputedly Chief of Staff of Soviet occupation forces in Germany 1952–53. Reduced in rank after Stalin's death (from General of the Army) and disappeared from public life for three years. Deputy Commander Volga Military District 1959–61. First Deputy Commander Transcaucasian Military District 1961–62. Chief of Main Staff of Soviet Ground Forces 1962–65. From 1965 Deputy Chief of General Staff. In 1968 appointed Chief of Staff of Warsaw Pact Forces.

Starinov, I. T. (1899–   ) Colonel. Russian. Son of railroad switchman. Entered Red Army 1918. Fought with engineer units in Civil War. Entered Party 1922. Graduate of school for military railroad technicians. Junior officer in engineering troops. Studied engineering in Central Institute of Labor 1928. In charge of training special detachments for guerrilla activities behind enemy lines 1929–33. On Staff of Military Intelligence Directorate of People's Commissariat of Defense 1933. Studied in Academy of Military Transport 1934–35. Deputy military commandant of railroad line 1935–36. Military adviser on mining and guerrilla warfare in Spanish Civil War 1936–37. Chief of military testing ground 1938–39. Took part in Finnish war 1939–40. Section chief in Military Engineering Directorate of Red Army 1940–41. Sent to Western, then Southwestern Army Groups to supervise construction of field fortifications and demolition of military and industrial objects in wake of Soviet reverses July–November 1941. For remainder of war served in Central Staff of partisan movement and directed a special forces school.

Stuchenko, A. T. (1904–   ) Colonel General. Ukrainian. Son of laborer. Entered Red Army 1920. Graduate of cavalry officer school 1926. Entered Party 1929. Platoon, squadron commander 1927–32. Chief, then Assistant Chief of Operations Section 4th Cavalry Division 1932–36. Attended Frunze Military Academy 1936–38. Chief of Operations 3rd Cavalry Corps 1938–39. Attended military pilots school 1939–41. Commander, cavalry regiment, division, rifle division, and corps during World War II. Commander of rifle corps 1947–51, 1953–54. Attended General Staff Academy 1951–53. First Deputy Commander, then Commander Northern Military District 1955–59. Commander Volga, then Transcaucasian Military District since 1961.

Telegin, K. F. (1898–   ) Lieutenant General. Russian. Entered Party and Red Army 1918. Political work during Civil War. Regimental and divisional political commissar in inter-war period. On staff of Main Political Administration of Red Army 1940–41. Chief of Political Administration, Moscow Military District June–July 1941. Member of Military Council Moscow Military District and Moscow Defense Zone during battle for Moscow 1941. Political commissar of Don Army Group in battle for Stalingrad 1942–43, of Central Army Group in battle for Kursk 1943, of 1st Belorussian Army Group in summer 1944 offensive and in assault on Berlin. With Soviet occupational forces in Germany after war. Member of Military Council of several military districts.

Timoshenko, S. K. (1895–   ) Marshal of S.U. Hero of S.U. Russian. Peasant origin. Village laborer. Private, non-commissioned officer in tsarist army World War I. Entered Red Army 1918. Entered Party 1919. Cavalry regiment and division commander during Civil War. Graduate of senior training courses 1922. Commander cavalry division 1924–28. Completed course for commander-commissars in Military-Political Academy 1930. Cavalry corps commander 1930–33. Deputy Commander Belorussian, then Kiev Military Districts 1933–37. Commander North Caucasian, Khar'kov, then Kiev Military Districts 1937–40.

Took part in occupation of Poland. In charge of Soviet winter offensive in Finland 1940. People's Commissar of Defense July 1940–July 1941. Deputy People's Commissar of Defense and Commander in Chief of Western, then Southwestern Strategic Sectors 1941–42. Commander and Supreme Headquarters representative in several operations 1942–45. Commander South Ural and Belorussian Military Districts 1946–60. From 1960 Inspector General of Ministry of Defense. From 1961 Chairman of War Veterans Committee.

Tiulenev, I. V. (1892–   ) General of the Army. Russian. Peasant origin. Private, non-commissioned officer in tsarist army 1913–17. Joined Red Guard 1917. Entered Red Army and Party 1918. Divisional cavalry commander during Civil War. Cavalry brigade, division, corps commander 1923–36. Deputy Inspector of Red Cavalry 1937. Commander Transcaucasian Military District 1938–41. Commander 12th Army in occupation of Poland 1939. Commander Moscow Military District January–June 1941. Commander Southern Army Group 1941–42. Commander Transcaucasian Army Group 1942–43. Commander Transcaucasian Military District 1944–45. Commander Khar'kov Military District 1946–53. On staff of Ministry of Defense 1953 until retirement from active service.

Tolbukhin, F. I. (1894–1949) Marshal of S.U. Russian. Peasant origin. Graduate of commercial school as accountant. Drafted into tsarist army 1914. Sent to officer school and ended World War I as battalion commander with rank of captain. Entered Red Army 1918. Took part in Civil War. Entered Party 1931. Divisional chief of staff 1922–31. Graduate of Frunze Military Academy with appointment as corps chief of staff 1934. Chief of Staff of Transcaucasian Military District 1938–41. Chief of Staff of Transcaucasian, then Crimean Army Groups 1941–42. Commander of 57th Army during battle for Stalingrad. Commander of Southern, 4th and 5th Ukrainian Army Groups consecutively 1943–45. Directed offensive in Crimea, then led Soviet troops into Bulgaria, Yugoslavia, Hungary, and Austria. Commander of Soviet troops in southeastern Europe 1945–47. Commander of Transcaucasian Military District 1947–49.

Vasilevskii, A. M. (1895–   ) Marshal of S.U. Twice Hero of S.U. Russian. Son of priest. Attended theological seminary. Officer in tsarist army during World War I. Ended war as battalion commander with rank of captain. Entered Red Army 1919. Fought in Civil War as deputy regimental commander. Head of divisional school, then regimental commander 1921–30. Began work in General Staff of Red Army in Moscow as section chief in Department of Combat Training 1931. Entered Party 1931. Chief of combat training in Volga Military District 1934–36. Attended Academy of General Staff 1936–38. After graduation appointed to work in General Staff. Year prior to German invasion promoted to Deputy Chief of Operations. Chief of Operations from August 1941, then shortly after appointed simultaneously Deputy Chief of General Staff. Replaced Marshal Shaposhnikov as Chief of General Staff June 1942. In this position, occupied almost to end of war, his time divided between work in Moscow and frequent and lengthy trips to armies in the field where as Supreme Headquarters representative he supervised preparation and execution of major operations and coordinated activities of large formations. Of 34 war months in post of Chief of General Staff, 22 were spent at the front. Replaced General Cherniakhovskii as Commander of 3rd Belorussian Army Group February 1945. Led assault of East Prussia. Commander in Chief of Soviet armies in Far East during August

1945 campaign against Japanese troops in Manchuria and Korea. Again assumed direction of General Staff in 1946. Simultaneously First Deputy Minister of Armed Forces. Minister of Armed Forces (renamed Ministry of Defense in 1950) from 1949 to Stalin's death in March 1953. First Deputy Minister of Defense 1953–57. Retired from active service December 1957.

Voronov, N. N. (1899–   ) Chief Marshal of Artillery. Russian. Son of clerk. Entered Red Army 1918. Entered Party 1919. Attended artillery training course. Battery commander in Civil War. P.O.W. in Poland 1920–21. Artillery battalion commander 1924–27. Studied in Frunze Military Academy 1927–30. Artillery regiment commander 1930–32. Military mission to Italy 1932. Chief of Divisional Artillery 1933. Commandant and Political Commissar of Artillery Officers School 1934–36. Military adviser in Spain during Civil War 1936–37. Chief of Artillery of Red Army 1937–40. Took part in Finnish War. First Deputy Chief Main Artillery Directorate of Red Army 1940–41. During Nazi-Soviet war member of Supreme Headquarters, Commander in Chief of Artillery of Red Army. As Supreme Headquarters representative took part in preparing and supervising several major operations, notably the Stalingrad counteroffensive. Commander in Chief of Artillery 1945–50. President Academy of Artillery Sciences 1950–53. Commandant, Artillery Academy from 1953 until retirement.

Voroshilov, K. E. (1881–   ) Marshal of S.U. Hero of S.U. Russian. Worker origin. Metallurgical worker. Underground Bolshevik from 1903. Active leader in revolutionary movement. Took part in 1905 and 1917 revolutions. One of creators of secret police 1917. Entered Red Army 1918. One of senior commanders in Civil War. Commander North Caucasian, then Moscow Military Districts 1921–25. People's Commissar of Defense 1925–40. Deputy Chairman of Defense Council of Soviet government 1940–41. Commander in Chief Northwestern Strategic Sector, then Commander Leningrad Army Group July–October 1941. Member State Defense Committee and Supreme Headquarters 1941–45. Simultaneously on Main Staff of partisan movement. Head of Soviet Control Commission in Hungary 1945–47. Deputy Chairman Council of Ministers 1947–53. Chairman of Presidium of Supreme Soviet (titular president of Soviet state, 1953–60. Member of Party's ruling Politburo 1926–60. Denounced by Khrushchev 1961 for alleged sympathy with Anti-Party Group of Malenkov, Molotov, et al. Removed from all official positions.

Voznesenskii, N. A. (1903–1950) Member of Academy of Sciences. Russian. Son of clerk. Entered Party 1919. Official in Young Communists League 1919–21. Studied at Sverdlov Communist University 1921–24. Party official in Donbas 1924–28. Studied at Economic Institute of Red Professors 1928–31. Instructor there 1931–34. Chairman City Planning Commission in Leningrad, Deputy Mayor of Leningrad 1935–38. Chairman State Planning Commission of USSR 1938–42. From 1939 until death Deputy Chairman Council of People's Commissars. During Nazi-Soviet war member of State Defense Committee. From 1939 member of Central Committee of Party. From February 1941 Alternate Member and from 1947 Full Member of Party's Politburo. Arrested 1949. Shot 1950.

Zakharov, G. F. (1897–1957) General of the Army. Russian. Peasant origin. Drafted into tsarist army 1915. Served as junior officer in World War I. Entered Red Army 1918. Company commander during Civil War. Graduate of infantry school, battalion then regimental commander 1923–29. Attended Frunze Military Academy 1930–33. Lecturer in tactics in Military-Engineering Academy 1933–37. Attended Academy of General Staff 1937–39. Chief of Staff of Ural Military District 1939–41. Chief of Staff of 22nd Army in northern sector July–August 1941. Chief of Staff Briansk Army Group in battle for Moscow. Deputy Commander Western Army Group December 1941–April 1942. Chief of Staff of North Caucasian Sector Command, then Deputy Chief of Staff of North Caucasian Army Group May–July 1942. Deputy Commander of Stalingrad Army Group August–December 1942. Commander of 51st Army from February 1943. Commander of 2nd Guards Army from July 1943. Took part in offensive in Don Basin and in Crimea. Commander 2nd Belorussian Army Group in summer 1944 offensive. Commander 4th Guards Army in Hungary November 1944–January 1945. Deputy Commander 4th Ukrainian Army Group 1945. Commander South Ural then East Siberian Military Districts 1945–53. Commandant, Marksmen Training Courses, then Deputy Chief of Main Directorate of Combat Training of Ministry of Defense 1953–57.

Zamertsev, I. T. (1902–   ) Major General. Russian. Entered Red Army 1920. Commander of 255th Rifle Division and 11th Rifle Corps 1941–45. Military Commandant of Budapest 1945–48. Lecturer in Frunze Military Academy then on staff of Soviet Ministry of Defense from 1949.

Zhukov, G. K. (1896–   ) Marshal of S.U. Four-time Hero of S.U. Russian. Son of village shoemaker. Apprenticed to furrier. Drafted into tsarist army 1915. Ended war as highly decorated cavalry sergeant. Entered Red Army 1918. Entered Party 1919. Squadron commander in Civil War. Squadron from 1920, then cavalry regiment commander 1923–30. Attended cavalry school 1925 and training courses for senior officers 1929. Cavalry brigade commander 1930. Assistant to Inspector of Cavalry of Red Army 1931–33. Commander cavalry division 1933–37. Commander cavalry corps 1937–38. Deputy Commander of Belorussian Military District July 1938–39. Commander of group of forces in Far East 1939–40. Led successful offensive against Japanese at Khalkhin-Gol in Mongolia August 1939. Commander Kiev Military District June 1940–41. Chief of General Staff January–July 1941. Commander Reserve Army Group in battle for Smolensk July 1941. Organized defense of Leningrad September 1941. Commander of Soviet troops in battle for Moscow October–January 1941. Commander Western Army Group and Commander in Chief Western Strategic Sector (4 Army Groups) winter–spring 1942. First Deputy Supreme Commander in Chief of Armed Forces August 1942–end of war. Key responsibility for Stalingrad and Kursk battles 1942–43. Coordinated 1st and 2nd Ukrainian Army Groups in winter offensive 1943–44. Commander 1st Ukrainian Army Group spring 1944. Coordinated 1st and 2nd Belorussian Army Groups summer offensive 1944. Commander 1st Belorussian Army Group in final assault on Germany 1945. Commander in Chief Soviet occupation forces in Germany 1945–46. Commander in Chief Soviet Ground Forces 1946. Commander Odessa then Ural Military District 1947–52. First Deputy Minister of Defense 1953–55. Minister of Defense 1955–57. Elected February 1956 to alternate membership in Party's ruling Presidium, the first and only military professional in Soviet history to reach this height. Elected to full membership June 1957. Removed from all positions, publicly disgraced for allegedly questioning Party leadership of armed forces October 1957. Retired from active service.

SELECTED BIBLIOGRAPHY
OF SOVIET WAR MEMOIRS

THE following list includes only books, and only those which have appeared in recent years. In all cases the latest edit ons were used. Unless otherwise indicated, all entries were published in Moscow by the Military Publishing House (Voenizdat).

Anthologies

Bitva za Moskvu. Moscow, Moskovskii rabochii, 1966. 624 pp. Battle for Moscow, by almost all key military participants and some political leaders and industrial managers.

Budapesht, Vena, Praga. Moscow, "Nauka," 1965. 383 pp. Action of 2nd and 3rd Ukrainian Army Groups in battles for southeastern Europe, by senior commanders.

Bug v ogne. Minsk, "Belarus'," 1965. 528 pp. June 1941 on western frontier and return of Red Army in 1944.

Cherez fiordy. 1964. 160 pp. Final stage of war in far north, by officers of Karelian Army Group and Northern Fleet.

Dorogoi bor'by i slavy. Moscow, Politizdat, 1961. 543 pp. Reminiscences on various periods of war, by participants including Marshal R>kossovskii and Generals Liudnikov and Telegin.

Eto bylo na Krainem Severe. Murmansk, Knizhnoe izdatel'stvo, 1965. 415 pp. Memoirs and documents concerning war in the Arctic Circle.

Final. Moscow, "Nauka," 1966. 350 pp. War with Japan, August 1945, by various authors including senior commanders.

Geroicheskaia oborona. 3rd ed. Minsk, "Belarus'," 1966. 598 pp. Defense of Brest fortress, summer 1941, by participants.

Iassko-Kishinevskie Kanny. Moscow, "Nauka," 1964. 280 pp. August–September 1944 battle near Iassy-Kishenev which permitted Soviet penetration of Balkans, under general editorship of Marshal Malinovskii, late Minister of Defense.

Ot Moskvy do Berlina. Moscow, Moskovskii Rabochii, 1966. 432 pp. Formation of Home Guard units in 1941 and their subsequent role, by Moscow Party functionaries and Home Guard officers.

Polki idut na zapad. 1964. 423 pp. Summer offensive in Belorussia, 1944, and annihilation of German Army Group Center, by various authors including key Army Group commanders.

Poslednii shturm. Moscow, Politizdat, 1965. 279 pp. Final assault on Berlin, by participants including commanders of Armies.

Razgrom nemetsko-fashistskikh voisk pod Moskvoi. 1964. 444 pp. Soviet counteroffensive near Moscow, winter 1941–42, by key commanders.

U chernomorskikh tverdyn'. 1967. 416 pp. Special Maritime Army in defense of Odessa and Sevastopol', 1941–42, by generals and officers.

V bol'shom nastuplenii. 1964. 496 pp. Soviet offensive operations in the Ukraine, 1943–44, by participants including Army Group commanders.

V ognennom kol'tse. Moscow, Politizdat, 1963. 214 pp. Defense of Leningrad, by military and civilian participants.

Voiuet Baltika. Leningrad, Lenizdat, 1964. 507 pp. Defense of Leningrad, by naval officers.

Individual Memoirs

Abramov, V. L. *Na ratnykh dorogakh.* 1962. 240 pp. Defense of Crimea and Caucasus 1941–42 and Kursk battle 1943, by rifle division commander.

Azarov, I. I. *Srazhaiushchaiasia Odessa.* Moscow, Politizdat, 1965. 127 pp. (2nd rev. ed., Moscow, Voennizdat, 1966.) Defense of the Black Sea port of Odessa, 1941, by senior political commissar.

Bagramian, I. Kh. *Gorod-voin na Dnepre.* Moscow, Politizdat, 1965. 160 pp. Battle of Kiev, 1941, by Marshal of S.U., then Chief of Operations of defending Army Group.

Beloborodov, A. P. *Ratnyi podvig.* Moscow, Politizdat, 1965. 110 pp. Battle of Moscow, by Commander of 78th Rifle Division.

Belov, E. E. *Syny otchizny.* Moscow, Politizdat, 1966. 263 pp. Account of wartime experiences, by Lieutenant General of armored troops.

Belov, P. A. *Za nami Moskva.* 1963. 332 pp. Battle for Moscow, by commander of cavalry corps.

Berezhkov, V. *S diplomaticheskoi missiei v Berlin 1940–1941.* Moscow, "Novosti," 1966. 159 pp. Soviet diplomatic activity on eve of war, by First Secretary of Soviet Embassy in Berlin.

Biriukov, N. I. *200 dnei v boiakh.* Volgograd, Knizhnoe izdatel'stvo, 1963. 159 pp. Stalingrad battle, by division commander.

Biriuzov, S. S. *Kogda gremeli pushki.* 1961. 280 pp. Initial retreat, battle for Stalingrad, and offensives in the Ukraine and Crimea, 1941–44, by an Army chief of staff.

———. *Sovetskii soldat na Balkanakh.* 1963. 336 pp. Soviet conquest of Balkans, 1944–45, by Chief of Staff of 3rd Ukrainian Army Group.

Blazhei, A. K. *V armeiskom shtabe.* 1967. 256 pp. Soviet offensive in the Ukraine, 1944, by an Army chief of staff.

Bobrenok, S. T. *Slovo o tovarishchakh.* 1961. 295 pp. June 1941 resistance of frontier fortress of Brest, by survivor.

Boldin, I. V. *Stranitsy zhizni.* 1961. 247 pp. First two years of war, by former Deputy Commander of Western Army Group and subsequently Commander of 50th Army.

Borisov, B. A. *Zapiski sekretaria gorkoma.* Moscow, Politizdat, 1964. 304 pp. Nine-month defense of Black Sea port and naval base of Sevastopol', by its Party Secretary.

Bychevskii, B. V. *Gorod-front.* 1963. 199 pp. Defense of Leningrad, by General in charge of its fortification.

Chuikov, V. I. *Nachalo puti.* 1959. 360 pp. Battle for Stalingrad, by Commander of 62nd Army defending city.

Egorov, F. I. *V oborone i nastuplenii.* Petrozavodsk, Karel'skoe knizhnoe izdatel'stvo, 1965. 164 pp. Defense of Leningrad and offensive operations against Finland in Karelia, 1941–45.

Eremenko, A. I. *Stalingrad.* 1961. 503 pp. Battle for Stalingrad, by Commander of Stalingrad Army Group.

———. *V nachale voiny.* Moscow, "Nauka," 1964. 511 pp. First year of war, by Marshal of S.U., then Commander of Western and Briansk Army Groups.

Eroshenko, V. N. *Lider "Tashkent."* 1966. 232 pp. War on Black Sea, by frigate commander.

Evseev, A. K. *Osazhdennyi Sevastopol'.* Leningrad, "Sovetskii pisatel'," 1959. 255 pp. Defense of Sevastopol', by Major General.

Fedorov, A. G. *Plata za shchast'e.* Moscow, "Molodaia gvardiia," 1963, 284 pp.

———. *Do poslednego starta.* 1965. 208 pp. Reminiscences 1941–45, by commander of dive bomber division.

Galkin, F. I. *Tanki vozvrashchaiutsia v boi.* 1964. 288 pp. Technical services in tank unit, by Major General.

Golovko, A. G. *Vmeste s flotom.* 1960. 270 pp. Diary of Commander in Chief of Northern Fleet 1941–45.

Guliaev, V. G. *Chelovek v brone.* 1964. 152 pp. Tank battles of 1941–43 near Moscow, Stalingrad, and Ukraine, by a senior political commissar in tank forces.

Gushchin, A. M. *Kurs prolozhennyi ognem.* 1964. 168 pp. War on Black Sea 1941–43, by Rear Admiral, Commander of cruiser *Red Caucasus.*

Iakovlev, A. S. *Tsel' zhizni.* Moscow, Politizdat, 1966. 543 pp. Life and career of leading aircraft designer and wartime deputy head of Soviet aircraft industry.

Iosseliani, Ia. K. *V bitvakh pod vodoi.* 1959. 272 pp. War in Black and North Seas on lend-lease submarine, by commander with 16 sunken ships to his credit.

Ivushkin, N. B. *Za vse v otvete.* 1965. 206 pp. Memoirs 1943–44, by divisional political commissar.

Kalinin, S. A. *Razmyshliaia o minuvshem.* 1963. 224 pp. Autobiography of senior Red Army commander who during war commanded field army and formed reserve units in interior.

Kazakov, M. I. *Nad kartoi bylykh srazhenii.* 1965. 224 pp. Autobiography of one of most respected Soviet generals, including his experience as an Army Group chief of staff 1941–43.

Kazakov, V. I. *Na perelome.* 1962. 191 pp. Battles for Moscow and Stalingrad, by Marshal of Artillery.

Krasovskii, S. A. *Zhizn' v aviatsii.* 1960. 264 pp. Autobiography of Soviet Air Marshal who commanded an air army during World War II.

Khizenko, I. A. *Ozhivshie stranitsy.* 1963. 104 pp. Rifle division's attempt to break out of encirclement in first weeks of war, by divisional political officer.

Kochetkov, D. I. *S zakrytymi liukami.* 1962. 254 pp. Diary 1941–45, by senior political officer of tank brigade, then tank army.

Kornev, A. S. *U nikh byli mirnye professii.* 1962. 183 pp. Construction of fortified defense lines, by commander in charge of unit.

Kozhevnikov, A. L. *Startuet muzhestvo.* 1966. 400 pp. Wartime experiences, by air force Lieutenant General, a fighter pilot with 27 downed planes to his credit.

Krivoshein, S. *Ratnaia byl'.* Moscow, "Molodaia gvardiia," 1962. 254 pp. Reminiscences, by famous tank corps commander.

Kumanin, M. F. *Otpravliaem v pokhod korabli.* 1962. 104 pp. Defense of Crimea and Caucasus, by Commander of the Poti naval base in Black Sea.

Kuznetsov, N. G. *Nakanune.* 1966. 427 pp. Soviet navy in years prior to war and in first period of war, by then Minister of Navy.

Kuznetsov, P. G. *Dni boevye.* 2nd ed. 1964. 327 pp. Diary of division commander near Leningrad 1942–43, later rifle corps commander in Ukraine 1943–44.

Lebedenko, P. P. *V izluchine Dona.* 1965. 176 pp. Retreat toward Stalingrad, summer 1942, by commander of a tank brigade.

Leliushenko, D. D. *Zaria pobedy.* 1966. 144 pp. First six months of war, by one of heroes of battle for Moscow, Commander of 30th Army.

Liudnikov, I. I. *Pod Vitebskom.* 1962. 223 pp. Belorussian offensive 1944, by Colonel General, Commander of 3rd Army.

Liudnikov, I. I. *Cherez Bol'shoi Khingan.* 1967. 120 pp. Offensive against Japanese Kwantung Army, by Commander of 39th Army.

Lobachev, A. A. *Trudnymi dorogami.* 1960. 336 pp. Battle for Moscow, by political commissar of Marshal Rokossovskii's 16th Army.

Luganskii, S. D. *Na glubokikh virazhakh.* 2nd ed. Alma-Ata, "Zhazushi," 1966. 194 pp. Five years of combat experience, by ace pilot and commander of fighter regiment.

Maiskii, I. M. *Vospominaniia sovetskogo posla.* Moscow, "Nauka," 1965. 407 pp. Memoirs, by Soviet Ambassador in London, 1939–43.

Maksimov, M. D. *Dorogami muzhestva.* Tula, Priokskoe knizhnoe izdatel'stvo, 1966. 236 pp. Defense of Tula 1941 and 1943 offensive west of Moscow, by Chief of Engineers of 50th Army.

Mednikov, A. M. *Berlinskaia tetrad'.* 2nd ed. Moscow, "Sovetskii pisatel'," 1964. 312 pp. Battle of Berlin, by war correspondent.

Momysh-uly, B. *Za nami Moskva.* Moscow, "Moskovskii rabochii," 1960. 191 pp. 1941 defense of Moscow, by regimental commander of legendary Panfilov division.

Monastyrskii, F. V. *Zemlia, omytaia krov'iu.* 1962. 228 pp. Fighting in Crimea 1942–43, by political commissar of Kerch naval base.

Panteleev, Iu. A. *Morskoi front.* 1965. 317 pp. Naval combat in the Baltic and defense of Leningrad, by Soviet Admiral.

Pavlovskii, M. P. *Na ostrovakh.* 1963. 94 pp. 1941 on Estonian islands, by an army major.

Pliev, I. A. *Cherez Gobi i Khingan.* 1965. 157 pp. War with Japan, August 1945, by Army commander.

Pokryshkin, A. I. *Nebo voiny.* 1966. 445 pp. Reminiscences, 1943–45, by top Soviet fighter ace.

Popel', N. K. *V tiazhkuiu poru.* 1959. 336 pp. Retreat, 1941–42, by political commissar of tank corps.

————. *Tanki povernuli na Zapad.* 1960. 381 pp. Victories, 1943–44, by same, now commissar of tank army.

Pukhov, N. P. *Gody ispytanii.* 1959. 87 pp. War experiences of officer who in last year of war commanded 2nd Assault Army.

Rodimtsev, A. I. *Na beregakh Mansanaresa i Volgi.* Petrozavodsk, Karel'skoe knizhnoe izdatel'stvo, 1966. 276 pp. Spanish Civil War and battle for Stalingrad, by Marshal of Armored Troops.

———. *Tvoi, otechestvo, synov'ia.* Kiev, "Radianskii pismennik," 1966. 381 pp. First months of war in the Ukraine.

Rzhevskaia, E. M. *Berlin, Mai 1945.* 2nd ed. Moscow, "Sovetskii pisatel'," 1967. 368 pp. First days of victory in Berlin, by translator attached to headquarters of capturing army.

Sandalov, L. M. *Perezhitoe.* 1966. 192 pp. Study at the Academy of the General Staff, service on the western frontier, and the beginning of the war, by the then Chief of Staff of 4th Army.

———. *Trudnye rubezhi.* 1965. 144 pp. Last year and a half of war, by Colonel General, Chief of Staff of 2nd Baltic Army Group.

Shatilov, V. M. *Znamia nad Reikhstagom.* 1966. 328 pp. Last year of war, by commander of rifle division which captured Reichstag.

Shchedrin, G. I. *Na bortu "S-56."* 2nd ed. 1963. 279 pp. Submarine S-56 from Pacific to Barents Sea and combat in Arctic conditions, by its commander, a Vice Admiral.

Shcheglov, D. A. *V opolchenii.* 1960. 286 pp. Diary of professional writer concerning Home Guard during Leningrad blockage.

———. *Upolnomochennyi voennogo soveta.* Moscow, "Sovetskii pisatel'," 1965. 312 pp. Soviet troops in Germany 1944–45, by writer who served in political department of an army.

Smirnov, N. K. *Matrosy zashchishchaiut Rodinu.* Moscow, Politizdat, 1962. 264 pp. Reminiscences, by commissar of Baltic Fleet.

Shutov, S. F. *Krasnye strely.* 1963. 272 pp. War reminiscences of tank brigade commander, twice Hero of S.U.

Solov'ev, V. K. *Pod Naro-Fominskom.* 2nd ed. 1966. 192 pp. Rifle division in battle for Moscow.

Starinov, I. G. *Miny zhdut svoego chasa.* 1964. 224 pp. Civil War in Spain and first month of Nazi-Soviet war on western frontier, by mining expert.

Starchuk, I. G. *S neba–v boi.* 1965. 183 pp. Paratroop unit in combat, by its commander.

Strel'bitskii, I. S. *Shturm.* 1962. 211 pp. Battles for Donbas and Crimea 1943–44, by Commander of Artillery of 2nd Guards Army.

Stuchenko, A. T. *Zavidnaia nasha sud'ba.* 1964. 256 pp. 1941–44, by cavalry division commander, later rifle division commander.

Sviridov, A. A. *Bataliony vstupaiut v boi.* 1967. 192 pp. 11th Army in defense of Soviet frontier, summer 1941.

Teremov, A. P. *Pylaiushchie berega.* 1965. 360 pp. War experience from Dnepr to Oder Rivers, by divisional commander.

Tiulenev, I. V. *Cherez tri voiny.* 1960. 256 pp. Combat experience of one of oldest Soviet generals in World War I, Civil War, and 1941–43 period of Nazi-Soviet war when he commanded an Army Group in the southern Ukraine and Caucasus.

Travkin, I. V. *Vsem smertiam nazlo.* 1964. 166 pp. Action in Baltic, by submarine commander.

Tributs, V. F. *Podvodniki Baltiki atakuiut.* Leningrad, Lenizdat, 1963. 335 pp. Baltic Fleet, by Admiral who served throughout war as its commander.

Umanskii, R. G. *Na boevykh rubezhakh.* 1962. 183 pp. Soviet fortifications on eve of war and experiences 1941–45, by colonel of sappers.

Veshchezerskii, G. A. *U khladnykh skal.* 1965. 149 pp. Combat in Arctic Circle.

Volynkin, I. T. *Nad piat'iu moriami.* 1964. 68 pp. Reminiscences, by naval pilot with Northern Fleet.

Voronov, N. N. *Na sluzhbe voennoi.* 1963. 437 pp. Combat in Spain, war with Finland, and Nazi-Soviet war until Stalingrad victory, by Chief Marshal of Artillery and member of Supreme Headquarters.

Vorozheikin, A. V. *Istrebiteli.* 1961. 230 pp.

———. *Nad Kurskoi dugoi.* 1962. 221 pp.

———. *Rassvet nad Kievom.* 1966. 200 pp. Soviet fighter division during initial defeats, in Stalingrad and Kursk victories, and 1943 offensive in Ukraine, by a foremost ace with 52 downed planes to his credit.

Zamertsev, I. T. *Cherez gody i rasstoianiia.* 1965. 198 pp. Memoirs, by military commandant of Budapest, 1945–48.

Zhdanov, N. N. *Ognevoi shchit Leningrada.* 1965. 294 pp. Artillery defense during siege of Leningrad, by Colonel General, one of its senior commanders.

Zhidilov, E. I. *My otstaivali Sevastopol'.* 2nd ed. 1963. 256 pp. 250 days of Sevastopol' defense, by Commander of 7th Marine Brigade.